LIBERTY AND FREEDOM

AMERICA: A CULTURAL HISTORY

LIBERTY AND FREEDOM

David Hackett Fischer

OXFORD
UNIVERSITY PRESS

2005

OXFORD
UNIVERSITY PRESS

Oxford   New York
Auckland   Bangkok   Buenos Aires   Cape Town   Chennai
Dar es Salaam   Delhi   Hong Kong   Istanbul   Karachi   Kolkata
Kuala Lumpur   Madrid   Melbourne   Mexico City   Mumbai
Nairobi   São Paulo   Shanghai   Taipei   Tokyo   Toronto

Published by Oxford University Press, Inc.
198 Madison Avenue, New York, New York 10016
www.oup.com

Oxford is a registered trademark of Oxford University Press

Library of Congress Cataloging-in-Publication Data
Fischer, David Hackett, 1935–
Liberty and freedom / David Hackett Fischer.
p. cm.
Includes bibliographical references and index.
ISBN 0-19-516253-6
1. United States — History. 2. United States — Politics and government.
3. National characteristics, American. 4. Liberty — History.
5. United States — History — Pictorial works. I. Title.
E179.F538 2004
323.44'0973 — dc22
2004005197

Book design and composition by Mark McGarry, Texas Type & Book Works
Set in Caslon

9 8 7 6 5 4 3 2 1
Printed in China
on acid-free paper

For Thea

This book is published in association with the Virginia Historical Society, organizer of the exhibition *American Visions of Liberty and Freedom*

EXHIBITION ITINERARY

Virginia Historical Society, Richmond
October 16, 2004–May 30, 2005

Senator John Heinz Regional History Center, Pittsburgh
July 17–December 31, 2005

Atlanta History Center
February 4–May 28, 2006

National Heritage Museum, Lexington, Massachusetts
June 24–October 16, 2006

Missouri Historical Society, St. Louis
November 18, 2006–March 11, 2007

CONTENTS

LIBERTY AND FREEDOM

INTRODUCTION

A Conversation with Captain Preston

I N THE YEAR 1843, a bright young scholar named Mellen Chamberlain was collecting evidence on the origins of the American Revolution. He interviewed Captain Levi Preston, ninety-one years old, a cantankerous Yankee who had fought on the day of Lexington and Concord.

"Captain Preston," the historian began, "what made you go to the Concord Fight?" The old soldier bristled at the idea that anyone had made him fight.

"What did I go for?" he replied. The scholar missed his meaning and tried again.

"Were you oppressed by the Stamp Act?"

"I never saw any stamps," Captain Preston answered, "and I always understood that none were ever sold."

"Well, what about the tea tax?"

"Tea tax? I never drank a drop of the stuff. The boys threw it all overboard."

"But I suppose you had been reading Harrington, Sidney, and Locke about the eternal principle of liberty?"

"I never heard of these men," Captain Preston said. "The only books we had were the Bible, the Catechism, Watts' Psalms, and hymns and the almanacs."

"Well, then, what was the matter?"

"Young man," Captain Preston replied, "what we meant in going for those Redcoats was this: we always had been free, and we meant to be free always. They didn't mean we should."[1]

In the study of history, every answer becomes another question. One might ask of Captain Preston, what did he mean by "always . . . free?" Was his thinking the same as ours? Has the meaning of that idea changed through time?

Here is a central problem in American history, as liberty and freedom are central values in American culture. Scholars have attempted to study it in many ways. The leading approach might be called the text-and-context method. It begins with American texts on liberty and freedom and fits them into an explanatory context that is larger than America itself.

Historians have discovered many different contexts by this method. They have variously told us that the meaning of American liberty and freedom is to be found in the context of Greek democracy, Roman republicanism, natural rights in the Middle Ages, the civic humanism of the Renaissance, the theology of the Reformation, the English "commonwealth tradition" in the seventeenth century, British "opposition ideology" in the eighteenth century, the treatises of John Locke, the science of Isaac Newton, the writings of Scottish moral philosophers, the values of the Enlightenment, and the axioms of classical liberalism.[2]

All of these approaches have added to our knowledge of liberty and freedom, but none of them comes to terms with Captain Preston. As he reminded us, the text-and-context method refers to books he never read, people he never knew, places he never visited, and periods that were far from his own time.[3]

Another method is the "coupling of concepts." That phrase appears in an excellent and useful book by Michael Kammen called *Spheres of Liberty,* which concludes that the "meaning of liberty in America has predominantly been explained in relation to some other quality," such as liberty and authority in the colonial era, liberty and property in the early republic, liberty and order through the nineteenth century, or liberty and justice in the twentieth century. Michael Kammen's coupling of concepts works very well for a study of conceptual writings, especially in constitutional law and political theory, but Captain Preston was thinking in more concrete terms.[4]

A third tool for the study of liberty and freedom might be called the philosopher's stone. It begins with a timeless abstraction that is the product of reflection rather than research. The leading example is Isaiah Berlin's essay "Two Concepts of Liberty," which attempts to organize the subject around a disjunction between "negative" and "positive" liberty, similar to the old German distinction between *Freiheit von* and *Freiheit zu.* Berlin's negative liberty is the idea that "no man or body of men interferes with my activity." His positive liberty "consists in being one's own master," by not being a slave to "unbridled passions" or possessions, or by achieving a "higher freedom" and helping or even forcing others to reach that state.[5]

Isaiah Berlin was writing in 1958, and his model was widely read as applying to the competing ideologies of the Cold War. Social scientists took it up with high enthusiasm, but philosophers and historians have not been happy with it. Eric Foner observes from long study that most ideas of liberty and freedom in America have tended to be positive and negative at the same time. Further, as we shall see, many ideas of liberty and freedom are larger than "noninterference with my own activity" or "being one's own master." Isaiah Berlin's "two concepts of liberty" are heuristically useful, but they are not mutually exclusive or collectively exhaustive. As organizing categories for the study of liberty and freedom they are mistaken.[6]

Eric Foner's *Story of American Freedom* takes a different and more historical approach to the problem. He begins with an idea of freedom as an "essentially contested concept," in W. B. Gallie's phrase, and studies it as a sequence of controversies that have shaped American history. The result is an excellent and large-spirited book, one of the best on its subject.[7] But it does not solve the problem of Captain Preston. To think of the history of freedom as a series of intellectual controversies is to center it on controversialists, which most Americans were not.[8]

Liberty and Freedom as Habits of the Heart

Without going against the text-and-context method, or the philosophical literature, or the scholarship of Michael Kammen, or the work of Eric Foner, we might try yet another approach in the hope of getting closer to Captain Preston. Most Americans do not think of liberty and freedom as a set of texts, or a sequence of controversies, or a system of abstractions. They understand these ideas in another way, as inherited values that they have learned early in life and deeply believe.

The only scholar who attempted to study the subject in this light was Alexis de Tocqueville. He observed that liberty and freedom were *habitudes du coeur,* "habits of the heart." He called them *moeurs libres,* by which he meant customs, beliefs, traditions, and folkways of free people.[9]

Tocqueville believed that liberty and freedom as "habits of the heart" had a special importance in the United States, more so than in other nations. To study their American history is to discover that they have been remarkably persistent but never constant. Like other folkways, they derive their meaning from their history and have changed profoundly from one generation to another, never more so than in our own time. Even at the start they varied from one group of Americans to another, and their diversity has increased through time. When they are studied, they are found to be ideas of surprising complexity.

The question is, how are we to study them? The answer is, by the same methods that any ethnographer would use to study any folkway. A folk belief can be studied from the inside and the outside. We know it from the inside by reenacting it in our minds, and we test the accuracy of that reenactment by studying it empirically from the outside.[10]

The empirical evidence comes mostly in the form of words, images, and actions. Let us begin with words, and two vital words in particular: liberty and freedom. They have a surprising history. In its origins, Captain Preston's language of liberty and freedom was unique to the Western world. A leading scholar of other cultures, Orlando Patterson, observes that "non-western peoples have thought so little about freedom that most human languages did not even possess a word for the concept before contact with the west."[11]

Other scholars have discovered that some ancient languages and texts had no words for liberty or freedom. A case in point was Hammurabi's Code. One leading student of that text was surprised to find "no special designation for a free man." There were many references to slaves, but the opposite of "slave" was not "free." It was "master," who was himself in thrall to a higher power.[12] Other ancient cultures were even more distant from ideas of liberty or freedom. Most were governed by tyrants, in the Greek sense of an absolute ruler whose will is law. The Greeks had a saying that in a tyranny only one person is free. In such a world, freedom as a general principle is difficult even to imagine.[13]

The Western world is unique not only in its invention of words such as liberty and freedom but also in having invented so many of them. These words have distinct origins and different shades of meaning. Consider the two leading terms in English usage: liberty and freedom. In early uses, both words implied a power of choice, an ability to exercise one's will, and a condition that was distinct from slavery. In all of those ways, liberty and freedom meant the same thing.[14]

But in other ways their original meanings were different. Our English word liberty comes from the Latin *libertas* and its adjective *liber,* which meant unbounded, unrestricted, and released from restraint. A synonym was *solutus,* from the verb *solvo,* to loosen a set of bonds. These words were similar to the Greek *eleutheria* and *eleutheros,* which also meant the condition of being independent, separate, and distinct.[15] The Greeks used these terms to describe autonomous cities, independent tribes, and individuals who were not ruled by another's will.[16] That ancient meaning survives in the modern era, where *eleutheros* has spawned scientific terms such as *eleutheropetalous* or *eleutherodactylic,* for separate petals or fingers or toes. *Eleutheria,* like the Roman *libertas,* always implied some degree of separation and independence.[17]

Freedom has another origin. It derives from a large family of ancient languages in northern Europe. The English word free is related to the Norse *fri,* the German *frei,* the Dutch *vrij,* the Flemish *vrig,* the Celtic *rheidd,* and the Welsh *rhydd.* These words share an unexpected root. They descend from the Indo-European *priya* or *friya* or *riya,* which meant dear or beloved. The English words freedom and free have the same root as *friend,* as do their German cousins *frei* and *Freund.* Free meant someone who was joined to a tribe of free people by ties of kinship and rights of belonging.[18]

A very similar meaning also appeared in the Sumerian *ama-ar-gi,* the oldest known word for anything like liberty or freedom, which appeared on clay tablets in Lagash before 2300 B.C. *Ama-ar-gi* came from the verb *ama-gi,* which meant literally going home to mother. It described the condition of servants no longer in bondage who returned to their free families.[19]

In that respect, the original meanings of freedom and liberty were not merely different but opposed. Liberty meant separation. Freedom implied connection. A person with *libertas* in Rome or *eleutheria* in ancient Greece had been granted some degree of autonomy, unlike a slave. A person who had *Freiheit* in northern Europe or *ama-ar-gi* in southern Mesopotamia was united by kinship or affection to a tribe or family of free people, unlike a slave.

The Roman idea of *libertas* as emancipation and independence has been studied at length by modern scholars.[20] The ancient idea of freedom as the rights of belonging in a free society is less familiar. We can observe it at a distance in the *Germaniae* of Tacitus and in sources such as the Lombard Laws and the Saxon Dooms. It appears most vividly in the Old Norse sagas, especially the Icelandic sagas. The free Norse families who colonized Iceland in the ninth century were refugees from kingship and

oppression. They carried into a new world their ancient folkways of freedom, which they understood as a complex set of rights and responsibilities. For them, freedom meant the rule of law, the power to choose one's
own chief, and the right to be governed and judged by a local assembly
called the *Thing*.[21]

The *Thing* was a gathering of free men, who in early years carried
weapons to the assembly and voted by "striking their shields or rattling
their spears," in what was called the *Vápnatak* in Old Norse, *Wapentake* of
Old English, and *Wappanschawing* of Old Scots. Icelanders also had an
Althing for their entire island, which included a council of chiefs, a court
of law, and a legislature, or *Lögrétta*. The *Lögrétta* was led by a *Lögsögu-
madr*, or lawspeaker, who was elected for three years. Each year the
lawspeaker stood by the *Lögberg*, or law rock, and recited one-third of the
laws from memory, before a highly critical audience of freemen. If the
freemen did not agree, the lawspeaker summoned five *lögmenn*, or legal
experts, to settle the question. A German historian in the eleventh century wrote of Iceland, "there is no king but only law."[22]

The meetings of the *Althing* and local *Things* had other functions that
tell us much about the meaning of freedom in northern Europe. They
were also social events, marriage marts, and family reunions for free families. They admitted sons of freemen to the freedom of the community by
a ritual gift of weapons and expelled freemen who broke the law. These
free societies suffered much from disorder, violence, and constant feuds.
The ultimate punishment was banishment, in which a freeman was
denied the right of belonging by the judgment of his peers.[23] By the
eleventh century, most men in Iceland were born free. This prior condition of freedom was a birthright that all freemen shared.[24]

In ancient Rome, the opposite was the case. Most people were born
in a condition of prior restraint, to which liberty came as a specific
exemption or release. The most common symbol of *libertas* in the ancient
world was the Roman goddess of liberty, holding a wand called a *vindicta*
in one hand and offering a cap called the *pileus libertatis* with the other, a
ritual by which slaves were released from bondage. A leading scholar concludes that "the Romans conceived of libertas as an acquired civil right,
not as an innate right of man."[25]

This led to another difference between freedom and liberty. The free-
born people of northern Europe were alike in their birthright of freedom,
however disparate they may have been in power, wealth, or rank.[26] In one
of the oldest lays of England the hero sings, "Lithe and listen, gentlemen,
that be of Freborn blood!" Among "folkfree" people, freedom created an

element of equality in the face of other inequalities.[27] The ancient rule was summarized by Frederick Pollock and Frederic Maitland: "All free men are equal before the law."[28]

In ancient Rome, liberty implied inequality. People were granted different liberties according to their condition. Some had many liberties. Others had few or none. When Rome was a republic, its citizens possessed the liberty of government by assembly, but in different ways according to their rank. Magistrates and senators had liberty to speak. Citizens had liberty to listen and vote. *Servi* had liberty to look on, but they could neither speak nor listen nor vote.[29]

Roman *libertas* gave rise to a complex vocabulary of stratification and mobility that still echoes in modern English speech. The Latin adjective *liberaliter* meant knowing how to behave gracefully and generously, in the manner of a highborn person who is secure in the possession of many liberties. It is the root of our word *liberality*. The noun *libertinus* meant an emancipated slave who had been granted liberties that he had not been prepared to use. Our modern word *libertine* preserves this ancient meaning.[30]

Within this social frame, ancient philosophers developed *libertas* and *eleutheria* as ethical ideas of high complexity. The leaders were the Stoics, who wrote at greater length about liberty than others in the ancient world, especially the slave Epictetus (A.D. 55–135) and the emperor Marcus Aurelius (A.D. 121–180). Both argued that to be truly free is to cultivate a spirit of independence from things that are not in one's control: bondage, tyranny, illness, pain, and death. This Stoic condition of liberty could be achieved even in a despotism. It is striking that the leading stoic philosophers of liberty in ancient Rome were an emperor and a slave.[31]

The condition of *libertas* in the Mediterranean civilizations was in some ways more limited than freedom in northern Europe, but it had a longer reach through a larger population. Freedom in Iceland and North Europe was more complete as a social condition, but it was more narrowly confined within a smaller sphere.

There was also another difference. Freeborn people in northern Europe had possessions that are called rights in English, or *rechte* in German. These words began as adjectives that meant straight, sound, correct, or good. They became nouns for specific entitlements that could be claimed as a matter of obligation, and also for the general idea of entitlement itself: rights as a matter of right. In northern Europe, rights were recognized as belonging to members of a particular folk. The laws of King Canute called them *folcrichts*.[32]

Ancient Mediterranean languages had no exact equivalent for rights. In archaic Greek, early references to *eleutheria* in Minoan Linear B referred not to rights but to an idea of "authorized concessions," as several scholars have observed.[33] In classical Latin, the nearest equivalent to an idea of a right was *ius,* which meant something permitted by law, or *fas,* which was something allowed by divine command. A careful student of this subject observes that *libertas* in Rome was "not an innate faculty or right of man" but the sum of liberties that had been "granted by the laws of Rome."[34]

Where North Europeans spoke of right or *richt* or *Recht,* citizens of Rome sometimes wrote of *privilegium* or *immunitas. Privilegium* meant literally a private law (from *privus,* private; *legis,* law). *Immunitas* was a formal exemption from a particular duty or obligation. Privileges and immunities were grants of special favor to particular individuals or groups. They were linked to liberty in their common idea of an exemption or release from prior restraint. In that respect, privileges were different from rights. A privilege or an immunity was something that might be given. A right was something that must be given.

It is interesting that the idea of *libertas* as *privilegium* coexisted with arbitrary rule in the Roman Empire and continued to be celebrated on Roman coins under even the most despotic emperors. But the freedom of North European tribes to rule themselves through their assemblies was the mortal enemy of kingship, and it was destroyed by monarchs in Europe during the medieval and early modern eras. It survived longest on remote impoverished islands and peninsulas in northwestern Europe, where self-governing *Lagtings* persisted in Norway until 1797, the *Althing* in Iceland until 1801, the Faeroese *Logting* until 1816, and British Parliaments to our own time.[35]

It is interesting (and urgently important for us to understand in the modern world) that these ancient traditions of liberty and freedom both entailed obligations and responsibilities. But they did so differently. The gift of *libertas* and *eleutheria* brought with it an obligation to act in a wise and responsible way—not as a libertine. A person with liberty was responsible for his own acts.

A person who was born to freedom in an ancient tribe had a sacred obligation to serve and support the *folk,* and to keep the customs of a free people, and to respect the rights of others on pain of banishment. In modern America too many people have forgotten this side of our inheritance. They think of liberty as license without responsibility, and freedom as entitlement without obligation. To think this way in the modern world is to remember only half of these ancient traditions.

With the coming of Christianity, ancient ideas of liberty and freedom acquired new imperatives and new layers of meaning. They were discussed in the four Gospels, and especially in the Book of John, which tells of a conversation between Jesus and a group of Jews. Jesus told them, "Ye shall know the Truth and the Truth shall make you free." They did not understand his meaning, and replied, "We be Abraham's seed, and were never in bondage to any man: how sayest thou, Ye shall be made free?" Jesus answered, "Verily, I say unto you, whosoever committeth sin is the servant of sin. . . . If the son therefore shall make you free, ye shall be free indeed."[36]

The English translators of the King James Bible rendered the word of Jesus as free, but in earlier texts it was the Greek *eleutheros* and the Latin *liber*. It meant a release from the bondage of sin. Roman Catholics later called this idea "Christian liberty" and linked it to a theology of absolution in the sense of "a formal release from guilt or obligation," remission in the meaning of "a release from sin," and deliverance as an idea of liberation from the world.

In another application, the teachings of Christ were taken in a different direction. They became the spiritual equivalent of North European freedom and came to mean a connectedness to Christ and an obligation to do His work in the world. The great example was Paul's triumphant cry: "Am I not an apostle? Am I not free? Have I not seen Jesus Christ our Lord? Are not ye my work in the Lord?"[37]

German Protestants and English Puritans were raised in this Pauline tradition of Christianity. Martin Luther was working within it when he wrote *Die Freiheit eines Christenmenschen*, "The Freedom of a Christian Person" (1520), which was the freedom to work for Christ in the world and to be joined to him and even to become one with Him. This also brought a great responsibility to a believing Christian. Luther summarized his idea of freedom in two sentences: "A Christian is a perfectly free lord of all, subject to none. A Christian is a perfectly dutiful servant of all, subject to all." To a modern reader, these two thoughts are contradictory. For Luther, with his ancestral idea of freedom, they were one.[38]

In the Protestant Reformation, Martin Luther developed this idea in another way that showed the persistent power of an old folkway. He was troubled by the conflicts that his ideas had caused and argued that the freedom of a Christian should be understood as love for others: *"Freiheit als Liebe,"* freedom as love, a bond between believers and the loving gift of God. This idea became a major theme in Luther's writing. It was taken up by Protestant reformers after him and has reverberated through the ages. Some of its strongest expressions appeared in English Puritan ideas of "soul freedom," which meant the freedom that grew from unity with

God and oneness with His Spirit. Soul freedom was thought to be a gift of God, which no mortal power could take away. Christian beliefs added a new imperative to old traditions in Western thought. The relationship of these ideas to one another might be summarized in a simple table.[39]

	The Mediterranean World	The North European World
general ideas	liberty, libertas, *eleutheria* (separation, release)	freedom, *Freiheit, folcfre* (kinship to free people)
legal possessions	*ius, fas, privilegium* (that which may be given)	right, *folcricht* (that which must be given)
religious belief	liberty of conscience (released from restraints)	soul freedom (becoming one with God)
social obligations	to use one's independence responsibly, i.e., not as a libertine	to serve and support a free folk, and to respect the rights of others who are free

Each term in the left column comes from Latin and Greek. Every word to the right is North European in origin. When the words in each column are joined, two constellations of thought emerge. North European traditions centered on freedom as a form of belonging and rights of connection to a community of free people. They imply tribal membership, and the existence of inalienable rights among all freeborn people. The Mediterranean tradition of liberty is an idea of separation and independence. It is an idea of hierarchy, in the variable possession of privileges that might be given or taken away by a higher power.

In analytic passages throughout this book we shall use the two words liberty and freedom in their original and literal meanings. Liberty will refer to ideas of independence, separation, and autonomy for individuals or groups. Freedom will mean rights of belonging and full membership in a community of free people (whether a tribe, a nation, or humanity itself). The phrase "liberty and freedom" will also appear. It refers to the entire range of modern ideas that combine elements of these ancient ideas in many different forms.

Other passages in this book include quotations from primary and secondary sources where liberty and freedom are used in other ways. In the nineteenth and twentieth centuries, writers in English often employed them interchangeably. But echoes of ancient origins have also persisted in a complex pattern of modern usage. They are the product of a long history, which is the unique heritage of English-speaking people.

Two Ideas to Many: The Importance of Having Been English

Every Western language has words such as liberty or freedom, but only one language employs them both in common speech. German, Dutch, and Scandinavian cultures have freedom but not liberty. Spanish, French, and Italian have liberty but not freedom. Philosopher Hannah Pitkin writes, "Speakers of English have a unique opportunity: they get to choose between 'liberty' and 'freedom.' No other European language, ancient or modern, offers such a choice."[40]

This heritage of English-speaking people has created a distinctive dynamism in their thought about liberty and freedom. At the same time, it is a stimulus to creativity, an invitation to conflict, and a driver of change. The people of early modern England spoke of liberty and freedom in the same breath, in phrases that ring strangely in a modern ear. One of Shakespeare's characters in *Julius Caesar* (ca. 1599) cried, "Liberty, freedom, and enfranchisement."[41]

During the English Civil Wars in the seventeenth century, men on both sides coupled freedom and liberty in the same way, even as they disagreed about their meaning. In 1649, King Charles I said defiantly of his subjects as they were about to cut off his head, "Truly, I desire their liberty and freedom as much as anybody whatsoever, but I must tell you that their liberty and freedom consists in having government." He used both words together in his last breath, but he was thinking mainly of a classical and hierarchical idea of *libertas* as specific privileges or exemptions that flowed from higher authority.

The King's Puritan opponents also coupled liberty and freedom in their speech, but with a different meaning. At the Putney Debates in Cromwell's New Model Army (1647–49), Colonel Thomas Rainborough declared, "The poorest man in England is not at all bound in a strict sense to that government that he hath not had a voice to himself under... if we can agree where the liberty and freedom of the people lies, that will do all." Colonel Rainborough's "liberty and freedom" meant the rights of all freeborn Englishmen and an idea of belonging to a community of free people. Here again, the use of "liberty and freedom" in one phrase was not a repetition for rhetorical effect. It engaged the entire heritage of English-speaking people in a single thought. Both Cavaliers and Roundheads laid claim to this dual legacy, with different ideas in mind.[42]

In the mid-seventeenth century, another usage appeared among English philosophers, who studied liberty and freedom as abstractions that existed apart from time and tradition. These writers had little interest in patterns of historical usage and gave those ideas new meanings of their own invention. In their works liberty and freedom were no longer yoked together but began to be used separately and interchangeably as "liberty or freedom," as two philosophical terms with the same meaning. This usage rapidly entered intellectual discourse.

A leading example is Thomas Hobbes, who wrote in his *Leviathan,* "Liberty or freedom signifieth, properly, the absence of opposition; by opposition, I mean external impediments of motion." Hobbes used liberty or freedom as synonyms. He created his own definition of both words for the particular purposes of his argument. Like many philosophers after him, he had no interest in the history of these ideas. Hobbes was entirely absorbed in the refinement of his own abstractions.[43]

But ancient differences between liberty and freedom were not so easily erased. Even as the distinction between them became blurred or disappeared altogether in Hobbes's *Leviathan,* older tensions of meaning persisted in the folk memory of English-speaking people. These tensions gave rise to a broad range of questions about the meaning of the singular abstraction that Hobbes called "freedom or liberty." Was it an idea of separation, or connection, or both, or neither? Did it belong to everyone, or to a chosen few? Was it tribal, or truly universal? Was it a right, or merely a privilege? Was it one general condition of liberty or freedom, or a bundle of specific liberties or freedoms? What did it include?

In folk traditions of liberty and freedom throughout the English-speaking world, these questions gave rise to a startling creativity of thought. What happened was not a persistence of two fixed ideas of liberty and freedom but something more complex and infinitely more interesting. Elements of both traditions began to be combined in different forms. Some, as we shall see, were very near the classical idea of *libertas.* Others were close to the North European tradition of *Freiheit.* Most were neither one thing nor the other but something new in the world. Altogether, English-speaking people invented many versions of liberty and freedom, which became folkways in their own right.

Many Ideas to One Tradition: Liberty and Freedom in America

This heritage of English-speaking people was carried to America by British colonists. It took root in the New World and persisted through many generations, from the earliest English settlements in the late sixteenth century to the War of Independence 190 years later. Ancient patterns of English speech were heard anew at Fort Ticonderoga early on the morning of May 10, 1775, when a band of Yankee farmers marched boldly toward the biggest fortress in British America, brushed its sentries aside, and captured its sleeping garrison in their beds. In a moment they were masters of the fort's hundred guns and a large supply of liquor. Their leader, Ethan Allen, wrote that they "tossed about the flowing bowl, and wished success to Congress, and the liberty and freedom of America."[44]

Here was that old double usage again, "liberty and freedom" in a new age of revolution. These taciturn New Englanders were not in the habit of rhetorical redundancy. They were known for thrift in words, but in 1775 they felt it necessary to invoke both words together. In their speech we hear the echo of a distant folk memory, and the special heritage of English-speaking people.

But what did those old words mean in the New World? To follow this line of inquiry is to find an astonishing variety of beliefs about liberty and freedom in early English settlements. Another inquiry, published as *Albion's Seed* (from which this work has grown), found evidence of at least four distinct ideas of liberty and freedom in Puritan New England, Cavalier Virginia, Quakers in the Delaware Valley, and North British borderers in the American backcountry. Once planted in the soil of the New World these ideas began to flourish, and American spaces provided growing room for many more. All were spoken of as "liberty and freedom," but they drew differently on that complex heritage.[45]

The diversity of these ideas and the complexity of their history compound our problem of coming to terms with Captain Preston. The confident ring of his speech and the boldness of his acts suggest that he was clear in his own mind about what freedom and liberty meant to him. Like Cromwell's russet-coated captain, Captain Preston "knew what he fought for, and loved what he knew." But how can we discover by an empirical method the ideas that were in his mind?

Visions and Images

Men such as Captain Preston did not write extended texts and treatises on liberty and freedom that might be analyzed by academic methods. But they left an abundance of evidence that might be studied in other ways. When Captain Preston and his comrades marched against the Regulars in 1775, they carried images of liberty and freedom into battle. Complex symbols of these ideas were painted on their battle flags, etched into their musket stocks, carved upon their powder horns, and embroidered on their coats and hats. Other images appeared in prints and paintings that hung on the walls of their homes.

In a strict and literal sense, Captain Preston and his comrades *envisioned* their ideas of liberty and freedom. They tended to represent their visions in the form of symbols and images. A symbol might be understood as a vehicle for thinking and as a device for transporting thought from one mind to another. More than that, an image does not merely communicate a vision. It can also create it, transform it, and persuade others to adopt it. Some images take on the character of sacred objects. When that happens, symbols become icons, which not merely signify but sanctify thought. They are regarded with reverence and protected from pollution.

Even as Captain Preston and many New England soldiers carried images of liberty and freedom, they were also able to read and write. In 1775, they were one of the first armies in history in which most of the rank and file were literate. Nearly all American images of liberty and freedom were invented by literate people. In their symbols, words and images often appeared together and became mutually explanatory. The old cliché that one image is worth ten thousand words also runs in reverse. Words such as liberty and freedom have inspired ten thousand images. It is certainly true, as Bazarov declared in Turgenev's *Fathers and Sons,* that "one picture will show me vividly something which a book would take all of ten pages to explain."[46] But to study a picture without a caption, and then to read the caption itself, is to discover that a few words can reveal the meaning of a picture as dramatically as the raising of a curtain. Images did not lose their importance with the growth of literacy. The more textual and hypertextual the modern world becomes, the more important are images in the explication of text, and the more useful is text for the understanding of images.

Further, words and texts have ways of becoming images. The great American documents of freedom and liberty are more often seen than read, and they have become icons in their own right. On the other hand, images have become texts, to be studied as closely as a written document. That is what we are about here. This inquiry is about the interplay of word and image, and about learning to decode their meanings by an historical method.

America's history has left a vast trove of materials for this project. An abundance of sources allows us to observe ideas and images in the process of formation. Most American images of liberty and freedom were deliberately and consciously invented. In many cases it is possible to discover the exact moment of invention, the identity of the inventor, and the intended meaning. Every American image of liberty and freedom has a story behind it. The purpose of this book is to tell those tales, one by one, in a way that centers on individual actions, deliberate choices, and contingent events.

At the same time, all of these stories come together in a larger story. It will be told here with several narrative lines, all braided together. One is about the continuing importance of liberty and freedom in all American generations. Another is about multiple meanings in every generation, and contested meanings in most. A third is about change and growth, as every American generation has enlarged the meaning of liberty and freedom.

Altogether, the central theme of this book can be summarized in two sentences. What made America free, and keeps it growing more so, was not any single vision of liberty and freedom but the interplay of many visions. Together, these many ideas made America more free than any one American ever was, or wished to be.

EARLY AMERICA
Visions of the Founders, 1607–1775

James Pike's Powder Horn, 1776. Chicago Historical Society.

THE LOYAL NINE AND THE LIBERTY TREE

New England Visions of Collective Rights and Individual Responsibilities

> Preserve the common Liberty. . . . The publick Liberty
> must be preserved though at the expense of many lives.
>
> —SAMUEL ADAMS, 1775[1]

IN THE WINTER OF 1775–76, a New England soldier named James Pike made himself a powder horn. It was a work of art, elaborately decorated in an old tradition of Yankee horn carving. On one side he carved his name and a scene that explained why he took up arms in the American Revolution. It showed the start of the war at Lexington and Concord as an attack by "Regulars, the Aggressors" against "Provincials, Defending." The first musket ball of the Revolution appeared in mid-flight, carefully marked with an arrow to show that a Redcoat had fired it. Directly in its path was an image labeled the "Liberty Tree."[2]

The meaning was very clear in every way but one. It is curious that James Pike thought of liberty as a tree. This is not a symbol that comes to modern minds, but it was popular in New England. To seek its origin is to find an old tradition of liberty and freedom, one of many that flourished in early America.

The story of the Liberty Tree begins in Boston, early on the morning of August 14, 1765. The inhabitants were up before the sun, as was their Yankee custom. It was Thursday, market day, and farmers were streaming into town. Heavy carts rumbled along Orange Street (now Washington) past the house of Deacon Jacob Elliott and his grove of old elm trees.[3]

In the half light of dawn, a passerby glanced at the largest of these trees and was amazed to see a body hanging from a branch. People began to gather around the tree. As the light improved, they discovered that the body was an effigy, marked with the initials A.O., which everyone took to be Andrew Oliver, a Boston merchant who had agreed to collect the new Stamp Tax that Parliament had levied on the colonies. Pinned to the effigy was a verse:

> *Fair Freedoms glorious cause I've meanly quitted,*
> *For the sake of self;*
> *But ah! the Devil has me outwitted.*
> *And instead of* stamping *others, I've* hangd *myself.*[4]

Beside the effigy was a big riding boot, which many recognized as a visual pun on the earl of Bute, a Scottish aristocrat who was thought to be the moving spirit behind the Stamp Tax. The boot was "stuffed with representation," according to one eyewitness. Climbing out of the boot-top was a grinning image of the Devil himself, with an evil gleam in his malevolent eye and the Stamp Act clutched in his sinister claw.[5]

Stitched to the bottom of the boot was a bright green sole. Green had long been the color of liberty and freedom in English folklore, since the day of Robin Hood and his Green Men in the fourteenth century. Rural rebels in Kent and East Anglia wore sprigs of greenery in their caps during the sixteenth century. The first English Whigs (as friends of liberty and freedom were called) organized themselves as the Green Ribbon Club in the seventeenth century.[6]

As the morning wore on, the crowd at Deacon Elliott's tree grew larger. Its size alarmed the governor, who sent for the lieutenant governor, who summoned the sheriff of Suffolk County, who ordered his deputies to cut down the effigy. They came running back to report they "could not do it without imminent danger to their lives."

The governor asked who had done this thing and was told that it was the work of a small club of Boston Whigs called the Loyal Nine. He would have known them, for they were men of property and standing. One was Benjamin Edes, printer of the *Boston Gazette*. The others included merchant Henry Bass and ship's captain Joseph Field, jeweler George Trott and painter Thomas Crafts, braziers Stephen Cleverly and John Smith, and rum distillers Thomas Chase and John Avery. They were town-born men, descended from the Puritan Migration. The Loyal Nine owed their loyalty not only to one another but to a close-knit community that was five generations old in 1765.[7]

The Loyal Nine were like many tavern clubs in that era. John Adams attended one of their meetings, though he was not a member. "We had Punch, Wine, Pipes and Tobacco, Bisquit and Cheese—&c," he wrote. "I heard nothing but such conversation as passes at all Clubbs among Gentlemen about the Times."[8]

The times were not good on the night of August 13, 1765, when these men met in Thomas Chase's distillery, across the street from Deacon Elliott's house. The colonies were caught in a world depression, and a hard-pressed British Parliament had imposed the new Stamp Tax without their consent, when they could least afford to pay. Every member of the Loyal Nine was directly threatened by it. For printer Benjamin Edes it meant a tax on every issue of his newspaper and another of two shillings on "every advertizement in any gazette," enough to put him out of business. The artisans and merchants would be hit with stamp taxes on every contract, indenture, and bill of sale. Distillers Thomas Chase and John Avery would owe a tax of four pounds on licenses to sell rum, and John Adams would pay ten pounds for a license to practice law. All of them would be liable for stamp taxes of two pounds on any school diploma, four pounds on any militia commission, and six pounds on "any grant of any liberty, privilege or franchise." Liberty itself was taxed by the new Stamp Act, which was more than a revenue measure. It was a crude attempt at social engineering by British leaders who believed that the American colonies had too many newspapers, schools, lawyers, and liberties.[9]

The Loyal Nine talked of these things on the night of August 13, 1765, and probably consumed some more than a little of Thomas Chase's rum punch. By morning, Deacon Elliott's tree was decorated with signs of their displeasure. Their work caused a sensation in Boston. Merchant John Rowe wrote in his diary, "A great number of people assembled at Deacon Elliot's corner this morning to see the Stamp Officer hung in effigy with a libel on the breast, on Deacon Elliot's tree."[10]

The spirit of the crowd was at first happy, even festive. Farmers who came to town were asked to have their goods stamped by the effigy, which was done in high good humor. The children were out of school, and hundreds began to parade around the tree. A spectator wrote, "You would have laughed to have seen two or three hundred little boys with a Flagg marching in procession, on which was the King, Pitt, and Liberty."[11]

Through the afternoon there was a carnival of laughter, and also much serious talk of "fair freedom" and "lost liberty." It is interesting that the Loyal Nine represented these ideas as the very opposite of Andrew Oliver's striving for "the sake of self." Here was a New England vision of "publick liberty," combined with "personal security, personal liberty and private property." It was a combination of collective rights and individual responsibilities, very different from our modern ideas of collective responsibility and individual entitlement.[12]

At sunset the crowd at the tree grew larger, and its mood changed. Fifty "gentlemen actors" appeared, "disguised in Trawsers and Jackets," the dress of day laborers. They cut down the effigy, stuffed it in a coffin, and carried it through the town in a funeral procession. Behind them marched a long column of Boston men, shouting "Liberty and Property," and stamping their feet in unity. They marched to the governor's mansion and gave a cheer so loud that the occupants came running out in alarm. Then they went to the Old State House, where the governor's council was meeting, and rattled its windows with three huzzas, the ancient British battle cry. The procession turned down King Street to Kilby Street, where Andrew Oliver had put up a building that was said to be his Stamp Office. In five minutes, the men of Boston pulled it to pieces with their bare hands and carried the pieces away. They marched on to Andrew Oliver's home, broke its windows, and burned the effigy in a bonfire made from the Stamp Office.

When that work was done, the "gentlemen actors" withdrew. Bottles began to fly from hand to hand, and the crowd became a drunken mob, dancing like Furies around the flames. When the liquor ran low, they returned to Andrew Oliver's house, broke into his wine cellar, and drank it dry. They also smashed his furniture and scattered his silver in an alcoholic fury but made a point of taking nothing except the wine. In Boston even this drunken mob was careful to respect the rights of property.

The sheriff and lieutenant governor tried bravely to intervene but were driven away in by a volley of stones. The governor ordered the militia officers to beat the alarm and was told that "all the drummers of the regiment were in the mob." The riot continued past midnight.[13]

The next morning Andrew Oliver asked to be excused from his office. Triumphant signs and shining lamps blossomed on Deacon Elliott's elm. The Loyal Nine became heroes in the town, and they grew into a much larger group called the Sons of Liberty. Hundreds of Bostonians became members. On September 11, 1765, they met in celebration beneath their tree and fastened a copper plate on its trunk with words in gold, "The Tree of Liberty." Each Son of Liberty was given a silver medal with an image of Deacon Elliott's elm.[14]

They called it a Liberty Tree, not a Freedom Tree. The logic of this movement against Parliament led the Revolutionary generation to speak

The Liberty Tree, engraving, 1774. Bostonian Society/ Old State House.

mostly of liberty in its classical sense of separation. Boston's town-born men understood that idea in terms of both individual rights of property and collective rights of self-government and the rule of law, which Samuel Adams called "the liberty of Boston," "the liberty of New England," and "the liberty of America."

As a symbol of that cause, the Liberty Tree instantly became a Boston institution. The open space beneath its branches was named Liberty Hall and used for many purposes, public and private. Tradesmen posted commercial notices on its trunk. One of the Loyal Nine invited his customers "to call and receive their respective dues of T. Chase at the venerable Liberty-elm."[15]

The example of Boston's "venerable Liberty-elm" inspired other Liberty Trees in New England. During the spring of 1766, John Adams was passing Brackett's Tavern in the town of Braintree when he came on an old buttonwood or sycamore tree with a sign, "The Tree of Liberty; Cursed is he who cuts this Tree." Adams wrote in his diary, "I never heard an Hint of it, till I saw it, but I hear that some persons grumble, and threaten to girdle it."[16]

Liberty Trees appeared in Cambridge, Petersham, Roxbury, Norwich, Newport, Providence, and many other towns. In southeastern New England some were buttonwoods. Connecticut preferred oaks. Boston, Providence, Roxbury, and Cambridge chose elms. Whatever the species, New England's Liberty Trees were giants of old growth, deeply rooted in the soil of the New World. The Liberty Elm in Providence was so big that it was dedicated from a large platform in its upper branches.[17]

They also spread to other colonies as far south as Savannah, Georgia.
Marylanders adopted a tulip tree in Annapolis. In 1766, the people of
South Carolina favored a live oak. Boston was their inspiration.
Charleston's *South Carolina Gazette* reported that "Mechanicks and other
inhabitants" met beneath "a most noble Live Oak Tree in Mr. Mazyck's
pasture, which they formally dedicated to LIBERTY, and drank toasts
to their colleagues in Massachusetts."[18]

Most Liberty Trees were in New England, and some were not pleas-
ing to the Whigs who invented them. Tory leader Thomas Hutchinson
observed that sometimes "the spirit of liberty spread where it was not
intended." When Harvard's faculty cracked down on chapel violations in
1768, the students gathered beneath a great elm in Harvard Yard, called it
their Liberty Tree, and resolved that the actions of the faculty were
"unconstitutional." Peaceful protest failed, and the students imitated a
Boston mob. They stoned the windows of their teachers, and the ring-
leaders were promptly expelled. Three undergraduate classes responded
by declaring their independence from Harvard. The fourth threatened to
transfer to Yale. That desperate act awakened the sleepy Harvard Corporation, who readmitted the rioters but kept the chapel rules in force. The
legitimacy of this academic insurrection was never acknowledged. Harvard's Liberty Tree would always be remembered as "Rebellion Elm,"
much to the gratification of Tories such as Thomas Hutchinson.[19]

The Iconography of the Liberty Tree

Why did old trees become symbols of liberty and freedom? Why New
England? Why Deacon Elliott's elm tree in particular? Part of the answer,
no longer obvious today, may be found in the appearance of a mature
American elm. Before the twentieth century, when Dutch elm disease
ravaged this species, an ancient elm was an inspiring sight. Its limbs
soared upward in long sweeping curves, like the tracery of a Gothic
cathedral.[20] A massive trunk and gnarled bark made it a symbol of great
age. Elms were thought to be more durable than most mortal things.
London Bridge was built of elmwood that was thought to last a thousand
years. Early Christians worshiped beneath elms that became emblems of
eternal life.[21]

In America, old elms also became symbols of community and were
used for public gatherings. William Penn made his treaty with the Indians beneath Shackamaxon Elm, a tree of "prodigious size." Artist Benjamin West wrote that it was "held in the highest veneration," and he

made it prominent in his paintings. The founders of Kentucky also met under a great elm, "surrounded by a turf of fine white clover," which served as their first "church, state-house, council chamber."[22]

In the English-speaking world, old trees of many species also had another meaning. They symbolized ancient folk-rights of freedom and liberty. The oaks of Sherwood Forest were emblems of Robin Hood's legendary struggle against the tyrannical sheriff of Nottingham. In 1450, Jack Cade's Rebellion in the east of England took an oak tree for its emblem. A century later, in the Norfolk Rising of 1549, Robert and William Ket administered justice under a great tree called "the Oak of Reformation." These events were remembered in Boston when Deacon Elliott's elm became the Liberty Tree. Massachusetts governor Francis Bernard wrote in 1768, "This tree has often put me in mind of Jack Cade's Oak of Reformation [sic]." The folk memory was strong even when the facts were garbled.[23]

Connecticut's Charter Oak, lithograph by E. C. Kellogg, ca. 1830–42. Connecticut Historical Society, Hartford.

New Englanders also had memories of Connecticut's Charter Oak, where the people of that colony were said to have hidden their fundamental laws from Royal Governor Sir Edmund Andros when he tried to take them away in 1687. Deacon Elliott's elm had a direct connection with the founders of Massachusetts. The plaque on its trunk noted that it had been planted in 1646 by the first settlers of the town.[24]

The builders of the Bay Colony had chosen a tree for their symbol as early as 1652, when they minted silver coins with crude images called the Willow, Oak, and Pine Tree designs. It was a bold act. The minting of money was a closely guarded prerogative of the Crown, and Charles II was angry with Massachusetts for usurping his authority. The colony's agent at court, Sir William Temple, used the tree on the coins as a defense. He tugged a Pine Tree Shilling from his pocket and showed it to the king, who asked what sort of tree it was. Temple explained it was "the Royal Oak which preserved your Majesty's life," a reference to the hollow tree in which the king had hidden after the battle of Worcester in 1651. That answer so pleased the king that he laughed heartily and called the New Englanders "a parcel of honest dogs."[25]

A tree remained the symbol of Massachusetts for many years. During the colonial wars, military colors in the province showed a green tree on a white canton. Sometimes the tree was cradled in the arms of a cross of St. George. Other flags displayed

Massachusetts Pine Tree Shilling, 1652, obverse and reverse. American Numismatic Society.

the tree alone and omitted the cross, which some believed to be idolatrous. These associations linked the Liberty Tree to the history of New England.[26]

The Liberty Tree also had an association with the American environment. An orator in Providence called it a symbol of "that Liberty which our Forefathers sought out, and found under Trees, and in the Wilderness." All of these meanings came together in a vision of liberty and freedom that was unique to New England.[27]

The Uses of the Liberty Tree

From the start, the Liberty Tree was a political instrument for uniting the communities of New England in the Patriot cause. In Boston it became a stage for political theatricals. During the winter of 1766, Whig leaders built a mock courtroom beneath the Liberty Tree, complete with a judge's bench, a jury box, a gallows with the Devil perched on the top beam, and effigies of Bute and Grenville chained to each post. A stamp in chains was indicted for "breach of Magna Charta," found guilty of "a design to subvert the British Constitution," and burned at the gallows before two thousand people.[28]

In the spring of 1766, Bostonians learned that the Stamp Act was at last repealed. The Liberty Tree was transformed into a symbol of loyalty to the Crown and decorated with Union Jacks. In the night 108 lanterns appeared on its branches to honor members of Parliament who voted for repeal.[29]

But in 1767 Parliament taxed the colonies again with the Townshend Duties and sent new customs officers to Boston. The Union Jacks were hauled down, and a red flag of alarm was raised on the Liberty Tree. The customs men were hanged in effigy on March 17, 1768. When these hated men confiscated John Hancock's sloop *Liberty,* a Boston mob seized their boat in retaliation, dragged it to the Liberty Tree, then burned it on the

Common. The crowds kept growing. On June 13, 1768, a Whig demonstration at the Liberty Tree attracted four thousand, which equaled the entire male population of Boston. Governor Francis Bernard thought it "a larger number than was ever known on any occasion." The scale of these events added another meaning to the Liberty Tree. It became a symbol of the town and its collective rights, in the old New England way.[30]

In the ebb and flow of politics, Boston Whigs used the Liberty Tree to regulate popular opinion. A balance was not easy to maintain. In 1765, 1770, and 1773, the Whig movement ran to excesses of violence that weakened the cause. At other times in 1766, 1771, and 1772, British policy became less

Liberty Tree Lamp, ca. 1766. Bostonian Society/Old State House.

threatening, and moderates lost interest. The rituals at the Liberty Tree were devices for maintaining continuity and preserving unity. The emblems of this idea were "union flags" that flew from Liberty Trees as symbols of a common identity and signals for collective action.[31]

Every year the Sons of Liberty honored the fourteenth of August as the birthday of the Liberty Tree, and the day became a Boston holiday. John Adams attended an annual celebration in 1769 that began at the Liberty Tree and moved to Dorchester's Sign of the Liberty Tree Tavern, where 355 Sons of Liberty dined together in an open field. Adams observed, "To the honour of the Sons, I did not see one person intoxicated, or near it," no small feat as they drank fourteen toasts at the Liberty Tree and forty-five more after dinner. He added, "This is cultivating the sensations of Freedom. . . . [James] Otis and [Samuel] Adams are politick in promoting these festivals, for they tinge the minds of the people, they impregnate them with the sentiments of liberty. They render the people fond of their leaders in the Cause, and averse and bitter against all opposers."[32]

"The Tree Ordeal": The Liberty Tree as a Device for Suppressing Dissent

From the beginning, Bostonians saw no contradiction between a fierce defense of their own rights and the persecution of aliens and dissenters.

A Tory View of the Liberty Tree: "The Bostonians Paying the Excise-Man, or, Tarring & Feathering," the ordeal of customs informer John Malcolm in a print attributed to Philip Dawe, London, October 31, 1774. Colonial Williamsburg Foundation.

A Whig View of the Liberty Tree: "The Bostonians in Distress," on the Coercive Acts that closed the port of Boston and were enforced by British troops and warships; copy of a print attributed to John Marlin Will, London, November 19, 1774. Image donated by Corbis/Bettmann.

That attitude had appeared in the banishment of Roger Williams, the exile of Anne Hutchinson, and the hanging of Quaker missionary Mary Dyer. It persisted into the American Revolution, and Loyalists became the leading victims. In Boston, the place of persecution was the Liberty Tree. It was a site for rituals of humiliation that Peter Oliver (brother of Andrew) called "the Tree Ordeal."[33]

In the fall of 1765, the Sons of Liberty heard that Andrew Oliver had talked of withdrawing his resignation as stampmaster. He was ordered to appear at the Liberty Tree and renounce his office forever. Oliver agreed to resign at the State House but was told that it must be done at the Liberty Tree. In fear of his life, Andrew Oliver went to the tree in a driving rain and made "public resignation under oath," while torrents of water descended through the Liberty Tree and rituals of shame were heaped upon him by a howling crowd of a thousand soggy but exultant Whigs.[34]

The Sons of Liberty of Boston did not have a liberal attitude toward their opponents. This New England town had a tribal spirit that was often xenophobic, sometimes anti-Catholic, and occasionally anti-Semitic. In 1766, a man refused to pay a creditor because a court order had not been stamped. The Sons of Liberty proposed to circumcise him, because "the man could not have been a Christian, and therefore, must have been a Jew." He quickly paid his debt.[35]

In 1774, customs officer John Malcom was tarred and feathered and carted to the Liberty Tree. The spout of a teapot was thrust down his throat, and he was forced to drink a toast in tea to every member of the royal family until he nearly exploded. Later he presented Parliament with a piece of his own skin, still tarred and feathered, in hope of winning a pension. Loyalist drawings of these events showed the Liberty Tree as an emblem of cruelty, terror, and mob rule. They made an argument that New England's vision of liberty and freedom was another face of tyranny.[36]

The Liberty Tree became so hateful to Loyalists that they vowed to destroy it. Their opportunity came in the summer of 1775, after the town passed under British control and many Whigs fled to the country. In their absence a mob of Tories and Regulars attacked the Liberty Tree and cut it down. It was so large that it yielded fourteen cords of firewood. A leader of the Tory mob was reported killed by a falling limb, which was thought by Whigs to be a sign. Nothing remained of the Liberty Tree but a broken stump.[37]

"The Battle of Bunker's Hill," a painting completed in 1786 by John Trumbull, an eyewitness to the battle. This is one of the few contemporary American images of a Liberty Tree flag. Yale University Art Gallery.

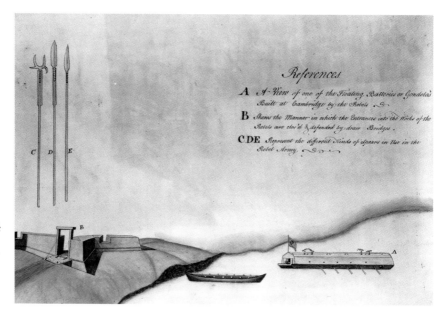

A New England floating battery, flying a Liberty Tree Flag at the siege of Boston, 1775, pen-and-ink drawing by British military cartographer Charles Blaskowitz. Library of Congress.

After the British army was driven out of Boston in 1776, the Whigs preserved what little remained of the tree and made it a landmark in the town. A broadside in 1782 was advertised as "to be sold near Liberty Stump." When Lafayette visited Boston he was taken to visit it. Many cultures have worshiped trees, but Boston was unique in its reverence for a shattered stump, which became a double symbol of American rights and British tyranny.[38]

The Liberty Tree as a Weapon of War

In the War of Independence, the Liberty Tree became the leading symbol of the Patriot cause in New England. Private soldiers carried its image as a talisman.[39] At Bunker Hill, the battle flags of Massachusetts regiments displayed liberty trees of several species. An eyewitness to that event was artist John Trumbull. His painting of the battle centered on a flag with a red field, white canton, and green liberty tree.[40]

The Provincial Council of Massachusetts adopted another Liberty Tree Flag as the official ensign of the colony. It showed a broad deciduous tree of great age, very much like Deacon Elliott's elm, with the motto, "An Appeal to Heaven." During the siege of Boston, a British sketch showed this flag flying over New England batteries. By October 1775, all American vessels in New England waters were ordered to fly Liberty Tree

Flags so that "they may know one another." Massachusetts ships adopted it as their naval ensign.[41]

The Liberty Tree in Other Cultures

As the fame of the Liberty Tree spread beyond New England, its symbolic meaning changed. An example appeared in Philadelphia on September 16, 1775, when Thomas Paine published a verse about the Liberty Tree. As a piece of poetry, it explains why we remember him for his prose. But the imagery is interesting:

> *In a chariot of light, from the regions of the day,*
> *The goddess of liberty came,*
> *Ten thousand celestials directed her way.*
> *And hither conducted the dame.*
> *A fair budding branch from the gardens above,*
> *Where millions with millions agree,*
> *She brought in her hand as a pledge of her love,*
> *And the plant she named Liberty Tree.*
> *The celestial exotic stuck deep in the ground . . .*

French arbres de la liberté *were often shown as small, fragile saplings unlike New England's sturdy old-growth Liberty Trees. © Photothèque des Musées de la Ville de Paris.*

Tom Paine was a British radical, recently arrived from London. His idea of a Liberty Tree was different from New England's. Where Boston's Liberty elms were old giants of great growth, Paine described the Liberty Tree as a newly planted "fair budding branch" and "celestial exotic."[42] That way of thinking came to be widely shared in Europe. During the French Revolution, many towns planted *arbres de la liberté* as young saplings in symmetrical rows. Irish and German radicals did the same thing.[43] In the French countryside, the *arbre de la liberté* was grafted on the peasant custom of the *mai sauvage* in which a young tree was stripped of its branches and used as a maypole in spring rituals of renewal. Historian Mona Ozouf observes that this rural folkway signified "taking leave of the old world and welcoming the birth of the new." In New England, the only people who associated Liberty Trees with maypoles and "the birth of the new" were Tories who cut them down. There was a double irony here. In the Old World, liberty was symbolized as something new,

Massachusetts Pine Tree and Liberty Tree Flags. Top left to bottom right: an unofficial civil flag of New England, ca. 1686–1707; Massachusetts Flag, 18th century; John Trumbull's Bunker Hill flag, 1775; the Appeal to Heaven Flag, 1775; Massachusetts Naval Ensign, 1775; Taunton Liberty and Union Flag, 1774; Standard of the Newburyport Militia, 1775?; Standard of the 13th Massachusetts Continental regiment, 1776. Courtesy of Whitney Smith, © 2003 Flag Research Center; the Newburyport and 13th Massachusetts standards, ca. 1775–76, from Edward Richardson, Standards and Colors of the American Revolution, with permission of the Pennsylvania Society of the Sons of the Revolution.

fresh, and fragile. In the New World it was thought to be old, tough, and very tenacious.[44]

French *arbres de la liberté* were unlike New England Liberty Trees in another way. In a nation that invented *bureaucratie*, they became highly rational symbols of modern society and were elaborately regulated by public authority. The French Convention published strict instructions on how to plant an *arbre de la liberté* and what species it should be, preferably "natural trees from the soil of our free brothers and friends of North America." French towns were ordered to surround their Liberty Trees with iron rails, stone walls, thorn hedges, and thickets of official regulations. French *arbres de la liberté* also inspired equality trees, decorated with masons' levels, which rarely appeared in the New World.[45]

The Old New England Way

The Liberty Trees of New England were distinctive in other ways. They were symbols of a tightly integrated traditional community. An example appeared on the colors of the Thirteenth Continental Foot, a Massachusetts regiment raised in 1776. It showed a Liberty Tree and two soldiers. One was gravely wounded, with blood streaming from his body. He pointed to three children and said, "For Posterity We Bleed." Here was an image of a free community as a bond among people, and between generations.[46]

To this idea New Englanders also added religious symbols, which rarely appeared in French *arbres de la liberté*. A case in point was the flag of the Newburyport militia in 1775, a green ensign with a white canton and a New England Liberty Tree in the center. Surrounding the tree was a chain of thirteen links, held by mailed fists that descended from the clouds, an old Puritan symbol of divine favor.[47] The same imagery appeared on the flag of the Bedford militia, a small crimson standard with a mailed arm descending from heaven, sword in hand. According to town tradition it was made in the seventeenth century and carried into battle on the day of Lexington and Concord.[48]

In 1775, New Englanders carried other old Puritan symbols that were similar in spirit to the Liberty Tree. The emblem of Connecticut was an old vine with three bunches of grapes, inscribed *Qui transtulit sustinet*: "He who transplants, preserves," a biblical reference to the carrying of vines into Israel. This symbol was adopted as early as 1656, to represent the original towns of Hartford, Windsor, and Wethersfield. By the eighteenth century it multiplied into three vines with nine bunches of grapes,

Old New England flags with Puritan motifs, carried in the American Revolution. Top left: colors, 2nd Battalion, 2nd Regiment, Connecticut Regiment, 1775–76; top right: ensign of the Connecticut Navy, 1776; bottom left: anchor standard of the Rhode Island Regiment, ca. 1781; bottom right: standard of the Bedford Militia, 1775–76. Courtesy of Whitney Smith, © Flag Research Center, after originals in Bedford Public Library and the Rhode Island and Connecticut State Houses.

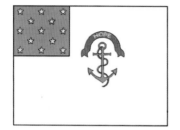

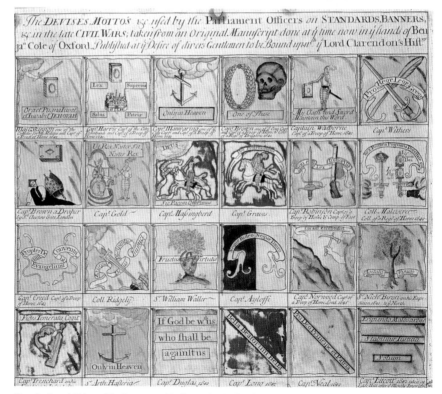

Standards and Colors of Parliamentary Regiments in the English Civil Wars, from a broadside for Clarendon's History of the Great Rebellion, *British Museum. Many of these motifs appeared in New England flags.*

when New Haven and Saybrook colonies joined Connecticut to form the modern state. Above the vines was the Puritan symbol of a disembodied hand that represented God's presence in the world.[49] In 1775, Connecticut men carried these emblems at Bunker Hill. When Dr. Joseph Warren rallied the New England men, he "reminded them of the mottos inscribed on their ensigns: an appeal to heaven and qui transtulit sustinet."[50]

Rhode Island regiments carried yet another Puritan emblem. Their symbol was a sheet anchor, the largest of a ship's anchors, used with its heavy hemp cable when all else failed. In the English Reformation, that symbol acquired a religious meaning. "Christ is the sheet-anker of salvation," Richard Montagu wrote in 1642.[51] In 1647, when the towns of Providence, Portsmouth, Newport, and Warwick united to form Rhode Island, their emblem was the sheet anchor of salvation, with the motto *In te Domine speramus*, "In God we hope," or simply "Hope." In the Revolution, this device appeared on the uniforms of the First Rhode Island Regiment, which included a battalion of former slaves who gave "hope" another meaning.[52]

All of these Puritan symbols had been used by Cromwell's New Model Army in the English Civil Wars. They became part of New England's complex imagery of liberty and freedom: old trees and ancient vines, divine hands and throbbing hearts, chains of unity and anchors of salvation, swords of righteousness and appeals to heaven. These elements shared a similar spirit. They were plain and very austere, without intricate motifs or classical embellishments. By 1775 they were folk symbols, firmly rooted in New England's ancestral ways.[53]

Together, they symbolized an old New England vision that had many names. John Cotton called it "well ordered liberty." Francis Higginson knew it as "soul freedom" and Nathaniel Ward as "free liberty." John Winthrop defined it as "civil or federal liberty to do that only which is good, just or honest."[54] It was a carefully balanced idea of individual and collective rights. John Wise began by proclaim-

Powder horn, with liberty-heart motif. Collection of William Guthman.

ing, "I shall consider every Man in a state of natural Being, as a Free-Born subject under the Crown of Heaven, and owing Homage to none but God himself." But he added quickly, "This Liberty does not consist in a loose or ungovernable Freedom, or in an unbounded license of Acting. . . . They alone live as they Will, who have learnt what they ought to Will."[55]

In New England minds, this vision of liberty and freedom was entirely consistent with the persecution of Quakers and Tories and others who challenged the "common liberty" and "publick liberty." As late as 1775, New Englanders were striving for their own rights, not those of all humanity.[56] But within its narrow limits, New England's vision of liberty and freedom was strong and deep, and difficult for outsiders to comprehend. When the imperial quarrel came to blows, long-serving British officers who thought they knew America discovered how little they understood of this old new world.

THE SONS OF NEPTUNE & THE LIBERTY POLE

New York's Pluralist Vision of a Free America

> It is now as common here to assemble on all occasions
> of public concern at the Liberty Pole and Coffee House
> as for the ancient Romans to repair to the Forum.
>
> —THOMAS GAGE ON NEW YORK CITY, 1770

EIGHT MONTHS after Boston's Loyal Nine invented the Liberty Tree, the Whigs of New York City created another symbol of their rights. It was similar to the Liberty Tree in some ways, but it represented a different tradition of liberty and freedom, as pluralist New York differed from Puritan Boston.

In 1766, these two small colonial seaports were much alike in their material condition, but far apart in their culture and history. Boston was still dominated by descendants of English Puritans who founded tight communities, shared a strong sense of ordered liberty and freedom, and fiercely defended their ancestral ways against outsiders. New York City had long been home to many ethnic groups, and by 1766 all of them were cultural minorities: old Dutch and new English, Germans and French, Irish and Scots, Moravians and Huguenots, a flourishing Jewish community, and one of the largest urban African populations in the New World.

New York's tradition of pluralism began with its Dutch founders early in the seventeenth century. It combined a policy of official toleration with intense ethnic rivalry and bitter religious conflict. Bonds within ethnic groups tended to be close and warm, but relations between them were distant and hostile. These patterns appeared as early as 1624 and still persist in New York City, which for sixteen generations has been a place of extreme ethnic diversity, conflicted class relations, turbulent politics, intense economic competition, enormous energy, abrasive manners, and abusive speech. In all of these ways, Manhattan in the twenty-first century is remarkably similar to descriptions of old New York in the eighteenth century, New Amsterdam in the seventeenth century, and even old Amsterdam in the sixteenth century. The urban folkways of New York City, for all its highly cultivated habit of historical amnesia, have strong linkages to a distant past.[57]

As early as the eighteenth century, New Yorkers shared a distinctive idea of liberty as the autonomy of groups, and of freedom as the right to belong to one's own group within an open society. This way of thinking appeared explicitly in William Livingston's *Independent Reflector* (1752–53), a journal that was "particularly adapted to the Province of New-York."[58] Some historians recognize the *Independent Reflector* for having made the first clear disjunction between "public" and "private" spheres. Livingston opposed "public aids" and "exclusive privileges" for "private parties" and "particular sects." He called this idea "impartial equity" and was thinking of a free society as a plural system in which no group had a hegemony over other groups. This idealized vision of an open society developed at an early date from the reality of life in New York City. It was far removed from the New England way.[59]

The First Liberty Pole

That diversity was evident on May 21, 1766, when New Yorkers celebrated the repeal of the Stamp Act. They organized a public procession, but there were arguments among ethnic and religious groups as to who should march first and "who should be the greatest." They all agreed to sponsor a congratulatory address to the governor, but when the heads of the established Church of England claimed to "speak in the name of the whole," others objected that the Anglicans were merely one "sect" among many and had no right to represent the others.[60]

As part of that celebration, the radical Whigs decided to erect a monument to liberty and freedom. Boston's Liberty Tree was an inspiration to them, but not a model. No self-respecting New Yorker was content to imitate a Yankee. Instead of adopting a tree as the Bostonians had done, the people of Manhattan went a different way. They erected a tall mast that rose high above the rooftops of their town and rigged it with stays and halyards. At its peak, New Yorkers hoisted "a large board fixed on a flag staff, with an inscription that read "George 3rd, Pitt—and Liberty." Other elements would be added later: a flag with the cross of St. George as an emblem of loyalty, a gilded weathervane with the word LIBERTY in large letters, and a liberty cap on top of the pole.[61]

"New York's Liberty Pole, Almshouse, Jail and Commons," drawing by Pierre Eugène Du Simitière, 1770. Library Company of Philadelphia.

This device was thought to be a new invention. Its novelty appeared in the fact that people did not know what to call it. A few spoke of it as New York's Liberty Tree, but that description did not fit. A Whig writer glorified it as the "monument of freedom," but that phrase was too grandiloquent for New Yorkers. A British officer contemptuously called it the "pine post," but this was no ordinary post. Seafaring men thought of it as a mast, which was the model for its construction, but landsmen began to call it the Liberty Pole. That simple name suited the blunt speechways of Manhattan. It quickly caught on.[62]

Inventors of the Liberty Pole: New York's Sons of Neptune

New York's Liberty Pole was largely the work of four Whig leaders: John Lamb, Joseph Allicocke, Isaac Sears, and Alexander McDougall. Their biographies were typical Manhattan stories. All were self-made men, humble in their origins and mixed in their ethnicity. John Lamb was a prosperous wine importer, the son of an English convict who had been transported to Virginia for burglary.[63] Alexander McDougall was a fiery Scottish immigrant who came to New York as a poor seaman, opened a secondhand slop shop on the waterfront, married a woman of means, and became a prosperous merchant.[64] Joseph Allicocke was described as the son of a "mulatto woman," an African American who worked as an employee of British provision contractors in New York and became a merchant in his turn. Isaac Sears was a Connecticut Yankee, the son of an

Alexander McDougall (1732–86), miniature on ivory by John Ramage. The New-York Historical Society.

John Lamb (1735–1800), engraving by Joseph Napoléon Gimbrede. The New-York Historical Society.

oysterman who followed his father's trade, became captain of a small sloop, married a tavernkeeper's daughter, and settled on the New York waterfront. He made a small fortune in privateering during the French and Indian War, became a prosperous merchant, and was called "King Sears" for his influence over sailors and dockworkers.[65]

These men made their own way in the world and earned their living from the sea. None had roots in New York City, but all of them had many friends among the floating population of mariners and merchants who worked along the waterfront. Their origins gave them a strong sense of class consciousness and class conflict, always more pronounced in New York than in other American cities. They had little formal schooling, but they read widely on politics and history and published literate essays with pen names such as Brutus, Plebeian, Vox Populi, and Son of Neptune—very different from Boston pseudonyms such as Puritan, Novanglus, and Publicola.

These young men of New York were radical Whigs, extreme in their devotion to rights of liberty and property within an open society. They were hostile to entrenched elites and not much concerned about law and order. In the words of Joseph Allicocke, they determined "to scourge the base Enemies of our Country and our greatest Darling LIBERTY." Raised in a hard and brutal world, they were quick to use violence against their enemies. The imperial elite in New York City regarded them with fear and loathing. They were highly skilled at the rough-and-tumble game of New York politics and masters at the art of political mobilization. In 1766, it was said that every mob in Manhattan was led by John Lamb, Isaac Sears, Joseph Allicocke, or Alexander McDougall.

Symbolic Associations of the Liberty Pole

These Sons of Neptune were also expert in the manipulation of incendiary images. Together they invented the Liberty Pole as a symbol of liberty and freedom that derived from their values, their experiences, and the character of the town in which they lived. The symbolism of the Liberty Pole began with an ancient image that was familiar throughout the English-speaking world in the eighteenth century. Political cartoons on both sides of the Atlantic commonly represented liberty as a Roman goddess of *libertas*, a timeless figure of great dignity, dressed in a long garment called a *stola* and a cloak called a *palla*. She was distinguished from other Roman goddesses by the things she carried: a long wand called a *vindicta* in one hand, and a soft cap called a *pileus* in the other. As we have seen, both were symbols of emancipation. Roman slaves were released from bondage by a ritual in which a *praetor* touched them with his wand and gave them a stocking cap as a token of their liberty.

This imagery had long been known in early modern Europe. It received fresh attention in the mid-eighteenth century, after German archeologist Johann Joachim Winckelmann found a bas-relief of the goddess of liberty in Roman excavations and published a description in 1766. Similar images often appeared in British publications and circulated through the American colonies. Cartoonists reduced their defining elements to a simple sketch of a liberty cap on the tip of a long wand. By 1766, this image of *libertas* was so familiar throughout the English-speaking world that artists did not need to label it.[66]

In a different form, this motif had also been widely known in the Netherlands at the time of the founding of New Amsterdam in 1624. A work called the *Neder Lantsche Gedenck-Clanck,* or Netherlands Commemorative Anthem, published by Adrianus Valerius in 1626, showed a gathering of Dutch leaders kneeling around a baroque pole that supported a broad-brimmed Dutch burgher's hat. This image became a symbol of Dutch liberty in the long struggle for independence from Spain. Later, a commemorative medal was struck for William of Orange and the Glorious Revolution in 1688. It showed a classical emblem of a tall liberty column, crowned by a liberty cap.[67]

New York's Liberty Pole resembled these models. Its inventors borrowed the Roman goddess's long wand of liberty, modernized it as the

A Dutch Liberty Pole, ca. 1626, from Adrianus Valerius, Nederlantsche Gedenck Clanck *(Haarlem, 1626). Houghton Library, Harvard University.*

Dutch had done, and expanded it in the New York manner into a gigantic Liberty Pole. On the top they placed a liberty flag or liberty vane, or sometimes the image of a large liberty cap carved from a block of wood. Several of these wooden liberty caps survive in a New York museum and private collections.[68]

It is interesting that New Yorkers chose the classical symbol of *libertas* as independence, autonomy, and separation. Their emblem was different from New England's trees and vines and rings and chains that expressed a more organic idea of liberty and freedom as something that belonged to a

Liberty Cap or Pileus, carved in wood and often carried on a pole or wand in public processions. Collection of Richard Hume.

tightly knit community. The Liberty Pole had a meaning that suited the condition of New York, where many ethnic groups lived side by side but never quite together. Their strongest bond was a common desire for liberty to keep their own customs, to worship in their way, and to be secure in their property.

Like most political emblems, New York's Liberty Pole combined its central symbolism with other meanings. It was constructed in the manner of a ship's mast by maritime artisans who represented a social class and had a strong sense of class consciousness. The Liberty Pole came to be associated with that idea, always stronger in New York than other American towns from the seventeenth century to our own time.[69]

Its origin also gave it another significance. Unlike the Liberty Tree, it was a human artifact. Its mast, spars, shrouds, stays, halyards, and blocks made it a human construction that was more mechanical and less organic than New England's favorite symbol.[70]

Further, a Liberty Pole had no roots. It could be constructed anywhere on the spur of the moment and in many different sizes. Some Liberty Poles were bigger than the tallest building in old New York. Others were small enough to be carried by a man or even a child. The Liberty Pole became a versatile symbol of autonomy for an individual, group, sect, class, party, guild, town, colony, or an entire country.

Iconography as History: The Liberty Pole Defined by Events

When the Whigs of New York City erected their Liberty Pole, they were not looking for trouble. It celebrated the repeal of the Stamp Act, and the sign at its peak honored George III, Pitt, and liberty. In the same spirit, New Yorkers also commissioned a statue of William Pitt to stand on Wall Street, and another of George III for New York's Bowling Green. These symbols were expressions of gratitude for recognition of their rights. They were also emblems of loyalty to an empire that New Yorkers believed to be founded in liberty.

At the same time, the Liberty Pole had another political message. The repeal of the Stamp Act had been accompanied by an American Declaratory Act (similar to a statute of the same name for Ireland), which avowed the right of Parliament to legislate for the colonies "in all cases whatsoever." The Liberty Pole was in its own way a colonial Declaratory Act on the other side of the question. It thanked the elder Pitt and the young king for a vindication of colonial rights but also was a reminder of the rights themselves.[71]

The Liberty Pole caused a collision with imperial authorities in New York. The events that followed became very violent and added another layer of meaning to this complex symbol that was defined by its history. The Whig leaders erected the Liberty Pole in an open space called the Fields, then north of the city, now City Hall Park in lower Manhattan. It was directly in front of a building called the Upper Barracks, then used by British troops.

During the summer of 1766, the radical Whigs of Manhattan met every day at the Liberty Pole and held "daily exercises" that were clearly meant to challenge the British garrison. The British commander-in-chief, General Thomas Gage, was an old hand at colonial politics and refused to be provoked. He responded with exemplary restraint. The Liberty Pole might have vanished into obscurity, had it not been for an unexpected turn of events.

In August 1766, a new British regiment arrived in Manhattan, the Twenty-eighth Foot, an ill-disciplined unit that had a long history of violence against civilians. At Montreal in 1764–65, it had caused much strife. When a Canadian magistrate tried to restore order, masked soldiers led by officers of the Twenty-eighth Foot beat him severely and cut off his ear. The regiment was transferred to Quebec, where more trouble followed. In 1766, General Gage ordered it to New York City, perhaps to keep an eye on it. The Twenty-eighth marched from Canada down the Hudson Valley and on the way got into yet another scrape with civilians. The regiment was asked to help local authorities deal with land riots of Yankee settlers against the great patroons. The British troops went to work with a will. Landlords expressed approval of their conduct, but settlers complained that the soldiers had burned farms, looted houses, and molested women.[72]

Early in August, the Twenty-eighth Foot marched into Manhattan and was billeted in the Upper Barracks. Much ill feeling already existed between soldiers and civilians in the town. New Yorkers reviled the Regulars and gathered round the Liberty Pole to tell them so. The Regulars made clear their contempt for the colonists and began to look upon the Liberty Pole as an affront to their honor. On the night of August 10, a party of soldiers from the Twenty-eighth Foot sallied from their barracks and cut down the Liberty Pole.

The Whigs were outraged. The next day they raised a new Liberty Pole at the same spot. Again the Regulars rioted against them. One soldier fired into the crowd and wounded a civilian. Another bayoneted a Whig leader near the Liberty Pole. British officers drove the troops back to their barracks and inflicted five hundred lashes on a soldier for assaulting a civilian.[73]

An uneasy peace was restored, but a month later, on the night of September 23, soldiers of the Twenty-eighth Foot attacked the Liberty Pole again and pulled it down. The Whig leaders put up yet another pole, and the Regulars wrecked it once more. On March 19, 1767, a crowd of

"Raising the Liberty Pole," engraving by John C. McRae, 1875, after a painting by F. A. Chapman. Library of Congress. This image shows black and white Americans working together. In the left foreground a well-dressed Tory turns away. In the background, Whigs are enlisting in the Patriot cause.

two thousand New Yorkers erected an armored Liberty Pole, covered with heavy iron plates around its base and set so deep in the ground that the Regulars could not chop it down, saw it off, dig it out, or blow it up.

General Gage transferred the Twenty-eighth Foot from New York to Ireland, but not before the regiment was involved in yet another fracas with civilians in New Jersey. Another regiment, the Sixteenth Foot, replaced it in Manhattan and inherited the hatred of the town. The new unit was also quartered in the Upper Barracks. Whigs shouted execrations across the Fields from the steps of Abraham Montayne's Tavern and Coffee House, which had become the headquarters for the New York's Sons of Liberty.[74]

British and colonial leaders tried to keep the peace, but the town was full of resentment against the Regulars and very angry with Parliament for passing a new Quartering Act that compelled the colonists to pay for the upkeep of troops who were dangerous to their liberty. Tempers rose dangerously through the winter of 1769–70. General Gage reported to London on January 8, 1770, "People seem distracted everywhere. It is now as common here to assemble on all occasions of public concern at the Liberty Pole and Coffee House as for the ancient Romans to repair to the Forum. And orators harangue on all sides."[75]

British soldiers began to be assaulted when they ventured out of their barracks. On the night of January 13, a party of Regulars responded by attempting to blow up the Liberty Pole with a charge of black powder.

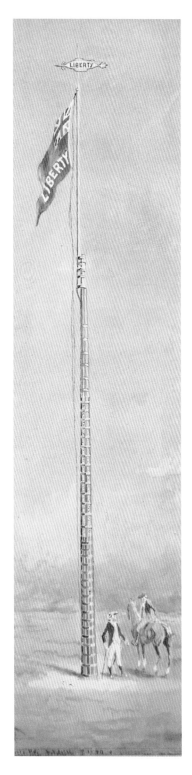

"The Fifth New York Liberty Pole," painting by Charles Lefferts. The New-York Historical Society.

They failed, but succeeded in cutting it down and sawed it into firewood, which they stacked neatly on the doorstep of Montayne's Coffee House.

Now the Sons of Liberty were outraged by an insult to their honor, and the town united behind them. More than three thousand New Yorkers rallied at the stump of the Liberty Pole and hurled abuse at the Redcoats. The troops swarmed out of their barracks. A pitched battle began between soldiers and civilians and spread rapidly through the streets of New York. Officers and magistrates lost control for two days, and order collapsed in the town. Gangs of soldiers armed with bayonets and cutlasses fought colonists who carried clubs and sharpened sleigh-rungs. Many were wounded in scenes of urban violence that were long remembered in New York as the battle of Golden Hill.[76]

Finally order was restored by civil and military authorities. General Gage banished the Sixteenth Foot to the fever-ridden swamps of Florida. The town fathers were appalled by the behavior of their own citizens, and the City Corporation refused to permit another Liberty Pole on public land in the Fields. But Isaac Sears bought an adjacent lot and exercised his private rights against public authority, in the spirit of New York. In defiance of the town fathers, the radical Whigs raised a new Liberty Pole, much larger than the others, and taller than any structure in the town.[77]

Its lower part was a ship's mainmast sixty-eight feet long, so big that six horses were required to haul it through the streets. It was surmounted by a topmast of twenty-two feet and crowned by a gilded vane with the gleaming word LIBERTY. From halyards it flew a large flag, probably the British Red Duster, which these seamen used at sea, with the word LIBERTY added in large letters.

The massive base of this new mast was heavily armored with iron bars, studded with nails, and bound with metal hoops. Thousands of New Yorkers escorted it to the Fields with weapons in their hands. To the people of the town it became a sacred object, baptized by the blood of its defenders. This Liberty Pole stood for six years, until the Revolution.[78]

The Spread of the Liberty Pole

The fame of New York's Liberty Pole grew with every fight and spread rapidly beyond Manhattan. Liberty Poles began to rise in many American colonies, but their greatest concentration was in the hinterland of New York City, a region that included Long Island, the Hudson Valley, western Connecticut, and East Jersey. On Long Island, Liberty Poles appeared at Hempstead, Huntington, Hampton, Easthampton, and other towns. In the country town of Brooklyn, a Liberty Pole was put up near the New Utrecht Dutch Church, now the corner of Eighteenth Avenue and Eighty-fourth Street. Others followed on that site through nine generations. One of them still stands, the sixth Liberty Pole in the same ground since the American Revolution. Others rose on the mainland in Westchester County. They spread up the Hudson River to Tappan Zee and Poughkeepsie, and west to the frontier town of German Flatts. Many would be erected after the Revolution in upstate towns such as Buffalo and Rochester, where the Liberty Pole is still a prominent landmark.

Liberty Poles were also very popular in East Jersey. One of them in Englewood, New Jersey, gave its name to an entire area, which is still called Liberty Pole. Others were built in Montclair, Morristown, Haddonfield, Pequannock, and many other towns. They also spread eastward into Connecticut, where towns competed for the honor of the tallest Liberty Pole in the world; a journalist reported in 1774 that "Liberty-poles, from 100 to 170 feet high, are erected and erecting in most of the towns of Connecticut."[79] Others were to be found in southern Rhode Island and on coastal islands from Long Island Sound to Martha's Vineyard and Nantucket. Throughout this large region, centered on New York City, Liberty Poles had their greatest density. They became rallying points for Whigs and places of punishment for Tories.[80]

Interesting things happened to the idea of a Liberty Pole when it spread into the heartland of New England. The device itself was redefined in ways that changed its symbolic meaning. Boston's Sons of Liberty made a gesture of solidarity with New York by raising a Liberty Pole in 1767, but in a special New England way. Boston's Liberty Pole was erected close beside the trunk of Deacon Elliott's Liberty Tree and rose among its branches, "through the tree and a good deal above the top of the tree," Governor Bernard reported. "Upon this they hoist a flag as a

A Tory suspended from a Liberty Pole, in an engraving by E. Tisdale for John Trumbull's poem "M'Fingal," published during the American Revolution. Library of Congress.

signal to the Sons of Liberty," he wrote.[81] The same thing happened at Newport, where a Liberty Pole was mounted on top of the Liberty Tree in 1770, and the two symbols became one.[82]

In 1774, the old Pilgrim town of Plymouth in Massachusetts also decided to erect a Liberty Pole. Instead of a freestanding structure on the New York model, they decided that their Liberty Pole should be built directly on top of Plymouth Rock. Further, to express New England's communal idea of liberty and freedom, it was agreed that this symbolic structure should stand in the center of the town. This was not easily done. Plymouth Rock was a big granite boulder at the water's edge, and the town center had moved inland. The town hitched forty oxen to Plymouth Rock and dragged it from its watery bed. As the great stone began to move, it suddenly cracked and broke apart, to the horror of the community. One piece was left by the shore, and the other was hauled to the center of town, where it became the base of the Plymouth Liberty Pole until 1881, when the pieces of Plymouth Rock were rejoined at the water's edge.[83]

The town of Concord in Massachusetts also put up a Liberty Pole. The place it chose was Meetinghouse Hill, next to a church that was the leading symbol of community in the town (New Yorkers had erected their Liberty Pole near a tavern). When British grenadiers arrived in Concord on the morning of April 19, 1775, they found a flag flying defiantly from the Liberty Pole. Scholars believe that it was probably the Liberty Tree Flag. The Regulars cut down the pole—the only act of deliberate destruction that their officers allowed apart from the burning of military stores, which was the object of their mission.[84]

Liberty Poles also appeared in other Massachusetts towns. Hadley in the Connecticut Valley had one of the tallest, at 130 feet. But when New Englanders went to war, the Liberty Tree remained their preferred symbol on flags and powder horns and official papers. New Yorkers, on the other hand, used the Liberty Pole and liberty cap as a revolutionary symbol more often than any other design. A flag captured by British troops at the battle of White Plains, New York, had a pole and cap with a crossed sword and the slogan "Liberty or Death." A similar design appeared on the flags of New York Regiments in 1777, which showed Liberty with her pole and cap on one side and Justice with her sword and scales on the other. In between was a rising sun. Flags carried by New York regiments in the Continental Army used the same symbols.[85]

Liberty Poles and wands were much favored in Rhode Island, but they were combined with the old Puritan imagery. In 1774, for example, Attorney General Henry Marchant wrote John Hancock to ask his help in hiring John Singleton Copley to paint a flag for the Rhode Island militia. Marchant submitted a design that combined a Liberty Pole or Staff with Rhode Island's old Puritan sheet anchor of salvation. The designer explained, "It is my idea to have a female figure representing the Genius of America standing erect with a staff in her right hand and the cap of liberty upon the top of it. In her left hand either the Bible or America's bill of rights, and under her feet, chains, the badge of slavery. The following motto in some proper place: Pater Cara Carior Libertas [Father(land) dear, liberty dearer]. And if a proper place can be found, to have the colony arms, being no more than a plain anchor."[86]

Henry Marchant's Rhode Island flag was completed by April of 1775, though not by John Singleton Copley. It no longer exists, but a surviving light infantry helmet of the Newport militia in 1775 shows exactly the same design. Like New York and more than Boston, Newport was a pluralist society, with a broad mix of ethnic and religious groups. The people of that town combined their old Puritan emblems with symbols of modern pluralism.[87]

Even as the symbolism of the Liberty Pole changed in all of these ways as it traveled to New England, it preserved the elements that its creators had given it in New York. It was no accident that New Yorkers invented the modern Liberty Pole and that Bostonians created the Liberty Tree. These emblems represented different visions of a free society, well matched to the communities that called them into being.

ISAAC NORRIS AND THE STATE HOUSE BELL
Quaker Visions of Reciprocal Liberty and Freedom

> Proclaim liberty throughout all the land unto all the inhabitants thereof.
>
> —ISAAC NORRIS'S INSCRIPTION FOR
> THE STATE HOUSE BELL, 1751

> It rang as if it meant something.
>
> —A PHILADELPHIAN, N.D.

WHILE YANKEES ADOPTED the Liberty Tree and New Yorkers invented the Liberty Pole, another symbol appeared in Quaker Philadelphia. We know it by the name that it acquired in the nineteenth century: the Liberty Bell. It has become a national icon in the United States, badly cracked and battered, but all the more beloved by the American people for its marks of hard use. In the city of Philadelphia, the Liberty Bell is carefully preserved in a modern shrine of steel and glass that grows more elaborate with every generation. Each year it is visited by millions of people, and it has become the center of a tourist industry in the Delaware Valley. Full-size replicas of the Liberty Bell, crack and all, have been commissioned by private donors and presented to the fifty states, where they are regarded with the same reverence as the original. They are displayed in every state except Oregon, which lost its Liberty Bell, when it was blown up by terrorists in 1970.

The Liberty Bell is often in the news. Many American presidents have come to visit it in Philadelphia since Abraham Lincoln did so on February 22, 1861. Liberals and conservatives both use it as a political symbol. Radicals and dissenters have made it a favorite site for demonstrations. Iconoclasts have tried several times to destroy it. In 1976, one idol-smasher attacked it in a very American way, with an automobile exhaust pipe. In 2001, it barely survived an assault by a self-styled middle-western "wanderer" from Nebraska, who wore camouflage pants, dreadlocks, and a Jesus

T-shirt. He tried to smash it with a five-pound sledgehammer, shouting "God lives" as he was subdued by tourists and rangers. After that incident, the National Park Service announced that the Liberty Bell would be surrounded by "heavily armed" guards, a sad irony in an open society.

Amid all the attention that swirls around this American icon, the Liberty Bell itself sometimes disappears from sight, and its origins are not well remembered.

The Liberty Bell is much older than its name, older even than the nation that celebrates it. From the start, it was meant to be the symbol of a free society, but in a special way. The great bell represented a vision of liberty and freedom that was unique to the people called Quakers. It symbolized a spiritual ideal, deeper than the secular memory of its modern guardians, and very different from visions that inspired Liberty Trees in New England and Liberty Poles in New York.[88]

The Pennsylvania State House Bell, 1752–53. Independence National Historical Park.

The Origin of the State House Bell

The story of the great bell begins in the year 1751. Philadelphia was then a handsome and flourishing town, increasingly diverse in its population, but still led by members of the Society of Friends. It was small enough that one of its citizens remembered that he knew "every person white and black, men and women & children by name." But the town was growing at a great rate and rapidly becoming the largest urban center in North America.[89]

A mark of its prosperity was a new State House that we know today as Independence Hall. In 1751 it was the biggest public building in North America, and still unfinished after twenty years of construction. The builders had just added a great tower and steeple. The tower was complete in 1750, but the steeple was empty and silent. The building had no bell.

The superintendent of construction decided to do something about it. He was Isaac Norris II (1701–66), one of the most powerful men in Pennsylvania. He and his father, Isaac Norris I (1671–1735), were rich Quaker merchants who expanded a capital of one hundred pounds into one of the largest fortunes in America. They also acquired great landholdings, including the manor of William Penn himself. Like most men of wealth in early America, they also became very active in politics. Both served many years in the Pennsylvania Assembly, and each was elected its speaker. The father also sat for twenty-five years on the governor's council, an unusual combination of offices. The son became an embattled leader of the antiproprietary Quaker Party, which was sometimes called the Norris Party after the family that led it.[90]

The Norrises were faithful members of the Society of Friends. For all their wealth and power, they never lost sight of the spiritual values in which they had been raised. In 1722, the father advised the son, "In thy Clothing be plain, and frugal, caring only to be decent and cleanly—and by thy return avoid the fluttering gaudy colors or show which the empty and weak heads appear in—which turns them to ridicule with people of sense and judgment." Both men shared a strong moral vision for their colony and a memory of its founding purposes. They were close students of the Bible and took its precepts as a practical guide to their daily decisions.[91]

In that spirit, the younger Isaac Norris turned to the task of ordering a bell for the State House. The year was 1751, and it was the fiftieth anniversary of an event in which his father had played a central role. Half a century earlier, in the year 1701, there was a moment of crisis in the affairs of Pennsylvania. The Quakers of that colony were deeply worried that their province might become a royal colony. Isaac Norris senior wrote of his concern that the colony might soon be "without laws or liberties" of the sort that the Quakers had given it. Worse, it might be run by Anglicans.[92]

As a precaution, the elder Norris helped to persuade William Penn to issue a Charter of Privileges that would guarantee the rights of the people. Norris worked to bridge the growing gap between a reluctant proprietor and antiproprietary leaders such as David Lloyd. Together they hammered out a document that established the rule of law, protected rights of property, guaranteed "civil liberties," and affirmed "liberty of conscience." It also recognized the freedom of a self-governing people to make their own laws, through the "powers and privileges of an Assembly according to the Rights of the Freeborne Subjects of England."[93]

Isaac Norris senior led the drafting committee, managed the difficult negotiations between the proprietor and the Assembly, and did his work well. In the end all parties came together, and the Charter of Privileges remained Pennsylvania's fundamental law until 1776. It created a system of rights that was more free and open than in any other colony.[94]

Fifty years later, in 1751, Isaac Norris junior had succeeded his father as a leader of the ruling Quaker Party and the Assembly. He took special pride in his father's work on the Charter of Privileges. Like his father, he was devoted to what he called the "Quaker cause" and the "cause of liberty and the rights derived to us by our charter and our laws."[95]

In 1751 the younger Norris persuaded the Pennsylvania Assembly to commission a great bell as an enduring symbol of that idea. He recommended that the bell should be ordered from England, inscribed with a suitable inscription about liberty, and hung in the State House, where it would call the Assembly into session and remind the people of their liberties.

The Assembly liked the idea. In 1750, exactly 75 percent of its members belonged to the Society of Friends.[96] The bell was very much a Quaker project, and it symbolized their values and purposes. Isaac Norris junior also chose the words for its inscription, and wrote it in his own hand: "Proclaim liberty thro' all the land to all the Inhabitants thereof." Norris took his text from the Bible. The verse in Leviticus 25:10 reads, in the King James version: "And ye shall hallow the fiftieth year, and proclaim liberty throughout *all* the land unto all the inhabitants thereof: it shall be a jubilee unto you; and ye shall return every man unto his possession, and ye shall return every man unto his family."

Here was a fitting passage for the fiftieth anniversary of Pennsylvania's Charter of Privileges. It also summarized a Quaker vision of liberty and freedom, which was different from beliefs in New England and New York. This Quaker idea began with an idea of liberty as a gift of God. Other Christians shared that belief, but Quakers understood it in a special way. They thought of it as an "inner light" that was given to all His children, not merely to the "elect," as Calvinists imagined, or to members of an established church, as Anglicans and Roman Catholics insisted. Quakers believed that this inner light dwelled within all Gods creatures. Sometimes they spoke of it as the light of liberty.[97]

Further, Quakers believed that God had given

The Liberty Inscription for the State House Bell, as ordered in 1751 by Isaac Norris II and written in his hand. It differs in detail from the inscription on the bell itself. Historical Society of Pennsylvania.

this gift for a purpose, so that His people might live in peace, and not oppress one another, and do His work of goodness and mercy in the world. This Quaker idea embraced everyone and bound them to treat others as they would wish to be treated. A central principle for the Society of Friends was the Golden Rule, which they regarded as a practical guide to the conduct of daily affairs. It held the promise of equality in the special sense of an evenhanded reciprocity of rights and Christian obligations.[98]

This large-minded vision of liberty and freedom was strong among the radical Protestants who settled the Delaware Valley. In Pennsylvania, West Jersey, and what is now Delaware, they genuinely tried to put it to work. The Quakers were among the few people in the world who extended to others the rights that they claimed for themselves. Their thinking was very different from the Puritan conception of ordered liberty and freedom for the Calvinist elect of New England, and even further from the unruly pluralism of New York.[99]

A perfect image for this Quaker idea was a bell that everyone could hear. The mere sight of such a bell became a metaphor for a dream of liberty and freedom that rang "throughout all the land." The sound of it deepened the symbol's meaning. Every peal of the great bell was meant to be a proclamation of universal liberty and freedom.

As a symbol, the great bell of liberty differed from Liberty Trees and Liberty Poles in another way. Like so many things in Quaker culture, its form followed the promise of function. One important Quaker value was a principle of utility. They did not approve of "needless" things. In 1751, the colony had need of a new bell. During the early years of settlement, William Penn had donated a small Province Bell, which was mounted in the crotch of a tree near the Delaware River. By the mid-eighteenth century, Philadelphia had grown so large that the Province Bell could no longer be heard throughout the town. A big bell was "needful," as Quakers liked to say. It was useful and instrumental in daily life, as well as emblematic of the cause that inspired it.[100]

The Making of the Great Bell

The younger Isaac Norris's idea for a great Quaker bell was a brilliant inspiration, but it proved difficult to execute. When the Pennsylvania Assembly commissioned the bell in 1751, no craftsman in America was able to make it. An order was sent across the Atlantic to the great Whitechapel Bell Foundry in London, an established firm that had cast Big Ben and the Bow Bells and many carillons throughout England.[101]

The Pennsylvania bell cost about £100 and was cast to a weight of a little more than one ton (2,080 pounds avoirdupois). By English standards it was a moderately big bell, but many churches and colleges had bigger ones. The bell called "Great Tom," which is still heard in Oxford's Christ Church College, weighed seven tons. By that comparison, Pennsylvania's great Quaker bell was on the small side, but it was large enough to do its work. The entire city of Philadelphia could hear it ring.

The Quaker bell was promptly made and shipped from London, but it suffered as many tribulations as did the Quakers themselves in the cause of liberty and freedom. The bell was damaged in transit, and a serious accident happened when it arrived in Philadelphia. Before the bell was properly secured, an attempt was made to ring it. To the horror of the workmen, it broke. Isaac Norris wrote, "I had the mortification to hear that it was cracked by a stroke of a clapper without any other violence, as it was hung up to try the sound."[102]

The Quakers wished to return the bell by the same ship that had brought it to America, but the captain refused to take it back. In desperation, the Quakers gave the ruined bell to a pair of "ingenious workmen" in Philadelphia, John Pass and Charles Stow, and asked them to recast it, which they had never done before. The two artisans hammered the bell into pieces, melted the metal, and remolded it. The work was done quickly. Isaac Norris wrote that the "mould was made in a masterly manner," and the molten metal ran well. The original Quaker inscription was carefully preserved, and the modeling of the letters was thought to be "better than the old one." Only the date was changed, from 1752 to 1753. The proud foundry workers added their own names and that of the town itself, to mark the first big bell that had been cast in British America.[103]

The result was yet another disaster. The American makers decided after testing several small bells to change the original bell-metal by adding an ounce and a half of copper to every pound of metal. The copper ruined the sound, which was so bad that the bell was thought to be useless. In Isaac Norris's words, the workers were much "tiezed with the witticisms of the town."

Undeterred, the craftsmen broke the bell yet again, changed the mix of metal once more, and recast it. This time the result was better. The great bell had a distinctive tone, deep and very heavy, almost a growl, which was not what Isaac Norris had in mind. "I own I do not like it," Norris wrote, and he ordered yet another bell from England. But others favored the gravitas of the great bell. One Philadelphian said that it "rang as if it meant something."[104]

The town warmed to the sound of the new bell. Isaac Norris noted that "some are of the opinion it will do," and in 1753 it was installed in the Pennsylvania State House. When Norris's replacement bell arrived by sea, the town observed that its sound was no better than the one they had. The remodeled bell of Pass and Stow appears to have remained in the steeple of the State House. For many years it announced each session of the Pennsylvania Assembly. Members who failed to appear within half an hour of its ringing were fined a shilling "for every such delinquency," and the money was given to the Pennsylvania Hospital. Another meaning was given to the bell by this association. It became an instrument of self-government in the province.[105]

The Great Bell and the American Revolution

Other layers of significance were added during the controversy over the Stamp Act, when the bell began to be heard more often, and in a different way. After the stamps arrived in 1765, the bell was "muffled and tolled" with much solemnity, for the funeral of American rights. On October 31, 1765, the day when the Stamp Act was to take effect, the great bell tolled again while a public meeting "mourned the death of liberty."

As the imperial crisis continued in 1767 and 1768, the great bell rang many times to summon freemen of the city to meetings against the Townshend Duties. It was heard again in 1770 for the Nonimportation Agreements. By 1772, the bell was ringing so often that "divers inhabitants ...living near the state house" complained that they were "much incommoded and distressed by the too frequent ringing of the great bell in the steeple of the state house, the inconvenience of which has often been felt severely when some of the petitioner's families have been affected with sickness, at which times, from its uncommon size and unusual sound, it is extremely dangerous, and may prove fatal."[106]

But the great bell kept ringing. On October 18, 1773, it summoned the people of Philadelphia to a meeting on the Tea Act. Two months later, when the tea ship *Polly* arrived, it rang again and drew what was said to be the largest crowd in Philadelphia's history, for a meeting that persuaded *Polly* to depart in peace. In 1774, the bell was muffled and tolled for the suffering of Boston under the Intolerable Acts, and on June 18 it called the people to another huge meeting, which collected food and money for hungry New Englanders.

The climax came on April 27, 1775. The great bell rang a tocsin for the dark news from Lexington and Concord. More than eight thousand people hurried to the State House yard and agreed unanimously (even some Quakers among them) to take up arms in defense of their "lives, liberty and property." All of these events added to the symbolic meaning of the bell.

One day when the bell did not ring was July 4, 1776. Very late on that Thursday afternoon, Thomas Jefferson's Declaration of Independence was adopted by the Congress. The weekend intervened, and independence was proclaimed at noon on Monday, July 8, 1776, with a reading by merchant John Nixon to another huge crowd. John Adams wrote, "The bells rang all day and almost all night. Even the chimes chimed away." The chimes were a carillon of bells at Christ Church. The many bells in the city pealed triumphantly in "great demonstrations of joy." It was remembered that the deep voice of the State House bell could be heard above all the other bells in the city.[107]

In 1777, the fortunes of war turned the other way, and an invading British army entered the city of Philadelphia. As the Regulars approached, the inhabitants moved quickly to save their beloved bells from the invaders—in fear that the British might take them away or melt them down. The big State House Bell was taken down and sent to safety in the countryside, not a small task. The wagon that carried it collapsed under the bell's great weight in the town square of Bethlehem, Pennsylvania. With great difficulty the bell was sent on to Allentown and hidden beneath the floor of a German Reformed Church.

All the bells of Philadelphia were sent into the countryside to keep them out of British hands. The result was a diaspora of bells that spread a symbol of liberty to other towns in the Delaware Valley and the interior of Pennsylvania. When the great bell came to Allentown, it reminded the

The State House Bell rescued from British troops. James Mann, "The Liberty Bell, Colonel William Polk's Overnight Bivouac, Quakertown, September, 18, 1777," mural, Allentown, Pa. Courtesy of James Mann.

Many town bells became symbols of liberty in Pennsylvania and the Delaware Valley, more than in other parts of the country. Six of these 18th-century Pennsylvania Liberty Bells were brought together in Philadelphia for the Sesquicentennial of the American Revolution. From John Baer Stoudt, The Liberty Bells of Pennsylvania *(1930).*

people of their own bell that had been cast in 1769 and hung in the stone church of the Zion Reformed Congregation. This Allentown bell was remembered to have been rung on July 8, 1776, for the Declaration of Independence. Like the great State House Bell in Philadelphia, it came to be associated with liberty and freedom.[108]

The town of York, Pennsylvania, had a bell in its St. John's Episcopal Church, the gift of a British donor in 1774. It rang for the great events of the Revolution in 1776 and summoned the members of the Continental Congress to their sessions when they took refuge in York from September 1777 to June 1778. This York bell also became a symbol of liberty.[109]

Other bells were cherished in same way through the old Quaker colonies of West Jersey, Delaware, and Pennsylvania. None appear to have been called Liberty Bells during the Revolution, but they were associated with that idea, as the State House Bell had been since its beginning. They were also linked to the spirit of reciprocal liberty that had become a regional tradition.

After the British troops departed, the great Quaker bell returned to Philadelphia. The steeple of the State House was found to be too rotten to support it, and for seven years the bell was stored in a munitions shed. By 1785, it was remounted and rang again on public occasions. Mostly it was called the Old State House Bell, but it also came to be known as the Bell of Independence, and the Pennsylvania State House was called Independence Hall.

The building and the bell were almost lost in 1816, when the state of Pennsylvania moved its capital to Harrisburg, and a proposal was made to sell Independence Hall to a developer who planned to divide the property into private building lots. The city intervened in the nick of time, bought the building for $70,000, and saved the great bell.

Its deep voice was often heard in the new republic, ringing for great public events, pealing on happy occasions, and tolling sadly for the departure of the Revolutionary generation. It tolled for the death of George Washington in 1799, Alexander Hamilton in 1804, Thomas Jefferson and John Adams in 1826, Charles Carroll of Carrollton, the last signer of the Declaration of Independence, in 1832, and Lafayette in 1834.

On several of these occasions, older inhabitants thought that its deep growl did not sound quite right. Subsequent study discovered that the bell was suffering from what would later be called metal fatigue, caused by "cooling strains" in the original casting. The city decided to replace it in 1828 and ordered a bigger one to be cast by the foundry of John Wilbank. The city fathers were an unsentimental lot and asked Wilbank to remove the old Quaker bell and get rid of it. He refused, not for patriotic reasons, but because the cost of hauling it away was greater than its salvage value. The city sought a court order for the removal of the bell, but a prudent judge ordered a compromise. John Wilbank was required to pay the court costs, and the city was told to keep the bell "on loan" from Wilbank, who had title to it. By law the bell belonged to the Wilbank heirs, who later agreed to allow it to remain in Independence Hall, on permanent deposit.

The great bell was still used on public occasions, but one Philadelphian remembered that on Washington's Birthday in 1835 a change in tone caused the ringers to inspect it, and they found a hairline crack in the metal. Another recalled that the crack grew larger on July 8, 1835, while tolling the death of Chief Justice John Marshall.[110]

Still, the cracked bell continued in use, because of an argument over public spending. In 1835, the city arranged for Christ Church to take over public ringing and be paid thirty dollars on each occasion. Other churches protested, and some taxpayers objected to any public spending. The broken State House Bell continued in service as a way of keeping the peace.[111]

Eleven years later, while pealing on Washington's birthday in 1846, the bell suddenly sprang a jagged crack from lip to crown. It was taken down from its mounting and began a second career as a silent symbol of liberty and freedom. People began to visit it in Independence Hall, where it became an American icon. The crack in the bell became part of its appeal, and its silhouette was enough to communicate a symbolic meaning.

In the mid-nineteenth century the State House Bell acquired its present name of the Liberty Bell. Its Quaker inscription, its linkage to the American Revolution, and its idea of universal rights were especially meaningful to the anti-slavery movement. In the 1840s, abolitionists called it the Liberty Bell and claimed it for their cause. This in turn revived memories of the Revolution. In 1851, Henry Watson published a collection of grandfathers' tales called *The Old Bell of Independence, at Philadelphia in 1776*. Benson J. Lossing's *Field-Book of the Revolution* included a highly embellished account of its history.[112]

In the twentieth century, as we shall see, it became an emblem of many different groups, and also a symbol of national unity. Today it is one of America's best-loved images of liberty and freedom. In its many associations, the great bell has preserved and enlarged its original meaning as an emblem of the generous Quaker idea of reciprocal liberty. The symbolism of the great bell, and the large meaning that Isaac Norris gave it in 1751, have made it one of the most enduring emblems of these great ideas.

THREE GENTLEMEN AND A GODDESS

Virginia Visions of Hierarchical Liberty

I am an aristocrat; I love liberty,
I hate equality.

—JOHN RANDOLPH OF ROANOKE, N.D.[113]

Freedom is to them not only an enjoyment, but a kind
of rank and privilege.

—EDMUND BURKE ON VIRGINIA, 1775[114]

IN THE SUMMER OF 1776, when Thomas Jefferson was toiling over the Declaration of Independence in Philadelphia, three of his friends in Virginia were hard at work on another assignment. The Virginia Convention on July 1, 1776, ordered Richard Henry Lee, George Mason, and George Wythe to "devise a proper seal for this Commonwealth."[115]

These men represented a small elite of Virginian gentlemen who had ruled their "Ancient Dominion," as they liked to call it, for more than a century. Their ancestors had been younger sons of English gentry and aristocracy, who emigrated to Virginia in the mid-seventeenth century. Their families were Anglican in religion, Royalist in politics during the English Civil War, and shared a pride of rank and ancestry, with coats of arms on file at the College of Heralds in London. In Virginia they became landowners, slavekeepers, and officeholders, and members of a close-linked cousinage who shared common interests and values. Even as much of their wealth rested on slavery, they had a highly developed sense of their own liberty and freedom.

On July 5, 1776, these gentlemen of Virginia recommended a design for a state seal, which represented their special vision of liberty and freedom. On the front (or obverse) they put two allegorical figures: "Virtus, the genius of the Commonwealth, dressed like an *Amazon*, resting on a spear with one hand, and holding a sword in the other, and treading on

George Mason (1725–92), left, portrait by Louis Mathieu Didier Guillaume (1857), after John Hesselius, 1750. Virginia Historical Society.

Richard Henry Lee (1732–94), portrait by Charles Willson Peale, ca. 1795–1805. National Portrait Gallery, Smithsonian Institution.

TYRANNY, represented by a man prostrate, a crown fallen from his head, a broken chain in his left hand, and a scourge in his right." Underneath they added the motto *Sic semper tyrannis,* thus always for tyrants.[116]

On the back (or reverse) of the seal was a figure of "LIBERTAS, with her wand and pileus." A familiar image of the Roman goddess was copied from a leading work of ancient iconography in their well-stocked libraries, Joseph Spence's *Polymetis.* She was given a Virginia meaning by the figures that surrounded her. On one side was the Roman harvest goddess, "CERES, with the cornucopia in one hand and an ear of wheat in the other." The stalk of wheat represented the cash crop that was rapidly replacing tobacco as the leading source of income on large Virginia plantations. The cornucopia was a symbol of abundance in the largest and richest American colony. In 1776, Virginia was nearly as large and rich and populous as the next two colonies combined.[117]

On the other side of Libertas was "AETERNITAS, with the globe and phoenix." The dynastic dreams of Virginia's gentleman-planters, and their hopes for their own estates, were expressed in this allegorical figure of eternity, with the earth in one hand and an emblem of eternal rebirth in the other.[118]

The most remarkable part of the seal, and a key to its special meaning, was the motto that Mason, Wythe, and Lee chose for the "exergon," or outer rim of the design. In a great arc around the central figures of Libertas, Ceres, and Aeternitas, they ordered that "In the exergon, these words appear: DEUS NOBIS HAEC OTIA FECIT," or "God has granted us this leisure."

The operative word was *otium,* which had a complex meaning in

classical Latin. It could be translated both
as "leisure" and "independence." Liberty, in the minds of these Virginia
gentlemen, was closely identified
with those ideas. It meant a release
from the tyranny of toil and liberty from dependence on
another's will. It signified not so
much the reality of a Chesapeake
planter's life but rather its driving
ideal. These men aspired to the
condition of an independent gentleman who was the lord of his plantation,
patriarch of his "people," ruler of his
county, and master of his time. In this coupling

*George Wythe (1726–1806),
engraving, 1807. Virginia
Historical Society.*

of *libertas* and *otium,* liberty and leisure and independence all became one.

In the Chesapeake colonies, *libertas* and *otium* were granted to people
in different degrees, according to their station. Independent gentlemen
were given many liberties and much leisure. Small farmers and tenants had
less of both. Indentured servants possessed few liberties, and slaves had
none. Liberty and leisure and independence were only for those who were
allowed "to enter into a state of society," as George Mason carefully put it
in his draft of Virginia's Declaration of Rights. The soaring phrases in that
document were meant to apply to some Virginians but not others. Here
was a very powerful idea of liberty that coexisted comfortably with slavery.

For us this idea of liberty and freedom is a contradiction in terms,
because we no longer share the assumptions of hierarchy on which it

*Virginia's seal, first design of
1776, obverse and reverse.
Library of Virginia.*

rests. But among the gentlemen of Virginia, and many others in their time, differences of social rank and condition were widely accepted and deeply believed. Similar ideas of hierarchy were widely shared by ruling elites throughout the Western world. In that respect, Virginia's hierarchical idea of liberty was also very similar to Roman *libertas*. But it was very far removed from the Puritan heritage of town-born New Englanders, and from the restless pluralism of New Yorkers, and most of all from the reciprocal rights of the Quaker colonies.

This tradition of liberty and freedom was established in Virginia during the seventeenth century. Chief among its many carriers was Sir William Berkeley (1606–77), a pivotal figure in the history of Virginia and its governor off and on from 1640 to 1677. Sir William Berkeley encouraged the migration of younger sons from Royalist families of the aristocracy and gentry. This small Cavalier elite arrogated to itself the wealth and power of Virginia and ruled the colony for many generations. It dominated the Royal Council of Virginia, which in turn controlled the distribution of land. Every member of that body in 1775 was descended from a councillor who served in 1660.

Sir William Berkeley and his small elite envisioned Virginia as a Cavalier utopia that would be Anglican in religion, hierarchical in its social relations, and governed by gentlemen of honor, courage, and breeding. This idealized society required large numbers of people who were willing to serve in lesser ranks, a role for which there were few volunteers. The gentlemen of Virginia tried to solve that problem by recruiting large numbers of indentured servants. When that supply ran low, they began to import African slaves.

The growth of slavery reinforced this hierarchical society and changed its vision of liberty and freedom to an idea of *laisser asservir* for slaveholders. It is certainly not correct, as some historians have written, that American freedom rose from American slavery.[119] But it is true that one American vision of liberty and freedom coexisted with slavery and even called it into being. "How is it," Doctor Samuel Johnson asked, "that we hear the loudest yelps for liberty among the drivers of negroes?" Here is a question that continues to echo in American history even to our own time.[120]

In 1775, Edmund Burke suggested an answer. He said of Virginia and Carolina, "A circumstance attending these colonies... makes the spirit of liberty still more high and haughty than in those to the northward. It is, that in Virginia and the Carolinas, they have a vast multitude of slaves. Where this is the case in any part of the world, those who are free are by far the most proud and jealous of their freedom. Freedom is to them not only an enjoyment, but a kind of rank and privilege."

Burke believed that the existence of slavery made masters more conscious of their own liberty and freedom. "Not seeing there, that freedom as in countries where it is a common blessing and as broad and general as the air, may be united with much abject toil, with great misery, with all the exterior of servitude, liberty looks amongst them like something that is more noble and liberal." He concluded, "These people of the southern colonies are much more strongly, and with a stubborn spirit, attached to liberty than those to the northward. . . . In such a people, the haughtiness of domination combines with the spirit of freedom, fortifies it, and renders it invincible." Slavery reinforced this idea of hierarchical liberty but did not create it. The temporal sequence is very clear. Hierarchy came first. Slavery followed.[121]

Not every gentleman of old Virginia shared this hierarchical idea of liberty and leisure. One of them dissented strongly. In 1776, Thomas Jefferson was asked to help with the engraving of the great seal, with its imagery of *libertas* and *otium*. So powerful was the ethic of *otium* in the Ancient Dominion that when the Virginia Convention voted to make an engraving of their design, the nearest industrious artisan who was able to do the work lived in Philadelphia.[122]

In hope of finding an engraver there, the design was sent to Jefferson, in the Continental Congress. He showed it to colleagues from other states and was "mortified" by their reaction, as Virginia gentlemen liked to say. Some expressed bewilderment at the linkage of *libertas* and *otium.* Others responded with raucous Yankee laughter that wounded the pride of Virginians. John Adams suggested another allegorical symbol that

Virginia's seal, second design of 1779, obverse and reverse. Library of Virginia.

showed America as young Hercules, climbing a northern mountain with the energetic maiden Virtue at his side, while a lascivious lady called Sloth tried to seduce him into lying with her in a vale below, which might have been the Valley of the Potomac or perhaps the Rappahannock.

Jefferson wrote home in high concern: "I like the device of the first side of the seal much. The second I think is much too crowded, nor is the design so striking. But for Gods sake what is 'Deus nobis haec *otia* fecit.' It puzzles every body here; if my country really enjoys that *otium*, it is singular, as every other colony seems to be hard struggling." He concluded, "This device is too aenigmatical, since if it puzzles now, it will be absolutely insoluble fifty years hence."[123]

Despite Jefferson's doubts, the design was endorsed by more than a hundred members in the Virginia Convention of 1776 and speedily adopted as the state seal. It was blazoned on its regimental flags, engraved upon its currency, and minted on its Indian medals.[124] But the part of the design that drew Adams's ridicule and Jefferson's displeasure became increasingly troublesome. The linkage between *libertas* and *otium* might have made sense to the gentlemen of Virginia in the heady days of 1775 and early 1776. But as the colonial rebellion became a social revolution, that hierarchical idea of liberty made no sense at all to people who lived outside the narrow circle of the Cavalier elite. And as the long struggle

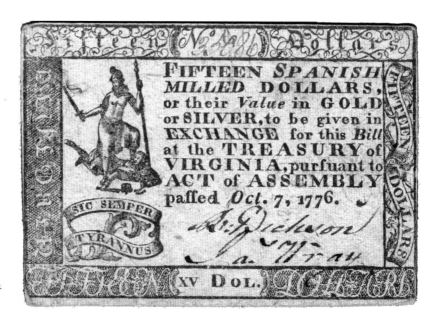

Virginia paper money.
Virginia Historical Society.

Virginia's seal, a variation on a pewter Indian peace medal, 1780. The original motto, "Sic Semper Tyrannis," has become "Rebellion to Tyrants Is Obedience to God." British Museum. Yet a third reverse design has appeared, with the motto "Happy While United."

wore on, *otium* seemed scarcely the word even for those weary few who were running the state of Virginia. In the dark days of 1779, Thomas Jefferson became governor of Virginia, and he succeeded at last in changing the state seal, quietly replacing *otium* with *perseverando*.[125]

But even with that change, Virginia's idea of liberty remained an expression of inequality and hierarchy for many in its ruling class. John Randolph of Roanoke gave it a classic expression when he said, "I am an aristocrat; I love liberty, I hate equality."[126] To those who did not share this way of thinking, Virginia's hierarchical idea of hegemonic liberty seemed false and even hypocritical, increasingly so as it faded into the past. But in its time and place it was a genuine ideal. A militant writer who signed himself "A Virginian" wrote with no sense of contradiction in 1774 that if Britain was determined to take away his liberty, "and from free born subjects supplant us slaves," the freemen of Virginia would prove that their colony has "Caesars as well as Ciceros" and "open in one day ten thousand graves."[127] It seems not to have occurred to him that the liberty he demanded for himself should be extended to his "people." But to liberty-loving slaveholders of old Virginia, this hierarchical idea of liberty was more dear to them than life itself. It lived on for many years, secure in its own world.

WILLIAM MOULTRIE'S LIBERTY CRESCENT

Lowcountry Visions of Liberty, Opportunity, and Fortune

> I had a large blue flag made with a crescent in the dexter corner. . . . This was the first American flag which was displayed in South Carolina. On first being hoisted, it gave some uneasiness to our timid friends.
>
> —COLONEL WILLIAM MOULTRIE, 1802[128]

IN 1776, a powerful British fleet entered the broad reaches of Charleston harbor in South Carolina. Its mission was to return that wayward colony to obedience. Standing between the great ships and their goal were two small palmetto-log batteries called Fort Moultrie and Fort Johnson. The British commanders studied the forts through their telescopes and discovered a strange flag flying above the ramparts. It was the color of indigo, one of the leading crops of the Carolina lowcountry. In the upper corner of the flag was a large white crescent of distinctive shape. Here was yet another emblem of liberty in the American Revolution, and a symbol unique to the Carolina lowcountry.[129]

Carolina's crescent flag of liberty was designed by Colonel William Moultrie, commander of the fort that bore his name. He was a charming man, with impeccable manners and a happy sense of humor. George Washington knew him well and described him as "brave" and yet "accommodating in his temper," the very model of a gentleman. An acquaintance in Charleston happily remembered that he was "a delightful host, could set the table in a roar, and was full of anecdote and pleasantry."[130]

One of William Moultrie's anecdotes was about the origin of the flag that flew in 1776. He wrote in his memoirs, "It was thought necessary, to have a flag for purpose of signals, as there was no national or state flag at that time. I was desired by the Council of Safety to have one made, upon which, as the state troops were clothed in blue, and the fort was gar-

Nicholas Pocock, "Attack by the British Fleet," 1776. South Carolina Historical Society. The crescent flag appears at the far left.

risoned by the first and second regiments, who wore a silver crescent in their caps; I had a large blue flag made with a crescent in the dexter corner, to be in uniform with the troops: This was the first American flag which was displayed in South Carolina. On its first being hoisted, it gave some uneasiness to our timid friends, who were looking forward to a reconciliation. They said it had the appearance of the declaration of war."[131]

Colonel Moultrie's memory was highly accurate. Two South Carolina regiments did indeed wear blue uniforms and light infantry helmets of an unusual shape. Each cap was blazoned with a silver crescent. An old portrait of Captain Charles Cotesworth Pinckney dimly shows this insignia on his uniform. With the crescent was a motto. The First South Carolina Regiment chose the words *Ultima ratio,* "Force as the final argument." Its sister regiment, the Second South Carolina, preferred "Liberty or Death," or simply "Liberty." Similar emblems also appeared on the flags of both

South Carolina's Crescent Flag, 1776, two versions. Courtesy of Whitney Smith, © 2003 Flag Research Center

Colonel William Moultrie (1730–1805), portrait by Charles Willson Peale, 1782. National Portrait Gallery, Smithsonian Institution.

South Carolina regiments, with the colors reversed: blue crescents against a silver background. Around each crescent was the motto *Vita potior libertas*, "Liberty above life." These insignia were the inspiration for Moultrie's flag.[132]

The distinctive element in all these designs was the crescent. It had long been favored in South Carolina. Ten years before the War of Independence, John Drayton described a blue flag with three white crescents that had been raised in Charleston during a protest against the Stamp Act in 1765.[133]

Why a crescent? What did that symbol mean to Colonel Moultrie and the Carolinians who adopted it for their emblem of liberty? Why did it become popular in their colony?

As so often in iconography, this device owed its success to a multiplicity of meanings. The crescent was an ancient symbol with many associations. It was an emblem of religious faith that had been used in the cult of Astarte and other ancient sects. It was also widely adopted by Byzantine Greeks, Ottoman Turks, and Islamic warriors. During the twelfth century, it was introduced to medieval Europe by returning Crusaders, who wore a crescent beneath the cross as a badge of Christian courage and honor.

The heralds of France and England developed the crescent into an elaborate set of symbols. At least three different designs appeared on medieval escutcheons. One version set the crescent on its back with its horns straight up. In heraldry this was called the "honourable ordinary," an emblem of chivalry and courage. Another design turned the horns of the crescent to the side and pointed them toward the wearer's left; this was called a crescent sinister, or decrescent, a dark badge of courage in adversity, and chivalry in defeat.

More often, the horns were bent in a third direction, toward the wearer's right, in a crescent dexter, or increscent, which was an emblem of courage and victory. In British heraldry, the crescent dexter also took on another meaning: it became the distinguishing mark of a younger son. By the rule of primogeniture he was unable to inherit his ancestral land, but he was entitled to wear the family's coat of arms. On his escutcheon, a crescent dexter was worked into the design to identify his rank within the family.

All of these crescents appeared in America during the eighteenth century. The horizontal crescent often appeared on military uniforms as a symbol of martial valor. This was the "honourable ordinary" with the horns pointing straight up, the old emblem of courage and chivalry. A Loyalist regiment called the Queen's Rangers adopted a horizontal crescent for its regimental badge in the American Revolution.[134]

The crescents on the caps and helmets of the First and Second Carolina Regiments appear to have been the crescent dexter, or increscent, in which the design was vertical and faced to the wearer's right. When William Moultrie designed his flag for South Carolina, he also used an increscent and explicitly described it in heraldic terms as a "crescent in the dexter corner."

This heraldic emblem of the younger son had a personal meaning for Carolina families, many of which were founded by younger sons. William Moultrie himself was the younger son of a younger son of an armigerous Scottish family. Charles Cotesworth Pinckney, who wore an increscent on his helmet, also came from the line of a younger son who came to America in search of land that was denied to him because of his birth.

The same thing happened in Virginia, where the Cavaliers who dominated that colony also tended to be younger sons. The most important of them, Sir William Berkeley, was a younger son who deliberately recruited many others of the same station. Richard Lee, founder of the Lee family in America, brought his coat of arms with him and proudly displayed it in a wood carving that was mounted above the front entrance of Stratford Plantation. Worked into the design was a heraldic crescent that signified the second-born son.

Colonel Moultrie's crescent flag combined many of these meanings. It preserved the associations of the "honourable ordinary" as an ancient sign of faith and a chivalric emblem of courage, honor, and chivalry. As a crescent dexter it was also a heraldic badge of rank that described the

The heraldic crescent as an emblem of a younger son appears in this 18th-century carving of the Lee arms, at Cobb's Hall, Northumberland County, Virginia. Courtesy of Clara C. Christophe and Bettie Lee Gaskins, through the R. E. Lee Memorial Association, Inc.

origins and memories of men such as William Moultrie and Charles Cotesworth Pinckney and the dreams of dispossessed younger sons.

The flag itself also made the crescent a symbol of liberty. In South Carolina, this was an idea with a special meaning. It had nothing to do with equality. Like the *otium* of Virginia's ruling elite, it was hierarchical and hegemonic. It existed in a world where highborn people had many liberties and defended them fiercely. "Baseborn" folk had few liberties, and slaves had none at all. There was no contradiction if one accepted an assumption of inequality.

The Carolina increscent had another significance. The Latin *crescens* meant growing or increasing. Like the crescent of a waxing moon, it was a symbol of prosperity and growth. More than that, these meanings were also associated with opportunity and fortune. It became an emblem of success in the present and optimism for the future. It implied that better times lay ahead. This expansive image of Carolina crescent-liberty was a little different from Virginia visions of a Cavalier utopia. But, as we shall see, a symbol of optimism would become a common American association with liberty and freedom.

Colonel Moultrie's banner was also very much a product of an American place. Its crescent motif was popular throughout the lowcountry of South Carolina and also tidewater North Carolina, where a similar emblem was also worn on military uniforms—more so than in any other colony. Moultrie gave his flag the color of indigo, which was an important cash crop. But he did not think that it stood for something unique to his own province. He called it "the first American flag to be displayed in South Carolina," and he thought of it as a symbol of the Continental cause. This paradoxical combination of a regional symbol with a national meaning was also true of Massachusetts's Liberty Trees, New York's Liberty Pole, and Philadelphia's Liberty Bell.[135]

The events of the Revolution added further meaning to Colonel Moultrie's indigo crescent banner. On June 28, 1776, the flag was flying above the

Charles Cotesworth Pinckney (1746–1825), portrait in the uniform of the 1st South Carolina Regiment. National Portrait Gallery, Smithsonian Institution. An original South Carolina metal cap badge, ca. 1776, is in the South Carolina Department of Natural Resources.

Colors of the 2nd South Carolina Regiment, with a drawing of the emblem. From Richardson, Standards and Colors of the American Revolution, *by permission of the Pennsylvania Sons of the Revolution.*

palmetto-log ramparts of his small fort when a large British fleet sailed into Charleston harbor. The warships mounted 170 guns against 25 in the fort. Experts warned Colonel Moultrie that his batteries would be reduced to ruin in half an hour. He replied that he would fight in the ruins until the day was won and ordered his men to stand by their guns.

The men of the second South Carolina Regiment waited behind the ramparts of Fort Moultrie for the attacking ships to come within range. The flag itself had an instrumental role. At the first sight of the British topsails, the crescent banner was hoisted to the top of its staff, then lowered quickly and raised again, as a signal to other batteries across the harbor and a message of defiance to the attacking British fleet.

A battle followed, and it contributed vivid images to the folklore of liberty and freedom in South Carolina. One of Fort Moultrie's defenders, Sergeant McDaniel, was mortally wounded by a cannon ball. As he lay dying, he cried, "Fight on, my brave boys! Don't let liberty expire with me today." His words were remembered in South Carolina, and Sergeant McDaniel became a martyr to the cause of liberty.[136]

Another long-remembered scene occurred as the battle approached its climax. The British warships anchored in line and fired full broadsides into Fort Moultrie. They took the crescent flag for an aiming point. An iron ball shattered the wooden flagstaff, and as the defenders watched in horror the crescent flag fluttered to the ground. Some feared that the attackers might think it was a sign of surrender. William Jasper, sergeant of grenadiers in the Second South Carolina Regiment, shouted to William Moultrie, "Colonel, don't let us fight without our colour." Jasper leaped on the parapet with a cannon sponge in hand. As British cannonballs crashed into the logs around him, he snatched up the fallen flag, ripped it from its broken pole, fixed it to the long staff of his sponge, and raised it above the rampart. The flag caught the wind, and the British ships increased their rate of fire. Jasper remained on the rampart, standing defiantly in the open, "gave three huzzas in the dangerous place where he stood," then returned to his gun.[137]

The British bombardment increased in fury but failed to damage the fort's palmetto logs. The Carolinians returned fire slowly and carefully, making the most of their meager supply of powder and recycling the British cannonballs. They began to do terrible execution on board the British ships. Masts were reduced to stumps and splinters, and two hundred men were killed or severely wounded. Among the casualties were the captains of the two largest British warships. Each lost an arm to a Carolina cannonball. The commander of the entire expedition, Sir Peter Parker, suffered a painful splinter wound in his backside. One British frigate, HMS *Actaeon*, was set ablaze and exploded. One Carolinian wrote that the ship blew up in a "grand pillar of smoke which soon expanded itself at the top, and to appearance formed the figure of a palmetto tree." To Carolina eyes, that image was yet another sign that Providence was on their side. It was an axiom of Horatio Nelson that "a ship's a fool to fight a fort." At last the British attackers came to the same conclusion and abandoned the fight. It was a rare victory for a handful of colonists against the assembled power of the mightiest navy in the world.

In South Carolina, the anniversary of the battle became a state holiday called Palmetto Day. Sergeant Jasper received a sword of honor as the reward for gallantry. At the American attack on Savannah he repeated his exploit, planting his regimental colors on the walls of the fort, but this time his luck ran out, and Sergeant Jasper was killed. His monument adorns one of Savannah's most handsome squares, near the place where he fell. Another monument was erected in Charleston for the centennial of the battle in 1876 and shows Jasper with the crescent flag attached to his cannon sponge. The memory of his courage remained alive for many generations and became part of the folklore of liberty and freedom in South Carolina and Georgia.[138]

After the fight in Charleston harbor, William Moultrie's gleaming crescent added yet another meaning to the many it already possessed. Now, to the people of South Carolina it became an emblem of courage and constancy in the cause of liberty and freedom. It was also a symbol of success at arms. As Moultrie explained in his memoirs, his generation were thinking broadly in terms of American liberty, but the emblem that he chose became the symbol of an American region.

RATTLESNAKES, HORNETS, & ALLIGATORS

Backcountry Visions of Liberty as Individual Autonomy

> Nemo me impune lacessit!
> [Nobody attacks me with impunity]
>
> —National Motto of Scotland

> Don't Tread on Me!
>
> —The Rattlesnake Motto, 1775

I N THE SPRING OF 1775, the western settlements were the last to hear the news of Lexington and Concord. We think of the West as the frontier, the forward edge of change in American history. But in the eighteenth century it was called the backcountry, and it was thought to be the most remote and isolated region in the colonies. The news of Lexington took nearly a month to get there. When it arrived, the back-settlers instantly perceived the fighting to be a struggle for their own liberty and freedom. Men in hunting shirts and buckskin leggings were soon on the march to Boston, with long rifles in their hands and tomahawks tucked under their belts.

One of these backcountry units was Captain John Proctor's Independent Battalion in Westmoreland County, Pennsylvania. It was raised in 1775 at Hannas Town, an area settled by North British and Scots-Irish emigrants on the far western fringe of the colony. Men in the battalion served through the war and fought at Trenton, Princeton, and Ash Swamp in 1777. For its colors, Captain Proctor's Battalion chose a new symbol of liberty and freedom. They carried a big crimson flag, made of heavy watered silk, six feet four inches broad by five feet ten inches high. It still survives at the Pennsylvania Museum in Harrisburg.[139]

The design and dimensions of the Westmoreland Flag exactly followed British regulations for regimental colors, even to a Union Jack in the upper corner, in every way but one. In the center of the flag, where a

dignified regimental crest and Latin motto would normally appear, the
backsettlers of Westmoreland County substituted a huge rattlesnake,
thirty-six by forty-two inches, painted yellow-brown with dark cross-
bands. The image was drawn with such accuracy that its subspecies can
be identified as a timber rattlesnake *(Crotalus horridus)*, which, like the
men who carried the flag, inhabited the wooded mountains and rocky
hills of the Appalachian highlands. The timber rattlesnake is often found
in that region today, tightly coiled and completely motionless, but with its
rattles erect and ready to strike, just as it appears on the flag.[140]

The Westmoreland men gave their rattlesnake a set of thirteen rattles,
with a fourteenth beginning to form in the hope that Canada would join
the cause. Beneath the rattlesnake was a blunt motto: "Don't Tread on
Me." Above was the cipher JP, for John Proctor, and the letters
I.B.W.C.P., for the Independent Battalion of Westmoreland County,
Pennsylvania.[141]

The design of the flag, its British Union Jack, and its hopeful allusion
to Canada all date it in the first months of the Revolution, probably in
mid-1775. This would make it one of the earliest rattlesnake symbols, but
others may have been earlier. Another rattlesnake flag was adopted by the
Pennsylvania Rifle Regiment, which had been raised in 1775. It was
recruited throughout the colony, but the leading authority writes that
"frontier areas had a disproportionately heavy representation." Its second
battalion came mostly from Lancaster, Cumberland, Northumberland,

York, and Westmoreland counties and drew largely from North British and Ulster families. The colonel of the regiment was Walter Stewart, also of North British descent. The regimental colors appear in his portrait, painted by Charles Willson Peale during the Revolution.[142]

Yet a third backcountry rattlesnake flag may (or may not) have been adopted in Culpeper County, Virginia, on the east slope of the Blue Ridge Mountains, by a unit that called itself the Culpeper Minutemen. They mustered three hundred men with bucktails in their hats and toma-hawks or scalping knives in their belts. One of its members wrote that they wore "strong brown linen hunting-shirts, dyed with leaves and the words 'Liberty or Death,' worked in large white letters on the breast." They mustered in 1775, armed themselves with "fowling pieces and squir-rel guns," and marched to Williamsburg, where tidewater Virginians were not thrilled to see them. One Culpeper man remembered, "The people hearing that we came from the backwoods, and seeing our savage-looking equipments, seemed as much afraid of us as if we had been indians."[143]

Part of the "savage-looking equipments" may have been their flag. A sketch of it by an historian in the mid-nineteenth century shows a design similar to the Westmoreland Independent Battalion's: the dark image of a timber rattlesnake, coiled and ready to strike, and the words "Don't Tread on Me." Also on the flag was another motto, which also appeared in large

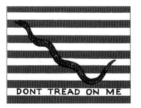

Six American rattlesnake flags as emblems of liberty. Top left to bottom right: standard, Proctor's Indepen-dent Battalion, Westmoreland County, Pa., ca. 1775; standard, Culpeper Minutemen, Virginia, 1775; stan-dard, Pennsylvania Rifle Regiment, later Stewart's 2nd Pennsylvania Regiment, before 1781; Christopher Gadsden's Continental Naval Ensign, 1776; South Carolina Naval Ensign (Rattlesnake Unity Flag, red and white stripes), 1776; South Carolina's Naval Ensign (red and blue stripes), ca. 1776. Courtesy Whitney Smith, © 2003, Flag Research Center.

white letters on their hunting shirts: "Liberty or Death." Their leader was Patrick Henry, who became colonel of the First Virginia Regiment, to which the Culpeper Minutemen were attached.[144]

This symbol of a singular rattlesnake which said "Don't Tread on Me" became very popular in the colonies. It spread so rapidly that its point of origin remains in doubt. The state of Georgia engraved rattlesnakes on its paper money. South Carolina briefly adopted the rattlesnake flag for its naval ensign in 1776. Purdie and Dixon's *Virginia Gazette* added a rattlesnake to its masthead from 1776 and 1777, along with many other symbols. Rattlesnakes appeared on Massachusetts treasury notes in 1777 and on a New Hampshire flag. In early 1776, it was proposed in Congress as a Continental flag.[145]

The rattlesnake symbol had two associations of particular importance. One was with the new American navy. In Congress a member of the marine committee, Christopher Gadsden, a South Carolina merchant who was the son of a British naval officer, proposed a yellow flag with a rattlesnake and "Don't Tread on Me" as the ensign of the Continental Navy. It was flown at sea in early 1776. Rattlesnakes were carved on the sterns of warships in the Continental Navy, which was sometimes called "the rattlesnake squadron." They were painted on the drums of the United States Marines. Gadsden also recommended a rattlesnake flag to the state of South Carolina, and its ships sometimes displayed an ensign with a rattlesnake stretched across a field of red and blue stripes. The flag was actively used, and in the mid-twentieth century the oldest ship in the United States Navy was authorized to fly a rattlesnake flag from its jackstaff.[146]

The strongest association was with the backcountry. This vast area of forested mountains and fertile valleys was dotted with new settlements in 1775. Most adults who lived there were not natives of the region. These backsettlers specially favored the rattlesnake emblem and were strongly drawn to the motto "Don't Tread on Me." How and why it was chosen is a story with more twists than a serpent's tail. To seek its origin is to find yet another vision of liberty and freedom in early America.

Origins: "America Typed as a Snake"

In a distant way, this new American symbol derived from an old European image that had a long history and a different meaning. As early as 1685, a French emblem book showed a serpent that had been cut apart, with a motto, *Se rejoindre ou mourir,* "Rejoin or Die."[147] In the mid-eighteenth century, when the British colonies found themselves in mortal danger of attack by their bellicose French neighbors, Benjamin Franklin borrowed this image of unity and used it to rally the English provinces against a common danger. In the *Pennsylvania Gazette* on May 9, 1754, Franklin published a cartoon of America as a serpent, sliced into eight pieces, representing separate colonies or regions. Beneath was a motto translated from the French original, "Join, or Die."[148]

Franklin actively promoted this image as a symbol of unity. He sent it to England for publication and encouraged its spread throughout the colonies. In 1754 the *Boston Weekly News-Letter* reprinted it, and the *Boston Gazette* added a more militant motto that came straight from the serpent's mouth:

The European serpent as an emblem of unity: "Se rejoindre ou mourir," rejoin or die; from Nicholas Verrien, Livre Curieux *(Paris, 1685). Duke University Library.*

"Unite and Conquer."[149] During the Stamp Act crisis in 1765, the serpent reappeared, once again as an emblem of colonial unity. After the Coercive Acts in 1774, Paul Revere engraved it for the masthead of the *Massachusetts Spy*, the newspaper of his friend Isaiah Thomas. Revere showed the American colonies as a large disjointed serpent (now in nine parts), facing a small, playful, and almost puppylike dragon of tyranny. Beneath was the old motto "Join or Die." The proportions that Paul Revere gave to the serpent of unity and the dragon of tyranny suggested that if America could get itself together, it had nothing to fear from its imperial ene-

J O I N, or D I E.

The European serpent borrowed by Benjamin Franklin as an emblem of American unity: "Join, or Die"; from Pennsylvania Gazette, *May 9, 1754. Library of Congress.*

mies.[150] Once again the symbol spread widely through the colonies. In Philadelphia, Whig printers Thomas and William Bradford used it for the masthead of the *Pennsylvania Journal.* New York's Tory printer James Rivington responded:

> *Ye sons of sedition, how comes it to pass*
> *That America's typed by a snake in the grass? . . .*
> *New England's the head, too—New England's abused—*
> *For the Head of the Serpent we know should be bruised.*

It was clever but not very wise. Rivington was hanged in effigy, his papers were burned, and his printing press was wrecked by a Whig mob. He fled the colonies for London.[151]

Transformation: The Rattlesnake as a Symbol of Natural Liberty

After the fighting began in 1775, the serpent became a rattlesnake and its symbolism changed in many ways. The serpent had been a generic European creature; the rattlesnake was an American species, unique to the New World. The European serpent had looked very weak and desperately wounded, even on the edge of death; the American rattlesnake was strong, healthy, and dangerous. His fangs were bared, his rattles were erect, and he was tightly coiled and ready to strike. Most important, the European serpent was an emblem of unity; the American rattlesnake became a symbol of liberty.

To observers from other cultures, it seemed a strange choice for a sacred emblem. Not many people have chosen to represent their most cherished principle as a poisonous reptile. Tories had a field day. A

Benjamin Franklin's American serpent was borrowed by Paul Revere as an emblem of unity in the revolutionary cause: "Join or Die," masthead for the Massachusetts Spy, *July 7, 1774. Courtesy of the Massachusetts Historical Society.*

Boston Loyalist observed that it was fitting for the Whigs to represent their cause as a snake in the grass. He added that the unkind thought that John Hancock might be understood as the rattle on the tail of Samuel Adams.

But Whigs rallied to the defense of the rattlesnake, with arguments that may help to explain why it was so popular among the British borderers who settled in the American backcountry. A writer in the *Pennsylvania Journal* explained, "The rattlesnake is solitary, and associates with her kind only when it is necessary for their preservation." He added that the rattlesnakes eye "excelled in brightness that of every other animal, and that she has no eyelids. She may, therefore, be esteemed an emblem of vigilance." He added that the rattlesnake "never begins an attack, nor, once engaged, ever surrenders. She is, therefore, an emblem of magnanimity and true courage." Moreover, he argued that a rattlesnake "never wounds till she has generously given notice, even to her enemy, and cautioned him against the danger of treading on her."[152]

The solitary rattlesnake symbolized liberty of a special kind. The motto summarized it in a sentence: "Don't tread on *me*." This was the only early American emblem of liberty and freedom to be cast in the first person singular. Here was an image of personal liberty, very different from the collective symbols of belonging that were widely used in New England but much like other backcountry expressions of liberty. The leading example was Patrick Henry's famous cry: "Give *me* liberty!"

It also warned the world, "Leave me alone, let me be, keep your distance, don't tread on my turf." This was an idea that had a strong appeal to settlers in the American backcountry, and especially to settlers who came from the borders of North Britain. These people came from northern Ireland, the marshes of Wales, the Scottish lowlands, and the six northern counties of England. They differed in ethnicity and religion but shared a common history and culture that had developed in the borderlands.[153]

For nearly a thousand years, they had lived between warring governments that turned their land into a bloody battleground. They had long been victims of incessant violence and brutal oppression. Liberty for the borderers meant a life apart from cruel rulers and the right to manage their affairs in their own way. Sometimes they called this idea "natural liberty."

The British borderers brought to America a fierce attachment to liberty, which they understood in that special way. Natural liberty meant the right of individual settlers to be left alone, especially by governments who

had brought them nothing but misery and exploitation. It also encouraged an idea of order as *lex talionis*, the rule of retaliation. Many centuries
of violence had also created a warrior ethic in North Britain and northern
Ireland. It taught the borderers that they must fight for their liberty, and
it encouraged a militant way of thinking about the world. Conditions in
the American backcountry reinforced these border folkways. In all of
these ways the image of the singular rattlesnake made a perfect symbol
for a highly articulated vision of liberty as the right to be free from government, and to live apart from others, and to settle differences with others in one's own way.[154]

Other Backcountry Symbols of Natural Liberty

The backsettlers also used other emblems to represent ideas of natural liberty and order. A leading example appeared in the small village of Charlottetown, today's Charlotte, the largest city in North Carolina. In 1775,
most of its inhabitants were North British and Scots-Irish settlers who were
fiercely attached to an idea of natural liberty. So strong were their beliefs
that on May 19, 1775, when an express rider reached Charlotte with news of
Lexington and Concord, Whigs in the town and surrounding Mecklenberg
County moved quickly. The next day, on May 20, by a "solemn and awful
vote they dissolved their allegiance to the hated Hanoverian King George,
created their own government, and resolved to "spread the electrical fire of
liberty" through the land. Their "Mecklenberg Declaration" was largely
invented after the fact, but the event itself actually happened.[155]

When a British army marched into the backcountry, they found that
the Scots-Irish settlers of Charlotte were among their most tenacious
opponents, so violent that even Banastre Tarleton complained of their
brutality. He reported that "the town and environs abounded with inveterate enemies" who harassed his foraging parties, killed his couriers, and

Another symbol of natural liberty in the American backcountry was this hornet's nest flag, a favorite emblem in Charlottetown, Mecklenberg County, North Carolina. Courtesy of Whitney Smith, © 2003, Flag Research Center

"fired from covert places" on his
troops. Lord Cornwallis wrote that
"Charlottetown" was "an agreeable
village, but in a damned rebellious
country." He wrote that "the people
were more hostile to England than
any in America" and called it the
"hornet's nest" of the American
rebellion.[156]

The people of Charlotte took

Cornwallis's words as a badge of honor and made the hornet's nest their own special symbol of liberty and freedom. An old North Carolina liberty banner showed a hornet's nest above the date May 20, 1775, for the Mecklenberg Declaration of Independence. Here was another symbol of natural liberty, very much like the rattlesnake in its meaning. A hornet, like a rattlesnake, was a creature that was not to be feared unless it was disturbed in its own home. It attacked to protect its territory.[157]

The people of Charlotte continued to use this symbol for many generations. During the Civil War, one of Charlotte's crack units was called the Hornet's Nest Rifle Corps. In 1996, a battlefield collector in Culpeper County, Virginia, dug up a brass button with a hornet's nest, and around it in that bloody ground he found "dozens of Ringtail Sharps and Gardner bullets." A similar emblem was worn by other North Carolina units in the Civil War. In the twentieth century, big downtown office buildings were decorated with big finials in the shape of hornets' nests. In the twenty-first century, the Great Seal of Charlotte combines a hornet's nest and a liberty cap. The city's first professional basketball team was called the Hornets, and police cars have a hornet's nest on the door.[158]

A hornet's nest finial, formerly mounted on a building in Charlotte, North Carolina. Charlotte Museum of History and Hezekiah Alexander Homesite.

Many other motifs of natural liberty appeared, mostly in the backcountry but also wherever Scots-Irish settled. An American powder horn in 1776 displayed the motto "Liberty or Death." With it was the image of a big

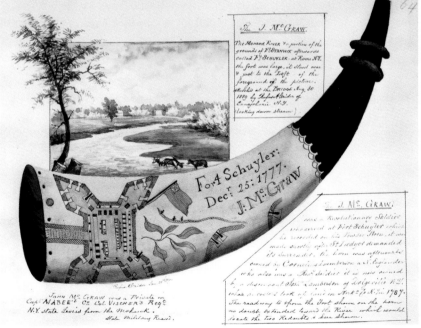

A Scots-Irish symbol of natural liberty in America: the powder horn of Private John McGraw, decorated with a flag combining American stripes with the Scottish Cross of St. Andrew. Drawing by Rufus Grider. The New-York Historical Society

American alligator with a small British lion on its back.[159] Another North Carolina image appeared on the colors of the militia of Bladen and Brunswick counties in the Cape Fear Valley, which had been heavily settled by Scottish immigrants. This ensign showed a coiled rattlesnake at the base of a pine tree, an interesting linkage of two symbols in colonial America.

In the American backcountry, Scottish and Scots-Irish borderers also introduced another symbol of liberty. It was the cross of Saint Andrew, an X-shaped white saltire on a blue field. It began to appear at the beginning of the Revolution. One example was engraved on the powder horn of John McGraw, a Scots-Irish private who lived and fought on the northern frontier; it showed a Union Flag with the cross of St. Andrew in its canton. The cross of St. George was omitted. Other backcountry flags added the Scottish national motto: *Nemo me impune lacessit,* which meant literally "No one attacks me with impunity." It might also be translated, "Don't tread on me."[160]

It is widely believed in America that western attitudes are a spontaneous product of the West itself, as if Daniel Boone smote the good earth of Kentucky with the stock of his long rifle and up sprang the American frontiersman. But before the West became the "frontier" it was the "backcountry," and the largest group of its inhabitants came from North Britain. Their idea of natural liberty was not invented in America. It derived from the ancient folkways of the British borderlands and flourished in the American backsettlements. The rattlesnake flag, with its motto "Don't Tread on Me," was a perfect symbol for this idea of natural liberty, and for a people who wished to be at a distance from government and free to go their own way.

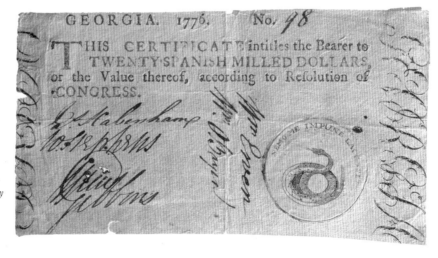

An American rattlesnake with the Scottish motto "Nemo Me Impune Lacessit." Georgia Revolutionary Currency, 1776. American Numismatic Society.

COL. MIDDLETON & THE BUCKS OF AMERICA

African American Images of Liberty as Emancipation
and Freedom as Belonging

> We are a freeborn Pepel . . . unjustly dragged by the
> cruel hand of power from our dearest frinds . . .
> brought hither to be made slaves for Life. . . . We
> therefore Bage [beg] . . . that we may obtain our Nat-
> ural right, our freedoms and our children to be set at
> lebety at the yeare of twenty-one.
>
> —"A GRATE NUMBER OF BLACKES" TO GOV.
> THOMAS GAGE, BOSTON, MAY 25, 1774

MERICANS OF AFRICAN ORIGIN also had distinctive visions
of liberty and freedom. In 1775, more than 96 percent of African
Americans were slaves. Very little hard evidence has survived
from the mid-eighteenth century about their ideas of liberty and freedom. Some images of liberty were forced upon them, as was slavery itself.
In South Carolina, for example, emancipated slaves were given "freedom
badges," which used the classic wand and pileus of the Roman goddess of
liberty.[161]

On other occasions slaves created their own iconography of liberty.
Carolina slaves in the Stono Rebellion carried flags that symbolized their
cause, but no descriptions of their banners have survived.[162] In Gabriel
Prosser's abortive Virginia Rebellion during the spring of 1800, the slaves
who were ready to follow him also designed a freedom flag. They took the
motto of their Virginia masters and turned it around. Patrick Henry had
said, "Liberty or Death." Gabriel's intended flag was reported to have
read, "Death or Liberty." That reversal communicated something of the
desperation that appeared in every slave rebellion. It was different from
the optimistic fatalism that appeared in many other American visions of
liberty and freedom.[163]

Among slaves, liberty always had one great meaning: the end of slavery itself. In the southern colonies, that idea inspired an underground
iconography of liberty as emancipation. One remarkable example sur-

Gabriel's flag; design for the banner of an incipient slave rebellion in Virginia, 1800; a modern construction from legal testimony. The flag appears never to have been made.

vives, dug out of the earth near the slave cabins on a plantation not far from Alexandria, Virginia. Some of the slaves in that area were highly skilled ironworkers, as their African ancestors had been for many centuries. They made a wrought-iron figure of a man standing strong and free. Many scholars have studied it. Sidney and Emma Kaplan conclude that it was done in a manner that "closely resembles the sculpture of blacksmiths in Mende Senegambia." Another scholar, Malcolm Watkins, observes that "it is a remarkable expression of African ironwork." At the same time, in the tone and posture of this iron man, there is a spirit of liberation. One might see it as a symbol of liberty as emancipation by an artisan slave.[164]

When the American War of Independence began in 1775, this vision of liberty as emancipation also guided slaves in their choice of sides. They chose differently in the northern and southern colonies, but always for emancipation. In the southern colonies many slaves became Loyalists, after Lord Dunmore and other imperial authorities offered emancipation to all who left their rebel masters. Some observers believed that an actual majority of southern slaves sympathized more with the Loyalists than with the Whigs. Crèvecoeur recorded a conversation in which an old Whig said to a young slave, "They say you are a good fellow, only a little toryfied like most of your colour."[165]

Thousands of slaves in the southern colonies fled to British forces at the first opportunity. Many were cruelly disappointed to discover that they had merely exchanged one master for another. British liberators sold some of them to West Indian plantations. Others were abandoned at the end of the Revolution to the cruelty of their former masters. But more than a few made good their escape from slavery and settled in Florida, the Bahamas, Canada, and England. These refugees and their friends turned American images of liberty and freedom against the Whigs who had invented them. An example is a song of doubtful origin, called "The Negroes Farewell to America" and sung to the tune of Yankee Doodle.

> *Farewell de Musketo farewell de black fly*
> *And Rattlesnake too who may sting me to dye*
> *Den negroe go 'Ome to his friends in Guinee*

Before dat old Englan' he 'ave seen'e.
Yankee doodle, &c
Den Hey! for old Englan' where liberty reigns
Where negroe no beaten or loaded with chains
And if negroe return O! may he be bang'd
Chain'd tortur'd & drowned—Or let him be hang'd
Yankee Doodle, &c[166]

Above the Mason-Dixon line another pattern prevailed. In the northern colonies 95 percent of African Americans were slaves in 1775. Most supported the Revolution because they believed that it would bring them emancipation, and they were right. On the day of Lexington and Concord, many slaves mustered with the Middlesex militia and fought against the Regulars. Within a few years, all were free.[167] In the northern colonies as a whole, the proportion of African Americans who were free increased from about 5 percent in 1775 to 56 percent in 1800, 74 percent by 1810, and 99 percent by 1840.[168]

Late in the war, former slaves in Massachusetts organized themselves as a military unit called "the Bucks of America," with strong support from Whig leaders. An account set down in 1855 noted that "at the close of the Revolutionary War, John Hancock presented the colored company, called the 'Bucks of America,' with an appropriate banner, bearing his initials, as a tribute to their courage and devotion throughout the struggle. The 'Bucks,' under the command of Colonel Middleton, were invited to a collation in a neighboring town, and *en route* were requested to halt in front of the Hancock mansion, in Beacon Street, where the Governor and his son united in the above presentation."[169]

"Yankee Doodle; or, The Negroes Farewell to America." Boston Public Library.

The banner survives today in the Massachusetts Historical Society. There is nothing African in its design, and little that is European, but much that is American. The canton is blue, with thirteen stars in an original arrangement. Four stars in the center probably represent the four New England colonies in 1776. They are surrounded by a circle of nine stars for the other colonies. Two scrolls contain the initials of the company's patron, John Hancock, and its commander-in-chief, George Washington. Below the canton is a white field with a New England Liberty Tree, and a big ten-point buck beneath it. At the bottom is the phrase "Bucks of America."[170]

A similar design appears on a surviving silver badge that was worn by members of the unit. It also shows a Liberty Tree with a prancing buck, thirteen stars at the top, and the French fleur-de-lis on the side. At the bottom is the inscription "The Bucks of America" and the letters M. W., which were perhaps the initials of the owner. This emblem is also in the collections of the Massachusetts Historical Society.[171]

The iconography of this piece shows a strong New England influence, with its Liberty Tree and the arrangement of its stars. It adds a different element in the prancing buck. The deer was a common symbol for America in the eighteenth century; colonists in Britain were called "buckskins" before the Revolution. But the image on the flag of the Bucks of America was distinctive in the strength and dynamism of its design. It might be taken as a symbol of pride and independence and

An African American image of liberty and freedom in the War of Independence: The Bucks of America, military colors and silver badge, ca. 1780. Courtesy of the Massachusetts Historical Society.

soul-freedom that became an important part of African American culture at an early date.

The spirit of this military company of former slaves appeared in the character of its commander, Colonel George Middleton. He saw active service at the battle of Groton Heights, and after the war he became a leader of Boston's African American community. Lydia Maria Child knew him and wrote a short sketch. Middleton was a man of the eighteenth-century Enlightenment, with many talents and skills. He was known for his expertise as a horse-breaker and for his virtuosity with a violin. Most of those who knew him spoke of his extraordinary courage. Mrs. Child remembered an occasion when the African community in Boston held their annual celebration of freedom on the anniversary of the end of the slave trade. They were attacked by a crowd of whites, and Colonel Middleton stood bravely against a howling mob of white rioters, while "clubs and brickbats were flying in all direction." Middleton came out of his house with a loaded musket, presented it at the mob, "and in a loud voice shrieked death to the first white who should approach." Other African Americans responded to his leadership. Together they faced down the mob and dispersed it, a rare event in the long and bloody history of American race riots.[172]

Colonel Middleton's character tells us something of the company that chose him for their leader. The Bucks of America, like many slaves in the northern colonies, shared a vision of both liberty and freedom. They sought liberty in the sense of emancipation from bondage. In the northern states, emancipated slaves also aspired to freedom in the sense of full rights of membership in a free society.

FIG TREES AND FREEDOM BIRDS

German Images of *Freiheit von* and *Freiheit zu*

> We cherish civil and religious liberty as a precious gift
> vouchsafed to us by God. Job says that the Lord has
> power to give and take away. If men turn priceless lib-
> erty into license and refuse to let the goodness of God
> lead them to repentance, hard times, chastisement or
> punishment will follow.
>
> —HENRY MELCHIOR MUHLENBERG, JUNE 2, 1775

GERMAN AMERICANS are today the largest ethnic group in the United States, and the least distinct as a cultural entity. In the Census of 1990, nearly 25 percent of Americans reported that they were of German ancestry, more than any other group by a large margin. That survey found the number of Americans of German origin to be nearly double the number of Irish Americans and greater than African Americans, Latin Americans, Asian Americans, Islamic Americans, and American Indians combined.[173]

German Americans do not have the same collective presence as other groups, partly because they have been divided by religion and politics. Most are Protestant, many are Catholic, and some are Jewish. Ethnic identity is blurred by these divisions, and also by a tendency of Germans to intermarry with other ethnic groups on religious lines, in a classic example of what has been called America's triple melting pot. German Protestants find spouses of British, Dutch, and Scandinavian stock. German Catholics marry Poles, Italians, and Catholic Irish. German Jews wed East European Ashkenazim and Hispanic Sephardim more often than they marry Germans who are not Jews.

Americans of German descent have also been divided in politics. They range from the radical "Red German" tradition on the left to extreme conservatism on the far right. Most are in the center. Their ancestors came to America in search of freedom and liberty and brought many different versions of those ideas.[174]

In the eighteenth century, a mass migration of nearly half a million Germans was set in motion by religious persecution in central Europe and by a religious revival that the Germans called *pietismus,* similar to the Great Awakening in America and the Evangelical Movement in Britain. Many German sects shared ideas of *Geistfreiheit,* or soul freedom, that were similar to those of English Quakers. These beliefs still flourish among Amish and Mennonite settlements in Pennsylvania and the Middle West, to the tenth generation. Strong currents of pietism also brought many German Calvinists and Lutherans to America, in search of religious liberty and soul freedom.

Other German immigrants were more secular in their purposes. Some spoke of *Freiheit von,* liberty from oppression. Others sought *Freiheit zu,* freedom to realize their own goals. More than a few wished to be what they called *vogelfrei,* free as a bird. In German popular culture, *Vogelfreiheit* implied a life beyond the reach of government, even outside the law. Here was an atomist idea of freedom, with a distinctive flavor of middle European *Wanderlust* and the spirit of the carefree *Glucksritter* who rides his luck wherever it takes him.

Other German immigrants were far removed from these ideas. Some were solid burghers, city people who settled in Philadelphia and Baltimore and the shire towns of the middle colonies. They flourished in commerce, excelled in education, supported the arts, and cherished the pleasures of urban life. Their distinctive way of life was organized around an old ideal of freedom that was called *Bürgerrecht,* by which inhabitants were accepted into the society of others and admitted to the freedom of an organized society.

Most German immigrants in the eighteenth century had yet another vision of freedom. They were peasants and farm workers who shared neither the communal *Geistfreiheit* of the pietistic sects nor the *Vogelfreiheit* of the rootless wanderers nor the *Bürgerrecht* of city people. The peasants, or *Bauernvolk,* of middle Europe were driven by an idea of *Freiheit* that grew from the suffering that had long been visited upon them in Europe. They came to America as refugees from a system of oppression that took many forms: religious conformity, compulsory military service, frequent wars, ruinous taxes, rapacious landlords, tyrannical princes, local bullies, and arrogant elites. Many fled the fatherland to be free of these afflictions.

At the same time that they wished to be free, these German peasants also had an exceptionally strong sense of order. Their households were

A German vision of living free in the New World. This fireback was made for German settlers by Isaac Zane in Frederick County, Va., ca. 1773–92. Collection of the Mercer Museum of the Bucks County Historical Society.

patriarchal, authoritarian, and highly disciplined. They dreamed of *Freiheit von* and *Freiheit zu* together, a freedom that would allow them to establish their own way of life in security and peace.

This vision of *Freiheit* inspired its own iconography. An example was a cast-iron fireback made for German settlers in the Valley of Virginia, circa 1773. It shows a vine and a fig tree, with a fractured German inscription: *einieglicher* [sic] *wird unter seinem weinstock und feigenbaum wohnen ohne scheu*, "every man shall live under his vine and fig tree without fear." This is a biblical passage from Micah 4:2–4: "And many nations shall come, and say, Come, let us go up to the mountain of the Lord. . . . And he shall judge among many people, and rebuke strong nations afar off, and they shall beat their swords into ploughshares, and their spears into pruning hooks: nation shall not lift up a sword against nation, neither shall they learn war any more. But they shall sit every man under his vine and under his fig tree; and none shall make them afraid."[175]

Here was an idea of *Freiheit von* and *Freiheit zu* in the same thought. It meant freedom from fear and freedom from war. At the same time, it was about the freedom of close-knit families and friends to live in peace with one another, secure in their property and their domestic autonomy. This idea was not political in the usual sense, but antipolitical. It sought freedom from governments, wars, taxes, and dynastic ambitions of powerful princes and great states.

Its dream of "everyone under his vine and under his fig tree" was an image of a world without violence, very different from the bellicose ways of British borderers but similar in a desire to be left alone by governments. Like the rattlesnake banners, this German vision referred to individuals and families rather than communities. The slogan that accompanied the image of the fig tree was cast in the singular—each under his fig tree. The German longing for the autonomy of highly disciplined families was different both from the natural liberty of North British borderers and the ordered liberty of New Englanders.

Like many ideas of liberty and freedom, this German vision of *Feigen-*

baumfreiheit was in some ways at war with itself. It demanded a system of government that was strong enough to preserve property, keep the peace, build roads, and preserve free markets, but it resented governors and resisted the taxes that governments require. An attitude of alienation from the state has persisted for many generations among German Americans, even to our own time. It would make them Democrats in the age of Jefferson and Jackson, and Republicans in the era of Reagan and Bush.

All of these German ideas of freedom and liberty, different as they may have been from one another, shared at least one quality that set them apart from the thinking of English-speaking people. British Americans thought of the world as fundamentally free. They wished to preserve ancestral rights and fought the Revolution to keep what they had. Immigrants from central Europe thought of the world as fundamentally unfree and came to America in search of freedom that had been denied to most people in Europe. In that respect, they were like other non-English-speaking immigrants. This attitude appeared in a Pennsylvania German broadside on May 19, 1766, in celebration of the Stamp Act's repeal. It showed a sun shining through heavy clouds on images of America and *Freiheit*:

> *Die sonne dringet durch, das Land wird fruchbarlich,*
> *Das Licht bestrahet [sic] den Sarg, die Freiheit richt sich auf!*

> *The sun breaks through, the earth becomes fruitful*
> *The light strikes the coffin, freedom arises.*[176]

PEDIMENT BUSTS AND GRAVEN IMAGES

Transatlantic Artisans and Their Visions of Anglo-American Liberty and Freedom

O thou whom next to heav'n we most revere,
Fair LIBERTY! thou lovely Goddess hear!
Have we not woo'd thee, won thee, held thee long,
Lain in thy Lap and melted on thy Tongue.

—A VERSE ON THE LIBERTY
OBELISK, BOSTON, 1766

OTHER SYMBOLS of liberty and freedom appeared in the high art that transatlantic craftsmen created for colonial elites. Some of these images are among the best-remembered emblems of the American Revolution. Others are very obscure but interesting for the coherence of their vision of a free society, and for their distance from folk images of liberty and freedom in the colonies.

The symbols that skilled artisans produced for American elites were bound by the conventions of high taste in eighteenth-century Anglo-America. Within those limits they were highly inventive, elaborately refined, and attentive to the latest fashions of the age. They represented currents of thought that flowed broadly through the Atlantic world. So intimate were these transatlantic connections that even experts have trouble identifying whether leading examples were made in London or Philadelphia. Some of the best work was done by migrant artisans who worked in both Europe and America. Their art reflected the tastes of wealthy patrons and the values of the makers in both places.

Philadelphia Finial Busts

A special iconography of liberty and freedom appeared among makers of fine furniture in Philadelphia, America's most cosmopolitan city on the eve of the Revolution. As the rococo style reached the peak of its refine-

ment in the mid-eighteenth century, skilled cabinetmakers added embellishments to their best and biggest work, especially the highboys, break-
fronts, bookcases, secretaries, and chest-on-chests that dominated an
entire wall of a Georgian room.[177]

These monumental pieces were often crowned with handsome neoclassical pediments. As baroque and rococo forms became more elaborate,
the triangular pediments of Greece and Rome were bent and broken and
curved in an infinite variety of inventive forms. Scroll pediments and
pitch pediments created central spaces that were filled with finials, and
sometimes with small sculptures called finial busts. In Europe these ornaments were made of plaster or marble, and commonly represented Greek
or Roman authors.

American and British furniture makers also used finial busts, but with
different motifs. At least nine examples survive on large pieces of furniture that are thought to have been made in Philadelphia during the
period from 1762 to 1775. They were carved in densely grained mahogany
by highly skilled craftsmen. None represented figures of classical antiquity. All of them touched on modern themes of liberty and freedom.
Most were portraits of writers who were associated with ideas of liberty.
One writer was preeminent: of eight surviving examples by at least three
craftsmen, five were busts of John Locke. Historians have challenged the
primacy of Locke's books in the philosophy of the American Revolution,
but Philadelphia's furniture makers had no doubt of his central role. The

*Finial busts of John Milton
(left) and John Locke, probably made in Philadelphia
before the American Revo-
lution. From the Metropolitan Museum of Art and a
private collection, with
thanks to Morrison
Heckscher.*

same pattern of Locke's primacy also appeared in the books that filled these cases. In libraries and book lists throughout the colonies, the writings of John Locke appeared more often than the work of any other modern author. Locke dominated the book collections of eighteenth-century America, just as his image dominated the final busts on the bookcases themselves.[178]

The carvings of John Locke were done in a modern spirit. In every case, Locke appeared as a contemporary figure in the clothing of the mid-eighteenth century, not the dress of Greece or Rome, and not even the fashions of his own generation. There was also a feeling of freedom and informality in the execution of the busts. On one of them the shirt and vest are unbuttoned and open at the neck to expose the throat and chest. Much attention is also given to the expression of individual character. John Locke appears as an intellectual figure with a high domed forehead and a deep furrowed brow. His strongest features are very large eyes, appropriate symbols for the generous vision of the *Essay Concerning Human Understanding* and the two *Treatises on Government*, which made him America's leading philosopher of a free society.[179]

Finial bust of Madame de Pompadour; Philadelphia, ca. 1770. The Metropolitan Museum of Art, John Stewart Kennedy Fund, 1918. (18.110.4) Photograph by Richard Cheek. Photograph © 1985 The Metropolitan Museum of Art.

After Locke, the favorite subject of Philadelphia furniture makers was John Milton (1608–74). He was known in the colonies not primarily as the poet of *Paradise Lost* but mainly as the political writer of *Areopagitica*, a passionate defense of liberty. Two surviving finial busts of Milton both stress his qualities of mind and character. He appears as the blind poet with large sightless eyes and a lofty forehead that is curved to reflect the light.[180]

An eighth finial bust introduced another theme of liberty. It represents Jeanne-Antoinette Poisson, marquise de Pompadour (1721–64), mistress of Louis XV. She appears as a symbol of sensual freedom, with bare swelling breasts and only the smallest suggestion of a dress. Below is an elaborately carved scene of spouting serpents and sensuous swans. Madame de Pompadour appears as a beautiful woman of autonomous spirit, untrammeled by the moral conventions of her age. Her image symbolizes a vision of hedonistic liberty that was very uncommon in early America. Here is another indicator of the distance that separated Atlantic artisans and elites from other colonial cultures.[181]

Charles Willson Peale's Allegorical Liberty Paintings

American painters also dedicated their art to the Whig cause and added another layer of complexity to the iconography of freedom. Among them was Charles Willson Peale (1741–1827), a gifted young painter from Maryland. In 1766, several gentlemen of Annapolis recognized his talent and raised a purse of eighty guineas, enough to send him to London for training. Peale traveled to England in the same ship that returned the hated stamps from the colonies and was in London when the Townshend Acts were passed. He was so incensed that he refused to doff his cap to the king.

In 1767, several Chesapeake gentlemen commissioned Peale to paint a portrait of William Pitt, who was much admired in America as a friend of liberty. Pitt was very ill and unable to pose, but Peale found an ingenious way to reconcile his subject with his commission. He did two heroic paintings of Pitt's statue, set in a garden of statuary that became an "allegory of liberty" in the words of the artist's biographer. The paintings were very large: eight feet high and five feet wide. One of them went to Richard Henry Lee in Virginia and still survives after many vicissitudes. The other was carried by the artist to Annapolis, where it is now kept in the Maryland State House.

Peale also made a mezzotint of the painting, scraped the plate himself, and sold it with a broadside that explained its iconography in elaborate detail. He explained his design as a struggle between two ideas of liberty. One idea was represented by what he called "the statue of British liberty, trampling under foot the petition of the Congress at New York." British liberty appeared as a melancholy lady in classical dress, who clutched a wand and pileus in one hand and a British shield in the other. The artist wrote, "Some have thought it not quite proper to represent LIBERTY as guilty of an Action so contrary to her genuine spirit." He quoted Montesquieu and others, that the "states which enjoy the highest degree of liberty are apt to be oppressive of those who are subordinate and in subjection to them."[182]

Charles Willson Peale, "Worthy of Liberty, Mr. Pitt Scorns to Invade the Liberties of Other People," mezzotint, London, 1768. Colonial Williamsburg Foundation.

The other idea of liberty was personified by William Pitt. The American painter elevated him to a condition of equality, called him Mr. Pitt, and represented him as neither English nor American but Roman, dressed in what the artist called consular dress. In one hand Mr. Pitt carries a copy of Magna Carta, set in Gothic script. With the other hand he points in the direction of the image of British liberty, but averts his eyes and looks the other way, toward the American viewer. Below, the artist adds an inscription: "Worthy of Liberty, Mr. Pitt scorns to invade the liberties of others."[183]

In front of Mr. Pitt is an altar with an eternal flame, to show that "liberty is sacred, and therefore they who maintain it not only discharge their duty to their king and themselves, but to GOD." On the altar are the heads of the martyrs Sidney and Hampden, both of whom were beheaded in Britain for their defense of liberty. In the background is Whitehall Palace, "not merely as an elegant piece of architecture but as a place where [Charles I] suffered for attempting to invade the rights of the British kingdoms." Below the statue of British liberty is a figure of America, an Indian with a bow in one hand and a dog by his side, "to shew the natural faithfulness and firmness of America." Peale's friends suggested that America should appear dejected. The artist disagreed. "In truth," he wrote, "the Americans being well founded in their principles and animated with a sacred love for their country, have never desponded."[184]

Peale's allegory of liberty is not much admired today even by historians who praise his other work. One critic has described the composition as less a painting than a political cartoon. But it was celebrated in its own time, which regarded historical and allegorical works as the highest expression of a painter's art. The mezzotint was widely discussed in British and American newspapers and did much to make the young artists reputation.

Liberty Pillars and Obelisks

In 1766, the Sons of Liberty in Dedham, Massachusetts, built a monument to celebrate the repeal of the Stamp Act. They called it their Pillar of Liberty. It was a sturdy classical column eight or ten feet high, on a heavy plinth of dark New England granite. On top was a bust of William Pitt. It was meant to commemorate not merely Pitt himself but all the members of Parliament who had repealed the Stamp Act and "saved America from impending slavery."[185]

The work was done by local artisans: the granite base by a Yankee "stonecutter" named Howard, the wooden column by Daniel Gookin, and the bust of Pitt by Simeon Skillin, a carver of ships' figureheads in Boston. A local physician, Dr. Nathaniel Ames, composed a classical inscription:

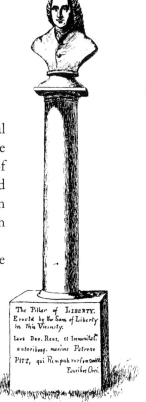

> *The Pillar of LIBERTY*
> *Erected by the Sons of Liberty in this Vicinity*
> *Laus DEO REGI, et Immunitatm autoribusq maxime Patrono*
> *PITT, qui Rempub. rursum evulsit Faucibus Orci*

A free translation might be "Praise God, the King, and the exceptional work of Pitt, the greatest benefactor, who plucked the republic from the jaws of Hell." On another side, Ames added in English, "The Pillar of Liberty, to the Honor of Willim Pitt, esqr, and other Patriots who saved America from impending Slavery & confirmed our most loyal Affection to Kg George III by procuring a Repeal of the Stamp Act, 18th March 1766."[186]

A "huge concourse" assembled on Dedham's Church Green for the dedication of the monument, which the town called Pitt's Head. It represented a moment when Americans celebrated liberty, loyalty, and renewed confidence in the young king and William Pitt as guardians of their rights. But within a few years, Parliament tried to tax the colonies again without their consent, and on May 11, 1769, the monument was "overthrown and defac'd" by parties unknown. Nothing remains but its granite base, still in the same place.[187]

Another strange device was an obelisk of liberty, erected on Boston Common on May 22, 1766, also to celebrate the repeal of the Stamp Act. It was designed by Paul Revere on the inspiration of an ancient Egyptian form, but it had nothing like the slender elegance of Cleopatra's Needle. This was a blunt Boston obelisk, as short, squat,

Dedham's Pillar of Liberty, 1766, sketch in Robert Hanson, ed., Diary of Nathaniel Ames. *Courtesy of the Dedham Historical Society.*

strong, and solid as the man who made it. It was a Yankee artisan's adaptation of a Georgian English version of a neoclassical idea of an Egyptian obelisk, at least four incarnations removed from the original.

Paul Revere applied himself to the design and construction of his obelisk with the same industry and attention to detail that he brought to all his labors in the cause of liberty and freedom. The obelisk's four sides were elaborately decorated with symbols, emblems, portraits, allegories, and long didactic inscriptions. The lower parts of the shaft told a story in four tableaus. The first showed America in deep distress, fearful that the Stamp Act would destroy her liberty. The second represented America appealing for the help of English patriots against the earl of Bute and Lord Mansfield. In the third, America "endures the conflict for a short season." The last tableau was a triumphant scene of liberty restored to America by the royal hand of the young patriot king, George III.

The top of the obelisk was adorned with the portraits of sixteen "worthy patriots" in England who were thought to have defended American liberty. Its midsection was covered with inscriptions about "fair liberty" and "honest freedom" that reveal another face of the American Revolution as part of the new Romantic movement that was stirring at Horace Walpole's Strawberry Hill:

> *O thou whom next to heav'n we most revere,*
> *Fair LIBERTY! thou lovely Goddess hear!*
> *Have we not woo'd thee, won thee, held thee long,*
> *Lain in thy Lap and melted on thy Tongue*

Paul Revere's obelisk was large but very fragile. It was made of translucent oiled paper on a thin frame and illuminated from within by 280 lamps. In the darkness of an eighteenth-century night, it must have gleamed like a great shaft of light on Boston Common. It was intended that after the celebration the obelisk would be moved to the Liberty Tree and given a permanent home there.

On May 22, 1766, the Sons of Liberty made Paul Revere's obelisk the center of an entertainment for the repeal of the Stamp Act. All day there were bells, cannons, flags, and parades. The houses were illuminated, and bonfires blazed on the hilltops. For a grand finale the Sons of Liberty mounted fireworks on the obelisk—pyrotechnic rockets, serpents, and revolving Catherine wheels.[188] At the climax of the celebration, as fireworks were flying in every direction, the oiled paper of the obelisk caught fire. The shaft of light became a column of flame and was consumed in an

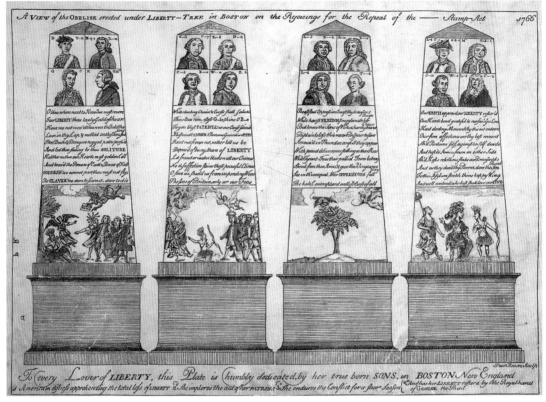

Obelisk of Liberty, 1766, design by Paul Revere to celebrate repeal of the Stamp Act, copperplate engraving. Library of Congress.

instant. Nothing survived but a meticulous copperplate engraving, also executed by the inexhaustible Paul Revere.[189]

Silver Medals and Liberty Bowls

Colonial silversmiths also contributed to the iconography of liberty and freedom—none more than Paul Revere. It may have been Revere who made the silver medals that Bostons Sons of Liberty wore around their necks on "publick occasions." The two sides of the medal displayed different motifs. On the front a strong arm held a liberty wand, surmounted by a cap of liberty. Beneath was the inscription "Sons of Liberty." On the back was the old New England symbol, a Tree of Liberty, and the name or initials of the man who wore it. The medal cleverly combined two iconographic traditions. Its outer side displayed the wand and pileus that were generally recognized as a symbol of liberty throughout the Western world. The inner side, closer to the hearts of the men who wore it, had the old New England emblem of freedom.

Paul Revere's Liberty Bowl, silver, obverse and reverse. Photograph © 2003, Museum of Fine Arts, Boston.

In another nice piece of symbolism, the wand and pileus were held in a workman's brawny arm, made strong by exercise. Many Sons of Liberty were mechanics in the eighteenth-century sense, men who worked with their hands and arms. This idea of liberty was not associated with an elite but with ordinary people. To drive home the point, the motto of the Sons of Liberty was "Equality Before the Law." This was not an idea of equality of condition but of equal rights among town-born men of an old New England community.[190]

Paul Revere also made one of the most handsome emblems of the Whig movement in America. It was a large silver Liberty Bowl that commemorated an event in 1768 when the Massachusetts legislature sent a circular letter to the other colonies protesting the Townshend Acts. The legislature was ordered in the name of the king himself to rescind the letter. Ninety-two members refused to do so, in an act of high courage.

The people of Boston regarded that event as a violation of their rights to self-government and freedom of speech. They were also conscious of a common cause with English Whig John Wilkes, a member of Parliament who in the forty-fifth issue of his magazine, *The North Briton,* had dared to accuse the king himself of uttering a falsehood. For this, the government issued a general warrant for the arrest of everyone involved in the publication of *Number 45 North Briton.* Wilkes himself was seized and secretly locked in the Tower of London so that a writ of habeas corpus could not be obtained for his release. He was brought to trial before Chief Justice Sir John Pratt (later Lord Camden), who released him on the grounds that a member of Parliament was privileged against arrest except for treason, felony, or breach of the peace.

Wilkes recovered his freedom and broadened the issue of his arrest to include the illegality of general warrants and the tyranny of arbitrary arrest. He sued the undersecretary of state for damages and won his case, as did his printer. But Britain's ruling parliamentary elite refused to accept those judgments. The House of Commons turned against its own member and voted (237 to 111) that Wilkes should be expelled from Parliament and tried for seditious libel. It also ordered that *45 North Briton* should be burned by the public hangman. At about the same time, Wilkes was severely wounded in a contrived duel that Horace Walpole took to be a deliberate attempt by the king's friends to murder him. When the indictment was brought against him, he fled the kingdom and became an outlaw in Britain and a hero in America.

Paul Revere's Liberty Bowl represented the two cases of John Wilkes and the Massachusetts legislature as a single cause. One side of the bowl was engraved with a short statement of the American case: "To the memory of the glorious Ninety-Two Members of the Honbl House of Representatives of the Massachusetts-Bay, who, undaunted by the insolent menaces of Villains in Power, from a strict Regard to Conscience and the Liberties of their Constituents, on the 30th of June 1768, Voted NOT TO RESCIND." Above was the liberty cap and wand, surrounded by a wreath of victory.

The other side was about John Wilkes. It centered on the inscription "No. 45. Wilkes and Liberty." Below was a torn paper marked "generall warrants." Above were Magna Carta, a Bill of Rights, and a wand and pileus. The symbolism was carried even to the size and weight of the bowl. When the bowl was first displayed on August 1, 1768, John Rowe noted that "the silver bowl; was this evening for the first time introduced, No. 45. Weighs 45 ounces, and holds 45 gills." The bowl was much admired for its proportions and gave rise to a classic design called the Paul Revere Bowl. Copies are still mass-produced in cheap silverplate with plastic liners by American silver companies.

All of these artifacts shared a common vision of liberty and freedom that set them apart from other American images. This was a transatlantic idea that linked British and American elements. It was responsive to the latest intellectual fashions in London and throughout the empire and made symbols of the great texts of liberty and freedom: Magna Carta and the writings of Locke and Milton. Of all the many American emblems of liberty and freedom before 1776, these are the closest to conventional historical scholarship on the coming of the American Revolution and to academic interpretations of liberty and freedom.

TORY ELITES

Imperial Visions of Liberty and Loyalty

> I think of the destruction and misery which awaits this once happy and flourishing people (who enjoy more liberty and freedom, than any other nation under heaven) which nothing short of a due submission to the parliament of great Britain can avert.
>
> —AMERICAN LOYALIST HARRISON GRAY, 1775

JOHN ADAMS reckoned that two-thirds of Americans supported the Revolution and one-third opposed it.[191] Both groups came to be remembered by names their enemies gave them: Whigs and Tories. *Whig* was originally a term of insult for Scottish Presbyterian cattle thieves and rebels who were hostile to Catholic princes. *Tory* was a word of abuse for Irish Catholic robber gangs who preyed upon Protestant neighbors. In the late seventeenth century, both words began to be used in English politics for enemies and supporters of the Catholic Stuarts. By 1775, Americans adopted them for foes and friends of their Revolution.[192]

Whigs and Tories both insisted that they were "*true* lovers of liberty" and faithful "friends to fair freedom's cause." Whigs, as we have seen, had many visions of these ideas. Tories had mostly one. They called themselves Loyalists and thought of liberty and freedom as the rule of law under the mixed or balanced government of king-in-Parliament, which they believed to be the freest system in the world.[193]

Some colonists in British America had particular reasons for feeling that way, and their feelings were linked to visions of liberty and freedom in the empire. Some Jewish colonists were Loyalists. Under British law, Jews throughout the empire were granted religious toleration, rights of marriage, and more liberties than in other European states.

In the southern colonies, African slaves were often sympathetic to the British cause. Many southern slaves fled their Whig masters in the hope that they would gain their freedom from British forces. Some American Indians were Loyalists during the War of Independence. The League of the Iroquois in particular, and other Indian nations, believed correctly that an independent American republic would be more dangerous to their liberty than the British Empire had ever been.

Highland Scots also tended to be Loyalists, perhaps because many of them had only just arrived in the colonies when the Revolution began. Americans not of English descent were slow to support a revolutionary movement that began as a demand for the rights of Englishmen.

The most prominent Loyalists were imperial elites who held high offices from the Crown, participated in commerce throughout the Atlantic world, and owned property in many parts of the empire. Most of these extended families and "kin-connexions" held imperial offices of trust and profit and had a

The Revolution as a battle of Tory and Whig images, detail from the French "Carte du Port de Havre de Boston," 1783. Society of the Cincinnati.

strong stake in the empire. They also deeply believed that the true path of liberty required the rule of law and sovereignty of the king-in-Parliament. Boston Loyalist Peter Oliver drew a distinction between the anarchic "natural liberty" of the Boston mobs who tormented his brother Andrew Oliver and the "civil liberty" that flourished under the British Crown.[194]

American Tories had a highly developed imagery of liberty and loyalty. Its elements were interlocking symbols of Church and Crown, Britannia and Libertas, a constitutional monarchy and the rule of law. The most common motif combined liberty and loyalty in a single image of Britannia with a wand and pileus in her hand and a lion at her side. Political drawings often contrasted this figure with European symbols of "universal monarchy" and absolute power.[195]

These emblems of liberty and loyalty appeared in celebrations of the King's Birthday, a Loyalist holiday of high importance during the American Revolution. In New York City, which remained under British control from 1776 to 1783, one Royal Birthday was celebrated with fireworks, of which the climax was a pyrotechnic portrait of "George Rex with a Crown imperial, illumined and finished with a globe of fire."[196]

A Loyalist image of liberty and freedom: George III as the guardian of Magna Carta and the Bill of Rights. The cornucopia on the left symbolized the fruits of liberty and freedom. Chimney Ornament. Collection of James C. Kelly.

Similar emblems appeared on the flags and uniforms of more than a hundred American Loyalist units that fought in the Revolution. One example was the guidon of the Kings American Dragoons (1768). Many others appeared on uniform buttons, cap badges, and officers' gorgets, which commonly included roses and thistles, lions and unicorns, and royal arms that expressed an idea of personal loyalty to the Crown.[197] Other Loyalist images were printed on broadsides and widely used by artists in Britain and British America. They also appeared on the mastheads of Loyalist newspapers such as James Rivington's *New-York Gazetteer*, which used the royal arms for its emblem. Loyalists linked these symbols to emblems of liberty. An interesting example was a chimney ornament that showed George III as the guarantor of British liberties in the Bill of Rights (1689) and Magna Carta (1215).[198]

After the war, many Loyalists fled the colonies—more in proportion to the population than emigrated from France after 1789. Many went to Canada, where they organized themselves as United Empire Loyalists. Wherever these refugees from the American Revolution settled, their symbols of liberty and loyalty took root and are still a living culture in British North America.

WHIG IMAGES OF PARTICULAR LIBERTIES

Visions of an "American Bill of Rights" before 1776

> Those RIGHTS which God and Nature mean,
> RIGHTS! which when truly understood,
> Are Cause of universal Good.
> RIGHTS! which declare, "That all are free,
> In Person and in Property."
>
> —PHILO PATRIAE, 1769

I N 1774, Henry Marchant designed a flag for the Rhode Island militia. He wrote, "It is my idea to have a female figure representing the Genius of America standing erect with a staff in her right hand and the cap of liberty upon the top of it. In her left hand either the Bible or America's Bill of Rights."[199]

Henry Marchant was the attorney general of Rhode Island. He knew well that in 1774 there was no such thing as a written Bill of Rights for America, only an English Bill of Rights, which had been part of the Revolutionary Settlement of 1689. With many Americans, he was keenly aware that Britain's Parliament had made very clear by repeated acts and usurpations that the English Bill of Rights did not apply to the colonies. But Henry Marchant had a vision of an American Bill of Rights that existed in another form. It was much like the British Constitution, a set of customs rather than written laws or charters.

To study these customary rights is to discover a history far removed from much American scholarship about constitutional rights and civil liberties in America. Customary rights were defined by their history, and mainly by acts of oppression. In particular, oppressive acts of British Parliaments and imperial officials were profoundly important in shaping these American traditions.

The result was a pluralist tradition of particular "liberties." It derived in a distant way from the liberties of ancient Rome and medieval Europe, which had been understood as specific exemptions from a condition of prior restraint or as special privileges for individuals and groups. But that was only its beginning. By the mid-eighteenth century, the English-speaking world had moved beyond this way of thinking. Writers such as John Trenchard and Thomas Gordon in *Cato's Letters* and *The Independent Whig* (1720–21) argued that liberties were not special privileges but inalienable rights.[200]

But what rights? And for whom? These questions had long been contested in the colonies, mainly in conflicts among elites. The great dissenters in early America were people of high rank: Anne Hutchinson and Mary Dyer, Roger Williams and William Penn, John Peter Zenger and Andrew Hamilton, Francis Makemie and James Otis. So also were their oppressors.

From the earliest colonial settlements to the American Revolution, every generation of American elites struggled over these questions. The most urgent rights were about religious liberty and freedom of conscience. There was a striking pattern here, even a universal tendency in colonial cultures. In most parts of the New World, colonists of many faiths became more intolerant of others in America than they had been in Europe. In Mexico, the Spanish Inquisition was more cruel than it had been in Spain itself, even though the colonial population was carefully screened for religious orthodoxy. The same thing happened in Quebec, where French Catholics established a system of religious surveillance and persecution that planted spies in every household. In Anglican Virginia, Sir William Berkeley and his Cavaliers were very cruel to Quakers and Calvinists, at the same time that Charles II was moving toward toleration in England. In New Netherland, Peter Stuyvesant abandoned the toleration of the Old Netherland and cruelly persecuted Jews and other groups. He resisted pressure from home to create a more open and tolerant regime. Puritanism in New England became a byword for bigotry at the same time that Puritans of the same stripe in old England embraced an idea of toleration. Rare exceptions to this rule of early American intolerance were Roger Williams in Rhode Island, the Catholic Lords Baltimore in Maryland, and most of all the Quakers, who extended to others the rights they claimed for themselves.

Here was a curious paradox in early American history. The anxiety of life in the New World made colonists of all faiths deeply fearful of dissent. At the same time, the New World attracted many dissenters. The result was a collision between two powerful movements, which led to bitter conflicts in most colonies, where rights of conscience were asserted and denied with equal passion.

Rights of Conscience

After 1760, these old struggles over religious liberty took on a new urgency in the expanding conflict between the colonies and the mother country. At the same time that an imperial controversy was developing over issues of property, taxation, and representation, Anglican Archbishop Thomas Secker tried to expand an Anglican establishment in America. His actions caused high outrage among colonists of many denominations. An engraving from 1769, "An Attempt to Land a Bishop in America," shows a bishop attempting to come ashore in America and being pushed away by an angry crowd. In the foreground is a Quaker, dressed in a broad-brimmed hat and a shadbelly coat. Behind him is a New England Congregationalist who has hurled a copy of Calvin's works at the bishop's head. Others hold the works of Locke and Algernon Sydney. One shouts, "No Lords Spiritual or Temporal in New England." Another carries a banner, "Liberty and Freedom of Conscience."

The engraving shows an interesting shift of thinking. The struggle for individual rights often began as a demand by dissenters for the freedom to establish their own hegemonies and to tyrannize others on their own terms. But in this eighteenth-century image we find a new vision of free society as a web of individual rights for people of all denominations.

An image of religious liberty and freedom of conscience: "Attempt to Land a Bishop 1769," a cartoon attacking the British government and Archbishop Thomas Secker for seeking to establish an Anglican episcopate in America. Library of Congress.

Rights of Free Expression

Another right of growing importance in the colonies was liberty of the press. The leading colonial case was fought out in New York. John Peter Zenger was a German immigrant who flourished in the New World and became publisher of the *New York Weekly Journal,* an opposition newspaper that opposed an increasingly arbitrary colonial regime. In 1734, Zenger's paper published articles that outraged the authorities. Even though they were not written by Zenger himself, he was arrested, thrown into jail, held incommunicado for nearly a year, and finally brought to trial in 1735 on a charge of seditious libel. Zenger was defended by Philadelphia lawyer Andrew Hamilton, with strong support from the city government of New York. Hamilton tried and failed to introduce truth as a defense against a charge of seditious libel but succeeded in winning acquittal. He had taken the case without fee. In thanks the Common Council of New York City gave Hamilton a gold box that celebrated the cause of liberty and law. In the center was the seal of New York. With it came the freedom of that city.[201]

In eighteenth-century America, ideas of a free press were more limited than they would later become. Liberty of the press often was thought to mean merely freedom from prior restraint, such as censorship before publication. It did not mean freedom from punishment after a work had been published, if it violated the common law of seditious libel. In the Zenger case, a larger idea of freedom of the press appeared in the arguments of counsel and the jury's finding. Both went beyond the doctrine of liberty from prior restraint.

Many other cases followed the older and more limited doctrine. Some historians have judged these ideas of freedom by our own standards and found them wanting. But images of freedom in these cases reminds us of the passionate belief that even these limited ideas inspired. It was from this passion that larger ideas of freedom would grow.

Rights of Property, Self-Government, and the Rule of Law

From the Stamp Act in 1765 to the Intolerable Acts in 1774, one of the most common rallying cries was "Liberty and Property." This idea was a bundle of individual rights. In general it meant the right to be secure in "the means of acquiring and possessing property," as some highly propertied Whigs put it in the Virginia Declaration of Rights. More specifically, it included the right to be secure from unlawful searches and seizures, the right to trial by jury "in controversies respecting property," the right against taxation of property without representation, and protections against the taking of property without due process of law or "just compensation."

Other individual rights were in dispute in Britain and America during the late colonial era. The *Writs of Assistance Case* in Massachusetts (1760) was a struggle over the right to be free from illegal searches and seizures. The *Parson's Cause* in Virginia (1762) was about the right to self-government. *McDougall's Case* in New York (1769) was about the right to a free

The Bloody Massacre perpetrated in King—t—Street BOSTON on March 5th 1770 by a party of the 29th REG.t

BUTCHER'S HALL

Engrav'd Printed & Sold by PAUL REVERE BOSTON

Unhappy Boston! see thy Sons deplore, | If scalding drops from Rage from Anguish Wrung, | But know, FATE summons to that awful Goal,
Thy hallow'd Walks besmear'd with guiltless Gore: | If speechless Sorrows lab'ring for a Tongue, | Where JUSTICE strips the Murd'rer of his Soul:
While faithless P—n and his savage Bands, | Or if a weeping World can ought appease | Should venal C—ts the scandal of the Land,
With murd'rous Rancour stretch their bloody Hands; | The plaintive Ghosts of Victims such as these; | Snatch the relentless Villain from her Hand.
Like fierce Barbarians grinning o'er their Prey, | The Patriot's copious Tears for each are shed, | Keen Execrations on this Plate inscrib'd,
Approve the Carnage and enjoy the Day. | A glorious Tribute which embalms the Dead. | Shall reach a JUDGE who never can be brib'd.

The unhappy Sufferers were Mess.rs SAM.l GRAY, SAM.l MAVERICK, JAM.s CALDWELL, CRISPUS ATTUCKS & PAT.k CARR
Killed. Six wounded, two of them (CHRIST.r MONK & JOHN CLARK) Mortally

Liberty as the right to life: Paul Revere's engraving "The Bloody Massacre Perpetuated in King Street," 1770. American Antiquarian Society.

and fair trial, and also the right to bail. In all of these cases lawyers such as Patrick Henry and James Otis, and defendants such as Alexander McDougall, became heroes of liberty and freedom. They became living symbols of the specific rights they were defending and also of the larger idea of a free society as a web of rights.

The most fundamental human right was to life itself, for without life there could be no other liberty. Whigs believed that this idea was threatened by imperial tyranny. A highly effective image was the engraving of the Boston Massacre in 1770 by Henry Pelham and Paul Revere. A learned literature dwells on inaccuracies of detail and misses the point. The print represents an actual event in which British troops destroyed the lives of American colonists and threatened the inalienable right to life itself. The Official Customs House is labeled "Butcher's Hall." At the bottom of the print is a passage from the Book of Psalms and a bolt of lightning descending from heaven to destroy a sword. The scene was widely copied and even engraved on powder horns.

When Americans began to draw up declarations of rights, they worked not from a theory of liberty or freedom but from an historical experience of tyranny and oppression and from a long memory of customary rights, which were more open, complex, and dynamic than written documents could ever be, and always with a deeper meaning. The great texts were a superstructure that rose on the foundation of this historical tradition.

LIBERTY OR DEATH!

America Becomes a World Symbol of Liberty and Freedom, 1775

> As for me, give me Liberty or give me Death!
> —A BACKCOUNTRY VERSION
> PATRICK HENRY, 1775

> Americans! Liberty or Death! Join or Die!
> —A NEW ENGLAND VERSION
> ISAIAH THOMAS, 1775

> They are all determined to die or [be] Free!
> —A LOYALIST LADY, 1775[202]

MANY VISIONS of a free society flourished in the American colonies. We have seen them in the ordered ways of town-born New England, the pluralism and materialism of New York, the reciprocal rights of the Quaker colonies, the hierarchical liberties of Virginia, the West Indian slavedrivers' dreams of unfettered opportunity in the Carolina lowcountry, the natural liberty of North British borderers, the *Vogelfreiheit* and *Feigenbaumfreiheit* of German immigrants, liberty as emancipation and freedom as rights of belonging among African Americans, Lockean liberty among transatlantic elites, Tory ideas of liberty as loyalty, and Whig ideas of an American Bill of Rights as early as 1774.

All of these ideas were interchangeably called liberty or freedom in 1775, often "liberty and freedom" in a single phrase. Some were closer to ancient ideas of liberty as independence on the model of Roman *libertas* or Greek *eleutheria*. Others were nearer to ideas of freedom as belonging to a community of free people, in the manner of North European *Freiheit* or Sumerian *ama-ar-gi*. All of them combined elements of these various traditions in original and highly inventive ways.

These early American ideas differed in many dimensions. Most restricted liberty or freedom to a tribe, class, religion, or race, but some reached out to many people, even to all people. The New England ideas were more communal or collectivist; backcountry visions were more individualist and even atomist. These various ideas of liberty and freedom were different in their mix of rights and responsibilities and in their enumeration of specific rights. They were by degrees religious or secular, material or spiritual, egalitarian or elitist. Most had inner tensions and even contradictions in their endless recombinations of ancient models of liberty-as-independence and freedom-as-belonging.

These traditions also differed in other ways, not least in regard to equality. As late as 1774, few American visions of liberty and freedom embraced universal conceptions of equality, or even equal rights. But some included elements of equality in special and limited ways. New Englanders inherited Puritan ideas of "parity" among the elect. New Yorkers adopted Livingston's idea of "impartial Equity" among different ethnic groups. Pennsylvanians shared Quaker visions of reciprocity and the Golden Rule. Others in Virginia and the Carolinas opposed equality in all its forms and thought of liberty and freedom as strenuously elitist and hierarchical in its relation to rank, race, and gender.

But for all their many differences, these American ideas shared important elements in common. All envisioned liberty and freedom as a union of ethical ideals and material interests. In England and America during the seventeenth century, a popular rallying cry was "Liberty and Property and No Wooden Shoes!" That spirit was strong among Americans of every rank and condition in the Revolutionary era. People of high and middling estates rallied to the defense of liberty and property. So also did the poor; in America their goal was not to condemn private property but to acquire it.[203]

"Liberty or Death," an iron fireback cast at Aera Furnace, York County, South Carolina by Isaac Hayne and his slaves, 1778. Hayne was hanged by British troops in 1781 for fighting in defense of his liberty. The Museum of Early Southern Decorative Arts, Winston-Salem, N.C.

Historians have variously argued (according to their politics) that the drivers of the American Revolution were colonial gentlemen, or yeoman farmers, or urban artisans, or mobs of "jack tars" and "saucy boys" in seaport cities. Others believe that the leaders of the Revolution were deists, or Calvinists, or evangelical Christians. Some think that the cradle of the Revolution was Boston, or Philadelphia, or New York, or Virginia, or the backcountry. All of these interpretations are right in assigning an important role to these various groups; wrong in arguing for a dominant role. The American Revolution was strong because it included so many ranks, regions, and religions, with visions of liberty and freedom.

Another common element was the depth of belief in all of these ideas. Throughout the colonies, Americans of many persuasions believed that liberty and freedom were more precious than life itself. When the fighting began, they took up the common cry, "Liberty or Death." That motto appeared everywhere in the American Revolution. It was flown from Liberty Poles, festooned on Liberty Trees, embroidered above backcountry rattlesnakes, and printed below lowcountry crescents.

In the southern backcountry, a staunch Whig entrepreneur named Isaac Hayne founded South Carolina's first ironworks in 1778 and called it Aera Furnace. He cast cannon and shot to fit, and also iron firebacks for American homes. One of them survives with the date 1778, marked with the initials of the makers, and the motto "Liberty or Death" cast in iron. The words were prophetic for Isaac Hayne. A British force destroyed the furnace and took Isaac Hayne prisoner. He was hanged at Charleston in 1781.[204]

In northern New England, New Hampshire's General John Stark played a major part at Bunker Hill, at Trenton, and as commander at the battle of Bennington, then refused public office and retired to his farm. His advice to his countrymen was as simple as his life: "Live free or die—death is not the worst of evils." Gentlemen of Virginia preferred to say it in Latin: *Vita potens libertas potior.* Rhode Islanders said, *Patria cara; carior libertas,* "The fatherland is dear, liberty is dearer." South Carolinians made it *Vita potior libertas.* People in Massachusetts cast it in collective terms: Isaiah Thomas proclaimed on the masthead of his *Massachusetts Spy,* "Americans! Liberty or Death! Join or Die!" The backcountry leader Patrick

"As for me, give me liberty, or give me death!" Patrick Henry's idea of individuated liberty was one vision among many in early America. Painting attributed to Asahel L. Powers, ca. 1820–30. Shelburne Museum.

Henry made it into an individual idea: "As for *me*, give *me* liberty, or give *me* death."[205]

Foreign observers of the Revolution noted this fervor for "liberty or death" and were astonished to discover that Americans really meant it. Among them was Lord Percy, who commanded a British brigade in heavy fighting on the day of Lexington and Concord. After the battle he wrote in amazement of "the spirit of enthusiasm" among New England militia who "advanced within ten yards to fire at me & other officers, tho' they were morally certain of being put to death themselves in an instant."[206]

In the same way, a Loyalist lady wrote to her English nephew, "All the Provinces [are] arming and training in the same manner, for It is not the low idle Fellow that fight[s] only for pay, but men of great property are Common Soldiers who say they are fighting for themselves and posterity."[207]

At the root of this way of thinking among American Whigs was an absolute and certain belief in the justice of their cause. There was no moral ambivalence here, absolutely nothing of the ethical relativism, alienation, anomie, and cynicism that flourished in other periods of American history, including our own. American Whigs of 1775 thought very clearly about great public questions in terms of white and black, right or wrong, liberty or slavery, freedom or tyranny. They were confident that right was on their side and that they were doing God's work in the world.

There was also a complete confidence that the cause of liberty and freedom would triumph in the world. Many emblems included an iconic expression of this optimism. A common motif was a rising sun. Carolina's waxing increscent was another symbol of the same idea, as were the signs that were hoisted on Liberty Trees, and the flags that flew from Liberty Poles, and the words that were inscribed on the great Quaker bell. All of these symbols shared a spirit of cosmic optimism, and even what H. G. Wells called an American attitude of optimistic fatalism.

These various elements came together to create the idea of a common cause, which appeared in a song that was written in 1770 and sung throughout the Revolution. Its composer was John Dickinson, a wealthy lawyer and landowner of Quaker ancestry. He brought the colonies together with his *Letters of a Pennsylvania Farmer* in 1768 and two years later composed a set of verses that was called "The Liberty Song" or "The Farmer's Song." It was sung to the tune of William Boyce's "Hearts of Oak," which was widely known throughout the English-speaking world. Primarily it was an appeal for liberty and unity in a common cause.

COME join Hand in Hand, brave AMERICANS all,
And rouse your bold hearts at fair LIBERTY's call.
No tyrannous Acts shall suppress your just claim,
Or stain with Dishonor AMERICA's Name

Eight stanzas of the song recited the acts of Parliament Americans believed to be destructive of their rights. After each stanza a chorus was sung.

In FREEDOM we're BORN and in FREEDOM we'll LIVE,
Our Purses are ready,
Steady, Friends, Steady
Not as SLAVES but as FREEMEN our Money well give. . . .
Then join hand in hand, brave Americans all!
By uniting we stand, by dividing we fall.

"The Liberty Song" was sung by the Sons of Liberty beneath Boston's Liberty Tree and by New York's Sons of Neptune at the Liberty Pole. It was heard from planters and mechanics of Charleston, South Carolina, beneath their crescent banners. It was printed in Williamsburg's *Virginia Gazette* and issued as a broadside by publishers in Philadelphia and throughout the colonies. Kenneth Silverman writes that "the Liberty Song became not a title but a type." It inspired many other songs and poems and broadsides that spread swiftly from America.[208]

In the late eighteenth century, new arteries of communication were opening rapidly throughout the western world. Most of them flowed with printers' ink. In Germany alone, 410 new magazines and newspapers were founded in the 1760s, 718 in the 1770s, and 1,225 in the 1780s.[209]

The news of the American Revolution traveled from one press to another with astonishing speed. Whig leaders in Massachusetts sent reports of the first shots at Lexington across the Atlantic by a fast-sailing Yankee schooner, which reached England two weeks before General Gage's version of events. This Whig interpretation of the American Revolution traveled from one print shop to another in France, Germany, Poland, and Russia. By the time it appeared in the *Warsaw Gazette,* the first shots at Lexington had become a major battle, and the issues were even more sharply drawn.[210]

The American Revolution awakened deep sympathy in Europe, even among ruling elites who had much to lose from large ideas of liberty and freedom. One observer wrote that the "fashion of the day" was to be "an aristocrat in Europe and a republican in America."[211]

The news from America went not only to Europe but throughout the world. In 1784, a British ship on a passage from India stopped at the Comoro Islands in the Mozambique Channel, off the coast of southern Africa. It found that the African inhabitants had risen in revolution against their Arab rulers. Their rallying cry was "America is free! Cannot we be?"[212]

By 1786, the news from America was traveling through Asia. One of the first American ships to trade with China called at the port of Macao, and the residents put on a dinner in their honor. After the main courses, the Americans were invited into an adjoining room for a "very elegant" dessert. Boston merchant Samuel Shaw was amazed at the events that followed. Shaw wrote in his journal, "The tables were ornamented with representations, in paper painted and gilt, of castles, pagodas, and other Chinese edifices, in each of which were confined small birds. The first toast was *Liberty!* and in an instant, the doors of the paper prisons being set open, the little captives were released, and, flying about us in every direction, seemed to enjoy the blessing which had just been conferred upon them."[213]

In Asia, Africa, and Europe, ideas of American liberty and freedom became a vision of a better world. After 1776, Americans began to struggle with the question of what that world might be. In the search for an answer, they created new and larger images of liberty and freedom, which are the next part of this story.

A REPUBLIC UNITED
The Search for a Common Vision, 1776–1840

"We Owe Allegiance to No Crown." This colorful image, often reproduced in the new nation, combines eight republican symbols of liberty and freedom. Can you find them? Lithograph. Library of Congress.

THE DECLARATION OF INDEPENDENCE

Jefferson's Ambiguous "Expression of the American Mind"

That's a hard mystery of Jefferson's.
What did he mean? Of course the easy way
Is to decide it simply isn't true.
It may not be. I heard a fellow say so.
But never mind, the Welshman got it planted
Where it will trouble us a thousand years.
Each age will have to reconsider it.

—ROBERT FROST[1]

ON JULY 4, 1776, after much talk and many votes, the Continental Congress approved the Declaration of Independence. That evening, the document was read aloud to small groups of "respectable people" in Philadelphia.[2] Through the night, printer John Dunlap set the full text on a handsome folio sheet. The next day, President John Hancock sent copies to every state and urged that "the People be universally informed." Philadelphia's Committee of Safety ordered gallopers to carry it through the country. In the weeks that followed, a new icon of liberty and freedom began to travel around the world.[3]

Americans received it with high enthusiasm. The Declaration of Independence was proclaimed on court days in Virginia, read at county polls in Pennsylvania, and discussed by town meetings in New England. It was celebrated with the same rituals that British colonists had used for the King's Birthday: fireworks and illuminations, cannonades and church bells, military parades and civil processions, dinners and toasts. To those old monarchical customs, new republican elements were added: readings of the document itself, and speeches on the meaning of liberty and freedom.[4]

The dates of these first celebrations in 1776 varied with the speed of the messengers: July 8 in Philadelphia, July 9 in New York, July 18 in Boston, mid-August on the far frontiers. In 1777, they began to happen on the Fourth of July, the date that appeared in John Dunlap's folio sheet.

In CONGRESS, July 4, 1776.

A DECLARATION

By the REPRESENTATIVES of the

UNITED STATES OF AMERICA,

In GENERAL CONGRESS ASSEMBLED.

WHEN in the Course of human Events, it becomes neceſſary for one People to diſſolve the Political Bands which have connected them with another, and to aſſume among the Powers of the Earth, the ſeparate and equal Station to which the Laws of Nature and of Nature's God entitle them, a decent Reſpect to the Opinions of Mankind requires that they ſhould declare the cauſes which impel them to the Separation.

We hold theſe Truths to be ſelf-evident, that all Men are created equal, that they are endowed by their Creator with certain unalienable Rights, that among theſe are Life, Liberty, and the Purſuit of Happineſs—That to ſecure theſe Rights, Governments are inſtituted among Men, deriving their juſt Powers from the Conſent of the Governed, that whenever any Form of Government becomes deſtructive of theſe Ends, it is the Right of the People to alter or to aboliſh it, and to inſtitute new Government, laying its Foundation on ſuch Principles, and organizing its Powers in ſuch Form, as to them ſhall ſeem moſt likely to effect their Safety and Happineſs. Prudence, indeed, will dictate that Governments long eſtabliſhed ſhould not be changed for light and tranſient Cauſes; and accordingly all Experience hath ſhewn, that Mankind are more diſpoſed to ſuffer, while Evils are ſufferable, than to right themſelves by aboliſhing the Forms to which they are accuſtomed. But when a long Train of Abuſes and Uſurpations, purſuing invariably the ſame Object, evinces a Deſign to reduce them under abſolute Deſpotiſm, it is their Right, it is their Duty, to throw off ſuch Government, and to provide new Guards for their future Security. Such has been the patient Sufferance of theſe Colonies; and ſuch is now the Neceſſity which conſtrains them to alter their former Syſtems of Government. The Hiſtory of the preſent King of Great-Britain is a Hiſtory of repeated Injuries and Uſurpations, all having in direct Object the Eſtabliſhment of an abſolute Tyranny over theſe States. To prove this, let Facts be ſubmitted to a candid World.

He has refuſed his Aſſent to Laws, the moſt wholeſome and neceſſary for the public Good.

He has forbidden his Governors to paſs Laws of immediate and preſſing Importance, unleſs ſuſpended in their Operation till his Aſſent ſhould be obtained; and when ſo ſuſpended, he has utterly neglected to attend to them.

He has refuſed to paſs other Laws for the Accommodation of large Diſtricts of People, unleſs thoſe People would relinquiſh the Right of Repreſentation in the Legiſlature, a Right ineſtimable to them, and formidable to Tyrants only.

He has called together Legiſlative Bodies at Places unuſual, uncomfortable, and diſtant from the Depoſitory of their public Records, for the ſole Purpoſe of fatiguing them into Compliance with his Meaſures.

He has diſſolved Repreſentative Houſes repeatedly, for oppoſing with manly Firmneſs his Invaſions on the Rights of the People.

He has refuſed for a long Time, after ſuch Diſſolutions, to cauſe others to be elected; whereby the Legiſlative Powers, incapable of Annihilation, have returned to the People at large for their exerciſe; the State remaining in the mean time expoſed to all the Dangers of Invaſion from without, and Convulſions within.

He has endeavoured to prevent the Population of theſe States; for that Purpoſe obſtructing the Laws for Naturalization of Foreigners; refuſing to paſs others to encourage their Migrations hither, and raiſing the Conditions of new Appropriations of Lands.

He has obſtructed the Adminiſtration of Juſtice, by refuſing his Aſſent to Laws for eſtabliſhing Judiciary Powers.

He has made Judges dependent on his Will alone, for the Tenure of their Offices, and the Amount and Payment of their Salaries.

He has erected a Multitude of new Offices, and ſent hither Swarms of Officers to harraſs our People, and eat out their Subſtance.

He has kept among us, in Times of Peace, Standing Armies, without the conſent of our Legiſlatures.

He has affected to render the Military independent of and ſuperior to the Civil Power.

He has combined with others to ſubject us to a Juriſdiction foreign to our Conſtitution, and unacknowledged by our Laws; giving his Aſſent to their Acts of pretended Legiſlation:

For quartering large Bodies of Armed Troops among us:

For protecting them, by a mock Trial, from Puniſhment for any Murders which they ſhould commit on the Inhabitants of theſe States:

For cutting off our Trade with all Parts of the World:

For impoſing Taxes on us without our Conſent:

For depriving us, in many Caſes, of the Benefits of Trial by Jury:

For tranſporting us beyond Seas to be tried for pretended Offences:

For aboliſhing the free Syſtem of Engliſh Laws in a neighbouring Province, eſtabliſhing therein an arbitrary Government, and enlarging its Boundaries, ſo as to render it at once an Example and fit Inſtrument for introducing the ſame abſolute Rule into theſe Colonies:

For taking away our Charters, aboliſhing our moſt valuable Laws, and altering fundamentally the Forms of our Governments:

For ſuſpending our own Legiſlatures, and declaring themſelves inveſted with Power to legiſlate for us in all Caſes whatſoever.

He has abdicated Government here, by declaring us out of his Protection and waging War againſt us.

He has plundered our Seas, ravaged our Coaſts, burnt our Towns, and deſtroyed the Lives of our People.

He is, at this Time, tranſporting large Armies of foreign Mercenaries to compleat the Works of Death, Deſolation, and Tyranny, already begun with circumſtances of Cruelty and Perfidy, ſcarcely paralleled in the moſt barbarous Ages, and totally unworthy the Head of a civilized Nation.

He has conſtrained our fellow Citizens taken Captive on the high Seas to bear Arms againſt their Country, to become the Executioners of their Friends and Brethren, or to fall themſelves by their Hands.

He has excited domeſtic Inſurrections amongſt us, and has endeavoured to bring on the Inhabitants of our Frontiers, the mercileſs Indian Savages, whoſe known Rule of Warfare, is an undiſtinguiſhed Deſtruction, of all Ages, Sexes and Conditions.

In every ſtage of theſe Oppreſſions we have Petitioned for Redreſs in the moſt humble Terms: Our repeated Petitions have been anſwered only by repeated Injury. A Prince, whoſe Character is thus marked by every act which may define a Tyrant, is unfit to be the Ruler of a free People.

Nor have we been wanting in Attentions to our Britiſh Brethren. We have warned them from Time to Time of Attempts by their Legiſlature to extend an unwarrantable Juriſdiction over us. We have reminded them of the Circumſtances of our Emigration and Settlement here. We have appealed to their native Juſtice and Magnanimity, and we have conjured them by the Ties of our common Kindred to diſavow theſe Uſurpations, which, would inevitably interrupt our Connections and Correſpondence. They too have been deaf to the Voice of Juſtice and of Conſanguinity. We muſt, therefore, acquieſce in the Neceſſity, which denounces our Separation, and hold them, as we hold the reſt of Mankind, Enemies in War, in Peace, Friends.

We, therefore, the Repreſentatives of the UNITED STATES OF AMERICA, in General Congress, Aſſembled, appealing to the Supreme Judge of the World for the Rectitude of our Intentions, do, in the Name, and by Authority of the good People of theſe Colonies, ſolemnly Publiſh and Declare, That theſe United Colonies are, and of Right ought to be, Free and Independent States; that they are abſolved from all Allegiance to the Britiſh Crown, and that all political Connection between them and the State of Great-Britain, is and ought to be totally diſſolved; and that as Free and Independent States, they have full Power to levy War, conclude Peace, contract Alliances, eſtabliſh Commerce, and to do all other Acts and Things which Independent States may of right do. And for the ſupport of this Declaration, with a firm Reliance on the Protection of divine Providence, we mutually pledge to each other our Lives, our Fortunes, and our ſacred Honor.

Signed by ORDER and in BEHALF of the CONGRESS,

JOHN HANCOCK, PRESIDENT.

ATTEST.
CHARLES THOMSON, SECRETARY.

PHILADELPHIA: PRINTED BY JOHN DUNLAP.

"The Declaration of Independence." John Dunlap's broadside was printed in Philadelphia on the night of July 4–5, 1776. It was reproduced on other presses and began to be displayed in American homes as an icon of a free republic during the first summer of independence. A census in 1976 located 21 surviving copies of the first printing. This one is in the Library of Congress.

By 1779, American expatriates honored the day in Europe. In 1782, American prisoners of war aboard the British hulk *Jersey* found ways to celebrate the Fourth of July, even in their terrible confinement. They hoisted thirteen small flags and sang "patriotic songs" until infuriated British guards drove them below with bayonets.[5]

Soon after the Revolution the Fourth of July became an American holiday, called the National Day, or Independence Day. On July 4, 1793, an irascible British traveler named Charles Janson happened to be in Boston and was awakened at dawn by guns and bells. He called for a soothing cup of tea, and demanded an explanation. The landlady's pretty daughter (whom he called a "pert virgin") told him that it was Independence Day, and insisted that he escort her to the public celebration. She refused to relent until he agreed, and led him to a hot and crowded hall. There he was made to endure the reading of the document and a torrent of "invective against England" by an "arrogant young Yankee." It was the maiden speech of a future president, John Quincy Adams.[6]

The Declaration's Double Meaning

At another of these early celebrations, in Worcester, Massachusetts, on July 22, 1776, gentlemen raised their glasses to the Declaration of Independence and drank a double toast: "George rejected and Liberty protected."[7]

From the start, Americans made Thomas Jefferson's great text into a national icon, always with that double meaning. It was celebrated on public occasions as an instrument of national independence and reverently displayed in private homes as a symbol of the rights of belonging to a free republic. In New York City, journalist John Holt reprinted it in 1776 on an extra sheet of his newspaper and urged his readers to "separate it from the rest of the paper and fix it up, in open view, in their houses." Many did so. Surviving copies of John Holt's broadside bear marks where they were nailed to walls or hung in frames.[8]

The same thing happened among America's friends in Europe. The marquis de Lafayette ordered a copy of the Declaration of Independence to be displayed on a wall in his home with an empty space beside it, "waiting the Declaration of Rights in France." On both sides of the Atlantic the text of the Declaration of Independence quickly became an international icon.[9]

But what exactly did it mean? On one level, the answer was clear enough. The Declaration's rejection of monarchy and its idea of national independence were self-evident from the start. But its ideas of liberty, free-

The first public reading of the Declaration in Philadelphia. This engraving by Edward Barnard, 1782, shows an early American union flag with thirteen red stripes. Library Company of Philadelphia.

dom, and equality were open to interpretation. Many scholars have tried to find their meaning by the text-and-context method. Some claim to have discovered the key in the writings of John Locke, or the treatises of Scottish philosophers, or other works that were written far from Philadelphia.[10]

The man who drafted the Declaration of Independence warned against that method. Thomas Jefferson wrote that he consulted "neither book nor pamphlet," nor "copied from any particular or previous writing," nor tried to frame any "new principles, or new arguments, never before thought of." He said that his text was meant "to be an expression of the American mind, and to give that expression the proper tone and spirit called for by the occasion." So it was, and we should take him at his word.

To that end, the text of the Declaration was conceived in creative ambiguity, in the hope that most Americans could support it, even as their visions of a free America were in some ways far apart. In that process, the Declaration of Independence itself became a new vision of liberty and freedom, larger and more open than any that had preceded it. It was the first of many enlargements in a process that would become a central theme of American history.[11]

The same creative ambiguity appeared in its idea of equality. Did the Declaration of Independence mean that "all men are created *equal*?" Or did it mean, in the words of Yankee Nathaniel Ames, that "all men are *created* equal, but differ greatly in the sequel"? Was it a vision of equality before the law, or equality of social rank, or equality of material condition? In Europe, these questions ignited an international debate between critics who thought that Mr. Jefferson had gone too far, or not far enough.[12]

Americans went a different way. In 1776, most of them found a middling position. They understood Jefferson's idea of "created equal" to mean "equal liberty," or "equality of rights" for all free men. George Mason wrote in Virginia's Declaration of Rights, "All men are, by nature, equally free and independent, and have certain inherent rights."[13] The backcountry leader Patrick Henry thought the same way. As governor of

Virginia in 1778, he ordered Colonel George Rogers Clark to introduce "equal liberty and happiness" to all the inhabitants of the Illinois country, even "Frenchmen and Indians." He added, "Let them see and feel the advantages of being fellow citizens and freemen."[14]

That same idea was shared by the most radical Whigs in America. Thomas Paine wrote in 1778, "Wherever I use the words *freedoms* or *rights,* I desire to be understood to mean a perfect equality of them. Let the rich man enjoy his riches, and the poor man comfort himself in his poverty. But the floor of freedom is as level as water. It *can* be no otherwise of itself and *will* be no otherwise till ruffled by a storm." This was not an idea of material equality. Thomas Paine assumed that the rich man would continue to "enjoy his riches" and that poverty would persist in the world. Here again, his idea of equality meant "equal freedoms" or "equal rights."[15]

In New England, a similar thought occurred to one of the most conservative Whigs. John Adams proclaimed in his first draft of the Massachusetts Constitution that "all men are born equally free and independent, and have certain natural, essential, and unalienable rights." Even that vision of equality was too much for Yankee Calvinists, who believed in the depravity of the natural man and salvation for a small elite. The Massachusetts Convention removed the word *equally* from Adams's draft. But still it meant the same thing, for if "all men are born free," then equal rights remained by implication. That interpretation was enforced by Massachusetts courts, which abolished slavery explicitly on the basis of what remained of John Adams's sentence. It is very interesting that conservative and radical Whigs both shared an idea of equal rights and rejected equality as a leveling of wealth. In the American Revolution, "created equal" meant equal liberty, and a broad distribution of rights for all free men.[16]

But which rights, and for whom? And what idea of liberty and freedom? On these great questions, other ambiguities appeared in the Declaration of Independence. Some were not of Jefferson's making. Several were added to his draft as it worked its way through the Congress.

One revision was important for New England. In 1776, Jefferson himself held an idea widely shared in the southern colonies and the backcountry, that liberty meant independence for nations and individuals. In his first draft of the Declaration he wrote that "all men are created equal and independant [*sic*]." His New England colleagues in the Congress agreed that the "united colonies" should be independent from Britain, but the idea that all men were created independent was inconsistent with New England's tradition of ordered freedom and its institutions of collective belonging such as the town meeting. After discussions with three native-born New Englanders on the drafting committee, Jefferson's idea that all men were "independant" disappeared from the document.

Another change made the text more acceptable to the "tone and spirit" of the Quaker colonies. Jefferson's first draft began with an assertion that "we hold these truths to be sacred and undeniable." Objections were raised to these words. Probably at Franklin's suggestion, Jefferson's "sacred and undeniable" became "self-evident," which was more consistent with ideas of religious liberty and separation of church and state in the Delaware Valley, and also with the Quaker idea of reason as a self-evident "light within."

A third change was demanded by men from the "southern" colonies, which in 1776 meant South Carolina and Georgia. Jefferson thought of liberty as inconsistent with slavery and included a strong attack on the slave trade in his first draft of the Declaration. That passage won broad support from New England and Pennsylvania, but it was unacceptable to South Carolinians, whose idea of crescent-liberty included the right to enslave others. Jefferson's condemnation of slavery was removed.

These changes made Jefferson's document generally acceptable to three large groups in the American republic. With great precision, the Declaration of Independence proclaimed many specific "rights of the people" as protections against acts that had actually been committed by Parliament and the king. With great passion, it affirmed the right of the "United Colonies" to be free and independent of the British Crown. It also created a larger and more generous "tone and spirit" of liberty and freedom than had existed anywhere in America before independence. But the final text of the Declaration, as revised in Congress, was careful not to contradict any major idea of liberty and freedom that existed in the American colonies. It did so by contrived ambiguities, studied evasions, and deliberate omissions on contested questions. In that way the Declaration of Independence was unfinished business in 1776, and so it remains today. But as Robert Frost observed, the Welshman got it planted. Good husbandman that he was, he also gave it room to grow. Through the ages it has kept on growing in ways that the framers never imagined.

But before that process could begin, there was some prior business for Americans in 1776. It was one thing to declare independence, and another to achieve it. It was necessary to win a war against one of the most formidable powers in the world. Visions of liberty and freedom became important weapons in that struggle. To that end, Americans urgently needed unifying symbols of their common cause.

THE SEARCH FOR A COMMON VISION

A Minimalist Solution: The Liberty Flags of Long Island

> There is likewise to be one Regimentary or Great Colour ... [and] four standards of the four companies. ... In the Colour and the standards must be embroidered the word liberty.
>
> —GENERAL CHARLES LEE, 1775

IN NEW YORK, on July 9, 1776, General George Washington ordered his army to form by brigades and hear a reading of the Declaration of Independence. As they stood together, these citizen-soldiers made an image of American diversity. They wore coats of many colors. The Virginia gentlemen of George Washington's own Fairfax Militia were elegant in hunting jackets of buff and blue. Several silk-stocking American regiments were resplendent in bright scarlet and gold lace. Haslet's Delaware Continentals were patriotic in blue coats, white waistcoats, and red facings. New England regiments preferred forest green and other "sadd colours" that had long been used in the Puritan colonies. Pennsylvania militia wore plain brown, and New York's contentious pluralists were able to agree upon gray. Backcountry riflemen wore linen hunting shirts, dyed a color that English speakers called phillymort (from the French *feuille mort,* dead leaf). Most units had no uniforms at all, and more than a few lacked coats and shoes. Altogether, Washington's command looked less like an army than a collision of thirteen armed mobs. They called themselves the Continental Army, but on July 9, 1776, they had no continental uniform or emblem. They carried no common flag except the Grand Union Flag, which gave general dissatisfaction and could no longer be used after independence.[17]

For Americans in arms, the lack of common emblems became a serious problem on the battlefield. In the confusion of combat, standards and colors were important instruments of command and control. Units formed and moved around them. The Continental Army needed highly visible flags for that purpose, and also to distinguish friend from foe in the fog of war.

In 1776 it was not easy to find an emblem that all American Whigs could share. Most agreed that they were fighting for a common cause of liberty and freedom, but no existing symbol could represent so many different visions of those ideas. Continental General Charles Lee reflected on that problem and proposed what might be called the minimal solution. He suggested that every regiment in the American army should carry simple flags of solid color, "embroider'd with the word liberty."[18]

His idea had much to recommend it. It was quick and easy to execute. American households had the skills and materials ready at hand. The design itself was generally acceptable to most Americans, even if its meaning was contested. No matter how American Whigs understood the idea of liberty, they agreed upon the word. Here was the common denominator of their cause.

A Liberty Flag, of the design recommended for the American army by General Charles Lee. Early accounts describe it as made of blue-green silk. Today the color can no longer be distinguished. Many such flags were carried at the battle of Long Island on August 27, 1776, as an emblem of a common cause that Americans understood in different ways. Schenectady County Historical Society.

General Lee's minimal solution was accepted by many American units, but not by all of them. Always a few cantankerous Continentals exercised their liberty to dissent from liberty itself: an eternal problem in a free society. At least one New England regiment stubbornly insisted on its right to substitute the word *Congress*. But *Liberty* became the term of choice. American regiments astonished their enemies by marching to the defense of New York City behind improvised military colors, hastily made from dress silk, window curtains, and upholstery fabrics, all proclaiming LIBERTY in large letters.[19]

The campaign that followed was disastrous for the American cause. Washington's army was nearly destroyed on Long Island, and many liberty banners fell into the hands of British and German troops. After the battle, Hessian Adjutant General Carl Leopold Baurmeister reported, "We came into possession of eleven enemy flags with the motto 'Liberty.'"[20] No two of these liberty flags were exactly alike. One of them, captured near the country village of Flatbush by

Hessian troops on August 26, 1776, was "made of red damask with the motto, LIBERTY." An American housewife appears to have contributed her draperies to the cause.[21] Another tattered flag survives in the Schenectady Historical Society. It proclaims "Liberty" in white silk letters on a handsome piece of blue-green silk that might have been a ball gown, with a simple hem to hold a flagstaff.[22] At least one liberty banner was a red ensign with the British Union Jack in the canton, to which the word LIBERTY was added. This was a recycled Red Duster that had been flown by British and American merchant ships before the Revolution. Maybe it was meant to show that some Americans were still fighting for liberty within the British Empire in the spring of 1776.[23]

Most of these liberty flags followed the recommendation of General Charles Lee. It is interesting to observe that Lee was an English officer who had joined the American cause shortly before the war. He had no roots in any of the regional cultures that were so highly articulated in early America, and no attachment to any particular idea of liberty and freedom. His minimal solution to the problem of a common symbol was a product of his own origins.

E PLURIBUS UNUM

Pluralist Solutions

Color est e pluribus unus
[many colors blend into one]

—Virgil, Minor Poems, "Moretum,"
A DESCRIPTION OF WHAT HAPPENS WHEN
A HEAD OF GARLIC IS GROUND TOGETHER

WHILE MANY AMERICANS were making General Lee's liberty banners, others were inventing common images of liberty and freedom in a different spirit: not a unitary symbol that sought a common denominator but an emblem of diversity that celebrated American pluralism. This process began at an early date in the Revolution. Its results included several emblematic disasters that might be a warning to designing multiculturalists in every generation.

Early in 1776, one of these experiments appeared in a portrait of Ezek Hopkins, the first commander of the infant Continental Navy. The artist, John Martin, painted Commodore Hopkins on the deck of a warship. In the background of the painting are two American men-of-war, both cleared for action and firing broadsides. One ship displays the official flag of Massachusetts: a Liberty Tree with the motto "An Appeal to God." The other vessel flies the naval ensign of South Carolina, a rattlesnake with the words "Don't Tread on Me." A scholar observes, "It could be assumed that . . . the two flags represented the northern and southern colonies united under Hopkins."[24]

This image was a noble attempt at a national iconography, but its elements did not come together. The two flags represented different ideas of liberty and freedom, and the tension between them was deepened by an accident of composition. The artist arranged the ships of Massachusetts and South Carolina so that they appeared to be firing at one another:

hardly an image of American unity, and a portent of things to come. A French engraving of the same painting removed the scene of combat but kept the theme of difference by juxtaposing the two flags below the portrait. Even so, it was not a convincing emblem of a common cause.[25]

Other pluralist experiments were even less successful. In 1774, a committee of the Continental Congress approved a complex symbol to represent the American cause. At the center was a fluted column. Its base rested on a copy of Magna Carta, and its capital was crowned by a liberty cap. The column was held upright by thirteen hands. Around the entire design was the Latin inscription *Hanc tuemur hac nitimur,* "This we protect; this we depend upon."

The Continental Congress placed this emblem on the title page of its journal. It was widely copied in 1774 and 1775, sometimes with strange results. An example appeared on the dedication page of John Norman's *Collection of Designs in Architecture,* published at Philadelphia in 1775. The designer borrowed the congressional seal and surrounded it with a serpent—not the new American rattlesnake but the old European symbol of unity. Inscribed on the serpent's skin was a poem:

John Martin's portrait of Commodore Esek Hopkins, the ranking officer in the Continental Navy, 1776. In the background are naval ensigns with two different symbols of liberty and freedom. Collection of Frank Mauran; photograph by the Society of the Cincinnati.

> *United now, alive and Free,*
> *Firm on this basis Liberty shall stand,*
> *And thus supported ever bless our land*
> *Till time becomes eternity.*

The designer's Whiggish intent was clear, but something went wrong in the engraving. The column lost its fluting, and the liberty cap was redrawn in a phallic manner so bizarre and even obscene that one wonders if the engraver was a secret Tory. Another problem also appeared. There was nothing American in this congressional emblem except thirteen grasping hands, a harbinger of Congresses to come.[26]

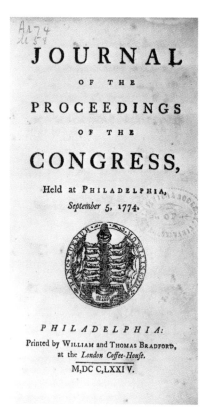

This seal of the Continental Congress appeared on the title page of its Journal of the Proceedings of the Congress, held at Philadelphia, September 5, 1774 *(Philadelphia: William and Thomas Bradford, 1774). Library Company of Philadelphia.*

Another version of the Continental seal. Engraving by John Norman. In Abraham Swan, A Collection of Designs in Architecture *(Philadelphia: Robert Bell and John Norman, 1775). New York Public Library.*

The National Seal and Motto: A Free Society as a Union of Differences

On July 4, 1776, the Continental Congress discussed the problem, and asked Benjamin Franklin, Thomas Jefferson, and John Adams "to be a committee to bring in a device for a Seal of the United States of America." These masters of the written word had dealt brilliantly with the task of writing a Declaration of Independence, but they were not so adroit in the manipulation of visual images. Each of them proposed an idea that came from a text. Franklin favored a Biblical image of Moses dividing the Red Sea and Pharaoh drowning in the waters. Jefferson had taught himself to read Anglo-Saxon in search of his ancestral rights, and he wanted to show the Saxon chiefs Hengist and Horsa as symbols of ancient British liberty and freedom, before it was corrupted by Norman conquerors, Plantagenet bullies, Tudor rogues, Stuart tyrants, and Hanoverian dunces. John Adams loved the classics and preferred an image of Hercules choosing between Virtue and Sloth, which was also his Yankee way of needling the master of Monticello.[27]

The impossible task of reconciling these ideas was assigned by the two older men to young Jefferson, who hired a Swiss scholar named Pierre Eugène Du Simitière to do the work. In consultation with the Virginian, Du Simitière came up with yet another version. He used Franklin's scene, incorporated changes by Jefferson, omitted Adams's idea altogether, and added the motto of the state of Virginia—a pointed reply to the gentleman from Massachusetts.[28] For the front of the seal, Du Simitière sketched a new American vision that centered not on a plurality of colonies but on a diversity of ethnic groups: a new idea in 1776. In the center he placed a shield with six quarters, symbolic of "the countries from which the states had been peopled": an English rose, Scottish thistle, Irish harp, French lily, German eagle, and Belgian lion. No reference was made to Indians or Africans. Around the rim Du Simitière put emblems of the thirteen colonies. He added a figure of Liberty with her wand and pileus, and

Justice with her scale. At the top he put "the eye of Providence in a radiant triangle," and at the bottom he inscribed another motto, *E pluribus unum,* "One out of many."[29]

The design did not succeed as a visual image. It was meant to be read rather than seen and was crowded to the point of chaos. Congress tactfully ordered it to "lie upon the table." But the work of the committee had one lasting result. It invented the national motto *E pluribus unum* to express a vision of unity and diversity in a free society.

The sources do not tell us which member of the committee proposed that graceful phrase. All would have known it, for it was the motto of *Gentleman's Magazine,* which circulated more widely in the colonies than any other periodical in the eighteenth century. It did not come from Thomas Jefferson, who favored an

Benjamin Franklin's proposed design for the Great Seal of the United States, a drawing by Benson J. Lossing for Harpers New Monthly Magazine, *July 1856. Virginia Historical Society.*

ornate Latin phrase with a complex cadence of six-syllable words: *insuperabiles si inseparabiles,* "insuperable if inseparable," and too clever by half. Certainly it did not come from Benjamin Franklin, who dropped out of Boston Latin School and did not think highly of classical learning. And it was unlikely to have been from John Adams, who did not think in terms of ethnic pluralism and shared conventional Anglo-Saxon attitudes on that subject.

That left Pierre Eugène Du Simitière, whose sketch for the national seal was a stronger celebration of ethnic pluralism than the work of

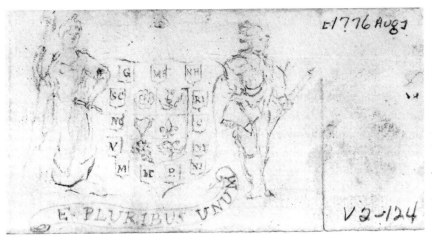

Pierre Eugène Du Simitière's design for the Great Seal of the United States, August 1776. Ms. sketch in the Jefferson Papers, Manuscripts Division, Library of Congress.

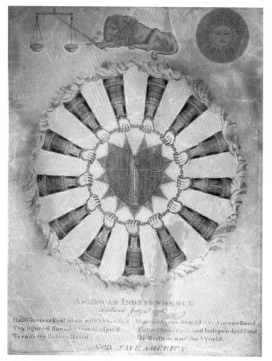

A New England vision of unity and pluralism: "American Independence Declared July 4th 1776," engraving and watercolor laid on paper, Boston, 1776. Winterthur Museum.

Franklin, Jefferson, or Adams. Du Simitière was a Swiss immigrant who contributed the perspective of his own country's diversity. We might think of his design for the Great Seal and the national motto as a gift from the ancient cantons of Switzerland to the new republics of the United States.[30]

The theme of *E pluribus unum* was taken up with high enthusiasm throughout America. It led to many pluralist images of a free society and inspired a wonderful range of regional variations. New Englanders went to work with images of mailed hands, clouds of divinity, and Liberty Trees. An engraving from Boston in 1776 celebrated continental unity with traditional New England elements: a throbbing heart with a burning flame and an inscription, "Warmed by One Hand, United in One Band." Around the heart were the mailed hands of Puritan iconography.[31]

Other emblems of *E pluribus unum* appeared on paper currency in different parts of the continent. In Philadelphia, Benjamin Franklin chose an instrumental symbol: a simple and "needful" image of a plain chain with thirteen links, with the motto "American Congress, We are One." New Yorkers favored a more materialist symbol: an opulent chandelier with thirteen candles. Backcountry Georgians preferred a rattlesnake in a Continental circle. Every American region had its own diverse ideas of *E pluribus unum.*[32]

The Golden Knot: A Free Society as a Plurality of Elites

American diversity in 1776 was not only a matter of region, religion, and ethnicity. It also appeared in variations by social class. New England and the Quaker provinces were the first modern societies where most people were of middling rank, a new phenomenon. In the southern colonies the majority were slaves, servants, tenants, convict laborers, or poor whites: the old story with a new twist. Every colony had its own elites, who were distinct in dress and decorum (more so than today). All colonies had underclasses and outerclasses.

Two visions of pluralism on American paper money: a utilitarian image of a simple chain with thirteen links in the plain style of Pennsylvania; and a gaudy, flamboyant New York City emblem of a chandelier with thirteen flames. Virginia Historical Society and American Numismatic Society.

In these complex colonial stratification systems (more complex than our own), the central ideas of the American Revolution were remarkable for the breadth of their appeal. People of many ranks invented pluralist visions of liberty and freedom, in different forms. Some of these images were in a popular style. Others were in the high style of colonial elites.

An opulent example of the high style appeared in the colors of the Philadelphia Light Horse, a silk stocking unit formed by twenty-one men of "independent means." All paid their own expenses in the Revolution and served actively in some of the heaviest fighting. They invested their entire pay in bank shares for a "lying in and foundling hospital" for female victims of the war.[33]

Their equipment gave full employment to Philadelphia artisans: chocolate brown uniforms with snow-white facings, high-topped riding boots, round black hats with silver cords and a jaunty buck's tail. They carried matched carbines and cavalry swords on blancoed belts, and horse pistols in saddle holsters marked with the unit's flowery cipher.[34]

The Philadelphia Light Horse took particular pride in their flag, which was designed by artist John Folwell and painted by James Clay-poole in September 1775. The original still survives, a cavalry standard of yellow silk with heavy silver fringe. In the upper corner is a small Union Jack, later painted over with thirteen blue and silver stripes. In the center is a set of interlocking symbols that explain what these gentleman-rebels thought they were fighting for. One emblem is the head of a high-bred

An image of America as a plurality of elites: the standard of the Philadelphia Light Horse, 1775. Reproduced by permission of the First Troop, Philadelphia City Cavalry, with thanks to Morrison Heckscher, John Heckscher, and Adjutant Thomas L. Farley, Jr.

chestnut horse. Another is the figure of an angel blowing a trumpet, the conventional eighteenth century symbol for honor, glory, and fame. A third is an American Indian holding the wand and pileus of liberty. Below those many emblems is the motto "For These We Strive." This linkage of liberty, nationality, privilege, and a gentleman's honor was favored by American elites in every colony.[35]

The dominant element in the design is a handsomely articulated baroque ribbon-knot with thirteen double-foliated ends, set in bright gold against a cerulean blue shield with a rolled rococo silver edge. The flowing ribbons represent the energy of thirteen colonial elites, and the golden knot signifies their unity in a common cause of liberty and freedom. Here is a pluralist symbol of the Revolutionary movement as a league of gentlemen from many colonies and cultures, striving together for their rights.[36]

LIBERTAS AMERICANA

A European Solution: The Franklin-Dupré Medal

Our mariners who know North America well claim
that a certain innate spirit of liberty is inseparable from
the soil, the sky, the forests and the lakes of that vast
and virgin land, and that this spirit of liberty marks it
off from all the other parts of the universe.

—GAZETTE DE FRANCE, APRIL 4, 1774

IN 1782, Benjamin Franklin turned to the task of finding a common emblem of American liberty. He was living in Paris as American minister to France and had formed the pleasant habit of walking for exercise on the banks of the Seine. One day he met a young French engraver named Augustin Dupré, and the two men strolled together along the river. Franklin remarked that his country needed an emblem to represent its cause, and Dupré offered his services. The result was a happy collaboration of a brilliant young French artist and a witty American sage. Together they created a gold medal that combined Dupré's elegance with Poor Richard's earthy humor.[37]

On the front of the medal they put a gorgeous blond goddess of liberty in what the French call *déshabille,* with tousled hair and an abundance of *décolletage.* Her appearance called to mind the ladies of France who pleased Doctor Franklin by receiving him in their *boudoirs* while they lay abed in elegant disarray. This golden goddess was looking west toward the New World. The theme of liberty was ingeniously introduced by the image of her unbound hair, blowing freely in the wind from America. In the background were the classical wand and pileus of liberty. Around the edge was a Latin inscription, *Libertas americana,* and the cabalistic date, "4 Juil[let] 1776."[38]

On the back of the medal Franklin and Dupré created an allegorical scene of combat between European powers. Britain appeared as a charg-

Benjamin Franklin and Augustin Dupré, "Libertas Americana," obverse and reverse, Paris, 1782. American Numismatic Society.

ing lion and France as a Roman warrior with a fleur-de-lis on his shield. Between them was young America as the infant Hercules, a small but muscular child with a look of fierce determination on his cherubic face. While Britain and France fought above his head, this American *enfant terrible* was killing two serpents by crushing their skulls in his little hands. This was an allusion to the myth of the infant Hercules and his stepmother Juno, who so feared that formidable child that she sent two serpents to kill him in his cradle. Young Hercules killed the serpents instead, in a triumph of innocence over evil and a harbinger of heroic feats to come.[39]

When Franklin commissioned the medal, his thoughts were centered on a difficult problem of diplomacy. Negotiations with France and Britain were full of pain and trouble. The old European monarchies were not happy to have a new American republic rising in their midst. The Franklin-Dupré medal was a warning: America was determined to be free, and ready in its infancy to defend itself from the British mother country, and also from its French stepmother if need be.

Franklin delighted in its design and celebrated it in a broadside titled "Explication de la médaille frappée par les Americains en 1782." Copies of the medal were struck in gold and presented to Louis XVI and Marie Antoinette. Silver versions went to French ministers. To a friend at home, Franklin wrote in his folksy way that the medals were "mighty well-received."[40] Professional medalists recognized the Franklin-Dupré liberty medal as a brilliant composition and celebrated it in Europe. It appeared on books, textiles, and coins, and helped to make young Augustin Dupré the leading medalist of his generation. After the start of the French Revolution, it was copied by a committee of medalists in their representation of "Liberté française" for the National Convention in 1792. Dupré went on to a distinguished career as chief engraver of the French Republic.

In America the medal had a very different reception. When the United States began to mint its coins, the large penny in 1793 followed the Franklin-Dupré design of liberty with flowing hair. On the reverse it added a chain of thirteen links. A Philadelphia journalist was quick to complain. "The American cents . . . do not answer our expectations," a correspondent wrote. "The chain on the reverse is but a bad omen for liberty, and Liberty herself appears to be in a fright." The next issue of the coin changed the face of liberty and replaced the chain with a wreath. Subsequent mint masters added a liberty cap, tinkered with the design, and made it worse. Finally it was abandoned altogether.[41]

A U.S. large penny, with a liberty motif inspired by the Franklin-Dupré Medal, obverse and reverse, Philadelphia, 1793. American Numismatic Society.

The Franklin-Dupré medal had a long reach in European numismatics, but it never became a popular symbol in the United States. The iconography of *Libertas americana* was admirable, but it was not American. It had no roots in the folkways of freedom and liberty that had taken root in the New World. The people of the United States needed an emblem that was closer to home.[42]

LIBERTY & FREEDOM AS NATIONAL IDEAS
The First American Solution: Indians as Symbols

> Here is Liberty in perfection.
>
> —SAMUEL PETERS ON AMERICAN INDIANS, 1781

> The only condition on earth to be compared with ours, in my opinion, is that of the Indians, where they have still less law than we. The European, are governments of kites over pigeons.
>
> —THOMAS JEFFERSON TO JOHN RUTLEDGE, 1787

O N BOTH SIDES of the Atlantic, artists searched for an emblem of liberty and freedom that was more distinctly American. A favorite solution was the image of an Indian. European artists had long personified America as an Indian figure. Engravers of maps and atlases often represented Europe, Asia, Africa, and America as women, all with the same classical features and Renaissance anatomies but different costumes and complexions. America commonly appeared as a female "Red Indian," sometimes fire-engine red, carrying a bow and arrow.[43]

A British image of colonial dependency: America as an Indian child. "Lord Chatham and America," Derby porcelain figurine, ca. 1767. Victoria and Albert Museum.

During the eighteenth century, political cartoonists borrowed this image of America as an Indian and modified it for polemical purposes. As they worked with this symbol, the Indian's age and gender changed in interesting ways. Early British prints represented the American colonies as a helpless Indian child, in the fostering care of a solicitous mother country or a fatherly William Pitt.[44]

When the colonial controversy grew more intense in the years from 1763 to 1775, American and European

140

America as a ravished Indian maiden: "The Able Doctor; or, America swallowing a Bitter Draught," London Magazine, *April 1774; copied by Paul Revere for the* Royal American Magazine, *June 1774. Library of Congress.*

artists portrayed the colonies as a beautiful and highly vulnerable young woman, wearing nothing but a feathered miniskirt, a shell necklace, and a small feather bonnet. Sometimes she carried a small bow and a quiver of arrows. Often she appeared as a maiden in distress, sexually abused by salacious European males of advanced age. In one brutal print, published both in London and Boston, her clothing is ripped away and she is held down by Justice Mansfield while Lord North thrusts the stem of teapot down her throat. Behind him, three lascivious European figures are peering under America's ruined skirt, while Britannia averts her eyes. But even in her distress, young America spits the tea into the face of her tormenter. She is an image of American liberty and defiance, against British tyranny and oppression.[45]

When the colonies began to fight for their rights, the emblematic Indian changed again. The young Indian maiden of 1774 became a more mature Indian princess and a more explicit symbol of liberty and freedom. The wand and pileus of classical Libertas were put at her side, or a Liberty Tree was added in the background, or the word *Liberty* was embroidered on her dress. One print called "Bunker's Hill, or the Blessed Effects of Family Quarrels" shows America and Britannia fighting with deadly weapons. Britannia is getting the worst of it, because she is also being stabbed in the back by her own ministers.[46]

Another print in 1776 made the theme of liberty more prominent. Britannia in court dress says, "I'll force you to Obedience, you Rebellious Slut." America in her Indian head dress replies, "Liberty, Liberty for ever

America as an embattled Indian princess with emblems of the old and new worlds: "The Female Combatants," January 26, 1776. John Carter Brown Library.

Mother, while I exist." In the foreground near America is a flourishing Liberty Tree. Next to Britannia is a rotten stump inscribed "for obedience." Two shields symbolize a war of alliances: America with enlightened France; Britannia with the autocrats of Germany.

A third print near the end of the war shows America and Britannia ending their quarrel. The Indian maid carries a wand, a liberty cap, and an American flag. She cries, "Dear Mama, say no more about it." Britannia replies, "Be a good girl and give me a Buss." In the background France and Spain try to separate them, and the Dutch look for a way to turn a profit.

After the American victories at Trenton, Princeton, Saratoga, and Yorktown, the emblematic Indian underwent a change in gender. In a French print, the Indian princess became a burly Indian brave who is armed, strong, and triumphant. Britannia was on her knees before him, begging for mercy, while France and Spain congratulate one another on her distress.

America as the prodigal Indian daughter, carrying the wand and pileus of liberty: "The Reconciliation between Britania and her daughter America." Colored engraving by Thomas Colley, London, 1782. New York Public Library.

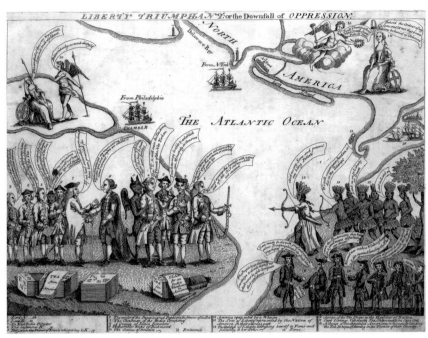

America as a band of victorious Indian warriors led by an Indian Queen: "Liberty Triumphant; or, The Downfall of Oppression." Society of the Cincinnati.

Another print in 1783 shows America as an Indian chief who has joined the European rulers as an equal and has learned to play the power game. A scatological English print shows these masculine figures urinating together into a common pot, which represents the Peace of Paris. England says, "I call this an honourable P[iss]." America replies, "I call this a free and independent P[iss]." France invites them to "freely make P[iss] with us." The parties have laid down their weapons but keep them close at hand for the next fight. For romantic souls who persist in believing that American history is about the "loss of innocence" in the twentieth century, it is interesting to see that all sense of American innocence had vanished in some quarters as early as 1783.[47]

Americans at home also used Indians as symbols of liberty and freedom, but in more knowing and particular ways. They adopted individual Indians as iconic figures and selected different figures according to their regional cultures. The gentlemen of Vir-

The gender change complete. America as an Indian chief: "The General P__s, or Peace," 1783. Library of Congress.

ginia identified with Indians of high rank such as the princess Pocahontas, the monarch Powhatan, or the council chiefs that Jefferson celebrated for their eloquence, dignity, and nobility of character. The Quaker colonies admired Tammany, the Delaware leader who made two peace treaties with William Penn and came to be called Saint Tammany for his virtue, humanity, and peace, until his image was tarnished by New Yorkers. The people of New England admired leaders of faith and learning such as Handsome Lake, spiritual leader of the Seneca, or Sequoyah, the creator of the first written Indian language in North America. Borderers and backsettlers, raised to a warrior ethic, had a fellow feeling for great Indian warriors such as Pontiac, war chief of the Ottawa, or Tecumseh, the Shawnee war leader. Later they would favor the images of Crazy Horse, Sitting Bull, Geronimo, and war chiefs who were known for their courage and endurance. In their different ways, all of these individual Indians became American images of liberty and freedom: the great warriors in their fierce determination to live free or die; the council chiefs with their proud spirit of autonomy and independence; the cultural heroes as symbols of soul freedom; and Saint Tammany in his respect for the rights of others.[48]

During the twentieth century, iconic Indians remained part of the iconography of freedom and liberty in America. They appeared on many artifacts such as the "Indian head" coins, which showed a heroic Indian profile and the word *Liberty* above his noble brow. Today, that vision still survives in the minds of many Americans.

THE AMERICAN EAGLE

The First Popular Solution: Animals as Symbols

> The Escutcheon is born on the breast of an American
> Eagle without any other supporters, to denote that the
> United States of America ought to rely on their own
> virtue.
>
> —CHARLES THOMSON AND WILLIAM BARTON,
> DESIGNERS OF THE NATIONAL SEAL, 1782

OTHER ICONOGRAPHERS represented America as an animal. In their efforts we can see a new concept in the process of creation: a vision of liberty and freedom as national ideas. Artists on both sides of the Atlantic experimented with many species, with bizarre results. Some animals were chosen to bring out themes of American diversity. The new republic variously appeared as a flight of birds, a flock of sheep, even a kettle of fish. In 1778, a British Tory represented the new republic as a zebra with thirteen stripes, each named for an American state. He arranged the states in geographic order from head to tail, with one exception. The offending state of Massachusetts was moved to the hind end.[49]

Other British Tories thought of the new American nation as a mongrel dog or a long-eared ass. Whig artists portrayed it more sympathetically as a thoroughbred horse that was throwing an incompetent royal rider, or a cow being milked by one British minister while another sawed off its horns—a cartoonist's cliché with many applications in English and European caricature. Several Whig artists showed America as a goose, primarily to attack the folly of British ministers who killed the bird that laid the golden egg. But these images had nothing particularly American in their symbolism, and they soon disappeared.

Other artists searched for an indigenous American animal of distinct character that was thought to represent the nation. In 1783, an English

engraver represented the new nation as a wild American buffalo that could not be controlled by its British keepers. But this image did not catch on. A ruminant beast as shaggy and stolid as the buffalo was not in keeping with American ideas of themselves. From time to time after the Revolution, the buffalo would be adopted as an American symbol for particular purposes, but it never found general acceptance as a national emblem.[50]

America as a kettle of fish: "State Cooks; or, the Downfall of the Fish Kettle." Engraving, December 10, 1781. British Museum.

A more popular choice in the eighteenth century was the white-tailed deer. That wild and graceful animal became a common symbol of America in the late colonial era. Young American expatriates wore deerskin leggings in British drawing rooms and were called "buckskins" in British slang. Pennsylvania regiments adorned their hats with bucktails in the American Revolution, a custom that continued into the Civil War. In New England, emancipated slaves called themselves "the Bucks of America." In all of these applications, a wild deer made a

America as a bison: "Amusement for John Bull and His Cousin Paddy; or, The Gambols of the American Buffalo." Engraving, May 1, 1783. Colonial Williamsburg Foundation.

graceful emblem of liberty and freedom, but it lacked the symbolism of strength that was wanted for a national emblem.[51]

Other Americans preferred the beaver. As early as 1705, Robert Beverley of Virginia wrote, "The admirable œconomy of the Beavers deserves to be particularly remember'd. They cohabit in one house, are incorporated in one House, something like a monarchy, and have over them a Superintendent, which the Indians call *Pericu*. . . . He . . . sees that every one bear his equal share of the burden; while he bites with his teeth, and lashes with his Tail, those that lag behind, and do not lend all their strength."[52]

The emblem of the Dutch colony of New Netherland was a black beaver, which those hardheaded businessmen valued less for its "admirable œconomy" than for the price of its pelt. The same symbol was adopted by New York City and is still used by organizations such as the Brook Club in that town. Early in the Revolution, New York's armed ships flew a flag that showed a black beaver on a white field. But this design did not find general support. It was not emblematic of liberty or freedom, unless it was the liberty to pursue a pelt.[53]

Others in the Revolutionary era admired the beaver in a different way. In the fall of 1775, Continental six-dollar bills

America as a beaver: A Continental Six-Dollar Bill, 1776. American Numismatic Society.

showed America as a very small beaver, gnawing down a very big tree. An essay explained that "the large tree represents the enormous power of Great Britain, which the persevering, steady-working beaver (America) is reducing within proper bounds." A French traveler found the same image copied on a tavern sign in Trenton: "a beaver at work, with his little teeth bringing down a large tree, and underneath is written *perseverando*."[54]

Other Americans in backcountry and the more militant southern states preferred to think of themselves as coiled rattlesnakes, angry hornets, infuriated alligators, and snarling wildcats. These symbols also failed in another way. They had popular appeal but lacked the *gravitas* of a national emblem. Something else had to be found.[55]

After independence, the Continental Congress struggled with this problem when it tried to design a national seal. Three committees were set to work on that task, and all failed to find a satisfactory symbol. In 1782, Congress asked its able secretary, Charles Thomson, to settle the question. He consulted a private citizen, William Barton of Philadelphia, who was an expert in "the laws of heraldry." The two men began by bringing together the various emblems that had been suggested for a Great Seal.

The result was what one might expect from the combined labors of three congressional committees, an early American bureaucrat, and an academic expert. A summary sketch included a maiden (for virtue), holding a dove (for peace), with a warrior in armor (military strength), an eagle (sovereignty), a harp (harmony), a pillar (fortitude), a cock (vigilance), two fleurs-de-lis (the French alliance), three emblems of liberty, and four national mottos. As if that were not enough, Barton added a small seal within the Great Seal that included an unfinished pyramid, as a symbol of "duration," and an all-seeing eye of Providence, for omniscient divinity and anything else that might have been omitted.[56]

This proposal worked its way through the legislative process. One by one the elements were stripped away by amendment, until nothing remained but the eagle, with thirteen arrows in one claw and an olive branch with thirteen leaves and fruits in the other. Above were thirteen shining stars. The eagle's head was turned toward the olive branch, and its breast bore a national shield. In its beak it held the first committee's motto, *E pluribus unum*, "out of many, one."[57]

Thus was born the eagle as an American emblem. Some citizens were not pleased. The most vocal dissenter was Benjamin Franklin, who complained to his daughter Sarah Bache that Congress had chosen "a bird of bad moral character; like those among men who live by sharping and rob-bing, he is generally poor, and often very lousy." Franklin preferred the turkey: "a much more respectable bird and withal a true original native of America. . . . a bird of courage and would not hesitate to attack a grenadier of the British Guards."[58]

Franklin's iconic turkey never got off the ground, but the eagle instantly took wing. It had dignity and grace, if not virtue or respectability. In solitary flight it was universally admired as a very beautiful bird, and when the eagle spread its great wings and soared high in the air of the New World, it became a powerful image of liberty. Its keen eye, dangerous beak, and sharp talons were exactly the symbols that Congress desired in the last years of the War for Independence. Doctor Franklin notwithstanding, a bald eagle of the species *Haliaeetus leucocephalus* was also "a true native," very much an American bird. Natural philosophers in Europe were pleased by the choice. The marquis de Chastellux thought that an eagle diving out of the sun was a perfect symbol for an American republic that was born of the Enlightenment. He wrote to the president of William and Mary College, "It would seem indeed that the English, in all fields, want only half-liberty. Let the owls and bats flutter about in the murky darkness of a feeble twilight; the American eagle must be able to fix its eyes upon the sun!"[59]

The eagle was adopted by Congress and quickly found favor in America as a popular symbol, more so than any other American emblem in the new republic. When George Washington made his national tour of the United States in 1789, Americans along the route covered their windows with soap or whitewash, traced the outlines of eagles on each pane, and illuminated them with candles. This spontaneous display expressed a new spirit of popular nationalism that began to appear in the last years of the eighteenth century.[60]

As late as 1775, the word *nation* itself had been used in a different way to describe any collectivity of human beings. At the University of Edinburgh, undergraduate classes were called "nations." The word *nationalism* before 1776 was a theological term for an obscure Calvinist heresy. Not until the era of the American Revolution did *nation* and *nationalism* acquire their modern meaning. They described an idea not of a sovereign state but a separate people, distinguished by various combinations of culture, land, blood, language, and most of all their history. By the time of Washington's inauguration in 1789, the American eagle became a national emblem in this sense, a symbol of the people of the United States, and the values they shared in common.[61]

As with most successful icons, the popularity of the eagle was rein-

The American eagle, painted panel of "The Arms of the United States," above the box pew used by George Washington in St. Paul's Chapel, New York City. This cherished American image was commissioned by the vestry in 1785 and narrowly escaped destruction on September 11, 2001. Trinity Church Archives, New York.

forced by many layers of symbolic meaning. People could identify themselves with it in different ways. For believing Christians who knew the Scriptures, especially New England Puritans, the eagle had a particular importance. In the Winthrop fleet that founded Massachusetts, the flagship *Arbella* had a biblical eagle for its figurehead. Many a Puritan preacher invoked that image and linked it to the words of the most Christian of Jewish prophets, the Deutero-Isaiah, who said: "They that wait upon the Lord shall renew their strength; they shall mount up with wings as eagles; they shall run and not be weary; and they shall walk and not be faint." It later inspired a Protestant hymn that many Americans knew very well. For readers of the New Testament, the eagle was also the symbol of John the Evangelist, and of evangelical Christianity in general.[62]

The gentlemen of Virginia knew the eagle in another way. In heraldry it had long been a symbol of honor. Many an armigerous English family carried an eagle on its coat of arms. In Anglican chapels and churches, the pulpit was often shaped in the form of an eagle. Several Virginians, including the Lee family and Sir William Berkeley, had a connection with Queen's College in Oxford, which adopted three silver eagles for its emblem.

On the American frontier the eagle had yet another set of associations. Indians had long regarded it as a symbol of courage and strength. An eagle's feather was an emblem of leadership, proudly carried by war chiefs. The Europeans who settled on the frontier borrowed these meanings for their own use.

In the new republic, Americans added other layers of meaning. An iconographic example was a painting by Boqueto de Woiseri of New Orleans, in which a huge American eagle spreads its protective wings over the rooftops of the town. Its beak bears a scroll with the inscription "Under My Wings Everything Prospers."[63] Woiseri represented the moment when New Orleans was acquired by the United States, much against the wishes of its French inhabitants. They were assured by American officials that their feelings would not be allowed to prevent them

The American eagle as a symbol of liberty and prosperity: J. L. Boqueta de Woiseri, "A View of New Orleans Taken from the Plantation of Marigny," 1803. Chicago Historical Society.

from enjoying the fruits of American liberty. They were destined to be free, whether or not they wished to be.[64]

The American eagle was linked directly to themes of liberty and freedom. This association became explicit in the use of interlocking symbols, which combined the eagle with a liberty wand and cap, or a banner in its beak, or all three. By the early nineteenth century, the American eagle signified a close affiliation of the nation with prosperity, democracy, liberty, and freedom.

This complexity of symbolic meaning expressed itself in a variety of iconographic forms. Some of the earliest American eagles were so stylized as scarcely to be recognizable as *Haliaeetus leucocephalus.* One early version appeared to have the legs of a frog, the body of a chicken, and the stance of a fighting cock. Gradually the American eagle became more anatomically correct. Typically it was a male eagle in the prime of life, but sometimes it was represented for special purposes as an eagle chick, a yearling eagle, or a gray eagle full of years and wisdom.[65]

It also appeared in as many postures as imagination could invent, and its demeanor changed with political events. During the War of 1812 the American eagle became more bellicose, a tendency that recurred in all subsequent wars from the defense of Baltimore to the liberation of Baghdad. In time of peace the bird became more domestic, even a household pet who lived quietly with Uncle Sam or perched gently on the arm of Miss Liberty.[66] All of these motifs were variations on an iconic theme of freedom and liberty as national ideas.

STARS AND STRIPES

A "New Constellation" of National Liberty and Freedom

> A thoughtful mind, when it sees a Nation's flag, sees not the flag only, but the nation itself . . . the Government, the principles, the truths, the history which belongs to the nation.
>
> —HENRY WARD BEECHER

R ICHARD HOFSTADTER once remarked that many nations have ideologies, but it was the fate of the United States to become one. He was thinking of its linkage with liberty and freedom. For better and for worse, a leading symbol of that association is the American flag. In the interior of West Africa, we saw a crowd of dancing youths, and many wore the Stars and Stripes as an article of dress. An elder turned to us and said, "See how your country is loved." In other places we have seen angry mobs burning the American flag, and people warned, "Look how your country is hated." No other flag in the world today is so celebrated and execrated. None carries such a weight of symbolic meaning.

The American flag is unique in its symbolism, and also in the process by which it was created. The Stars and Stripes were not copied from an ancient source, or handed down by a single leader or a small elite. As a national symbol of liberty and freedom, the flag was invented in an appropriately free and open way. Many Americans played instrumental roles: Sons of Liberty, an American Indian, seamen, soldiers, their commanding general, a widowed seamstress, members of Congress, state officials, and others of every rank and region.[67]

The Continental Congress was slow to adopt an American flag, partly because it was busy with other questions, but mostly because the problem of design was very difficult. How could one find a symbol of unity for a nation of such diversity? What would be an acceptable emblem of a free society in a country that had so many different visions of liberty and freedom? Congress did not settle on an official design until June 14, 1777, and it did not address the question by statute until the Flag Act of 1818. The form and function of the American flag remained remarkably fluid until President William Howard Taft laid down the law in 1912. Even to our own time, the cultural uses of the flag have continued to change in every generation. This endless process of invention is itself an artifact of liberty and freedom.[68]

Stripes Without Stars:
The Sons of Liberty and Their Union Flags

In the design of the American flag, the first elements to emerge were the red and white stripes. They first appeared in Boston before the Revolution, when the Sons of Liberty hoisted Union Flags on their Liberty Tree as early as 1773, perhaps earlier. These banners probably took different forms. One large Union Flag, seven by twelve feet, survives in the collections of the Bostonian Society and is believed to have flown from the Liberty Tree. It consisted of nine red and white stripes, vertical in their arrangement.[69] The number may have been inspired by the segmented serpent of Paul Revere, who counted New England and the Quaker colonies as single units and divided his American snake into nine parts.[70]

Another striped flag was improvised by the militia of Manchester, Massachusetts, perhaps in 1775, and still survives in a remarkable state of preservation. It is roughly five feet square, similar in size to British regimental colors, and made of red silk. Its original canton was replaced with another piece of red silk with seven pieces of white silk to create thirteen horizontal stripes. Many flag historians and textile experts have examined the flag, and all conclude that it is authentic. Some believe that the red and white stripes replaced a British Union Jack. It is the oldest surviving striped American flag that may have been used in the Revolution, even on the day of Lexington and Concord.[71]

During the siege of Boston, the American army adopted another unity flag of a different design: thirteen red and white horizontal stripes with the British Union Jack in the corner. It was variously called the Union Flag or the Continental Colors and symbolized colonial solidarity in the struggle for rights within the British Empire. Later it would be called the "Grand Union Flag," a term that was probably not used at the time.[72]

On New Year's Day, January 1, 1776, George Washington ordered it to be raised on Prospect Hill in Cambridge, Massachusetts, where it could be seen by the British garrison in Boston five miles away. The reaction was not what he expected. General Gage's officers studied the new flag through their spyglasses and puzzled over its meaning. They concluded that the "peasants" of New England had at last come to their senses and had hoisted a quaint provincial idea of the British Union Jack as a token of surrender. The American commander reported to Congress that the Continental Flag was "received in Boston as . . . a signal of submission."[73]

Later in 1776, the Union Flag was flown at sea by the Continental sloop of war *Reliance* when she carried an American diplomat to the

Origins of the American Flag: Stripes Without Stars. Top left to bottom right: Sons of Liberty Flag with vertical stripes, 1765–66; Union Flag with horizontal stripes, ca. 1774–75; Fort Mifflin Flag with red, white, and blue stripes, 1777; Forster Flag, Manchester, Mass., 1775(?); Delaware Militia Colors, 1777; the Continental Colors or Union Flag, 1776; John Paul Jones Flag with Liberty Tree, 1776–77; General Sullivan's Rattlesnake Union Flag; Philip Schuyler's Eagle Flag, probably after the Revolution, but a similar design appears on early diplomas of the Society of the Cincinnati. Courtesy of Whitney Smith, © 2003 Flag Research Center.

French island of Martinique. As she entered harbor she was intercepted by a British warship, HMS *Shark*. The British captain wrote that he saw "a sail in the offing with colours which I was unacquainted with (being red and white striped with a union next the staff)." He took the flag to be "the property of His Brittanick Majesty's rebellious subjects in North America" and instantly attacked. The attack of the *Shark* was beaten off with timely help from the French fort, but the Americans were not pleased to be perceived as "His Majesty's rebellious subjects." Yet that was the literal meaning of their flag.[74]

The Union Flag also proved unsatisfactory in another way. It was very similar to the ensign of the British East India Company, which combined the Union Jack with nine horizontal red and white stripes. For all of these reasons, some Americans began to remove the Union Jack from their Union Flag and kept only the thirteen red and white stripes. Contemporary prints show such flags in 1776.[75]

"The Taking of Miss Mud Island," W. Faden, Charing Cross, 1778, an English satire on the fall of Fort Mifflin, October 1777. An American flag appears with vertical stripes and a snake. Courtesy of the John Carter Brown Library at Brown University.

Other striped flags multiplied in profusion. At the siege of Fort Stanwix in 1777, the American troops contributed their own clothing to make a flag of red, white, and blue stripes and no stars at all. Other designs combined the stripes with Franklin's serpent of unity, a backcountry rattlesnake, a New England Liberty Tree, or an eagle.[76]

Stars Without Stripes: Washington's Headquarters Standard

While stripes were gaining popularity, George Washington chose another design for standards and colors in the Continental Army. He favored a flag of Continental blue with thirteen white stars, six-pointed in the style of English heraldry. An original survives in the Valley Forge Historical Society. It is made of faded blue silk with a homespun linen header, 27.5 by 35.5 inches, the size of a cavalry or artillery standard.

For many years this very handsome banner remained in the Washington family. In 1912 it was donated by Frances Lovell, a descendant of

Betty Washington Lewis, the sister of George Washington, who said that it was "known in the family as Washington's Headquarters Flag." Flag scholars did not take her account seriously until a careful flag scholar, Edward Richardson, made an examination and found that "the heading material appears to be the same as that of Washington's marquee," which also survives. Richardson concluded that the flag "is exactly what [the family] claimed it to be—Washington's Revolutionary-era command standard." It may have been handed down from Lieutenant George Lewis, Washington's nephew. He was an officer in the Headquarters Guard and may have served as its Ensign and carried its standard.[77]

The date of the standard is uncertain, but Washington may have used it as early as the battles at Trenton and Princeton in the winter of 1776–77. The artist Charles Willson Peale thought so. He would have known, for he fought at Princeton as an infantry officer in Cadwalader's brigade. Later he served as the General's aide. In January 1779, while on leave from the army, Peale was asked to do a portrait of Washington at Trenton and Princeton. He visited the battlefields with his brother James Peale and his pupil William Mercer, a deaf-mute son of the American general who had been killed at Princeton. The three artists did sketches and two paintings. Both showed Washington's headquarters standard in use during the campaigns of 1776 and 1777.

One painting is a small scene of the battle at Princeton, attributed to James Peale but probably the work of William Mercer. The work has the naiveté of a folk painting, combined with close and very accurate attention to detail. It shows the artist's father falling mortally wounded on the

Origins of the American Flag: Stars Without Stripes. Three images of Washington's headquarters standard survive: a blue silk flag of uncertain date, ca. 1776–83, in the Valley Forge Historical Society (left); the standard at the battle of Princeton on Jan. 3, 1777, painted by James Peale and William Mercer, ca. 1779–86 (center); and the standard at the battle of Trenton, December 26, 1777, painted by Charles Willson Peale in 1779 (right). The Valley Forge standard measures 27.5 inches on hoist, and 35.5 inches on the fly. Courtesy of Whitney Smith, © 2003 Flag Research Center.

field, and Washington rallying the men of Mercer's and Cadwalader's brigades. Behind Washington is a trooper of the Philadelphia Light Horse and an ensign carrying the blue standard with thirteen scattered stars, exactly like the headquarters flag that passed from Washington's family to Valley Forge Historical Society.[78]

In January 1779, Charles Willson Peale also painted a full-length portrait of Washington at Princeton, on a commission from the Pennsylvania Council. Washington sat for it between January 20 and February 2 of that year. At Washington's feet are captured German and British colors. Behind him is the headquarters standard, of a different design from that in the Mercer painting, with thirteen six-pointed stars in a circle on a blue field. Peale was known to be meticulous in matters of historical detail, so much so that he was permitted to use captured Hessian flags and guns as models for the painting.[79]

Peale's heroic painting of Washington was a great success, and his studio was asked to produce many copies. The central figure was always the same, but the details varied with the commission. Sometimes the background was the battle at Princeton, and sometimes Trenton. General

Charles Willson Peale, "George Washington at Princeton," 1779. Pennsylvania Academy of Fine Arts.

James Peale and William Mercer, "The Battle of Princeton," ca. 1779-86. Historical Society of Pennsylvania Collection, Atwater Kent Museum.

Rochambeau ordered a copy for his chateau with the battle of Yorktown in the background. Buyers in the 1780s asked for the Stars and Stripes rather than the headquarters flag, and the painters obliged.[80] But if the early paintings were correct, Washington's headquarters standard was in use before Congress settled on the Stars and Stripes in 1777, not afterward as some flag scholars have believed.[81]

The headquarters standard might have been adopted as early as the spring of 1776, when Washington created his headquarters guard. He ordered every regiment to send him four men, chosen for "sobriety, honesty and good behavior." Every man was required to be between five feet eight and five feet ten inches tall, "handsomely and well made," and "neat and spruce." Officially it was called the Commander-in-Chief's Guard, and unofficially the Life Guard, a title that Washington disliked for its monarchical associations. Sometimes he called it "my regiment." The unit, which began with 180 men and grew to 250 in 1779, had many duties of security, ceremony, and administration. It also fought as an elite unit, often in the post of greatest danger.[82]

Washington took great pride in his guard and gave close attention to the smallest details of drill and discipline. He was especially interested in their appearance and probably chose a standard to match their uniforms of Continental blue, for he thought that the colors of a unit should "bear some kind of similitude to the uniform." Flag historian Edward Richardson collected all of Washington's writings on the subject and concluded that "the blue flag with stars was probably Washington's choice."[83]

In the spring of 1776, Washington was much concerned about flags, standards, and colors for the army. On May 28, he wrote to Major General Israel Putnam, "I desire you to speak to the several Colonels and hurry them to get their Colors done." Washington wrote that letter from Philadelphia, where he was consulting with Congress from May 23 to June 5. While he was there he also consulted about flags, if Betsy Ross is to be believed.[84]

Stars and Stripes Together:
The True Story of Betsy Ross, Free Quaker

Learned opinion is divided on the legend of Betsy Ross. Many filiopietists believe that the story is entirely true. Iconoclasts and dissenters (another American tradition) insist that it is totally false. One scholar dismisses it as a "fantasy," another as a complete "fiction," a third as a family legend. Close attention to primary sources suggests a mediating judgment. This historian is persuaded by the evidence that the legend of Betsy Ross is partly mistaken but mostly true.[85]

Among those who knew her, Betsy Ross became a Philadelphia legend in her own time, not primarily for the flag that posterity remembers but for her "uncommon beauty," independence, and remarkable success in business. She was born Elizabeth Griscom, probably on January 1, 1752, on a farm in New Jersey and raised in Philadelphia among the Society of Friends, the seventh of eighteen children. Her Quaker forebears were carpenters and housewrights in the Delaware Valley for three generations, and her father helped to erect the steeple for the Liberty Bell at Independence Hall.[86]

She had a better education than most women of her age, at the excellent Friends School in Philadelphia, and in her teens was sent out from a crowded household to learn needlework and upholstery in another family. There she met and fell in love with John Ross, an upholsterer's apprentice. To the horror of her Quaker family he was an Episcopalian, son of the assistant rector of Christ Church. When the family objected, Betsy and her lover eloped to New Jersey, and she was disowned by the Society of Friends in May 1774. The young couple opened an upholstery shop and worshiped every Sunday at Christ Church. According to the family legend, they became acquainted with George Washington, who sat next to them at services during his attendance at the Continental Congress.[87]

The Revolution suddenly shattered her world. Early in the war Betsy's husband was killed by an explosion of gunpowder. She took over the upholstery shop, hung out a small tin sign on the little house that still stands in Arch Street, and built a business as a seamstress. She employed several women to work with her and earned a reputation for honesty and industry. Many testified that she was held in high respect by friends and neighbors, but in June 1776, the beautiful young widow Ross, twenty-four years old, was struggling to make ends meet.[88]

Then came the event for which she is best remembered. She told the story to her family, and her grandson William Canby wrote it down in 1870. His account was confirmed by three of Betsy's daughters, and also by other family members in affidavits that were solemnly affirmed in the Quaker style.[89] Betsy Ross told her family that early in June 1776, George Washington appeared in her shop. Her daughter Rachel remembered hearing that Washington had "often been in her house on friendly visits, as well as on business," and that Betsy Ross "had embroidered ruffles for his shirt bosoms and cuffs." This time he brought his close friend Robert

Morris and Colonel George Ross, who was Morris's powerful political ally and Betsy Ross's rich uncle-in-law.[90]

By daughter Rachel's account, the callers asked Betsy Ross if she could make a flag. She answered that she had never done one but could do it from a pattern. Washington produced a rough sketch. Rachel remembered her mother saying that it was a "square flag," with six-pointed stars "scattered promiscuously over the field."[91] Her mother suggested several changes: a rectangular shape, an arrangement of the stars in lines, or a circle, or a star, and she also said that five-pointed stars were more easily cut and sewn. To make her point she folded a piece of paper and cut a star with a single snip.[92] Betsy Ross told her children that "General Washington seemed to her to be the active one in making the design, the others having little or nothing to do with it." She also said that Washington himself drew another sketch on her advice, and she made a prototype of the flag.[93]

Many have read this evidence as a statement by Betsy Ross that she made the first Stars and Stripes. They probably misunderstood her. To study her daughter Rachel's affidavit carefully is to find no mention of a flag with stripes. To read the original documents is to discover that the flag they describe is a square military standard with scattered stars, closer to Washington's headquarters standard than to the Stars and Stripes.

Further, to read Washington's papers on colors and standards is to learn that he was unhappy with the Union Flag in the spring of 1776, and in subsequent papers favored a design for Continental military colors similar to his headquarters standard. A painting of the Continental Army at Yorktown shows his regiments carrying these flags, larger than the headquarters standard and differently proportioned, some blue with white stars, and others white with blue stars.[94] The Peale paintings suggest that these flags may have been done in a variety of designs. Some had a scattering of six-pointed stars. Others had a more refined design of six-pointed or five-pointed stars in linear or circular patterns, which Betsy Ross remembered.

In short, it is highly probable that Betsy Ross and George Washington actually met in the spring of 1776 and that they did work together on a design for military colors that later became part of the Stars and Stripes but were not the Stars and Stripes themselves. We find a strong congruence of interlocking evidence in Washington's correspondence, in his surviving headquarters standard, in the provenance of that flag through the Lewis family, in descriptions of the flag that was shown to Betsy Ross by descendants who had no knowledge of the headquarters standard, and in testimony of others who knew her.[95]

It is remotely possible that Betsy Ross may also have created a prototype of the Stars and Stripes in June 1776, but that is not what the most
important affidavits in her family actually say. Scholars agree that not one
scrap of supporting evidence has been found that the Stars and Stripes
were authorized or approved by Congress at that time or flown anywhere
in the spring and summer of 1776. By contrast, a flood of evidence began
to flow a year later, after the Flag Resolution of June 14, 1777.[96]

The family remembered that the meeting with Washington was the
beginning of a new career for Betsy Ross as a flagmaker. Her uncle gave
her a note for a hundred pounds and an open line of credit to get started
in that business. Betsy Ross said that she never wanted for employment
after the flag business began to grow. She employed men to paint silk
flags and women to do the sewing. By 1777, she was making ensigns for
the Pennsylvania Navy, which from newly discovered evidence may have
been another combination of stars and stripes: a large blue field with
white stars, and a small canton of red and white stripes in the upper corner. For many years she continued to make Stars and Stripes and other
flags. A receipt survives for a "large ensign" by Elizabeth Claypoole as late
as 1813. A granddaughter remembered that she continued in the business
until 1827, and the family kept it going until 1856.[97]

Betsy Ross's life was difficult in the Revolution and the new republic.
Two of her husbands died in the war. A third was severely wounded and
became an invalid. She supported her family for many years and did very
well, acquiring several houses in the city and an estate of 190 acres in the
country, which she managed with great success. Betsy Ross lived for sixty
years after 1776 and was one of the last survivors of the Revolutionary
generation. She became a living icon of liberty and freedom and earned
that image in many ways. Betsy Ross supported the Revolution and the
War for Independence when her Quaker relatives went another way.
Even when British troops occupied Philadelphia she remained steadfast
in her principles. British officers who occupied her house called her "the
Little Rebel." She also maintained the freedom and independence of her
family in very hard times.

In 1785, Betsy Ross was a founding member of a new religious society
of "Free Quakers," who had been "disowned" by their meetings for supporting the American War of Independence. She signed a declaration of
principles that is the nearest statement we have to her own vision of liberty and freedom. The Free Quakers aspired to a religion without dogma
and a church without discipline. They had "no desire to form Creeds or
Confessions of faith" and proposed to leave every member free "to think

and judge for himself," subject only to his "sole Judge and sovereign Lord." The Free Quakers reached out to "all nations, kindreds, tongues and people." Their meeting was open equally to "brothers and sisters." Many of Philadelphia's most prominent Quaker families joined, and their handsome meetinghouse still stands in Philadelphia. Betsy Ross became one of its two managers, with Samuel Wetherill. The two of them were the last of the Free Quakers, and they closed the meeting in 1834, shortly before her death. In the meeting's safe was found the five-pointed star that Betsy Ross cut with one snip for George Washington. With the star was a note from Samuel Wetherill affirming its authenticity.[98]

The children and grandchildren of Betsy Ross remembered her in old age as a small woman, still very beautiful, with a charming manner. Even after her retirement, she wore on her dress the emblems of her calling: a silver hook with two chains, a small pair of scissors, and a silver-ringed needle ball. Betsy Ross died in 1836, surrounded by a loving family, esteemed by her friends, and secure in the memory of her nation.

How an Indian Prodded Congress to Adopt the Stars and Stripes

A year after Betsy Ross's meeting with General Washington, Congress still had not settled on an American flag. The absence of an official design began to cause practical difficulties. It became a matter of life or death for an American Indian who signed himself Thomas Green. In the spring of 1777, the leaders of his nation wanted to send a diplomatic mission to Philadelphia, a journey of great danger for an Indian in time of war.

Thomas Green sent an urgent letter to the president of the Pennsylvania Council. He asked for "a flag of the United States," which he could "take to the chiefs of the nation, to be used by them for their security and protection," so that they would not be killed on the road to Philadelphia. Given the condition of the Continental treasury, the Indians expressed concern about the expense. To pay for an official flag of the United States, Thomas Green thoughtfully enclosed three strings of wampum.[99]

On June 3, 1777, the president of the Pennsylvania Council referred Thomas Green's letter to the Continental Congress. Ten days later, on June 14, Congress at last passed a resolution that "the flag of the United States be 13 stripes alternate red and white; that the Union be 13 stars, white in a blue field, representing a new constellation." Nothing was said about the arrangement of the stars, or other details.

The resolution, with its poetic flourish at the end, was the probably the work of Francis Hopkinson of New Jersey, chairman of the Marine Committee. He is thought to have brought the elements together: the stars on a true blue field, with the red and white stripes of the Grand Union Flag. Hopkinson also may (or may not) have invented the circular arrangement of stars, which first appeared on a Continental forty-dollar bill that he designed in 1778.[100]

Later, he claimed full credit for designing the Stars and Stripes and asked Congress for a quarter-cask of "public wine" in payment. When that request failed, he asked for money (£9 sterling). Congress looked into the question and concluded that many people had helped to design the flag. It denied Hopkinson's claim for money but did not dispute his claim to an important role in the process.[101]

If we put these elements together, a history of the flag emerges that is closer to the national folklore and the memories of Betsy Ross's family than to many academic histories. The Stars and Stripes developed from the striped flag of Boston's Sons of Liberty, and the blue and white star-spangled standards of George Washington's army. It evolved from the advice of a Quaker seamstress, the prompting of an American Indian, the timely intervention by Pennsylvania politicians, the inspiration of Francis Hopkinson, and a resolution of the Continental Congress.

These Americans were part of a process of mixed enterprise that combined public effort and private initiative in a way that was typical of the new republic. An American Indian was not reluctant to instruct the rulers of the colonies on what should be done, and they were quick to respond to his suggestion. A Philadelphia seamstress did not hesitate to criticize the commander-in-chief of the Continental Army, and he was open to her advice. The Continental Congress accepted these contributions in the spirit of the open society that America was becoming.

The Flag Resolution of the Continental Congress in 1777 was clear enough in a general way but vague in its details. American citizens received it not as a fixed instruction but as an invitation to creativity. The result was an outpouring of stripes and stars in many designs.[102] In Europe, John Adams and Benjamin Franklin gave their blessing to an American flag with thirteen red, white, and blue stripes and six-pointed heraldic stars. Later, a wonderful American flag in Vermont had seven-pointed Masonic stars, arranged in an arc above the cabalistic number 76, in a design reminiscent of the insignia of freemasonry.[103]

The stars were distributed in many ways during the War of Independence. Early flags often used a linear arrangement of rows (3,2,3,2,3). Others placed the stars in a circle or in an elegant ellipse that became the most fashionable design in the new republic. John Adams, as always, had his own ideas. He observed that by a resolution of Congress the stars represented a "new constellation," and the constellation Lyra might serve as a model. That idea became a tradition in the Adams family. In 1820, Secretary of State John Quincy Adams ordered a new design for passports: an American eagle holding in its beak the constellation Lyra, with the motto *Nunc sidera ducit,* by which he meant to say, "Now he reaches to the stars."[104]

Nothing in the Flag Resolution of 1777 prohibited the addition of other elements. Eagles sometimes appeared among the stars or replaced

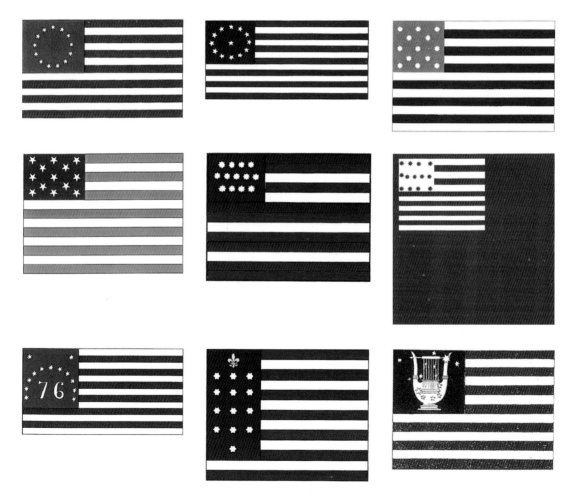

Origins of the American flag: The Stars and Stripes Together, 1777–83. Top left to bottom right: Betsy Ross Flag, ca. 1777; Elliptical flag, date uncertain; Alliance Flag, 1779; Fort Mercer Flag, 1777; Serapis Flag, 1779; Brandywine Flag, 1777; Bennington Flag (19th century?); French Alliance Flag, ca. 1781–82; an artist's idea of the Lyra Flag, proposed by John Adams and adopted by John Quincy Adams for use on American passports. Courtesy of Whitney Smith, © 2003, Flag Research Center.

them altogether on the diplomas of the *Cincinnati*. After the French alliance other American flags may have included a fleur-de-lis. Often, regional symbols of liberty and freedom were added: a New England Liberty Tree, a backcountry rattlesnake, or the word *Liberty* itself. A silk flag "displayed at the rejoicing for peace" in New Haven on April 24, 1783, added three words on a scroll: "Virtue, Liberty, Independence."[105]

The Flag as an Instrument of Liberty and Freedom

In the early years of the republic the Stars and Stripes were rarely flown by private citizens, except on ships at sea. The flag was used mainly for naval ensigns, military colors, and installations of the new federal government. It was primarily a symbol of sovereignty. That pattern of use changed during the administrations of John Adams (1797–1801), Thomas Jefferson (1801–9), and James Madison (1809–17). The catalysts were the "quasi-wars" of the early republic, when predators of other nations seized hundreds of American ships and thousands of sailors on the high seas. The piratical Barbary Powers of North Africa not only captured American ships but also made slaves of American crews. The worst predators were press gangs of the British navy, which captured as many as six thousand Americans and held them against their will in conditions worse than slavery.

As a consequence, the infant United States Navy found itself fighting France (1797–1801), the Barbary Powers (1803–5), and Great Britain (1812–15). At issue were "free trade and sailors' rights," which American leaders extended to all who sailed under the American flag. Events at sea dramatized these issues and gave rise to hero-tales, which often became flag stories. A case in point was a story about a young naval officer named Thomas McDonough (1783–1825). In 1806–7 he was serving aboard the small brig of war USS *Syren* in the Mediterranean. One day his vessel was at anchor in Gibraltar. McDonough watched with growing anger as a boat from a British frigate impressed a seaman from an American merchant brig that was flying the Stars and Stripes. McDonough ordered away a boat, intercepted the British press gang, and rescued the seaman at gunpoint. An infuriated British captain came aboard *Syren* and threatened to sink her on the spot. McDonough was unmoved. "While she swims," he said of his ship, "you shall not have the man. He was under the protection of my country's flag."

The British officer said, "Would you interfere if *I* were to impress men from that brig?"

"You have but to try," McDonough answered.

The British officer retreated, and the tale was told to many generations of American schoolboys. It had two morals. One was about courage and resolve in the face of a blustering bully. The other was about the flag, which became an emblem of liberty for all who sailed under its protection. In these stories the Stars and Stripes was not merely an icon but an instrument. The American sign became a guarantee of individual seamen's rights. In the words of Congressman Peter Wendover, it also became a "banner of freedom" that protected the rights of all American citizens. More than that, the flag became a talisman against tyranny throughout the world. Of all those many conflicts, the War of 1812 had a special importance in changing the symbolic meaning of the Stars and Stripes.

American sea chest, ca. 1840–50, with painted symbols of liberty and freedom as sailors' rights and free trade in the early republic. To the left is Hope with her anchor; to the right is Liberty with a wand and pileus. The central scene shows the victory of USS Constitution *over the HMS* Averriere, *August 19, 1812. Peabody Essex Museum, Salem, Mass.*

THE STAR-SPANGLED BANNER

Francis Scott Key's Vision of "The Land of the Free"

> I saw the flag of my country waving over a city, the
> strength and pride of my native state. . . . I saw the
> array of its enemies as they advanced to the attack. I
> heard the sound of battle. The noise of the conflict fell
> upon my listening ear, and told me that the brave and
> the free had met the invaders.
>
> —Francis Scott Key's memory of
> the battle at Fort McHenry, 1814

Most Americans know the story of the flag that flew over
Fort McHenry when a British army attacked the city of Baltimore in 1814. With a little help, many citizens can sing the
first verse of the freedom song that it inspired. But nobody remembers
the vision of freedom that its author had in mind.[106]

Francis Scott Key was a very American figure, but of a special kind.
He was a young gentleman of old Maryland, born to wealth and privilege
on the western shore of the Chesapeake Bay, where his family owned
plantations and slaves in five counties. Key was himself a slaveowner and
master of a plantation called Terra Rubra after its fertile red clay. Always
he loved his beautiful native land of Maryland and felt himself to be a
part of it. One of his pleasures was to canter a high-bred horse across the
green rolling estates that his family owned.[107]

As a young man, Francis Scott Key had lived with his grandmother
Ann Ross Key in a manor house called Belvoir on Maryland's beautiful
Severn River, while he studied at St. John's College in Annapolis. He had
a romantic sensibility, and in spare moments he formed the habit of scribbling poetry on scraps of paper that he carried in his pockets—love sonnets, light verse, political ditties, and devotional poetry.[108]

In 1802, Francis Scott Key married Mary Tayloe Lloyd, daughter of
Colonel Edward Lloyd, one of the richest planters in the United States
and owner of many slaves, among them later Frederick Douglass. The

bride and groom moved to an elegant town house in Georgetown, where they raised six sons and five daughters. Key practiced law with his uncle Philip Barton Key, joined the local militia, was an active layman in the Episcopal church, and became a member of the Federalist Party. Some of his family had been high Tories during the Revolution; Philip Barton Key had fought for the British and remained an officer on half pay in the British army even while he practiced in the courts of the new republic.[109]

Francis Scott Key (1779–1843), engraving. Maryland Historical Society.

Maryland Federalists such as Francis Scott Key were an odd breed in American politics. They combined the manners of southern gentlemen with very strong feelings of national identity. In the early republic, the strongest American nationalists were apt to be southern Federalists and northern Republicans.[110]

In 1814, Maryland Federalists were caught in a dilemma. They disliked Mr. Madison's war and despised his incompetent administration, but they had no sympathy for the secessionist talk of New England Federalists. They were strongly anglophile, but they watched in dismay as British warships seized control of the Chesapeake Bay and British troops marched deep into their beloved Maryland countryside. Key regarded the invaders as trespassers on his turf. When a British force attacked Washington, he joined the militia at the battle of Bladensburg, where American forces suffered a humiliating defeat. He was appalled when Tory British officers burned the Capitol and the President's House, which he regarded as a wanton act of criminal folly.

In that campaign, one of Key's acquaintances, an elderly physician named William Beanes, had an altercation with British troops and was taken prisoner aboard a ship of the Royal Navy. The friends of Doctor Beanes went to Key, knowing his family's British connections, and asked him to visit the British under a flag of truce, in hope of obtaining the doctor's release.

Key and an associate went aboard the British flagship under a flag of truce. They were received as gentlemen and welcomed to the admiral's table. But they were appalled by the treatment of Doctor Beanes, when at last they "found him in the forward parts of the ship, among the soldiers and sailors; he had not had a change of clothes from the time he was seized; was constantly treated with indignity by those around him, and no officer would speak to him."

For a man of honor this treatment was more galling than whips and chains. It was not something that one gentleman would inflict upon another. Francis Scott Key, anglophile though he had always been, was deeply disillusioned by his meetings with officers of the Royal Navy. He wrote his friend John Randolph of Roanoke, "Never was a man more disappointed in his expectations than I have been as to the character of the British officers. With some exceptions they appeared to be illiberal, ignorant and vulgar, and seem filled with a spirit of malignity against everything American." Key added in his gentlemanly way, "Perhaps, however, I saw them in unfavourable circumstances," but his encounter fundamentally changed his thinking.[111]

Francis Scott Key persuaded the British commanders that Doctor Beanes had treated wounded British officers with more humanity than he received, and the doctor was given his release. The British fleet was preparing to attack the city of Baltimore, and the Americans were ordered to remain aboard a British sloop until the battle was over. The British warships sailed up the Chesapeake Bay and anchored in the Patapsco River. Francis Scott Key and Doctor Beanes could make out the low ramparts of Fort McHenry, and they could see a large national ensign that had been raised by the fort's commander, a Virginian named George Armistead.

Major Armistead was not hopeful of the outcome. Fearing that the city of Baltimore would fall to the British fleet, he sent his pregnant wife, Louisa, to the safety of a peaceful country town called Gettysburg. But he and his men were determined to put up an honorable fight, and he ordered a big battle flag as a symbol of their resolve. "It is my desire to have a flag so large that the British will have no difficulty in seeing it from a distance," Major Armistead wrote.

His instructions were carried to Mary Pickersgill, who supplied maritime ensigns and house flags to the merchants of the town. She made Major Armistead a flag so big that it overflowed her workshop and had to be stitched on the floor of a brewery. Altogether it took 350,000 stitches, many of them made by Mary Pickersgill's slave and by a free black woman who worked for her. In the end, the flag was thirty feet high and forty-two feet long—large enough that Francis Scott Key and Doctor Beanes could see it eight miles away.[112]

As Key and Beanes watched, the British ships began a massive bombardment of the American fort. Five British bomb-ketches, a large part

The attack on Fort McHenry, September 13–14, 1814, colored aquatint by J. Bower, Philadelphia. Maryland Historical Society.

of all the heavy naval siege artillery in the world, hurled huge explosive shells into the small mud-brick ramparts. A new British rocket ship, the latest in military technology, sent terrifying projectiles with flaming tails screaming through the air.[113]

The bombardment continued into a dark and rainy night. As the weather grew worse, Major Armistead replaced his big battle flag with a "storm flag," smaller than his best ensign but still very large, seventeen by twenty-five feet, also made by Mary Pickersgill. From time to time the flag appeared in the white light of a bursting shell or the red flash of an exploding rocket. Then it would vanish again into smoke, rain, and darkness. In the middle of the night the great guns fell silent, and Key and Beanes were alarmed to hear the rattle of small arms, rising to a crescendo and then dropping away. Beanes's old eyes were not strong, and he kept asking, "Is the flag still there?" Key could not tell.[114]

At four o'clock in the morning the bombardment ceased. The two Americans did not know who had won and waited impatiently for dawn, fearing another British victory. At first light they were amazed to see the Stars and Stripes still flying defiantly above the shattered ramparts. A British assault in small boats had been beaten back by the musketry they had heard in the night. On land a makeshift force of green Maryland militia had met a British army of Wellington's invincibles, inflicted many casualties, killed its able commander, and disrupted its command. A British officer was heard to say, "These Americans are not to be trifled with."[115]

Early in the morning, the admiral ordered a retreat. In the moment of American victory, the men of Fort McHenry lowered their storm flag and hoisted their big battle ensign. Even the attackers were moved by the sight of it. On board HMS *Hebrus* British midshipman Robert Barrett wrote, "As the last vessel spread her canvas to the wind, the Americans hoisted a most superb and splendid ensign on their battery."[116]

Francis Scott Key's romantic feelings were overwhelmed. He pulled a letter from his pocket and "in the fervor of the moment" began to draft a poem. Later in the morning, he and Doctor Beanes were released and made their way to Baltimore. The streets were full of triumphant militia, and an exaltation of victory was in the air. Key went to an inn called the Indian Queen, and that night wrote out a fair copy of his poem, which was first called "The Defence of Fort M'Henry."[117]

Key matched his meter to a familiar melody. It was an English song called "Anacreon in Heaven," written for a high-toned musical society in

"The Star-Spangled Banner," a draft in the handwriting of Francis Scott Key, ca. September 16, 1814. Maryland Historical Society.

London called the Anacreontic Club, but Key knew it in another way. In the American republic it was best known as a political song called "Adams and Liberty," the anthem of the Federalist Party. It was sung at party rallies and frequently published in political newspapers and broadsides.

Francis Scott Key took the song of a political party that in 1814 was identified with peace and sectionalism and made it a hymn to martial courage and national unity. At the same time, he linked courage and national pride to a particular idea of freedom that came naturally to a young gentleman of old Maryland. Its elements appeared in the poem's refrain:

> *Oh say, does that star-spangled banner yet wave*
> *O'er the land of the free and the home of the brave.*

His theme became more visible in stanzas that are rarely sung today:

> *And where is the band that so vauntingly swore*
> *That the havoc of war and the battle's confusion,*
> *A home and a country shall leave us no more?*
> *Their blood has washed out their foul footsteps' pollution....*

> *O thus be it ever when freemen shall stand*
> *Between their lov'd homes, and the war's desolation.*
> *Blest with vict'ry and peace, may the heav'n rescued land,*
> *Praise the Power that hath made and preserv'd us a nation!*[118]

This was not the revolutionary idea of universal rights that appeared in the Declaration of Independence. Francis Scott Key's freedom song was about the right of possessing people to be safe in their "lov'd home" and sovereign in their "heav'n rescued land." Most of all it was about defending the sanctity of their own sacred soil from the "foul footsteps' pollution" of a foreign invader. Francis Scott Key's freedom was not an abstraction that reached out to all humanity. It was something tangible and concrete, a species of property that belonged to people such as himself, secure in "the land of the free, and the home of the brave."[119]

In Baltimore, Francis Scott Key's new song was first printed as a handbill and published in the *Baltimore Patriot* on September 17, 1814. Probably it was first sung by militiamen in Baltimore taverns where they met to sip their "early mint juleps."[120] By October the song was performed in public concerts and widely reprinted with a new title, "The

Star Spangled Banner," from Key's own line. The sentiments of the song were strongly favored in the middle states and the South. It had less appeal in New England, and its printing history shows that it was rarely published there until the era of the Civil War, when (as we shall see) Oliver Wendell Holmes wrote other lyrics that added an idea of freedom that was far removed from the thinking of a young gentleman of old Maryland, Francis Scott Key.[121]

All of these flags, eagles, and Indians represented something new in the world: liberty and freedom as a national idea. As late as 1776, national consciousness was so little developed that our most common words for it did not exist with the meanings we use today.[122]

Our modern language of nationality began to develop rapidly during the American Revolution and its immediate aftermath. The logic of the Revolution led Americans to think of liberty as a condition of national independence and of freedom as a set of rights that came with national citizenship. The interaction of these ideas changed all of them. American nationalism, in its association with liberty and freedom, took on a special meaning that was different from other forms of national identity. In many countries nationalist movements were hostile to democracy and individual rights and strongly associated with the authority of a strong state. That was not the American pattern. In the United States the idea of the nation centered on the people and their rights, not primarily on the nation state, or national institutions of power and authority.

At the same time, freedom and liberty were also changed by their new association with nationalism. These ideas became more broad in some ways but less so in others. In early America, as we have seen, folkways of freedom and liberty were often tribal ideas, limited by rank, religion, and place. The new national visions reached beyond those boundaries but also had their limits. In that way, they were less inclusive than the large thinking of the Declaration of Independence, which envisioned liberty and freedom as universal ideas for all humanity.

Many Americans rejected both tribal ideas and universal principles. They found a middle ground in the idea of a nation, which they applied in different ways. Some thought in terms of liberty and freedom in one nation. They believed that the best way to support liberty and freedom was to promote the welfare of the United States. The converse of this idea, for some Americans, was the proposition that what was good for America was good for liberty and freedom everywhere in the world. That doctrine became a cloak that covered a multitude of sins.

Other Americans took a different view. For them, freedom and liberty would be stronger if these ideas grew in other nations through the world. During the nineteenth century, they showed a distant sympathy for liberty and freedom in Greece, Hungary, Ireland, and Latin America. But few believed that the United States should or could proselytize other nations. They had problems enough at home, making a republic.

The Stars and Stripes became a symbol of these ideas, and after 1815 it began to be displayed in a new way. No longer was it only an emblem of sovereignty for ships and public buildings and armies. Voluntary associations adopted it as their emblem. Individual Americans began to fly the flag over their homes, and some even began to wear it. After the War of 1812 American artist William Birch made flag brooches for American women to wear as a badge of belonging to a nation of free people. The Stars and Strikes gained a double meaning—an emblem of liberty as national independence and a symbol of freedom as the rights of citizenship in a true nation.

Flag Brooch, William Birch, ca. 1820. Philadelphia Museum of Art, purchase, Joseph E. Temple Fund.

REPUBLICAN VISIONS OF LIBERTY & FREEDOM

Thomas Paine's Common Sense of the Subject

> Government, like dress, is the badge of lost innocence;
> the palaces of kings are built on the ruins of the bowers
> of paradise.
>
> —THOMAS PAINE, COMMON SENSE,
> NEW EDITION, FEBRUARY 14, 1776

BEFORE THE REVOLUTION, most Americans were staunch monarchists, amazingly so in light of their subsequent acts. When George III came to the throne in 1760, his colonial subjects outdid themselves in expressions of loyalty to the Crown. On June 4, 1766, after the repeal of the Stamp Act, the people of Philadelphia celebrated the King's Birthday with a joyous Handelian chorus:

> *Happy! Happy! Happy we,*
> *To GEORGE our Father and our King*
> *True-Born Sons of Loyalty.*[123]

This was less than a year after the Americans had been rioting against Parliament and mobbing the king's officers.

After the repeal of the Townshend Acts it was the same again. New Yorkers erected a gilded equestrian monument to George III on a marble pedestal fifteen feet high. Americans wanted desperately to believe that their quarrel was not with the king himself but with his evil ministers. Loyalty to the Crown persisted even after the fighting began at Lexington and Concord and Bunker Hill. As late as December 6, 1775, the Continental Congress insisted that they had no intention of challenging their royal sovereign, even as they were creating their own army and navy, conducting a foreign policy, and issuing their own money. To read their

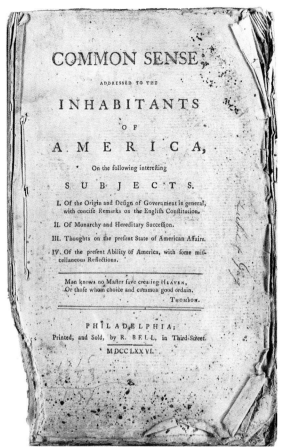

Thomas Paine, "Common Sense," 1776, an instrument and icon of liberty and freedom. A much-used copy in the American Philosophical Society.

abundant correspondence is to discover that these protestations of loyalty were genuine and deeply believed.[124]

Then suddenly the bonds of loyalty snapped. A flurry of royal proclamations persuaded Americans that George III was deeply hostile to their liberty and freedom. The king's decision to send foreign troops against them had a major impact, for Americans thought that the imperial dispute was a family affair. The language of British leaders made a difference, always referring to the Americans as "them" and "our subjects," as if all Americans were the subjects of each Briton.

The crystallizing event came on January 9, 1776, with the publication of Thomas Paine's *Common Sense*. This British radical incendiary invented a new language of politics and used it to persuade Americans that kingship itself was the root of their trouble. Throughout the colonies, people petitioned Congress for a Declaration of Independence from the British Crown and Parliament. Historian Pauline Maier has found evidence that independence developed as a broad popular movement, not a decision by a small elite. When the American people chose independence, they also became republicans and never looked back. Their rejection of monarchy was sudden, total, and permanent. On July 9, 1776, the same day that the Declaration of Independence was read in Manhattan, New Yorkers pulled down their statue of George III, smashed the metal to small pieces, and sent it to the women of Connecticut, who molded it into forty-two thousand musket balls.[125]

The break with monarchy was so complete that, in comparison with other revolutions, there was little rage against kings or kingship in America—nothing like the fury of the French Revolution against Louis XVI and Marie Antoinette, which shocked Americans by its violence. A rare exception was the American sculptor Patience Wright, who lived in London during the Revolution. She made a reputation for remarkably lifelike wax replicas of British monarchs and also for outspoken republicanism even to the point of regicide. British artist John Downman painted her portrait in 1777 and called it "the famous Wax-Woman and Republican from America." Her son Joseph Wright also painted the "Wax-Woman" in the studio, working on a severed head of Charles I, with the heads of George III and Queen Charlotte waiting nearby. The portrait caused an uproar at the Royal Academy Exhibition in 1780.[126]

After 1776, most Americans had little interest in tearing down a distant monarchy. They were more absorbed in building a new republic on a continental scale, a supremely difficult task. Experts in eighteenth-century political science such as the baron de Montesquieu pronounced it not merely difficult but impossible. He proved that large republics had always been unworkable and incapable of holding the support of a numerous people. Monarchy was

Thomas Paine (1737–1809), the "Common Sense Man," as he was called by the Continental Army, in which he served as a volunteer aide in 1775. Library of Congress.

Destruction of a statue of George III in New York City, July 6, 1776, from an old print in the collections of the New-York Historical Society.

thought to be more efficient. It was also believed to inspire personal loyalty in a way that solved critical problems of identity, legitimacy, and succession.

In a world of monarchy and despotism, Americans struggled to create a broad political base for a large republic and a moral imperative for republicanism. These problems were solved in several ways. One part of the solution was the development of federalism and representative government. Another was the invention of a pantheon of republican heroes and patriots who inspired identity, loyalty, and legitimacy. These men became surrogate figures for kingship. They clearly understood the roles they had to play as symbols as well as leaders, and began to function that way even while the Revolution was still in progress. Many became living icons of constitutional liberty and republican freedom.

REPUBLICAN HERO: GEORGE WASHINGTON

Icon of Virtue in a Free Society

> W itness, ye sons of tyrant's black womb,
> A nd see his Excellence victorious come!
> S erene, majestic, see he gains the field!
> H is heart is tender, while his arms are steel'd.
> I ntent on virtue, and her cause so fair,
> N ow treats his captive with a parent's care!
> G reatness of soul his ev'ry action shows,
> T hus virtue from celestial bounty flows,
> O ur GEORGE, by heaven, destin'd to command,
> N ow strikes the British yoke with prosp'rous hand.
>
> —"A YOUNG LADY," PENNSYLVANIA
> EVENING POST, JANUARY 7, 1777

THE FIRST AND GREATEST of these republican figures was George Washington. In his own time he became a living monument of flesh and blood, even before he was petrified in granite and marble. In public appearances during the 1780s, he was regarded not merely with respect but with reverence. By the 1790s, graven images of Washington were produced in quantity and displayed in households throughout the United States. These icons represented Washington in many ways. Most of them centered on visions of liberty and freedom.[127]

One of the first images appeared on a linen scarf that has been called America's "first political textile." It was made in Philadelphia by John Hewson, at the request of Martha Washington. In the center it shows the general on horseback, with the motto "George Washington, Esq., Foundator and Protector of America's Liberty and Independency." In the corners of the scarf are flags that symbolize the diversity of America: a rattlesnake flag with the slogan "Don't Tread on Me," a New England Liberty Tree Flag, a Union Flag with thirteen horizontal red stripes, and a curious flag with thirteen radiant red stripes in a design that calls to mind the Japanese "rising sun" naval ensign. Washington appears as the leader who unites all of these different visions of liberty and freedom in a common cause.[128]

Another early image emerged after the battles of Trenton and Princeton. It also represented Washington the Soldier of Liberty. Leading examples were portraits by Charles Willson Peale and John Trumbull, who actually served in the Continental Army and painted Washington as they had known him in the war: a strong commander, a superb horseman, and a man of courage who led from the front on many a desperate field. Their portraits celebrated his energy and decision and most of all his depth of character that sustained the American cause in its darkest moments. They also represented him as a charismatic leader of free men.[129]

At the end of the war another iconography was invented. This was Washington the Victor, crowned with laurels, surrounded with the trophies of war, dressed in Roman clothing or a glittering European uniform. Above his forehead buzzed the conventional flying figures of Fame with her trumpet and Liberty with her wand and pileus. Benjamin Franklin helped to promote this idea with his gift of wit and good humor. A story is told of a state dinner in Versailles. The British minister gave a toast in which he compared George III to the sun. The French minister rose and likened Louis XVI to the moon. Franklin got to his feet and said, "George Washington, Commander of the American armies, who like Joshua of old, commanded the sun and moon to stand still, and they obeyed him."

In the peace that followed, a different image appeared: Washington as Cincinnatus, a stoic soldier who had no ambition for conquest or dominion and preferred the quiet retirement of country life. He was shown

"George Washington, Esq. Foundator, and Protector of America's Liberty and Independency." Linen Scarf, printed in Philadelphia by John Hewson, 1776. It combines many American symbols of liberty and freedom and has been called America's first political textile. Winterthur Museum.

with a plow at his side and weapons at a distance, but always near enough to be taken up again. In the early republic, Americans bought engravings and mezzotints of Washington as Cincinnatus. Many soldiers modeled themselves on his example.[130]

In the years of Washington's presidency yet another vision emerged: the president as a republican citizen, first among equals. He was portrayed in a plain suit of black cloth, a symbol not of power or majesty but of liberty, virtue, justice and republicanism. Sometimes he had a sword at his side, a symbol of a willingness to use force if necessary to preserve a free republic. But most of all he was a guardian of the laws.

Toward the end of his administration, more exalted images appeared of Washington as the god of liberty. A print by Robert Field in 1795 showed Washington as an immortal spirit who was borne above the world on the back of an eagle. Above him was a sword surmounted by a liberty cap. For anyone who missed the point, the artist added the word *libertas*, set within a laurel wreath.

The most popular images appeared in pamphlet biographies, written mainly for the young and centered in Washington's private life, as a model of virtue for citizens of a free nation. The most important work in this genre was Mason Locke Weems's imaginative *Life and Memorable Actions of General George Washington* (1800). The author was a Chesapeake clergyman who told his publisher that the object was to display Washington's "Great Virtues. 1 His Veneration for the Deity, or Religious Principles. 2 His Patriotism. 3 His Magnanimity. 4 His Industry. 5 His Temperance and Sobriety. 6 His Justice, &c &c." To that end Weems told the tale of Washington and the cherry tree, Washington and the school bullies, Washington refusing a duel and apologizing when in the wrong, Washington at Braddock's defeat, Washington in prayer at Valley Forge, and many more. Some of these stories (the duel, the school) were founded in fact. Others passed current in the oral culture of the Chesapeake. A few may have been invented by Weems, and all were much improved by him. Every story had a moral about a private virtue that was thought to be fundamental to a free republic.[131]

All of these images came together after Washington's death in 1799. Americans produced a flood of mourning pictures in many different genres: paintings, prints, sculptures, textiles, rings, ceramics. One mourning picture showed Washington as the soul of virtuous simplicity, dressed in the plain suit of a republican citizen, without decorations or adornments. Below him were allegorical figures of poetry and history and a weeping Indian woman who represented the sorrow of America. In the clouds above were three figures that represented justice, virtue, and especially liberty.[132]

These images of George Washington became icons in every sense. They were reproduced in lithographs and chromos, hung on the walls of American homes, and regarded with a reverence that other people reserved for religious images. They were also political instruments of high importance. The image of Washington became the great guide to conduct in American politics. In the early republic Americans deeply distrusted open displays of political ambition and despised men who lusted after public office. Candidates for the presidency were expected not to seek the job, or even to desire it. Those who acted otherwise paid a price at the polls.

Washington's impact was especially great on the political right. After the War of Independence, officers in the Continental Army formed an association called the Society of the Cincinnati and chose that Roman republican and their modern American Cincinnatus as their models. Their medal was an American eagle hanging from a ribbon that was blue and white for honor, truth, and loyalty. Other Americans noted the new society with alarm, mainly because it made itself a hereditary organization that descended through the male line, at first on the rules of primo-

"Freiheit, Gleichheit, Eintracht und Bruder liebe" Freedom, Equality, Unity and Brotherly love," a Pennsylvania German image of George Washington with a stylized folk image of a liberty cap and liberty pole, 1842. Illuminated fraktur art. Philadelphia Museum of Art, Titus C. Geesey Collection.

geniture. Ironically, an association that was understood by its members as binding them to a self-denying idea of republican virtue was regarded by others as an attempt to create an American aristocracy. But even as the Society of the Cincinnati was attacked by radical republicans, its function was to reconcile the officer corps of the army to the republic. The image of Washington as Cincinnatus was their model. The history of other republics demonstrates the importance of this example.

The way it worked to create identity and legitimacy may be observed in the politics of the early republic. The Federalist and Whig parties made heavy use of Washington as a republican symbol, more so than did the followers of Jefferson and Jackson. On April 30, 1814, the twenty-fifth anniversary of George Washington's inauguration as president, the Federalists put on a grand parade in Boston. In spirit it was closer to a saint's procession than to a party rally. The main body of the procession was led by twenty-one youths, with silk banners that represented the acts of George Washington and the principles for which he stood. Next came a sacred relic of the great man himself, the gleaming gorget that he had worn in battle, borne reverently on a satin cushion. Then came the rank and file of Boston's very large Federal Republican Party, marching in divisions four abreast, a mile and a half long. The most memorable part of the procession was a large company of Federalist children, all dressed in white and bearing wreaths and garlands. Each child had a chain around its neck. Suspended from the chain was a small sacred book called "Washington's Legacy," which contained the text of the United States Constitution and Washington's Farewell Address.[133]

These children were the next generation of Boston's leaders. The cult of Washington was very strong among American elites, especially military officers and men of wealth who destroyed republican institutions in many other countries. The strength of this process was important to the stability of America's free institutions. George Washington's iconography retained its influence for many years in American politics. Most of all it expressed a central idea in his generation: that liberty and freedom could only survive in a republic of virtue, which in turn required virtuous rulers and a virtuous people. Washington was the great prototype and moral example.

REPUBLICAN SAGE: BENJAMIN FRANKLIN
A Living Symbol of Liberty, Knowledge, and Wisdom

> A Bible and a newspaper in every house, a good school
> in every district . . . are the principal support of virtue,
> morality, and civil liberty.
>
> —BENJAMIN FRANKLIN

ANOTHER LIVING SYMBOL of liberty and freedom was Benjamin Franklin, an iconic figure even before the American Revolution. This ingenious American offered many images to the world. Most were his own inventions, self-made symbols of a self-made man. They also had a large meaning for the history of liberty and freedom.[134]

The first of these images was Poor Richard, an ordinary American and homespun philosopher, full of practical folk wisdom. Franklin himself consciously created this image in 1732 and polished it for twenty years in annual editions of *Poor Richard's Almanac* (1733–51). He offered an abundance of advice in form of pithy proverbs, which he made a popular genre of philosophical discourse. They were a form of packaged wisdom, for people on the go. They passed from mouth to mouth in early America, and some of the most memorable have been rarely reproduced. "Force shites upon reason's back," said Poor Richard in 1736. Here was an earthy celebration of an open society, and of liberty from arbitrary power.

Many of Poor Richard's sayings were about liberty and freedom. They began with a very old-fashioned idea of a free society and a limited vision of liberty: "The Magistrate should obey the laws; the People should obey the Magistrate" (1734). "If you ride a Horse, sit close and tight, If you ride a man sit easy and light" (1734). "Nothing brings more pain than too much pleasure; nothing brings more bondage than too much liberty" (1738).

Gradually Poor Richard became more libertarian and egalitarian: "No longer vertuous no longer free; is a maxim as true with regard to a private person as a Common-wealth" (1739). "All Blood is Alike Ancient" (1745). By the 1740s, Franklin was speaking strongly for liberty and freedom, not by lofty appeals to reason but in the skeptical folk spirit of Poor Richard, who believed that no man was fit to rule another.[135]

Another self-created image appeared in Franklin's two books, *The Way to Wealth* and his unfinished *Autobiography,* which became steady sellers for many generations. They celebrated the ideal of the "self-made man" who achieved material success and happiness through individual striving in a free country. Franklin's autobiography was a braided narrative with many didactic themes. One was about how Poor Richard became rich. Another was about how the benighted son of Boston Puritans found happiness in the free air of Philadelphia. Yet a third was a civic story about a young man who helped himself by helping others. Many American lives were consciously modeled on these images, which spread rapidly beyond America itself. The French called Poor Richard "le bonhomme Richard." By the end of the eighteenth century he was an international symbol of self-liberation.

Another set of images was about Doctor Franklin, scientist, discoverer, and symbol of the practical benefits of free inquiry. An engraving in 1762 showed him at his table in Philadelphia, surrounded by the imagined apparatus of his experiments on lightning: a lightning rod, an electroscope, and bells that rang when an electrical current passed through the apparatus. It was a symbol of Franklin's standing as an inventor, scientist, and philosopher. The icons of Doctor Franklin celebrated the triumph of enlightenment over darkness and of reason over irrationality in all its forms. His discoveries promised to liberate humanity from chains of ignorance and superstition.[136]

A fourth image developed in France when Franklin arrived to represent his nation. It represented him as "le bon Quaker," a symbol of virtue that was thought to be the vital principle of a free republic. Franklin allowed his French friends to report that he was a native of Philadelphia and a member of the Society of Friends. It was entirely false, and highly effective. He did not advertise the darker truth that he had been born in Boston of Puritan stock, and belonged to no church or sect.[137]

A fifth image represented Franklin as a noble savage who lived in the wilderness and personified the freedom that existed in a state of nature. This also was a humbug. All his life Franklin was a sophisticated city slicker. He was born and raised in Boston, made his reputation in Philadelphia, lived eighteen years in London, and spent much of the Revolution in Paris. But he permitted others to represent him as a natural

Benjamin Franklin as a free spirit of the American forest, engraving by August de St. Aubin, after a ca. 1777 drawing by Charles Nicolas Cochin. The original is in the American Philosophical Society.

Benjamin Franklin as a man of science and liberty, print by Marguerite Gerard after a ca. 1778 design by Jean Honoré Fragonard after an epigram by Anne-Robert-Jacques Turgot, Baron de l'Aulne: "Eripuit Coelo Fulmen Sceptrumque Tirannis." Philadelphia Museum of Art.

phenomenon who miraculously emerged from the American forest. Franklin himself cultivated this idea by wearing a symbolic bearskin cap that delighted the people of France. An engraving by Johann Martin Weill improved the effect by putting him in a full-bodied fur coat that made him look like the bear itself.[138]

The sixth image was Franklin as a leader of the Revolution. This idea was combined with iconic elements from other images. A leading example was a celebrated epigram of the French philosopher Turgot, who said of Franklin that "he seized the lightning from the heavens, and the scepter from tyrants." This saying was much repeated in Paris. The court painter Fragonard created an iconic work that phrased Turgot's epigram in Latin, dressed Franklin in a toga, and put him in the role of Jupiter, directing the lesser gods. With his left hand he guided the shield of Minerva to deflect a bolt of lightning. With his right hand he ordered Mars to strike at tyranny. Sitting by his lap was America, with a crown of stars and a bundle of fasces, symbols of republicanism and civic virtue.

Fragonard's image of Franklin, and others like it, was widely reproduced in Europe, not always in a positive way. King Louis XVI was infuriated by this celebration of a republican leader. He was even more jealous of the affection that Franklin inspired in the charming and beautiful Comtesse Diane de Polignac. The king gave her a chamber-pot of Sèvres porcelain, with the face of Franklin on the inside bottom, an indelible image of antirepublicanism.[139]

Extravagant as this imagery became, yet another icon of Franklin became even more exalted. In 1778, the French court artist Joseph Duplessis painted a portrait that contemporaries judged to be one of the best and most accurate paintings that was ever done of the American sage. But it was more than merely a "likeness." Duplessis represented Franklin as a symbol of humanity itself. The iconography of the painting was made explicit in a sumptuous gold frame. At the top of the frame was a snake—not the American rattlesnake of liberty but the European serpent of unity, in this case the unity of all humanity. At the bottom was a single Latin word, *Vir*, man. It meant man in general, Franklin as the archetype of universal mankind. In its classical associations, it also meant a man of virtue and what the Italians called *virtu*, a strength of character and leadership and presence in the world.[140]

At the end of Franklin's life, all of these themes were brought together in an iconography of high complexity. A printed cotton textile, made in Britain for the American market after the Revolution, shows an image of Dr. Franklin in a European academic gown, with an American bearskin on his head. He is striding toward the Temple of Fame, with two gorgeous young women in classical gowns. One of his escorts represents America, with a starry shield and a sunburst behind her head. She floats beside him on a cloud. The other young woman is the goddess of liberty with her wand and pileus. She is closer to Franklin and keeps his feet firmly on the ground. Franklin himself holds a flowing scroll that reads, "Where liberty dwells, there is my country." In these interlocking symbols, we find another theme that Franklin personified. A republic was thought to require

Benjamin Franklin as Vir, an archetype of humanity; portrait by Joseph Duplessis, 1778. The Metropolitan Museum of Art, Friedsam Collection, Bequest of Michael Friedsam, 1931. (32.100.132) Photograph © 1981 The Metropolitan Museum of Art.

"The Apotheosis of Franklin and Washington," English copper-plate-printed cotton-linen textile, ca. 1785–90. Tennessee State Museum, Nashville. Reproduction courtesy of Scalamandré.

wisdom and knowledge in its leaders and the people. Franklin became the great exemplar of this idea.[141]

Other leaders of the early republic were not happy about the adulation of Washington and Franklin. John Adams wrote, "The history of the revolution will be one continued lie from one end to the other. The essence of the whole will be that Dr. Franklin's electrical rod smote the earth, and out sprang General Washington. That Franklin electrized him with his rod—and henceforward these two conducted all the policy, negotiation, legislation and war."[142]

For most Americans, Washington and Franklin were republican models who rose above the partisanship of the new republic and inspired a complex iconography that linked ideas of liberty and freedom to other themes. In the image of Washington, liberty was connected to virtue, character, courage, and gravitas, and freedom with his service in the republic. With Franklin, liberty was associated with the striving of a self-made man; freedom with his civic spirit; and both ideas with his passion for useful knowledge, science, reason, and enlightenment. Always, liberty and freedom were at the center of this republican iconography.

Franklin continued this image-building even into the grave. When he was in France, he was given a handsome walking stick, with a gold top in the shape of a liberty cap. In a codicil to his will, he left it to George Washington with these words: "My fine crab-tree walking-stick, with a gold head curiously wrought in the form of a cap of liberty, I give to my friend, and the friend of mankind, General Washington. If it were a sceptre, he has merited it and would become it." It made a small but enduring memorial of these two extraordinary men.[143]

REPUBLICAN STATESMEN AS SYMBOLS
Madison, Adams, Hamilton, and Jefferson

> If men were angels, no government would be neces-
> sary. If angels were to govern men, neither external nor
> internal controls on government would be necessary.
>
> —JAMES MADISON

A MERICANS also cherished the memory of the Founding Fathers,
the generation who had launched the American republic. Chief
among them were John Adams, James Madison, Alexander
Hamilton, and Thomas Jefferson. All were tough and hardened practical
politicians, and each became an American icon. Their images appeared
on commemorative pitchers and plates and artifacts that were mass-produced in Britain for the American market. In the nineteenth century,
artists and sculptors found a strong market for paintings, engravings,
prints, and busts. Many of these images included symbols of liberty and
freedom with a range of meanings.

Through the full span of American history, the reputations of all these
men ebbed and flowed in a long rhythm of declension and revival. The
central figures changed from one period to another, in very interesting
ways. Four periods of revival might be identified. The first came in the
1820s. The leading figures were Thomas Jefferson and John Adams, especially after July 4, 1826, when both men died on the same day, which was
also the fiftieth anniversary of the Declaration of Independence. Many
Americans received that extraordinary event as a warning and a sign.
They responded by returning to the example of the founders as models of
republican virtue and civic spirit.

Another revival came after the era of the Civil War and Reconstruction. In two-thirds of the country, the urgent question of the age was

about the preservation of the Union and the construction of a strong nation-state, all in the cause of liberty and freedom. Two founders were predominant: George Washington and Alexander Hamilton, who were associated with those purposes.

A third revival came during the struggle against Fascism and Communism (ca. 1935–65), when Americans became more mindful of the founders as apostles of democracy and individual rights. Two founders in particular were prominent in this period: Thomas Jefferson and James Madison.

Yet another period developed in the last decade of the twentieth century and the early twenty-first century. After many scandals in high office, Americans returned to the founders as moral leaders. The central figures in 2001, thanks to David McCullough's wonderful biography, were John and Abigail Adams, who set an example for honesty, authenticity, and sterling character. Together, the Adamses became exemplars of integrity, unyielding moral principle, public service, and private virtue.

Even as the reputations of individual men and women rose and fell, the founders themselves preserved their collective identity as symbols of liberty and freedom. The memory of these leaders legitimated America's republican institutions. At the same time, four individual founders were remembered in another way. Hamilton, Jefferson, Adams, and Madison also came to personify distinctive ideas of a free republic. Each inspired a popular iconography that had great importance in the early republic and a long reach in American history.

Congress: James Madison's Free Republic as a Vision of Representative Government

When the republic was young, one of its leading symbols of liberty and freedom was the Congress. The calling of the First Continental Congress in Philadelphia during the summer of 1774 inspired broadsides, songs, and a poem called "Hope":

> *LIBERTY, great LIBERTY, yet lives,*
> *Lives a HEROIN[E], by Schuykill's wat'ry side;*
> *Known is her worth, and FREEDOM is her pride.*[144]

With the Declaration of Independence, the Second Continental Congress also became the symbol of a free republic. An example was John Trumbull's painting of the Declaration of Independence. It began as a small oil sketch at the urging of Thomas Jefferson in 1786 and grew into a great project that occupied the artist for thirty years. Trumbull expanded his original painting into an enormous canvas of twelve by eighteen feet. After its completion in 1818, it toured the country for two years and drew large crowds. An engraving by Asher Durand in 1823 extended its reach, and it has been reproduced in many forms: a steel engraving on the back of the two-dollar bill, a transfer print on ceramic plates, and a polychrome wood carving reminiscent of religious icons.[145]

Trumbull's painting does not represent the actual signing of the Declaration of Independence but the submission of a text by the drafting committee, perhaps on June 28 or more likely July 2, when Congress went into a committee of the whole and devoted the better part of three days to revising the document.

Pauline Maier has written that "what generations of Americans came to revere was not Jefferson's but Congress's Declaration, the work not of a single man, or even a committee, but a larger body of men."[146] Trumbull's painting affirms that idea. It celebrates the central role of Thomas Jefferson, Benjamin Franklin, and especially John Adams, who is the strongest figure in the painting. But mainly it represents that "larger body of men" who made up the Second Continental Congress: not exactly the signers, of whom ten are missing, but the leading members of Congress, including four who did not sign the Declaration.[147]

Trumbull made at least thirty-six life studies of the men who appear in the painting. Many details bring out their differences of region, rank, religion, and politics. We see Stephen Hopkins in his broad-brimmed Quaker hat, and John Witherspoon in the dress of a Presbyterian minister. Connecticut shoemaker Roger Sherman is in a plain homespun suit. The Virginia gentleman Thomas Jefferson wears a scarlet waistcoat that was a badge of high rank in the eighteenth century. New Englanders appear in "sadd colours" such as snuff brown and dark gray that preserved the austerity of their Puritan forebears. Southern gentlemen are painted in fine linen and elegant suits of the latest London fashion. Political differences are evident too. Richard Stockton skulks in the background; he would be the only signer to renounce the Declaration when British troops approached his home in New Jersey. John Adams, the driver of independence, appears at the center of the painting, hand on hip, in a posture of defiance, resolve, and strength.

Trumbull's image of the Continental Congress symbolized a free republic that functioned on a large scale through the election of represen-

Congress as a symbol of a free republic: John Trumbull, "The Declaration of Independence," 1786–94. Yale University Art Gallery.

tatives. At the same time, it expressed a distinctive idea of representation that was central to American republicanism and implicit in the eighteenth century idea of Congress. The word itself derived from the Latin verb *congredior,* which meant to meet together in hostile combat, or to dispute or argue. In the early modern era, *congress* was a word for the meeting of differences or even the collision of opposites. It was a common term for sexual intercourse in the eighteenth century. It also described a meeting of people from different countries or states or places. The idea of a Congress was very different from a Parliament, which meant literally a group of people who came to talk things over.

When the American colonies began to work together, they called their meetings Congresses in the eighteenth-century meaning of the word. This was the case in the Albany Congress in 1754, the Stamp Act Congress in 1765, the First Continental Congress in 1774, and the Second Continental Congress.

American Congresses and British Parliaments were both representative bodies, but they rested on different principles of representation. Members of Parliament did not as a rule consider themselves bound by the wishes of their constituents. They thought of themselves as elected to do what they thought best for the good of the realm. Americans expected their representatives to act in another way, as ambassadors from their constituents. This idea appeared early in the eighteenth century and was developed at length by Daniel Dulany as early as 1765.

It was not at first a democratic idea. In the beginning it bound representatives to local elites. Americans introduced many devices to make representatives responsible to their constituents: open legislative sessions, public galleries, recorded votes, printed debates. It was generally believed that constituents could instruct their representatives and that representatives had a duty to obey. In the early republic, American representatives were recalled for not obeying: John Quincy Adams for one. Rotation in office and term limits were required of all members of the Continental Congress under the Articles of Confederation. After independence, Congress lacked the powers to govern effectively, and acquired a reputation for weakness. But Americans never turned away from the congressional idea.

One member of Congress invented a new vision of a free republic as a system of representative government on the Congressional model. James Madison (1751–1836) came of age in the Revolutionary era and thought that its turbulence was normal and natural in politics. That experience taught him to think of a free society as open, pluralist, disorderly, and ridden with "faction." He asked how the dangers of faction and tyranny could be controlled, and his answer was clear and consistent: enlarge the system. He proposed to create an empire of liberty, a system of representative government so large and diverse that no faction could tyrannize the rest. The instrument and image of that idea was a Continental Congress.

Madison's solution became one of the great American visions of freedom and liberty. It was prominent in the debate over the Federal Constitution in 1788. During the 1790s, Madison put it to work by leading the development of national political parties. Always, his key to the preservation of liberty and freedom in a republic was to keep the union large and strong. This was the theme of his final "advice to my country," which urged above all "that the Union of the States be cherished and perpetuated. Let the open enemy to it be regarded as a Pandora with her box opened; and the disguised one, as the Serpent creeping with his deadly wiles into Paradise."

James Madison (1751–1836), the fourth president of the United States, as a symbol of a free republic: portrait by Thomas Sully after Gilbert Stuart, 1856. Virginia Historical Society.

Later James Madison's vision gave rise to a school of American history and a theory of political science, called "Madisonian" in honor of its author. In the twentieth century it was taken up by writers on American pluralism, and it flourishes in the multicultural metaphors of our own time.[148]

The Constitution: John Adams's Free Republic as a Government of Laws

In 1795, the Washington administration selected names for a new class of large frigates in the infant United States Navy. Their choices were unique in the naval nomenclature of that age. British men-of-war celebrated kingship and aristocratic pride: *Royal George, Royal Savage, Royal Sovereign, Royal Oak, Majestic, Superb, Inflexible,* even HMS *Arrogant.* French warships, after the Revolution of 1789, were named *Ça Ira, Droits de l'Homme, Egalité, Fraternité, Insurgent, Peuple Souverain,* and *Révolutionnaire.* Spanish ships of the line commemorated Catholic piety: *San Agustín, San Francisco de Asís, Santísima Trinidad.* The new American frigates were named *Congress, President, United States, Constellation,* and *Constitution.*[149]

One of these ships, USS *Constitution,* still survives in Boston, the oldest commissioned warship afloat and one of America's most cherished icons. She is visited every year by millions of visitors. Today, many Amer-

Harold Wylie, "US 44 Gun Frigate Constitution." Reproduced with permission from the Thomas Ross Collection.

icans remember her as an image of patriotism and military strength. In the beginning she also had another significance. Her name made her the symbol of a free republic, bound by a fundamental written Constitution that became an ark of liberty and a covenant of freedom.

The early American republic was distinctive that way, in the strength of its conviction that freedom and liberty required the protection of fundamental written laws that are superior to presidents, congresses, and courts. In the seventeenth century, most English colonies in the New World had constitutional documents of that sort: the Great Fundamentals in Plymouth (1636), the Fundamental Orders of Connecticut (1639), the Body of Liberties in Massachusetts Bay (1641), the Rhode Island Constitution (1647), the Fundamental Constitutions of Carolina (probably drafted by John Locke in 1669), the Concessions and Agreements of West Jersey (1677), the Charter of Liberties in New York (1683), and the Charter of Privileges in Pennsylvania (1701).

These documents became the foundation of another American tradition. In the eighteenth century, every colony that became part of the United States operated under a written constitution. After independence, every new state framed a new constitution or renewed its colonial charter. All of these documents were designs for a free republic of laws.

The man at the center of America's constitutional tradition was John Adams. In the Second Continental Congress, a delegate from North Carolina was about to draft a constitution for his state and asked Adams for a "sketch" of his ideas. The result was a short essay called "Thoughts on Government." Other congressmen asked for a copy, and Richard Henry Lee of Virginia had it printed in Philadelphia. Adams's pamphlet had a major impact on constitution-making in America. Adams himself put it to work in his draft of the Massachusetts Constitution of 1780, now the oldest in the world. He also wrote a three-volume treatise called *Defence of the Constitutions of Government of the United States of America* (London, 1787).

All of his work developed from a very clear vision of a free republic. On the basis of wide reading in Aristotle, Machiavelli, James Harrington, and many authors, Adams believed that a free republic was best maintained by preserving a constitutional balance between social orders, especially the *aristoi* and the *demos*. To that end, he designed a constitution in which the few and the many were represented by separate branches of the legislature, and the balance was maintained by a strong and independent executive, operating within a system of fundamental law.

Few Americans read John Adams's *Defence of the American Constitu-*

tions, but many used his "Thoughts on Government" as a blueprint for constitution-making. Among American elites in the 1780s, Adams became a symbol of his own ideas, and he was true to them through his long career. As president, he thought his duty was to preserve his independence and shift his weight back and forth to preserve the balance. Adams did exactly that in his own administration. He believed in 1797 that the worst danger to freedom came from unbridled democracy, and he threw the weight of his presidency to the other side. By 1799, he was convinced that the danger was now coming from the Hamiltonian right. He shifted his weight and suddenly began working against the *aristoi,* to the horror of his Federalists and the destruction of his own chances for reelection. High Federalists thought he had taken leave of his senses, but Adams was always true to his own principles. Single-handed, he called off a war with France because he thought that it threatened the destruction of a free republic, and he may have been correct. He did so at the cost of his own career. It was one of the great moments of courage and conviction in American history.

In 1820, Adams held his last public office as a member of another Massachusetts Constitutional Convention. His final effort was to propose a radical measure for complete religious freedom in Massachusetts. The convention heard him with respect, celebrated his integrity, and voted against him. Fourteen years later, Massachusetts saw the error of its intolerant ways and did just what Adams had recommended. His public service ended as it began, in the cause of liberty, freedom, and a balanced constitution.

John Adams with the Goddess of Liberty, Justice, and Abundance, creamware pitcher. Collection of David J. and Janice L. Frent; image from Corbis/Bettmann.

In the new republic most Americans created a popular image of this abstract idea. They began to represent the balanced constitution as a full-rigged ship. In many American towns, the ratification of the Constitution was celebrated by a "Grand Federal Procession" in which a large part of the community marched behind a model of a full-rigged ship, as big as a small house, and drawn by matched teams of ten or twelve horses. These emblematic Federal ships had many names: *Hamilton* in New York, *Union* in Philadelphia, *Federalist* in Portsmouth, Virginia, *Constitution* in other towns. But everywhere the

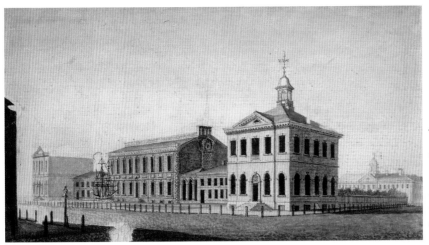

James P. Malcolm, "The Ship 'Union' before the State House and Congress Hall," watercolor, ca. 1792–94. Collection of H. Richard Dietrich, Jr.; photograph by Lynn Rosenthal, Philadelphia Museum of Art.

imagery was the same. A full-rigged ship was the largest and most complex machine in that era, and it became the symbol of the complex constitutional machinery that was thought to be fundamental to a free republic.[150]

The imagery persisted for many years. In Philadelphia the ship *Union* remained in front of Congress Hall for four years as a symbol of the Constitution and a vision of free government. Cartoonists often used the image as a constitutional emblem in the early republic. And then came the USS *Constitution*, which still survives today as a symbol of republican freedom and the vigilance and strength and courage that are needed to maintain it.

Commonwealth: Alexander Hamilton's Free Republic as a Hive of Commerce and Industry

On July 23, 1788, the Federalists of New York City held a festival to celebrate the ratification of the new Constitution by ten states. They also meant to send a message to their own reluctant state politicians who had not yet agreed to join the new Federal union. The festival was a great event, full of colorful imagery on the theme of a free republic. The leading event was a grand parade of New Yorkers, who mustered in seventy-six groups (every number had a cabalistic meaning) and marched down Broadway to the Bowling Green.

At the head of the procession was Christopher Columbus on a horse, followed by four "foresters" with felling axes who symbolized the taming of the land. Then came the industrious artisans and craftsmen of the city,

marching behind big banners crowded with emblems and symbols. Many
of the artisans pulled floats on which their brethren were busily at work in
their trades. The printers carried a banner that showed Benjamin
Franklin and the goddess of liberty, with her wand and pileus. On their
float was a printing press, on which they were running off copies of a
poem specially written for the event and handing them to spectators.

The coopers had a float on which they were making a handsome new
keg labeled "the New Constitution." The upholsterers were finishing a
gigantic "Federal chair." The bakers carried a Federal cake made from an
entire barrel of flour. Musical instrument makers displayed Apollo playing his lyre in celebration of republican harmony. The scholars of the
New York Philological Society led by Noah Webster carried emblems
celebrating "the principles of a federal language."

The Society of Pewterers marched behind a handsome banner that still
survives at the New-York Historical Society. It showed four artisans at work
in their shop with examples of their wares. Over their heads was a verse:

> *The Federal Plan Most Solid and Secure*
> *Americans Their Fredom Will Endure*
> *All Arts Shall Flourish in Columbia's Land*
> *And All Her Sons Join as One Social Band.*[151]

*Banner of the Society of
Pewterers, 1788. New-York
Historical Society.*

The festival ended in a great dinner for six thousand citizens at tables 440 feet long, arranged in an elegant federal fan.[152]

Similar festivals were organized in Boston, Baltimore, Philadelphia (the biggest of all), and many smaller commercial towns. More people may have participated than the number who voted in the elections of that year. These events were important demonstrations of support for the new government and may have made a difference in the outcome. In Boston, Paul Revere's mobilization of the mechanics and artisans may have persuaded Samuel Adams and John Hancock to accept the new system. In New York, a hostile convention of Anti-Federalist state politicians finally agreed to ratify the constitution three days after the Grand Federal Procession in New York City, which made credible a threat by Alexander Hamilton that Manhattan would secede from the state and join the Union if need be.

The festivals were also important in another way. They represented yet another vision of a free republic that was strong in most commercial cities and towns. The man at the center was Alexander Hamilton (1755–1804), who developed an idea of a free republic as a great commonwealth, a hive of industry, commerce, and individual enterprise, sustained by a strong nation-state and supported by "energy in government" in alliance with moneyed men for the common good. This idea was shared by merchants and mechanics in the country, who wanted a republican government to encourage commerce, promote industry, and protect property. It was a dynamic image of economic growth, political stability, and social harmony. Men of property in the seaport cities and shire towns strongly supported it.

The Federal Processions of 1788 were symbols of this vision, which was an idea of a free republic. Many images were used to communicate this idea. One of them in New York was a new version of the wand and pileus, in which the liberty cap was transformed into a beehive, a common emblem on the mastheads of Federalist newspapers. For these men, the free republic was a hive of industry, stratified and specialized like a community of bees themselves.

Alexander Hamilton (1755–1804), portrait by Charles Willson Peale, ca. 1791. Independence National Historic Park.

This republican vision of liberty and freedom cannot be understood in the categories of the twenty-first century. It accepted inequalities of wealth but condemned aristocracy, supported the rights of free labor, and was deeply hostile to slavery. It fiercely defended private property, commerce, and industry but favored active public regulation of the economy in a system of mixed enterprise, public and private together. Here was a vision of a republic as a commonwealth of free men who combined individual rights with a strong sense of community. The imagery of the great urban festivals symbolized this Hamiltonian idea in the early republic.

Heralds of Liberty: Thomas Jefferson's Republic as System of Free Expression

In 1700, there were no newspapers in the American colonies. The first appeared at Boston in 1704, and their numbers began to grow at an exponential rate: 5 in 1725, 13 in 1750, 23 in 1764, 201 in 1800. Most were very small operations. A young printer and a few ink-stained apprentices worked at a hand press in a dingy office to produce a four-page weekly that reached a few hundred subscribers.[153]

These little newspapers had a large presence in the new republic. Liberty and freedom of the press was protected by the Federal Constitution

The Goddess of Liberty holding a portrait of Thomas Jefferson, unknown artist, Salem, Massachusetts, January 15, 1807. Yale University Art Gallery, Mabel Brady Garvan Collection.

and guarded by the laws of every state. Every leader in the new republic supported it. Thomas Jefferson was its most eloquent champion. After 1790 he developed an idea of a free republic as representative democracy with minimal government and as much liberty as possible for thought, speech, and the printing press. He and his Democratic supporters were not always consistent in their libertarian acts. But when they were goaded into attempts to restrain their own critics, Alexander Hamilton and the Federalists took up the idea of a free press and became its strong defenders. Hamilton did so from 1775, when he defended the right of Tories to publish opinions that which he despised, to his defense of a scurrilous newspaper called the Hudson *Wasp* from a Jeffersonian prosecution for seditious libel in 1804. Many prominent politicians in the new nation felt the sting of scandal sheets such as the *Wasp*, and many tried to control the worst excesses of the press. But in cooler moments most agreed with Jefferson that "error of opinion may be tolerated where reason is left free to combat it."[154]

In the generation after independence, a free press became both an instrument and a symbol of American republicanism. Many American newspapers published an iconography of that idea in their own mastheads. An example was a small country newspaper, published every Monday in the western hamlet of Washington, Pennsylvania, during the late 1790s. It called itself *The Herald of Liberty*. Its masthead was a crude image of a woman in a classical gown. She combined two motifs: the old symbol of fame and honor, a winged angel with a trumpet in her right hand; and the goddess of liberty in ancient dress with a wand and pileus in her left hand. This was a Jeffersonian newspaper, and from the mouth of the trumpet came an egalitarian motto: "Man Is Man, Who Is More." The herald of liberty was floating in heavenly clouds, which in early American were an emblem of divinity.[155]

The Herald of Liberty, *March 18, 1799, newspaper masthead. American Antiquarian Society.*

Similar themes appeared in many newspaper mastheads from one end of the republic to another: the Augusta *Herald of Liberty* and Saco *Freeman's Friend*, the Exeter *People's Advocate* and Keene *New Hampshire Sentinel*, the Bennington *Ploughboy* and Burlington *Northern Sentinel*, the New York *Spirit of '76* and many more. Other papers were more aggressive in partisan tone: the Federalist Hudson *Wasp* and its Republican rival the Hudson *Bee*, the Boston *Scourge*, which was no man's friend, the Baltimore *Porcupine* and the Cooperstown *Switch*, which summarized its vision of a free press in a stanza:

> *To seek, to find the kennel'd pack,*
> *To lacerate the Rascals back.*
> *Detect their crimes, expose their pranks,*
> *And put to flight their ragged ranks.*

Other papers cultivated a more lofty tone: the Knoxville *Impartial Observer* was true to its title. A few kept apart from politics. The Edenton *Post Angel, or Universal Entertainment* declared on November 12, 1800, that "too many politicians is no blessing to a country."[156]

Some politicians felt the same way about publishers. But for better and for worse, a free press was firmly established in the new American republic. It was so important to the life of the nation that it became virtually a fourth branch of republican government. At the same time, it became an enduring vision of a free and open system.

REPUBLICAN PARTIES

Contested Visions of Liberty and Freedom

> The public is the judge, the two parties are the combatants, and that party which possesses power must employ it properly, must conduct the government wisely, in order to ensure public approbation. . . . While the two parties draw different ways, a middle course is produced that is generally conformable to public good.
>
> —ROBERT GOODLOE HARPER, FEDERALIST LEADER, CONGRESS, JANUARY 19, 1798

I N 1789 a revolution began in France, and a new republic was inaugurated in the United States. Most Americans welcomed both events, but as the French Revolution became more violent and less stable, and the American republic faced many hard choices, Americans divided into political parties. The Federalists turned against the French Revolution after the Terror began. They favored "energy in government" at home, and looked to the leadership of George Washington, John Adams, and Alexander Hamilton. The Democratic Republicans sympathized with the Revolution in France, favored less active government, and followed Thomas Jefferson and James Madison.

Both parties claimed to be the true defenders of liberty and freedom. A Federalist mug showed a likeness of George Washington, supported by allegorical figures of justice and liberty who spoke the words, "My Favorite Son." The mug added a curse against Washington's critics:

> *Deafness to the ear that will patiently hear*
> *And dumbness to the Tongue that will utter*
> *A calumny against the immortal Washington.*

The followers of Thomas Jefferson insisted that he was liberty's "chosen son." An elegant piece of electioneering pottery had a portrait of their hero on one side and a verse on the other:

Hail Columbia happy land
Hail ye patriotic band
Who late oppos'd oppressive laws
And now stand firm in freedom's cause.[157]

Even as the parties agreed on their devotion to liberty and freedom, they differed on how to preserve these ideals. Federalists believed that liberty required the rule of law and a strong republican government. They feared that American liberty was in danger of dissolving into anarchy, and communicated that idea in simple drawings. An early example was a print called "A Peep Into the AntiFederal Club," drawn by an anonymous New York Federalist in 1793. It showed a meeting of a Democratic Society, many of which were founded in that year. Presiding is Thomas Jefferson himself, who argues for "knocking down a government." A follower with his pistol in his belt says, "Damn governments I shall never be worth a dollar as long as there is any government at all." On a wall appears the "Creed of the Democratic club," which held that "the people are all and we are the people, government's but another name for aristocracy" and "liberty is the power of doing anything we like."[158]

Jeffersonian Republicans feared that the danger was not anarchy but tyranny. One of their drawings attacked William Cobbett, an English writer who lived in Philadelphia and contributed his angry prose to the

"A Peep into the AntiFederal Club," New York, 1793, a Federalist critique of the "Creed of Democratic Clubs" as destroying liberty by making it "the power of doing anything we like." Historical Society of Pennsylvania.

Federalist cause under the pen name of Peter Porcupine. He appears as a maniacal porcupine with quills erect, frantically scribbling libels against decent citizens. Supporting Cobbett is the Devil, who says "More scandal. Let us destroy this idol liberty." The British lion with a crown of monarchy on his head says, "Go on dear Peter, my friend, I will reward ye." In the background the goddess of liberty weeps over a monument to the Declaration of Independence and Dr. Franklin, while the American eagle hangs its melancholy head.[159]

The Defeat of the Federalists: Infant Liberty and Mother Mob

After the Democratic Republicans won the election of 1800, Federalists went two ways. A few angry men turned against democracy and even liberty and freedom. An example was John Richard Desborus Huggins, a Manhattan barber who called himself "empereur du Frisseurs and Roi du Barbieres." His obsession was politics, and he wrote actively for the conservative press in New York. In 1808, he pulled together his writing into a little book called *Hugginiana; or, Huggins' Fantasy* and hired some of the best engravers in New York to illustrate his anti-Jeffersonian polemics.

"See Porcupine in Colours just Portray'd," a Jeffersonian critique of Federalist William Cobbett as the destroyer of liberty by his libels on Republicans and his defense of monarchy. Historical Society of Pennsylvania.

"Infant Liberty nursed by Mother Mob," a Federalist attack on liberty and democracy after the election of 1800, a rare theme in American politics, commonly fatal to those who use it. Engraving by William Leney after a drawing by Elkaneh Tisdale, for John Huggins, Hugginiana; of Huggins' Fantasy *(New York, 1808). Library of Congress.*

One of the most striking scenes was called "Infant Liberty Nursed by Mother Mob." It shows the mother of all Jeffersonians nursing a dirty baby at her swollen breasts, which are marked "whisky" and "rum." At her side, a democratic brood amuse themselves by burning the laws of the republic, while a winged imp fans the flames with falsehoods, and a mob in the background dances around the "pinnacle of liberty." Jeffersonian leaders in New York were outraged by these images. Tammany sachem Brom Martling was so infuriated that he attacked Huggins and gave him a public flogging with a rope's end.[160]

For a brief period, this conservative fringe of the Federalist Party became one of the few groups in American history who put themselves outside the broad tradition of liberty and freedom. Others in generations to follow, as we shall see, included the proslavery movement and the right wing of the southern secessionist movement, small bands of Communists and Fascists in the early twentieth century, and elements of the academic left in American universities during the late twentieth century.

These arguments against democracy and even liberty were disastrous for the Federalists. A party that was defeated in 1800 found itself nearly destroyed by 1804. But they learned from their losses, and by 1808 younger Federalists were learning to play the game of popular politics. They also came to terms with political democracy, and some discovered that ideas of minimal government could enlarge the power and privileges of elites. The result was a fierce competition for possession of symbols of liberty and freedom.

The young Federalists challenged the Jeffersonian claim to the Declaration of Independence. An example was a Fourth of July Dinner in Raleigh, North Carolina. The Declaration of Independence was read aloud, and Joseph Gales, Democratic Republican editor of the *Raleigh Register,* proposed a toast to Jefferson as "the sage and patriotic author of the Declaration of Independence." He was challenged by William Boylan, Federal Republican printer of the rival *Raleigh Minerva.* Boylan insisted that John Adams had helped draft the Declaration of Independence and deserved part of the credit. The dispute ended in a fistfight between the two editors. The Jeffersonian journalist was severely beaten, and the Federalists identified themselves with the principles of the Declaration of Independence.[161]

"The Providential Detection," a Federalist defense of Republican liberty and freedom before the election of 1800, etching by James Akin, ca. 1797–1800. American Antiquarian Society.

After the War of 1812, this process was carried a step further. The Federalist Party suffered another round of disastrous defeats in the election of 1816, and this time the blow was fatal. Washington's lieutenant James Monroe was elected president with more than 80 percent of the electoral vote. After a triumphal tour of the United States, Monroe won a second term with all but one vote in the electoral college.

This period of American politics was called "The Era of Good Feelings." The old parties disappeared, and most Americans came together around ideas of American liberty and freedom that were at once democratic and republican. A symbolic event occurred in 1817, when leaders of both parties in Congress came together to commission a huge copy of Jonathan Trumbull's painting of the Declaration of Independence for display in the new U.S. Capitol, which had risen from the ashes of the War of 1812. The great canvas was finished in 1818. It became his best-loved work. On its way to the Capitol it attracted large crowds in Boston, New York, Philadelphia, and Baltimore.

Congress also ordered Secretary of State John Quincy Adams to make a facsimile of the Declaration of Independence. The copy was made by a "wet press" process that did serious injury to the original document, but facsimiles were successfully produced and distributed in large numbers through the country. Private printers issued their own engraved copies. The text of the Declaration of Independence became a nonpartisan icon of freedom and liberty for Americans of all parties. It symbolized a new spirit of national unity that flourished briefly after the War of 1812.[162]

Jacksonians and Whigs

The Era of Good Feelings came to an end in the elections of 1824 and 1828. The old Jeffersonian Republicans divided into National Republicans, who followed John Quincy Adams and Henry Clay; and Democratic Republicans, who went with Andrew Jackson. Once again both parties claimed to be the best friends of liberty and freedom. One of the few electioneering emblems for John Quincy Adams used the slogan "Peece [*sic*] & Liberty, Home Industry, J. Q. Adams." Andrew Jackson's followers also deeply believed that their hero was the true defender of liberty and freedom. They claimed the mantle of the Revolution, and wrapped themselves in its rhetoric. For their symbols, they used both the Liberty Tree and the Liberty Pole, and gave both emblems a distinctive Jacksonian twist.

The presidency of Andrew Jackson deeply divided American opinion. Many were troubled by his duels and fights, his execution of militiamen under his command, his abuse of martial law in Louisiana, his arbitrary imprisonment of Judge Dominick Hall, who dared to issue a writ of habeas corpus against him, and his summary execution of two British subjects without trial after his unlawful invasion of Spanish Florida in pursuit of runaway slaves. As president, Jackson vetoed more congressional bills than all of his predecessors combined and defied the Supreme Court.

David Claypoole Johnston, Andrew Jackson as Richard III, engraving. American Antiquarian Society.

Many Americans began to think of Jackson as a slaveholder, a bully, and a tyrant who was dangerous to the liberties of the republic. A lithograph by David Claypoole

Johnston represented Jackson as Richard III. His features were composed of the bodies of his victims, and the fringe on his epaulets were the corpses of the men he had killed. On his chest were prison bars from which two prisoners waved a rejected petition for habeas corpus. Below was a Shakespearean line: "Methought the souls of all that I had murder'd came to my tent." This image was not original with Johnston. The same motif had been used in an English caricature of Napoleon, but it had a powerful impact on American politics.[163]

Another cartoon, which must have infuriated Old Hickory, represented him as Lady Macbeth in a red white and blue dress with a bowie knife in his girdle, engaged in the destruction of liberty and free trade.[164] The most common anti-Jackson motif appeared on a Whig handbill in 1834, which showed him in royal robes, with a scepter in one hand and a veto message in the other. It is titled "King Andrew the First, Born to Command." A bill of indictment follows of "a king who has placed himself above the law."[165]

In 1834, Jackson's opponents founded a new political party, dedicated to the preservation of American liberty and freedom. They had little in common beyond their hostility to Old Hickory, but that impulse gave them a message and a party name. They claimed a kinship with the American Whigs of 1776 in their opposition to a military despot and a monarchical tyrant. For their party emblem, the Whigs adopted the liberty cap. A student of Whig buttons, badges, tokens, and ribbons observed that "nearly all of the clothing buttons featured the Whig symbol, a liberty cap upon a pole." By their name and insignia they claimed the symbols of the revolution in their struggle against "King Andrew I." Some of their badges read, "True Whigs of 76 and 34."[166]

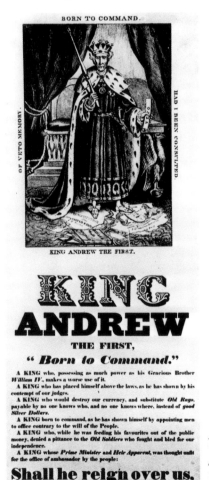

Edward Clay Williams, "King Andrew the First," engraved cartoon, 1834. Tennessee State Library.

The leader of the Whig Party was Henry Clay, who was made into a political symbol of liberty and freedom. In 1846, the Whig Ladies of Tennessee presented him with a large silver urn. It was surmounted by the figure of Liberty with a staff and cap. Below was the figure of Diogenes with his lamp, searching for a free and honest man, and finding Henry Clay.[167]

On the other side, Jacksonians saw the Whigs as tyrannical enemies of American liberty, and friends of monopoly. They also claimed the old Revolutionary symbols, but in a different way. In the War of 1812, the western militia who fought with Andrew Jackson had called him "Old Hickory" for his toughness and tenacity.[168] That name followed him into presidential politics and inspired new Jacksonian hickory trees and hickory poles. A Jacksonian election ribbon read,

> *Freemen, Cheer the Hickory Tree*
> *In Storms Its Boughs have Sheltered Thee.*[169]

During the election of 1834, French traveler Michel Chevalier was halted in his tracks by an enormous hickory pole in Philadelphia. "I stopped involuntarily at the sight of the gigantic liberty poles, which made their solemn entry on eight wheels for the purpose of being planted by the democracy on the eve of the election. I remember one of these poles, its top still crowned with green foliage, which came on to the sound of fifes and drums, and was preceded by ranks of Democrats, bearing no other

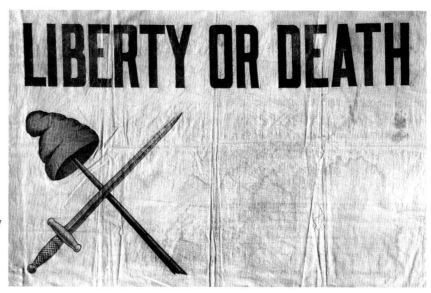

Liberty or Death, Whig campaign banner, in the second American party system, 1834–52, when both Whigs and Democrats claimed to be heirs of the American Revolution and true defenders of liberty and freedom. National Museum of American History, Smithsonian Institution.

badge than a twig of the sacred tree in their hats. It was drawn by eight horses, decorated with ribands and mottos. Astride the tree itself were a dozen Jackson men of the first water, waving their flags with an air of anticipated triumph and shouting, *Hurrah for Jackson!*"[170]

Hickory poles continued to be used by the Democratic Party long after Andrew Jackson himself had left politics. They appeared in the presidential election of 1844, when Democratic candidate James K. Polk won by identifying himself as "Young Hickory." In 1852, it was the same again for New Hampshire Democrat Franklin Pierce, who was called "Young Hickory of the Granite Hills." The Democratic Party was still erecting hickory poles in the election of 1860.[171]

The zeal of the party faithful rivaled religious movements and created an iconography of political devotionalism. Michel Chevalier witnessed an election-night rally of Jacksonians in New York City. "The procession was nearly a mile long," he wrote. "The Democrats marched in good order to the glare of torches; the banners were more numerous than I had ever seen in any religious festival."

In every electioneering campaign during the 1830s and 1840s, images of liberty and freedom were very prominent. The Whig motto in 1840 was "Harrison, Tyler and Constitutional Liberty." The Democrats responded with "Van Buren and Johnson, Enlightened Heroes of Patri-

otic Liberty." In both Whig and Jacksonian hands, these ideas of liberty were mostly hostile to active government and strong leadership. Andrew Jackson himself supported them, and his strong attacks on government in the Monroe and Adams administrations carried him to the White House. Once there, he became the object of the same arguments that he had used against his predecessors.

Each party claimed to be the true defender of American liberty and accused its opponents of tyranny. As party battles continued, consensual ideas about the nature of liberty and freedom began to emerge.[172]

The Constitution and Declaration of Independence were also increas-

A Whig Party icon showing Diogenes with his lamp searching for a free and honest man and finding Henry Clay; silver urn by William Gale and Nathaniel Hayden, "Presented to Henry Clay by the Whig Ladies of Tennessee," 1846. Tennessee State Museum.

ingly celebrated by all parties as sacred texts that together became the great ark of American liberty. A striking example was a printed cotton textile that reproduced the entire signed text of the Declaration of Independence, with facsimiles of all the signatures. The images of Washington, Adams, and Jefferson were surrounded by many symbols: trumpets of fame, cornucopiae of abundance, flags and eagles, seals of the thirteen states, and emblematic scenes of the Boston Tea Party and the surrender of Burgoyne at Saratoga.

This idea of liberty meant the rule of law. Every party took up that theme, especially when it was in opposition. Parties in power were kept on a short leash, with opponents and the press scrutinizing every act for the slightest tendency toward tyranny.

The opposition press, no matter whether Jacksonian or Whig, also reinforced an association between liberty and minimal government. Liberty came to be increasingly identified with the defense of private rights and local interests. Almost any assertion of public power or presidential leadership brought cries of corruption and tyranny. This was the case with George Washington and Jay's Treaty, John Adams and the Quasi-War with France, Jefferson on Louisiana and the Embargo, Madison and the War of 1812, Monroe and public spending, John Quincy Adams and his alliance with Henry Clay, and almost any act by Andrew Jackson.

The second American party system was very short-lived. It began when the Whigs first competed as a political party in 1834 and ended with the collapse of their party in 1852. Altogether it spanned a period of only eighteen years. But while it lasted, competition between the two parties had an extraordinary intensity. Fierce party rivalry in the age of Jackson did much to establish a consensual vision of liberty and freedom. This American tradition was a national idea but protective of local autonomy and regional cultures. It was democratic but attentive to the interests of propertied minorities. It was consciously modern but rooted in a republican past. It became the creed of the "venturous conservatives" who were Tocqueville's archetypical Americans.

ORDINARY PEOPLE

Liberty and Freedom as Democratic Ideas

AMERICAN LIBERTY, OR A SPECIMAN
OF DEMOCRACY

—SIGN ON THE BACK OF THOMAS DITSON,
TARRED AND FEATHERED BY BRITISH
TROOPS, BOSTON, MARCH 9, 1775.
HE SURVIVED TO FIGHT AT CONCORD.

WHILE PARTIES BATTLED in the early republic, Americans were inventing other visions of liberty and freedom. They began to represent these ideas as images of ordinary people. These American folk figures were not heroes in the classical sense. None of them was remarkable for great achievements, brave deeds, or immortal words, which was precisely the point. They were meant to be broadly representative of the people, a word that changed its meaning in the early republic. When John Adams spoke of the people, he meant the "lower order" of humanity, a common usage in the eighteenth century. By the generation of John Quincy Adams, most Americans understood "the people" as all the people. A new set of icons represented liberty and freedom as something that belonged to everyone.

This theme appeared in popular figures that were invented in a span of about half a century, from 1758 to 1814. Most of them first appeared in New England or were inspired by New Englanders. At the start they were figures of satire. Most of all, they mocked New England's combination of high ideals and low manners. In the process, they succeeded in capturing qualities that many Americans recognized in themselves, and the entire nation took them to heart with affection and self-deprecating humor. Hostile critics of American culture used them in other ways as emblems of American vices but never changed their fundamental character.

These folk images of ordinary people as the personification of a free society expressed a vision of liberty and freedom as a democratic ideas. This was something new in the world. In Western political thought democracy had long been thought to be the enemy of a free society. But in the early American republic, a new set of popular symbols communicated the opposite idea that ordinary people were the best protectors of everybody's rights.

Here was another linkage that connected liberty and freedom to equality in a new sense. To an older idea of equal rights, it added a new vision that J. R. Pole has called "equality of esteem." Free-born Americans expected others to treat them with respect. This became a matter of right, and a question of freedom.[173]

YANKEE DOODLE

A "Simple American" Becomes a "Favorite Air of Liberty"

O Glory is a Pretty Toy—
'T is that for which I bawl so;
And Freedom, Friends, a clever Thing,
And Liberty is—also.
Yankee Doodle, &c

—Loyalist satire of "Yankee Doodle," 1770

T HE FIRST and most enduring of these folk characters was Yankee Doodle. He was not a corporeal being. Yankee Doodle was a song, a puff of wind, a creature of the air. Nobody recognized his face, but every American knew him at a distance, with a feather in his cap, riding on a pony.

Yankee Doodle made his appearance in the American colonies during the middle decades of the eighteenth century. There are as many legends of his origin as there are verses of his song. The oldest story is still credible, though some scholars do not agree. More likely than not, this most American of songs was invented by Richard Shuckburgh, an amiable English surgeon in the French and Indian War.[174]

Doctor Shuckburgh (as Americans called him) was a delightful eighteenth-century character who might have stepped from the pages of Fielding or Smollett. Born in Britain early in the eighteenth century, he received a gentleman's education but no large share of worldly goods. Sometime before 1735, he emigrated to the colonies in search of fortune and settled in the Delaware Valley. Success eluded him, and he moved to New York, where he bought a commission as a military surgeon in the British army and served in two colonial wars. He also became a good friend of Sir William Johnson, one of the most powerful imperial British officials in America, and in 1767 he was appointed Johnson's secretary for Indian affairs.

Doctor Shuckburgh was a convivial man who enjoyed music, laughter, and conversation. An acquaintance described him as "a gentleman ... of infinite jest and humour."[175] He organized clubs on dreary frontier posts and was welcomed for his wit in country houses throughout the Hudson Valley. Near the end of his life he wrote in his good-natured way, "I am apt to say somewhat like Scarron when he was dying, that I may have made more People laugh in my lifetime in this World of America than will cry at my departure out of it."[176]

"Yankee Doodle American Satan," an early image of Yankee Doodle in the era of the Revolution. This ironic engraving is a self-portrait of Joseph Wright, an American in London. It represents Yankee Doodle as an ordinary American youth, very far from the Devil Incarnate of Tory imagery. Library of Congress.

Something of Richard Shuckburgh's laughter survives in the song called "Yankee Doodle," which has long outlived its author. According to the testimony of at least three New Yorkers, it was written by Doctor Shuckburgh in a military camp near Albany during the French and Indian War. A likely date may have been 1759 or 1760, when large British and colonial forces under the command of Lord Jeffrey Amherst gathered near Albany and prepared to attack Canada.[177]

The Regulars laughed at the antics of the Yankee militia. Their quaint clothing, curious speech, and clumsy manners became the butt of British humor. Some of the British and colonial troops camped on the land of the Van Rensselaer estates along the Hudson River. Members of the family later remembered that Doctor Shuckburgh was there. One recalled that he sat on the stone curb of an old well at Green Bush Manor and dashed off a satirical song about the Yankee soldiers who were camped nearby. His original verses may have included the opening quatrain that is best remembered today:

> *Yankee Doodle came to town*
> *Upon a little pony.*
> *He stuck a feather in his hat*
> *And called it Macaroni.*

Macaroni was eighteenth-century English slang for a foolish young fop or dandy.[178] Other verses may also have been of Doctor Shuckburgh's invention, and several hint at autobiography:

There is a man in our town,
I pity his condition,
He sold his oxen and his sheep,
To buy him a commission.

The verses were set to a song called "Fisher's Jig":

Lucy Locket lost her pocket
Kitty Fisher found it.
Not a bit of money in it,
Only binding round it.

Lucy Locket was a lost soul in John Gay's *Beggar's Opera* (1728) and Kitty Fisher was Catherine Maria Fischer (d. 1767), a beautiful German courtesan who rose to such eminence in London that her lovers commissioned three portraits by Joshua Reynolds. All of the paintings are unfinished, perhaps because Kitty Fisher's amours never lasted long enough see them through. Her entire career was very short and reached its peak in 1759, as did "Fisher's Jig," just when Shuckburgh was composing "Yankee Doodle."[179]

Within a few years Kitty Fisher was forgotten, but the English tune that she inspired began to be called "the Yankee Doodle song" in America, and it became very popular. In 1767 it turned up in an opera by Thomas Forrest and was published in New York—its first appearance in print.[180] When the British Regulars landed at Boston in 1768, it was reported that "the Yankee Doodle song was the capital piece in their band of music." It was often played by British troops as an expression of contempt for the colonials.

On April 19, 1775, when Lord Percy's brigade marched to the support of the Concord expedition, the regimental fifes and drums played "nothing...but Yankee Doodle" as they left Boston. That evening the brigade returned to Charlestown with many casualties. An American asked a British officer "how he liked the tune now." The officer replied, "Damn them, they made us dance it until we were tired." The American remarked, "Since then, Yankee Doodle sounds less sweet in their ears."[181]

Like "Dixie" in the Civil War and "Lili Marlene" in World War II, "Yankee Doodle" was sung by both sides in the American War of Independence. New material was added in such profusion that the playwright Royall Tyler made one of his comic characters confess that he knew only 199 verses, but his "sister Tabitha at home can sing it all."[182] With many

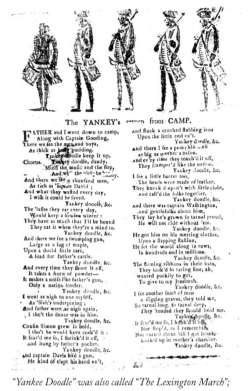

additions, "Yankee Doodle" became a ballad history of the American Revolution. Some of its verses were about the fight at Lexington and Concord:

> *And Captain Davis had a gun,*
> *He kind of clapt his hand on't.*
> *And struck a crooked stabbing iron*
> *Upon the little end on't.*

This was Captain Isaac Davis, the Yankee gunsmith whose company of Acton Minutemen were put in the front of the American formation at Concord's North Bridge, because they were one of the few units with bayonets. Davis was shot dead at the head of his men and became an American hero. Other stanzas of "Yankee Doodle" celebrated the siege of Boston but were not so sure about the man who commanded the American army:

> *And there was Captain Washington,*
> *And gentlefolks around him*
> *They say he's grown so tarnal proud*
> *He will not ride without 'em.*

> *He got him on his meeting cloathes,*
> *Upon a slapping stallion,*
> *He set the world along in rows,*
> *In hundreds and in millions.*

Leaders as exalted as George Washington received little respect in the song, and no deference whatever. The heroes were Yankee Doodle himself and ordinary people, more than "Captain Washington and gentlefolks around him." The northern expedition against Canada inspired verses that took a baleful view of Benedict Arnold, even before his treason:

> *Arnold is as brave a man*
> *As ever dealt in horses,*
> *And now commands a numerous clan*
> *Of New-England Jack-asses.*

American troops laughed at this satire and became very fond of "Yankee Doodle." In defeat it raised American spirits. In victory, it became a march of triumph:

> Sing Yankee Doodle, that fine tune
> Americans delight in.
> It suits for feasts, it suits for fun;
> And just as well for fightin'.[183]

After the battle of Saratoga in 1777, the American fifes and drums played "Yankee Doodle" while the defeated British army laid down its arms. A British officer at the scene wrote, "Yankee Doodle is their paean, a favorite of favorites—played in their army, and esteemed as warlike as the Grenadier's March. It is the lover's spell, the nurse's lullaby." He added, "We held the Yankees in great contempt. So it was not a little mortifying to hear them play this tune, of all others, when our army marched down to surrender."[184]

American poet Joel Barlow added, "In the course of the war it became a favorite air of liberty, like the present *Ça Ira* of France." Barlow was in Paris when the French Revolution began. He wrote, "It is remarkable that after the taking of the Bastille, and before the introduction of *Ça Ira*, the Paris guards played Yanky-doodle."[185]

When new immigrants began to enter the United States in large numbers, they claimed the song as their own. Many insisted that their ancestors had composed it. Germans asserted that "Yankee Doodle" was a Hessian folk dance. Irish scholar William Grattan Flood announced that it "can rightly be claimed as a product of Ireland." A professor in Spain identified it as a "danza esparta" from the "the music of the free Pyrenees." Hungarians were sure that it had been invented in their country. An Iranian claimed that it was an old Persian tune called "Jengee Duniah." A Netherlander proclaimed that it was an old Dutch harvest song that went:

> Yanker didel, doodel down,
> Didel, dudel lauter,
> Yanke viver, voover vown,
> Botermith und Yauther.[186]

In the Civil War, "Yankee Doodle" was played so often that General Ulysses Grant, who was severely tone-deaf, once remarked that he only knew two tunes: one was "Yankee Doodle," and the other wasn't.

All of this might have amused that amiable English gentleman Doctor Richard Shuckburgh, who loved a laugh and was fond of happy endings. He died at Schenectady, New York, in 1773, two years before the American Revolution, and did not live to see the many uses to which his song was put. It changed with time and circumstance but always kept its original spirit. Yankee Doodle remained an ordinary American, awkward in movement and clumsy in speech, but high-spirited, good-natured, and full of life and laughter. Even with a musket in hand he was not a great warrior, but he was fiercely independent and ready to fight for his freedom. The song satirized his manners but celebrated an idea of freedom and liberty as something that belonged to all ordinary Americans.

Yankee Doodle as a national symbol, chromolithograph by Thomas Nast, ca. 1871–74. American Antiquarian Society.

The lyrics of "Yankee Doodle" are unique in the history of nations. Most national songs are as portentous as "Deutschland über Alles" or "Rule Britannia." Here was something new, a patriotic song about an ordinary person with a self-deprecating sense of humor. Yankee Doodle has lived in the American imagination for many generations. Children still sing of him with laughter and delight.

BROTHER JONATHAN
"A True Blue Son of Liberty"

> Jonathan: Du you call this a land of liberty, where I cannot larrup my own nigger without being ordered out of the house? Du explain to me the principles of the British constitution!
>
> —R. B. Peake, Jonathan in England; or, Americans Abroad, British comedy, 1824

THEN THERE WAS Brother Jonathan, a figure now vanished from the national Pantheon but more eminent in the early republic than Yankee Doodle.[187] Some believe that he first appeared in the American Revolution and was modeled after Jonathan Trumbull (1710–85), a wise and well-respected governor of Connecticut. According to legend, George Washington regularly urged his subordinates to seek Governor Trumbull's advice and told them, "Let us consult Brother Jonathan."[188] It makes a good story, especially in the state of Connecticut, but it cannot be true. The phrase "Brother Jonathan" was in common use before Washington and Trumbull began to work together. It was circulating in England as early as the mid-seventeenth century, as a city dweller's term of affectionate contempt for a country bumpkin. An example survives from London in 1643.[189]

In the eighteenth century, British Regulars began to speak of New England militia as Brother Jonathan in a way that implied both kinship and condescension. The fighting around Boston in 1775 and 1776 produced the first firmly documented use of this image in America. When the British army evacuated Boston on March 17, 1776, they left a set of scarecrow-sentinels with signs that read, "Welcome Brother Jonathan."[190]

The siege of Boston also inspired what may have been the first published image of Brother Jonathan. During the winter of 1775–76, a crude British cartoon was published with the title "The Yankee Doodles

Intrenchments near Boston." It showed a ragged band of Yankee soldiers, wearing tattered coats and stocking caps marked "Death or Liberty," and carrying a Liberty Tree Flag. One Yankee says to the others, "It's plaguey cold Jonathan; I don't think they'll attack us. . . ." A faint-hearted Jonathan replies, "I fear they'll shoot again." Another says, "I don't feel bold today." But a third is made of stronger stuff and cries, "Blast their eyes, we'll have no excise." With them is a sinister Puritan minister in collar and bands who says, "Tis old Oliver's cause, no monarchy or laws."[191]

As the fighting spread beyond New England, British troops began to speak collectively of Americans as Jonathan, much as American troops in Vietnam called the Viet Cong Charlie and Allied infantry in World War II referred to Germans as Jerry.[192] In 1780, a Loyalist newspaper in New York reported a skirmish in which "Col. Delancey with a party of his loyal refugees . . . took and destroyed a piece of cannon, which the Jonathans in vain endeavored to defend."[193]

These early usages were mostly pejorative but tinged with a tone of affectionate disapproval. As the war continued, the image of Brother Jonathan became more positive, even in British hands. A British cartoon in 1778 showed John Bull in a fashionable tricorne and Brother Jonathan

Brother Jonathan as a New England Yankee in the American Revolution: "I swear its Plaguey Cold Jonathan," engraving ca. 1776. British Museum.

in a broad brimmed-country hat. They were sitting together, drinking and smoking amicably. The title, a line from *The Beggar's Opera*, reads, "Brother, brother, we are both in the wrong."[194] The pairing of Brother Jonathan and John Bull became increasingly common, and by 1778 they were used as symbols of two kindred but separate nations.[195]

After the war Jonathan became a stock character on the American and British stage. At the same time, he became a symbol of American liberty and freedom. One called himself "a true blue son of liberty."[196] In the United States, the most widely known of these stage Jonathans appeared in Royall Tyler's comedy *The Contrast*, which centered on two American figures, a "brave and sentimental" hero of the Revolution called Colonel Manly and his honest, plain-speaking Yankee servant called Jonathan. In the third act, Jonathan stole the show with his straight talk and his steadfast resistance to the "devil's devices."

On the other side of the Atlantic, Joseph Atkinson's comic opera *A Match for a Widow; or, the Frolics of Fancy* had a similar American manservant named Jonathan, whose rustic honesty became a vehicle for satire of prevailing fashions. Jonathan was a Yankee and commonly a sympathetic character—more so than the corrupt figures who were set against him.[197]

The literati were quick to borrow Jonathan from the dramatists. In 1812, James K. Paulding wrote a book called *The Diverting History of John Bull and Brother Jonathan*. Brother Jonathan was introduced as the younger son of John Bull, "very large for his age . . . a tall, stout, double-jointed, broad-footed cub of a fellow, awkward in his gait, and simple in his appearance, but showing a lively shrewd look, and having the promise of great strength when he should get his full growth." Paulding's Jonathan was "a peaceable sort of careless fellow, that would quarrel with nobody if you would only let him alone." The author made him into a clumsy, awkward country bumpkin, much like Yankee Doodle: "He used to dress in homespun trousers with a huge bagging seat, which seemed to have nothing in it. This made people to say he had no bottom, but whoever said so lied, as they found to their cost whenever they put Jonathan in a passion." A later edition of this book added cartoons of plucky young Jonathan, standing up for his rights.[198]

Brother Jonathan was originally a New England Yankee, but after 1815 he became the personification of Americans in general. Novelists developed that theme at great length and associated Jonathan with every region of the United States. John Neal published a three-volume novel called *Brother Jonathan; or, the New Englanders* (1825). Frances Trollope produced another three-volume work, called *The Life and Adventures of*

Jonathan Jefferson Whitlaw, or, Scenes on the Mississippi (London, 1836), which made a westerner of him. And an anonymous author produced yet another three volume work called *Jonathan Sharp; or, The Adventures of a Kentuckian* (London, 1836), which turned him into a southerner.

Journalists and dramatists did the same. Two popular twelve-penny weeklies in the nineteenth century were called *Yankee Notions; or, Whittlings of Jonathan's Jack-Knife,* and *Brother Jonathan.* The popular actors James Hackett and George Hill often played Jonathans on the nineteenth-century American stage: Jonathan Doolittle in William Dunlap's *A Trip to Niagara* (1831), Jonathan Ploughboy in Samuel Woodworth's *The Forrest Rose* (1832), and Jedidiah Homebred in Joseph Jones's *The Green Mountain Boy* (1833).

In these various works, Jonathan's reputation began to change for the worse. A folk figure who had possessed many virtues in the early republic became a dark and even villainous character. An example was *Jonathan Doubkins; or, Jonathan in England* (1824). The leading character was no longer a simple and upright country character but devious, crude, corrupt, and violent.[199] Many stage Jonathans were closely associated with slavery and racism and were used to attack the hypocrisy of American ideas of liberty and freedom. One work had a scrap of dialogue between Jonathan and his Uncle Ben:

> "Uncle Ben," says I, "I calculate you have a Nigger to sell."
>
> "Yes I have a Nigger I guess. Will you buy a Nigger?"
>
> "Oh yes! if he is a good nigger, I will, I reckon; but this is a land of liberty and freedom, as every man has a right to buy a Nigger, what do you want for your Nigger?"
>
> "Why, as you say, Jonathan," says Uncle Ben, "this is a land of freedom and independence, and as every man has a right to sell his Nigger, I want sixty dollars and twenty-five cents."[200]

British writers never wearied of mocking Jonathan and America in these same terms. He was also associated with extreme hostility to Catholics and Jews.

Others identified Jonathan with dishonesty and corruption. He appeared on the stage as an unscrupulous businessman, or a corrupt politician, or an empty braggart who could not be counted to keep his word. An anonymous British novel called *The Playfair Papers* (1841) was subtitled *Brother Jonathan, the Smartest Nation in All Creation.* It made much of the dishonesty of Yankee trading and the brutality of southern slavedriving.

Brother Jonathan as a southern slave driver in the American Republic with his foot on the fallen bust of Washington. Above are scenes of cruelty in the Mexican War, the desecration of a church, slave-trading, lynching, theft, and murder. "The Land of Liberty," Punch, 1847. Library of Virginia.

Another common theme was violence. Jonathan in the nineteenth century was armed to the teeth, with weapons such as daggers and derringers, which gentlemen regarded as less than honorable. In the British press he was associated with foreign adventures that were dangerous to the peace of the world. In 1856, *Punch* published a cartoon called "Spoilt Child," which represented Jonathan as an ill-behaved younger brother. He was shown as a spoiled brat, breaking his own toys and beating a small drum with a pistol butt, while John Bull looked on in a kindly but disapproving way and said, "I don't like to correct him just now, because

"Petit Jonathan," the view from Quebec: "Imprudence du petit Jonathan," ca. 1850. American Heritage Publishing Company, with thanks to Fred Allen.

he's about his teeth, and sickening with the measles—but he certainly deserves a clout on the head."[201]

The French did not recognize kinship with brother Jonathan, but they kept the pejorative image and changed his name to "le petit Jonathan l'Américain." A French Canadian cartoon (ca. 1837) showed Jonathan as a lean, sharp-featured Yankee with an imbecile smile on his ugly face and a big old-fashioned six-barreled pistol on his hip. "Petit Jonathan l'Américain" held the American flag in one hand, twisted the British lion's tail with the other, and snarled in the general direction of Europe.[202]

By the mid-nineteenth century, *Jonathan* had become a generic noun for an American. A visitor to the United States in 1841 described a country lad with a strong American accent as "a Jonathan of the first water." In Europe he also became an *ism*. A British political writer referred to "Brother Jonathanism" to describe any sort of exaggerated expression of American national prejudice, without any awareness of his own.[203]

In the years before the Civil War, Jonathan took on a new meaning in America. Southern writers made him an image of all they despised in the North. In 1860, when South Carolina left the Union, a Confederate published a poem called "Caroline's Farewell to Brother Jonathan."

> *Farewell, we must part, we have turned from the land*
> *Of our cold-hearted brother with tyrannous hand. . . .*

O Jonathan, Jonathan, vassal of pelf,
Self-righteous, self-glorious, yes, every inch self. [204]

By the beginning of the Civil War, Brother Jonathan's reputation was in tatters at home and abroad. He had become an image of moral decline of the American republic, and the symbol of an idea of liberty that had decayed into license.

As a folk character, this new Jonathan became a casualty of the Civil War. After the Union victory he faded rapidly and soon disappeared from the American scene. For a time he lingered in British plays and humor magazines. Writers on both sides of the water lost interest in him as the sense of kinship between Britain and America faded. America was moving to the city, and a country bumpkin was increasingly remote from the realities of American life. By the end of the nineteenth century, Jonathan had no place in American hearts, and he was soon forgotten.

But in his own time he was an important symbol of the linkage between liberty and individual striving. In the early republic he represented the spirit of individual autonomy. Later he came to stand for individual self-seeking. In both ways he represented an image of American liberty that embraced Yankee traders, western pioneers, and southern slaveholders in the early nineteenth century.

THE ORIGINAL UNCLE SAM

An Affectionate Symbol of Free Government

> In his political creed he was strictly Republican and was warmly attached to the democratic party.... In his religious creed he was tolerant to all.... and he has left a pleasing assurance both to the church and his friends.
>
> —OBITUARY FOR SAMUEL WILLSON,
> THE ORIGINAL UNCLE SAM, IN THE TROY
> NORTHERN BUDGET, AUGUST 1854

MORE DURABLE than Brother Jonathan was Uncle Sam. He also began as a New England Yankee, but in a different way. Unlike Yankee Doodle and Jonathan, the original Uncle Sam was the genuine article: a red-blooded, white-skinned, blue-eyed son of liberty and freedom who actually existed in the early republic. His name was Samuel Willson (his family favored two l's when he was born).[205] Everybody called him Sam. He was a wonderful character, perfectly American but in so unpredictable a way that no novelist could have invented him.

Sam Willson came of old New England stock. He was born in 1766 in a country village called Menotomy, now the suburban town of Arlington, Massachusetts, ten miles west of Boston. His Yankee family were yeoman farmers who owned the covenant in their Congregational church and scratched a precarious living from New England's stony soil. When the American Revolution began in the neighboring town of Lexington, young Sam Willson was eight years old. His kinsmen went to war that day, and the heaviest fighting occurred very near his home. Later his brothers joined a Continental regiment, and Sam himself may have enlisted as a "service boy" in Washington's army. He was an eyewitness to the great events that created the American nation.

After the Revolution, his family left Massachusetts in search of land, and settled in the town of Mason, New Hampshire, where Samuel Willson came of age. He was a likely young man and won the heart of pretty Betsey Mann, daughter of the leading family in town. A life of farming in a New England hill town was not for him. In 1789, Sam and his brother Ebenezer Willson moved west to a village that took the hopeful name of Troy, New York. It lay at the head of tidewater navigation on the Hudson River, where the Mohawk flowed in from the west, and looked to be a good place for business.

Samuel and Ebenezer Willson acquired a brickyard, went into commercial farming on a large scale, set themselves up as merchants, operated sloops on the river, built stockyards, and founded a meatpacking business. It was said that Samuel Willson "prosecuted, successfully, at least four distinct kinds of business, employing about 200 hands constantly." One who knew him wrote, "His tact for managing laborers was very peculiar; he would always say 'come boys' instead of 'go,' and thereby secured a greater amount of labor than ordinary men."[206]

In 1797, Sam Willson returned to New Hampshire, married his beloved Betsey, and brought her west in a sleigh. Other relatives settled around him—so many that Sam Willson was said to be kin to several hundred people in the neighborhood, who began to call him Uncle Sam. He and Aunt Betsey were much loved in the town. An historian writes, "An atmosphere of jocularity seems to have pervaded Samuel Willson's operations wherever he went. Part of this can be traced to Uncle Sam himself, who according to the testimony of his relatives and friends, would go to considerable length to make a good joke."[207]

When the War of 1812 began, Sam Willson supplied provisions to American troops on the northern frontier. The meat was shipped in barrels branded with the initials U.S. According to local legend, a soldier asked an Irishman what "U.S. stands for," and was told. "Why, Uncle Sam Willson. It is he who is feeding the army." New York militia began to speak of their rations as Uncle Sam's. The name caught on and was soon attached to the government itself. As early as September 7, 1813, the *Troy Post* observed, "This cant name for our government has got almost as common as John Bull."[208]

After the war, Americans throughout the country began to call the federal government Uncle Sam, and foreign travelers picked up the expression. In 1823, British travel writer William Faux wrote of the post office as "Uncle Sam's western mail" and Harper's Ferry as "Uncle Sam's grand central depot of arms and ammunition." For British readers he added a slash of sarcasm in the American idiom: "Uncle Sam is a right slick, mighty fine, smart, big man."[209]

That image of Uncle Sam was commonly the view from abroad, but Americans always thought of him in a different way. Uncle Sam was not primarily a figure of power and authority but an emblem of kinship and affection. Americans may be unique that way. Many people think of their nation state as a stern father, as in the Roman *patria* or the German *Vaterland.* Others regard it as matriarchal or at least maternal. The English speak of Britannia as the mother country; Moscovites talk of Mother Russia. The American republic is unique in its idea of the nation-state as a kindly old uncle, to whom Americans feel attached but not dependent.

Through the years, his image changed. Cartoonist Art Young observes that "the figure of Uncle Sam, like the Constitution, has had to submit to amendments."[210] People today would not recognize his earliest likenesses. In one of his first lithographs, called "Uncle Sam in Danger" (1832), he was stout, round-faced, and clean-shaven, much like Samuel Willson. His dress was also different from what it would later become. In 1832, Uncle Sam wore a dressing gown with stars and stripes and a liberty cap. A similar image appeared in another cartoon, dated 1852 but probably earlier, by Whig cartoonist Frank Bellow. It showed an ailing Uncle Sam, suffering from Jacksonian "mint drops and gold pills." His democratic physicians, Old Hickory himself, Thomas Hart Benton, and "Aunt

"Uncle Sam in Danger," 1832, one of the earliest images of Uncle Sam in a liberty cap and striped gown; his health is ruined by Jacksonian physicians, who are draining him of his life's blood. Unsigned lithograph. Alton Ketchum, Uncle Sam: The Man and the Legend, *61.*

Matty" Van Buren offer him the "juice of humbug." Uncle Sam replies, "If you don't leave off ruining my constitution with your quack nostrums, I'll . . . call in Doctor Biddle," a reference to Nicholas Biddle, the Jacksonian nemesis. Uncle Sam wears old-fashioned knee britches, leather moccasins, a dressing gown with stars and stripes, and a cap marked "liberty." By his side is a hungry American eagle who says, "I must fly to Texas, for I shall be starved out here."[211]

In the second quarter of the nineteenth century, Uncle Sam changed his appearance. Knee britches yielded to pantaloons, dressing gowns to a swallow-tail coat, and the liberty cap to a beaver hat. A high-collared shirt, vest, and cravat completed Uncle Sam's outfit, which was that of an ordinary American. The entire costume was lavishly adorned with red and white stripes on stockings or trousers. The white stars on a blue field migrated from one article of clothing to another, finally settling on the hatband. His features were equally varied, but usually he was clean-shaven before the Civil War.[212]

"Uncle Sam Sick with La Grippe," cartoon by Whig artist Frank Bellow. Hand-colored lithograph by Henry R. Robinson, 1838. Collection of Gerald E. Czulewicz, Sr.

Foreign artists adopted Uncle Sam for their own purposes, often pejorative, and changed his appearance. European cartoonists replaced the stars with dollar signs. A pistol was put on his belt, and a slaveholder's whip went into his hand. His handsome features became ugly, even nasty. America's favorite uncle tended to be intensely irritating to others in the world.

At home, Uncle Sam was held in high esteem. This American folk figure personified the union of liberty and freedom with equality and democracy. In their different ways, Yankee Doodle, Uncle Sam, and Brother Jonathan all symbolized an idea of liberty and freedom as eternally connected to the sovereignty of the people.

At the same time, Uncle Sam was an affectionate symbol of a democratic government. This was a very rare attitude. Other people around the world have great pride of nationality, but few are warmly attached to their national governments. Americans thought differently. They actively exercised their sovereign right to rage against national administrations, but in the early republic they took great pride in their political institutions, and except for a few recalcitrant elites they were warmly attached to the American system of government. Uncle Sam was the icon of this American attitude. Much of it still survives, despite prolonged efforts by slaveholders in the nineteenth century, and right-wing Republicans in the twentieth century to persuade the American people that the government of the United States is their mortal enemy.

Most Americans don't buy that argument, despite its incessant repetition. They believe that the American government belongs to them. On the Fourth of July more than a few dress as Uncle Sam, and when they march in the town parade, crowds cheer the symbol of a free government that belongs to the people. As we shall see, the image of Uncle Sam was modified many times by later generations, but the more he changed, the more beloved he became. The iconic shadow of Samuel Willson is still America's favorite uncle.

THE MANY FACES OF MISS LIBERTY

Visions of Freedom and Liberty as Contemporary Ideas

> Whether in long curls, coiffured, Liberty Capped or
> crowned, whether feathered, draped or gowned, this
> supreme icon of America has always been . . . a con-
> stant reminder to all that America is "still at liberty."
>
> —NANCY JO FOX, LIBERTIES WITH LIBERTY

POPULAR as Uncle Sam and Yankee Doodle may have been, the
most appealing images of liberty and freedom have always been
female. It is interesting to observe how these feminine figures have
changed through time. They descended from the ancient goddess of liberty, a timeless figure who represented an idea that derived its authority
from an aura of eternal truth. In the early American republic, they
became something very different—a symbol of modernity, endlessly redefined by the whirl of contemporary fashion—and they gained new meaning from their relevance to the present.

Let us begin with the goddess of liberty. Even before the American
republic was born, she was more than two thousand years old. A Roman
temple had been raised to her on the Aventine Hill as early as the third
century before Christ. The Graachi renewed the Temple of Liberty in 135
B.C. Often she appeared on the coins of the Roman Republic, and later
on those of the Roman Empire as well. Surviving images show her as
woman of maturity with the stylized features of Greco-Roman temple
sculpture and an abundance of ancient gravitas.[213] She was instantly recognizable as a figure of liberty by the symbols around her. At her feet
were the broken chains of bondage, or a smashed pitcher that symbolized
the end of servitude. Sometimes she was accompanied by a cat, the
animal that acknowledged no master. In her hands she offered the wand
and pileus.[214]

The Roman goddess of liberty became a familiar figure in the political iconography of the early modern Europe. Addison celebrated her in the *Tatler,* as did many European writers. She appeared in Cesare Ripa's *Iconologia,* a major work that was much reprinted in early modern Europe. European artists and engravers often reproduced her image in highly stylized ways.[215]

The goddess of liberty appeared as an ageless and immortal figure who existed outside time. Her features were carefully detailed, but in an abstract way. There was nothing individual about her. She symbolized an idea of liberty as an ancient, eternal, and universal principle, inherited from the distant past and applicable to the present and future without change. The goddess of liberty belonged to the ages.

Liberty as Columbia, Mother of the Republic

After the American Revolution, this ageless figure began to change. By degrees, the ancient goddess was transformed into new female images of liberty and freedom. Many distinctive features persisted: the wand and pileus, and the white flowing robes of antiquity. But other elements disappeared. Among the first to go were the cat, the shackles, and the broken pitcher. Those changes were symbolic of a new way of thought. After 1776, liberty and freedom were seen not so much as release from bondage but as a condition of natural rights which free people gained at birth and preserved by their own efforts. Cats and chains and smashed pots were no longer appropriate to that expansive vision.

As those elements faded away, others appeared in the United States. They tended to associate liberty and freedom with the idea of a nation. In the 1780s, feminine images of liberty and freedom began to carry an American flag, or a shield with the national arms, or a bald eagle. Often they wore a distinctive American headdress, with stars and stripes, or Indian feathers, or the needles of the northern white pine (*Pinus strobus*), or the leaves of the southern live oak (*Quercus virginiana*).

With these changes, the goddess of liberty became Columbia, an American image of liberty and freedom. She appears in Samuel Jennings's painting *Liberty Displaying the Arts and Sciences,* done for the Library Company of Philadelphia in 1792. The artist represents liberty as a female figure who is less abstract and more animated than the Roman goddess had been. Her features were softer, more human. She is not standing but seated, inclining gracefully toward others. The grim gravitas of the Roman goddess is gone. Columbia is young, blond, beautiful, and has a

"Liberty Displaying the Arts and Sciences," painting by Samuel Jennings, 1792. Library Company of Philadelphia. Another version, different in detail, is in the Winterthur Museum.

pleasant smile. She wears a white gown of simple dignity and carries a wand and pileus of distinctive color. It is not the blood-red bonnet of the French Revolution, or the true blue of British iconography. Columbia's American liberty cap is white for virtue, innocence, and hope.

Behind this American figure are the sturdy columns of a Roman temple. In the foreground is a globe, with the New World foremost. In the background, a group of slaves are rallying around a liberty pole. Another group who have been emancipated from bondage are surrounded by books, papers, a painter's palette, a sculptor's bust, a musician's lyre, scientific instruments, and other symbols of the arts and sciences. Here is a new idea of universal freedom, as contingent on modern learning and enlightenment. It also represents liberty as secular rather than sacred, a product of human effort rather than the gift of a goddess.

In the early nineteenth century, other artists represented Columbia in another way. Her images often combined elements of the goddess of liberty with Minerva, the Roman goddess of wisdom and war. Minerva's helmet and spear were added to make Columbia appear more bellicose and better able to defend her own freedom and independence.

When Columbia's new image was complete, Americans raised her on a pedestal, high above their public buildings. She became a figurehead on sailing ships, a finial on storefronts, a decorative zinc statue in private homes, a monument on public buildings, and a familiar figure in the American republic.

Liberty as Hebe, Goddess of Youth

While Columbia was settling into her long career, another female image of liberty appeared. She sprang from the palette of British artist William Hamilton, who in 1791 painted a graceful watercolor on a classical theme called *Hebe Offering a Cup to the Eagle (Jove)*. The painting told the old story of Hebe, a young woman who had a special place in Greek mythology. Zeus came to her in the form of an eagle. She fed him from an upraised bowl and won the favor of the gods.

Hamilton's work inspired American artist Edward Savage to do a painting called *Liberty in the Form of the Goddess of Youth Giving Support to the Bald Eagle.* The central figure is a

beautiful young woman in a diaphanous dress with deep décolletage of the Directory style. Her dark hair is loose and curly, in the mode that was popular in the 1790s. She is a vision of simplicity and innocence, with flowers in her hair and a bright garland of blossoms on her shoulder. With an outstretched arm this goddess of youth offers a cup of nourishment to an American bald eagle who is hovering above her. In the clouds over her head are the wand and pileus of liberty, with an American flag attached. Above the eagle, rays of divine light emerge from dark clouds. Below are broken symbols of tyranny: a smashed scepter and a key to the Bastille, which Lafayette had sent to George Washington.

In the background is a warning to despots. Edward Savage has painted his goddess of liberty on a hill near Boston, at the end of the campaign that drove General Gage's army from the town. A bolt of

"Liberty in the Form of a Goddess of Youth," painting on glass by Abijah Canfield, ca. 1800. Greenfield Village and Henry Ford Museum.

Jove's lightning descends from the cloud of liberty and strikes the spire of Old North Church, as the British Regulars flee to ships in the harbor. The young American goddess crushes beneath her foot a star and garter, the proud emblem of British kingship and aristocracy. Tyrants beware!

Americans loved Edward Savage's vision of American liberty as a goddess of youth. Many artists, amateur and professional, copied it in oil and watercolors, on paper and canvas, velvet and glass. So popular did it become that Chinese artists reproduced it for the American market. One of the most successful copies was a handsome reverse painting on glass by American artist Abijah Canfield, who closely followed Savage's design and reinforced its major themes. Canfield's Liberty became even more youthful and innocent; his warning to tyrants grew darker and more dire.[216]

Liberty as Anne Willing Bingham, Philadelphia's Feminist "Queen of Beauty"

In 1796, the United States Mint at Philadelphia began to issue a new set of coins that featured the head of a woman, surrounded by a galaxy of silver stars and the word LIBERTY in bright shining letters. At first sight, they looked much like earlier American coins that had used a stylized image of *Libertas americana*. But this image was something new. It was the fresh face of a young American, Anne Willing Bingham of Philadelphia.

Nancy Bingham, as her family and friends knew her, is not widely remembered today, but she was one of the most eminent women of her age. An oil sketch by Gilbert Stuart shows strong fine-boned features, deep chestnut eyes, firm mouth, and full chin, all framed by a bright cascade of auburn hair. Her figure was said to be as striking as her face. French officers described her as "ravissante et charmante." Even a Loyalist lady wrote, "Speaking of handsome women brings Nancy Willing to my mind. She might set for the Queen of Beauty."[217]

Born in Philadelphia, Anne Bingham was raised in a transatlantic family of great wealth and schooled in the Quaker tradition that gave serious attention to the education of women. She was admired for her "very ingenious" intellect and her "conversational cleverness in French and English." She read widely, was deeply interested in public questions, and corresponded with Thomas Jefferson as an intellectual equal.[218]

She was also a decided feminist. Jefferson, thinking to please her, made the mistake of complaining about the women of Paris. She replied,

Anne Willing Bingham, a lost oil sketch by Gilbert Stuart (1794–95), published in Robert C. Alberts, The Golden Voyage: The Life and Times of William Bingham *(Boston, 1969).*

"We are irresistibly pleased with them, because they possess the happy art of making us pleased with ourselves.... Their education is of a higher cast, and by great cultivation they procure a happy variety of Genius, which forms their conversation, to please either the fop or the Philosopher. We are therefore bound to admire and revere them, for asserting our privileges, much as the friends of the Liberties of Mankind reverence the successful struggles of the American patriots." No wonder Abigail Adams wrote, "Taken altogether, Nancy Bingham was the finest woman I ever saw."[219]

If women could have held office in the new republic, one wonders how high Anne Bingham might have gone, but her only career could be marriage and family. At the age of sixteen she married William Bingham, a Philadelphia financier who made himself one of the richest men in America. Her husband took her to London with a retinue of servants. Abigail Adams watched as Anne Bingham turned every head at the Court of St. James. The crowd murmured in amazement, "Is she an American?" Abigail Adams thought of Pope's line, "She moves like a goddess and looks like a queen," and wrote home, "I felt not a little proud of her." Her picture was painted by Sir Joshua Reynolds, and cheap prints were sold in London shops as an image of beauty. She was twenty-one years old.[220]

The Binghams returned to Philadelphia, built a huge mansion, and entertained lavishly. Anne Bingham was called "queen of the republican court." Abigail Adams wrote from Philadelphia on 24 December, "Mrs. Bingham has certainly given laws to the ladies here, in fashion and elegance; their manners and appearance are superior to what I have seen."[221]

In 1796, she was at the pinnacle of her fame when the U.S. Mint needed a new design for its coinage. Chief engraver Robert Scott found a model for American coins in Gilbert Stuart's portrait of Anne Bingham.[222] The design was very simple: a profile with a draped bust and loose flowing hair. Above her head was the single word LIBERTY. This new image represented liberty not as an ancient goddess but as a modern

American woman. It was not abstract and
general but highly individuated and as
free-spirited as Anne Bingham herself. It
was also a celebration of her femininity
and her independent spirit. The design
was well received, and the Mint adopted it
for all denominations of American silver
coins.

*American "draped bust"
coin, modeled by chief
engraver Robert Scott of the
U.S. Mint on Anne Willing
Bingham in 1795. American
Numismatic Society.*

Anne Bingham herself was now in her
thirties, and more beautiful than ever. Her
life was crowded with events. Having married at sixteen, she became a
grandmother in 1799 at the age of thirty-five. In 1800, she gave birth to a
son, and her friends became concerned about her health, which was
described as increasingly "delicate." She was suffering from tuberculosis,
which grew into a galloping consumption. Her husband hired the best
physicians, chartered a special ship, and took her to sea in hope of a cure.
All of his wealth availed nothing. On May 11, 1801, Anne Willing Bingham died in Bermuda and was buried beside St. George's Harbor, beneath
a stone inscribed with Tudor roses. She was thirty-seven years old.

The liberty coins that bore her likeness continued to be minted in
many denominations until 1807 and were issued for special occasions as
late as the 1830s. Altogether, her features appeared on more than twenty-
three million coins, in a nation of six million people. They became the
most widely distributed emblem of liberty in the new republic. An historian of American numismatics writes, "In the late 18th and early 19th century, all America had Anne Bingham in their pockets and purses." She
remained a vision of American liberty long after her story was forgotten.

The Modernization of Miss Liberty:
Freedom and Liberty as Contemporary Ideas

Nancy Bingham's image was followed by many fresh new faces, who were
collectively called "Miss Liberty" during the nineteenth and twentieth
centuries. Miss Liberty was very different from the grim Roman goddess,
and also distinct from Columbia and even Anne Bingham. Unlike those
more matronly figures, she was young, pretty, and sexy in a virginal way.
Miss Liberty was an all-American girl, innocent and pure, the girl next
door, an ordinary young person with democratic attitudes, egalitarian
manners, and popular tastes.

America's Miss Liberty was also different from the Statue of Liberty,

"Liberty," oil on canvas, American, ca. 1800–20. Gift of William and Bernice Chrysler Garbisch. Image © 2004 Board of Trustees, National Gallery of Art, Washington.

Miss Liberty, pointing with her sword to the Declaration of Independence, painted fire engine panel by Thomas Curlett, ca. 1842, Baltimore. Maryland Historical Society.

with which she is sometimes confused. That great Gallic symbol, with her upraised torch and book of laws, beckoned to all humanity. Miss Liberty was not the sort of girl to carry a torch for anyone, and she was rarely seen in the company of a book. Except in time of war, she was not much interested in events beyond America and was happy to live in her own world, at peace with her surroundings. Always Miss Liberty was lively and carefree, with a smile on her cherry-red lips, a bloom on her alabaster cheeks, and a twinkle in her bright blue eyes.

Miss Liberty kept up with the latest fashion. In the early republic, she wore loose high-waisted diaphanous gowns in the neoclassical Directory style. Later her costume became more romantic, with a fitted bodice, puffed sleeves, and flounced skirts. By the mid-nineteenth century she was a buxom Victorian beauty with a narrow waist, full breasts, plump arms, and sensual shoulders. A little later she wore tight corsets and a bustle. In the early twentieth century, Miss Liberty became a Gibson Girl with fine-boned features and a handsome Anglo-Saxon profile. Her flowing hair was elegantly coiffed. Her high-collared blouse and the long lines of her skirt bespoke the beauty of refinement. But always there was a spirit of strength and independence in her features.

During the 1920s, Miss Liberty rolled her stockings, bobbed her hair, and put on rouge and lipstick. She liked to kick up her high heels and often showed a flash of thigh. A cigarette dangled from a Cupid's-bow mouth, and a cocktail glass was sometimes within reach. In the Depression era, some of the most striking paintings of Miss Liberty were created by Howard Chandler Christie, the American artist who was known for fantasy paintings of beautiful young women in transparent party gowns. Others in the late 1930s made Miss Liberty into a pin-up girl, with a two-piece red, white, and blue bathing suit that showed a bare midriff and Betty Grable legs.

When the Second World War began, the party dresses were packed away and Miss Liberty put on her work clothes. She wore overalls, high-topped safety shoes, even a welding helmet, and pitched in at the factory or the shipyard. The rouge vanished, and her cheeks were smudged with paint and grease. During the war, Norman Rockwell painted another face of Miss Liberty as a busy bobby-soxer in red-and-white-striped trousers, tucking up her blue sleeves and going to work with a plumber's wrench, a

trainman's oil can, a milkman's bottle rack, a bus driver's coin changer, a gardener's hoe, a pilot's headphones, a nurse's cap, a trainman's lantern, a fireman's shovel, a watchman's time clock, and a mechanic's oil can that suggested the many roles women assumed in the war.[223] When the troops came home, Miss Liberty became more feminine. She was as American as ever, wholesome, sweet, and sexy— every man's domestic dream. But she was also autonomous and high-spirited—no man's domestic slave.

In the 1960s and '70s, when the nation was deeply divided, Miss Liberty offered several images to the world. Some Americans saw her as an angry rebel with tousled hair and a

Miss Liberty, ca. 1850–60, ornament on a painted wood boathouse, Tuftonborough, New Hampshire. Private Collection.

dark light in her deep mascaraed eyes. Other images in that divided era made Miss Liberty into a go-go girl with childlike features, plucked eyebrows, white lipstick, long hair, tight miniskirts, high plastic boots, and heavy jewelry. She actually became a Barbie doll called "Lady Liberty," in "a silvery metallic gown with long sleeves and a sweeping train at her feet" and "a full length acrylic sweep of rhinestones and stars and silver pumps."[224]

In the narcissistic nineties, Miss Liberty reinvented herself yet again. She worked out on weight machines and developed fabulous abs and buns of steel. In 1990, a photograph by Jock Macdonald called *American Girl* showed her as a young woman with a perfectly sculpted body, wearing nothing but spike heels and a flag on her head. She clenched her fists and flexed her biceps. Her taut skin was covered with body tattoos of stars and stripes. More than ever, the all-American Miss Liberty of the 1990s was a bundle of paradoxes. She was an emancipated woman, cool and hip but hungry for love. Miss Liberty was strong and tough, but feminine and always free.[225]

This dizzy whirl of fashion symbolized a new idea in the long history of liberty and freedom. From ancient Rome to early modern Europe, the goddess of liberty represented an eternal idea that came from the distant past and existed outside of time. The American image of Miss Liberty is different in all those ways. She is very much a modern miss, and her supple figure resembles the willow more than the oak. She changes with the times, and her time is always now. Her fresh face and current fashions represent liberty and freedom as contemporary ideas, continuously updated in an ever-changing world. Miss Liberty is the symbol of a principle that derives its power not from its roots in the past but its relevance to the present. This is how Americans have come to understand their visions of liberty and freedom, as contemporary ideas.

But there is yet another irony here. These visions of liberty and freedom as contemporary ideas emerged in America more than two centuries ago. The more they change, the more they preserve the founding impulse: never quite *le même chose* but always true to the spirit of Oscar Wilde's epigram that "the youth of America is its oldest tradition." In every new incarnation, it expresses an idea of modernity that was born during the eighteenth century, developed in the time of Edward Savage's Hebe, flourished in the generation of Nancy Bingham, and still appears in the many faces of Miss Liberty.

COMING TOGETHER

Emblems of Unity and Diversity in a Free Republic

> Make the word American mean, not a man born on this soil or on that, but a free and accepted member of the grand republic of men. Such is what has been boasted as the principle and destiny of this New World.
>
> —ORESTES BROWNSON, 1844

WHILE NEW VISIONS of liberty and freedom were invented in the early republic, old symbols continued in circulation with a change of meaning. The history of the Liberty Pole is a case in point. In the party battles of the 1790s, it was revived as a symbol of Republican resistance against a tyrannical federal government. The Whiskey Rebels who rose against the federal excise tax used this revolutionary symbol. The *Baltimore Daily Intelligencer* reported on September 8, 1794, "They threaten to march to Middletown and Funks-town and put up Liberty poles at those places."[226]

After the party battles subsided, small towns throughout the republic continued to raise liberty poles in the mid-nineteenth century. A lively watercolor of an Independence Day celebration at Weymouth, Massachusetts, in 1853 shows a Liberty Pole in a grove of elm trees.[227] Liberty Poles were still being constructed in major cities during the mid-nineteenth century. In 1858, the people of New York City raised a two-hundred-foot Liberty Pole on West Broadway.[228]

Liberty Trees also acquired new meanings: national, republican, and democratic. In Massachusetts, the town of Cambridge had its "old elm," where Washington took command of the American army on July 3, 1775. James Russell Lowell wrote a poem about it for the centennial ceremony of 1875. The town of Weston, Massachusetts, cherished its ancient "Burgoyne elm," where the captured army of General John Burgoyne camped

Emblems of liberty and freedom as symbols of rights of belonging: Susan Torrey Merritt, "Anti-Slavery Picnic on Weymouth Landing," watercolor, ca. 1845–53. © Art Institute of Chicago; gift of Elizabeth R. Vaughan.

after their defeat at Saratoga. The towns of New Haven and East Hampton and many others in New England planted their commons and main streets with elms in the early republic. Baltimore's "Rochambeau elms" graced the corner of Charles and Mulberry streets until the mid-twentieth century. In New Hampshire a great elm stood on the bank of the Merrimack River. The owners of the huge Amoskeag mills wanted to cut it down. The millworkers resisted, telling the owners that the old elm was "a connecting link between the past and present." All of these trees became popular sites for republican rituals. Local communities preserved them as symbols of a common struggle for liberty and freedom, and turned the memory of that revolutionary past into an instrument of republican unity.[229]

The great Quaker bell of liberty also took on a broad range of symbolic meanings during the nineteenth century. It became a national symbol of "liberty in one country," a republican symbol of liberty as self-government, a democratic symbol of liberty for everyone, and a contemporary symbol of an idea that was renewed in every generation. A leading role was taken by Samuel Francis Smith, a Baptist minister who lived in Newton, Massachusetts. In 1832, while still a seminary student, he wrote a hymn to American liberty and freedom. Most Americans know its first stanza by heart:

> *My country! 'tis of thee, sweet land of liberty, of thee I sing.*
> *Land where my fathers died! Land of the pilgrims' pride!*
> *From ev'ry mountain side let freedom ring.*

Smith wrote the song in half an hour on a scrap of waste paper. He matched its lyrics to a melody that he found in a German music book and liked for "its simple and natural movement, and by its special fitness for childish voices, and children's choirs." Not until later did he learn that the same tune was sung in Britain as "God Save the King."

A single metaphor runs through the song: "let freedom ring." It was similar to the imagery of the Quaker bell, but not precisely the same. The images were different, in the same way that the faith of a New England Baptist was distinct from that of a Pennsylvania Quaker. Samuel Francis Smith began with an idea he shared with the Quakers, that liberty was the gift of God; but he took it in a different direction. His idea of freedom was strongly nationalist, something unique to America and its chosen people. In his image of the "pilgrims' pride" and the "land where our fathers died," he borrowed something of New England's tribal sense and expanded it to the American nation. The old text "proclaim liberty throughout the land" became an image of freedom in one nation.

At the same time, Samuel Francis Smith added another new element when he wrote the hymn in the first person singular. His friend and Harvard classmate Oliver Wendell Holmes wrote, "If he had said, 'Our Country' the hymn would not have been immortal, but that 'My' was a master stroke. Everyone who sings the song feels at once a personal ownership in his native land. The Hymn will last as long as the Country." Here was another new idea of individuality that scarcely existed in 1751 when the Quaker bell was proposed.[230]

When Samuel Francis Smith died in 1895, the people of his town built a bell tower and a chime of bells in Newton Center, Massachusetts. They dedicated it to the memory of the man himself, and also to his vision of freedom, ringing through the nation "unto all the inhabitants thereof."

In their different ways, party builders, community boosters, and denominational ministers all did much to establish consensual images of liberty and freedom. This American tradition was national but protective of local autonomy and regional cultures. It was democratic but attentive to the interests of propertied minorities. It was consciously modern but rooted in a republican past. It became the creed of the "venturous conservatives" who were Tocqueville's archetypical Americans. But no sooner was this consensus established than it began to be challenged in a new way. The result was yet another American revolution, which Abraham Lincoln called "a new birth of freedom."

A NATION DIVIDED
Freedom against Liberty, 1840–1912

"Freedom to the Slave," a lithograph thought to be printed at Philadelphia in 1863. It combined an image of liberty for slaves on the right, with a vision of freedom for the emancipated on the left. National Museum of American History, Smithsonian Institution.

THE FRIENDS OF UNIVERSAL REFORM

New Visions of Liberty and Freedom

> All literature worthy of the name is and must be on the
> side of freedom. . . . [W]ithout freedom no good liter-
> ature can be born or long exist.
>
> —FRANKLIN BENJAMIN SANBORN,
> CONCORD REFORMER AND ONE
> OF JOHN BROWN'S SECRET SIX

I N 1840, Ralph Waldo Emerson left the quiet of his Concord home
for a stormy meeting in Boston. It called itself a Convention of the
Friends of Universal Reform, and it was a wild affair. "If the assembly was disorderly," Emerson remembered, "it was picturesque. Madmen,
madwomen, men with beards, Dunkers, Muggletonians, Come-outers,
Groaners, Agrarians, Seventh Day Baptists, Quakers, Abolitionists,
Calvinists, Universalists, Philosophers—all came successively to the top,
and seized their moment, if not their hour, wherein to chide, or pray, or
preach, or protest."[1]

The avowed purpose of the convention was to reform the Sabbath
laws of New England, but its members had larger goals in mind. Most
were inspired by new visions of liberty and freedom that reached far
beyond the American Revolution. Like Emerson himself, these Friends
of Universal Reform were grandchildren of the Revolutionary generation. They deeply cherished the achievement of independence, but sixty
years after the Revolution they believed that many Americans were not
yet free.[2]

The universal reformers meant to do something about that. Some
sought to enlarge the circle of liberty and freedom by including Americans who had been left behind by the Revolution. That was the purpose
of the abolitionists, who had two goals in mind: liberty for slaves and
freedom for the emancipated. It was also the object of feminists who

An Abolition Convention,
Harper's Weekly, *May 28,*
1859. Virginia Historical
Society.

expanded the circle to include women, with the same double purpose of liberty from oppression and freedom to share full rights of citizenship.

Other reformers sought to emancipate Americans who had been born to liberty and freedom but were in fetters of their own making. Temperance workers tried to liberate people from the bondage of addiction. Others labored to free the deaf and blind and the insane from the chains of cruel affliction. Prison reformers hoped to transform hardened criminals into free citizens. Debt reformers worked to release debtors from confinement: more than a thousand debtors in the jails of Baltimore alone, mostly for debts of less than ten dollars.

Among the most successful reformers were the founders of free schools and common schools, mainly as instruments of individual liberty and republican freedom. The most radical were economic reformers who worked for a more free and equal distribution of land, work, wages, and wealth. The most ambitious envisioned the entire reconstruction of society on the model of Fourierist phalansteries, Owenite communities, and homegrown American utopias. The most profound were Transcendentalists such as Ralph Waldo Emerson and Henry David Thoreau, who urged Americans to reform their inner selves in the cause of liberty and freedom. Thoreau wrote, "Is not our own interior white on the chart? Inward is a direction which no traveller has taken. . . . O ye Reformers, here in your own realms . . . is the application to be made."[3]

These movements deeply divided the American republic. The reform-

A Women's Rights Convention, Harper's Weekly, June 11, 1859. Virginia Historical Society.

ers were always a small minority of Americans. Most were descendants of Puritans and Quakers. Among leading abolitionists, 85 percent came from the Northeast, and 60 percent from New England, which had only 21 percent of the national population. Two-thirds were Congregationalists, Friends, and Unitarians (altogether 7 percent of Americans). Half were clergy or the children of clerical families, who were less than 1 percent of the population. Similar patterns appeared in other reform movements.[4]

Like their Puritan and Quaker ancestors, the reformers met strong opposition from opponents who also claimed to be heirs of the American Revolution and true defenders of liberty and freedom. When Horace Mann and his friends insisted that tax-supported common schools were fundamental to a free society, others argued with equal fervor that no man's property could be used to educate another man's children without consent. One citizen in southern Indiana ordered that his tombstone should proclaim that he died an enemy to free schools, in the cause of liberty.[5]

Of all the great reforms, the most bitterly contested was the antislavery movement. It directly challenged many Americans in their material interests, racial prejudice, and regional pride. Here again the struggle was mainly between competing visions of liberty and freedom. Southern planters insisted that they were striving for their absolute liberty to keep a slave. They also invented a new idea of freedom that restricted rights to the "white race," and passionately believed that the greatest danger to a free republic came from meddlesome Yankee reformers. The conflict over slavery led to the most severe test of American institutions in the nineteenth century.

All of this developed from the driving purposes of men and women who called themselves Friends of Universal Reform. In the end, they were remarkably successful in enacting their programs. At the same time, they succeeded in starting a process of permanent reform that continues today. Trotsky's Marxist dream of permanent revolution never happened in any nation, but Emerson's Transcendental idea of permanent reform is part of every free society in the world. The great reformers of Emerson's generation became enduring symbols of their own expanding visions of liberty and freedom. They are still with us in that iconic role.

EMERSON'S CONCORD

Transcendental Ideas of Fate and Freedom

If you cannot be free, be as free as you can.

—RALPH WALDO EMERSON

I F THE FRIENDS of Universal Reform had an intellectual capital, it
was the town of Concord in Massachusetts. If they had an inner
sanctum, it was the study of Ralph Waldo Emerson. Today that
entire room has been moved to the Concord Museum and maintained as
a living shrine, frozen in Transcendental time, as if the sage of Concord
had laid down his papers for a moment and gone to greet some of his
friends in the next room.[6]

Emerson made his study the center of an intellectual circle that spread
outward from his writing table like ripples on the deep waters of Walden
Pond. Some say that the circle formed when he moved to Concord in
1835. Others date its origins from Emerson's essay "Nature" in 1836, which
Bronson Alcott regarded as the instrument of his own awakening, or
from *The American Scholar* in 1837, which the poet Oliver Wendell
Holmes remembered as "our intellectual Declaration of Independence."
Many believe that Emerson's circle began with the founding of the Tran-
scendental Club, a gathering of sympathetic thinkers who met formally
from 1836 to 1840 and informally all their lives: Bronson Alcott, Margaret
Fuller, Elizabeth Palmer Peabody, Theodore Parker, and Henry David
Thoreau. All looked to Emerson as their teacher, patron, and friend.[7]

Bronson Alcott observed that the members of this circle were "each
working distinct veins of the same mine of Being."[8] They modeled themselves on Emerson's peculiar habits of thinking. Convers Francis wrote,

253

The iconic "Mr. E": Ralph Waldo Emerson (1803–82) at the writing table in his Concord study, 1879 photograph. By permission of the Ralph Waldo Emerson Memorial Association and the Houghton Library, Harvard University.

"Mr. E is not a philosopher, so called, not a logic-man, not one whose vocation is to state processes of argument; he is a seer who reports in sweet and significant words what he sees; he looks into the infinite of truth, and records what passes before his vision: if you see it as he does, you will recognize him for a gifted teacher; if not, there is little or nothing to be said about it."[9]

Most members of his circle were seers in that same Transcendental sense. If there was a passage in Emerson's works that most inspired his friends and appalled his critics, it would be the two famous (or infamous) sentences in his "Nature." "Standing on the bare ground," Emerson wrote, "my head bathed in the blithe air and uplifted into infinite space—all mean egotism vanishes. I become a transparent eyeball; I am nothing; I see all; the currents of the Universal Being circulate through me; I am part or parcel of God."[10]

The Transcendentalists of the Concord Circle were all inspired by the image of Emerson's transparent eyeball and by his vision of liberty and freedom. Theodore Parker, who knew him well, observed that even when Emerson did not use the words *liberty* and *freedom,* all of his work was about those ideas. To set his thinking in that context is to discover how very original it was, and how different from some of his most fervent admirers and detractors.[11]

Emerson is celebrated and condemned as a philosopher of individual
liberty and self-reliance. Much of his
language lends itself to that understanding of his thought. "In all my lec-
tures," he wrote in 1840, "I have taught
one doctrine, namely the infinitude of
the private man." The lapidary sentences of his essay "Self-Reliance" have
shaped his reputation: "Trust thyself;
every heart vibrates to its own iron
string. Whoso would be a man, must
be a nonconformist."[12]

But to dig beneath the surface of
those words is to discover a deeper
vision. This high priest of individualism was preeminently a social being.
The man who wrote "Self-Reliance"
lived all his life among others, deeply embedded in his town, family, and a
complex web of social relationships. Henry David Thoreau observed of
Emerson's circle, "All these friends & acquaintances & tastes and habits
are indeed my friend's self."[13]

Ralph Waldo Emerson as a "transparent eyeball," caricature by Christopher Cranch, ca. 1837–39. Houghton Library, Harvard University.

Emerson's vision of living free developed not as a solitary exercise in
self-reliance but in a collaboration with others. Even his essay "Self-
Reliance" emerged from conversations with his brilliant aunt Mary
Moody Emerson and many Concord friends. Emerson celebrated "the
infinitude of the private man," but he also wrote, "Each of us has need of
all." In his paradoxical way he believed that those two ideas were one, and
they became for him a synergy of liberty and freedom.[14]

Emerson always condemned the simple-minded ideas of individualism
and extreme individual liberty others ascribed to him. He wrote that the
"vice of the age is to exaggerate individualism." He complained at length
of his own era in those terms: "It is the age of severance, of dissociation, of
freedom, of analysis, of detachment. Every man for himself. The public
speaker disclaims speaking for any other; he answers only for himself. The
social sentiments are weak; the sentiment of patriotism is weak; veneration
is low; the natural affections feebler than they were.... There is a universal
resistance to ties and ligaments once supposed essential to civil society."[15]

He complained that the spirit of "dissociation" was too strong in his
own generation. "The new race is stiff, heady, and rebellious," Emerson

wrote; "they are fanatics in freedom; they hate tolls, taxes, turnpikes, banks, hierarchies, governors, yea, almost the laws. They have a neck of unspeakable tenderness; it winces at a hair."[16]

Two keys to Emerson's thinking are his essays called "Fate" and "Power," which offer a vision of life as struggle, in which "all things are double, one against another." This was one of his favorite themes: "All the universe over," he said, "there is but one thing, this old Two-Face." He often wrote of the "dual constitution of things," and the "twofold nature in every individual."[17] Most of all he understood this "dual constitution" as a vision of individual liberty within a free society. Emerson's idea of liberty was a state of consciousness that allowed individuals to realize their own inner nature. It was joined to a conception of freedom as a right of belonging to a just society that helped individuals to reach that end.

If one returns to his essay "Self-Reliance" with this "dual constitution" in mind, its phrases take on a deeper meaning. Emerson wrote, "We want men and women who will renovate life and our social state." He added, "A greater self-reliance must work a revolution in all the offices and relations of man." His individualism was a social idea. It was very much in the town-born New England tradition of ordered freedom and individual responsibility.[18]

In his own time, many of Emerson's generation understood the originality and complexity of his thought. They celebrated the man himself as the center of his Transcendental circle and the leading citizen of Concord. Both the circle and the town itself became images of his ideas. They set his individualism within a community of individuals, bound together in mutual support of their individuality. All this appeared not only in Emerson's words but also in his acts.

That way of understanding Emerson faded after his death in 1882. For people who did not know him, and could not read his works at length, he was understood through some of his epigrams, which made him appear to be the image of unrestrained individual autonomy. This mythic Emerson became the favorite philosopher of Henry Ford and John D. Rockefeller, who claimed Emerson's ideas as a justification of their business buccaneering.

By the 1930s, that image was turned upside down by critics who used the same epigrams to condemn him for what others had praised. During the Great Depression, American literati took turns attacking Emerson for a simpleminded optimistic celebration of individual autonomy. A gloomy southern writer named Allen Tate complained that Emerson was "the

light-bearer who could see nothing but light, and was fearfully blind."
This was complete miscomprehension of his thought.[19]

The pendulum of these interpretations continued to swing back and
forth for many generations. During the 1940s and 1950s, Emerson
returned to favor, and his quotations were celebrated as expressions of
individualism against Fascism and Communism. The inevitable reaction
came in the 1960s and 1970s, when writers complained that Emerson had
created a monster that one of them called the "imperial self," another profound misunderstanding of his life and work. In the 1980s and 1990s, self-
reliance came back into fashion. Emerson was celebrated in a commercial
for the Nike Corporation that recited passages from "Self-Reliance" while
it showed images of beautiful young narcissists doing their own thing,
with Emerson's words on their lips and Nike shoes on their feet.

In the twenty-first century, Emerson's iconic image is changing yet
again, at last in a more informed and constructive way. His works have
become available on thousands of web pages. A voluntary association
called the Ralph Waldo Emerson Society has dedicated itself to a more
accurate understanding of his thought. A new generation of Emerson
scholars such as Joel Myerson, Phyllis Cole, Wesley Mott, Robert
Richardson, and Len Gougeon have given us "the most thoroughly
Emersonian Emerson to date," in the words of Ronald Bosco. Today,
Americans are visiting Emerson's study in Concord in larger numbers
than ever before. They are reading his essays and finding new meaning in
his thought. Many are drawn to his creative synthesis of liberty and freedom for individuals as social beings.[20]

THOREAU'S CABIN

A Naturalist's Vision of "Absolute Freedom and Wildness"

> As long as possible live free and uncommitted. It makes but little difference whether you are committed to a farm or the county jail.
>
> —HENRY DAVID THOREAU

ANOTHER VISION of liberty and freedom appeared in the life and work of Emerson's protégé, Henry David Thoreau. His biographer Robert Richardson gives us a memorable image of this extraordinary man as his neighbors saw him, on the road in Concord. Richardson writes: "He walked with a long ungainly stride that reminded people of an Indian's. His eyes rarely left the ground. He wore old corduroys, stout shoes and a straw hat." Often a crowd of children swarmed after him. Adults toiling in their fields looked up as he passed by, and shook their heads in affectionate disapproval. Even those who were not his admirers saw him as a living image of civil liberty and soul freedom. Emerson wrote that Thoreau was "the only man of leisure in his town; his independence made all others look like slaves."[21]

Today Thoreau has become an iconic figure in American culture. Every year three million people make a pilgrimage to Walden Pond. They peer into the cloudy windows of Thoreau's reconstructed cabin, which has become an American icon. It stands by the side of a busy highway, incongruously guarded by helpful young men and women in uniforms that would have surprised the sage of Walden. Many visitors walk the path to the cabin's original site in Walden Woods and add a small stone to a cairn that has grown larger than the cabin ever was. To stand on that site, and to watch the wind as it moves across the waters of Walden Pond, is to feel the stirring of a spirit.

Many Americans know Thoreau in another way. At school they are required to read passages from *Walden* and "Civil Disobedience," and they study snatches of his prose, as if his writings were books of quotations. These selections represent him as a nature-loving hermit who sought solitude in Walden Woods, and also an anarchist who invented the idea of civil disobedience. Thoreau himself rejected these understandings of his life and work. "I am naturally no hermit," he wrote. "I love society as much as most." He was very active in the life of his beloved town and became, in Emerson's phrase, "*the* man of Concord." Thoreau also insisted that he was no anarchist. "I ask for, not at once no government, but *at once* better government," he wrote in "Civil Disobedience."[22]

To follow Thoreau's thinking through time is to find a highly original synergy of liberty and freedom. He began with a restless feeling that the American Revolution had been incomplete. "Do we call this the land of the free?" he wrote in 1851. "What is it to be free from King George the Fourth and continue slaves to prejudice? What is it [to] be born free and equal, and not to live? What is the value of any political freedom, but as a means to moral freedom? Is it a freedom to be slaves or a freedom to be free of which we boast? We are a nation of politicians, concerned with the outermost defenses of freedom."[23]

With those thoughts in mind, Thoreau dedicated himself to a second American Revolution. "It is our children's children who may perchance be essentially free," he wrote. The question was how to achieve this condition, which Thoreau called "moral freedom." Like Emerson he was a romantic idealist who believed in the power of ideas as instruments of liberation. To that end, he undertook to persuade others to think anew, that they might act anew.[24]

One line of Thoreau's thought started in the genteel circle of the Transcendental Club, took him into the woods, and led to the book called *Walden* (1854), which he addressed to the people of his town. Thoreau tried to persuade the freeholders of Concord that they were "serfs to the soil," with less liberty or freedom than the beasts in their fields. He said to them, "Men are not so much the keepers of herds, as herds are keepers of men, the former so much freer." Thoreau lectured his long-suffering neighbors that they were prisoners of their possessions, captives of their work, and slaves to the despotism of good behavior. He told them, "It is hard to have a southern overseer; it is worse to have a northern one; but worst of all if you are the slave driver of yourself."[25]

Thoreau insisted that everyone is free to choose differently, to find "freedom in his love, and in his soul be free." That vision of liberation had

An American symbol of living free: Henry David Thoreau (1817–62), photograph. Image donated by Corbis/Bettmann.

many dimensions. One was what we would call social. He never wanted to be apart from others. His argument was not with society itself but with the tyranny of a false society that enslaved people to purposes other than their own.

Thoreau's ideal of social freedom was an idealized image of Concord at its best. On a warm midsummer night in 1851 he wrote, "8:30 P.M. The streets of the village are much more interesting to me at this hour of a summer evening than by day. Neighbors, and also farmers, come a-shopping after their day's haying, are chatting in the streets, and I hear the sound of many musical instruments and of singing from the various houses. For a short hour or two the inhabitants are sensibly employed."[26]

Another dimension of his thought was environmental. It was a vision of liberation by thinking and acting anew in the natural world. *Walden* was only the beginning of Thoreau's evolving thought on this subject. In later work, especially posthumous publications such as "Wild Apples" and the final text of his essay called "Walking" (1862), he argued that it was not enough to study nature. One must seek to become one with it. Only in that way could one achieve what he called "absolute freedom." He wrote, "I wish to speak a word for nature, for absolute freedom and wildness, as contrasted with a freedom and culture merely civil." He concluded, "In wildness is the preservation of the world."[27]

But that idea was not the end of his quest. Within the span of his short life, Thoreau discovered the paradox that "wildness" was something that needed to be protected and even preserved by human effort. Thus, his search for "absolute freedom" through "wildness" led him back to others. In *Walden* he wrote that he did not wish to think or act alone but always welcomed the company of "honest pilgrims who came out to the woods for freedom's sake." He added later, "I left the woods for as good a reason as I went there," even for the same reason.[28]

Yet another part of Thoreau's vision was a dream of a new politics. It appeared in the essay later called "Civil Disobedience" (1847–48), which proclaimed the right and duty of every individual to stand against an unjust government. Thoreau's first thoughts on that subject are prominent in his quotations: "Disobedience is the true foundation of liberty. The obedient must be slaves. . . . If the law is of such a nature that it requires you to be an agent of injustice to another, then I say, break the law. . . . Let your life be a counterfriction to stop the machine."[29]

This was not an expression of hostility to politics but a hunger for a higher politics. In 1854 he wrote, "It is not any such free-soil party as I have seen, but a freeman party—i.e., a party of free men,—that is wanted."[30] But that

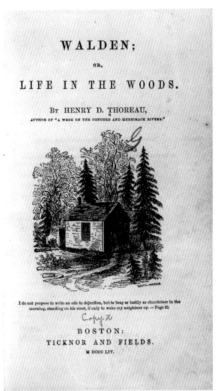

Walden, *title page of the first edition, with Sophia Thoreau's sketch of Thoreau's cabin, the only known contemporary image of this American icon. Concord Free Public Library.*

idea was only his starting point. The continuing expansion of slavery during the 1850s taught Thoreau that something more was needed than civil disobedience or party politics. We can follow his thinking as it developed in later works such as "Slavery in Massachusetts" (1854) and "A Plea for Captain John Brown" (1859), and the long soliloquy in his journal on slavery and the Harper's Ferry Raid. He became more active against slavery, moving from petitions and tax refusals to instrumental acts such as aid for fugitive slaves and his strong support for John Brown in Kansas and Harper's Ferry. All this took him far beyond his starting point in the Transcendental Club. A leading Thoreau scholar writes, "What Thoreau ultimately discovered is that reform of individuals, through the development of a virtuous self-culture, can only occur in an environment where personal freedom is guaranteed."[31]

These visions made Thoreau himself into a living symbol of liberty and freedom, even in his own time. The legend that he languished in obscurity and neglect is not correct. The first edition of *Walden* received more than a hundred reviews and nearly sold out within a year. A clergyman in Worcester, H.G.O. Blake, became the self-appointed promoter of

Thoreau, with high success. In the nineteenth century, many Americans were his admirers. One of them was the industrialist Henry Clay Frick. Many years ago this historian visited the ornate library of Frick's New York mansion, now the Frick Collection Museum. In the place of honor beside Frick's desk was a sumptuous leatherbound set of Thoreau's writings. One wonders what Thoreau would have thought.

Thoreau's international reputation began to grow in 1886 with an English edition of *Walden* and an excellent biography by British socialist Henry Salt, who introduced "Civil Disobedience" to Gandhi. Thoreau's ideas were put to work in India's National Independence movement. They were tried again (and failed miserably) in European resistance movements against Fascism during the Second World War. In the 1950s they were deployed once more in the American civil rights movement, with triumphant success.

During the 1950s, the American beat writers Jack Kerouac and Allen Ginsberg discovered Thoreau in another way, as a prophet of existential freedom. He became a hero to the young in the 1960s and 1970s, and a play called *The Night Thoreau Spent in Jail* by Jerome Lawrence and Robert Lee was a great success. His nature writing made him an icon for the environmental movement, and his phrase "In wildness is the preservation of the world," became the motto of the Sierra Club. In the 1980s, a rock musician named Don Henley led a major campaign to save Walden Woods from Concord developers. The circle of Thoreau's followers continues to grow in unexpected ways, as people find new meanings in this iconic figure.

How does one see such a seer as Henry David Thoreau? One can see him through the eyes of others, or as he saw himself, or by envisioning his visions, or by seeking to see beyond him in ways he inspired but could not have imagined. To approach Thoreau in any of those ways is to discover that there is more to this man than even his warmest admirers have made of him, and especially in his vision of liberty and freedom. Every generation has reinvented Thoreau by its own revision of his ideas. As long as that process continues, his legacy is a living thing. "Perchance," Thoreau wrote, "when in the course of ages, American liberty has become a fiction of the past—as it is to some extent a fiction of the present—the poets of the world will be inspired by American mythology."[32]

MARGARET FULLER'S PARLATORIO

A Feminist Vision of "Perfect Freedom, Pure Love"

> If the negro be a soul, if the woman be a soul, appareled in flesh, to one master only are they accountable.
>
> —MARGARET FULLER

ROM THE START of English settlement in America, women asserted their rights to liberty and freedom. At first they did so not by arguments to equality but the very opposite. In Massachusetts Bay as early as 1637–38, Mistress Anne Hutchinson asserted her superior right and duty as one of God's elect to teach His word to unregenerate males whom she regarded as living examples of depravity. By 1647, Maryland's highborn Mistress Margaret Brent demanded a "place and voyce" in the Assembly as the privilege of her exalted rank, which made most men her inferiors. In the same spirit, female Virginians claimed the special entitlements of free-born "She-Britons," as one plantation mistress proudly called herself, over less fortunate mortals who were theirs to command. All of these arguments rested on a claim to superiority over most men, not merely equality.[33]

The American Revolution changed that way of thinking. It inspired a different vision of liberty as equal rights for women. Among the first to put this egalitarian idea on paper was Judith Sargent Stevens Murray, who signed herself Constantia and published a series of essays "On the Equality of the Sexes" in the *Massachusetts Magazine* during the spring of 1790, two years before Mary Wollstonecraft's *Vindication of the Rights of Woman*.[34]

In the nineteenth century, the writings of Murray and Wollstonecraft inspired a second generation of feminists, who were the first to take that

263

Frontispiece to the Ladies Magazine and Repository of Entertaining Knowledge, I *(1792), the first American printing of Mary Wollstonecraft's* A Vindication of the Rights of Woman. *Library of Congress.*

name. One of the strongest voices belonged to Sarah Margaret Fuller (1810–50). In her short life she created one of the most large-minded visions of liberty and freedom in her generation and became a symbol of her own ideas.[35]

Nobody who knew Margaret Fuller was neutral about her. Her strong-boned features were variously described as beautiful and ugly. Her sinuous neck brought comparisons to a swan and a serpent.[36] Her piercing but very near-sighted eyes attracted and alienated in the same glance. Ralph Waldo Emerson wrote of their first meeting, "Her extreme plainness,—a trick of incessantly opening and shutting her eyelids,—the nasal tone of her voice,—all repelled, and I said to myself we shall never get far."[37]

But Emerson was won over by her qualities of thought, and to read her work is to make the same discovery. Here was one of the most powerful and creative minds of her generation. Margaret Fuller owed her eminence to her intellect, reinforced by character and temperament. Even when she was a little girl, her father watched her walking in an orchard with "such an air and step" that he turned to her sister and, remembering his Virgil, said, "*Incedit regina,*" she moves like a queen.[38]

He was Timothy Fuller, a prominent lawyer and Congressman in Cambridge, Massachusetts. Like many men of his generation, he made the private education of his daughter a special mission. As a child Margaret Fuller studied six languages, translated Horace at the age of seven, gained full access to the library at Harvard College, grew more learned than some of its faculty, and came down with a bad case of what might be called the Cambridge Consumption with its twin symptoms of arrogance and angst. Once she remarked, "I know all the people worth knowing in America, and I find no intellect comparable to my own." At the same time, she was consumed by nervous headaches that she compared to a bird of prey, fastening "iron talons in my brain." Perry Miller writes that she was "as tormented and anguished a soul as any in America."[39]

In her teens she was taken in hand by Eliza Rotch Farrar, a woman of wealth and refinement who brought Margaret Fuller into her home and undertook to "make her less abrupt, less self-asserting, more *comme il faut*" in ideas, manners, and even dress. Fuller's father had educated her as an intellectual of exceptional power; Eliza Farrar made her a woman of extraordinary presence.

A transforming moment in her life came in 1836, when she went to visit Emerson in Concord, stayed for three weeks, and emerged with the sense of purpose that he instilled in others. She became part of his Transcendental circle, edited *The Dial,* published her first book, called *Summer on the Lakes,* in 1844, inspired Thoreau to try his hand at nature writing, persuaded Horace Greeley to make her a literary critic, and became roving reporter for the *New York Tribune.* She went to Europe as its first female foreign correspondent, joined Mazzini's radical movement, took part in the Revolution of 1848, became the lover of a radical aristocrat, the Marchese Giovanni d'Ossoli, bore him a child in 1848, may have married him in 1849, and embarked with her family for America in 1850. As they approached New York, a great storm wrecked their ship, and Margaret Fuller drowned with her husband and child in the surf on Fire Island.

Margaret Fuller (1810–50), from a daguerreotype. Image donated by Corbis/Bettmann.

In the few years that were given her, she had a great impact on others. Her kinsman James Freeman Clarke wrote, "To those of her own age, she was a sibyl and a seer—a prophetess revealing her future, pointing the path, opening their eyes to the great aims only worthy of pursuit in life."[40]

Much of Margaret Fuller's short career as "sibyl and seer" centered on a vision of freedom, which she developed in her writings and exhibited in her life. She is remembered mainly for her devotion to the rights of women, the subject of her most important book, *Women in the Nineteenth Century,* and the theme of many essays which argued that "as the principle of liberty is better understood, and more nobly interpreted, a broader protest is made in behalf of women." Her feminism was part of a larger Transcendental vision of liberty and freedom.[41]

In 1839, that vision flourished in a new setting, when Margaret Fuller organized a series of "conversations for a circle of women in Boston." They attracted a large number of highly educated women to the parlor of Elizabeth Peabody. Emerson called them "Margaret's Parlatorio." In the center sat Margaret Fuller herself, "a living image of Beauty and Truth." One wrote, "Margaret, beautifully dressed (don't despise that, for it made a fine picture) presided with more dignity and grace than I would have thought possible."[42]

A stenographic record was kept of the Parlatorio on March 22, 1841, which centered on a discussion of freedom. The question of the day was "What Is Life?" Margaret Fuller opened the conversation and turned to her lively friend Caroline Sturgis.

"Caroline, what is life?" she asked.

"It is to laugh, or cry, according to our organization," Caroline answered.

"Good," said Margaret, "but not grave enough."

Other answers began to fly. Ralph Waldo's wife, Lidian Emerson, said very gravely, "We live by the will of God, and the object of life is to submit," and she led the group into a thicket of Calvinist theology. This brought a strong reaction from a lady who replied that "God created us in order to have a perfect sympathy from us as free beings." Another said, "The object of life is to obtain absolute freedom."

Margaret Fuller warmed to that thought and was asked about her own vision of freedom. She answered with a torrent of words that overwhelmed the stenographer, who noted that "she began with God as Spirit, Life so full as to create and love eternally... by becoming more ourselves... we attain to absolute freedom, we return to God... we become Gods, and able to give the life which we now feel ourselves able only to receive."[43]

Fuller divided her idea of absolute freedom in two parts. First was "the liberty of law," a condition of "independence of the encroachments of other men," which she also called "outward freedom" or "external freedom." Only then could one achieve the inward freedom that transcended rights and became "a sacred duty to become one's self" and "to be one with God," even "to become God." In that union one could achieve "a state of perfect freedom, pure love."[44]

In her writings, Margaret Fuller developed this idea of "perfect freedom, pure love" for "woman as much as for man" and for all humanity. Like much of Emerson's thought, it was a mystical idea that transcended reason and could never be translated into rational terms. But this was not another mystic fatalism. Margaret Fuller's vision of freedom was a call to action. Her thinking had a long reach in that way.

Margaret Fuller served this vision of "perfect freedom, pure love" all her life. After her death she became an icon of her own ideas for the generation that had known her as "sibyl and seer." Thoreau, who had a difficult relationship with her, journeyed to Fire Island and searched the surf for remains. He found a single coat button. Emerson published a glowing memoir, and Transcendental friends issued collections of her writings.

After their passing she drifted into obscurity for a time until she was rediscovered in the twentieth century. By 2001, there was a Margaret Fuller Society in Texas, a Margaret Fuller Home Page in Kentucky, a Margaret Fuller National Historic Site in Massachusetts, and an International Margaret Fuller Conference that met every year in Italy. Writings about her life and work poured from the presses: hundreds of volumes, thousands of papers, and 132,000 Web pages.

Most of this literature celebrates Margaret Fuller as a feminist, but Perry Miller reminds us that "her interest in women's rights was only a subordinate part of the most comprehensive program of nineteenth-century liberation. She was a great radical and so we should remember her." Her idea of "perfect freedom, pure love" embraced all humanity in a romantic vision of universal reform.[45]

Perhaps her greatest contribution came not through her writings but in the many lives she touched. Among the many women who attended Margaret Fuller's Parlatorio was Lydia Maria Child (1802–80), another "great radical" who developed the same large-spirited idea of "perfect freedom, pure love" in the antislavery movement. As a prolific writer and editor of the *National Anti-Slavery Standard* from 1841, Child led the abolitionist movement to a deep concern for the rights of former slaves. Her books and pamphlets argued for the integration of "Americans called Africans" in the life of the great republic. Her many causes were equal rights for all and equality of opportunity. Her antislavery appeals were written not in anger but love, the same idea of "perfect freedom, pure love." Margaret Fuller and Lydia Maria Child were two souls who vibrated on the same string.[46]

Another woman who attended Margaret Fuller's Parlatorio was Elizabeth Cady Stanton (1815–1902), who joined the antislavery movement, married abolitionist Henry Brewster Stanton, and went with him to the World's Anti-Slavery Convention in London in 1840. A transforming moment happened when she and the American Quaker Lucretia Mott were refused seats in that meeting, because of their sex. They decided to organize a Women's Rights Convention in the United States. The result was a gathering at the Wesleyan Methodist Church in Seneca Falls, New York. Elizabeth Stanton was the organizer of that event and author of its Declaration of Sentiments, which became another

Lydia Maria Child (1802–80), carte de visite photograph. Wayland Historical Society.

Elizabeth Cady Stanton (1815–1902), photograph.
Image donated by Corbis/Bettmann.

iconic text of liberty and freedom, on the model of the Declaration of Independence.[47]

Five generations of feminists have celebrated Stanton's radical leadership on women's rights and especially her work for women's suffrage. Against the judgment of her friend Lucretia Mott, Stanton included a demand for women's suffrage in the Declaration of Sentiments. She ran for Congress in 1866 and won twenty-four votes, then joined Susan B. Anthony in starting the journal *Revolution* (1868) and founded the National Woman Suffrage Association (1869).

Stanton also had a largeness of spirit that set her apart from some other feminists, and sometimes against them. While her friend Susan Anthony preferred to center her efforts on women's suffrage, Elizabeth Stanton took a broader view of women's lives and the human condition. She worked closely with her husband and other male reformers and combined her public role with private life as wife and mother of seven children. She actively supported other causes and founded the Women's Loyalty League to support the Union in the Civil War. Always she put the freedom of each individual above the interest of class or gender. That idea was the theme of her most widely admired work, "The Solitude of Self," with its celebration of "the individuality of each human soul." These women, Margaret Fuller, Lydia Maria Child, and Elizabeth Cady Stanton, shared the same feminist vision of liberty and freedom for all humanity. All were driven by the same dream of "perfect freedom, pure love."[48]

JOSEPH BRACKETT'S SONG

A Shaker Vision of Freedom as the Simple Gift

> 'Tis the gift to be simple, 'tis the gift to be free
> 'Tis the gift to come down where we ought to be.
>
> —JOSEPH BRACKETT, 1848

WHILE EMERSON was toiling in his study, and Thoreau was walking the woods with his long Indian stride, and Margaret Fuller was presiding over her Parlatorios, other American reformers were inventing many new ideas of liberty and freedom. Most were not part of the Transcendental circle, but they shared the same idealism, the same originality of thought, and the same idea that liberty and freedom were moral absolutes that reached far beyond the realm of law and politics.

One of the most creative visions came from the people called Shakers. American historians commonly link them to the great reform movements but not to liberty or freedom. A religious society that required its members to give up private property and live in close-ordered communities appeared the very opposite of what most Americans would understand as liberty or freedom. But the Shakers themselves believed that they had found a better way of living free.

Their American story might begin on May 19, 1780, long remembered in Yankee folklore as the "Dark Day." At high noon the sun vanished from the sky above New England and New York. The Dark Day was caused by forest fires, which shrouded the American Northeast in a pall of smoke so dark that birds went to roost and animals cried out in terror. Not knowing the cause, people fled to their churches, thinking that the Last Judgment had come.

On that very day a small immigrant sect of dissident English Quakers happened to be holding their first public testimony in the frontier village of Niskayuna, New York. They were called the Shaking Quakers from their form of worship, and they had not been flourishing in America. In 1780, nearly two-thirds of the congregations in the United States were Calvinists who kept the cruel creed of limited atonement, natural depravity, and predestination for God's elect. The Shaking Quakers had a different faith. They believed in "free grace, freedom from sin, and the coming end of the world." These ideas did not at first find a warm welcome in America, but new currents were stirring in the Revolution, and Calvinists were beginning to lose ground.[49]

Then came the Dark Day, and suddenly the Shakers began to make converts. Their matriarch, Mother Ann Lee, invited Americans "to live together, every day, as though it was the last day you had to live in this world." Some were drawn by her promise of salvation through free grace. Others were attracted by her ideas of celibacy and individual perfection. More than a few liked the Shakers' strong sense of community and delighted in their way of worship by "agitations . . . akin to a dance." Within a few years after the Dark Day their numbers grew to four thousand members in sixteen villages, mostly in New England.[50]

As they multiplied, many Shakers joined their faith to the culture of New England. Those elements came together to create an ethic of honesty, industry, austerity, and extreme simplicity. They also combined their

ideal of sharing with a reality of internal strife, a pattern painfully familiar to members of Protestant denominations and inhabitants of New England towns.[51]

This interplay of Shaker faith and Yankee folkways appeared in the life of Joseph Brackett, a great American character who was much loved by those who knew him. A lifelong resident of Maine, he was born in the town of Cumberland on May 6, 1797, and died at New Gloucester on the Fourth of July 1882. His portrait still hangs in the last surviving Shaker community at Sabbathday Lake.[52]

Joseph Brackett (1797–1882), photograph. Collection of the United Society of Shakers, Sabbathday Lake Shaker Community, Maine.

Like many Shakers, Joseph Brackett loved to write the songs and dances that became a form of worship and an instrument of community. Thousands of songs were composed in Shaker settlements. In 1848, Brackett himself wrote the one that is best remembered today. Many Americans know it by heart:

> 'Tis the gift to be simple, 'tis the gift to be free;
> 'Tis the gift to come down where we ought to be.
> And when we find ourselves in the place just right
> 'Twill be in the valley of love and delight.
>
> When true simplicity is gain'd
> To bow and to bend we shan't be ashamed
> To turn, turn will be our delight
> Till by turning, turning we come round right.

Joseph Brackett meant it to be a song for dancing, a "quick dance" as Shakers called it. Its lyrics describe the motions of bending and turning that were performed in unison. There are many accounts of Shakers "singing and jumping with very exact time. . . . every person jumped quite round but without moving out of the spot." Joseph Brackett was said to have danced to his own tune with his coattails flying.[53]

Brackett was asked how he came to write the song and answered that it came to him by divine inspiration. It centered on the Shaker idea of "the

Shaker Dance, watercolor by Benson Lossing. Huntington Library, San Marino, Calif.

gift," a theological doctrine of high complexity, inspired by the teachings of St. Paul and Mother Ann Lee. For Shakers a gift was a spiritual emanation from God, which could appear in many different forms. A gift could be a revelation, a power, a teaching, and sometimes a communal ritual. Like other Christians, they spoke of gifts of prophecy and faith. They also talked of their own special "whirling gift" and "shaking gift" that became their way of worship, and they celebrated Mother Ann Lee's "sweeping gift." Among Shakers a gift was also "a sense of divine direction." Joseph Brackett's quick dance was a gift song in all of those senses.[54]

At the same time, it was a song of freedom. For Joseph Brackett, the "gift to be free" had many meanings. It was the gift of free grace and eternal life, open to all who exercised the will to believe. It was also an idea of gaining freedom "in the world" by the Shaker method of stripping away useless possessions, and cultivating a simple life of high austerity. Yet another layer of meaning came from the communal ritual of the dance, which was a vision of freedom as the gift of belonging to a community of people who shared free grace.

Joseph Brackett's quick dance was also a song of simplicity. In that respect his Shaker vision was reinforced by New England ways. The founders of the Puritan colonies had cultivated an attitude that Max Weber called "worldly asceticism," an idea of living "in the world but not of it" and of freeing oneself from useless and needless encumbrances. Shakers converted this ascetic tradition into an aesthetic idea and carried it to a high level of development in their houses, furniture, and clothing. The beautiful austerity of these objects was not an end in itself but a means to the greater end of "freedom from the world" and "the gift to be free."

The simple melody of Joseph Brackett's song expressed this vision in a musical form that gave it great appeal. A leading historian of the Shaker experience finds evidence that it caught on quickly and became popular in their communities during the nineteenth century. By the early twentieth century it was discovered by people who were not Shakers, among them antique collectors Edward and Faith Andrews, who made many friends among Shakers in Maine. In 1940, Andrews published a book of Shaker tunes called *Simple Gifts*, with Joseph Brackett's quick dance as the title piece.[55]

The book passed into the hands of the American dancer Martha Graham, and she asked her friend Aaron Copland to compose an American ballet around it. Copland erroneously called the result *Appalachian Spring*. He was a cosmopolitan New Yorker, at home in London and Paris, but a little shaky on American geography beyond Manhattan. For this piece

Aaron Copland turned away from the cold dissonance and harsh cacophony of his European training and wrote a warm and happy American score with appealing harmony and a strong melodic line. His central theme was the melody of Joseph Brackett's "Simple Gifts," which appeared in the prologue to the ballet and was repeated in many variations. Martha Graham was delighted. She matched the music to dances of extreme simplicity, with an austere Shaker chair as her only prop.[56]

Appalachian Spring won a Pulitzer Prize and became so popular that Aaron Copland rewrote the music in many other forms, mostly centered on Brackett's melody. In 1970, folk singer Judy Collins began to sing the Shaker words of Joseph Brackett's dance song, and Americans discovered that it was a song of freedom. Its popularity continued to grow. Brackett's simple song began to be used in ways that would have amazed its creator. Detroit journalist David Crumm made a wonderful study of its career in the twentieth century. He described the use of "Simple Gifts" by the General Motors Corporation to promote an ill-fated luxury car called the Oldsmobile Aurora. Crumm writes, "The ad showed a driver floating through the galaxy while astronauts constructed his dream car to the strains of *Appalachian Spring*." A spokesman explained, "We wanted music that spoke to the grandeur, elegance and luxury of the vehicle. And we wanted something that inspired patriotism, because this was an American car going head-to-head with foreign luxury cars."[57]

Stranger things happened in the city of Washington, where the Shaker song was scored for military band and performed with ruffles and flourishes at the inaugurations of Ronald Reagan and Bill Clinton, before crowds of fund-raisers, lobbyists, and specialists in military procurement. These scenes might have set Joseph Brackett's coattails flying in more ways than one. But they did not define the meaning of his song. It belongs to the American people, and they understand it better than some of their leaders. The more complex their world becomes, the more relevance they find in his Shaker vision of freedom as a simple gift.[58]

'MOTHER ANN'S WORK'

"Simple Gifts," words and music for Joseph Brackett's quick dance, in Shaker notation; a 19th-century manuscript in Edward Deming Andrews, The People Called Shakers *(New York and Oxford, 1953), p. 173.*

SLAVERY ATTACKED

Liberty for the Enslaved, Freedom for the Emancipated

> Those who profess to favor freedom, and yet depre-
> cate agitation, are men who want crops without plow-
> ing up the ground, they want rain without thunder
> and lightning.
>
> —FREDERICK DOUGLASS

O F ALL the great reforms, the most urgent was the abolitionist movement. It also had the hardest task. By the nineteenth century, Americans had developed the largest and most profitable system of race slavery in the world. On the eve of the Civil War, returns to capital on southern plantations were greater than in northern factories. American slavery was growing rapidly, and it was the only large system of forced labor in modern history that expanded at a high rate by natural increase. By 1860, four million human chattels were the personal property of four hundred thousand masters and mistresses in the southern states. Many of the master class, and others who hoped to join them, were ready to fight and die for this "peculiar institution," which they defended in the name of southern honor, states' rights, and liberty to keep a slave.[59]

At the same time that slavery was flourishing in the southern states, Americans in the northern states created the world's largest and most dynamic antislavery movement. In 1860, nearly two million people in the northern and western states voted for candidates who condemned slavery and demanded an immediate end to its expansion. Many were deeply offended by the moral wrong of slavery. Some were ready to lay down their lives in the cause of abolition.

In 1861, these two great American forces, slavery and antislavery, met in a violent collision that shook the republic to its foundation. The result was the bloodiest war in American history, and something else that

274

Abraham Lincoln called a new birth of freedom. Each side claimed to be the true defender of liberty and freedom. Both deployed images that defined their visions of a free society. Specially interesting in that respect is the antislavery movement. For many generations it struggled to find a vision of liberty and freedom that could persuade others to join its cause. Much can be learned from its many failures, and ultimate success.

The first known English-speaking abolitionist in the New World was a Puritan named Samuel Rishworth, who took a strong stand against slavery in the colony of Providence Island as early as 1638. The first attempt to abolish slavery was a sweeping but short-lived law in Rhode Island and Providence Plantations in 1652. The first antislavery tract in English was Samuel Sewall's *The Selling of Joseph*, published at Boston in 1700. Sewall attacked slavery as a sin against God and defended liberty as a divine design for the world. Sewall wrote, "Forasmuch as Liberty is in real value next unto Life: None ought to part with it themselves, or deprive others of it, but upon the most mature Consideration." None of those early efforts succeeded. Samuel Rishworth failed to stop slavery in his colony, the Rhode Island law became a dead letter, and Sewall was

unable to win converts to his cause. One Boston slave-seller answered Sewall by publishing the first defense of slavery in British America. But in these early failures, slavery was on the moral defensive in the English-speaking world.[60]

In the eighteenth century, Quakers John Woolman and Anthony Benezet, and others such as Benjamin Lay, bore witness against slavery with appeals to the teachings of Christ, the Golden Rule, and an idea of reciprocal rights. The Quakers were the first to expand the antislavery cause into a double movement that sought liberty for slaves and freedom for the emancipated to share rights of membership in a free society. These arguments persuaded the Philadelphia Yearly Meeting to expel members who refused to free their slaves, but failed to win many converts beyond the Society of Friends.

The imagery of Puritan and Quaker

Benjamin Lay (ca. 1681–1759), lithograph by Sinclair after ca. 1760 engraving by Henry Dawkins. Society Collection, The Historical Society of Pennsylvania.

antislavery reflected its religious inspiration. Much of it centered on the souls of masters and slaves, rather than slavery itself. Some of it was about the souls of antislavery figures themselves. An iconic example is an engraving of Benjamin Lay, in which a slave nowhere appears. Mainly it centers on the conscience of the antislavery advocate, and the emblems of his faith and resolve.

During the Revolutionary era, another antislavery movement appeared among European and American *philosophes* such as Benjamin Franklin, Benjamin Rush, James Otis, and Thomas Jefferson. Its values were of the Enlightenment, its tone was secular, its spirit was at once neoclassical and romantic, and its arguments were humanitarian appeals to reason and emotion. Now the slave moved to the center. A leading symbol was Josiah Wedgwood's antislavery medallion of an African in chains, who reached out to others and asked, "Am I Not a Man and a Brother?" This image was invented in Britain and widely adopted in the American Republic. It centered on ideas of humanity, fraternity, and decency.[61]

Humanitarian antislavery had remarkable success in the United States. During and after the American Revolution, it succeeded in ending slavery in eight northern states and all the northwest territories between 1776 and 1800. These were not small victories. In Rhode Island and other northern communities, the relative size of the slave population approached the proportions of African Americans in the entire United States during the twentieth century. These were the first general emancipations in the world, and the foundation of the free states within the Union. Humanitarian antislavery also put a stop to the transatlantic slave traffic from Africa to the United States in eleven of thirteen states, and in 1807 by federal statute. It was unable to end bondage below the Mason-Dixon Line, but it failed in the largest slave states of Virginia and Maryland by a narrow margin.[62]

Within the southern states, enlightened masters attempted to end slavery in another way. They organized voluntary manumission societies and invited others to free their slaves by appeals to conscience. This

"Am I Not a Man and a Brother," Jasperware medallion by Josiah Wedgwood, ca. 1787. Photograph by Gavin Ashworth; courtesy Chipstone Foundation.

movement won over men such as George Washington, who freed all his slaves by his will, and Robert Carter, who emancipated one of Virginia's largest slaveholdings by an individual act. The most dramatic manumission was that of Edward Coles (1786–1868), who inherited a plantation and twenty slaves in Albemarle County, Virginia. In 1819, Coles sold his land and loaded his slaves into covered wagons without telling them their destination. He led them to the Ohio River, put them aboard flatboats, and explained his purpose only after they had left the southern shore. He later wrote, "I proclaimed in the shortest and fullest manner as possible, that they were no longer Slaves but free—as free as I was, and were at liberty to proceed with me, or go ashore at their pleasure." They stayed with him and went to a new settlement called Edwardsville, Illinois, where Coles gave each family 160 acres, and protected them from the rapacity of neighbors who did not share his philanthropy. Afterward, Coles was elected governor of Illinois and played a decisive role in defeating strong attempts to reintroduce slavery into the Old Northwest. This extraordinary event inspired many others, but most masters did not respond to the

"Slave Trade Abolished," colored mezzotint, published by T. Hinton, London, 1808. New York Public Library.

call of conscience. In the early republic, more slaves were born into bondage than released by manumission.[63]

In 1816, yet another antislavery movement was the American Colonization Society, which was founded to free slaves and return them to Africa. In its own time it had a large following. A large proportion of future abolitionists began as colonizationists. So also did free blacks such as Paul Cuffe, a New Bedford merchant who freed thirty-eight slaves out of his own pocket. The colonization movement attracted prominent political leaders of all parties, from Madison and Monroe to Lincoln and Grant. Altogether it succeeded in sending about fifteen thousand former slaves to Liberia, but it failed to make a difference in slavery itself. In the southern states, colonization was an advance toward liberty for the enslaved, but a retreat from freedom for the emancipated.[64]

All of these early forms of antislavery relied mainly on voluntary action. To that end they invented new forms of persuasion and created powerful antislavery images, but they failed to have much impact on a slave society in the southern states. That failure gave rise to a more militant form of antislavery, which drew heavily on radical reform and evangelical Christianity. One version flourished among western revivalists such as Theodore Weld, who indicted slavery as sin. In a book called *Slavery As It Is,* Weld drew upon advertisements of runaway slaves to create horrific images of physical cruelty: instruments of torture such as metal gags and head vises and cages; evidence of deep scars on a whipped slave's back and of maimings and slashed hamstrings and castrations that were meant to make slaves more "manageable"; accounts of slave quarters and slave clothing; descriptions of professional slave-catchers and slave-jailers and slave-breakers; brutal treatment of slave women; the abandonment of old and ill slaves whose suffering shattered the myth of paternalism.[65]

An even more extreme form of evangelical antislavery was a Manichaean movement led by William Lloyd Garrison, who demanded immediate emancipation of all slaves. He launched a bitter campaign of personal attacks on slaveowners, their allies in high office, and moderates who did not join him. Garrison also joined militant antislavery to other radical causes including feminism, anarchism, socialism, and pacifism. He demanded that the northern states should secede from a union with slaveholders. On the Fourth of July 1854, Garrison rose before an abolitionist meeting in Framingham, Massachusetts, gave a public reading from his Bible, then burned a copy of the U.S. Constitution, calling it a "covenant with death" and crying out, "So perish all compromises with tyranny."[66]

In thirty years, Garrison succeeded in attracting more attention to abolition than anyone else had done. He also shattered the antislavery movement, alienated potential supporters, disrupted its leading organizations, and sharply reduced membership in abolitionist societies from a peak in the 1830s. Garrison's tactics outraged many in the North and made slavery stronger in the South.[67]

The failure of Garrison persuaded other enemies of slavery to adopt different tactics. Many tried to persuade Americans of moderate and rational opinions to support an antislavery movement within the political system. This approach sought to demonstrate that slavery was not merely wrong in itself but also dangerous to the rights of free people in the United States. This theme had long appeared in the rhetoric of the antislavery movement, but in the 1830s it took a new and more urgent form. After the appearance of Garrison's *Liberator,* angry conservatives in the South and North increasingly invaded the fundamental rights of free citizens. A series of events dramatized this issue with growing clarity and force.[68]

The first was the Gag Rule. For many years, Congress had received many petitions against slavery and had routinely referred them to committees or allowed them to disappear quietly into legislative limbo. This was not enough for angry southerners. In 1836, they were able to pass a "Gag Resolution" in the House of Representatives, which ordered that petitions on slavery could not be printed or referred to committee and that "no further action whatever shall be had thereon." Congressman John Quincy Adams insisted that the Gag Rule was a "direct violation of the Constitution . . . of the rules of this house, and the rights of my constituents." Many northerners agreed. The Gag Rule caused a flood of petitions. Every year from 1836 to 1844, angry southern representatives and their northern friends defiantly reenacted the Gag Rule in even more stringent forms, which inspired yet more petitions. In Concord, Massachusetts, the first names on the petitions were Ralph Waldo Emerson and Henry David Thoreau, followed by most of their townsmen. Many moderate northerners joined this campaign. It inspired them to think of their own liberty and freedom as directly threatened by slavery.[69]

A more dramatic issue appeared in 1837, with the suffering of Elijah Lovejoy, a Presbyterian minister in Alton, Illinois, and editor of a religious newspaper that supported gradual emancipation. Proslavery mobs destroyed his printing presses three times, and a committee of leading citizens asked him to leave town. Lovejoy answered, "Is this not a free state? . . . Have I not a right to claim the protection of the laws?" He installed yet another press. The slavery mob attacked again, and Lovejoy was murdered.[70]

John Quincy Adams described the response as "an earthquake throughout the continent." An outpouring of speeches, pamphlets, and pictures identified abolition of slavery with the civil liberties of free people everywhere. One iconic image showed the classical goddess of liberty with a printing press and an inscription to the martyred memory of Elijah Lovejoy. In all of these events, slavery appeared not only as destructive of Africans in bondage but as a menace to everyone's rights. This linkage had two consequences. It broadened the base of the abolitionist movement and enlarged ideas of liberty and freedom.[71]

Yet another iconic event was the Fugitive Slave Act of 1850, which required citizens in the northern states to return runaway slaves. This was nothing new. The Constitution explicitly bound every state to return runaway slaves to their masters, and a Fugitive Slave Act was passed in 1793. But the new law showed little regard for civil liberties. It denied trial by jury to fugitives and refused to admit their testimony. The result was yet another linkage of slavery to the violation of civil liberties. Riots and rescues of fugitive slaves followed in New England, New York, Pennsylvania, Maryland, and the Old Northwest. These events had a powerful symbolic meaning. They brought the question of southern slavery into the northern free states.[72]

Ceramic plate, invoking the First Amendment to the Federal Constitution in defense of rights of abolitionists to speak and write against slavery. From the collection of Rex Stark; photograph by Gavin Stark; courtesy Ceramics in America.

Another effect of the Fugitive Slave Law was to inspire Harriet Beecher Stowe's antislavery novel, *Uncle Tom's Cabin*. First serialized in an antislavery newspaper, the *National Era*, in 1852, it became a bestseller with more than 1.2 million copies in print by 1853. Mrs. Stowe moved millions of readers with her intimate descriptions of the suffering that slavery afflicted on parents and children. The impact of the book appeared in accounts of Queen Victoria weeping over the fate of Uncle Tom, and in the writings of a bitter southern plantation mistress who confided bitterly to her diary, "Mrs. Stowe did not hit the sorest spot. She makes Legree a bachelor."[73]

Even more powerful was antislavery

speaking and writing by African slaves themselves. An iconic example was Henry Box Brown, who escaped from slavery in Virginia by mailing himself to Pennsylvania. He frequently appeared at abolitionist meetings with his shipping box, which became a symbol of individual effort by slaves to escape their bondage. More than four hundred other slave narratives were published before the Civil War, many with graphic scenes of slavery.[74]

The strongest voice was that of Frederick Douglass, a fugitive slave from Maryland who became a leader of the antislavery movement. He was also an icon of liberty and freedom. An example was a pair of dolls, made in or near New Bedford, Massachusetts, in the 1850s. One of them shows Frederick Douglass as a slave. The other shows him as a free man. Together they bring out the most powerful antislavery message: a double theme of liberty as emancipation from slavery and freedom as the right of former slaves to become full members of a free society.[75]

Abolitionists worked hard at developing this dual iconography of liberty and freedom. Their favorite emblem was Isaac Norris's great Quaker

Frederick Douglass (1817–95), a fugitive slave who became a journalist and leader of the antislavery movement. The author of an autobiography now recognized as a major work of American literature, in his own time he became a living symbol of liberty from bondage and freedom for former slaves to share in the civil rights of American society. Daguerreotype, ca. 1850. National Portrait Gallery, Smithsonian Institution.

A pair of cloth figures made by Cynthia Hill, ca. 1850–60. They represent Frederick Douglass as a slave and a free man and also show him as an American icon of liberty and freedom, even before the Civil War. Courtesy of the New Bedford Whaling Museum.

bell that promised to "proclaim liberty throughout all the land unto all the inhabitants thereof." The breadth of that universal idea of liberty made it a perfect symbol for the antislavery movement. It first appeared in 1839, when William Garrison's *Liberator* published a poem about the Quaker bell, which it began to call "the Liberty Bell," the first documented use of that name.

New England abolitionists Maria Weston Chapman and Lydia Maria Child published every year an anthology of antislavery writings called *The Liberty Bell*. From 1839 to 1846, each volume was bound in sturdy cloth with an elaborate gold-stamped iconography. In the center was a great Liberty Bell and two African Americans, one in the chains of slavery, the other kneeling to liberty. The editors introduced other iconic elements to this image. On top of the bell they added a pineapple, a popular American symbol of success, which frequently appeared on doorways, fences, and canopy beds. In the iconography of antislavery it became a symbol of inevitable triumph. The editors included another iconic element, a bell rope dangling from the crown of the Liberty Bell, with its lower end hanging loose for helping hands to grasp, a symbol of voluntary effort and the vital importance of individual participation in the antislavery movement.

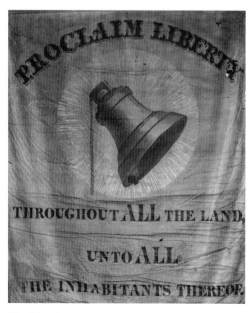

"Proclaim Liberty Throughout All the Land," antislavery banner. Massachusetts Historical Society.

Abolition quilt by Theresa Baldwin Hollander, ca. 1853, embroidered silk. Society for the Preservation of New England Antiquities, Boston.

Some of the annual *Liberty Bell* books also showed the Liberty Bell hanging from the Liberty Tree, nicely combining a folk emblem of Congregationalist New England with a symbol of the Quaker tradition. Another motif appeared as a frontispiece in the volumes for 1839 and 1840, which showed a female figure of liberty, surrounded by Africans in chains. Behind her was a bright light, and above was the motto "Truth shall make you free." Light was a common motif in a movement that was confident that truth and enlightenment were on its side.

Behind this iconography of the antislavery movement was a vision of freedom that sprang from Puritan and Quaker roots. It expanded in the Enlightenment and the American Revolution, found a broader meaning in the values of the American republic, and was reinforced the moral precepts of evangelical Christianity and the American revivals. The abolitionists drew upon images such as the Great Quaker Bell, and in the process they enlarged their meaning. The antislavery movement did not invent the name of the Liberty Bell, as some historians have written, but they popularized it and gave it a new purpose that it had not possessed before.

SLAVERY DEFENDED

Liberty for Slaveholders

> How is it that we hear the loudest yelps for liberty among the drivers of negroes?
>
> —Dr. Samuel Johnson, 1775

I N T H E Y E A R 1852, a Louisiana cotton farmer named Edwin Epps hired a Canadian carpenter named Samuel Bass to build a new plantation house. As the two men worked side by side, they fell into an argument over slavery.

"I tell you what it is, Epps," the carpenter began, "it's all wrong—all wrong, sir—there's no justice nor righteousness in it. . . . What *right* have you to your niggers when you come down to the point?"

"What *right!*" answered Epps with a laugh, "Why, I bought 'em and paid for 'em."

"Of *course* you did," said Bass. "The law says you have a right to hold a nigger, but . . . suppose they'd pass a law taking away your liberty and making you a slave?"

"Oh, that ain't a supposable case," replied Epps, laughing again. "Hope you don't compare me to a nigger, Bass."

"Well," said the carpenter, "no, not exactly. But . . . what is the difference, Epps, between a white man and a black one?"

"All the difference in the world," said Epps. "You might as well ask what the difference is between a white man and a baboon. Now I've seen one of them critters in Orleans that knowed just as much as any nigger I've got. You'd call them feller citizens, I s'pose," and laughed out loud at his own joke.

"Look here, Epps," said the carpenter, "you can't laugh me down that

284

way. Some men are witty, and some ain't so witty as they think they are. Now let me ask you a question. Are all men created free and equal as the Declaration of Independence holds they are?"

"Yes," said Epps. "But all men, niggers, and monkeys *ain't.*" He laughed again.[76]

Egalitarian Visions of Herrenvolk Democracy: Liberty for the Master Race

Many masters have invented rationales for slavery, but American slave-holders such as Edwin Epps did so in a peculiar way. They passionately defended slavery at the same time that many of them deeply believed in the doctrines of the Declaration of Independence. They began by justifying the keeping of slaves as an exercise of their own liberty. When Epps was challenged to defend slavery, he thought first of his property rights under the law. When he was asked to justify the law itself, he introduced the subject of race and his belief that slaves were incapable of liberty. Other ideas were often added. Southerners knew their Scripture and were well aware that slavery was justified in both Testaments: "especially commanded by God through Moses, and approved by Christ through his apostles," one of them said.[77]

This linkage of liberty, slavery, race, and religion was widely shared throughout the Old South, more widely than slavery itself. Many a poor white in the southern states accepted the institution of slavery, and some became enthusiastic defenders of slavery. But even as these attitudes were generally a part of southern culture, southerners were not of one mind on the subject.[78]

One way of thinking was that of Edwin Epps himself, who believed that all white men were created free and equal. William L. Yancey of Alabama declared to a Boston audience in 1860, "Your fathers and my fathers built this government on two ideas: the first is that the white race is the citizen, and the master race, and the white man is the equal of every other white man. The second idea is the Negro is the inferior race."[79]

Further, many southerners believed that race slavery was necessary to maintain liberty, equality, and democracy for whites. Governor Henry Wise of Virginia asserted, "Break down slavery, and you would with the same blow destroy the great democratic principle of equality among men."[80] A spokesman for this idea was J.D.B. DeBow, editor of *DeBow's Review,* the most widely read magazine in the South, who argued that the main benefit of slavery came to nonslaveholding southern whites.

DeBow was a self-made southerner who bought a few slaves after he made a success of himself by defending slavery. In a famous essay called *The Interest in Slavery of the Southern Nonslaveholder,* he wrote, "No white man at the South serves another as a body servant, to clean his boots, wait on his table, and perform the menial services of his household. . . . He is a companion and an equal."[81]

In the Old South, this vision was sometimes called "Athenian democracy," from the idea that the democratic constitution of Athens and the achievements of its citizens were made possible by an underclass of slave-helots.[82] In the twentieth century, sociologist Pierre van den Berghe called it "Herrenvolk Democracy," the democracy of the master race, after systems that developed in South Africa and the southern United States.[83]

The operative word was race. A new ideology of racism developed rapidly in the nineteenth century, with a novel "science" of cephalic indices and a theology of "polygenesis." To planters such as Edwin Epps, this way of thinking justified a system of slavery in which liberty was extended more fully to whites and denied more completely to blacks than in any other society. The linkage of liberty, race, and slavery changed the meaning of liberty itself. It became the southern dream of liberty as *laisser asservir,* the inalienable right of one person to enslave another of an inferior race. The logic of that idea carried its believers to extreme libertarian ideas of minimal government, maximal protection for private property, and autonomy for the individual slaveowner.

This idea always had its limits. The existence of slavery sometimes required the intervention of the state, but that happened rarely in the daily life of the Old South. Slavery was sustained mainly by private means. Masters had broad latitude in the discipline of slaves, and when they were unable to control "their people," private means were deployed to help them: the private slave jail that Nathan Bedford Forrest ran, or private slave-breakers, or entrepreneurial slave-catchers. The murder of slaves was prohibited, but even those laws were rarely enforced. Many narratives tell of masters who were so angry or alcoholic or sadistic that they killed their slaves and were punished only by the disapproval of their neighbors. The powers of state were mobilized only when all else failed, as in the suppression of Maroon communities after the Revolution and the War of 1812, the great Louisiana slave rebellions in the early republic (the greatest and least studied in American history), and Nat Turner's Rebellion in 1831. The prevailing culture of most southerners associated slavery with liberty, equality among whites, and minimal government.

Elitist Visions:
An Oligarchic Republic of Great Slaveowners

A very different way of linking slavery to liberty was shared among south-ern elites, who were few in numbers but large in power and wealth. A very small number of families owned most of the slaves and much of the land in the Old South. These elites existed in every southern state and were specially strong in the state of South Carolina. They did not believe in democracy or equality and rejected the Declaration of Independence outright. James Henry Hammond wrote, "I repudiate, as ridiculously absurd, that much lauded but nowhere accredited dogma of Mr. Jefferson, that 'all men are created equal.'" So also did Chancellor William Harper and John C. Calhoun, who wrote that "great and dangerous errors have their origin in the prevalent opinion that all men are born free and equal; than which nothing can be more unfounded and false."[84]

At the same time that they rejected democracy and equality, they believed deeply in republicanism and liberty—for a small elite. Harper wrote, "The love of liberty is a noble passion—to have the free uncon-trolled disposition of ourselves, our words and actions. But alas! It is one in which we know that a large portion of the human race can never be gratified."[85]

These men concluded that "inequality of condition" was "a necessary consequence of liberty" and "indispensable to progress." They favored government by an elite such as themselves and believed that democratic currents in the modern world threatened their hegemony. In 1860, South Carolina was the only state in the Union that did not choose its governor and presidential electors by popular vote. Slavery became a way of increasing the wealth and power of a ruling class and controlling the bal-ance of power among the free population. They insisted that slavery was necessary to preserve the liberty of the few and to protect the many who are incapable of exercising it. In that way they concluded, with Governor William McDuffie of South Carolina, that "slavery is the cornerstone of our republican edifice."

Patriarchical Visions: Justice without Liberty

A third defense of slavery came very close to rejecting outright ideas of liberty, equality, democracy, republicanism, capitalism, and an open soci-ety. It centered on a root-and-branch rejection of a liberal culture and cre-ated a vision of a slave plantation as a system of patriarchy in which father

"God bless yer, Missis." A southern answer: slaves as happy volunteers. Engraving from J. Thornton Randolph, Cabin and Parlor: or, Slaves and Masters *(Philadelphia, 1852). Virginia Historical Society.*

knew best. In some ways it was reminiscent of old works that justified absolute monarchy, such as Robert Filmer's *De Patriarcha* (1680). But it recast this theme in nineteenth-century terms and took many forms. Some of defenses of slavery consisted mainly of an attack on "the failure of a free society." The leading example was George Fitzhugh's *Cannibals All! or, Slaves Without Masters*, which drew heavily on Filmer, rejected Locke, the Glorious Revolution, the Enlightenment, the American Revolution, constitutionalism, and minimal government, and told Americans that "their liberty is merely a modification of slavery."[86]

Other patriarchical visions flourished in the Old South: theological elaborate writings by James Henley Thornwell, secular works by Henry Hughes and George Holmes, and in Zephaniah Kingsley's utopian ideal of the South as a patriarchical system of slavery without racism.[87] These visions of the proslavery right have fascinated academic writers on the American left, who share a common revulsion of liberalism and capitalism.[88]

The Descent of the Cotton Curtain: Slavery and Civil Liberties

The more that southerners tried to defend slavery, the greater their distance from the ways of a free society. Their attempts to reconcile slavery with liberty and freedom could not survive close criticism, as many southerners knew well. Judge Nathan Green said of slavery in 1858, "I have long considered it an evil. Until the last twenty-five years I never heard any well-informed Southern gentleman give expression to any contrary sentiments. About that time, Mr. Calhoun first announced the opinion that the institution was a desirable one. Now many southern men following Mr. Calhoun—and pressed by aggressive attacks from the North—hold the same opinion."[89]

Southern opponents of slavery fell silent after the events of 1831–32, when the publication of *The Liberator* and the rebellion of Nat Turner put an end to open debate. A few brave souls continued to speak against slavery: a Virginian named John Underwood attended the Republican National Convention in 1856, Professor Benjamin Hedrick kept talking against slavery in North Carolina, and a newspaper called *The Free South* kept publishing in Newport, Kentucky, as late as 1858. But Underwood was run out of his own home, Hedrick was forced to flee from his state, and the *Free South* office was wrecked by an angry mob.[90]

Southern ideas of liberty as the power to enslave could not coexist with a free press, or free speech, or open discussion. Southerners tried to stifle dissent by brute force and to shut down the flow of ideas from the North. In 1856, the *Richmond Examiner* raged against "Our Enemies, the Isms." The result was a Great Repression, which Clement Eaton has compared to the descent of a "cotton curtain" around the South. Increasingly the southern states became a closed society that seemed as threatening to northerners as slavery itself.[91]

TEXAS AND THE EXPANSION OF SLAVERY
Visions of Lone Star Liberty

> I consider the cause of Texas as the cause of freemen &
> of mankind.
>
> —STEPHEN F. AUSTIN, APRIL 19, 1836

JOHN C. CALHOUN spoke for many southerners when he declared that their peculiar institution must either grow or die. They watched with alarm as slavery began to shrink along its northern edges. In the early nineteenth century, it slowly disappeared from counties abutting the Mason-Dixon line. In Delaware, the proportion of African Americans who were slaves fell from 97 percent in 1770 to 8 percent by 1860.[92]

But at the same time that slavery lost Delaware, it gained Texas. This great expansion of slavery was done by design. Its leaders were two rival slaveholders, Stephen Austin (1793–1836) and Sam Houston (1793–1863). Both were born in the state of Virginia and moved to Mexico in search of land for their families and space for slavery to grow. The government of Mexico at first encouraged their settlement, but in 1829 the Mexican republic abolished slavery. In 1830 Austin and Houston led a movement for a separate state of Texas. Their purpose was to create a safe haven for a slaveholder's liberty.[93]

At the battle of San Jacinto, on April 21, 1836, the Texas army of Sam Houston defeated the Mexican army of Santa Anna on the west bank of the San Jacinto River, near Galveston Bay. One of the Texas banners was a liberty flag, which had been given to Sidney Sherman by the women of Newport, Kentucky. It is made of bright white silk, with gold fringe. It shows a young bare-breasted female figure of Liberty. In one hand she holds a long wand. With the other she aims a cavalry saber at the enemies of Texas. Draped across the blade of the sword is Patrick Henry's motto, "Liberty or Death." The flag still survives and was presented by the Sherman family to the people of Texas. Today it is proudly displayed in the Texas House of Representatives, behind the speaker's desk, as a sacred relic of the old Republic of Texas.[94]

The flag was carried on the field at San Jacinto by James A. Sylvester, another Kentuckian. Before he left for Texas, he attended a ball in his home state and asked his dancing partner for a memento. She "drew a long red glove from her arm and gave it to him." Before the battle, Sylvester put the red glove on the tip of his flagstaff. In place of the pileus of emancipation and the *bonnet rouge* of equality, he held high an emblem of the Old South with its legend of gauntlet and glove. It made a perfect symbol of southern liberty. In the fighting that followed, Sylvester was one of three men who captured the Mexican leader Santa Anna, but he lost his lady's glove, and it was never found again.[95]

The Flag of San Jacinto inspired many Texans. Daniel Cloud wrote, "Since Texas has unfurled the banner of Freedom, and commenced a warfare of liberty or death, our hearts have been enlisted in her behalf. . . . If we succeed, the country is ours, it is immense in extent and fertile in its soil. If we fail, death in the cause of liberty and humanity is not a cause for shuddering."[96]

Many other battle flags were carried by Texans in their war against Mexico. Their banners are a rich source of symbolism for a vision of liberty that was deeply rooted in the American past, but very different from other American beliefs in its own time. Many were lone star flags. The standard of Captain William Scott's company at the battle of Concepción shows a lone star on a blue field, with one word, "Independence." The Lone Star Flag that is the present state banner of Texas appeared as early as 1839. Others were explicitly liberty flags. The Goliad Flag showed a lone star with Patrick Henry's Motto, "Liberty or Death." A blue flag that was hoisted over the Alamo by the first company of Texas Volunteers from New Orleans displayed a spread eagle with a motto in its beak: "God and Liberty."[97]

The San Jacinto battle flag, 1836, an icon of liberty displayed in the Texas State House, Austin. Courtesy of the State Preservation Board, Austin, Texas; photograph by Fonda Thompson.

These flags celebrated a world of violence and struggle. One of the most striking is a flag carried by Captain William Brown's Texas Company at the siege of San Antonio in 1835. It has thirteen red and white stripes and a blue field, but instead of the stars or even a lone star it shows a strong arm with a bowie knife, dripping blood on the shoulder of the man that holds it. Inscribed on the stripes is a one-word motto: "Independence." Another flag was flown by a Texas garrison at Gonzales in 1835. They had earlier borrowed a cannon from the Mexican government, and the Mexicans demanded its return. The flag is white with an image of the cannon, the lone star again, and the motto "Come and Take It."

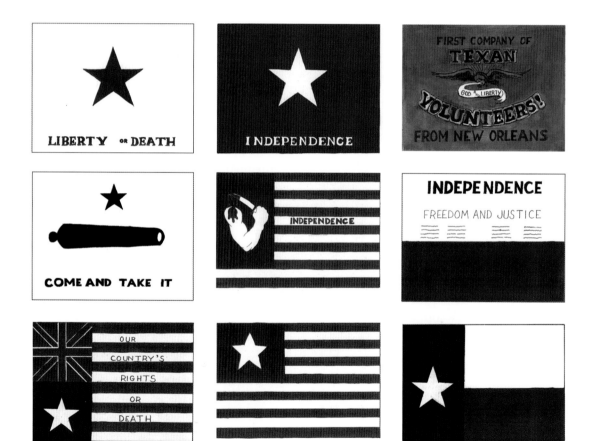

In the Texas War of Independence, many battle flags communicated distinctive visions of Lone Star liberty. Among them, top left to bottom right: the "Liberty or Death Flag" of Ward's battalion; the Independence Flag of Scott's Liberales; the spread eagle "God and Liberty Flag" of the First Company of Texan Volunteers from New Orleans; the defiant "Come and Take it" Gonzales Banner of 1835; Brown's Flag of Independence, with a brawny arm and blood-soaked bowie knife; the Fredonian Rebellion Flag of "Independence, Freedom and Justice"; Captain Baker's Flag that proclaimed "our country's rights or death"; the striped naval ensign of the Texas Republic; and the Lone Star Flag of the Texas Republic. From Charles E. Gilbert, Flags of Texas *(Gretna, La., 1989); reproduced by permission of the publisher.*

After the Mexicans attacked and were driven off, the flag entered Texas folklore as "Old Come and Take It."[98]

Most of these flags were carried by men who had been born and raised in the southern highlands and the Mississippi Valley. Their idea of liberty was closely akin to the backcountry images of the American Revolution, and they were fighting for a vision of natural liberty as independence, the right to practice slavery wherever they pleased, and the survival of the strongest.

The battle of San Jacinto ended in the defeat of the Mexican army, the capture of Santa Anna, and a treaty in which the president of Mexico was forced to agree to the independence of Texas. The Texas Republic moved quickly to proclaim liberty and slavery, two causes that became one in Texas minds. After annexation by the United States, Texans practiced slavery on an ever larger scale, until they were conquered by northern armies in the Civil War and forced to stop, much against their will. But the Texas idea of Lone Star Liberty survived long after the Civil War.

Its symbol is a huge sculpture that stands atop the statehouse in Austin, the "Texas Goddess of Liberty." She has a grim, masculine, belli-cose appearance and holds a sword in her hand. In place of the wand and pileus or an uplifted torch, she holds high the lone star of liberty. The statue was cast of "white bronze" (zinc), and Texas schoolchildren are made to memorize her statistics. She weighs three thousand pounds and stands fifteen feet, seven and a half inches tall. Texans brag that her height makes their state capitol taller than the U.S. Capitol in Washing-ton. Yankees are not convinced.[99]

When this statue was erected in 1888, the Civil War had come and gone. Slavery was formally abolished, later in Texas than any other state. But the old Texas idea of Lone Star Liberty flourishes even in our own time. It is one of the most strongly held visions of liberty in the United States, an uncompromising idea of individual liberty and minimal government.

Lone Star Liberty is a utopian vision of a world with low taxes, inactive regulators, and minimal restraints of law. It thinks of life as struggle and celebrates the survival of the strongest. Texans combine a Darwinian idea of how the world works with a fundamentalist idea of how the world began. They identify with winners in every field of endeavor and have little sympathy for losers. They preserve a custom of unstinting hospitality with an unforgiving creed of *lex talionis,* the rule of retaliation against any wrong. They believe in the right to life, but not for evildoers. Texans pride themselves on thinking big and serving large purposes. They have the largest state in "the lower forty-eight" and the weakest government. Many (not all) still share a vision of Lone Star Liberty, even to our own time.

THE CONTAINMENT OF SLAVERY
The Visions of the New Republican Party

Free Soil, Free Speech, Free Men, Free Labor, Free
Kansas, Frémont

—REPUBLICAN PARTY SLOGANS, 1856

AFTER THE MEXICAN WAR, the expansion of slavery became
the great polarizing question in the American republic. One by
one, the great national institutions began to break apart on sectional lines during the 1840s and 1850s. The churches, sadly, were among
the first to divide. The Baptists split on sectional lines in 1843, Methodists
in 1844, New School Presbyterians in 1847, and Old School Presbyterians
in 1861. Education became more sectional. Southern youths stayed home
for their schooling, and those who had gone to northern colleges were
summoned home after John Brown's raid on Harper's Ferry. Southern
colleges of liberal arts became military academies. The American economy also became more sectional. Two railroad systems developed in
the North and South, with only a few tenuous linkages between them
by 1860.

National leaders desperately tried to hold political parties together by
adopting omnibus symbols of American liberty and freedom. In the presidential election of 1844, Democratic candidates Polk and Dallas promised to "Enlarge the Boundaries of Freedom," in a spirit that embraced
both Oregon and Texas. Their Whig rivals, Henry Clay and Theodore
Freylinghuysen, championed a national vision of "Liberty and Union."
But a small group in the North took the name of the Liberty Party and
promised to stop the expansion of slavery. It won only 2.3 percent of the
vote, but that was enough to determine the winner, by shifting the bal-

ance from Clay to Polk in the pivotal state of New York. Ironically, the antislavery Liberty Party caused the election of a slaveholding president, who led the nation into the Mexican War, expanded the territory for slavery, and created the issue that led to the Civil War.

Four years later, the election of 1848 was another three-cornered struggle. This time a new third party called itself the Free Soil Ticket. It nominated Martin Van Buren and Charles Francis Adams, and its campaign badges carried mottos such as "Free Soil, Free Speech," and "Vote the Land Free." Democrats Lewis Cass and William Butler stood for "Liberty, Equality & Fraternity, the Cardinal Principles of True Democracy." The Whigs tried to reach both northern and southern voters by nominating a military hero of the Mexican War, Zachary Taylor, whose campaign avoided references to liberty and freedom, which were becoming bitterly contested concepts. He won the election for the Whigs with safe slogans such as "Neither Faction nor Party nor Individual Interest, but the Common Welfare of every Man in the Union."[100]

In 1852, both major parties tried desperately to escape the sectional question. Whigs attempted to repeat their success with another military man, General Winfield Scott. Democrats called their candidate General Franklin Pierce. Both avoided sectional images, but the free soil issue would not go away. It shattered the Whig Party, and nobody could put the pieces back together again.

Then came an attempt by southern Democrats and their northern ally Stephen Douglas to repeal the ban on slavery in the lands of the Louisiana Purchase. The reaction of the northern states to the Kansas-Nebraska Act in 1854 was much like the response of the colonies to the Stamp Act in 1765. A great wave of anger spread across the country. The same symbols of liberty and freedom were deployed, and the same rituals were reenacted. Liberty Poles rose once more on Broadway in New York City, and Liberty Trees returned to fashion in New England. Stephen Douglas was hanged in effigy, much as Andrew Oliver had been. Douglas said, "I could travel from Boston to Chicago by the light of my own effigy. All along the Western Reserve of Ohio I could find my effigy upon every tree we passed."[101]

The Republican Party was born of this event. In public meetings throughout the North, Republicans borrowed the old mottos of the Liberty Party and the Free Soil Party and created a new American idea of liberty and freedom. In 1856, it was summarized in campaign slogans that rang through the North: Free Soil, Free Speech, Free Labor, Free Press, Frémont. Each of these simple terms held a new vision of a free America.

THE UNION

SHALL BE PRESERVED.

COL. FREMONT,

Free Speech! Free Men!!
Free Kansas!

STAND
FOR THE
RIGHT.

FREEMEN!
REMEMBER
NOVEMBER 4th 1856.

Here was another new vision of liberty and freedom in the founding of the Republican Party—a campaign ribbon for John C. Frémont, the first Republican nominee for the presidency (1856). Collection of David J. and Janice L. Frent.

"Free Soil" promised an end to the expansion of slavery, and an "empire of freedom" from the Mississippi to the Pacific. More than that, free soil meant that slavery would have no room to grow and therefore would die. It also entailed a political revolution. If it succeeded, the "Slave Power" would inevitably shrink to a minority that could no longer elect a president, control a Congress, or dominate the Supreme Court.

"Free Labor" was the vision of work without bondage. For some it was an idea of untrammeled industrial capitalism. For others, including Abraham Lincoln, it meant that "labor is prior to, and independent of capital." For most who used that phrase, it meant that all free and honest labor was equally honorable. Free labor meant no slaveholding class who lived on the toil of others.[102]

"Free Speech" meant an open society where civil liberties were respected, and also open discussion, which promised to speed the end of slavery. Republicans believed that slavery could not live in the light and survived only in a dark regime of tyranny and repression that was dominant in the southern states. Free speech was about liberties for the press, debate, petition, and assembly, which the southern states were opposing.

"Free Men" meant civil rights for citizens and voters, and an idea that all people were entitled to rights in a free society. It meant that no freeman could be denied citizenship, as Dred Scott had been, by slaveholding justices on the Supreme Court. It also meant Homestead Acts, and free schools, and federal aid to education, which southern voters had blocked.

"Frémont" meant "vote Republican." The man himself was born and raised in the South, a Democrat and a Roman Catholic, and an odd choice for a Republican standard-bearer. But Frémont was a hero of the

Mexican War and a man of the Great West. He was chosen to broaden the appeal of the Republican ticket and to enlarge its vision of freedom by separating the Republican Party from the Native American movement. Always he was a symbol, more than a leader. Sometimes his name was written FreeMont. Another element was added to his campaign. Republican banners proclaimed, "Free Soil, Free Speech, Free Labor, and Eternal Progression," making freedom and liberty into a teleological idea and an optimistic vision of inevitable progress.

The Democratic candidate, James Buchanan, had nothing to compare with this broad vision of a free America. He ran two different campaigns, above and below the Mason-Dixon line. In the North he claimed the legacy of "Jackson and Liberty." In the South, Buchanan's backers printed angry ribbons that showed fugitive slaves running to the Rocky Mountains, and added the sarcastic slogan, "Frémont! Free Niggers!" This political iconography was something very rare in American politics. In 1856, Buchanan Democrats in the South were one of the few major political parties in American history to campaign against liberty and freedom.

Buchanan won the election of 1856, but without a majority of the popular vote. He carried every state below the Potomac but only five states in the North. Victory came to him because northern voters divided between the antislavery Republicans and the anti-immigration Native American Party. The election of 1856 was a dark omen for southern slaveholders. The national Whig Party was gone, the Democrats could not compete in the North, the demographic balance in the nation was shifting to the free states, and sectional lines were hardening.

In 1856, Democratic nominee James Buchanan ran two different campaigns. Above the Mason-Dixon line his slogan was "Jackson and Liberty." In the slaveholding South his supporters distributed angry ribbons that attacked the Republican Party, appealed openly to race hatred, and reviled "free niggers." This was one of the few elections in American history in which a major political party attacked liberty and freedom. Corbis/Bettmann; collection of David J. and Janice L. Frent.

CONTESTED IMAGES OF THE CAPITOL DOME

Freedom Triumphant or Armed Liberty?

> Mr. Davis says that he does not like the cap of liberty
> introduced into the composition. That American lib-
> erty is original and not the liberty of the freed slave.
>
> —Secretary of War Jefferson Davis to
> northern sculptor Thomas Crawford

T HE RISE OF the Republican Party caused a surge in southern militancy. Even small questions flared into sectional conflicts. A case in point was a symbolic controversy that suddenly erupted at Washington in 1855. The construction of the Capitol was entering its final stage. Ironically, at a moment when the sectional crisis was threatening to tear the republic apart, a huge iron dome began to rise above the Houses of Congress as a symbol of national union.[103]

All parties agreed that the Capitol dome should be crowned with a monument to liberty and freedom. The commission went to Thomas Crawford, a talented young Irish American sculptor. He had been born in New York during the War of 1812, married Louisa Ward, the sister of Julia Ward Howe, and entered a circle of Yankee reformers who were strongly hostile to slavery.[104]

Crawford proposed to crown the Capitol with a colossal female figure, nearly twenty feet tall, which he called "Freedom Triumphant in War and Peace." His preliminary sketches showed a female figure with a short sword in one hand and a long olive branch in the other. Around the base were wreaths, which the artist explained as "indicative of the rewards Freedom is ready to bestow upon distinction in the arts and sciences."

When Crawford submitted his design, the supervisor of construction for the Capitol was Secretary of War Jefferson Davis, a graduate of West Point, hero of the Mexican War, Mississippi slaveholder, and militant spokesman for southern rights. Jefferson Davis was not happy with Crawford's image of "Freedom Triumphant in War and Peace." It looked weak to his southern eyes. There was too much peace about it. He demanded a more bellicose symbol.[105]

Four months later Crawford delivered a second design, called "Armed Liberty." The classical female figure became muscular and militant. In one hand she held a naked sword. With the other she grasped the shield of the republic and a laurel wreath for a nation that had never lost a war. The olive branch of peace disappeared. Instead of rising from emblems of the arts and sciences, she bestrode the globe in a posture of triumph.

She was very close to Jefferson Davis's ideas in every way but one. On her head the artist placed a crown of stars "to indicate her heavenly origin." Above the crown he added a liberty cap, the old Roman symbol of an emancipated slave. It seemed a direct affront to a militant slaveholder, and Jefferson Davis exploded with rage. The northern sculptor and the southern slaveholder had already clashed over a liberty cap in the interior decoration of the Capitol. He sent his aide, Captain Montgomery Meigs, with peremptory orders to remove the Roman pileus. Davis wrote that "its history renders it inappropriate to a people who were born free and would not be enslaved."[106]

Jefferson Davis knew exactly what he wanted: a vision of liberty not as an emancipated slave but as a warrior who had been born free. In a drawing class at West Point he had done a sketch of Minerva, the Roman goddess of war and wisdom, wearing a soldier's helmet. Crawford was ordered that "armed liberty should wear a helmet." Davis also insisted that an acceptable symbol of liberty should be more American in its motif and was not to be associated with radical symbols of the French Revolution or Roman emancipation.

The sculptor did as he was told. He replaced the liberty cap with a helmet of distinctly American design. Its crest was "composed of an Eagle's head and a bold arrangement of feathers suggested by the costume of our Indian tribes." He also remodeled the female figure to make her yet more militant and less feminine, with thick wrists and a bull neck. He also

A war of images for the Capitol dome: northern sculptor Thomas Crawford's "Freedom Triumphant in Peace and War." Engraving, 1855. Library of Congress.

A slaveholding secretary of war, Jefferson Davis, demanded a figure of "Armed Liberty" and ordered the removal of a liberty cap because it was associated with emancipation in ancient Rome. Photograph. Office of the Architect of the Capitol, Washington, D.C.

covered her classical drapery in what looked to be an Indian robe and brutally carved the initials "U.S.A." into her breasts. One wonders if this was the sculptor's revenge.[107]

Jefferson Davis approved this version and ordered it cast in bronze. The colossal statue was many years in the making. Eric Foner tells of an irony in its construction. The final version was cast in Rome, but it was so big that had it to be shipped in pieces, for assembly in America. When it arrived, only one man in the Washington area could put it together. He was Philip Reed of Bladensburg, a highly skilled metalworker who was himself a slave.[108]

There was yet another irony in this tale. The casting and assembly of the statue was a work of many years. The statue was finally installed and dedicated on December 2, 1863, after the Emancipation Proclamations and the great Union victories at Vicksburg and Gettysburg. It was deliberately turned to the South, "rebukingly toward Virginia" and the failed Confederacy that was led to defeat by Jefferson Davis.[109] The figure of "Armed Liberty" that a militant slaveholder had demanded became an emblem of conquest over a slaveholder's rebellion. The Civil War transformed it from Jefferson Davis's "Armed Liberty" to the northern sculptor's original vision of "Freedom Triumphant in War and Peace." Today, after many vicissitudes, Thomas Crawford's statue still stands on top of the Capitol dome, wearing the peculiar costume that was designed to placate a defender of slavery, but with a new meaning that nobody could have imagined in 1855.

THE PRESIDENTIAL ELECTION OF 1860

Four Visions of a Free Republic

> Lincoln and Hamlin—say you shan't; Breckinridge and Long—say shall; Douglas and Johnson—say as you please; and Bell and Everett—say nothing!
>
> —FOUR POSITIONS ON SLAVERY
> IN A POLITICAL JINGLE OF 1860

I N T H E S P R I N G O F 1860, the nation moved closer to disunion. The Democratic Party came apart in a convention at Charleston, and the Republicans found unity on an antislavery platform in Chicago. "What do you think of matters now?" one disconsolate southern Unionist asked another. Alexander Hamilton Stephens replied, "Why that men will be cutting one another's throats in a little while. In less than twelve months we shall be in a war, and that the bloodiest in history."[110]

The mood of the country was heavy with foreboding as four political parties took the field in 1860. All of them nominated candidates of high principle who stood for liberty and freedom, but their visions of a free republic were farther apart than ever. All spoke also of honor. Much has been written of southern honor, but there were northern versions of that idea, and both made it difficult for the parties to resolve their differences. The campaigns of 1860 revealed the visions of liberty and freedom that divided them, and also the principles of honor that kept them apart.[111]

John Bell and Constitutional Rights: The Cause of Public Liberty

The first candidates in the field led a coalition of moderate conservatives who called themselves the Constitutional Union Party. Their man for president was John Bell, a wealthy Tennessee slaveowner and a founder of

In 1860, the Constitutional Union Party stood for the old republic and the middle way: "Bell, Everett, Union and Liberty." Tennessee State Museum.

the old Whig Party. He had supported the great compromises and was the only southerner in Congress to vote against the Kansas-Nebraska Act. His running mate was Edward Everett of Massachusetts. They did not agree on slavery but shared a common horror of secession, which John Bell condemned as neither a right nor a remedy. Their convention in an old Baltimore church displayed many symbols of liberty and freedom as national ideas. Reporter Murat Halstead observed "a full length painting of Washington, surmounted by an American eagle," and the walls were "covered with an assortment of star spangled banners."[112]

Their platform had a single plank: "the Constitution, the Union and the enforcement of the laws," which they called "the great principles of public liberty and national safety." This was public liberty in the literal meaning of *res publica*, the things of the republic. These men were deeply attached to a civic ideal, to the old republic that they loved, and to a principle of honor as fidelity to the Constitution. They ran a dignified campaign, with carefully worded slogans such as "John Bell and the Constitution; Edward Everett and the Union." Many of their contemporaries despised them as the "Old Gentlemen's Party," but they found strong support among moderate voters in the upper South and lower North, who shared their vision of liberty and freedom as constitutional rights under the old republic.[113]

Breckinridge and Southern Rights

John C. Breckinridge, the presidential nominee of southern Democrats, was the youngest candidate in the field, thirty-nine years old. Baron de Rothschild met him in 1860 and described him as "a young man, charming, full of fire, intelligent, and, what is rare, a perfect gentleman."[114] He was a Kentuckian, much liked even by his opponents, and a living symbol of southern honor. Abraham Lincoln was his friend and said, "I was fond of John, and regret that he sided with the South."[115]

Breckinridge was the sitting vice president in 1860. He refused to run an electioneering campaign and stood for office in the old-fashioned way, making no speeches after he accepted the nomination. But earlier speeches made his position very clear. He was not a secessionist in 1860 and spoke strongly in support of the Union, but in a southern states'-rights way. In accepting the nomination, he declared," The Constitution and the equality of the states! These are the symbols of everlasting Union." At the same time he was outspoken for strict construction of the Constitution, limited government, "states' rights," "southern rights," and absolute protection of "personal property rights" in slaves and anything else. He also opposed "negro equality" and warned that if the Republicans did not relent on these issues, the result would be disunion. Here was a heartfelt idea of the Constitution and Union that protected hegemonic liberty for white southerners.[116]

Southern Breckinridge Democrats demanded liberty to enslave others: "Our Country and Our Rights" and "No Submission to the North." Collection of David J. and Janice L. Frent.

If Breckinridge was not a secessionist in 1860, every secessionist was a Breckinridge man, and they joined the campaign with symbolic politics of their own. The slogans of his supporters were "No Submission to the North" and "Our Country and Our Rights." In the Deep South, Breckinridge men organized military organizations called Minute Men, heavily armed and dressed in uniforms of gray homespun. They used brute force to suppress any sign of sympathy for the Republican Party. In New Orleans, a vendor of campaign badges displayed his stock, which happened to include a Lincoln-Hamlin badge. A crowd of Breckinridge supporters turned into a lynch mob and chased him down Royal Street, shouting, "Hang him! Hang him!" This idea of southern liberty and states' rights did not include the right of dissent within the South.[117]

Douglas and Popular Rights:
The Cause of "Democracy Liberty"

The most prominent candidate in 1860 was Stephen Douglas of the National Democratic Party. He has been much misunderstood as a "pragmatist in politics" and a man of "dim moral perceptions," even "morally deaf" in the judgment of one very hostile historian. Douglas had strong ethical principles and was faithful to them all his life. "I am a radical & progressive democrat," he wrote in 1852. He believed deeply in an idea of "popular rights" and what he called "the cause of Democracy Liberty," a phrase peculiar to himself. His idea of "popular sovereignty" spanned his entire career.[118]

Douglas was a strong nationalist and a leader of Young America, a romantic movement similar to Young Italy, Young Ireland, Young Russia, Young Germany, Young England, Young Dalmatia, and others throughout the Western world in his generation. Douglas believed in a strong nation but a weak national government. He thought that the American people were destined to dominate the Western Hemisphere and that governments should get out of their way. He had little interest in civil liberties and regarded those of different opinions as "traitors."[119]

He was also a strict constructionist, a factor in his attitude toward slavery. Douglas regarded slavery as "a curse beyond computation to both white and black." But he added, "We exist as a nation by virtue of the Constitution and under that there is no way to abolish it."[120] Douglas was strongly racist, and many of his followers were even more racist in the campaign. In Ohio one man remembered that in 1860 "a favorite democratic exhibition was a large wagon, drawn by six white horses. On the wagon were young girls, dressed in white, bearing banners—'White Husbands or None.' On one occasion the daughter of a prominent Republican was on one of those wagons. The father got crazy. He jumped on the wagon and by force dragged her off. A fight followed but she did not continue in the parade."[121]

Stephen Douglas had a vision of what he called "Liberty Democracy": "Vox Populi," "Popular Sovereignty," "Intervention Is Disunion," and "MYOB" [Mind Your Own Business]." This "donut" ferrotype from the election of 1860 shows Douglas on the front and his running mate, Hershel V. Johnson, on the reverse. Collection of David J. and Janice L. Frent.

Douglas conducted his politics according to his democratic creed. "I live with my constituents," he wrote, "eat with my constituents, drink with them, lodge with them, pray with them laugh, hunt, dance, and work with them; I eat their corn dodgers and fried bacon and sleep two in a bed with them." He believed that a politician should "adapt his laws to the wants, conditions and interests of the people to be governed by them." His campaign was an expression of his democratic principles. In 1860, two of his slogans were "Vox Populi" and "Popular Sovereignty." An important Douglas theme was summarized in another slogan: "Intervention is Disunion, 1860/ MYOB [Mind Your Own Business]."[122]

Douglas was the only candidate in 1860 who campaigned actively in every part of the United States and tried to reach the people in every region. He spent much of his time in the South, speaking actively against secession with a courage and conviction that impressed his opponents but did not win their votes. An historian highly critical of his career, Allan Nevins, writes that his attempt to dissuade the southern people from disunion was his finest hour. Honor for him meant fidelity to his democratic principles.

Lincoln and Equal Rights

Abraham Lincoln, fifty-one years old, campaigned very actively throughout the northern states for more than a year, but he was not on the ballot in most of the southern states. In many speeches he made a few simple points over and over again. Some had never been said before by a presidential candidate: that "Negroes have a share in the Declaration of Independence,"[123] that the great question was "slavery or freedom," that slavery was "morally wrong" and freedom was the "eternal right,"[124] that he would not interfere with slavery in states where it existed but would stop its expansion. Lincoln had no sympathy for southern slaveholders. "They say they are tired of slavery agitation," he declared. "We think the slaves, and free white laboring men, too have more reason to be tired of slavery." But he pledged to obey the Constitution and to execute the laws, even the fugitive slave laws. He broke with his fellow Republicans on these questions. "I agree with Seward in his 'Irrepressible Conflict,'" Lincoln wrote, "but I do not endorse his 'Higher Law' doctrine."[125]

Many of Lincoln's supporters were more militant. They invented a new style of symbolic politics in their Wide Awake Clubs, which first appeared in Hartford, spread rapidly through the North, and filled southern slaveholders with alarm. The Wide Awakes were able-bodied men of

Abraham Lincoln and his Republican Wide Awakes: a vision of freedom as equal rights. Harper's Weekly, October 13, 1860. Virginia Historical Society.

military age. One western detachment consisted entirely of men six feet, four inches tall, which was Lincoln's estimate of his own stature. They mustered in military formations, and Ulysses Grant served as their drill-master in Illinois. They marched at night with massive coal oil torches and dressed in glistening black oilskin capes and military kepis to protect their clothing. In northern cities the Wide Awakes rallied in huge numbers. They turned Broadway into "a river of flame" and Boston Common into "a sea of light." Signs and transparencies proclaimed their ideals with mottos such as "Lincoln and Liberty Forever" and "Free Speech, Free Homes, Free Territory." One Wide Awake banner in Chicago showed an all-seeing eye with the slogan "Union, Liberty and Honor." Honor was as important to these men as to southerners, but in a different way.

The torchlight marches of the Wide Awakes sent a spasm of fear through the South. So also did the rhetoric of Republican candidates. Charles Sumner promised to surround slavery with "a ring of fire." Reports of arson multiplied in the South and were attributed to slaves and "Black Republicans." The sight of thousands of Wide Awakes in shiny black capes and kepis with burning torches in their hands was the South's worst nightmare. It was a vision of the slaveholder's apocalypse.[126]

The candidate promised not to interfere with the domestic institutions of the southern states. But some of the Lincoln imagery sent a different message to the southern states.

When the votes were counted in the presidential election of 1860, Bell and the Constitutional Unionists carried Virginia, Kentucky, and Tennessee and won 13 percent of the popular vote. Breckinridge swept the lower South but took only 18 percent of the popular vote, a measure of how small was the base of secession in the Republic. Douglas won 30 percent of the popular vote but carried only Missouri and three electors in New Jersey. He ran a weak second in the North and a distant third in most southern states. Abraham Lincoln received only 39.8 percent of the popular ballot; more than 60 percent of Americans voted against him. But he swept every electoral vote in the North except three in New Jersey. It was enough to make him president, even though he lost every electoral vote in the South.

In one state, no popular ballots were cast for president. South Carolina's electors were selected by state legislators who had already resolved that a "Black Republican" could never be their president. "It is the loss of liberty, property, home, country—everything that makes life worth having," commented the *Charleston Mercury*. Even before the presidential electors met, the slaveholders of South Carolina left the Union to preserve their idea of liberty.[127]

A political image unique in American history was this Lincoln-head percussion rifle, ca. 1863, by Hiram Berdan. Winchester Arms Collection, Buffalo Bill Historical Center, Cody, Wy.

SOUTHERN LIBERTY AND INDEPENDENCE

Robert Barnwell Rhett and the Secession of South Carolina

Southern Civilization. . . . separate and free.

—ROBERT BARNWELL RHETT

T HE EPICENTER of southern secession was South Carolina, the only American state where most white families owned black slaves in 1860. From an early date in the eighteenth century, free South Carolinians were staunch defenders of slavery and states' rights. Their defense of what Calhoun called the "peculiar institution" inspired some highly particular images of liberty.

South Carolinians combined old symbols of the Revolutionary War with new emblems of the War for Southern Independence. This process of invention continued from 1846 to 1861. The most important of their new emblems was invented during the Mexican War. For many southerners the purpose of that conflict was to win more land for slavery. The people of South Carolina were quick to raise a military unit for service in Mexico and called it the Palmetto Regiment. Its emblem was the palmetto tree, a graceful fan palm of distinctive appearance that is native to the Carolina coast. Each company in the regiment was given a flag that bore the silhouette of a palmetto against a field of Carolina blue. These banners were carried into battle at Contreras and Cherubusco. One of them was said to have been the first U.S. flag flown over Mexico City in 1846. Another, the palmetto flag of Edgefield County's Company D, is still proudly displayed in the state capital of Columbia, South Carolina.[128]

After the Mexican War, South Carolinians led a movement for southern autonomy, or even independence. An emblem was needed for their

cause, something that represented the symbolic union of
a principle and a place. In
1851, a solution was found by a
new secessionist newspaper
called *The Palmetto Flag*. On
its masthead it displayed a
banner that combined three
symbols in a single design.
The banner itself was white.
Its canton was the old Fort

*The secessionist movement
in South Carolina used a
combination of old symbols
to communicate a new
vision of liberty for slaveholders: the rattlesnake, a
lone star, and the Palmetto
Tree. Textile. Benjamin and
Susan Shapell Foundation.*

Moultrie flag from the American Revolution, a blue field with a white
crescent. In the center of the flag was a Carolina palmetto tree, with a rattlesnake coiled dangerously around the trunk. The design united lowcountry and upcountry emblems of liberty and independence.

Immediately after the election of Abraham Lincoln, a secession convention met in Charleston's Institute Hall and voted unanimously to
leave the Union. In the streets outside the hall, palmetto emblems were
invoked as symbols of the secessionist cause. Young men of Charleston
wore blue cockades and plaited palmetto leaves in their lapels.

Inside the hall, the ordinance of disunion was signed beneath a great
iconic "banner of secession" that was meant to represent a new southern
republic. In the center of the secession banner was the palmetto tree with
a coiled rattlesnake. Above the tree was a triumphal arch of fifteen stone
blocks, to represent the fifteen slave states. The keystone of the arch was
South Carolina, sagging dangerously beneath a massive marble monu-

*An old symbol was given
new life in this secessionist
serpent and its motto.
Museum of the Confederacy.*

A South Carolina secession banner, 1860. South Carolina Historical Society, Charleston.

ment to John C. Calhoun. Below the arch was a pile of rubble that represented the disintegration of the old Union. The design included two defiant secessionist cannon that were aimed in the general direction of New England and the Old Northwest.[129]

Four days after the act of secession, a resolution was introduced in the South Carolina legislature for a "distinguishing ensign or flag" of "sovereignty and independence." Many designs were suggested. One was called the "sovereignty flag of South Carolina." It was a red banner with a blue cross of St. George and fifteen white stars for the southern states. In the upper corner was a palmetto tree and a white crescent. On January 20, 1861, this flag was raised in the unlikely setting of New Haven, Connecticut, by Yale undergraduates who sympathized with the South. The sight of a Carolina secession banner flying above the crenellated tower of Yale's Alumni Hall caused a campus riot and spread the fame of the sovereignty flag throughout the world. But it never caught on in South Carolina, perhaps because its many elements blurred its symbolic meaning.[130]

Another state legislator suggested a blood-red flag with a green palmetto tree. This design was strongly resisted. The red flag smacked of revolutionary radicalism, which was far from the politics of South Carolina. A member of the legislature also objected that the green palmetto would fade in the strong southern light to a cowardly yellow. The blood-red flag with a green-yellow palmetto tree as a symbol of secession was lost for the want of a second.

The winning idea for a South Carolina sovereignty flag came from secessionist leader Robert Barnwell Rhett. His lowcountry family had a flair for the invention of tradition. It had changed its name from Smith to Rhett to present a more romantic image to the world and embraced the mystique of Carolina culture with an enthusiasm that belied its bourgeois origins in, of all places, the hated Yankee state of Massachusetts.

Young Barnwell Rhett studied the problem of a Carolina banner and invented a simple flag with a white palmetto tree and a white crescent on a deep blue field. His design had the merit of symbolic economy. It neatly linked the old Fort Moultrie flag of the American Revolution with the palmetto flag of the Mexican War.

The legislature rapidly approved Rhett's design as the state flag of South Carolina. As copies began to be made, an error was introduced by accident in the design of the crescent. The Carolina flag statute called explicitly for Colonel Moultrie's right-facing increscent, a heraldic emblem with many meanings—among others, a symbol of success. In the manufacture of the flag, this emblem was inadvertently changed, and a confusion of crescents continued through the Civil War. Some Carolina flags displayed a left-facing decrescent, an emblem of decline—not at all what southern fireaters such as Barnwell Rhett had in mind. Others used a horizontal crescent with upraised horns, the "honourable ordinary." Its use in the Crusades made it an emblem of heroic courage in the face of defeat.

The display of this Carolina Secession Flag at Yale caused a riot in New Haven, Connecticut. Harper's Weekly, *1861.*

With these unlucky changes, Barnwell Rhett's design became the state flag of secessionist South Carolina. It flew above the Confederate batteries that fired the first shots of the Civil War at Fort Sumter in 1861. Today, it remains the state's official banner. The original increscent has been restored, and it flies above a southern state that is more prosperous than ever and fiercely proud of its leading role in secession and the Civil War.

THE CIVIL WAR AS A CLASH OF SYMBOLS
Liberty and Independence Against Freedom and Union

Freedom and Union

—MOTTO ON VERMONT'S STATE SEAL

Let us alone

—SLOGAN ON A DESIGN FOR
FLORIDA'S STATE FLAG

THE WORLD REMEMBERS the American Civil War as a struggle between liberty and slavery. It began in another way, as a conflict between irreconcilable visions of liberty and freedom. Both sides used the same words, but in different combinations with distinct meanings. Abraham Lincoln observed in 1864, "The shepherd drives the wolf from the sheep's throat, for which the sheep thanks the shepherd as a liberator, while the wolf denounces him for the same act as the destroyer of liberty.... Plainly the sheep and the wolf are not agreed upon the definition of the word liberty."[131]

Confederate leaders always insisted that they were fighting for liberty or freedom and used both words more or less interchangeably to mean a condition of independence and autonomy. "Our cause is just and holy," President Jefferson Davis declared in 1861. "We will continue to struggle for our own inherent right to freedom, independence and self-government." In the same spirit, General Robert E. Lee issued a general order to his army: "Let each man resolve to be victorious, and that the right of self-government, liberty and peace shall in him find a defender."[132]

Inside the South, this Confederate idea of liberty was not for everyone. The master class had many liberties. Slaves had none. Southern liberty and freedom implied inequality. Alexander Hamilton Stephens, vice president of the Confederacy, told a meeting of Savannah's leading citizens in 1861, "Our new government...rests upon the great truth that the

312

negro is not equal to the white man; that slavery, subordination to the superior race, is his natural and moral condition." Many Confederates agreed with Stephens that ideas of liberty in the old Union were "fundamentally wrong," in that "they rested upon an assumption of the equality of races" and "were attempting to make things equal which the Creator had made unequal."[133]

When northerners explained why they were fighting, they also used liberty and freedom interchangeably but coupled them with another word: union. In that association, these words came to imply an idea of belonging and an equality of rights and obligations among those who belonged to the union. This northern way of thinking resembled ancient European traditions of *Freiheit* in its idea of freedom as a connection to other free people. But it was no longer a tribal idea. Now it referred to a nation.

These northern and southern visions had emerged long before the first shots were fired. One can observe them in symbols that were chosen by states above and below the Mason-Dixon line. In 1845, Florida was admitted as a slave state. A design for its first flag included the national stars and stripes in the canton at the upper corner and five bands in brilliant colors. The most striking element was its motto in capitals: "LET US ALONE!"[134]

In 1846, Iowa became a free state. Its first state seal and the flags that followed showed an American eagle and other national emblems, with the image of an ordinary citizen, and the motto, "Our liberties we prize; our rights we will maintain." Here was a vision of liberty and freedom that stressed universal rights in union with others. Many states above and below the Mason-Dixon line showed the same contrast. The state seal of Vermont in 1777 struck a New England note: in the center was a tree and the motto "Freedom & Unity." In the same year the slave state of Delaware preferred the motto "Liberty and Independence."[135]

 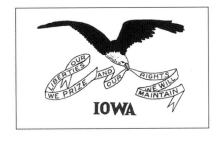

Different visions of liberty and freedom appeared in proposed flags for the slave state of Florida in 1845, with the motto "Let us alone," and the free state of Iowa in 1846, with the slogan "Our liberties we prize; our rights we will maintain." Courtesy of Whitney Smith, © 2003 Flag Research Center.

During the Civil War, both sides developed new versions of those old ideas. Northerners expanded their ideas of freedom and union into a universal principle. Southern notions of liberty and independence went the other way. They became more exclusive in terms of race, rank, and region. As the war continued, both sides became acutely aware of the growing distance between them. Abraham Lincoln wrote in 1864, "We all declare for liberty; but in using the same word we do not all mean the same thing. With some, the word liberty may mean for each man to do as he pleases with himself, and the product of his labor; while with others the same word may mean for some men to do as they please with other men, and the product of other men's labor. Here are two, not only different, but incompatible things, called by the same name—liberty."[136]

Visions of liberty and freedom made a difference in the conduct of the war. The North was at first deeply divided by the radical implications of its cause. As the war went on, many people rallied to its expanding principles of union and universal rights. Others in the world were inspired by the long reach of these large ideas.

Supporters of the Confederacy were at first united by their passion for secession, but as the struggle continued their idea of liberty as independence became disruptive of the southern cause. Some turned this principle against the Confederacy itself. Others demanded privileges for themselves that they denied to others. Southern liberty became a divisive idea that weakened the Confederacy in its internal cohesion and external appeal. In the end, the South was defeated not merely by material difficulties but by the moral weakness of its cause.

To communicate competing ideas of liberty and freedom, both sides made heavy use of symbols. Old emblems were put to work, and new ones were invented in great variety: new flags and badges, new songs and slogans, new iconic leaders and emblematic events, new images of the past and intimations of the future. The visions that were awakened by the Civil War retained their power long after the fighting ended. Some are still with us today.

EMBLEMS OF THE SOUTHERN CAUSE

A Plurality of State Symbols

Noli me tangere
Independent Now and Forever

—MOTTOS ON ALABAMA FLAGS

THE SLAVEHOLDING STATES of the Confederacy revived many emblems of liberty and combined them with new symbols of their cause. The first flag of Confederate Alabama was a case in point. The front of Alabama's flag showed a goddess of liberty with bright blond hair and a flowing scarlet gown. In one hand she carried a naked sword. In the other she held a banner with a lone star that said "Alabama." Over her blond hair was a bright golden motto, "Independent Now and Forever."

The back of the flag was interesting in its iconography. It showed a lush green cotton plant with many fertile blossoms and bolls. Emerging from the foliage was a rattlesnake, erect and poised as if to strike. Beneath was the Latin motto *Noli me tangere,* which might be translated "Touch me not," or loosely "Don't tread on me." Here in the southern highlands was an updated, modernized, romanticized, slaveholding version of the old backcountry rattlesnake banner of liberty.[137]

The Ancient Dominion, as always, went its own way. For many months, Virginia held back from the brink of secession. But when President Lincoln called for armed volunteers, Virginians met on April 17, 1861, and voted to leave the Union rather than holding it together by force, which was thought to be an act of tyranny.

On April 30, 1861, Virginians adopted a state banner as an emblem of sovereignty and a symbol of their cause. Its color was true blue, the same as the Bonnie Blue Flag. But in place of the lone star, the state of Virginia preferred a highly refined classical symbol of a female figure, wearing the ancient Phrygian cap of liberty and independence. This was not the conventional goddess in a long flowing robe. In 1861, Virginians represented liberty as an Amazon warrior, with a bared breast and a blue military kilt. This fighting lady carried a spear in one hand and a sword in the other. She stood in triumph over a fallen tyrant, her foot planted on his lifeless chest, and his crown in the dust. Beneath the figure was the explanatory motto *Sic semper tyrannis*, "thus always for tyrants."[138]

This motif was adapted from Virginia's Revolutionary seal, with several changes. *Otium* and even *perseverando* had disappeared entirely. What

Many symbols of southern liberty and independence appeared in flags of the slaveholding states. Top left to bottom right: A South Carolina flag in 1861 with the old crescent, palmetto, blue cross, white stars and red field; the South Carolina crescent and palmetto flag; the Virginia state flag of resistance to tyranny; in the southern backcountry, an early Alabama lone star flag and another Alabama flag with a blond goddess of liberty on the obverse; and on the reverse of the same flag, a snake emerging from a cotton patch with the Latin motto "Noli me tangere," which might be translated freely as "Don't tread on me." A Mississippi flag combined the lone star of independence with a magnolia tree, and a North Carolina flag linked sucession in 1861 to the Mecklenberg Declaration of Independence in 1775. Louisiana favored the pelican as its symbol. These flags are drawn from Devereux D. Cannon, Jr., Flags of the Confederacy (1994), with the permission of the Pelican Publishing Company, Gretna, La.

remained was a militant idea of liberty, linked to a rule of retributive justice. The motto *Sic semper tyrannis* meant that the stain of tyranny must always be expiated by the destruction of the tyrant. This ancient rule was called by the Romans *lex talionis,* the law of retaliation. In the American South it was more than merely a rhetorical flourish, as the world learned to its horror in 1865, when a fanatical southern sympathizer assassinated Abraham Lincoln in the hour of the nation's triumph. John Wilkes Booth shot the president, leaped to the stage, and shouted to the assembled crowd, "Sic semper tyrannis!" Some in the audience thought he also said, "The South is avenged."

The cry of John Wilkes Booth is remembered as a theatrical gesture. It was more than that. Before the fatal act, Booth left a letter with his brother-in-law. "People of the North," he wrote, "to hate tyranny, to love liberty and justice, to strike at wrong and oppression, was the teaching of our fathers." Here was a Manichaean idea of liberty and tyranny, with liberty as independence and justice as retribution against the tyrant. It was an idea that John Wilkes Booth had inherited from his forebears and that was widely shared in the South.[139]

In 1861, southerners also searched for a symbol of the entire Confederacy. A Confederate seal was designed to bring out a large theme of liberty. It quickly inspired mock Confederate seals, which centered on the cruel and selfish hypocrisy of a slaveowner's cry for liberty: a contradiction that dogged the Confederacy throughout its short life.

Another task was to agree on a Confederate flag. Popular opinion favored a simple blue flag with a large white star in the center. This was the lone star of liberty—an emblem of independence, separation, and apartness that had been used by three secessionist movements in the American South.

The Lone Star of Liberty first appeared in the West Florida Revolution of 1810, when English-speaking inhabitants in the panhandle of that province seceded from Spanish East Florida. They issued a Declaration of Independence and demanded to be annexed by the United States, which on October 10, 1810, Virginia-born President James Madison was happy to do. The flag of the West Florida Revolution was a single white star on a blue field.

A similar flag was used again after 1836 when Texas seceded from Mexico. It came to be called the "Lone Star Flag" and became the banner of the independent republic of Texas. After Texas entered the Union, it adopted the lone star as its state flag. It is widely flown today as a defiant emblem of liberty as autonomy, in a spirit that is still very strong in the "Lone Star State."[140]

When the state of Mississippi left the union in 1861, its convention also adopted the lone star flag as a symbol of sovereignty, secession, liberty, and independence. Later, Mississippians designed another flag, which showed a magnolia in "natural colors," blazoned on a white background. The lone star remained on a blue canton in the upper hoist, with a vertical red stripe along the fly.

The symbolism of the lone star spread swiftly through the South. In 1861, Florida, Mississippi, Alabama, Louisiana, and Texas all adopted lone star flags as an emblem of independence. When the Civil War began, the lone star flag was also adopted unofficially as the banner of the Confederacy itself. Part of its popularity came from a song called the "The Bonnie Blue Flag," written by an Irish actor named Harry McCarthy in 1861. The first performance of the song was in New Orleans. The audience were men from Texas and Louisiana, who responded with what was called "a riot of joy."

Before the war began, lone star flags also became the unofficial banner of the Confederacy itself. One of the first was called the States' Rights Flag, a red star on a white field. It flew over public buildings in Columbia, South Carolina.[141] More popular was a simple blue flag with a large white star in the center, the Bonnie Blue Flag of southern legend. The flag became very popular throughout the Southern states, and its colors were thought to symbolize southern liberty. During the Civil War, this historian's great-grandfather, then a small boy in Baltimore, was taken for a stroll in a suit of blue satin, with many white and blue rosettes. Federal troops who occupied the city sent him home, with orders to remain there until a small red center was sewn on each rosette as a symbol of Union.[142]

After much discussion, on March 4, 1861, the Confederate Congress adopted an official flag, a blue canton with a circle of seven stars and three broad horizontal bars, red over white over red. It was called the Stars and Bars and was soon flying throughout the South. Its display caused one of the first acts of deadly violence in the war.

On May 24, 1861, the day after Virginia seceded, Abraham Lincoln looked south from the White House and saw the Stars and Bars flying defiantly over a hotel in Alexandria. He called it an insult. With him was Colonel Elmer Ellsworth, a dashing young officer and a personal friend of the president. Ellsworth had recruited a regiment from the New York City Fire Department and dressed them in red and blue zouave uniforms. For northern reporters, Colonel Ellsworth and his Fire Zouaves were good copy, and they were much in the news. The President ordered Ellsworth and his Fire Zouaves to occupy Alexandria. They stormed the hotel and cut down the Confederate flag. The hotel's proprietor, a hot-blooded Virginian named James Jackson, was so infuriated that he attacked them single-handed, killed Colonel Ellsworth at close range, and was put to death by the Zouaves.[143]

Political ceramics in the northern states commemorated the death of Colonel Elmer Ellsworth, ca. 1861, and expressed contempt for the flags of the Confederacy, even to printing them on the bottom of spittoons. Similar attitudes of contempt appeared in the Confederacy against symbols of the Union cause. Charles F. Gunther Collection, Chicago Historical Society.

The event caused a sensation and gave each side a flag martyr. Colonel Ellsworth's body lay in state at the White House, and the president himself was among the mourners. The corpse was carried to New York by a special funeral train. Poets mourned Ellsworth's loss; towns and babies were named Ellsworth from downeast Maine to the Old Northwest. The South also gained a hero in the martyred hotelkeeper Mr. James Jackson. Flags were lowered to half-mast throughout the Confederacy. The Stars and Bars had been washed in the blood of a patriot and became a sacred symbol of southern liberty and honor.

Even as the Stars and Bars became an emblem of the southern cause, its design never gave general satisfaction in the Confederacy. In the first big battle at Manassas, southern soldiers discovered that the Stars and Bars were impossible to distinguish at a distance from the Stars and Stripes. Both armies suffered losses from "friendly fire," partly because their flags looked so much alike. Northern troops protested that Confederates deliberately fought under Federal colors to mislead their opponents. It wasn't so, but southerners were stung by this insult to their honor.

After much discussion General Pierre G. T. Beauregard and several Confederate congressmen designed a new Confederate banner: a small red square with a blue cross of St. Andrew, and a white star for every state that should have joined the Confederacy. Three prototypes were stitched together by the Cary sisters of Virginia: Constance, Hettie, and Jennie, who became heroines in the South. The fabric was said to have come from their dresses.

Thus was born the battle flag of the Confederacy. First reactions were not uniformly favorable. A Confederate congressman complained that the star-studded cross of St. Andrew looked like the backside of a brace of suspenders. But the army was pleased with the design. Its square shape was instantly distinguishable from the rectangular American flag. Its cross of St. Andrew, the Scottish national emblem, also found favor with the many southerners of North British and Scots-Irish descent, who were a large part of the Confederate population and a larger part of its fighting men. In September 1861, General Joseph Johnston ordered that the new Confederate battle flag should be issued to every regiment in the Army of Northern Virginia. The ladies of the South rustled through their wardrobes for silks of a suitable color and got busy with their needles. By November 1861, the new battle flags were carried by Confederate military units in the East.

In the Army of Northern Virginia the design was elaborately standardized. Battle flags were to be four feet square for infantry, three feet for artillery, and thirty inches for cavalry. For added visibility, the edges of the battle flag were given a colored border, at first bright yellow. Later the border was changed to orange, and after Chancellorsville to white or an incongruous shocking pink.[144]

Confederate armies in the West were less orderly in their flag discipline, as in other things. Some bid defiance to regulations and carried battle flags of their own invention. Several units in Missouri preferred an upright Christian cross. Others in Polk's Army of the Tennessee favored a horizontal cross of St George. Richard Taylor's command in western Louisiana accepted the Confederate cross of St. Andrew, but with colors reversed. Some of Earl Van Dorn's trans-Mississippi troops who had migrated from South Carolina added a white crescent to a field of stars.

The battle flags of the Confederacy were made at home by southern women, who presented them to regiments in solemn ceremonies that were heavy with symbolism.[145] They were entrusted to chosen color bearers, an assignment that combined high honor with low prospects for survival. The colors made a rallying point for each regiment and an aiming point for the enemy. At Antietam, the First Texas lost eight color bearers in one day. At Gettysburg, the Twenty-sixth North Carolina lost fourteen. Bell Wiley writes that "most units had similar tales to tell." But such was the honor of carrying the colors that volunteers stepped forward, even in the face of certain death.[146]

Each Confederate regiment was authorized to paint its battle honors on its colors. As the list of battles grew longer, the colors of veteran regiments became so ripped and torn by shot and shell that they resembled pieces of old lace. A special aura surrounded these sacred emblems. The Confederate battle flag began to be called the Southern Cross. In 1863 it became the canton of a new Confederate flag, with a pure white field, called the Stainless Banner. It was an icon of enormous power. These two flags became leading symbols of all the things that southerners were fighting for, and one thing most of all: their vision of southern liberty as independence. They were also emblems of honor, blood, and sacrifice, which gave an old idea of liberty new meaning in southern hearts. Even its most implacable northern foes were moved by the courage and devotion that they inspired.

The most powerful symbols of the Southern cause were the flags of the Confederacy. They drew heavily upon lone star motifs of liberty as independence, the example of the stars and stripes, and the Scottish cross of St. Andrew in areas where much of the free population came from the borderlands of North Britain. Top left to bottom right: the unofficial "Bonnie Blue Flag," which was popular at the start of the war; the Stars and Bars, which were officially adopted on March 4, 1861; the Scottish Cross of St. Andrew, which with colors reversed became a Confederate battle flag in East Tennessee; the flag proposal of the Joint Committee on Flag and Seal, April 19, 1862; the square Confederate Battle Flag issued in November 1861 and later called the Southern Cross; the Battle Flag of Bishop General Leonidas Polk's Corps in the Army of Tennessee; the rectangular Battle Flag of the Army of Tennessee, 1864; the official flag of the Confederacy, May 1, 1863 to March 4, 1865, called the Stainless Banner; and the last official flag of the Confederacy, adopted March 4, 1865. From Devereaux D. Cannon, Jr., The Flags of the Confederacy *(1994), with permission of the Pelican Publishing Company, Gretna, Louisiana.*

NORTHERN VISIONS OF FREEDOM & UNION

New Meanings for the Eagle, Old Glory, and Uncle Sam

Did a man ever fight for a holier cause,
Than Freedom and Flag, and Equal Laws?

—NORTHERN RALLYING CRY

THE NORTH also searched for emblems of its sacred cause, and found them in the old American symbols. The eagle, the Stars and Stripes, and Uncle Sam were all enlisted in the northern war effort. In the process these old symbols took on a new meaning during the Civil War. They were linked to large ideas of national union and universal freedom. At the same time, they became the particular property of the northern cause and the Republican Party.

The American flag was the most important of these emblems. It acquired new significance in northern hearts when infuriated southerners went out of their way to revile it by ingenious insults of their own invention. In 1861, a party of secessionists in Murfreesboro, Tennessee, covered a ballroom floor with American flags and danced merrily upon them as a gesture of contempt that was bitterly resented above the Mason-Dixon Line. The Confederates of Memphis staged a flag burial of the Stars and Stripes. The citizens of Liberty, Mississippi, organized a ritual flag-burning on May 10, 1861, in a ceremony that may have been the first deliberate provocation of its kind.[147]

Southern insults to the Stars and Stripes awakened a passionate devotion to the flag throughout the North. Angry crowds compelled merchants and householders of doubtful loyalty to fly the banner of freedom or risk destruction of their property. National flags were blazoned with patriotic mottos, Republican Party slogans, and electioneering rhetoric.

Each northern regiment was sent to war with its own set of national and regimental flags. They were called "the colors" and had many important military functions. Regimental encampments were laid out around a "color line." On the march, units were trained to "guide on the colors." In battle, every regiment aligned its long fighting ranks on its colors, which marked the tactical center of its position. Many armies observed the ritual of the trooping of the colors, in which the flags were carried slowly past every man in the regiment, so that all would become familiar with them and could rally round the flags in the confusion of combat. Battles in the Civil War often became fierce melees around the colors. To capture the enemy's flag was a feat of high valor. To lose one's colors was a regiment's deepest disgrace.

The regimental flags were carried by two color sergeants and protected by a color guard of eight to ten corporals, specially selected for skill, size, and military bearing. The position to the right of the flag in the line of battle belonged to the color company, a post of honor and responsibility that was given as a reward of merit. The size and strength of the color guard and color companies were testaments to the importance of the flag on the field.

In February 1862, the Union Army authorized every regiment to inscribe its national flag with "the names of battles in which they have borne a meritorious part." As the war went on, the names of many great and terrible battles were written in white and red on the stripes of union. The banners themselves came to be called Old Glory. That name had first appeared thirty years before the Civil War. It is thought to have been coined in 1831 by William Driver, a Yankee ship captain in the South Pacific, who carried some survivors of HMS *Bounty* from Tahiti to Pitcairn Island. His passengers presented him with a new American flag for his ship. As Captain Driver hoisted it he said, "I name thee Old Glory."[148]

The Civil War gave Old Glory a new meaning in its association with the terrible losses of the men who carried it into battle. It also became a symbol of the

An image of freedom and union in the northern states: a polychromed wood drum made by William Bridget of Belfast, Maine. Collection of Michael and Pat Del Castello.

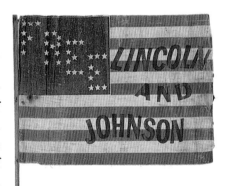

The American Flag took on new meaning in the Civil War. An example was this Republican election banner in the 1864. The names of Abraham Lincoln and the war Democrat Andrew Johnson were overprinted on the stripes. The stars were arranged to spell the word "Free," thus joining a vision of freedom and union to the Republican party and the northern war effort. Collection of David J. and Janice L. Frent.

Republican idea of an indissoluble union. The national colors carried by blue-clad regiments had at least thirty-four stars for all the northern and southern states, a symbol of their determination to restore the republic. A popular design promoted that idea by the arrangement of the stars. One of the most popular designs grouped the stars in tight concentric circles or ovals, which became another symbol of union. Another combined the thirty-four stars into one large star. Poet George Pope Morris captured the sentiment in a stanza that continues to echo in American culture:

> *A song for our banner! The watchword recall*
> *Which gave the Republic her station:*
> *United we stand, divided we fall!*
> *It made and preserves us a nation!* [149]

The American eagle also took on new meaning in the Civil War. After President Lincoln's call for volunteers, eagles multiplied throughout the northern states. They appeared on flags, drums, banners, broadsides, pamphlets, prints, and newspapers. Artists gave them many forms: screaming eagles, spread eagles, soaring eagles, diving eagles, and perched eagles. Some were highly articulated. Others were simple folk images. They carried a complex iconography of sovereignty and nationality, courage and sacrifice, freedom and union, and eternal vigilance in the protection of human rights.

This new meaning was explained by Mrs. Josephine Wilcox, who helped make a unit flag for the Fourth Michigan Volunteers. When the regiment received its colors on June 21, 1861, Mrs. Wilcox gave a speech on what she called "the eagle of American liberty." She told the assembled regiment, "The eagle of American Liberty from her mountain eyrie has at intervals during the past few years given us faint warnings of danger. Now she swoops down on spreading pins with unmistakable notes of alarm; her cries have reached the ears of freemen and brave men rush to arms. She has perched on this banner which we now give to your keeping." [150]

The emblem became so popular that several Union regiments adopted live eagles as mascots. The most renowned of these warbirds was Old Abe of the Eighth Wisconsin Volunteers. [151] The regiment made him a portable perch with small American flags at each end and carried him on parade. At one regimental review, Old Abe became so excited by the crowds that he let out an unearthly scream and took one of the little flags in his beak, to the delight of his keepers. The men of the Eighth Wisconsin began to call themselves the Eagle Regiment. When they marched south to war they carried Old Abe along. He caused a sensation in

The Union Eagle, Old Abe, was the mascot of 8th Regiment of Wisconsin Volunteers, ca. 1863. Wisconsin Historical Society.

Chicago and started a riot in St. Louis when a mob of spectators tried to get a view of him.

The Army forbade mascots to be taken into battle, but the Eighth Wisconsin defied that rule, and many war stories began to be told about Old Abe. In the fight at Farmington, it was said that the regiment was ordered to lie down, and the eagle did the same, dropping from his perch into the grass and staying out of sight. When the regiment was ordered to its feet, Abe fluttered up to his perch again and advanced with them. At the battle of Corinth, Old Abe was wounded. He jumped from his perch and tried to hide behind the legs of his bearer. It was observed that "he was thoroughly demoralized and the same feeling suddenly extended itself to the line and they broke and ran . . . the carrier of the Eagle picking him up and carrying him under his arm as fast as he could run."[152]

Some said that Old Abe disliked the sound of musketry and slumped low on his perch when volley firing began. But the heavy crash of artillery aroused him. In a cloud of white smoke, he would "stand erect, screaming and flapping his wings. When the fighting was hot, he would give a series of five or six especially shrill screams, ending in a startling trill," which was said to be "perfectly inspiring to the soldiers."[153]

Old Abe soldiered on until the summer of 1864, when the regiment's time expired. Now a veteran with a snow white head, the eagle was carried home to Wisconsin, discharged from the service, and given a room of his own in the State House. After the war, he became a living symbol of the Union cause. In 1868, Old Abe made an appearance at the Republican national convention. He was seen by huge crowds at the Great

Encampment of the Grand Army of the Republic in 1875, and again at
the Philadelphia Exposition in 1876. The end came in 1881, when a fire
broke out in the Wisconsin State House and Old Abe perished in the
smoke. He was mourned throughout the nation.[154]

Uncle Sam also acquired a new role in the Civil War. When the fighting began in 1861, he instantly became a symbol of the Union cause. An
example was a lithograph by C. F. Morse called "Yankee Volunteers
Marching into Dixie." It represented the Union forces as an entire army
of identical Uncle Sams. Each soldier wore striped pantaloons, a star-
spangled shirt, a swallow-tailed coat, and a white top hat. They were
young and confident of victory. Every Uncle Sam had a smile on his face
and a spring in his step. Their appearance expressed the spirit of union in
the cause of freedom.

This army of identical Uncle Sams formed a column that stretched as
far as the eye could see. In the background was a city on a hill that looked
like Boston, with the gold dome of the Bulfinch State House and the
Bunker Hill Monument. The foreground was a desolate southern landscape, the symbol of the moral decay of a slave society. This northern
army of Uncle Sams advanced inexorably into a southern desert, in what
appeared to be a march of material progress and spiritual freedom, two
ideas that became one in northern iconography.[155]

*Uncle Sam goes to war:
C. F. Morse, "Yankee Vol-
unteers Marching into
Dixie, 'Yankee Doodle Keep
It Up, Yankee Doodle
Dandy.'" Chromolithograph
by J. H. Bufford, 1862.
Photograph courtesy of
Philadelphia Print Shop.*

During the war, Uncle Sam was given a new face by northern cartoonists such as Thomas Nast, a strong supporter of the Union cause and the Republican Party. After 1861, Nast and other artists made many changes in the appearance of Uncle Sam. He acquired a fashionable beard, a lanky frame, and gaunt features. He became a Lincolnesque figure, a man of the hour, and a symbol of freedom and union in the northern cause.

At the same time, he remained a man of the people, an emblem of liberty and democracy. In 1866, Thomas Nast did a powerful drawing called "Why He Cannot Sleep" in which Uncle Sam tosses restlessly in his bed. Behind him is a ghostly figure of Liberty. Beside him is a skeleton. In the background are scenes of the terrible slaughter of the war. The features of Uncle Sam are those of the martyred President Abraham Lincoln.[156]

Thomas Nast, Self-Portrait with Uncle Sam, "Watch and Pray." Virginia Historical Society.

For some Americans Uncle Sam and Abraham Lincoln became one. In Charleston, South Carolina, a correspondent of the *New York Tribune* was in the street when news of Lincoln's assassination reached that battered southern town. He wrote:

> The colored people—the native loyalists—were like children bereaved of an only and beloved parent. I saw one old woman going up the street wringing her hands, and saying aloud, as she walked looking straight before her, so absorbed in her grief that she noticed no one,
>
> "O Lord! O Lord! O Lord! Massa Sam's dead! Massa Sam's dead! O Lord! Massa Sam's dead!"
>
> "Who's dead, Aunty?" I asked her.
>
> "Massa Sam!" she said, not looking at me,—renewing her lamentations: "O Lord! O Lord! Lord! Massa Sam's dead!"
>
> "Who's Massa Sam?" I asked.
>
> "Uncle Sam!" she said, "O Lord! Lord!"
>
> I was not quite sure that she meant the President, and I spoke again:—"Who's Massa Sam, Aunty?"
>
> "Mr. Lincum!" she said, and resumed wringing her hands and moaning in utter hopelessness of sorrow.[157]

THE MUSIC OF THE CIVIL WAR

Songs of Southern Rights Against the Battle Cry of Freedom

> Let me write the songs of a nation, I don't care who writes the laws.
>
> —ANDREW FLETCHER

THE MEANING OF these symbols became more explicit in the songs that they inspired. The two sides shared many songs that had nothing to do with liberty or freedom. Still a hit in 1861 was "Listen to the Mockingbird," written before the war for President Buchanan's beautiful niece Harriet Lane. "Dixie" was a favorite in both armies; it came to be associated with the Confederacy but was never relinquished by the Union. Near the end of the war, when Lincoln visited Richmond, he ordered the bands of the Army of the Potomac to play "Dixie." "It's a fine tune," he said. "And now it belongs to the nation."[158]

Sentimental ballads were always a favorite in that high romantic age. Some war songs were very dark, even early in the war, and a few seemed to belong to another era:

> *Have you sharpened your swords for the war that's begun?* . . .
> *Have you sharpened your swords for the red carnival?*[159]

But most Civil War songs had a positive tone and a message of high purpose. Many were about liberty and freedom. A great favorite in the South was "The Bonnie Blue Flag," which, as we have seen, was probably written in 1861 by a traveling English-born actor named Harry McCarthy and set to a drinking song called "The Irish Jaunting Car." It was received with high enthusiasm throughout the Confederacy and was soon identified with the southern cause in the war. The words to the song communicated the purposes for which southerners were fighting.

> *We are a band of brothers and native to the soil,*
> *Fighting for the property we gained by honest toil;*
> *And when our rights were threatened the cry rose near and far:*
> *Hurrah for the Bonnie Blue Flag that bears a single star.*

> *Hurrah! Hurrah! For Southern Rights hurrah!*
> *Hurrah for the Bonnie Blue Flag that bears a single star!*

The song celebrated the unofficial flag of the Confederacy with a poetic phrase that had originally described the flag of Scotland. It spelled out the southern idea of liberty as independence from the North, property rights for slaveowners, and "southern rights" for a "band of brothers," who were "native to the soil."[160]

The same idea of liberty appeared in "Maryland, My Maryland," one of the most widely sung southern songs of the war. It was written on April 23, 1861, at Poydras College in Louisiana by a young Maryland-born professor named James Ryder Randall, after he learned that a close friend had been wounded in street fighting between southern sympathizers in Baltimore and the Sixth Massachusetts Regiment. Later the song was set to the German Christmas song "O Tannenbaum" by Jennie Cary of Baltimore. Its vision of southern liberty centered not on a universal abstraction, but on the defense of southern soil.

> *The despot's heel is on thy shore,*
> *Maryland, my Maryland!*
> *His torch is at thy temple door,*
> *Maryland, my Maryland!*
> *Avenge the patriotic gore*
> *That flecked the streets of Baltimore,*
> *And be the battle queen of yore,*
> *Maryland, my Maryland!*

The song ends:

> *I hear the distant thunder-hum,*
> *Maryland, my Maryland!*
> *The Old Line's bugle, fife, and drum*

Maryland, my Maryland!
She is not dead, nor deaf, nor dumb;
Huzza! She spurns the northern scum—
She breathes! She burns! She'll come! She'll come!
Maryland, my Maryland!

Here was a song of liberty as states' rights, and the right of southerners to be free from the despot's heel that had polluted their sacred ground. Yankees were condemned as "northern scum." Privately, Randall called them a "mangy race" of "codfish poltroons." Randall's idea of southern liberty centered on local rights and an idea of what the South against, more than what it was for.[161]

Northern songs had very different visions of freedom. A lively song called "The Why and the Wherefore" resembled a catechism:

Why, why, why, and why
And why to the war, young man?
Did a man ever fight for a holier cause,
Than Freedom and Flag and Equal Laws?
Just speak your mind quite freely—Now reely.

Here was a universal idea of freedom and equality before the law.[162]

Perhaps the most popular marching song in the North was "Battle Cry of Freedom," with words and music by George F. Root:

Oh, we'll rally 'round the flag, boys,
We'll rally once again,
Shouting the battle cry of freedom . . .

We will welcome to our numbers the loyal, true, and brave,
Shouting the battle cry of freedom,
And we'll fill the vacant ranks with a million freemen more,
Shouting the battle cry of freedom.

Root dashed it off a few hours after hearing a proclamation for volunteers by Abraham Lincoln. The first public performance was at a war rally in Chicago in 1862. It was so successful that the firm of Root and Cady reported sales of 350,000 copies of the sheet music by 1867.[163]

A Confederate officer remembered the first time he heard it, at the end of the Seven Days campaign in the summer of 1862. Just before Taps, a Union soldier began to sing it, and "others joined in the chorus until it seemed to me the whole Yankee army was singing." Another Confederate said to him, "What are those fellows made of, anyway? Here we've licked 'em six days running, and now on the eve of the seventh, they're singing 'Rally 'Round the Flag.'" The officer recalled, "I am not naturally superstitious, but I tell you that song sounded like the 'knell of doom,' and my heart went down into my boots."[164] A second version was written as a battle song. Northern regiments actually sang it on the battlefield from the Seven Days to the Wilderness where it played a part in the battle.

The greatest northern freedom song was Julia Ward Howe's "Battle Hymn of the Republic." It derived from an army ballad, said to have been invented (or more likely improved) in a Massachusetts regiment as a "jibe" against a sergeant named John Brown who came from Boston. It spread rapidly through the army in 1861 and 1862, and many soldiers thought that they were singing about John Brown of Harper's Ferry. Other words were added to the same tune. The most popular lyric was "We'll hang Jeff Davis from a sour Apple Tree."[165]

In the fall of 1861, Julia Ward Howe was in Washington with her husband, Samuel Gridley Howe, working with the Military Sanitary Commission. They visited camps around the capital and heard the soldiers singing "John Brown's Body." A New England minister, James Freeman Clarke, suggested to Mrs. Howe that she write new verses that explained the purpose of the war. That night she found her inspiration in the sight of the soldiers' watch-fires in "a hundred circling camps" around the city. She awakened in "early dawn," and later remembered that "the long lines of the desired poem began to twine themselves in my mind." She wrote them down with "an old stump of a pen which I remembered having used the day before." It was so dark she could barely see the sheet that she was writing on. "I scrawled the verses almost without looking at the paper."[166]

Mrs. Howe said that she had been brought up "after the strictest rule of New England Puritanism," and that creed became her theme. She also constructed her song like a Puritan sermon, on a text from Isaiah: "I have trodden the wine press alone, and of the peoples there was none with me for I will tread them in mine anger and trample them in my fury, and their blood shall be sprinkled upon my garments and I will stain all my raiment. For the day of vengeance is in my heart, and the year of the redeemed is come."[167]

It began as Puritan sermons so often did, by affirming God's omnipotence and omniscience, his eternal presence in the world, his wrath with the sins of humanity.

Mine eyes have seen the glory of the coming of the Lord;
He is trampling out the vintage where the grapes of wrath are stored;
He hath loosed the fateful lightning of His terrible swift sword,
His truth is marching on.

It proclaimed a conviction of guilt.

I have seen Him in the watch-fires of a hundred circling camps;
They have builded Him an altar in the evening dews and damps;
I can read His righteous sentence by the dim and flaring lamps,
His day is marching on.

Then came the miracle of grace.

I have read a fiery gospel writ in burnished rows of steel;
"As ye deal with my contemners, so with you My Grace shall deal";
Let the Hero born of woman, crush the serpent with His heel,
Our God is marching on.

It became a song of salvation, and dedication to God's work in the world:

He has sounded forth the trumpet that shall never call retreat;
He is sifting out the hearts of men before His judgment-seat;
Oh! be swift, my soul, to answer Him, be jubilant, my feet!
Our God is marching on.

And it ended in a soaring vision of freedom.

In the beauty of the lilies Christ was born across the sea;
With a glory in His bosom that transfigures you and me;
As He died to make men holy, let us die to make men free,
While God is marching on.

Mrs. Howe sent her verses to the *Atlantic Monthly* in Boston. Editor James Fields paid her five dollars, gave them the title of "The Battle Hymn of the Republic," and published them in February 1862. The song's fame swiftly rapidly through the northern states. Northern churches used it as a song of worship. Soldiers sang it in the darkest moments of the war. At Richmond's Libby Prison in 1863, a Confederate jailer told Union prisoners that the Battle of Gettysburg had ended in southern victory. In a moment of despair a slave whispered the truth, and the prisoners responded by singing "The Battle Hymn of the Republic." Here was a song that transformed an idea of freedom into a vision of divine purpose, human suffering, and inevitable triumph. The Confederacy had nothing like it.

THE ICONOGRAPHY OF EMANCIPATION
Changing Meanings of Freedom

> As I would not be a slave, so I would not be a master.
> . . . Those who deny freedom to others deserve it not
> for themselves.
>
> —ABRAHAM LINCOLN

THE EMANCIPATION of the slaves turned the Civil War into a social revolution. It happened not as a single event but in a long process that continued through four years of war. As early as 1861, southern slaves began to be freed by military emancipation as "contraband of war." Others were liberated by congressional emancipation in the Confiscation Acts. Many gained freedom by presidential emancipation, through executive proclamations. The question was finally settled by constitutional emancipation in the Thirteenth, Fourteenth, and Fifteenth amendments. In the course of the war many slaves emancipated themselves, and more than two hundred thousand freedmen took up arms to emancipate others.[168]

Of all these many acts, the most prominent were Abraham Lincoln's emancipation proclamations, which were issued under the authority of the Confiscation Acts and carefully qualified to keep within the law. Many historians have stressed the limits of these documents, but they were large in their symbolic meaning, and they inspired a complex iconography.

In the spring of 1862, Abraham Lincoln wrote the first draft of an emancipation proclamation in the secrecy of the War Department's telegraph office, which was more secure than the White House. Deeply worried about the response of the country, he hid it away in a desk drawer and showed it only to a few trusted advisors behind closed doors. In the summer he consulted his cabinet and party leaders, who warned that it could bring defeat in the fall elections and urged the president to wait for a military victory.[169]

After the battle of Antietam, the president moved quickly to issue his Preliminary Emancipation Proclamation. Opinion was as deeply divided as he feared. In the fall elections, the Democrats gained thirty-two seats in the House of Representatives. The reaction to the proclamation inspired many cartoons and political caricatures. Most were hostile to emancipation, contemptuous of Abraham Lincoln, and grossly racist. One Democratic electioneering print was called the "Abolition Catastrophe." It represented the proclamation as a train wreck. As a Republican locomotive smashed into a pile of rocks labeled "emancipation" and "confiscation," Abraham Lincoln and a slave were hurled high into the air. The slave cried out, "Lor Amighty massa Linkum is dis wot yer call 'Elewating de Nigger?'"[170]

It was crude stuff, but it clearly expressed a strong sentiment that was shared by most southern Confederates, many northern Democrats, and voters in the border states who together constituted a majority of white Americans in 1862. When Abraham Lincoln issued his preliminary proclamation, the enemies of emancipation outnumbered its friends among the free white population of the United States. That painful fact is

"The Abolition Catastrophe; or, The November Smash-Up," lithograph by Bromley & Co., N.Y., 1864. Courtesy of Special Collections, Musselman Library, Gettysburg College, Gettysburg, Pa.

forgotten by those who still criticize the president for moving slowly. The early cartoons against emancipation remind us how far the republic had to travel on a long hard road.[171]

Even as these attacks continued, the Emancipation Proclamation inspired a second wave of paintings and drawings that were more thoughtful, and more studied in their symbolism. They also divided for and against emancipation. Two examples, pro and con, make a striking study in contrasts.

A strongly positive iconography appeared in a painting of the Emancipation Proclamation by northern artist David Gilmour Blythe. It portrayed the president in shirtsleeves and carpet slippers, sitting in his study, surrounded by the scales of justice, piles of paper, and many symbols of morality and law. Lincoln appears hard at work: studying the Constitution, consulting several volumes of American history, reviewing the writings of Webster, Calhoun, and Randolph, and reading petitions, protests, and letters against slavery. The window curtain is an American flag, pulled back to admit the light of reason. In the background is the text of Lincoln's presidential oath. Beneath his feet are a map of the South and a fallen handbill that represents the failure of Peace Democrats in the North. On the wall is a bust of James Buchanan with a traitor's noose around his neck. Around the edges of the print are supporting symbols of Christianity, Freemasonry, and the International Order of Odd Fellows.[172]

A very different iconography appears in a drawing of the same scene by Adalbert Volck, a southern sympathizer in Baltimore. Volck's "Writing the Emancipation Proclamation" shows a diabolical Abraham Lincoln sprawled over his writing desk, trampling the Constitution beneath his foot. The Devil holds his inkwell, and the president is surrounded by symbols of tyranny, corruption, and violence. A strange image of Columbia appears with the national shield in her hand and the head of a baboon. Behind Lincoln are bloody scenes of the slave revolt in Santo Domingo and a portrait of John Brown, labeled "St. Ossawatamie," with a pike in his hand. Flying through the window are swarms of bats, and the tieback of the curtain is a vulture's head. In the background is a sideboard with glasses and a decanter, to express the Confederate canard that Abraham Lincoln was a drunkard (in fact he was a teetotaler).[173]

The two iconographers, northern and southern, both appealed to ideas of liberty and freedom. Union sympathizer David Blythe represented Abraham Lincoln as the herald of universal freedom. Confederate supporter Abalbert Volck, saw him as a tyrant who violated the liberty of

The Emancipation Proclamation, a view from the North: "President Lincoln Writing the Proclamation of Freedom," *lithograph after David Gilmour Blythe, 1863. Library of Congress.*

The Emancipation Proclamation, a view from the South: "Writing the Emancipation Proclamation," *etching by Adalbert Volck, ca. 1863–64. National Portrait Gallery, Smithsonian Institution.*

white masters. The only iconographic element common to both works is the all-seeing, all-knowing eye of God. Both artists were equally convinced of the eternal righteousness of their respective causes.

Opinion began to shift rapidly in 1863, and the Final Emancipation Proclamation became a national icon in the last years of the war. Abraham Lincoln donated his working draft of the Final Proclamation to the ladies of the Western Sanitary Fair, who sold it at auction in 1863 to raise money for the Sanitary Commission. The purchaser, Charles Bryan, gave it to the Chicago Soldiers Home. Copies were lithographed and widely sold to support that institution. The original was lost in the Chicago Fire of 1871, but other drafts and manuscript copies survive, some in Lincoln's hand. All have become cherished documents of liberty and freedom in the United States.[174]

In the last year of the Civil War, the iconography of emancipation began to inspire major works of art. The result was a series of big paintings and major sculptures, and a large flow of engravings and lithographs. This material represented a strong change in American opinion. Most of these images strongly supported emancipation, but they represented the event in different ways.

The most important of these works was a painting called *The First Reading of the Emancipation Proclamation,* by American artist Francis Carpenter in 1864. The painting caused a great stir. Several books were written about it, including one by the artist himself. Francis Carpenter was a complex character, part idealist, part entrepreneur. According to his

Francis Carpenter, "The First Reading of the Emancipation Proclamation," painting, 1864. U.S. Senate Collection.

own account, the idea of the painting came to him in a divine voice that said, "Behold, how a Man may be exalted to a dignity and glory almost divine, and give freedom to a race."[175] Carpenter proposed the idea to the president through a friend, and Lincoln agreed. The artist was invited to visit the White House and stayed six months. Lincoln gave him the state dining room for a studio.

Carpenter resolved to paint Lincoln's first reading of the Emancipation Proclamation to his cabinet. The president and the artist also visited Mathew Brady's studio, where a series of photographs was taken on the painter's instructions. For many weeks, the artist toiled away at painstaking portraits of every cabinet member. The result was a huge canvas, nine feet high and fourteen feet, six inches long. Lincoln appears sitting to the left of center with the proclamation in his hand. On the far left are the two most radical members of the cabinet, Treasury Secretary Salmon Chase and Secretary of War Edwin M. Stanton. To the right are five more conservative men. The most prominent figure is not the president but Secretary of State William H. Seward. The artist was a New Yorker and a strong admirer of Seward. He centered his painting on the moment

John Quincy Adams Ward, "The Freedman," 1863–65. Boston Athenaeum.

John Rogers, "The Fugitive's Story," 1869. The New-York Historical Society.

when Seward urged Lincoln to wait for a major union victory before issuing the proclamation. Most of the cabinet and the president himself were
looking toward Seward, who appears as a stronger leader than the President himself.[176]

Most icons of emancipation centered on Lincoln. A leading example
was Thomas Ball's emancipation statue that was erected in Washington
in 1875, with a copy in Boston (1879). Lincoln appears as the Great Eman-
cipator, extending the gift of freedom to a passive slave who cringes
beneath his hand. This work celebrated the northern principles of liberty
and union but was slow to embrace ideas of racial equality.[177]

During the Civil War, other iconographic works began to take a different approach to emancipation. The former slaves became more visible,
and more active in the pursuit of freedom. An early example was *The
Freedman* (1863), a bronze statuette by John Quincy Adams Ward, who
gave strong support to the abolitionist movement. He made a figure of a
slave, raising himself to freedom by his own effort. To make his point, the
sculptor broke decisively with the neoclassical conventions of American
sculpture and created a realistic image. It also became a symbol of pride,
resolve, and self-liberation.[178]

A more radical sculpture by Joseph Pezzicar went further and showed
a muscular and nearly naked male slave in a militant posture, with strong
tones of sexuality and violence. It
caused an uproar when it was
exhibited in the centennial celebrations of 1876.

Another theme of self-eman-
cipation appeared in a portrait
group by John Rogers, a prolific
American sculptor who specialized in narrative works that
became very popular after the
Civil War. One of the favorites
was a group sculpture on the
theme of emancipation. Called
The Fugitive's Story (1869), it
shows a former slave woman with
a child in her arms, telling the
tale of her flight from bondage to
three antislavery leaders: Henry
Ward Beecher, William Lloyd

*Francesco Pezzicar, sculptor,
"The Abolition of Slavery
in the United States; or, The
Freed Slave." Engraving by
Miranda in* Frank Leslie's
Illustrated Newspaper,
*August 5, 1876. Library of
Virginia.*

Garrison, and John Greenleaf Whittier. Each figure is a meticulous portrait-sculpture. The strongest figure is the slave.[179]

The most renowned of these works was the Shaw Memorial in Boston, a large bronze sculpture in high relief by American artist Augustus Saint-Gaudens. The subject of the work is Colonel Robert Gould Shaw, who was killed at the head of the Fifty-fourth Massachusetts Regiment at Fort Wagner. The strongest figures in the piece are not the white officer but the black soldiers who march beside him. Saint-Gaudens carefully modeled them in individual portrait busts of great power. They survive in the Saint-Gaudens home and studio, now a National Historic Site in Cornish, New Hampshire, and at the National Gallery in Washington.[180] All of these sculptures centered the story of emancipation on African Americans.[181]

Augustus St. Gaudens, Robert Gould Shaw Memorial, Boston, 1884–97. Photograph by Judith Fischer, 2003. The sculptor's full-scale plaster cast, painted gold, is in the National Gallery, Washington.

THE LONG "SHADDOW" OF ABRAHAM LINCOLN

A Living Symbol of Liberty & Freedom in the Camera's Eye

> Our David's good sling is unerring,
> The slavocrat's giant he slew,
> Then shout for the freedom preferring,
> For Lincoln and Liberty, too.
>
> —"LINCOLN AND LIBERTY," 1860

A CENTRAL THEME in the Civil War was the emergence of Abraham Lincoln as the leader of a free republic, and a symbol of liberty and freedom. It was a remarkable transformation. When Lincoln came to the presidency, few people expected great things from him. In 1861, Americans did not expect their presidents to be leaders. Four presidential failures in a row had taught them to think otherwise, and Lincoln seemed even less promising than his predecessors. His early life offered few hints of greatness. During the presidential election, Lincoln won the Republican nomination as a dark horse after strong contenders had eliminated one another. His party was entirely sectional in its appeal, and most American voters cast their ballots against him. When he came to office, Lincoln was mocked by journalists, scorned by rivals, snubbed by his own generals, and despised by enemies of the Union cause.

Lincoln's weakness was compounded by his appearance, which seemed strange, awkward, and unpresidential even to his friends. When he visited New York in 1860, some of his supporters met him for the first time. "His form and manner were indeed very odd," one wrote, "and we thought him the most unprepossessing public man we had ever met." They were appalled by his western twang, rough manners, dark moods, rumpled clothing, clumsy movements, and bad jokes.[182]

Lincoln himself made a joke of his appearance. "Nobody has ever expected me to be President," he said in 1858. "In my poor, lean, lank face, nobody has ever seen that any cabbages were sprouting out." Later, he was accused of being two-faced. He replied, "If I had another face, do you think I'd be wearing this one?"[183] It was typical of the man that he laughed at his appearance and invited the world to laugh with him.

Laugh they did. In the early years of the new administration, cartoonists were very cruel. The British magazine *Punch* began by portraying Lincoln as a burlesque of Brother Jonathan. Its cartoons grew more vicious as the war progressed. Through the dark years of 1862 and 1863, *Punch* used caricatures of Lincoln's features to attack him as an incompetent fool, a cowardly bully, a dishonest lawyer, a primitive clown, and a party hack. The assault continued to the hour of Union victory and the moment of Lincoln's assassination. Then suddenly a chastened editor of *Punch* issued a public apology:

> *Yes, he had lived to shame me from my sneer,*
> *To lame my pencil, and confute my pen—*
> *To make me own this hind of princes peer,*
> *This rail-splitter a true-born king of men.*[184]

Many Americans also made a mockery of Lincoln in his early administration, but slowly they awakened to the extraordinary character of their president and his genius as a political leader who guided an ungovernable nation through its deepest crisis.

One of Lincoln's political strengths was his skill in the manipulation of imagery, including his own image. His instrument was the camera's eye, which he was among the first to use in a systematic way for political purposes. Photography itself was not new. At least eight American presidents had been photographed before Lincoln. Daguerreotypes had been made in the field during the Mexican War. But as late as 1860, most American leaders and events were seen primarily through the medium of paintings, engravings and lithographs. After 1865, Americans saw their leaders mainly through the camera's eye, a major shift in the imagery of politics.[185]

Abraham Lincoln was a transitional figure, who spoke of photography in the language of a prephotographic era. As late as 1858, he described a session with Matthew Brady as having his "shaddow" taken, as if a photograph were a silhouette. But Lincoln was very quick to see the political uses of Mr. Brady's "shaddows," and he exploited them with high success. In the course of his presidency, he took a very active part in the photographic construction of his own image. In the process, he made himself a symbol of liberty and freedom.[186]

Lincoln's first use of political photography occurred before the Civil

War, when he was preparing to challenge Democratic leader Stephen Douglas for a Senate seat in Illinois. In 1857, Lincoln was a prosperous corporate lawyer, and a member of the conservative Whig party for many years. To have any chance of success in a frontier state, he had to cultivate the common touch. Before the campaign began, he went to Chicago and had a photograph taken by Alexander Hesler, in a very special way. The photographer brought out the angular irregularity of his homely features. Lincoln wore a plain shirt and a badly rumpled suit. Specially striking was his hair, which Lincoln carefully disarranged, explaining that the people would not recognize him unless he gave his scalp a "bad tousle." The result was a carefully contrived image of a rough, homespun frontiersman, a tribune of the people.[187]

Mary Todd Lincoln was appalled, but Lincoln was very pleased. He wrote that the Hesler portrait "was taken from life, and is, *I* think, a very true one, though my wife and many others do not. My impression is their objection rises from the disordered condition of the hair."[188] Lincoln encouraged his backers to use the Hesler portrait. Its invented image of a folksy frontiersman was widely distributed to voters and convention delegates. Historian Harold Holzer observes that it was chosen "because Lincoln's 'wild Republican hair,' in the descriptive words of one of his admirers, seemed especially suitable for illustrating the Log-Cabin-to-White House image his supporters were cleverly crafting in the candidate's behalf."[189]

Reproductions of Lincoln's Hesler portrait were also embellished with emblems of liberty, notably the wand and pileus of the Roman goddess of liberty. In the political iconography of the 1850s, these symbols did double duty. The wand and pileus were emblems of the Whig Party and helped Lincoln to claim the mantle of his hero, Henry Clay. At the same time, they represented the spirit of liberty that flourished on the western frontier. Never mind that Lincoln himself was a corporation attorney who represented banks and railroad companies, married into the western

Alexander Hesler, portrait photograph of Abraham Lincoln, Chicago, February 28, 1857. Lincoln Museum, Fort Wayne, Ind.

ascendancy, and owned one of the largest houses in the rising city of Springfield, Illinois. Despite all that, the image of Honest Abe as the awkward, uncombed rail splitter rapidly acquired a reality of its own.

By the beginning of 1860, Lincoln had become a serious contender for the presidency. The folksy Hesler image of Lincoln was suitable for the rough-and-tumble politics of frontier Illinois, but other parts of the country expected a candidate to look more presidential. To that end, another photographic image of Lincoln was carefully contrived in 1860. Lincoln was in New York to give his "House Divided" speech at the Cooper Union. He visited the studio of Mathew Brady for a photograph, which in the words of David Donald was a "work of art," in more senses than one.

Brady was highly skilled at the manipulation of images. He placed Lincoln against a classical column in a pose that created a feeling of presidential gravitas. Lincoln's hands were carefully arranged in repose, with the left hand resting on a stack of books. A shiny satin waistcoat added a touch of refinement, and Lincoln's Prince Albert coat was pulled snug and smooth to create an air of neatness and refinement.[190]

That was only the beginning of Brady's image-making. He made a photographic negative of Lincoln in that pose, then developed a print and improved it in detail. Brady was expert at retouching, and he put his skill to work on Lincoln's behalf. The line of Lincoln's drooping right eye was corrected. The angular jaw and cheekbones were made softer and more symmetrical. Seams and wrinkles were removed from Lincoln's face by retouching, and the rough texture of Lincoln's skin was smoothed. Lincoln's features remained recognizably his own but were polished into a presidential image. The result was widely reproduced during the election of 1860. Later, Lincoln remarked that "Brady and the Cooper Institute made me president."[191]

Mathew B. Brady, portrait photograph of Abraham Lincoln, New York City, February 27, 1859. Lincoln Museum, Fort Wayne, Ind.

After the election, Lincoln developed yet another image problem, which was made painfully clear by an incident on his journey to Washington. On February 18, 1861, the president-elect arrived by train in Albany, where a friendly crowd had gathered at the station to welcome him. *Tribune* reporter Henry Villard was there and described the mood of the people as one of "intense excitement." As the train arrived, the people of Albany were ready to cheer their new president. Then Lincoln appeared on the platform. The bystanders began a cheer, which quickly sputtered into silence. The man who appeared on the platform looked very little like a president, and not much like Brady's photograph. "The president-elect was barely recognized by the crowd . . . ," wrote the *Tribune* reporter. "Tired, sunburned, adorned with huge whiskers, [he] looked so unlike the hale, smooth-shaven, red-cheeked individual who is represented upon the popular prints and is dubbed the 'rail splitter' that it is no wonder that the people did not recognize him until his extreme height distinguished him unmistakably."[192]

Once in office, Lincoln created yet another image that was very different from the Hesler and Brady photographs. It was highly distinctive—so much so that by 1862 nobody could fail to recognize him. Lincoln began by letting his whiskers grow into a full beard. The satin waistcoat disappeared, and he made a point of wearing the plain black suit of an ordinary American citizen. He also exaggerated his great height by his headgear. Before the war, Lincoln had worn a top hat of conventional proportions.[193] By the fall of 1862, his topper had grown into a stovepipe hat that made this very tall man nearly a foot taller, between seven and eight feet high. Lincoln's exceptional height was mostly in his legs and his hat. Seated and bareheaded, he looked to be of ordinary stature, but when he rose to his feet and put on his hat, he towered above other men.

The president employed this new image as a political instrument. One of its first uses was in a meeting with General George McClellan and intelligence chief Allan Pinkerton. Both were difficult and fractious men who may have caused Lincoln more anxiety than Jefferson Davis and Robert E. Lee combined. The president had himself photographed standing beside McClellan and Pinkerton, towering above them in a long coat, high boots, and stovepipe hat.[194] It was not easy to be photographed that way, standing motionless in an open field during the long exposures that photographers then required. In some of these shots, Lincoln's image was a little blurred by his movements while the photograph was taken, but these blurry "shaddows" created a commanding image of presidential leadership. Lincoln appeared at the center of a standing group, with others turned toward him. His exaggerated height and ramrod posture made him appear a giant among lesser men. It is interesting to note that he was most apt to use this posture with his most fractious subordinates.

In these photographs, Lincoln's plain black middle-class civilian suit made another point. He always appeared as an ordinary citizen of a free republic, a man of the people, a symbol of republican government, and an instrument of civil supremacy over the military in time of war. He gave himself a unique identity in that role, with such success that by the end of 1862 a cartoonist had only to hint at a long face, lanky frame, dark beard, plain dress, and stovepipe hat. All the world recognized the image of Abraham Lincoln and associated it with the cause of freedom and union.[195]

In 1863 and 1864, yet another photographic image of Lincoln began to appear. After three years of war, the president's dark hair and beard were turning gray, and his angular features were taking on the fullness of age. His face became deeply lined with the anxieties of office, and his sad eyes showed his profound sympathy for the suffering that the war had caused. An artist remarked of Lincoln's appearance in 1864, "In repose it was the saddest face I ever knew. There were days when I could scarcely look at it without crying."[196]

In the same period, other qualities also became evident in Lincoln's changing appearance. As the war went on, the president's demeanor

Photograph of Abraham Lincoln with General George B. McClellan and Allan B. Pinkerton, 1862. Library of Congress.

showed growing strength and steadiness. The line of his jaw suggested firmness of purpose, and the set of his eyes showed a clarity of vision in this extraordinary man. His appearance increasingly displayed qualities of character, integrity, and moral leadership that were the source of his greatness.

In 1863 and 1864, the president often visited Brady's studio in Washington and had many portraits taken by Alexander Gardner and Anthony Berger, two very able portrait photographers. Both were attentive to the qualities of character that increasingly appeared in Lincoln's face and used every trick of their art to make them more evident. In 1863 and 1864, Gardner and Berger made much use of tight close-ups. Gardner was known for his pathbreaking work in the use of photo-enlargement. Berger was highly skilled in the manipulation of light. Both men used these techniques to emphasize the facial lines that Brady had removed by retouching in 1860. They also set the camera below the plane of Lincoln's head to create a monumental feeling and reinforced the shadows above his eyes to add depth and texture to the face.

Alexander Gardner, portrait photograph of Abraham Lincoln, November 8, 1863. Library of Congress.

The results are among the most powerful and moving images of character that portrait photographers have ever achieved. One of them was a photograph of Lincoln by Alexander Gardner after the battle of Gettysburg, in the period when the president was writing his address. Lincoln appears full face. The camera is very close and slightly below the sitter's head. The features are dark and worn. The face of Lincoln is an image of pain and worry and exhaustion. At the same time one is made to feel the presence of a strong resolve to see the struggle through to victory.[197]

In the fall of 1864, with a critical election at hand, Anthony Berger created an image of Lincoln as a wise and experienced leader, with an aura of growing strength and confidence. But the deep lines and shadows are still there and are made more visible by the photographer's technique. Other photographs by Alexander Gardner on February 5, 1865, showed

Alexander Gardner, portrait photograph of Abraham Lincoln, April 1865. National Portrait Gallery, Smithsonian Institution.

the toll that the war had taken of this man, but also a feeling that it was not in vain.[198]

On March 4, 1865, Abraham Lincoln delivered his second inaugural address, which many thought the greatest speech of his career. Frederick Douglass remarked that it was "more like a sermon than a state paper." The nation was deeply moved by its strength of resolve, and also by the spirit of reconciliation, in its great climax: "with malice toward none; with charity for all; with firmness in the right, as God gives us to see the right, let us strive to finish the work we are in; to bind up the nation's wounds."[199]

The scene was captured by Alexander Gardner in a blurry photograph, one of the most extraordinary in American history. In the center is the president himself, towering above other men, intent upon his speech. In the background the camera has caught the assassin John Wilkes Booth, watching and waiting for his opportunity. The crowd is listening silently, even reverently. Many are wearing photographs of Lincoln, small prints of Gardner's portrait of February 15, 1865, hanging from plain ribbons without captions or slogans. No words were necessary, for by 1865 America and all the world recognized the features of Abraham Lincoln.[200] As the Civil War approached its end, with the restoration of the Union and the emancipation of the slaves, Lincoln himself became the leading symbol of that great struggle, and an image of the suffering that it caused. That idea appeared in Alexander Gardner's photograph of April 1865. Lincoln began to be seen as spiritual leader: first a Moses for his nation, then, after his assassination on Good Friday, 1865, a Christ-like figure who died that others might live in freedom.

All of this appeared in the great photographs of Gardner, Berger, and Brady during the last year of the war. They carefully created the image of Lincoln that still lives in the hearts of the American people. The war-ravaged face of this man became the image of the nation's greatest leader and the symbol of its largest cause. It was also a new vision of freedom, with a depth of sympathy for the suffering of others. Even today one can "scarcely look at it without crying."

IMAGES OF ROBERT E. LEE

A Stoic Vision of Liberty Through Self-Mastery

He acted out a paradox; duty set him free.

—EMORY THOMAS

AFTER APPOMATTOX, the personification of the southern cause was another iconic figure, Robert E. Lee. The South was slow to think of him in that way. Historians of this subject were amazed to discover that "the Confederacy failed to produce a single separate sheet print portrait of its greatest hero during the entire course of the war." By a count of images, the most celebrated southern soldiers during the Civil War were Stonewall Jackson and Jeb Stuart.[201]

Lee himself was unpopular in the first year of the war. He was scorned as "Granny Lee" during his first cautious campaign in West Virginia. After a few months of undistinguished service in that theater, he was transferred to the southern coast, where he gave so much attention to defensive fortifications that bellicose South Carolinians contemptuously called him "the King of Spades" and demanded his removal. He was kicked upstairs to a staff job in Richmond.

The break came in 1862 when General Joseph Johnston was severely wounded and Jefferson Davis appointed Lee commander of the Army of Northern Virginia. His stature began to grow during the weeks that followed, when his aggressive generalship defeated McClellan in the Peninsula Campaign. Then came the victories that secured his reputation: second Manassas, Fredericksburg, and Chancellorsville. Even Lee's defeats against heavy odds at Sharpsburg-Antietam and Gettysburg, and the defensive battles in the Wilderness, added to his reputation.

As Lee grew more prominent as a military leader, he also became a symbol of southern liberty. Men who were close to him, such as Armistead Long in his *Memoirs of Robert E. Lee,* described Lee as "a firm supporter of Constitutional Liberty," who detested slavery as "a moral and political evil" and freed his own slaves in 1862 but insisted on every state's right to control its own domestic institutions.[202] Lee himself often declared that the pursuit of liberty and freedom was the cause for which he was fighting. After the bloody battles of the Peninsula Campaign, he

Robert E. Lee, photograph by Matthew Brady, 1865. Virginia Historical Society.

wrote of the Confederate dead, "let us not forget that they died nobly in defence of their country's freedom."[203] He regarded northern ideas of freedom and union as another name for tyranny. "Is it not strange," he wrote, "that the descendants of those Pilgrim Fathers who crossed the Atlantic to preserve their own freedom have always proved most intolerant of the spiritual liberty of others?"[204]

After the war, Lee wrote to Captain James May on July 9, 1866, "I had no other guide, nor had I any other object than the defense of those principles of American liberty upon which the constitutions of the several States were separately founded, and unless they are strictly observed, I fear there will be an end to republican government in this Country."[205] Lee's republican model was George Washington. Governor Henry Wise once said to him, "General Lee, you certainly play Washington to perfection." Like Washington, whose sword he carried through the war, Lee understood liberty in classical terms and framed it within the values of a Stoic tradition.[206]

That conception of liberty began in ancient Greece with a school of philosophers who did their teaching near a colonnade, or stoa, in the painted market of Athens and drew their inspiration from the interplay of Eastern and Western philosophy in the wake of Alexander's Asian conquests. Their ideas were developed in imperial Rome by the courtier Seneca, the emperor Marcus Aurelius, and especially the Phrygian slave Epictetus.

Eleutheria, the Greek idea of liberty, had a central place in Stoic thought, more than in other ancient schools of philosophy. A philologist has discovered that the words *eleutheria* and *eleutheros* appeared more often in Epictetus than in any other ancient writer. The Stoics believed that happiness and peace could be attained only through liberty and virtue. True liberty was to be found in independence and self-mastery. True virtue lay in living "according to nature, and in submission to a higher power." Epictetus wrote, "He is free (*eleutheros*) who lives as he wills, who is subject neither to compulsion, nor hindrance, nor force, whose choices are unhampered, whose desires attain their end, whose aversions do not fall into what they would avoid."[207]

In this Stoic tradition there were three paths to liberty: to defend one's independence against the will of others, to become independent of one's passions and material possessions by strict self-discipline, and to achieve the annihilation of desire. For Lee as for the ancient Stoics, these three ways were one: the more free one became of external controls, the more important it was to control oneself through self-mastery, discipline, and duty. Historian Emory Thomas writes, "He acted out a paradox; duty set him free."[208]

Robert E. Lee matched his life to this Stoic vision of liberty and self-discipline. Those who knew him celebrated his "calm self-reliance" and complete "self-possession."[209] This role was not easy for Lee to play, for it went directly against his own temperament. Intimate friends noticed that he often had trouble keeping his explosive temper in check. In moments of frustration and anger, the back of his neck would turn bright red, and his head would begin to jerk in uncontrollable spasms as he struggled to master himself.[210] Lee himself was burdened by a sense of failure to control his passions, when all the world had the opposite impression. He worried often about his transgressions and his "unworthiness," but he kept trying to keep his own creed. In his diary he wrote, "The main thing to be acquired consists in habits of industry and self-denial." To a student at Washington College he wrote, "You will find it difficult at first to control the operation of your mind under all circumstances ... but the power can be gained by determination and practice.... If it had not been for this power, I do not see how I could have stood what I had to go through with."[211]

Lee modified this ancient Stoic idea by linking it to Christianity. His struggle for self-mastery was translated into Christian terms of sin and redemption. It was also a Christian idea of selfless service to others, but always without an idea of equality.[212]

These Stoic values framed his thinking about slavery and race. Lee never defended slavery and always believed that "slavery as an institution is a moral and political evil in any country." But he owned slaves for many years and in 1857 suddenly found himself responsible for three plantations and at least 150 slaves, on the death of his father-in-law, George Washington Parke Custis. Lee was executor of the estate, with instructions to pay its debts, distribute its property to heirs, and free the slaves within five years. The estate was in extreme disorder. Lee finally paid its debts, distributed its assets, and emancipated all the Custis slaves by proclamation on December 29, 1862, ironically three days before Lincoln's Final Emancipation Proclamation took effect. He had earlier emancipated his own personal slaves, and they continued with him, working for wages. In this episode one finds Lee struggling to do his duty and trying to get clear of slavery.[213]

After the war Lee developed his Stoic creed into an idea that his duty was to accept defeat and his task was to help rebuild the South. On a slip of paper he wrote a monitory maxim: "The gentleman does not needlessly and unnecessarily remind an offender of a wrong he may have committed against him. He can not only forgive, he can forget. He strives for that nobleness of self and mildness of character which impart sufficient strength to let the past be but the past."[214]

Lee took upon himself the duty of training a new generation of leaders for the South. He turned down offers of lucrative employment and became president of Washington College in Lexington, Virginia, with that larger purpose in mind. Lee also devoted himself to the task of training a new generation of southern leaders to his Stoic and Christian vision of liberty and self-mastery. At Washington College he was asked for a copy of the rules of the institution and answered, "We have but one rule here, and it is that every student must be a gentleman."

In his papers Lee left a short summary of his idea of a gentleman: "The forbearing use of power does not only form a touchstone; but the manner in which an individual enjoys certain advantages over others, is a test of a *true gentleman*. The power which the strong have over the weak, the magistrate over the citizen, the employer over the employed, the educated over the unlettered, the experienced over the confiding, even the clever over the silly; the forbearing and inoffensive use of all this power or authority, or a total abstinence from it, when the case admits it, will show the gentleman in a plain light.... A true man of honor feels humbled himself, when he cannot help humbling others."[215]

Many southerners responded to Lee's example and made him an image of this ideal. Books and papers began to appear on Lee as a war leader, written by men who served with him. Most celebrated his idea of Stoic liberty. Many are still in print, and some are widely read today.[216] Another wave of books and images appeared for Lee's centennial in 1907. Monuments were raised to him in Richmond and throughout the South. In one iconic photogravure, called "Lee and His Generals," made him appear half a head higher than the rest. He stood out among them by his stoic air of calm and gravitas.[217]

Former slaves had a different image of him. In 1866, a communication was published in the *National Anti-Slavery Standard* by one of the Custis slaves at Arlington who testified that Lee ordered some to be whipped and instructed the "overseer to wash their backs in brine." This incident had a major impact on attitudes of African Americans.[218] In 1907, a Lee monument was opposed by John Mitchell Jr., editor of the *Richmond Planet*, an African American leader of great courage who fought lynching in rural Virginia, revolver in hand. He also led a nonviolent boycott that bankrupted a segregationist streetcar company in Richmond half a century before Martin Luther King. In 1907, Mitchell spoke out bravely against Jim Crow and racism, but his voice was not heard by most Americans.[219]

Lee's reputation continued to grow in the mid-twentieth century, and he became a national figure, mainly through the effort of Douglas Southall Freeman, a Richmond journalist trained as a professional historian at Johns Hopkins, who wrote a great biography of Lee in four volumes, and three volumes more on Lee's Lieutenants. Every page linked Lee's generalship to his Stoic character. Freeman wrote of Lee as an example of "leadership in adversity." His account of Lee's "forebearing use of power" and leadership by moral example came to be much admired in the United States as a method of command. Many American leaders modeled themselves on Freeman's Lee. Dwight Eisenhower kept a portrait of Lee in his office and wrote, "He was thoughtful yet demanding of his officers and men, forbearing with captured enemies.... He was noble as a leader and a man."[220]

In the late twentieth century, the image of Robert E. Lee changed yet again. From 1976 to 1999, revisionist historians began to criticize him. Some challenged his generalship. Others analyzed his Stoic idea of liberty and self-mastery as a personality disorder. Many criticized his record on slavery.[221] Similar trends appeared in the public life of the South. In Richmond, when a Canal Walk was opened in the waterfront district in 1999, a biracial group decorated it with a mural that carefully included Indians, blacks, and Robert E. Lee. Most people approved, but a city councillor named Sa'ad El-Amin demanded the removal of Lee's image. "If Lee won," he said, "I'd still be a slave." El-Amin was voted down seven to one, and the mural remained. But on Lee's birthday, January 17, 2000, it was destroyed by a Molotov cocktail. In the same year, a small number of radical students at the University of Virginia demanded that Lee be banished to the "scrap heap of history."[222]

The revisionists and iconoclasts succeeded in deepening the shadows in Lee's image, but other historians began to construct a "post-revisionist" interpretation that appears in works by Emory M. Thomas and Gary Gallagher.[223] In the twenty-first century, Lee survives and even flourishes as an iconic figure in the South and throughout the United States. On the Internet in 2001, sixty-four thousand Web sites offered Lee prints, portraits, statues, and memorabilia. Many Americans believe that even as one condemns slavery and racism, one can admire the qualities of Lee's character. Some also remember that he was the central figure in a tradition that gave America several of its greatest leaders, from George Washington to George Marshall, who shared the same Stoic vision of American liberty and freedom.

RECONSTRUCTION AND ITS ENEMIES

Freedom Triumphs, Liberty Endures

> Slavery is not abolished until the black man has the ballot.
>
> —FREDERICK DOUGLASS

WHEN THE WAR WAS OVER, a dream of national reunion and reconstruction was widely shared in the northern states. American artists went to work on this great theme. In 1867, one of them invented an elaborate iconography of reconstruction. It shows a panorama of the restored nation—its cities, countryside, rivers, and mountains. In the foreground Americans work together to rebuild a temple of national union, with pillars to symbolize the return of the southern states and the reconstruction of the Federal Edifice. Above the temple are clasped hands with the words "Liberty and Union Forever." High in the clouds are the departed shades of Puritans and Cavaliers, Quakers and western settlers, Washington and Lincoln, Adams and Jefferson, Webster and Calhoun, all watching the reconstruction of the Union with an air of satisfaction. On one side is the goddess of liberty with her wand and pileus. On the other is Justice with her sword and scales. At the very top is Christ with his crown and the Golden Rule: "Do to others as you would have others do to you." Around the temple are cradles with white and black babies, and a motto, "All Men Are Born Free and Equal." Inside the temple are hundreds of individual northern and southern leaders, shaking hands. In the distance, every region is flourishing.[224]

Unhappily, the reality of Reconstruction was very different. Northern ideas of freedom, union, and equality triumphed in 1865, but southern ideas of liberty, independence, states' rights, and racial hierarchy endured.

"*Reconstruction," lithograph by John Lawrence Giles, published by Horatio Bateman, New York, 1867. Library of Congress.*

The struggle between them continued in new forms. In some ways, the two sections moved farther apart in Reconstruction than they had been before the Civil War.

A year after Appomattox, a Virginia secessionist named Edward Pollard published an unrepentant book called *The Lost Cause: A New Southern History of the War of the Confederates.* The work was soon forgotten, but its title caught on. The legend of the lost cause was born in the hour of Confederate defeat, and it flourished longer in the South than the Confederacy itself, even to our own time.[225] Iconography was one of its major vehicles. A leading example was a lithograph called *The Lost Cause, or Deo Vindice.* Its author, Lewis Simons, reproduced a ring of worthless Confederate dollars that symbolized the losses of the lost cause. On one surviving copy of the lithograph, the owner pasted actual Confederate dollars. The rest of the lithograph centered on the cause itself, which was remembered as a struggle for liberty:

> *Representing nothing on God's earth now,*
> *And naught in the waters below it,*
> *As a pledge of a nation that passed away,*
> *Keep it dear friend and show it.*
>
> *Show it to those who will lend an ear*
> *To the tale this trifle will tell,*
> *Of Liberty born of a patriot's dream,*
> *Of a storm cradled nation that fell.*

In the upper corner was the goddess of liberty with her wand and pileus.[226]

Behind the romantic image of a lost cause was intense bitterness and hatred in the South. A case in point was Major Innes Randolph, who in his own words "followed Marse Robert for four years" and was "wounded in three places." After the war he wrote a dark ballad called "The Good Old Rebel." Innes scored it to be played "slow" and sung "defiantly."

Lewis R. Simons, "The Lost Cause," lithograph. Library of Congress.

Oh, I'm a Good Old Rebel, now that's just what I am.
For this "Fair Land of Freedom" I do not give a damn!
I'm glad I fit against it, I only wish we won.
And I don't want no pardon, for anything I done.

I hates the Constitution,
This Great Republic too,
I hates the freedman's Buro,
In uniforms of blue;
I hates the nasty eagle,
With all his brag and fuss,
The lyin' thievin' Yankees,
I hates 'em wuss and wuss.

I hates the Yankee nation
And everything they do.
I hates the Declaration
of Independence too;
I hates the "glorious Union,"
'Tis dripping with our blood,
I hates their striped banner,
I fit it all I could.

It continued through many angry verses that systematically reviled every Yankee image and symbol of freedom and union.

> *I can't take up my musket,*
> *And fight 'em now no more,*
> *But I ain't a-going to love 'em*
> *Now that is sartain sure;*
> *And I don't want no pardon*
> *For what I was and am.*
> *I won't be reconstructed*
> *And I don't care a damn.*[227]

The song was probably written in 1866, ironically dedicated to Thaddeus Stevens, and sung throughout the South for many years. It shows what the architects of Reconstruction and reunion were up against. The most difficult task of reconstruction was not in the public life of the Old South but in the hearts of unrepentant southerners.

At the same time that southerners such as Innes Randolph were slow to change their minds, and unwilling to surrender their old liberties, former slaves were quick to claim their new freedom. The result was an angry conflict that continued more than a century after the Civil War.

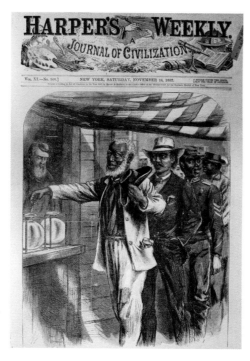

A hopeful image of black voters in the South. "The First Vote," Harper's Weekly cover, November 16, 1867. Virginia Historical Society.

The lines were drawn differently. The politics of the Old South were about masters and slaves. The politics of the New South were about white against black.

Two iconographies were created by this conflict in the years just after the war. One of them centered on former slaves who were now freedmen. The cover of *Harper's Weekly* on November 16, 1867, showed a sketch by Alfred Waud called "The First Vote." The Reconstruction Act of 1867 forbade states to deny the right to vote on grounds of race. In that year many former slaves went to the polls for the first time. The sketch shows four African American freedmen at the ballot box. One is a skilled crafts-man with his tools in his pocket. Another is a merchant with a bundle of papers in the pocket of his business suit. The third is a sergeant of Union cavalry with a medal on his jacket. The fourth appears to be a minister in a black hat. There is a sense of social order and material independence in the scene. It is an image of economic freedom as well as political rights.[228]

This iconography grew more elaborate as Reconstruction continued. A chromolithograph by Thomas Kelly called "The Fifteenth Amend-ment" (1870) shows many scenes of progress for the former slaves. The central image is a parade celebrating the Fifteenth Amendment, which prohibited racial restrictions on the right to vote. It is surrounded by images of former slaves who are tilling their own fields, serving in the militia, sitting in Congress, going to school, marrying without impedi-ment, and exercising freedom of worship and the right of association. Four white men appear: Abraham Lincoln, Ulysses Grant, Schuyler Col-fax, and John Brown. Black leaders are at the center.[229]

Yet another chromolithograph was called "The Shackle Broken by the Genius of Freedom." It has a similar composition but a different theme. It centers on an image of Robert Elliott, an African American leader in South Carolina speaking in Congress for the Civil Rights Act of 1875.

Below is a black farming family with the inscription, "American Slave Labour is of the Past—Free Labour is of the Present—We Toil for Our Children and Not for Those of Others." In all of these works, freedom appears as an idea that embraced all humanity, and the great test is equal rights for former slaves.[230]

Some of these images were clearly designed to remind former slaves of a debt to the Republican Party. The cover of a deposit book from the Freedman's Bank in Mobile, Alabama, was covered with the faces of Lincoln, Grant,

This unreconstructed image openly celebrates Klansmen in the act of lynching a black voter. The ballot is trans-formed into a skull, as a symbol of death. "Ku Klux Klan," sheet music cover, ca. 1884, published by James A. McClure, Nashville, Ten-nessee. Virginia Historical Society.

*"The Fifteenth Amend-
ment," chromolithograph
by Thomas Kelly, 1870.
Virginia Historical Society.*

Sherman, Stanton, Oliver O. Howard, and Farragut, with the iconography of flag and eagle, perched on the "Freedman's Safe" above the inscription "Lincoln and Freedom." It was a doubtful advantage to the
Republicans. The Freedman's Bank failed in 1874, and many former slaves
lost savings.[231]

Southern democrats were quick to develop counterimages. An example is a drawing called "Murder of Louisiana, Sacrificed on the Altar of
Radicalism." The prostrate state is stretched on a block by two former
slaves; the Radical Republican Governor William P. Kellogg cuts out the
heart of the state while a crowd of carpetbaggers looks on from the left
and beautiful young white women in chains watch in horror from the
right. Presiding over the scene is "Ulysses I," who is President Grant.
Attorney General George H. Williams stands behind him in the shape of
the Devil. Here was a symbol of southern liberty, trampled by Yankee
tyranny.[232]

The speed with which these images appeared after Appomattox
strongly suggests that no period of forgotten alternatives existed between
the Civil War and Reconstruction. The depth of hostility also indicates
that the root of the problem was not to be found in material things—not
in the absence of material support for former slaves. Its root was a head-
on collision between two ways of thinking about the world—both deeply

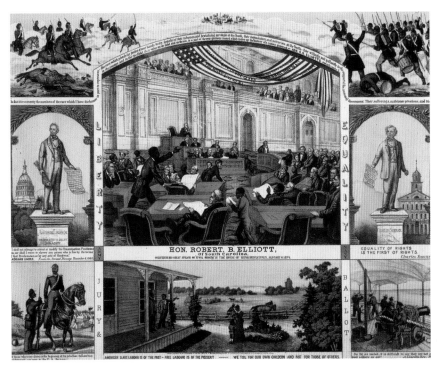

"The Shackle Broken," chromolithograph by E. Saachse & Co., Baltimore, 1874. Wadsworth Atheneum, Hartford.

believed. One was a vision of southern liberty and white supremacy, which was stronger than it had been before the war. The other was an ideal of freedom for former slaves, the rule of the law, which was larger than ever. Reconstruction became a domestic war between these two causes. It was more brutal in some ways than the Civil War and created a reign of terror throughout the South. The results were very mixed. The Reconstruction regimes ended in defeat. African Americans in the South soon lost the vote and became victims of Jim Crow, and violence could strike anytime in the night. But in the midst of all those troubles, freed slaves slowly and painfully inched ahead. Within a generation, most learned to read and write. Approximately 25 percent became landowners in the South. Most built families and communities and churches and voluntary associations. Radical reconstruction failed, but a deeper process moved forward entirely by the efforts of the former slaves.

RIGHTS FOR ALL, OR WHITE MAN'S RULE?
Emblems of Freedom and Liberty in the Election of 1868

Union, Now and Forever

—MOTTO OF REPUBLICANS FOR
ULYSSES GRANT IN 1868

Liberty: This is a White Man's Government

—MOTTO OF DEMOCRATS FOR
HORATIO SEYMOUR IN 1868

IN THE ELECTION OF 1868, the Union soldier who had defeated Robert E. Lee became the Republican candidate for president of the United States. In Hartford, Connecticut, hundreds of Union veterans showed their support for Ulysses S. Grant by marching through the town in a torchlight parade. Many wore their faded blue uniforms. More than a few carried the scars of a long and bloody war. But a feeling of victory was in the air, and these triumphant Union men were in a mood for celebration. An eyewitness remembered that whenever they came to "a specially illuminated house the leader turned and marched backward, keeping time with his sword, and the men shouted: 'ONE! TWO! THREE! U! S! G! HURRAH.'"

At one house a little girl watched the torchlight parade in wide-eyed wonder. She herself became part of the event. Her family dressed her as the goddess of liberty, and she stood immobile as a statue in the doorway of her home, the living symbol of a sacred cause. As the long column of men in blue passed by, they turned toward her and gave her a mighty cheer, and another, and another. Many years later, when that small child had grown to womanhood, she still remembered that moment with the clarity of total recall. "In every one of our tiny window-panes we had stuck a candle," she wrote. "In the full light of those lamps stood a Goddess of Liberty—eight years old! A white dress, a liberty cap, a liberty pole (which was a new mop-handle with a red-white-and-blue sash tied on it and a cornucopia of the same colors on its tops), and a great flag draped around me—there I stood—Living. One crowded hour of glorious life, that was to a motionless, glorified child."

The child was Charlotte Perkins Gilman. She later became a leader in the movement for women's rights and a heroine to three generations of American feminists. Her life was crowded with great events, but one of her most vivid memories was that evening of marching soldiers and flaming torches. "I can hear them now!" she wrote in her old age. In

A Republican vision of freedom and union in the election of 1868: "Lincoln, Grant, Colfax, Union Forever," textile by Elizabeth Holmes.

her memoir we hear them too, those men in faded blue cheering a little girl who symbolized the idea for which they fought.[233]

In the presidential campaign of 1868, the Republican and Democratic candidates stood once again for different ideas of freedom and liberty. Republicans united behind Grant and Colfax and demanded freedom and civil rights for the former slaves. This universal idea was picked up through the northern states. An appropriate symbol, widely celebrated in the northern states, was a marble sculpture, completed in 1867 and widely reproduced in that election year. It represented an African slave with broken chains at his feet and the remains of a fetter still hanging from his left hand. His right hand rested upon the shoulder of an Indian woman, her hands clasped in prayer. The sculptor was Mary Edmondia Lewis, who was herself the daughter of an African American father and a Chippewa Indian mother. She first titled the work *The Morning of Liberty*. It was renamed *Forever Free* and today is in the collection of Howard University.[234]

The resurgent Democratic Party went a different way. In reaction against ideas of universal freedom that had gained strength during the Civil War, a coalition formed between unreconstructed southern Confederates, northern ethnic groups that had not supported the war, and conservatives in every region. Together they supported the Democratic candidate, New York's Horatio Seymour (1810–86), a conservative country gentleman and a disciple of Jefferson and Jackson. He combined a plat-

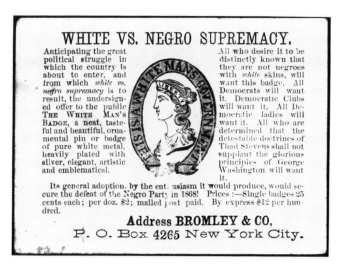

A Democratic vision of liberty in 1868: "Liberty; This Is a White Man's Government," a Horatio Seymour campaign badge and card. Collections of Scott Dolson; David J. and Janice L. Frent.

form of liberty with a campaign of open racism. Seymour's electioneering badges in 1868 showed the Roman goddess of liberty, surrounded by the defiant words, "This Is a White Man's Government."[235]

Seymour and the Democratic Party in 1868 revived the old hierarchical idea of liberty and redefined it in terms of race. This was liberty for white people only. In the late nineteenth century, racial attitudes of that sort hardened into a formal ideology of racism. In other forms, racial prejudice had long existed throughout American history, as in most other cultures. Racism was not unique to the United States, but it was highly distinctive in its American expressions. Only in America was racism strongly linked to a tradition of liberty.[236]

The election of 1868 was a close-run thing. In the end the Republican Party won by a very narrow margin. Political historians have calculated that of 5,717,246 ballots cast, a shift of merely one half of 1 percent of the votes (29,862 votes to be exact) would have made Horatio Seymour president of the United States.

The presidency of Ulysses Grant is remembered for its many failures. One of the most successful generals in the Civil War proved to be among the worst chief executives in American history. His administration became one of the most corrupt in the history of the republic. But for all its many flaws, it kept alive an idea of freedom and union through the bitter years of Reconstruction.

THE CENTENNIAL CELEBRATIONS OF 1875-76

Old Images Renewed

> The Grand Centennial Wedding of Uncle Sam and
> Liberty
>
> —AN ARTIST'S IDEA OF THE
> CENTRAL THEME, 1876

URING THE ERA of Reconstruction, triumphant symbols of freedom and union became more visible throughout the prosperous northern and western states. Every Independence Day called forth a vast display of banners and bunting, screaming eagles, and Lincolnesque Uncle Sams. Images of Columbia became so popular throughout the North and West that the De Muth Company mass-produced large zinc lawn figures and sold them at $105 apiece.[237]

A new national holiday was added after the Civil War, variously called Memorial Day or Decoration Day. It began in 1868, when General John Logan of the Grand Army of the Republic proposed that the thirtieth day of May should be set aside "for the purpose of strewing with flowers or otherwise decorating the graves of comrades who died in defense of their country during the late rebellion." Gradually every northern state made it a public holiday, variously called Memorial Day or Decoration Day. It was observed with parades and speeches that celebrated the great national themes of freedom and union.

The southern states appointed their own holidays to mourn the Confederate dead and commemorate their cause of southern liberty and states' rights. Typically, they were unable to agree on a date. Louisiana, Tennessee, and Arkansas had their Decoration Day on June 3, the birthday of Jefferson Davis. Alabama, Florida, Georgia, and Mississippi preferred April 26, the date of Joseph Johnston's surrender. North Carolina and South Carolina preferred May 10. Virginia adopted the national date of May 30 but called it Confederate Memorial Day and created another holiday on January 19 to commemorate Robert E. Lee and Stonewall Jackson.

At the same time, a series of national centennial celebrations from 1875 to 1892 revived images of national identity. For the Revolutionary centennial of 1875, New England gave the nation the iconic figure of the Minuteman, an embattled Middlesex farmer with a musket in one hand and a plow by the other. The sculptor was Daniel Chester French, a gifted young artist who was himself a native of Concord, Massachusetts. The Minuteman was in one way a highly particular figure, a plain Yankee farmer in his ordinary working dress. At his side was an old-fashioned East Anglian moldboard plow of the sort that Puritans had brought from the east of England to America. It was quickly adopted as an icon of American nationality and a symbol of universal freedom.

A second Centennial Exposition was staged at Philadelphia in 1876, on a much larger scale. Its logo was the Liberty Bell, a symbol widely reproduced in souvenirs and keepsakes of that event. The bell itself was moved to a more prominent place in the vestibule of Independence Hall and suspended from the original beam that had supported it in 1776. The

head of the organizing committee, Colonel Frank Etting, added, "We deemed it appropriate to inscribe upon its base the whole scriptural text, a part of which had been moulded upon the bell in 1753, as it, even then, so essentially predicted and ordained: first 'Liberty throughout all the land,' and secondly the Centennial celebration thereof."[238]

In 1876, the old bell preserved something of its Quaker spirit at the same time that it acquired a new meaning that it had not possessed before. After the centennial celebration, the Liberty Bell began to travel through the country. Some of its most interesting journeys took it to the states of the former Con-

Daniel Chester French, "The Concord Minuteman of 1775," bronze statue, 1875. Photograph by Judith Fischer.

federacy. The Liberty Bell was sent to New Orleans in 1885 for the Cotton States Industrial Exposition, with stops along the way in southern towns and cities. Even Jefferson Davis rose from his sickbed to honor the bell in another symbolic gesture of reunion. The Liberty Bell visited Chicago for the World's Fair in 1893. It went to Atlanta in 1895, Charleston in 1902, Boston in 1903, and San Francisco in 1915. Everywhere crowds came to see it. Blind children were held up to feel the bell's raised inscription. Old people knelt before it. The sick and the lame touched it in hope of a cure.[239]

A new spirit of national unity appeared in these events, but below the surface the old differences ran deep. In Boston, the Liberty Bell was exhibited with John Brown's Bell, which had summoned the slaves to resistance. In the southern states, the Liberty Bell became a symbol of national reunion, with tolerance for regional differences. Even as the Liberty Bell was widely perceived primarily as a national symbol, regional difference persisted in the meaning of those images, but within a more narrow range.

Thomas Nast, The Centennial Liberty Bell, Harper's Weekly, June 27, 1885. Virginia Historical Society.

NEW VISIONS OF UNIVERSAL FREEDOM
Laboulaye, Bartholdi, and the Statue of Liberty

The Gospel's daughter, the sister of Justice and Mercy,
the mother of Equality, Abundance and Peace

—EDOUARD DE LABOULAYE'S IDEA OF
LIBERTÉ, WHICH INSPIRED THE STATUE

IN THE SPRING OF 1865, a small party of French politicians dined together in a country house near Versailles. Their host was a distinguished historian, Edouard-René Lefebvre de Laboulaye, professor at the Collège de France. He was a man of many liberal causes: chairman of the French Anti-Slavery Society, advocate of religious liberty, expert on constitutional law, and one of America's best friends in Europe. Laboulaye had just finished his largest publication, a three-volume history of the United States. The thesis of his work was that the birth of the American republic was "the dawn of a new world" in which "liberty arose on the other side of the Atlantic to enlighten...the universe."[240]

Laboulaye was described as "le plus américain de tous les Français," the most American of all the people of France. He had never been to America but loved the idea of it, perhaps all the more so because he observed it from a distance and could see the lights but not the shadows. All his life he dressed as he thought an American might do, in a plain high-necked Republican tunic of gray or black, with a thin line of white at the top. A writer in *Le Figaro* observed that he looked like a Quaker. Americans flocked around him in Paris. One observed him lecturing at the Sorbonne in 1873 "with hundreds of pretty American girls at his feet."[241]

Laboulaye was a charming man who combined a generous spirit with the exquisite manners of his family's aristocratic origins. He dropped the

French Medal honoring Abraham Lincoln and presented to Mrs. Lincoln in 1866. Lincoln Papers, Manuscript Division, Library of Congress.

Edouard René Lefebvre de Laboulaye, the French liberal historian who proposed the Statue of Liberty and led the campaign. Statue of Liberty National Monument.

particule de noblesse from his name, threw himself into liberal politics, and attracted a circle of centrist political leaders. He and his friends strongly supported the Union in the American Civil War. After the death of Abraham Lincoln they raised money for a gold medal and sent it to the president's widow with the inscription "Lincoln, an honest man, he abolished slavery, restored the union, saved the republic, without veiling the statue of liberty."[242]

At his dinner party in the spring of 1865, Laboulaye urged that something more should be done. He suggested that the people of France might commission a monument in the United States to celebrate the triumph of liberty and to commemorate the friendship of the two nations. Seated at his table was Frédéric Auguste Bartholdi, an accomplished young sculptor and a chevalier of the Legion of Honor. Bartholdi was a Lutheran from Alsace, a Freemason, and a liberal who loved large causes. He volunteered to design the monument.[243]

In 1871, Bartholdi went to America to study the question. With introductions from Laboulaye, he met President Grant, Senator Charles Sumner, Henry Wadsworth Longfellow, and many antislavery leaders who gave him strong support. Bartholdi found himself attracted and appalled by the scale of American life. "Everything is big here," he wrote; "even the petits pois are larger." Bartholdi decided to design a monument on a scale appropriate to the New World. In a flash of inspiration he

Frédéric Auguste Bartholdi, sculptor of the Statue of Liberty, portrait. Statue of Liberty National Monument.

identified Bedloe's Island in New York harbor as the appropriate place for a colossus of liberty.[244]

Laboulaye and Bartholdi shared an interest in the French Revolutionary tradition of Boullée's *architecture parlante*, structures that speak. Laboulaye defined the message of this statue, which was to be "truly liberty, but American liberty. She is not liberty with a red cap on her head and a pike in her hand, stepping over corpses. Ours in one hand holds the torch—no, not the torch that sets afire but the *flambeau*, the candle-flame that enlightens. In her other hand, she holds the tablets of law." This was to be a monument to "the liberty that lives only through Truth and Justice, Light and Law."[245]

Laboulaye's idea of liberty was balanced and centrist. It was also very broad. A friend wrote that for him "freedom was an individual thing [*chose individuelle*], the right belonging to everyone as a human being to exercise and develop one's body and mind without the intervention of the state, except to maintain peace and justice." This was liberty as it was understood by classical liberals in the late nineteenth century. It was carefully limited in its substance, yet also enlarged into a universal idea that embraced all humanity. The Statue of Liberty was deliberately designed to be became the symbol of this vision.[246]

Bartholdi faithfully followed Laboulaye's ideas and added other themes. Among the most important appeared in his female figure of liberty. The model was his mother, Anne-Marie-Auguste Charlotte Beyssar, a woman of great presence, described as "handsome" and "statuesque." The resemblance was said to be striking, so much so that in 1876, when the sculptor introduced his friend Senator Jeannotte Bozérian to his

Philip Ratner, bronze sculptures of Bartholdi and Laboulaye that stand on Bedloe's Island. Courtesy of Philip Ratner.

mother, the senator exclaimed, "That's the Statue of Liberty!" The sculptor preserved the likeness but generalized and abstracted the features to create an image of universal liberty. A linkage of the particular with the general was an important message of this *architecture parlante*.[247]

Yet another theme emerged in the pose of Bartholdi's figure. Liberty is represented as moving forward. It is a dynamic image of an idea in motion, advancing through the world. Bartholdi developed this kinetic theme in his choice of the monument's site. In New York harbor he placed the monument in such a way that the impression of movement is strongest when the statue is seen from ships entering the harbor. As one comes abreast of the statue, the illusion changes from dynamism to stability, with America behind her. Then, as one continues on toward Manhattan and sees the statue from the Battery, she appears to be looking outward from America to the world. The result is an ingenious integration of figure, pose, setting, and message. The effect is also to create a double dynamic: one in the monument itself; the other in the observer, moving from one perspective to another.[248]

Bartholdi and Laboulaye added other symbolic details to reinforce these larger themes of ordered liberty, universal liberty, and dynamic liberty. The liberty cap, a radical symbol in France, was replaced by a starry crown, radiating outward like rays of light. The liberty pole or wand was also removed to make way for a torch, symbolic of liberty enlightening the world. And a tablet was added in the other hand to represent the rule of law. The torch, book, and crown were all emblems of Freemasonry, to which Bartholdi belonged. He also put broken shackles at the base of the statue, which made it an image not only of liberty but liberation. This *architecture parlante* had many messages.

For the construction of the statue Laboulaye recruited the leading structural engineers of his generation. The first was Eugène Emmanuel Viollet-le-Duc, who proposed a light copper skin, hammered by the method called *repoussé* until it was barely 2.5 millimeters thick, less than a tenth of an inch. The copper sheets were to be fastened by metal bars to a rigid structure of massive sand-filled stone compartments.

Philip Ratner, sculptures of Gustave Eiffel and Joseph Pulitzer. Courtesy of Philip Ratner.

Viollet-le-Duc died in 1879, and Laboulaye replaced him with Gustave Eiffel, who specialized in large metal railroad bridges and structures
such as the Eiffel Tower, which was for many years the tallest in the
world. Eiffel kept the copper skin but changed the supporting structure
to an iron pylon ninety-six feet high, made of light trusses, flat bars,
springs, and bolts. It was designed as a dynamic engineering structure of

*"La Statue de la Liberté,
Rue de Chazelles," painting
by Paul-Joseph-Victor Dar-
gaud, 1884. © Photothèque
des Musées de Ville de
Paris.*

high resilience and great strength. It was a brilliant conception, at the cutting edge of applied mathematics, metallurgy, and building design. If the appearance of the statue derived from the ancient goddess of liberty, its structure was prophetic of modern architecture with its curtain walls and flexible skeleton.[249]

Fund-raising was another difficult problem. This liberal monument was not to be created by the state. Laboulaye recruited the great promoter Ferdinand de Lesseps, who built the Suez Canal, to help rally support. Together they raised part of the money by subscription and much of it by lottery.

The Statue of Liberty was twenty-one years in the making. Its huge components were made separately. With a flair for showmanship Laboulaye and de Lesseps staged a dinner for donors inside the completed right foot of the statue, and later an intimate gathering inside the knee.

In 1881, the statue was finally completed. It was put together in a test assembly. One of the most charming paintings of the statue shows it rising high above the rooftops of Paris, higher than the Vendôme Column. In that setting it was an image of a new spirit emerging from an old world.[250]

While French workers made the statue, Americans prepared the base. The pedestal was a massive granite pile designed by an American architect trained in France, William Morris Hunt. The foundation was the largest concrete structure in the world at that time. It was built by General Charles Stone, for whom the Statue of Liberty had a personal meaning. Early in the Civil War, General Stone had been made a scapegoat for the Union defeat at Ball's Bluff. He was seized by government agents at midnight, arrested without charge, and imprisoned without trial for 189 days on an island in New York harbor, probably to protect the real culprits, who had friends in high places. Laboulaye's idea of liberty as the rule of law had a special significance for the man who laid its foundation.[251]

General Charles Stone, the engineer who constructed the base of the Statue of Liberty and had his own idea of its meaning. Statue of Liberty National Monument.

On October 28, 1886, the monument was ready for dedication by President Grover Cleveland. The harbor was crowded with shipping, colorfully decorated with flags and

Edward P. Moran, "The Unveiling of the Statue of Liberty, Enlightening the World," 1886. Museum of the City of New York, J. Clarence Davies Collection. Moran did two earlier paintings on the Statue of Liberty: "Commerce of Nations Rendering Homage to Liberty," and "The Statue of Liberty at Night."

bunting. Warships greeted the president with thunderous salutes, and the entire harbor was covered with rolling clouds of dense white smoke. As the president's vessel sailed across the upper harbor, nothing could be seen above the smoke but the monument itself, a gigantic figure of Liberty with a torch in her upraised hand.[252]

Not everybody liked it. Philadelphians thought that it belonged on the Delaware River. New England Yankees complained that the Statue of Liberty was too big, too vulgar, too foreign, too French, and too New York. The conservative Boston poet James Russell Lowell wrote that it was overdone, and he could not see the point of it.[253]

At the opposite end of the political spectrum was a Russian radical, Aleksandra Kollontai, who thought it was "pitiful" and "shrunken" and even "powerless," a "tiny figure shrinking before the all powerful gigantic skyscrapers" in Manhattan, which were symbols of rapacious capitalism. The Roman Catholic clergy were hostile in yet another way. They raged against a pagan female idol of liberty, which gave them four reasons to dislike it.[254]

But these naysayers were small minorities in the Great Republic. Most Americans accepted the gift of a sister republic with gratitude and took it warmly to their hearts. They were deeply moved by Laboulaye's conception of American liberty, inspired by Bartholdi's dream of universal rights, amazed by Eiffel's brilliant construction, and delighted by its grace. This noble, generous, and large-spirited symbol of liberty demonstrated the power of an image to transform an idea. American visions of liberty and freedom would never be the same again.

THE GOLDEN DOOR

Immigrant Visions of Universal Freedom in the North

> Give me your tired, your poor,
> Your huddled masses yearning to breathe free.
>
> —EMMA LAZARUS

> O Liberty, white Goddess! Is it well
> To leave the gates unguarded?
>
> —THOMAS BAILEY ALDRICH

NO SOONER WAS THE Statue of Liberty erected than its meaning began to change. It quickly acquired a new significance from its location on Bedloe's Island in New York harbor. Nearby was Ellis Island, which in the late nineteenth century became the largest point of entry for immigrants to the United States. In the moment of their arrival, they shared a common experience that became part of the mythology of the republic.

The journey to America was an ordeal for many immigrants. The agony of parting and the anxiety of an unknown future were very painful for some of them. The long sea voyage was difficult, and sometimes dangerous. Then at last they reached the New World, and had their first sight of Liberty with her upraised torch.

Many seaborne immigrants retained an indelible memory of the moment. Edward Corsi, who came from Italy, never forgot the instant when his ship sailed into New York harbor and the Statue of Liberty suddenly came into view. He remembered that a great silence fell suddenly across the deck of the immigrant ship—a silence filled with awe and hope and glorious inspiration. Parents reached down and raised their children above the rails to see the Statue of Liberty, "shadowy through the mist." He recalled the feeling that Liberty was beckoning to each of them, bidding them welcome in the great republic that was to be their home.

On Edward Steiner's immigrant ship the decks were quiet as the new

Immigrants on Ellis Island, looking at the Statue of Liberty, photograph, ca. 1930. Library of Congress.

land came into sight. Then, he remembered, "slowly the ship glides into the harbor, and when it passes under the shadow of the statue of liberty, the silence is broken, and a thousand hands are outstretched in greeting to this new divinity to whose keeping they now entrust themselves." Immigrants embraced the Statue of Liberty as their own. Italian Catholics bought votive statues, which they called Santa Liberata. Hungarian Jewish immigrant Louis Pulitzer devoted his life to its welfare.[255]

In 1919, a history pageant was organized in Milwaukee, Wisconsin, by a radical Jewish labor organization called Poale Zion Chasidim. A photograph of the event shows a tall young lad dressed as Abraham Lincoln, and by his side a handsome young woman as the Statue of Liberty, with a torch in her hand and a gleam in her eye. At her feet, a sign reads "The Wanderer Finds Liberty in America." Her name was Goldie Mabovitz Myerson. She had emigrated from Kiev to Milwaukee as a small child. In 1921, she moved again from Wisconsin to a collective farm in Palestine. Later she changed her name to Golda Meir and became prime minister of Israel.[256]

Golda Meir was always ambivalent about her American experience, and with reason. Jewish immigrants from eastern Europe met a mixed reception in the United States. In the period when the Statue of Liberty was rising on Bedloe's Island, the Congress was busily raising new barriers to immigration. In 1882, Congress prohibited the entry of paupers, lunatics, idiots, criminals, and any incapacitated person who might become a public charge. More sweeping restrictions followed in the next forty years.

Arguments for exclusion were made in terms of protecting liberty. In Boston, Thomas Bailey Aldrich wrote a powerful poem called "Unguarded Gates."

> *Wide open and unguarded stand our gates,*
> *And through them presses a wild motley throng, . . .*
> *O Liberty, white Goddess! is it well*
> *To leave the gates unguarded?*

Aldrich explained to a friend that he had "looked in on an anarchist meeting" and heard "such things spoken by our 'feller citizens' as made my cheek burn." He added, "I believe in America for the Americans; I believe in the widest freedom and the narrowest license, and I hold that jail-birds, professional murderers, amateur lepers...and human gorillas generally should be closely questioned at our gates."[257]

Similar attitudes appeared throughout the United States. In Clinton, Louisiana, southerners founded the American Protective Association to stop the flow of immigrants and especially Roman Catholics. On the West Coast, mobs brutally maimed and murdered Chinese immigrants. In one of the darker ironies of American history, Congress acted in 1882 to forbid the entry of laborers from China, on the ground that their arrival "endangers the good order of certain localities." The same law also declared that Chinese could not become citizens of the United States. This was the first federal law to impose a racial test for citizenship. Congress did not act on its own initiative.

The Chinese Exclusion Act of 1882 was a response to heavy pressure from public opinion in the Pacific states. It was passed while Chinese laborers were actually at work on Bedloe's Island, helping to build the pedestal for America's great icon of liberty. Saum Song Bo wrote angrily in 1885, "The word liberty makes me think of the fact that this country is the land of liberty for men of all nations except the Chinese. I consider it as an insult to us Chinese to call on us to contribute toward building in this land a pedestal for the Statue of Liberty." Saum Song Bo wondered "whether this statute against the Chinese or the Statue to Liberty will be the more lasting monument."[258]

To this great question every American generation has made a different answer. Here again, two conflicting visions of liberty and freedom met in collision. One was a universal idea of rights for all. The other was a tribal idea of rights only for the citizens of one nation. In the late nineteenth and early twentieth centuries, the tribal idea began to be enacted by the Congress, enforced by presidents, and upheld by the courts.

But the larger vision took on a life of its own. In New York City a young

Jewish History Pageant in Milwaukee, with Golda Meir as the Statue of Liberty, 1919. Wisconsin Historical Society.

Jewish woman found the words for it. Emma Lazarus was the daughter of a wealthy sugar refiner in New York, a poet of talent, and a translator who was fluent in six languages. She also worked as a volunteer in the hospital for indigent immigrants on Ward's Island and was deeply moved by the suffering she saw there. In 1883, Emma Lazarus was asked by a friend to write a poem for an auction to raise money for the pedestal of the Statue of Liberty. She drew upon her experience of Ward's Island to compose a sonnet called "The New Colossus." Most Americans know its last lines:

> *"Keep, ancient lands, your storied pomp!" cries she*
> *With silent lips. "Give me your tired, your poor,*
> *Your huddled masses yearning to breathe free,*
> *The wretched refuse of your teeming shore.*
> *Send these, the homeless, tempest-tost to me,*
> *I lift my lamp beside the golden door."*

The poem did not at first make a public impression. Other poets were among the first to notice it. James Russell Lowell, who shared the New England prejudice against the monument, wrote the author, "I like your sonnet about the statue—much better than I like the statue itself. But your sonnet gives its subject a raison d'être which it wanted before quite as much as it wants a pedestal."[259]

A few months later, Emma Lazarus was stricken with cancer, and died in 1887 at the age of thirty-eight. Her poem was published posthumously

in a volume of collected works and was nearly forgotten until the turn of the twentieth century. Her friend Georgina Schuyler stumbled on it in a secondhand bookstore and was so deeply moved that she persuaded others to set the poem on a bronze tablet at the base of the Statue of Liberty as a memorial to its author.

In the years that followed, it became much more than that. Other writers, many of them immigrants or the children of immigrants such as the Slovenian American writer Louis Adamic,

Emma Lazarus (1849–87), photograph. American Jewish Historical Society.

"The New Colossus," 1883, Emma Lazarus's poem about the Statue of Liberty. American Jewish Historical Society.

wrote about the poem, and its fame began to spread. In 1941 it was read in a film called *Hold Back the Dawn*, about the suffering of a refugee played by Charles Boyer. During the Second World War the poem was set to music and became a part of Fourth of July concerts throughout the nation.

But mostly it gained its popularity from its association with a symbol of the Statue of Liberty. Every new immigrant enlarged this idea of universal freedom. In the process, the monument itself changed, too. New York's great green lady and her gilded torch became a beacon for all humanity.

ROSE OF SHARON, STAR OF ZION

Afro-American Visions of Universal Freedom in the South

> O Freedom, O Freedom,
> O Freedom, after a while. . . .
>
> There'll be shouting, There'll be shouting,
> There'll be shouting, after a while.
>
> —"O Freedom," southern spiritual

A PARALLEL MOVEMENT for universal freedom also happened in the old Confederate states. After Reconstruction, whites regained control of the South, and Jim Crow spread through the region. Rigid systems of racial segregation were enacted by every southern legislature and ratified by the Supreme Court in *Plessy v. Ferguson* (1896). Black men lost the right to vote merely because of the color of their skin, and the federal government did nothing to help them. Violence increased, and lynching became an instrument of racism. As late as 1884, 211 people were lynched in the United States, and three out of four were white. In 1892, 230 people were lynched, and three out of four were black. By 1902, more than 90 percent of lynching victims were black.

The South returned to its hierarchic ideas of hegemonic liberty. Images of white supremacy were cast in terms of the rights of the master race. When Carter Glass was told that Jim Crow was a form of discrimination, he answered defiantly, "Discrimination! Why that is precisely what we propose; that exactly is what this convention was elected for."

But even in this dark era of racial injustice, freedom as a universal idea continued to expand. Its primary defenders were African American people themselves, who never stopped striving for their rights. This side of the story is to be found in the chronicles of African American churches and newspapers and schools and colleges.

African American iconography of freedom was different from that of

Emancipation Day, Richmond, Va., photo by Cook, ca. 1880s. Valentine Richmond History Center.

white Americans. Many symbols of freedom and nationality in the United States looked very different to former slaves. At New Bern, North Carolina, in 1896, a black housewife and journalist, Sarah Dudley Pettey wrote that the American eagle sheltered "beneath his mighty wings all of his white children: while with his talons he ruthlessly clawed all who are poor and especially those who trace their lineage to ebony hued parentage."[260]

Other images of freedom flourished among African Americans in the South. They were drawn from the Bible, the words of the Gospels, and the music of hymns and spirituals. They multiplied in the nineteenth century, especially in times of trouble.

Some of these symbols began to appear in the last years of bondage. One of them emerged in Texas, where slavery was a long time dying. Two months after Robert E. Lee surrendered at Appomattox, Union troops entered Galveston and found that Texas slaves were still in bondage, as if the war had never happened. On June 19, 1865, Union commander Gideon Granger immediately issued a general order to masters and slaves:

"The people are informed that in accordance with a proclamation from the Executive of the United States, all slaves are free. This involves an absolute equality of personal rights and rights of property between former masters and slaves, and the connection heretofore existing between them, becomes that between employer and hired labor. The freed are advised to remain at their present homes, and work for wages. They are informed that they will not be supported in idleness either there or elsewhere."[261]

Union troops with weapons in hand read General Granger's blunt military order as a public proclamation. It struck the Lone Star State with shattering force. Many slaves had no knowledge of the war's end, or the beginning of emancipation. To them the news came as revelation. Many downed tools and celebrated their freedom. Some left in search of families that had been broken by slavery. Masters and mistresses fled in fear that the cruelty of slavery would be visited upon them. Slaves ripped off their rags and helped themselves to the clothing of their former owners.

The emancipated slaves in Texas always remembered that day of liberation, June 19, 1865. The next year they celebrated it as the anniversary of their emancipation, and kept on keeping the Day each year. They called it by many names: Emancipation Day, Freedom Day, Jubilee, Jamboree. Children began to speak of it as Juneteenth, and the name caught on.[262]

Its growth owed much to the miserable conditions in which the former slaves lived. White Texans abused them without mercy, even more so than in slavery itself. In 1866, a defiant state legislature enacted a Black Code that fell cruelly on former slaves, even returning some of them to bondage. A Texas Homestead Act gave land to whites but denied it to blacks. Racial violence increased. In the first years of freedom, many freed slaves died of hunger, disease, and brutality.

In the face of continued oppression, African Americans kept the spirit of freedom alive in annual celebrations of Juneteenth, which grew steadily larger in big Texas towns. White authorities responded by repression. The use of public land was refused for Juneteenth celebrations. Former slaves reacted by raising money and buying their own land for the event. In Houston they raised a thousand dollars for the purchase of a tract called Emancipation Park, to be used as a place for Juneteenth celebrations. In the town of Mexia, former slaves founded Booker T. Washington Park by 1898; on Juneteenth celebrations it drew crowds as large as twenty thousand people. Every year the former slaves of Texas celebrated their freedom that way.

In some ways Juneteenth resembled the Fourth of July. It often included a parade, marching band, speeches, picnics, songs, rodeos, barbecues, and dances. But in one way it was different. This was a celebration not of liberty as independence but of freedom as the rights of belonging to other free people. Juneteenth had its own character that way. Sometimes it included a ritual of removing ragged work clothes, throwing them into the river, and putting on one's best clothes, in memory of what happened on the first Juneteenth. Always there were prayers of thanks for the end of slavery, prayers of dedication for the challenge of freedom, and prayers of resolve against racism and strength against violence.

A favorite symbol was the Rose of Sharon, from the Song of Solomon 2:1: "I am the Rose of Sharon and the lily of the valleys, as the lily among thorns." A "traditional prayer" began: "Father, I stretch my hand to thee—for no other help I know. Oh my rose of Sharon, my shelter in the time of storm. My prince of peace, my hope in this harsh land." It ended, "When I come down to the river of Jordan, hold the river still and let your servant cross during a calm down. Father, I'll be looking for that land where Job said the wicked would cease from troubling us and weary souls would be at rest . . . and we can say with the saints of old, Free at Last, Free at Last, thank God almighty, I am free at last."[263]

Another image of freedom was the Star of Zion. Black newspapers called themselves by that name, and it inspired an iconography of freedom on their mastheads. The Star of Zion was a symbol of light. The book that the freed slaves knew best was the gospel of light. Spirituals celebrated it as the light of freedom.

> *I've got the light of Freedom, Lord,*
> *And I'm going to let it shine,*
> *Let it shine, let it shine, let it shine!*

The Star of Zion also had another meaning. Its rays reached out to everyone on God's earth. This was an image of universal freedom, and it was taken up by former slaves of the Old South, still dispossessed of the rights to liberty and even life itself that the Constitution promised them. They embraced the idea of universal freedom with a large and generous spirit, and they did so at a time when southern whites went another way.[264]

ORGAN OF THE AFRICAN METHODIST EPISCOPAL ZION CHURCH IN AMERICA.

ıme XXIII.   Charlotte, N. C., Thursday, January 5, 1899.   Number 1.

Charlotte, N.C., Star of Zion, *newspaper masthead. Library of Congress.*

The Star of Zion also promised victory and triumph in a dark time of suffering and defeat. In the sorrowful days of southern decline, when the children of the Confederacy lost their way, the former slaves sang of light and kept the faith of universal freedom. The greatness of America's dream passed to them, and it was nourished by a forgotten generation of African Americans who lived in the valley of the shadows between the Civil War and the civil rights movement in the twentieth century. It should always be remembered that they never lost faith in the light of freedom to come.[265]

BRIGHT EYES AND STANDING BEAR

American Indians and Universal Freedom in the West

> Let us alone and keep away from us.
>
> —BLACK HAWK, 1832

> Let me be a free man.
>
> —CHIEF JOSEPH, 1879

SOME OF THE most striking visions of liberty and freedom were created by American Indians. In the eighteenth century, as we have seen, Indians had been a European symbol of liberty in the New World. The Indians themselves had their own ideas on that subject and incorporated a version of this idea in their own cultures. Its meaning can be observed in the evidence of Indian sign language. A common gesture for liberty or freedom was a hand sign that meant alone, or by oneself, or solitude. When combined with a presentation of a gift, it also meant that nothing was expected in return. It represented a vision of liberty as the desire to be left alone, free to go one's own way. This was one Native American response to European presence in the New World.[266]

That vision of liberty was put into words by many Indian leaders during the eighteenth and nineteenth centuries. A leading example was Makataimeshekiakiak (1767–1838), war leader of the Sauk and Fox nations. White settlers in Illinois called him Black Hawk. In 1832, he explained his idea of liberty to J. M. Street at Prairie du Chien: "We told them to let us alone and keep away from us; but they followed on, and beset our paths, and they coiled themselves among us, like the snake. They poisoned us by the touch. We are not safe. We live in danger. We are becoming like them; hypocrites and liars, adulterers, lazy drones; all talkers and no workers." He fought for the liberty to be let alone.[267]

Similar visions were shared by many Indian leaders, such as the brilliant chief Inmuttooyahlatlat (ca. 1840–1904) of the Nez Perce people. He was known as Joseph to the United States Army, which his people defeated in every battle but the last. In 1879, Joseph came to Washington and was invited to give a speech in the Capitol, which was later printed by his many admirers. Some of his thoughts were similar to Black Hawk's. Joseph said, "Let me be a free man, free to travel, free to stop, free to work, free to trade, where I choose, free to choose my own teachers, free to follow the religion of my fathers, free to think and talk and act for myself—and I will obey every law, or submit to the penalty." This was the same vision of living free as the right to go one's own way.

But Joseph was beginning to think differently in 1879. He added, "If the White Man wants to live in peace with the Indian he can live in peace." Joseph explained how it could be done. "Treat all men alike," he said. "Give them all the same law. Give them all an even chance to live and grow. All men were made by the same Great Spirit Chief. They are all brothers. The earth is the mother of all people, and all people should have equal rights upon it."[268]

After the great wars on the western plains, that idea began to spread among Indian leaders. They accepted the hegemony of the United States as an inexorable fact and began to develop an idea that Indian nations should seek their own way by claiming the rights of free citizens in the American republic.

Standing Bear, chief of the Ponca Indians, who found a new way to fight for his people and became a living symbol of universal rights in the American West. Nebraska State Historical Society.

A leading example was a movement led by Chief Standing Bear and the people of the Ponca Nation in what is now Nebraska. They had been badly used by land-hungry white settlers, fought back in bloody struggles, and were confined on a reservation in Nebraska. Then that land was taken, too, and they were forcibly removed to Indian Territory in what is now Oklahoma. A deeply corrupt Bureau of Indian Affairs made it impossible for them to support themselves and failed to supply sufficient food or shelter to keep them alive. Many Ponca died. Standing Bear, after losing his own son, decided that he would lead his people home again. After a terrible journey they joined the kindred people of the Omaha Nation in Nebraska.

Generals William Tecumseh Sherman in Washington and Philip Sheridan in Chicago ordered that the Ponca be arrested and returned to Oklahoma. Given the corruption of the "Indian Ring" in the Bureau of Indian Affairs, that order amounted to a death sentence for the Ponca Nation. Other army officers in Nebraska protested against it. One of them at Fort Omaha reported that the Indians and their horses were so ill and weak that they could not survive the journey to Oklahoma.

The senior officer in Nebraska, General George Crook, also sympathized with the Indians but knew better than to challenge Sherman and Sheridan. Crook dealt with the problem in another way. He quietly contacted a journalist, Thomas Tibbles, and said, "I've been forced many times by orders from Washington to do most inhuman things in dealing with the Indians, but now I'm ordered to do a more cruel thing than ever before." Tibbles in turn talked with Indian leaders on the Omaha Reservation, including a young woman named Bright Eyes. Whites knew her as Susette La Flesche, member of a highly educated Indian family. She began to write essays. With encouragement from Tibbles, La Flesche, and Crook, the Ponca Nation decided to sue in federal district court.[269]

The result was the case of *United States ex ret. Standing Bear vs. George Crook* (1879), brought by twenty-six members of the Ponca Nation who sought to win their freedom by a writ of habeas corpus. The U.S. district attorney appeared against them, insisting that Indians were not citizens and had no right to sue in federal court, an argument reminiscent of Dred Scott. The case was heard by Judge Elmer Dundy, who observed that in fifteen years he had never heard a case that "appealed so strongly to my sympathy as the one now under consideration." His ruling found for the Indians on every point of law. In a ringing phrase he wrote that "an Indian is a PERSON within

Bright Eyes, Susette La Flesche (here seen with her brother), who joined in the struggle for rights of the Ponca People. Nebraska State Historical Society.

the meaning of the laws of the United States," and has a right to sue for Habeas Corpus in all cases "where he is restrained of liberty in violation of the Constitution or laws of the United States." Further, he found that the government had no constitutional right to remove the Poncas to Indian Territory in the first place, and he added that Indians have an "inalienable right to life, liberty, and the pursuit of happiness."[270]

The government considered an appeal but decided against it. The case caused a sensation throughout the West, and much of the press coverage was sympathetic to the Indians. The St. Paul *Pioneer Press* observed that the ruling "should be as good for Indians as Negroes. The protection of habeas corpus is not superfluous for any class under government."[271]

The Ponca Nation won their case. Standing Bear visited his lawyers in Omaha and made them a speech of thanks. "You and I are here," he said. "Our skins are of a different color but God made us both." He said that for many years, more than a century. white men had been abusing his people, and they replied by going to war. "We took our tomahawks and went to kill," he said, ". . . but you have found a better way. You have gone into the Court for us and I find our wrongs can be righted there. Now I have no more use for a tomahawk. I want to lay it down forever." Standing Bear laid it on the ground, then presented it to his lawyer.[272]

In the late nineteenth century, this dream of universal freedom for all people to go their own way was taken up by other Indian nations. It appeared among the western Navaho and Apache in the Southwest, the Arapaho and Shoshone in the Great Basin, and the Nez Perce and the nations of the Northwest. It flourished among the Sioux and the Crow and the Cheyenne on the Great Plains.

These were the last Indian nations to be conquered. During the late nineteenth century and immediately afterward, their art and culture changed in striking ways. All of these nations preserved their aesthetic traditions and combined them with the ways of people they fought against. The art of the American Indians had always made heavy use of iconic emblems and symbols—some of their own heritage, some borrowed from other cultures.

Prominent among these borrowings in the late nineteenth century were the emblems of American nationality and universal freedom as they had emerged from the Civil War. The Stars and Stripes became a great favorite in Indian arts and crafts. Much use was made of red, white, and blue shields, lone stars, and American eagles. A remarkable example was a leather bag made by a Plateau Indian in the late nineteenth or early twentieth century. It was cut out of native tanned hide, and the front of the bag was entirely covered in beadwork. In the center were two American flags, a spread eagle, a national shield, and a lone white star with a red center. At the bottom were an Indian and a white settler, both armed with rifles and fighting against one another. The Indian artist appealed to the symbolic meaning of the flag, even as he commemorated the armed struggle of the Indians to be free of domination.[273]

The arts and crafts of many Indian nations made heavy use of the same devices. The Stars and Stripes and the national eagle frequently appeared on Iroquois breastplates, Cheyenne banners, Navaho blankets, Oglala vests, and the pouches and tobacco bags and gauntlets and cuffs of Indian nations throughout the continent. Among the most dra-

American Indian beaded bag. American Hurrah Antiques, courtesy of Joel Kopp.

matic artifacts were the ceremonial horse masks of the Lakota Sioux. These were large leather facings that entirely covered a horse's head and neck, with openings for eyes, ears, and nose. One handsome Lakota horse mask was made of brightly colored beads, with two dozen American flags in red, white, and blue repeated over a glistening white background in fine-textured beadwork.[274]

Howard Bad Hand, a Lakota Sioux who grew up on the Rosebud Reservation, observed that "today any visitor to a Lakota gathering will be struck by what appears to be a zealous showing of patriotism and love for the American flag and its many symbolic variations." He asks why that is so, after "many atrocities, injustices and destructive aggression were committed against the Lakota by the United States." An answer appears in the flag songs of the Lakota Nation. One anthem begins: "The President's flag [literally, the staff of the one they call the grandfather] will stand without end. Under it the people will grow."

The American flag was perceived as a universal symbol that protected the Lakota people, as it did other groups. It appeared in Lakota crafts, linked to Indian symbols such as the morning star, a symbol of rebirth and prosperity. It was also combined with birds, flowers, and geometric symbols that represented eternal life and happiness, harmony, and balance. American Indians integrated themselves into the symbolic life of the republic even as they preserved their own culture.[275]

In the next century, visions of liberty and freedom would come together in a more complex idea of Indian rights. One was the National Congress of American Indians. Kiowa-Navajo John Belindo, executive director of that organization, testified to Congress in 1969, "I think this is essentially the song of every Indian and Indian tribe, a certain feeling of freedom, a chance to be free to manage their own affairs."[276]

Another was the American Indian Movement, founded in Minneapolis in 1968. Its inspiration was the civil rights movement, and its first purpose was to protect the rights of Indians in American cities, where they suffered from racial prejudice and poverty. The goals of the movement grew larger and led to annual events that were designed to draw attention to Indian rights: the takeover of Alcatraz Island (1969), the march on Washington and Takeover of the Bureau of Indian Affairs (1971), the "Trail of Broken Treaties" (1972), the takeover of Wounded Knee (1973), the "Longest Walk" from San Francisco to Washington (1978), and the takeover of the Black Hills in 1981.

These trends began among many minorities in the North, South, and West during the late nineteenth century. As white Americans abandoned the promises of universal rights that were part of the Civil War and Reconstruction, others took up those ideas and kept them growing.

Indian rights inspired many movements in the America during the 1960s and 1970s. They were influenced by the struggle for civil rights and by the long heritage of struggle by Indian Nations. An example was the American Indian Movement. Its occupation of the Village of Wounded Knee, South Dakota, from February to May 1973, expressed a vision of liberty and freedom through strength and autonomy. Wounded Knee, Pine Ridge Indian Reservation, S.D., March 3, 1973. Image donated by Corbis/Bettmann.

THE REVIVAL OF LIBERTY

The Growth of Classical Liberalism in the Gilded Age

> Liberty is not a means to a higher political end. It is itself the highest political end.
>
> —LORD ACTON

ANOTHER NEW MOVEMENT appeared in American politics during the presidential election of 1872. Its leaders were both Democrats and Republicans. They included gentleman scholars such as Charles Francis Adams and Henry Adams, gentleman journalists such as Samuel Bowles and "Marse Henry" Watterson, and gentleman reformers such as Samuel Tilden ("a Democrat *and* a gentleman," said a Philadelphia lady in amazement).[277]

Many of these reform-minded men had supported Grant's administration, but they were offended by its corruption, appalled by the spread of scandal in the states and cities, and amazed by the effrontery of the Tweed Ring in New York. The reformers concluded that both parties were hopeless as instruments of change and nominated Horace Greeley as a candidate for the presidency. Their slogan was "Liberty, Equality, Fraternity, Universal Amnesty, Impartial Suffrage."

The reformers knew who they were against and what they were for, but they did not know what to call themselves. In the South they were known as Conservatives, or Reform Democrats. In the northern states they were called Liberal Republicans, or simply Liberals, and that name caught on. In 1872, they became the first self-styled Liberal party in American politics.[278]

These first American Liberals defined their purposes primarily in terms of liberty. One of them summarized their party's goals in a phrase:

The Liberal idea and the rebirth of liberty: Horace Greeley, the Liberal Republicans and the Reform Democratic movement in the election of 1872, chromolithograph. Library of Congress.

"the largest liberty consistent with public order." To many, the "largest liberty" meant the smallest government that could keep the peace. Another said that they were committed to "the reformatory work of Mr. Jefferson," and to that end they favored a dismantling operation on the state.

Government meant to them the corruption of the Grant presidency, the tyranny of the Tweed Ring, the failure of military reconstruction in the South, and the misery of Indian reservations in the West. Their idea of liberal reform was a reduction of public spending, removal of federal regulation, expansion of local control throughout the republic, an end to military reconstruction, no more public favors for private corporations, and strong protections for property and civil rights.

In the election that followed, the Liberal Republican candidate, Horace Greeley, also became the nominee of the Democratic party. He

"The Flag, Liberty and Prosperity," by Jacob G. Baumann. Private Collection, through David Wheatcroft.

won 2.8 million popular votes, no small achievement, but not enough to defeat Ulysses Grant's 3.6 million. Greeley died shortly after the election, and the new party disintegrated. Grant was reelected to a second term, which proved to be even more corrupt than the first.

The Liberal Republicans failed in their immediate object but succeeded in another way. They were unable to turn the rascals out, but they were highly successful in giving new life to their vision of liberty. This was nineteenth-century liberalism. In economics, they favored free markets and free trade. In politics, they sought free, open, and honest elections. This was an American vision of untrammeled individual liberty and strict restraints on constitutional government, combined with a strong civic sense of public service and private integrity, all for the common good. Within the ancient framework of classical *libertas,* this modern liberal idea set the tone for a new age. It also created a new problem about the relationship of classical liberty to freedom for all and social order in a free republic.

Liberty of Commerce and Economic Order

"All Hail Liberty!" was a Liberal election cry in 1872. One of the most fertile fields for this impulse was liberty of commerce. Some Americans thought of that idea as a strict rule of laissez-faire and minimal government in all cases whatsoever. Other people understood laissez-faire as minimal government in most cases, with the exception of aid to an enterprise in which they had a stake. More than a few believed (correctly in this author's estimation) that America's true genius was a pragmatic gift for mixed enterprise, which combined elements of public and private

The American Indian also became an image of prosperity, liberty, and free commerce, as in this Indian princess wrapped in the flag, selling five-cent cigars. Judith A. Lowry, "American Indian Tobacco Girl." Peabody Essex Museum, Salem, Mass.

initiative within a framework of liberty-as-separation and freedom-as-belonging.[279]

In the late nineteenth century, political leaders actively encouraged private enterprise with all the public instruments at their disposal. At the same time, American entrepreneurs learned to use the opportunities that a strong republic and a stable polity presented to them. They availed themselves of the corporate form, a classic application of mixed enterprise, which armed private capitalists with powers and protections of the state. They made heavy use of tariffs, subsidies, land grants, and public assets of many kinds.

In the same spirit, private businesses also made heavy use of public symbols. They often used the most sacred emblems of the republic to advertise their wares. Private companies printed American flags with their own trademarks and advertisments stenciled across the stripes. The most mundane products were adorned with emblems of liberty. In Chicago, Old Glory was used to advertise "bicycles, belts, breweries, burlesque shows, door mats, ballet dresses." It was flown from saloons and brothels. In New Jersey, two breweries added flags to their advertisements with the slogan "Stands for the best beer." Americans wiped their feet on flag doormats and blew their noses into flag handkerchiefs. In Washington, American flags were printed on toilet paper and stamped on the surfaces of urinals, and American eagles were cast on the front of porcelain toilet bowls. Many protested against these practices. Booker T. Washington complained that commerce had turned the flag into an "emblem of the dollar, rather than an emblem of liberty."[280]

Molded vitreous porcelain toilet with American eagle, ca. 1900. National Museum of American History, Smithsonian Institution.

A deeper controversy developed over the balance of public and private control in America's system of mixed enterprise. This question was framed in terms of liberty and regulation in economic affairs, and it became increasingly urgent with the growth of the American economy in the late nineteenth century. Liberty of commerce in combination with the fostering hand of government had greatly encouraged the growth of corporate enterprise. As corporations grew larger, they controlled broad sectors of the American economy, and in the name of free trade they began to restrain the liberty of others.

Here was one of the great public questions in the late nineteenth century, and one that persisted through the twentieth century as well. On one side of the question were corporate leaders and company managers who fiercely defended their economic liberty to run their businesses as they pleased. They insisted that the new forms of private economic organization made a free society stronger than ever before. On the other side were economic reformers who argued that the great corporations were increasingly operating in restraint of trade and were abusing their own property rights to infringe the rights of others.

Like most public issues in American life, this great question rapidly became a debate over the meaning of liberty and freedom. Both sides claimed to be the defenders of those ideas and appealed for public support. It is interesting that they used the same iconographic symbols to represent very different ideas of liberty and freedom.

On one side of the question were images of unfettered corporate enterprise as instruments of liberty. One example appeared in a business

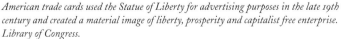
American trade cards used the Statue of Liberty for advertising purposes in the late 19th century and created a material image of liberty, prosperity and capitalist free enterprise. Library of Congress.

Thomas Nast, "The Home of the Trusts and the Land of the Plutocracy," 1889. New York Public Library.

advertisement for the Holmes and Coutts Company of New York, large commercial bakers who were known for their "famous seafoam wafers." Their trade card featured the Statue of Liberty, standing on a large box of Holmes and Coutts wafers. In her upraised hand she holds another wafer box, which is open and upside down. From it, a shower of seafoam wafers descends toward the upraised arms of the people below. Above the scene are the words "Liberty feeding the world."

On the other side of the question were visions of reformers such as Thomas Nast, who in 1889 attacked the growth of large corporations and trusts in America as subversive of American liberty. A Nast cartoon shows the Statue of Liberty completely covered with trusts and sinking into the sea beneath their accumulated weight. Even Liberty's torch is now taken over by the "Light Trust." In the background is the skyline of Manhattan, each building representing another trust. The people appear as a ship that has been wrecked by the "Monster Trust."

Religious Liberty and Republican Order: Catholics and Mormons

Another controversy developed at the same time in regard to religious liberty and public order. Catholic immigrants complained bitterly that public schools throughout the nation required students to read the King James Bible and even to recite Protestant prayers. In New York as early as 1840, Bishop John Hughes had opposed Protestant instruction in the schools of New York City and attempted to remove Catholic children from the Public School Society. In 1868, the Democratic Party gained control of the New York state legislature, with strong Catholic support. It used its power to give public money to private schools, many of which were Roman Catholic.

The Republican cartoonist Thomas Nast contributed his pen to this controversy, always strongly supportive of common schools and virulently anti-Catholic. He did a famous drawing that turned Bishop Hughes and Catholic prelates into predatory reptiles. Their mitred hats became the sinister jaws of crocodiles, attacking the children of the republic.

Thomas Nast fiercely defended the separation of church and state. He did another drawing that showed priests and preachers of many denominations, all with little churches mounted on wheels, appealing for public support, while Union troops bar the way, and Liberty waves them away from the public door.

Here were two ideas of religious liberty. One demanded protection for every creed and sect but also sought support for separate parochial

Thomas Nast: "The American River Ganges; The Priests and the Children," Harper's Weekly, *September 30, 1871. Library of Virginia.*

Thomas Nast, "Religious Liberty is Guaranteed," drawing on scratchboard. Library of Congress.

schools. The other insisted on separation of church and state but also favored the suppression of denominations that were thought to be dangerous to the faith and morals of the republic. Both tried to balance liberty and order, but in different ways.

Nast attacked Protestant denominations, too, when he thought that they threatened America's republican order. Some of his sharpest quills were reserved for the Mormons. Their practice of polygamy was thought by many Americans to threaten the institution of marriage and the family. The Mormons were entirely home grown, but their tabernacles,

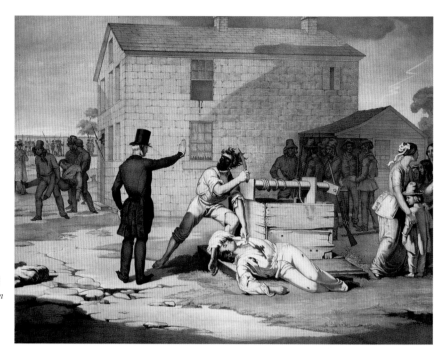

The Martyrdom of Joseph and Hiram Smith, colored lithograph by C. G. Crehen after G. W. Fasel, N.Y., 1851. Library of Congress.

polygamous families, and defiance of the federal government seemed entirely foreign to Protestants such as Nast. Another of Nast's drawings showed a Roman Catholic crocodile and a Mormon snapping turtle climbing onto the dome of the U.S. Capitol. Nast added the inscription: "Religious Liberty is guaranteed, but can we allow foreign reptiles to crawl all over US?"

On the other side of the question, Mormons were the objects of violent persecution by Protestants of other denominations. They claimed the protection of the Constitution and the Bill of Rights. One of the most powerful images of religious freedom was a vivid engraving of a masked assassin in the act of murdering Joseph and Hiram Smith. Both sides claimed to be striving for religious liberty. Each attacked the other for tyranny.

Free Love and Sexual Order:
The Claflin Sisters against the Beecher Clan

The most sensational controversy between liberty and order swirled around the figure of Victoria Claflin Woodhull. For some she was one of the free spirits of the age. For others she was thought to be the mortal enemy of ordered liberty and republican freedom. Victoria Claflin was born in the frontier town of Homer, Ohio, and named after Queen Victoria. Her mother was a spiritualist and her father an eccentric who was accused of arson and run out of town. Victoria and her sister, Tennessee Claflin, became professional clairvoyants and faith healers. She married an alcoholic physician named Canning Woodhull and bore him two children. Then she took a second husband, Colonel James Blood, who introduced her to radical causes.

With Colonel Blood's encouragement, Victoria and Tennessee moved to New York City. They made a convert of Commodore Vanderbilt, who helped them to open a brokerage office and make a killing in the market. In the same year Benjamin Butler invited her to give a speech on women's suffrage before the House Judiciary Committee. Victoria was herself converted by a utopian socialist movement called the Pantarchy, which preached economic radicalism and free love. The sisters were handsome, articulate, and charismatic. They began to attract a large following, and in 1872 the Equal Rights Party nominated Victoria for the presidency. She tried to cast a vote but was turned away from the polls.

The sisters also founded a newspaper called *The Woodhull and Claflin Weekly,* which strongly supported the rights of women, published Marx's Communist manifesto, and tirelessly advocated a vision of "free love." Others attacked this idea as promiscuity. To the Claflin sisters and their legion of admirers it meant something very different: an idea that various forms of coercion between women and men destroyed the freedom of true love.

Victoria Woodhull campaigned against prostitution, abortion, sexual slavery in marriage, and especially sexual hypocrisy. She spoke openly of her sexual affairs and lived with both of her husbands at the same time. Her life became more complex when she grew very close to a handsome young journalist, Theodore Tilton, and was thought to be his lover. Tilton and his wife belonged to the Brooklyn church of Henry Ward Beecher, America's leading evangelical minister and a figure of enormous moral stature in the republic. His sisters, Harriet Beecher Stowe and Catherine Beecher, both staunch defenders of domestic respectability, began to attack Victoria Woodhull. Victoria responded by publicly accusing Henry Beecher of adultery with Elizabeth Tilton, the wife of Victoria's friend Theodore Tilton. A huge national scandal followed, which became a severe test for liberty and sexual order. Elizabeth Tilton confessed to her adultery. Theodore Tilton sued Beecher for adultery, and a show trial ended in a hung jury. Beecher went on preaching to even larger audiences until his death in 1887. Victoria Woodhull and Tennessee Claflin went to jail for "issuing obscenity," then moved to England, where they were married yet again, Victoria to a rich banker and Tennessee to a

*Victoria Woodhull
(1838–1927), photograph.
Image donated by
Corbis/Bettmann.*

Thomas Nast, "Get Thee Behind Me, (Mrs.) Satan," Harper's Weekly,
February 17, 1872. Virginia Historical Society.

nobleman. They went on publishing a journal called *The Humanitarian* with the help of Victoria's daughter, sensationally named Zulu Woodhull, and continued to outrage respectable opinion on two continents until Tennessee Claflin died in 1923, and Victoria in 1927.

The career of Victoria Woodhull created a continuing controversy about free love and sexual order in the United States. Many Americans regarded her as a menace to the republic. Among her enemies was Thomas Nast, who attacked her relentlessly. One of his drawings showed her as a bat, preaching the Devil's gospel, "Be Saved by Free Love," while an honest woman turns away, preferring domestic misery to Victoria Woodhull's satanic message, with the words "I'd rather travel the hardest path of matrimony than follow your footsteps."[281]

Others defended her with equal passion, and Victoria Woodhull was always eloquent in her own defense. More than a century later she remains a national heroine in the cause of sexual liberation. In the twenty-first century, a Victoria Woodhull Web site sells iconic portraits of her in a plum-colored dress, with a white rose at her wrist. It also offers badges, buttons, and bumper stickers that still proclaim, "Victoria Woodhull for President."

"FREEDOM, THE SYNONYM OF EQUALITY"

Populist and Progressive Visions of a Free America

> Freedom, the synonym of equality, has been the stimu-
> lus and condition of progress. . . . They acknowledge
> the equality of right between man and man, just as
> they ensure to each the perfect liberty which is
> bounded only by the equal liberty of every other.
>
> —Henry George, Progress and Poverty

IN THE YEAR 1881 or thereabout, a small boy named Vernon Parrington sat by a kitchen stove in a farmhouse on Pumpkin Ridge in
Kansas. His family broke the prairie sod, planted many acres of
corn, and discovered to their horror that they had no market for their
crop. The cost of shipping was greater than its value. "Many a time," Parrington recalled, "have I warmed myself by the kitchen stove in which
ears were burning briskly, popping and crackling in the jolliest fashion.
And while we sat around such a fire watching the year's crop go up the
chimney, the talk sometimes became bitter."[282]

Many farming families shared that bitterness in the late nineteenth
century. Their fields were parched by drought, and their crops were ravaged by insects. Farm prices had fallen for thirty years, and what little
they earned went to the railroads and bankers. Many families abandoned
their farms, and moved to the city. American farmers had long thought of
themselves as the strength of the republic. In 1776, about 90 percent of
Americans worked in agriculture. A century later, the Census of 1880
showed that farm workers had fallen below 45 percent of the American
labor force. For the first time in American history, farmers were a minority of the population.[283]

Throughout the country the farmers began to organize political movements. First came the Grangers in the 1870s, then the Farmers Alliances
in the 1880s, and a new national organization called the People's Party in

1891. In the election of 1892, it nominated a presidential ticket of James Weaver and James Field, who had worn blue and gray in the Civil War. Together they won a million votes. By 1893 the press called them Populists, and they became a major force in American politics. They never won a national election, though the Populist Democrat William Jennings Bryan came close in 1896, but they did very well in state and local elections. At various times, the Populists controlled the legislatures of every state in the South and many in the West.

In political cartoons, both friends and enemies represented the Populist movement by a stereotypical figure of a farmer with a straw hat, plaid shirt, patched overalls, muddy boots, and a hayseed dangling from his mouth. Other symbols of the movement were its colorful leaders, who carefully cultivated an image of rural rebellion. A symbol of populism in Texas was "Cyclone" Davis, "tall and thin as a southern pine, with eyes kindled from the fire of the prophet, a voice of far reach," and a vocabulary "drawn from the gospels." In the South, the iconic figures were "Pitchfork Ben" Tillman and redheaded Tom Watson, a "rebel by temperament." Other major figures were "Bloody Bridles" Waite in Colorado, "Calamity" Weller in Iowa, and Congressman "Sockless Jerry" Simpson on the middle border. One of the most striking Populist orators was Mary Elizabeth Lease, the daughter of an exiled Irish revolutionary, a fiery beauty known as Mary Ellen to her friends and Mary Yellin to her many enemies. She gave 160 Populist speeches in the Kansas election of 1890 and was known throughout the southern plains for telling farmers to "raise less corn and more hell." The rhetoric of these Populist leaders was marked by violence, bitterness, and the despair that was felt by many of their followers.[284]

Historians have long been divided in their understanding of the Populists. Some have condemned them in very harsh terms as narrow and intolerant reactionaries. Others have written of them as broad-minded, forward-thinking democratic reformers. To study the Populists in the context of the American history of liberty and freedom is find a new vision of a free society for a modern world.[285]

The Populists were part of a large reform movement in the late nineteenth century, which included Henry George's Single-Tax cause, Edward Bellamy's democratic socialism, and many other groups. All shared a common purpose, which was to link equality with liberty and freedom. This connection was closer and tighter in their thinking than in any movement that preceded them, so close that these ideas became one. Henry George, in *Progress and Poverty* (1877–79), wrote that freedom was

"The Slave Market of Today," Puck, *1884. Chicago Historical Society.*

"the synonym of equality" and that the two ideas together were the leading "stimulus and condition of progress." Many farmers did not think well of Henry George's single tax on land, but they shared his larger vision that joined freedom to equality.[286]

For Populists, freedom and equality meant equal rights, equal votes, equal treatment, equality of esteem, and also greater equality of wealth. Their experience taught them that the enemies of a free America were private groups who had gained control of public institutions. Their remedy was to make government more responsive to the people and more active in their behalf. They believed that governments could make a difference in the economy by creating the conditions of prosperity. Their hope was to achieve these goals by "Fraternity and Unity" among all the American people, in a web of popular alliances between the South and West, white and black, Republican and Democrat, labor and farmer.

These ideas appeared in their party manifestos: the Omaha Platform in 1892 and the St. Louis Platform in 1896. Both offered many specific suggestions on how to achieve those ends. Populists favored monetization of silver to create a more open and expansive monetary system as a key to growth and welfare, an idea that developed into a major school of neoclassical economics in the twentieth century. They urged programs of public spending in periods of "industrial depression." One of their major goals was a system of mixed enterprise, which combined private owner- ship of the means of production with nationalization of railroads, to pro- tect "political rights and personal liberties." They backed democratic reforms such as direct election of senators, abolition of the electoral col- lege, initiatives and referenda, ballot reform, and term limits. An impor- tant demand was a graduated income tax so that "aggregated wealth shall bear its just proportion of taxation." They strongly opposed private forces of "mercenary police" and favored a new idea of "constitutional liberty," with protections for unemployed Americans, including the repeal of vagrancy and loitering laws and "the right to go freely from place to place in search of employment." These Populist measures were means of reach- ing a larger goal, which was a vision of equality, liberty, freedom, and uni- versal rights. It was an idea that a democracy could govern actively and fairly in the interest of all the people.[287]

The People's Party did not succeed in enacting these reforms. It failed because it was unable to make good its hope of unity and fraternity. The party was destroyed by divisions between the South and West, between black and white, between ethnic and religious groups, and between the Republican and Democratic parties. But many Populist ideas were later taken over by Progressive movements, and some were put into effect. The Populist impulse became part of American culture, always with strong supporters and opponents.

After the demise of the People's Party in 1904, populism became a general noun in America, with opposite meanings. Often it was used to mean regressive politics of popular resentment against established institu- tions and elites. In that mistaken sense it was applied to Joseph McCarthy, George Wallace, and other dark spirits in American life.

Populism also acquired another meaning in America: a broad-based and large-spirited democratic reform movement, with broad popular sup- port, strong hostility to corrupt elites, and a determination to restore power to the people and rights to all. In public opinion polls at the end of the twentieth century, most Americans described themselves as populists. Here is a deeply rooted American folk tradition of universal liberty, free- dom and equality.

LIBERTY, FREEDOM, AND ORDER
Francis Bellamy's Pledge of Allegiance, 1892

> What does that vast thing, the Republic mean? . . .
> Here arose the temptation of . . . "Liberty, equality, fra-
> ternity." No that would be too fanciful. . . . But we as a
> nation do stand square on the doctrine of liberty and
> justice for all.
>
> —FRANCIS BELLAMY ON HIS
> PLEDGE OF ALLEGIANCE, 1892

IN 1833, the French government sent a young engineer named Michel
Chevalier to study the construction of canals and railroads in America. Like many intellectual travelers in the United States, he became
deeply interested in American institutions. Chevalier was surprised by the
stability of America's free society and amazed that it did not degenerate
into anarchy or tyranny. He reflected at length on that puzzle and wrote a
book about it, *Lettres sur l'Amérique du Nord* (Paris, 1836).

To explain the stability of American institutions, Chevalier framed a
theory called a law of equilibrium, between liberty and order. He summarized it in a few sentences. "Both order and liberty are essential to human
nature," he wrote. ". . . It is impossible to establish a society on one of these
principles alone! If you abandon a portion of social institutions exclusively
to the spirit of liberty, be assured that the principle of order will take no
less exclusive possession of some other portion. . . . Such are the laws of
equilibrium which govern nations and the universe of worlds."[288]

Chevalier's Law held that every expansion of liberty must be balanced
by an extension of order. In the late nineteenth century, something like
that idea was much on American minds. A leading historian, Robert
Wiebe, believes that the central theme of that era was the "search for
order" in a free society. His work shows how businessmen and politicians,
conservatives and radicals, all worked in different ways to solve the problem of ordering an open system.[289]

Other ordering solutions were meant to operate internally within individual citizens of a free republic. One of them is still with us today, a device that that was meant to bind young people to a free society. An American socialist invented it in 1892, and it came to be much loved by political conservatives in the twentieth century. It is the Pledge of Allegiance, and every American citizen knows it by heart.[290]

The story of the Pledge of Allegiance began in the Boston offices of a magazine called *The Youth's Companion,* which had one of the largest circulations in the United States, 650,000 for its World's Fair edition in 1893. Its publisher was Daniel Ford, a Baptist businessman with a strong sense of public duty. The magazine promoted many civic causes. Ford's nephew and partner, James Bailey Upham, adopted one civic cause in particular. He proposed to distribute American flags to every school in the country and sought to create a ceremony that every child would perform every morning in every class, a salute to the Stars and Stripes and a pledge of allegiance to a free republic.

Upham turned to a staff member of the magazine, Francis Bellamy, and asked him to draft a pledge of allegiance and to promote it with the help of the magazine and school superintendents in the National Education Association. Bellamy was a Baptist clergyman and a Christian socialist, who ministered to poor congregations of laborers and immigrants in Boston. His principles were close to those of his cousin Edward Bellamy, who wrote the utopian novels *Looking Backward* and *Equality.* Francis Bellamy himself wrote and sermonized on similar themes. Historian John Baer writes that Francis Bellamy's first idea was a pledge of allegiance to liberty, equality, and justice for all. It was decided on second thought that equality would divide Americans, but liberty and justice would unite them. And so it was done. Upham and Bellamy together added the idea that every American child should salute the flag while reciting the pledge, and they designed a special way: right arm and hand extended straight toward the flag, with the palm up. The National Education Association strongly supported the Pledge, and superintendents began to adopt it. The states passed laws requiring every classroom to display an American flag and every child to begin the day with the Pledge of Allegiance.

The words changed in detail. Bellamy had originally written "I pledge allegiance to my flag." In 1924, patriotic and veterans organizations proposed a change to "the flag." In 1954, the Catholic Knights of Columbus asked that the words "under God" be added, and Congress agreed. From time to time, challenges were mounted to that phrase, and in 2002 a federal court found that it violated First Amendment. A furious reaction

Schoolchildren pledging allegiance in Hampton, Virginia, with the straight-arm salute recommended by Upham and Bellamy. Photograph by Frances Benjamin Johnston, 1899–1900. Library of Congress.

followed, and many members of Congress appeared on the steps of the Capitol and swore their allegiance under God. The words remained.[291]

In symbolic rituals such as the Pledge of Allegiance, Chevalier's Law operated very powerfully in the United States. It reinforced an idea of order that descended from Puritan New England and spread through the country in the late nineteenth century. At the same time, it encouraged the growth of freedom and liberty. Every expansion of one brought an increase in the other. That paradox of dynamic equilibrium was at the heart of the American system.

FREE SILVER AND SOLID GOLD

The Contested Visions of McKinley and Bryan

> In form, the struggle is on the currency question. But these are only symbols, and behind them are gathered the world-opposing forces of aristocratic privilege and democratic freedom.
>
> —HENRY GEORGE

IN 1896 AND 1900, American politics centered on two hard-fought presidential elections. The leading candidates were the same in both campaigns: the Republican Civil War hero William McKinley, fifty-three, against an eloquent young Democratic country lawyer, William Jennings Bryan, thirty-six years old. Both men were broadly within a nineteenth-century liberal tradition, but their differences were profound. They represented different classes, different interests, and different ideas of liberty, freedom, and order. McKinley appealed to prosperous urban conservatives of the upper middle class and celebrated the "Full Dinner Pail." Bryan spoke for struggling farmers who were caught in the long deflation of the late nineteenth century. They also had different ideas of America's place in the world. The Republican standard-bearer strongly supported a vision of American imperialism in Panama and elsewhere; Bryan opposed it.

The candidates also differed in religion, which as always was profoundly important to American ideas of liberty and freedom. Bryan was a Christian fundamentalist, and his rhetoric had an evangelical spirit. McKinley was a mainstream Methodist Episcopal churchman who believed deeply in Christianity as a code of conduct and morals.

The campaign degenerated into a contest over monetary nostrums. The Republicans staunchly defended the gold standard. Bryan, the "silver-tongued orator" from the River Platte, demanded free coinage of

A campaign poster for the Democratic and Populist candidate William Jennings Bryan. Collection of David J. and Janice L. Frent.

A campaign poster for the Republican candidate William McKinley, 1900. Library of Congress.

silver. In one of the most vivid electioneering images in American history, he preached political sermons on his own text: "You shalt not press down upon the brow of labor this crown of thorns. You shall not crucify mankind upon a cross of gold."[292]

Bryan ran three times for the presidency, in 1896, 1900 and 1908, and won strong support in the South and West. McKinley ran in 1896 and 1900 from his front porch in Canton, Ohio, and carried both elections in the Northeast. The campaigns were rich in political iconography. Colorful and highly detailed electioneering posters offered two graphic images of a free America. Two examples from 1900 show McKinley standing on a sound-money platform of solid gold. He is literally wrapped in the American flag, with many visual images of prosperity at home and "prestige abroad." In the foreground is an exaltation of capitalism and labor. Bryan used some of the same images: the flag most of all. But his campaign's tone and substance were very different: strong symbolic appeals to liberty and justice, support for a genuinely free Cuba, and opposition to the trusts. His symbols were a silver dollar, a farmer's plow, and a rooster that was the emblem of the Democratic Party. All of Bryan's campaigns used these images as a vision of "equal rights to all, special privileges to none."[293]

THE PRESIDENTIAL ELECTION OF 1912

Four Progressive Visions of Liberty and Freedom

> Of course, we want liberty, but what is liberty?
>
> —WOODROW WILSON, 1911

IN THE CAMPAIGN OF 1912, something extraordinary happened in American politics. Four first-class candidates competed for the presidency. All were men of intelligence and integrity, and each had a creative vision of a free society. The result was another great debate on the meaning of liberty and freedom, and one of the most important elections in American history.

The event was driven not merely by the candidates themselves but by fifteen million voters who were deeply worried about the future of the republic. In 1912, many Americans believed that their nation was in peril. The times seemed out of joint, and the economy had been not working well. The deflation of the late nineteenth century had come to an end. A long inflation had begun in 1896, and the cost of living was rising more rapidly than wages. A financial panic, short but very sharp, had disrupted the American economy in 1907, and unemployment had increased. Most worrisome was the growing concentration of wealth and power in a few large corporations and trusts, who were thought to be dangerous to liberty and freedom.

At the same time, the "new immigration" reached the highest recorded levels in American history. Cities struggled to deal with severe urban problems. State governments became more active in passing social legislation but less successful in solving social problems. In Washington, congressional leaders of the Republican and Democratic parties were increasingly corrupt, out of touch, divided among themselves. These many interlocking problems created a sense of social crisis.

Historians have written about the election of 1912 mainly as a discussion of the economic role of government, but it was more than that: a debate about the nature of a free society. At issue were four competing ideas of American liberty and freedom: the New Conservatism of William Howard Taft, the New Socialism of Eugene Debs, the New Nationalism of Theodore Roosevelt, and the New Freedom of Woodrow Wilson.[294]

William Howard Taft's New Conservatism: "Personal Liberty and the Right of Property"

The least studied of these visions was the progressive conservatism of President William Howard Taft (1857–1930), who was running for a second term in 1912. Taft's historical reputation has been obscured by the brilliance of his adversaries and by his manner and appearance. In his

own time, his huge girth made him the object of much low humor about snapshots of Mr. Taft on horseback and photographs of his custom-made bathtubs in Washington and Manila, filled with large numbers of Americans and Filipinos. He deserves to be treated with more respect.[295]

Taft was a man of character and intellect, second in his class at Yale, a great scholar of the law, the only person to serve as president and also chief justice of the Supreme Court. He believed deeply in a republic of laws under the Constitution and summarized his vision of a free society in a sentence. "Next to the right of liberty," he wrote, "the right of property is the most important right guaranteed by the constitution and the one which, united with that of personal liberty, has contributed more to the growth of civilization than any other institution established by the human race."[296]

Taft's vision was conservative and very old-fashioned in its idea of protecting

William Howard Taft, portrait by Anders L. Zorn. White House Historical Association.

property, preserving personal liberty, upholding the Constitution, and supporting the existing structure of American society. At the same time it was also progressive in its idea of a small but highly efficient government that intervened actively for the general good.

One of his leading goals was to protect "the spirit of commercial freedom" against monopolistic trusts. Taft strongly supported antitrust legislation, in what he called "the effort of a freedom-loving people to preserve equality of opportunity." His administration brought twice as many antitrust suits as had Theodore Roosevelt's (ninety against forty-four), and it broke up some of the most powerful trusts in the country: Standard Oil, the Tobacco Trust, and the Steel Trust. Taft also favored federal (rather than state) statutes of incorporation as regulatory instruments. He was a free trader in a protectionist Republican Party and worked for moderate tariffs. As president he brought order and efficiency to public administration and proposed the first comprehensive modern budget for the national government. Altogether, William Howard Taft's progressive conservatism combined new instruments of modern government with old ideas of liberty of contract, property rights, personal liberty, and commercial freedom.[297]

Eugene Debs's New Socialism: "Social Self-Rule and Equal Freedom for All"

At the opposite end of the spectrum was Eugene Victor Debs (1855–1926), a great American socialist, who believed that the revolutionary moment had come in 1912. "This is our year!" he told his supporters. "Let us make the numerals *1912* appear in flaming red in the calendar of this century."[298]

Eugene Debs was a son of the Middle West. His parents were Alsatian immigrants who settled in Terre Haute, Indiana, where Debs was born in a small shack. Even in extreme poverty, there were books in his home, and one book in particular that made a great impact: Victor Hugo's *Les Misérables*. After a few years of school Debs went to work on the railroad as a locomotive fireman, became active in the fireman's union, and rose rapidly to national leadership. He tried to found a general railway union and was sentenced to jail for violating a court injunction against labor activity. He entered prison as a trade unionist and came out a Socialist who transformed his American Railway Union into the American Socialist Democratic Party. Debs was its candidate for president five times. He was a brilliant speaker, a gifted writer, and a man of legendary decency and kindness, much loved even by people who hated his ideas.[299]

Debs was a Christian, a socialist, and a staunch democrat. In his thinking these three creeds became one, and they produced a very special idea of liberty and freedom. For Debs, the true measure of a free society was the condition of its least advantaged members. He declared: "Years ago I recognized my kinship with all living things, and I

Eugene Victor Debs.
Library of Congress.

made up my mind that I was not one bit better than the meanest on the earth. I said then and I say now, that while there is a lower class, I am in it; while there is a criminal element, I am of it; while there is a soul in prison, I am not free."

His socialism consisted in an idea that "liberty is emancipation from wage slavery," that "the tools of labor belong to labor," and that "wealth produced by the working class belongs to the working class." Debs believed that the land should belong to those who lived on it and worked it, and he wished to "transfer the title deeds of the railroads, the telegraph lines, the mines, mills and great industries to the people in their collective capacity." He wrote: "We shall then have industrial democracy. We shall be a free nation whose government is of and by and for the people."[300] This Christian, socialist, democratic idea of a free nation had deep appeal to mining towns in the Far West, factory villages in New England, and labor camps in the Deep South.

Theodore Roosevelt's New Nationalism: "Free Government" as the Guardian of "Healthy Liberty"

The boldest American vision in 1912 belonged to Theodore Roosevelt (1858–1919), a man much loved in the United States even today and vividly remembered for his largeness of spirit. He was born to wealth and privilege in New York. The shaping event of his childhood was the Civil War. In 1865, a street photograph of Lincoln's funeral procession in New York City happened to catch Theodore Roosevelt at the age of seven, looking on. As a small boy, Roosevelt was inspired by the large purposes of liberty and union, impressed by the massive mobilization of national strength, deeply moved by stories of courage and glory, and uplifted by the example of Abraham Lincoln.

His political thought took its inspiration from the Civil War. The impact of that event appeared in his idea of life as struggle, his strong nationalism, his concern for social justice, his comfort with large institutions, his lifelong fascination with war, and his soldier's code of courage, duty, and honor.

Theodore Roosevelt developed these values into a political creed, which appeared in a collection of speeches called *The New Nationalism* (1910). The title piece in that book was a speech to an audience of Civil War veterans at Osawatomie, Kansas. Roosevelt began with a vision of American life as a "struggle for healthy liberty." He said to the veterans, "The essence of any struggle for healthy liberty has always been, and must always be, to take from some man or class of men the right to enjoy power, or wealth, or position, or immunity, which has not been earned by service to his or their fellows. That is what you fought for in the Civil War, and that is what we strive for now."[301]

Roosevelt believed that a large part of this striving for "healthy liberty" was a political struggle by "free men to gain and hold the right of self government as against special interests, who twist the methods of free government into machinery for defeating the popular will." Another piece of it was a struggle for economic freedom "between the men who possess more than they have earned and the men who have earned more than they possess." A third component was a social struggle for "equality of opportunity."[302]

To further the cause of liberty in these struggles Roosevelt proposed his idea of a New Nationalism, to operate "mainly through the national government" as a "steward of social welfare." He believed that large organizations were an inexorable fact of modern life. His object was not to break them apart but to regulate them for the public good as instruments of "healthy liberty."[303]

Theodore Roosevelt, portrait by John Singer Sargent. White House Historical Association.

A fundamental goal of his program was to make the national government more responsible to the people by political reforms such as national primaries, popular election of senators, a short ballot, and anticorruption laws, which established "the right of the people to rule." In economics, he sought a national government with "complete power to regulate and control all the great industrial concerns" and national legislation of living wages, decent hours, good safety conditions and fair business practices.[304] On social questions he said in this speech, "I stand for the square deal. But when I say that I am for the square deal, I mean not merely that I stand for fair play under the present rules of the game, but that I stand for having those rules changed so as to work for a more substantial equality of opportunity and of reward for equally good service."[305]

He broke with Taft on a question about the priority of rights. Roosevelt declared, "We cordially believe in the rights of property, but we feel that if in exceptional cases there is any conflict between the rights of property and the rights of man, then we must stand for the rights of man." Here was a new vision of a great nation-state intervening actively to promote liberty and freedom in an open society.[306]

Woodrow Wilson's New Freedom: "Freemen Need No Guardians"

In 1912, the most subtle vision was that of Woodrow Wilson (1856–1924). Born in Virginia and raised in Georgia, he witnessed as a child the horror of the Civil War, which filled him with loathing for what he called "the terrible wreckage and ruin of war." A minister's son, Wilson was brought up in a deeply religious household and schooled at Presbyterian Princeton. He chose the path of teaching and scholarship, became a highly creative historian, and was a brilliant teacher. After a troubled term as a reforming president of Princeton, he became a successful progressive governor of New Jersey, who took on the bosses and business leaders and defeated them.

In 1912, Wilson framed a program that he called the New Freedom. It was a complex idea, which he explained in a metaphor. "If you want the great piston of an engine to run with absolute freedom," he wrote, "give it absolutely perfect alignment and adjustment with the other parts of the machine so that it is free, not because it is let alone or isolated, but because it has been associated most skillfully and carefully with the other parts of the great structure."

Wilson argued that "human freedom consists in perfect adjustments

Woodrow Wilson, portrait by F. Graham Cootes. White House Historical Association.

of human interests and human activities and human activities and human energies." His New Freedom put that idea to work in public affairs, by a seeking a series of adjustments between "individuals and the complex institutions," and also "between those institutions and the government." All this required an active role for government to keep the machinery of a free society running smoothly. "Freedom to-day is something more than being let alone," he said. "The program of a government of freedom must in these days be positive, not negative merely. . . . Without the watchful interference, the resolute interference, of the government there can be no fair play between individuals and such powerful institutions as the trusts."

But the main purpose of Wilson's New Freedom was to create a system in which individuals could live free without the constant presence of government in their lives. "Freemen need no guardians," said Wilson. "America is never going to choose thralldom instead of freedom." He believed that Roosevelt's New Nationalism would "put us in leading strings to the special interests."

Wilson's method was to change the scale of institutions, both private and public. An example was the decentralized structure of the Federal Reserve System for the regulation of the nation's banking and monetary system, and also his policy for the banking industry itself, which he wished to divide into a very large number of small institutions. Wilson favored a new approach to antitrust regulation, not merely to break up "monopolistic trusts" as Taft had done, or "bad Trusts" as Roosevelt sought to do. The Wilson Clayton Anti-Trust Act went after big trusts that had interlocking directorates in corporations with a capital above a million dollars. Most of all Wilson wanted political reforms that increased the transparency of government and made it more responsive to the popular will, so that the people themselves became the government and would have no need of stewards or guardians. It was an old idea, which Wilson renewed for the twentieth century.[307]

The Election of 1912

In the campaign that followed, these four remarkable men attracted strong support from loyal followers. Taft appealed strongly to the possessing classes. Debs won a following among the dispossessed in many parts of the country and from many Americans who sympathized with their plight. Wilson and Roosevelt divided the broad middle class, but in the end it was Wilson's New Freedom that had the greatest appeal. It carried all but eight states, and every major region of the country, and was strongly supported in the Congress.

Woodrow Wilson's large idea had its limits. Many Americans were not included in his New Freedom. Wilson had southern attitudes on race and did very little for African Americans in an age of Jim Crow: less than Roosevelt or Debs or Taft. But in other ways, the New Freedom inspired a strong wave of progressive legislation. A century later, the election of 1912 is still remembered as one of the great debates in American history and one of the deepest national discussions of liberty and freedom.

A WORLD AT WAR
A Free Society and Its Enemies, 1916–1945

"America's Bit," James Montgomery Flagg, cover of Leslie's Illustrated Weekly, *January 19, 1918. Library of Congress.*

THE STATUE OF LIBERTY IN A NEW LIGHT

Woodrow Wilson's New Freedom as a Vision for the World

Let there be light.

—WOODROW WILSON'S SLOGAN
FOR THE NEW FREEDOM

O N DECEMBER 2, 1916, the presidential yacht *Mayflower* dropped anchor near Bedloe's Island in New York harbor. On board was Woodrow Wilson, in a triumphant mood. He had just won a second term in the White House and a mandate for his New Freedom. A good place for a celebration was the Statue of Liberty, which was thirty years old that year. It had survived three decades of neglect, which nearly ended in her ruin. Thereby hangs another tale of liberty and freedom.

The story began in 1886, when the people of France presented the Statue of Liberty to the United States. President Grover Cleveland accepted the gift with gratitude, but worried about how he could maintain it. He believed in minimal government and strict construction of the Constitution. So rigid were his principles that as governor of New York in 1884 he vetoed an appropriation of $50,000 for the Statue of Liberty on the ground that it was an unconstitutional use of the people's money and therefore dangerous to liberty itself.

As president, Grover Cleveland faced the same question on the national level. He studied the Constitution and the acts of Congress and concluded that his only course was to declare the Statue of Liberty to be an aid to navigation under a Congressional Resolution of 1877, and he ordered the U.S. Lighthouse Service to maintain it as a beacon.[1]

That strange arrangement solved Mr. Cleveland's constitutional problem, but it did nothing good for the Statue of Liberty. On Bedloe's Island, the lighthouse keepers were sometimes unable to keep the torch burning, and the monument began to fall apart. In less than fifteen years, a much-loved symbol of universal freedom was threatened with destruction by an idea of constitutional liberty.

The statue decayed so rapidly that in 1901 President Theodore Roosevelt was warned it might collapse during his administration. Mr. Roosevelt did not share Grover Cleveland's constitutional principles. He was the first president of a new Progressive generation who favored active government for a free society. Instantly he took action. By executive order he transferred the Statue of Liberty from the Lighthouse Service to the War Department and ordered the secretary of war to make an emergency survey of its condition.

The wheels ground slowly in Washington. Five years later, Secretary of War William Howard Taft delivered his emergency report. He concluded that "the condition of the statue is such that it may collapse unless repairs are made soon." That warning, from so weighty a civil servant as Mr. Taft, concentrated the collective mind of Congress. Repairs were reluctantly authorized, but only where urgently needed to prevent collapse. The great lady still languished in the weeds of Bedloe's Island.

New York publisher Joseph Pulitzer learned of her condition and published an exposé in his newspaper, the *New York World.* He also urged improvements such as a set of Thomas Edison's new electric flood lamps and offered to raise the money by public subscription if the federal government would pay the upkeep. Once again the government was slow to act. Little was done until Woodrow Wilson took office in 1913.

Wilson shared Theodore Roosevelt's idea of active government, even as he differed on its role. He also thought that the Statue of Liberty made a perfect emblem for his New Freedom, and the new flood lamps symbolized his reform motto, "Let There Be Light." A Democratic Congress was quick to agree, and the work was done by the General Electric Corporation.

On the night of December 2, 1916, all was ready. From the deck of the *Mayflower,* Wilson issued a command. A signal rocket soared into the dark sky, and on Bedloe's Island another rocket rose in reply. Suddenly a battery of lamps snapped on, and the monument was bathed in a flood of golden light. Even a cynical reporter for the *New York Times* (no friend of Mr. Pulitzer) was overcome by the sight. "As if touched by a magic hand," the *Times* reporter wrote, "the great statue sprang into view, the pedestal a beautiful brown and Liberty a great green figure."[2]

She looked different in the light. The lamps at her feet made her seem taller, stronger, more majestic, more serene, and all the brighter and more beckoning against the darkness of the night. Suddenly this great image of universal rights was visible in a new way. Woodrow Wilson turned the occasion into a festival of his New Freedom and a symbol of Progressive government. In a speech at the Waldorf-Astoria, he spoke of an immigrant who saw the Statue of Liberty for the first time. "I wonder," the president asked, "if, after he lands, he finds the spirit of liberty truly represented by us? I wonder if we are worthy of that symbol."[3]

The Statue of Liberty in a new light. Central News Service Photo, December 22, 1916. Local History Collection, New York Public Library.

The lighting of Liberty in 1916 was also symbolic in another way. It made this American monument more visible for the world to see and was emblematic of a sweeping change in the relationship between the United States and other nations. In 1916, the republic was being drawn inexorably into world affairs, but it acted in its own particular way. Since the early years of the republic, ideas of freedom and liberty had guided American attitudes toward foreign affairs. Not that the United States was always on the side of the angels. The motives of the great republic were never pure, and its actions were not always wise or just. Sometimes its founding principles had been used to justify acts of tyranny, greed, and oppression. But for better and for worse, large ideas of liberty and freedom were always near the center of American approaches to world affairs.

When these principles were applied to foreign relations, the result was an invitation to struggle with other nations. In 1916, American ideas of liberty and freedom were alien to most cultures, and anathema to more than a few. Many rulers lived in fear of these ideas, and some sought to destroy them. The consequence was a series of world wars, which pitted the United States against enemies of liberty and freedom.

Americans did not start any of these conflicts and tried to stay out of them. As late as December 1916, Woodrow Wilson was struggling to keep America out of war. In New York City, he remarked that the Statue of Liberty should send two messages to the world: liberty and peace. But the American people were drawn inexorably into the fighting, as in every general European war in the modern era. American involvement changed these conflicts into what Wilson called world crusades for liberty and freedom.

The English noun *crusade* is an iconographic term. Like the Spanish *cruzada,* the French *croisade,* and the German *kreuzzug,* it comes from the Latin verb *cruciare,* which means to mark with a cross. By definition, a crusade requires sacred symbols of its cause. These iconic emblems have often made a difference in the outcome of events, sometimes in unexpected ways.

THE GREAT WAR AND MR. WILSON

A European Conflict Becomes a World Struggle
for Liberty and Freedom

> The right is more precious than peace, and we shall
> fight for the things we have always carried in our
> hearts.
>
> —Woodrow Wilson's War Message,
> April 2, 1917

AMERICA'S FIRST CRUSADE in the twentieth century began on April 6, 1917, when the United States entered World War I. None of the belligerents knew it by that name. In their innocence they called it the Great War, as if none could be greater. It started in 1914 as a European conflict between the Central Powers (Germany, Austria, and Italy) and the Allied Powers (Britain, France, and Russia). Some historians think that its cause was extreme militarism and nationalism in a dysfunctional European state system. Others are convinced that it rose from the ruthless ambition of Kaiser Wilhelm II and a small group of German leaders who wished to dominate Europe. Many believe that the war was deliberately provoked (or permitted to happen) by entrenched European elites who feared the rising tide of democracy, liberty, and freedom in their own nations. All of these ideas are correct. Each was a necessary condition of the war.[4]

It began with an outpouring of national pride, martial ardor, and high hopes for quick victory on both sides. After a century without a major conflict, the European generation of 1914 had forgotten the horror of war and had yet to discover the destructive power of modern weapons. The result was a ghastly slaughter. Millions of young men were marched to their deaths, increasingly against their will. For three years, neither side could gain a decisive advantage.[5]

In 1917, the long stalemate was broken by a sudden turn of events that

"United We Stand": Symbols of American liberty, freedom, and unity in the First World War. Collection of David J. and Janice L. Frent.

brought Germany to the edge of victory. On the eastern front, Russia collapsed and withdrew from the war. Millions of German troops were released for service on the western front, more than France and Britain could match. The German navy mounted a campaign of unrestricted submarine warfare that threatened to starve Britain into submission. The United States was caught up in the growing violence of the war. German U-boats killed many American citizens with reckless disregard for neutral rights. The German government also organized violent and bloody attacks on American factories that were thought to be supplying the Allies.[6]

In the face of these provocations, and in fear of impending German victory, President Woodrow Wilson brought the United States into the war on the side of Britain and France, which he saw as defending freedom and democracy. He was almost too late. In the spring of 1918, while the United States was struggling to mobilize its resources, Germany mounted a great offensive that nearly broke the French and British armies. Then at last American troops began to enter combat in large numbers, attacking into the German advance. The Allies rallied to a rising hope of victory. All along the western front German troops were stopped, driven back, and defeated.[7]

Wilson's decision to intervene determined the outcome of the war and also changed its purpose. The president told the Congress: "we shall fight for the things which we have always carried in our hearts—for democracy, for the right of those who submit to authority to have a voice in their own governments, for the rights and liberties of small nations, for a universal dominion of right by such a concert of free peoples as shall bring peace and safety to all nations and make the world itself at last free."[8]

More than any other leader, Wilson transformed a rivalry among European powers into a movement for a free and democratic world order. In the process he gave new meaning to those ideas, and new images to their meaning. Wilsonian symbols of liberty and freedom had a unique character in the First World War. So also did the ideas themselves.

MOBILIZING A FREE REPUBLIC

George Creel's Committee on Public Information

> Ideas, for whatever reason they were held, took us into
> the war and kept alive the fiercely burning fires of
> industrial and military and naval activity.
>
> —James R. Mock and Cedric Larson, 1939

To HIGH OFFICIALS in the Wilson government, visions of liberty and freedom became tools of war. To control their use, the president created a new agency called the Committee on Public Information. It had four members: the secretaries of state, war, and navy, and its chairman, George Creel, a friend of the president and one of the most colorful characters in his administration.[9]

Like many of Woodrow Wilson's friends, George Creel was a southerner, the son of a Virginia officer in the Civil War. Born in Missouri, he became a crusading journalist in Kansas City, full of energy and enthusiasm for Progressive causes. He gloried in the name of muckraker and published a highly successful exposé of child labor, *Children of Bondage*, in 1914. Creel combined the principles of Woodrow Wilson with the temperament of Teddy Roosevelt. Barely five feet seven inches tall, he boxed with professional prize fighters, married a prominent actress, played the lead role in a western movie, and vastly enjoyed the excitement of politics. In 1916 he worked hard for the reelection of President Wilson. The Committee on Public Information was his reward.[10]

The committee itself met only a few times. A journalist observed, "The Committee on Public information was George Creel. It continued to be George Creel after a hundred and fifty thousand people were taking part in its incredibly varied activities."[11] Creel hurled himself into the work with his prodigious energy. He hired Chicago promoter Donald

Ryerson to organize a program of speakers to give four-minute speeches (many written by Creel himself) about American purposes in the war. Altogether seventy-five thousand "Four Minute Men" were carefully chosen (three letters of recommendation were required). They were trained by speech teachers and evaluated by a corps of inspectors. Creel, who had a passion for statistics, reported that they gave 755,190 speeches to 314,454,514 people in theaters, colleges, and clubs. There were Army FMMs on military bases and junior FMMs in schools.

One of their first tasks was to win public support for conscription, which they did with high success. Then they addressed the question of "Why we are fighting," and their answer was clear and simple. The war became a great crusade of American liberty, freedom, democracy, and civilization, against militarism, despotism, and barbarism. The American people were told they *must* join this great movement. Here was a new vision of America's role in world affairs, as the leader of a moral and spiritual movement to save other nations by converting them to liberty and freedom. It was also a new vision of those ideas.[12]

The Speakers Program was merely one of nineteen divisions in Creel's organization. A Film Division produced movies in support of the war effort and generated a profit that supported other ventures. The Division of Civic and Educational Cooperation flooded the country with seventy-five million pamphlets. An Advertising Division distributed copy to newspapers. The Division of News issued a torrent of press releases. More than four thousand historians were recruited to check accuracy and to contribute their own work to the war effort. The Division of Syndicated Features distributed human-interest stories and opinion pieces about the war. Creel recruited the American artist Charles

James Montgomery Flagg. "Wake Up, America!" Poster, 1917. Library of Congress.

Dana Gibson to head the Division of Pictorial Publicity, which mass-produced an American iconography of liberty and freedom for the war effort.[13]

Much of the committee's work was aimed at world opinion. George Creel hired an international team of pitchmen and advertising agents and claimed to have opened offices in "every capital of the world outside of the Central Powers." They made heavy use of radio, with the Eiffel Tower in Paris as an antenna. George Creel wrote with only a little exaggeration that "the official addresses of President Wilson, setting forth America's position, were put on the wireless at the moment of delivery, and in twenty-four hours were in every language in every country." That at least was the goal. The American war aims were converted into advertising slogans and broadcast on radio, fliers, and billboards.

The problem was that President Wilson's prose did not lend itself to the methods of modern advertising. The committee's man in Russia cabled home, "If President will restate anti-imperialistic war aims and democratic peace requisites of America, thousand words or less, short almost placard paragraphs, I can get it fed into Germany in great quantities in German translation, and can use Russian version potently in army and elsewhere."

George Creel went to the president, who responded with "the dry comment that he had never tried his hand at slogans and advertising copy." Creel persisted, and a few days later Wilson delivered a summary of "war aims and peace terms" in placard paragraphs that became the Fourteen Points. Creel's men broadcast them from the Eiffel Tower, sent them into Germany, and "plastered them on billboards in every Allied and neutral country."[14]

At the start, Creel tried to take the high road. He favored open debate, disliked atrocity stories, and strongly opposed

Images of a Great Crusade: "Weapons for Liberty," poster for the Third Liberty Bond Drive. Liberty Memorial Museum of World War I, Kansas City, Mo.

attacks on German Americans (his mother was of German ancestry). But the committee soon abandoned this approach. Films appeared with titles such as *The Kaiser: Beast of Berlin*. German Americans were reviled, dissenters were attacked, and newspapers were censored. The Creel Committee came under heavy attack from critics such as H. L. Mencken, who called them "Star-Spangled Men."[15]

The Creel Committee came to a bad end. After President Wilson's peace policy was opposed by Senator Henry Cabot Lodge, Creel made the fatal mistake of attacking Congress. The result was a sharp reduction in his appropriations. When the war ended, Congress cut off funds so quickly that Creel was unable even to wind up his operations in an orderly way. Accusations of mismanagement multiplied. But in its prime, Creel's committee had a major success in rallying a divided nation. It also gave a special character to images of liberty and freedom during the First World War.

I WANT YOU!

Authoritarian Images: Ordered Liberty, Conscripted Freedom

Get behind the Government

—WAR POSTER, 1917

VISIONS OF FREEDOM and liberty had a unique tone during World War I, different from those in other American generations. Woodrow Wilson's government did not invite Americans to join the war effort. It ordered them to do so. For a liberal administration, its images of a free world had a strong authoritarian thrust. This distinctive tone was not imposed by the president himself, though he was quick to adopt it. Similar patterns were evident in the United States and other nations during the early twentieth century. They began to color the imagery of liberty and freedom even before America joined the war. The leading example was a new image of Uncle Sam, which appeared the year before the United States went to war. On July 6, 1916, *Leslie's Weekly* ran a cover portrait of Uncle Sam. He appeared as an angry and authoritarian leader who fixed the reader with a formidable stare and demanded, "What are YOU doing for Preparedness?"[16]

The artist was American illustrator James Montgomery Flagg. He liked to say that he used himself as a model for Uncle Sam so that he did not have to pay a modeling fee, but he also had another model. Montgomery Flagg's Uncle Sam bore a striking resemblance to British Field Marshal Horatio Herbert Kitchener, whose portrait appeared on recruiting posters throughout the United Kingdom. Lord Kitchener did not merely ask the young men of Britain to fight for king and country. He

Uncle Sam as a new authoritarian image of Liberty and Freedom. James Montgomery Flagg, "I Want You." U.S. Army recruiting poster, 1917–18. Liberty Memorial Museum of World War I, Kansas City, Mo.

commanded them to do so. With a lowering brow and a rigid glare, he pointed his finger and said "I want you!"

James Montgomery Flagg closely followed this design and replaced Kitchener with Uncle Sam. In the process the artist gave a new spirit to that American symbol. Earlier incarnations of Uncle Sam had looked old and sickly, or weak and perplexed, or kindly and well meaning. Flagg painted him in a different light. The new Uncle Sam lost his avuncular air and became the forceful leader of a world power. He looked strong, stern, righteous and militant. Like Britain's Lord Kitchener, Uncle Sam pointed a warning finger directly at the viewer's eye and demanded to be obeyed. This American icon of liberty and freedom also became an image of national authority, as he had never been before.

When the United States entered the war, the Army conscripted James Montgomery Flagg's magazine cover and turned it into a recruiting poster that was even closer to the British model. Now Uncle Sam resembled Kitchener not only in his appearance but also in his language. The War Department's Uncle Sam said, "I want *you* for the U.S. Army." Four million copies of the poster were distributed by the War Department alone and many more by other agencies. James Montgomery Flagg's authoritarian Uncle Sam became the leading image of the American war effort.

A similar authoritarian flavor was given to other symbols of liberty and freedom. A leading example was the Statue of Liberty. In 1917, Treasury Secretary William G. McAdoo invented "Liberty Bonds," as a way of persuading Americans to pay voluntarily for the war and to feel invested in the war effort. A huge campaign was organized, with much iconography that centered on the Statue of Liberty. A poster by artist C. R. Macauley for the first bond drive in the United States (1917) showed the Statue of Liberty in a new mood. She brandished her torch as if it were a weapon. From her pedestal she looked down with an angry stare, pointed her right hand in the manner of Lord Kitchener, and said imperiously, "YOU buy a Liberty Bond lest I perish." Some paintings added yet another imperative: "Get Behind the Government!"[17]

Other posters addressed new immigrants in the same imperative tone. One proclaimed, "Remember your first thrill of American Liberty. Your Duty— Buy United States Government Bonds." Another read, "You came here seeking freedom. You must now help preserve it." A third showed a sailor telling a scholar, "Don't Write American History, Make It!"[18]

The Statue of Liberty also became of symbol of authority in the great crusade. C. R. Bond, "You! Buy a Liberty Bond!" Poster, 1917. Liberty Memorial Museum of World War I, Kansas City, Mo.

Altogether, Creel's Division of Pictorial Publicity distributed more than seven hundred war posters, which used these bellicose and authoritarian images in a cause of liberty and freedom. Miss Liberty was transformed from the girl next door into an Amazon warrior. In one poster a Boy Scout on his knees hands her a massive Highland broadsword. As in many posters in the First World War, the Boy Scout appears in a submissive posture of deference and obedience. Here again Miss Liberty had a very different feeling than she had in other generations.[19]

Historians have attributed the tone of the war effort to Woodrow Wilson himself and high officers in his administration, but it had a broader base. On the right, even more authoritarian attitudes were shared by Republican opponents such as the president's inveterate enemy Senator Henry Cabot Lodge. To the left, the same authoritarian spirit also appeared in antiwar images that were published by Max Eastman in radical journals such as *The Masses*. It characterized the work of many American artists in that era.

This paradox of authoritarian visions of liberty and freedom had a complex cause. Partly it rose from that generation's deep concern about social order in a free republic. Another part of it derived from a diversity of deeply felt beliefs about the nature of social order. In the early twentieth century, liberals, conservatives, radicals and reactionaries were far apart on those questions. A third factor was the depth of division on the war itself. In 1917, fifty-six members of the House and Senate voted against the War Resolution. By comparison, only one member of Congress dissented from the Declaration of War in 1941, and two opposed the Tonkin Gulf Resolution in 1964.

Perhaps the most important factor was something else. American adults in 1917 had been raised in a world of moral certainties and found themselves living in a very uncertain time. Conflict, uncertainty, and anxiety bred the authoritarian spirit that was unique to this generation. This attitude was combined with a sense of extreme urgency, not only about the fighting in Europe but for the future of liberty and freedom in the world. A leading example was Joseph Pennell's poster "That Liberty Shall Not Perish From the Earth," one of the most widely reproduced posters in the war effort. It showed New York under attack and the Statue of Liberty beheaded. These works had an apocalyptic theme that had not appeared in the darkest moments of the Civil War or the American War of Independence.[20]

This imagery became more elaborate as the war went on. The climax came in the Fourth Liberty Bond Drive during the fall of 1918. It centered on the idea of a world alliance of free people against militarism and tyranny. Every day of the drive was dedicated to a different Allied nation, from September 18, which was Belgium Day, to October 19, United States Day. In New York City, Fifth Avenue was renamed the Avenue of the Allies. Each block was devoted to an Allied nation, in alphabetical order from Belgium to Siam. Large flags of every country were interspersed with the Stars and Stripes. The flag paintings of the American impressionist Childe Hassam celebrated the swirl of color and movement in an atmospheric haze of patriotic feeling.[21]

On Fifth Avenue at Madison Square, an enormous altar of liberty was constructed, forty feet high. It became a site for the performance of Liberty Oratorios by Liberty Choruses, Liberty Dramas by Liberty Theaters, and huge Liberty Parades. The artists pitched in, with a working Liberty Studio in front of the New York Public Library on 42d Street. Crowds gathered to watch artists at work, painting big canvases from live models. The finished works were displayed in store windows on Fifth Avenue, which became an enormous art gallery from 23rd Street to 59th Street.

Many of these works centered on themes of liberty and freedom, which the artists interpreted in interesting ways. Much admired was

Frank Benson's poster called "Liberty Bonds Guarantee Immunity from Frightfulness." It showed children fleeing from the destruction of war and was an early idea of what would later be thought of as freedom from fear. Other paintings centered on dark images of tyranny and oppression. An example was George Bellows's very powerful painting of German militarism, a common theme. Here again, the Wilson administration sponsored a total mobilization of the nation's creative resources. Every artist was conscripted in a crusade for freedom.[22]

The Altar of Liberty, Fifth Avenue, New York City, ca. 1917. Hulton Archive/Getty Images.

Living Tableaus

A curious ritual was often repeated in army camps during the First World War. Large numbers of draftees were mustered on parade grounds and ordered to form living tableaus of liberty and freedom. For that purpose, many American icons were called into service as symbols of a great struggle against the Kaiser. A favorite was the Liberty Bell, with its symbolism of a ringing ideal for all humanity. At basic training camps in 1917, American conscripts were made to form a living Liberty Bell, crack and all, composed of hundreds of individual doughboys.

Another popular emblem was the Statue of Liberty. At Camp Dodge, Iowa, eighteen thousand officers and men were carefully arranged in a large field on the open prairie to create a khaki image of that great icon. These tableaus were photographed from the air, and copies were widely distributed to the nation and the world, as a way of explaining why millions of young Americans were being sent to the trenches in Europe.[23] The Navy, not to be outdone, ordered ten thousand and men at its Great Lakes Naval Training Station to form a gigantic living flag, with stars and stripes waving in a nautical breeze. Photo-engravings were distributed by the Navy Relief Society in 1917.[24]

Human flags, Liberty Bells and Statues of Liberty became a national craze. Entire communities were mobilized to create them. At county fairs and Fourth of July festivals, thousands of fellow citizens formed living tableaus of liberty and freedom, before enormous crowds. These highly

Conscripted Images of Liberty: "Human Statue of Liberty," 1918.
National Archives.

regimented celebrations of liberty and freedom communicated the unique spirit of America's first world crusade in the early twentieth century. They captured an irony that was typical of American involvement in the First World War.[25]

These ordered images of regimented liberty and freedom were more highly developed in that era than in any other period of American history. They symbolized a vision of liberty and freedom that belonged to the nation more than to its individual citizens.

This idea had a long pedigree. It descended from the ordered freedom of the Puritans and the "publick Liberty" of Samuel Adams. Similar ideas also appeared in the thinking of Theodore Roosevelt and many Progressive leaders.

Images of authoritarian liberty and ordered freedom had particular appeal to that generation. At the same time they represented a theme that spanned the full range of American history and is still with us today. It is a complex idea, far removed from the values of other Americans who think of liberty as autonomy for individuals. This is a vision of freedom as a right and obligation of membership in a community of free individuals who are parts of a larger whole. Ordered freedom in that sense is sometimes understood by its critics as the opposite of individual liberty, but it has also functioned as an instrument of individual rights. In the heritage of English-speaking people, these complex ideas—liberty and freedom, rights of independence and rights of membership—have always been linked, even in the minds of people who desire one of them more than another. That larger truth appeared yet again in the human tableaus of conscripted freedom and regimented liberty during the First World War.

LIBERTY AS THE FIRST CASUALTY

The Strange Case of *U.S. v. Spirit of '76*

> It was a fight for the minds of men, for the "conquest
> of their convictions," and the battle-line ran through
> every home in every country.
>
> —GEORGE CREEL, 1920

EHIND THESE SYMBOLS of ordered liberty and authoritarian freedom were emotions that ran deep in Woodrow Wilson's America. There was always an angst about liberty and freedom in every American generation, but never more so than in the era of the First World War. Strong tensions were tugging at the fabric of American life in that troubled time. Some were ethnic conflicts caused by new migrations from Europe to the New World. Others rose from racial strife, which spread through the United States with migration from the rural South to northern cities. Ideological conflicts developed over anarchism and socialism. Material problems came with the growth of cities, factories, and markets. All of these stresses were reinforced by conflicts related to the war itself.

Most Americans supported President Wilson's decision to enter the war, but fifty-six members of Congress voted against it, and a large minority became strong opponents of the war. Some were immigrants of German descent who were more sympathetic to the *Vaterland* than to the Allied cause. Others were socialists such as Eugene Debs and Victor Berger. Many were pacifists, led by Congresswoman Jeanette Rankin. A few were Communists and anarchists of violent inclination. Among the most outspoken were liberals who opposed military conscription. A brave stand was taken by social worker Roger Baldwin, who refused to register for the draft. He said, "I regard the principle of conscription of

437

life as a flat contradiction of all our cherished ideals of individual freedom, democratic liberty, and Christian teaching."[26]

Woodrow Wilson in his early years had shown respect for rights of dissent, more than most Americans of his generation. As late as 1899, he had strongly opposed "schoolrooms full of children going through genuflections to the flag." Wilson insisted that the flag stood for "liberty of opinion" and the right to dissent from rituals of that sort. "We have forgotten the very principle of our origins," he wrote, "if we forget how to object, how to resist, how to agitate, how to pull down and build up, even to the extent of revolutionary practices if it be necessary." But the president and most other Americans deeply believed that military conscription was right and necessary when the republic was at war. They also became less tolerant of dissent when they believed that vital principles of liberty and freedom were in mortal danger.[27]

The result was a bitter conflict, in which both sides became intensely intolerant, highly militant, and sometimes violent to the full limit of their powers. The difference was that the patriots had the government on their side, and the biggest mobs. President Wilson allowed his administration to establish a program of severe repression, with support from both parties in Congress. An Espionage Act in 1917 punished "disloyalty," and even incitement to disloyalty. The Supreme Court unanimously upheld the law in *Schenck v. U.S.* (1919). Even more sweeping was a new Sedition Act (1918), which made a felony of "disloyal, profane, scurrilous, or abusive language" against the Constitution, flag, armed forces, and American institutions.

The Wilson administration actively enforced this statute, which became more invasive of individual rights than the Federalist Sedition Act of 1798 had ever been. For speaking against the war, Eugene Debs and Victor Berger went to prison, with other socialists and pacifists. Woodrow Wilson himself was a party to these persecutions. He said to Josephus Daniels, "Suppose every man in America had taken the same position Debs did. We would have lost the war and America would have been destroyed. No, I will not release him." Later he said, "This man is a traitor to his country, and he will never be pardoned during my administration."[28]

This spirit of repression in the name of freedom and liberty came not only from the Wilson administration. Many states passed their own sedition laws, and state courts enforced them with a rigor that exceeded federal prosecutions. Prosecutions in the name of liberty and freedom were mounted in every region by local governments. In Montana, a dissenter named E. V. Starr refused a mob's demand to kiss the flag. He was arrested and sentenced to ten to twenty years at hard labor in the state penitentiary. The case was appealed to a federal district court where, Justice George M. Bourquin described the sentence as "horrifying" and observed that it was the mob who deserved to be prosecuted, not their victim. But he ruled that a federal court had no power to intervene in a state case, and Mr. Starr remained in prison. George Bernard Shaw observed that French courts during the war were "severe," English courts were "grossly unjust" and American courts were "stark, staring, raving mad."

Symbols became deeply important to both patriots and dissenters. The consequence was a domestic war of images and icons between infuriated nationalists and Progressives on one side and outraged anarchists, pacifists, socialists, and internationalists on the other. A case in New York City involved a radical dissenter named Bouck White, who called himself a minister in the "Church of the Social Revolution." In 1916, before the United States joined the war, White distributed handbills that showed the Stars and Stripes and a moneybag on the ground, encircled by a snake called "war." For this he was arrested under a state law that prohibited desecration of the flag and sent to jail for thirty days by an angry judge who asked him, "Why don't you go off and live in some other country?"[29]

Shortly before the trial, the *New York Times* reported that Bouck White had joined a ritual in which the American flag was burned in a kettle marked "melting pot," while hymns were sung to international unity. He was tried again, found guilty of flag burning, and jailed for another thirty days. The judge said he would have sent White away for thirty years if the law had allowed it. Bouck White did his time in the Tombs. As part of his punishment he was compelled to raise the Stars and Stripes over the jail every morning.[30]

A great wave of prosecutions for flag desecration followed in the period from 1914 to 1920. Earlier cases had been mainly about commercial use of the flag. During the era of World War I most were acts of political protest.[31] Prosecutors and patriotic organizations could never quite agree on what constituted desecration of the flag. In 1916, the Daughters of the American Revolution warmly endorsed flowerbeds in the shape of American flags. Two years later they condemned floral "flag parks" on the ground that Old Glory "must never touch the ground," and flowerbeds might be "trod upon." In both cases there was the same uncompromising spirit.[32]

All parties abused the rights of their opponents, and the worst cases were outside the law. In St. Louis, an American of German descent spoke out in defense of his fatherland. A mob stripped him naked, wrapped him in an American flag, and lynched him. The roles were reversed in Milwaukee on September 9, 1917, when a mob of Germans later described as anarchists attacked a loyalty rally and tore down an American flag. A fight followed and grew into a gun battle. Two "anarchists" were killed and several policemen were wounded before order was restored.[33] Nobody's hands were clean in this era when the victims became tyrants in their turn. The same spirit appeared among patriots and pacifists,

Flags as emblems of freedom: Ezio Anichini, "The Love of Freedom," lithograph, 1917. Collection of Gerald E. Czulewicz.

nativists and aliens, anarchists and conservatives. It rose from the culture of an age.[34]

One of the most bizarre cases happened in California. In 1917, a film opened in Los Angeles. Its producer was Robert Goldstein, a California businessman who had supplied the costumes for D. W. Griffith's eighteen-reel epic *The Birth of a Nation*. The success of that extravaganza inspired Goldstein to become a movie producer himself. As the country moved closer to war, he saw an opportunity for what he called "Yankee Doodle, Wave the Flag" films. The result was *The Spirit of '76,* a shameless commercial exploitation of patriotic symbols and scenes such as Patrick Henry's "Liberty or Death" speech, Paul Revere's midnight ride, Washington at Valley Forge, and the fight for liberty and freedom by heroic American colonists against cruel British oppressors.

Goldstein finished *The Spirit of '76* in the spring of 1917 and congratulated himself on his timing. It seemed the perfect moment for his patriotic film, and he expected a box office bonanza. To his amazement, federal agents descended on his office, seized the prints of his film, and arrested him under the Espionage Act on a charge of giving aid and comfort to the enemy. A trial followed in a case that was officially called *U.S. v. Spirit of '76*. The prosecutor argued that Goldstein's scenes of Redcoats killing colonists were calculated to "excite and inflame the passions of the people" so that "they will be deterred from giving that full measure of cooperation sympathy, assistance and sacrifice, which is due Great Britain . . . as an ally."

Never mind that Britain was not by law or treaty an actual ally of the United States in the First World War. The Wilson administration had insisted on joining the war as an "associated power." And never mind that the First Amendment guaranteed Goldstein's rights to speech and the press, which certainly extended to cinematic prints. The Wilson administration believed that constitutional rights did not protect acts or thoughts that were threatening to its crusade for liberty and freedom. Goldstein was found guilty, and an outraged federal judge sentenced him to ten years in prison. He actually served three years, and his business was ruined in one of the strangest acts of federal tyranny in American history. Woodrow Wilson could have intervened, but he chose not to do so. Here was the dark side of his vision for a free America. The case of *U.S. v. Spirit of '76* rested on an idea that freedom and liberty were moral absolutes, and that any threat to that sacred cause must be suppressed in the name of a free republic.[35]

WEELSIN! VIELSOHN!

Woodrow Wilson Becomes the Symbol of a Free World

> The truth of Justice, of Liberty, and of Peace
>
> —WOODROW WILSON ON HIS GOALS
> IN PARIS AND VERSAILLES, 1919

> Never has a king, never has an emperor received such a welcome.
>
> —L'EUROPE NOUVELLE, 1919

ON OCTOBER 29, 1918, as the war approached its bitter end, a drama was enacted on the forecastle of the German battleship *Markgraf.* The admirals of Kaiser Wilhelm's imperial navy ordered the High Seas Fleet to leave its moorings and make one last desperate fight against the combined strength of the Royal Navy and United States Navy. There was no hope of success. The object of the admirals was not victory but heroic defeat. They hoped to inspire German generations yet unborn by a Wagnerian death ride into the North Sea.

War-weary German seamen who were called upon to make this sacrifice did not share the death wish of their officers. The day before the fleet was to sail, they rose in a mutiny that spread swiftly through the fleet. Aboard the dreadnought *Markgraf,* angry sailors gathered on the forecastle and denounced their own officers. To make their point, they displayed an image of Woodrow Wilson and cheered the American President as a symbol of *Freiheit* and democracy.[36]

By the autumn of 1918, Woodrow Wilson had become a living icon of those ideas, even in the armed forces of his enemies. Many nations turned to him in that same spirit. Wilson's words were translated into every major language. Boulevards and babies were named in his honor. Bridges and buildings bore his name. When he came to Europe he was received with an outpouring of emotion by the largest crowds that the Old World had ever seen, all shouting for "Weelsin" and "Vielsohn." Millions who

442

The First World War becomes a world movement for liberty and freedom: a smiling Woodrow Wilson leads the procession that followed the signing of the Treaty of Versailles, Versailles, France, June 28, 1919. Image donated by Corbis/Bettmann.

could not pronounce his name looked to him not only as a triumphant war leader but as a spiritual figure. In a war-torn world, he represented a hope for peace, democracy, liberty, and freedom.

In 1918, Woodrow Wilson made a very odd icon of those ideas. With his compressed features, severe expression, tight lips, and pince-nez spectacles, he was to some Americans an image of strict morality, strong self-righteousness, and rigid authority. The authoritarian tone of Wilson's politics and diplomacy derived from a deeply held belief that freedom and liberty were moral imperatives that could never be compromised. This was his greatest strength and gravest weakness. Wilson's unyielding moral courage was at once the source of his appeal and also the cause of his defeat in the Conference at Versailles and the United States Senate.

After the catastrophic failure of the peace, Woodrow Wilson's vision of liberty and freedom came to be much criticized, but in its own time it was a great and noble idea of a free and open world. Of the President's Fourteen Points that defined his war aims and peace program, nine dealt with liberty, freedom, and self-determination as an absolute moral right of all people. Wilsonian ideas of world freedom centered not on the rights of individuals but on the destiny of nations. Individual people were the instruments of his idea rather than its beneficiaries. This way of thinking derived from his own temperament, inclinations, and experiences. He once remarked, "I have a sense of power in dealing with men collectively, which I do not always feel in dealing with them singly."[37]

Woodrow Wilson's vision had great appeal to a generation that sought to combine liberty and order, democracy and authority, throughout the world. His vision of liberty and freedom, for all its limits, had a universal quality that raised it far above his American critics. Wilson's ideal of a free world reached beyond the thinking of leading opponents such as Henry Cabot Lodge, a narrow and vindictive partisan who cared only for his own nation, class, and party. Lodge's vision of liberty and freedom descended from the tribal ideas of the distant past.

After the president's defeat in the American fight over the League of Nations, Wilsonian ideas passed rapidly out of fashion. Another generation of American historians took turns mocking his "politics of morality." Some held him personally accountable for the authoritarian approach to liberty and freedom that prevailed in his own time. To think that way is to misunderstand his high idealism and his enormous appeal to his own contemporaries. It is also to miss the tensions and anxieties that were deeply embedded in his age.

NEW DIRECTIONS IN THE TWENTIES

Expanding Visions of Liberty and Freedom

> Our constitution . . . is an experiment, as all life is an experiment.
>
> —OLIVER WENDELL HOLMES,
> in ABRAMS V. U.S., 1919

> If there is any principle of the constitution that more imperatively calls for attachment than any other it is the principle of free thought—not free thought for those who agree with us but freedom for the thought we hate.
>
> —OLIVER WENDELL HOLMES,
> in U.S. v. SCHWIMMER, 1928

WILSONIAN IDEALS of liberty and freedom had a way of growing during the First World War. Some Americans began to think about applying them at home. After the defeat of the Kaiser, journalist Walter Lippmann wrote that America must turn "to our own tyrannies—to our Colorado coal mines, our autocratic steel industries, our sweatshops and our slums."[38]

Many American workers agreed. The First World War greatly stimulated the growth of the labor movement. Union membership doubled during the war, and immediately after the armistice workers became more militant than before. The postwar years were marked by what Eric Foner has called "the greatest wave of labor unrest in American history." Major strikes occurred among textile workers in the Carolina Piedmont, coal miners in West Virginia, and other industries. Throughout the country, workers applied the ideas and images of Woodrow Wilson's world crusade to problems at home. Foner describes parades of workers "in doughboy uniforms with Liberty buttons, denouncing their employers and foremen as 'kaisers' and demanding 'freedom in the workplace'" for wage earners to organize unions and to seek a living wage.[39]

The possessing classes had a very different vision of "freedom in the workplace." They deeply believed that employers had an inalienable right to manage their own property and that workers should be free to work without having to join a union. Many regarded the labor movement as a

"The Four Hour Day," by Hermon F. Titus, radical leader in Seattle, pamphlet cover. Courtesy of MSCUA, University of Washington Libraries, Seattle.

revolutionary conspiracy to overturn American liberty. This was not merely the view of capitalist elites. It was widely shared by middle-class Americans.

The distance between these visions of a free America appeared with stark clarity in the city of Boston when the police went on strike in 1919 and a surge of crime and violence followed. Boston, like many American cities, was bitterly divided by differences of class, ethnicity, religion, and ideology. In 1919, those divisions grew deeper than ever. When Massachusetts governor Calvin Coolidge acted quickly to restore order, he was strongly supported by the broad middle class and opposed by many in the working class. Harvard undergraduates volunteered to keep the peace in Boston. They were praised as guardians of the republic and condemned as scabs and strikebreakers. The conflict also had an ethnic dimension. National Guardsmen, many of

"Patriotism and Loyalty Presuppose Protection and Liberty." African American Protest March, New York, 1917. Library of Congress.

them Yankee farm boys, patrolled sullen neighborhoods of Irish and Italian immigrants.

African Americans also laid claim to Wilsonian ideals. Leaders as radical as William Monroe Trotter and W.E.B. Du Bois had urged African Americans to support the war effort, and most did so. Many served in France and discovered a world without Jim Crow. Feelings of anger and militancy began to grow rapidly in African American communities.

Throughout the country, African Americans demanded for themselves the freedom that Wilson had promised to others. The first result was a huge backlash in many parts of the nation. In East St. Louis, the worst race riot in American history broke out on July 2, 1917. After the armistice, conflicts multiplied when African American soldiers came home and did not hesitate to fight for their rights. In the "Red Summer" of 1919, twenty-five

Here the Klan appears as the defender of liberty. Ku Klux Klan sheet music, chromolithograph, 1924. Virginia Historical Society.

major race riots broke out. The official death toll was seventy-seven African Americans, some of them still in uniform. Lynching began to increase. Most of it happened in the South, and in the northern states, such as Oregon and Indiana, where the Ku Klux Klan revived.

So entrenched was segregation in the South that individual African American families had only one choice: to move away from it. During the war itself, a huge flow of migration went from the rural South to cities and factory towns in the North and West. African Americans thought of it as a second emancipation. The railroads that carried them north were called "liberty trains."[40]

In communities throughout the United States, African Americans staged large nonviolent marches, demanding their rights and drawing the attention of the nation. Even in the South, newspapers and magazines supported them. The glare of publicity fell upon dark scenes of violence and cruelty. Photographs of lynchings began to appear in print. These vivid images of oppression began to awaken the conscience of the nation. Slowly, the tide of opinion turned. Wilson's war helped to turn it, beyond the intentions of the president himself.

WOMAN'S SUFFRAGE

Feminist Visions of Carrie Catt and Alice Paul

> There are two kinds of restrictions upon human liberty-the restraint of law and that of custom. No written law has ever been more binding than unwritten custom supported by public opinion.
>
> —CARRIE CHAPMAN CATT

> I never doubted that equal rights was the right direction.
>
> —ALICE PAUL

THE MOST SUCCESSFUL freedom cause in America after the First World War was the movement for woman's suffrage. It had long been active in the United States, but with very few victories to show for many years of effort. Four western states granted women the right to vote, but the Supreme Court ruled against woman's suffrage in 1875, and a constitutional amendment was defeated in 1878. The energy of the movement was scattered through many feminist groups with different purposes and methods.

In 1890, Susan B. Anthony succeeded in organizing the National American Woman Suffrage Association. Its leadership passed to a new generation of Progressive leaders, and by the early twentieth century it began to get results. The movement presented two faces to the public. One of them belonged to Carrie Chapman Catt (1859–1947), a middle westerner who became president of the Woman Suffrage Association in 1900. She was an excellent organizer and worked to build a broad coalition of women's groups throughout the country. At the same time, she reached out to male Progressives. Catt and her supporters cast their appeal in terms of fundamental principles of inclusion, in the hope that women and men would back them. Mainly they appealed to images of liberty and justice.

In 1915, suffrage leader Katherine Rauschenberger purchased a replica of the Liberty Bell and named it the "Women's Liberty Bell," or the "Jus-

tice Bell." She bound the bell's clapper with a chain so that it could not
be rung and promised to remove
the chain only when women won
the right to vote. The Women's
Liberty Bell became a leading icon
of the suffrage movement. Much
use was also made of the original
Liberty Bell. Its old Quaker promise of liberty to all the people made
it a perfect symbol of the movement
for women's rights and helped place
them in the mainstream of American culture and institutions.[41]

*Woman's suffrage, liberal
visions: Carrie Catt
(1849–1947) and suffrage
marchers in New York.
Image donated by
Corbis/Bettmann.*

Carrie Chapman Catt encouraged the use of mainstream symbols
in peaceful rallies, meetings, and orderly demonstrations. She centered
her efforts on persuading state legislatures, with high success. By 1914,
women won the right to vote in six states, and momentum was building
throughout the nation. Catt also became head of the International
Woman Suffrage Alliance.

Another wing of the suffrage movement was more militant. Its leader
was Alice Paul, who chose the path of confrontation and provocation.
She broke with Carrie Catt, seceded from the Woman Suffrage Association, and founded her own group in
1913. A large part of her method
might be called the politics of
expressive action. Alice Paul
launched furious attacks on President Woodrow Wilson during the
First World War, compared him to
Kaiser Wilhelm, set fire to his
speeches, and chained herself to the
White House fence. She sought
publicity by outrageous acts, and
the Wilson administration was pre-
dictably outraged. Paul and some of
her followers went to prison. In
confinement they resorted to
hunger strikes. Wardens responded

Woman's suffrage march in Baltimore. Maryland Historical Society.

Woman's suffrage, radical visions: Alice Paul toasts Tennessee's ratification of the 19th Amendment (with grape juice, due to the 18th Amendment), Washington, D.C., August 17, 1920. Image donated by Corbis/Bettmann.

with forced feeding. Stomach tubes were rammed down women's throats by male jailers in scenes of horror and revulsion that Alice Paul used as symbols of her cause.

A later generation of feminists made Alice Paul into an iconic figure, and after her death she became a radical heroine. In her own time, other suffrage leaders did not approve her tactics. Most worked within the pragmatic tradition of American Progressivism. Their method was to win by persuasion rather than by confrontation. Their goal was to get results by gaining the right to vote, which they expected to be an instrument of other reforms to follow.

In 1917, Carrie Chapman Catt and most suffrage leaders supported the Wilson administration in its decision to enter the war and invoked the president's rhetoric in their own behalf. They demanded that rights of self-determination should extend to the women of America. The active participation of women in the war effort was used by the suffrage movement as an argument for their cause

An interesting question is the effect of these various tactics and images on the movement for women's suffrage. Historians disagree: some believe that Alice Paul lost more support than she gained and gravely weakened her cause. Others take a more positive view of her work. The efforts of Carrie Catt and her national association are thought to have had more success, but radical feminists still complain of her moderation. Jane Addams, who observed the suffrage campaign at first hand, believed that the decisive factor was the conduct of American women in the First World War. Woman's suffrage, she wrote, came as "a direct result of the war psychology." It was an extension of ideas of liberty and freedom that kept expanding in America, during and after the war.[42]

Radical suffrage leaders burning Woodrow Wilson's papers in front of the White House. Library of Congress.

In 1919, Congress at last passed the Nineteenth Amendment to the Constitution, giving women the right to vote. Strong support came from President Wilson and his administration. State legislatures in the North and West (but not the South) quickly ratified the amendment. It became law on August 18, 1920, just in time for the presidential election. Much to the surprise of Progressive feminists—and also conservatives, who had opposed women's suffrage—American women cast their first ballots mostly for Warren Harding. In 1920, their visions of liberty and freedom were more conservative than those of men. Half a century later, the reverse would be the case.

The War and Women's Rights: "Help Her Carry On! 'Miss America reports for service, Sir,'" a poster for the National League for Woman's Service, September 1917. Library of Congress.

Anti-Suffrage imagery in Tennessee: the Nashville headquarters of the Southern Woman's League for Rejection of the Susan B. Anthony Amendment, August 1920. Tennessee State Library.

THE RED SCARE AND CIVIL LIBERTIES
The Palmer Raids and Roger Baldwin's Liberty Union

> Liberty is always dangerous but it is the safest thing we have.
>
> —Harry Emerson Fosdick

I N T H E A F T E R M A T H of the Great War, the limits of liberty and freedom were severely tested by a political panic that overswept the Western world. Its cause was the Bolshevik Revolution in Russia and the growth of anarchist and communist movements in Europe. Radical groups and leaders also operated in the United States. Prominent among them were Emma Goldman and Alexander Berkman, who edited an anarchist journal called *Mother Earth*. In 1919, other radical leaders organized the Workers Party, which later became the American Communist Party. These groups attacked constitutional democracy as an instrument of capitalist oppression. They were outspoken in their determination to destroy the values and institutions on which the American system was based.[43]

Every American generation has struggled with the question of what to do about aliens and dissenters who use the open institutions of a free society to attack liberty and freedom. In quiet times, the great republic has tended to adopt Jefferson's hopeful rule that error should remain free where truth can correct it. But in critical moments many Americans have gone the other way. When they believe that their republic is in mortal danger, they have never hesitated to suppress opinions, groups, and movements that they regard as a menace to a free society.

Other Americans have opposed these efforts at suppression. For them, an effort to preserve a free society by restricting liberty and freedom is not merely mistaken but absurd. They believe that such an effort destroys what it seeks to defend. Both parties to this old American argument believe deeply in their cause, and each grows by reaction to the other. In a free society, the stronger the effort at repression, the greater the resistance that it inspires. That resistance in turn inspires more repression.

These trends have created a powerful rhythm in the American history of liberty and freedom. Every major war has caused a great repression of liberty and freedom, always for the avowed purpose of protecting a free society. These repressions inspired a reaction that revived and expanded liberty and freedom.

As a consequence, every American war began by diminishing liberty and freedom, and it ended by enlarging them. This pattern recurred in the American Revolution, the Civil War, both World Wars, the Cold War, and the War on Terror, but never twice in the same way. In general, repressions were most severe in the earliest American wars; they became progressively less so with each succeeding conflict. The worst repression in every sense was the treatment of Tories in the American Revolution. Also very severe was the treatment of dissenters in the Civil War, both northern Copperheads, and southern Unionists. The least repressive conflict (notwithstanding a large literature to the contrary) was the Cold War. The two world wars were in between.

Reactions against repression also varied from one conflict to another, but in a different way. As the repressions themselves grew weaker, the reactions grew progressively stronger through time, from weak responses to the persecution of Tories in the Revolution, to strong campaigns for civil liberties in the Cold War.

Other patterns also appeared. The agents of repression were both liberals and conservatives, but liberals have often been cruelly repressive in times of stress. The worst tyrants are true believers in one single vision of liberty or freedom that rigidly excludes other visions. In moments of danger they tend to be very careless with other people's rights and utterly unscrupulous about their own methods. It matters little if they are true believers of the left, right, or center. They share an idea of a higher law and do not hesitate to break lower laws, even the Constitution itself.

A leading example of all these trends was the Great Repression of 1918–19. Its leader was A. Mitchell Palmer, a Progressive Democrat who became Woodrow Wilson's attorney general. With his leadership, federal agents raided the offices of the International Workers of the World (IWW) as early as 1917 and 1918 and took many leaders into custody. In 1919 Palmer launched a campaign to arrest communists and anarchists such as Emma Goldman and Alexander Berkman. He borrowed the military transport *Buford* and used it to deport 249 leaders, including Goldman and Berkman. The climax of this campaign came on January 2, 1920, when government agents took into custody 2,700 people in thirty-three cities. Most were seized without being arrested, and held without being charged. Their homes were searched and property taken without warrant. They were punished without trial, sometimes for acts that were the work of an *agent provocateur* who worked for the government.

Attorney General Palmer and the Bureau of Investigation (later the FBI), and employees of the Justice Department violated virtually all the protections in the Bill of Rights, for thousands of aliens and citizens. Even worse things were done by state and local governments, who actively enforced criminal syndicalist laws, red flag statutes, and state sedition acts with a heavy hand. Much of this repression was done by Progressive Democrats in the cause of liberty and freedom. Many of their victims had nothing to do with anarchism or communism.[44]

President Woodrow Wilson did not restrain this activity. Congress justified it after the fact in the Immigration Act of 1920, which authorized the arrest and deportation of aliens for owning radical books, speaking in defense of radical causes, associating with others who were under suspicion, or merely holding radical beliefs. The Supreme Court affirmed the constitutionality of these acts. In the case of *Schenck v. U.S.* (1919) it unanimously upheld the conviction of a socialist who had opposed conscription. Oliver Wendell Holmes, speaking for the entire Court, declared that the Bill of Rights did not protect speech or publications that were a "clear and present danger," a judicial doctrine that echoed in American law for many years. The court also allowed the jailing of a German editor who challenged the constitutionality of conscription. It unanimously upheld the imprisonment of Eugene

"The Strike Has Failed." Uncle Sam appears as a strikebreaker in this image of the links between class and ethnicity that frightened Mitchell Palmer after the First World War. Advertisement, Pittsburgh Chronicle Telegraph, October 6, 1919. Historical Society of Western Pennsylvania.

Debs for speaking against the war, and Debs ran for the presidency in 1920 from a federal cell in Atlanta. The photograph of a presidential candidate in his prison uniform became one of the great iconic images of civil liberties in American history.[45]

Eugene Debs campaigned for the presidency in his prison uniform from Atlanta Penitentiary. This campaign button is from the collection of David J. and Janice L. Frent.

After the armistice the war fever diminished, but the abuses of Mitchell Palmer's Great Repression increased in his raids on radical groups. The result was a very strong reaction. Two Supreme Court justices, Oliver Wendell Holmes and Louis Dembitz Brandeis, began to issue strong dissents. In *Abrams v. U.S.* (1919), a case that rose from the indictment of Jacob Abrams and four Bolshevik supporters on New York's Lower East Side, Holmes asserted that "the test of truth is the power of the thought to get itself accepted in the competition of the market." It was a phrase that only a lawyer could love, but in an age of materialism it began to have an impact. Holmes was working within a judicial system that had become more attentive to rights of property and laissez-faire than to other ideas of liberty and freedom. His argument by analogy that government should not restrain competition in the marketplace of ideas began to find a following.[46]

Others went far beyond Holmes. As early as 1917, when federal agents were arresting critics of the war, several groups came together to defend what they began to call "civil liberties." They were a mixed coalition of pacifists, conscientious objectors, lawyers, and Progressives. Together they founded a group called the Civil Liberties Bureau and made common cause against the Sedition Act and the Espionage Act. In 1920, after the Red Scare and the Palmer Raids, they reorganized themselves as the American Civil Liberties Union. Their founder and director was Roger Baldwin, a Progressive social worker and pacifist who had strongly opposed conscription.[47]

The Palmer Raids ended in 1920, and the Red Scare diminished after Warren Harding promised a "return to normalcy," which meant an end to the Great Repression. But the American Civil Liberties Union continued to function through the 1920s and made itself a major institution in American life. It took up many causes: the release of "political prisoners," support of free speech and freedom of the press, the defense of due process, protection of procedural rights in courts of law. In the early years,

Roger Baldwin at an antiwar rally, Columbia University, April 12, 1935. Image donated by Corbis/ Bettmann.

Roger Baldwin centered its efforts mainly in support of the labor movement to organize, protest, and strike. Through the decade of the 1920s, he estimated that 90 percent of the work of the Civil Liberties Union supported the labor movement "in its contests with employers or with civil authorities."[48]

The growing reaction against the Great Repression began to awaken the conscience of a nation. In every political party, it inspired leaders such as William Borah, George Norris, Robert LaFollette, and Burton Wheeler to take leading roles in support of civil liberties. Public pressure began to increase on courts, police, and local governments to act within the Constitution. The result was a new campaign to expand civil liberties, at the same time that other Americans were seeking to curtail them in the name of liberty and freedom.

These impulses continued through the 1920s, which became one of the most important periods in the history of liberty and freedom. It was a time of cross-purposes. The great repressions continued, but new and very powerful visions of liberty and freedom developed against them. Some were extensions of Wilson's Progressive ideas. Others were reactions against the intolerance of his administration. Many had their own imperatives.

These new visions of a free society after the First World War were different from one another, and even opposed. But all of them shared an abiding belief in liberty and freedom, and a determination that America should become more free. These movements developed great momentum in the United States during the 1920s. Their growing strength in America during that decade made all the difference in the Great Depression and the Second World War, when many nations lost their freedom to dictatorships of the left and right.

A history of liberty and freedom opens a new perspective on the 1920s. That era is remembered in popular culture as the age of flappers, jazz, and bathtub gin. In historical scholarship it is too often interpreted as the aftermath of the First World War or the precursor of the Great Depression. But in the history of liberty and freedom, it was an era that had its own distinct character and was truly a pivotal moment. Without the strength that those ideas developed in America, the history of the world might have been very different in the troubles that followed. Let us consider four new visions of a free world that developed very rapidly in this transitional period.

PROHIBITION

Experiments in "Orderly-Liberty" Inspire New Visions of a Free Society

> The objection to Puritans is not that they try to make us think as they do, but that they try to make us do as they think.
>
> —H. L. MENCKEN

I N T H E 1920s, an epic battle was fought over a social experiment in the United States. On December 18, 1918, Congress voted the Eighteenth Amendment to the Federal Constitution, prohibiting the manufacture, sale, and transportation of alcoholic beverages. It was ratified very quickly by the states on January 29, 1919, and took effect a year later. A National Prohibition Enforcement Law, known as the Volstead Act, was vetoed by Woodrow Wilson, who as a liberal Democrat favored moral liberty and economic regulation. It was passed over his veto by conservative Republicans and southern Democrats who wanted moral regulation and economic liberty. These ideological divisions persisted through the next century.

The movement for moral regulation was justified as necessary for the maintenance of a free society. Theodore Roosevelt told the Catholic Total Abstinence Union, "We recognize as the first and most vital element in Americanism the orderly love of liberty." He added, "I put the two words together: 'Orderly-Liberty'; and we recognize that we feel that absolutely, without regard to race, or origin, or different creeds."[49]

This idea of "Orderly-Liberty" became a common theme in Roosevelt's speeches. At Bangor, Maine, in 1902, he declared that "the permanence of liberty and democracy depends upon a majority of the people being steadfast in morality." Many Americans agreed. They also believed moral standards should be legislated, to preserve a free society in the

United States. This argument was invoked to justify many kinds of moral regulation. It became a rationale for Sabbath laws, which Theodore Roosevelt himself actively enforced as police commissioner of New York City. It also appeared in the movement for the prohibition of alcohol.[50]

Others deeply disagreed and insisted that moral legislation infringed the rights that it claimed to be protecting. This question deeply divided the American people. Many polls in the twentieth century found something near to 50 percent of Americans on each side of the

Prohibition: "Wet or Dry?" Cover art from Francis Nichol, A Brief, Candid Examination of the Moot Question in American Life (Mountain View, Calif., 1932). National Museum of American History, Smithsonian Institution.

question. In company with many politicians, Theodore Roosevelt assessed the national mood and stood firmly on both sides of the issue, at various moments in his career.

The national champion of Prohibition was Captain Richmond Pearson Hobson, a hero of the Spanish-American War and a highly paid orator for the Anti-Saloon League. One of his favorite speeches was called "The Great Destroyer." Its central argument was that drink was dangerous to liberty.

> As young as our nation is, the deadly work of Alcohol has already blighted liberty in our greatest cities. . . . If no check is put upon the spread of alcoholic degeneracy, the day cannot be far distant when liberty in great States must go under. It will then be but a question of time when the average standard of character of the nation's electorate will fall below that inexorable minimum, and liberty will take her flight from America, as she did from Greece and Rome.[51]

On the other side of the question, arguments against Prohibition were also cast in terms of liberty. The leading spokesman was H. L. Mencken, the Sage of Baltimore, who attacked the Eighteenth Amendment as an act of tyranny, and made two prophecies that rapidly came to pass. He

warned that Prohibition would turn a large part of the American population against its own democratic institutions. Further, he predicted that
the hopeless task of enforcement would lead to massive violations of civil
rights. "What disturbs me, of late," Mencken said in 1924, "is the tendency to abandon the Bill of Rights. The Supreme Court seems very
careless of it. The Volstead Act drives immense holes through it, and
nine-tenths of the Federal Judges appear unconcerned."[52]

Mencken became a leader of a powerful movement, which demanded
that every freeborn American had a sovereign right to pick his own poi-
son. He enthusiastically practiced what he preached, describing himself as
"omnibibulous," in one of his own inimitable words. Mencken's home
state of Maryland supported him and took the name of the Free State,
not for its support of the Revolution, as some of its sober citizens still
earnestly believe, but for its stubborn defense of the inalienable right to
wash down a Maryland oyster roast or crab supper with a schooner of
Baltimore's pilsner beer. Here was a Chesapeake vision of liberty to lift a
glass, and freedom to share the *gemütlichkeit* of kindred spirits.

Other Americans opposed Prohibition in a different way, but always in
the name of liberty and freedom. Some were leaders of the Democratic
Party in the northeastern states such as Al Smith and John Raskob, both
Roman Catholics and self-made sons of immigrants. Others were liberal
Republicans of old-stock families such as the du Pont brothers: Pierre,
Irénée, and Lammot. With them were Thomas W. Phillips (president of
Phillips Gas), Edward Harkness, and members of the Belmont and Har-
riman families. This improbable coalition of urban Democrats and silk
stocking Republicans came together to form the Association Against the
Prohibition Amendment. They raised large sums of money and worked
tirelessly for repeal in the cause of "Constitutional Liberty."[53]

Arrayed against them was another unlikely coalition. The friends of
Prohibition included New England Calvinists and southern Baptists, radical feminists and Methodist bishops, urban reformers and conservative
middle westerners, Imperial Wizards of the Ku Klux Klan, and born-
again Christians of many denominations. The same groups joined
together in support of other prohibitions at the same time: the prohibition of prostitution and sexual deviance and prohibition of narcotics, as
well as alcohol. Here was a twentieth-century trend, which reached its
apogee in the era of the 1920s. The Western world in the years of Queen
Victoria had been more tolerant of all these practices, as long as they did
not disturb the peace or "frighten the horses."

This conflict of coalitions was about something more than Prohibition itself. It was a collision between two ideas of liberty and freedom. One of these American visions combined the "orderly-liberty" of Theodore Roosevelt with the "publick liberty" of old New England. The other descended from the natural liberty of the backcountry, the reciprocal liberty of the Quaker colonies, and the *Feigenbaum Freiheit* of German immigrants. It created something new from those old materials. Patterns of ethnic and regional support were very complex.[54]

The Anti-Prohibition movement claimed the imagery of the American Revolution in this repeal textile. Virginia Historical Society.

In the election of 1932, Prohibition became a major issue. Democratic posters featured Franklin Roosevelt and John Nance Garner, with an overflowing mug of beer. The beer was in the center. The nation responded enthusiastically to the slogan of "Roosevelt and Repeal," and the noble experiment came to an end in 1933. Victory went to a coalition in which ethnic Democrats supplied the votes, liberal Republicans put up the money, and H. L. Mencken contributed the rhetoric.

Prohibition proved a costly failure for the American people. It put a heavy strain on the social fabric and caused a surge of crime and social disorder. But something constructive came from that experience. The failure of Prohibition established the limits of moral regulation in a free republic. The result was a major defeat for attempts to legislate morality. It was also a heavy blow against authoritarian visions of liberty and freedom. The spirit and substance of most movements to come would be very different.

A SOCIETY OF PORCUPINES

Arthur Garfield Hays, Civil Liberties, and "the Protection of the Unpopular"

> History is largely a struggle for the right of each individual to be damned in his own way.
>
> —ARTHUR GARFIELD HAYS, 1928

GERMAN PHILOSOPHER Artur Schopenhauer liked to tell a story about a band of porcupines who huddled together for warmth in the winter. When they got very close, their quills would prick one another, so they would move apart until they felt the cold. Then they would huddle again, and move apart once more, until at last they found a middle way.[55]

Schopenhauer's parable of the porcupines became very popular in America during the 1920s. In New York City, a lawyer named Arthur Garfield Hays often used it as a way of describing an American dilemma. How could one create a society of cantankerous individuals who were at least as prickly as Schopenhauer's porcupines and yet also in need of each other's warmth? How could they come together and yet remain apart? The parable of the porcupines suggested that the only solution was a middle way.

Hays found a solution in a vision of America as a system of civil liberties that combined the two goals of *civis* and *libertas*. This way of thinking changed the idea of civil liberties from a maximal autonomy of each individual to an optimal balance between an assertion of one's own rights and a respect for the rights of others. The result was a centrist idea of civil liberties that began to spread very rapidly through America in the mid-1920s. It first established itself not in Congress or the Supreme Court but in the court of public opinion. Its leading advocate was Hays himself. More than any other individual, he helped to popularize a new vision of individual rights and civil liberties as a *unifying* principle of American society.[56]

Arthur Garfield Hays (1881–1954) seemed to be everywhere in America during the 1920s. Many knew him by sight, "thick-set, stocky, demo-cratic-looking." He was born in Rochester, the son of affluent German Jewish immigrants who prospered in the clothing business and were so devoted to their adopted country that they gave their son the name of three American presidents (and misspelled one). Hays went to Columbia University, became a commercial lawyer, and made a fortune by rescuing the rich and powerful from results of their own follies. While earning large fees from his law practice, he also became deeply interested in civil liberties and took many cases without fee, tirelessly defending clients of spectacular unpopularity.[57]

Hays was a brilliant courtroom lawyer, highly skilled in the art of swaying hostile judges and juries in civil liberties cases. But his greatest contribution was to convince a larger public to accept his vision of a free society as a web of individual rights and mutual forbearance. The progress of civil liberties has never been easy that way. Americans have never responded warmly to the idea that they should support the rights of people they detest. Hays was able to persuade others that civil liberties were a matter of fundamental freedom for everyone. He had a gift for dramatiz-ing civil liberties in that way, and drew broad support from the general public. In the process he transformed the cause of civil liberties from the domain of a small sect of radical liberals to a popular movement with strong appeal in the United States.[58]

This happened in a series of hard fights that occupied the front pages of American newspapers through the 1920s. One of them was fought in the Bible Belt, as H. L. Mencken called the evangelical South, and it was about liberty to teach. In 1925, the state of Tennessee passed a law that forbade any teacher in any school or university to teach "any theory that denies the story of divine creation of man as taught in the Bible, and to teach instead that man has descended from a lower order of animals."[59]

The Scopes Trial, intellectual freedom, and liberty to teach: Arthur Garfield Hays stands by as his client, John T. Scopes, seated with his father, Thomas Scopes, confers with Dudley Field Malone, Tennessee, July 16, 1925. Image donated by Corbis/Bettmann

A young science teacher named John T. Scopes challenged the law. He was an attractive and modest figure, popular in his community, a leader in school athletics, "clean-cut, typically American." Many compared him to Charles Lindbergh. Scopes believed deeply in his cause, which he defended as the "ideal of academic freedom."[60] For his trial, the American Civil Liberties Union assembled a team of top lawyers, with Arthur Garfield Hays as strategist, Clarence Darrow as the master of cross-examination, and Dudley Field Malone as the eloquent courtroom orator whose soaring appeals to "fundamental freedom" won accolades even from the opposition. Counsel on the other side were a colorful team of highly skilled lawyers and public figures led by William Jennings Bryan, a born-again fundamentalist and a close student of the Bible.

Thousands came to hear the trial. The audience was so large that it threatened to collapse the courthouse, and the trial was adjourned to an open stage outside, with the defense on one side, the prosecution on the other, and the judge in between. The vast audience sat under the trees, cheering their champions. Young people in the latest fashions rooted strongly for Scopes, evolution and academic freedom. Older farming families in overalls were for Bryan and the Bible. Looking on was an international press corps led by Henry Mencken of the *Baltimore Sun,* whose colorful reports riveted the attention of the nation.[61]

The trial began badly for the defense. The judge and jury deeply believed in the Bible as a fundamental truth that required no interpretation. As the trial approached its climax, Arthur Garfield Hays suddenly proposed that Darrow should cross-examine William Jennings Bryan as an expert on the Bible. Later Hays wrote, "I have never yet discovered whether this was a greater surprise to Darrow or to Bryan." Darrow relentlessly forced the fundamentalist to concede that much of his reading of the Bible was interpretation, a concession fatal to his cause. The next day the judge ordered the entire examination to be stricken from the record, but it had already flashed around the world. Scopes was found guilty of teaching evolution by a Tennessee jury and fined one hundred dollars, but his lawyers won in the court of public opinion. They made an attempt at classroom censorship appear not merely mistaken but absurd. The moderate majority of American opinion rallied to the cause of civil liberties.[62]

In the following year, Hays went to Boston for another case, this time about freedom of the press. Self-appointed censors called the Watch and Ward Society, with help from the police and the courts, had long suppressed the sale of publications they disliked, including H. L. Mencken's irreverent magazine *The American Mercury.* Mencken hired Arthur Hays, and it was agreed that the author and his publisher, Alfred Knopf, would sell the magazine on Boston Common, in hope of arrest. The Watch and Ward Society took the bait, and the result was a civil liberties circus. On April 5, 1926, Mencken and Knopf appeared at the corner of Park and Tremont streets, where a wild crowd of thousands had gathered, waving money and demanding to buy the magazine. Mencken was duly arrest-

Upton Sinclair selling his book Oil!: A Novel *(1927), in the streets of Boston. With the help of his lawyer, Arthur Garfield Hays, the author mocked the censors by peddling a "fig leaf edition" of his book, in which the offending pages were replaced by large fig leaves. From Arthur Hays,* Let Freedom Ring *(1928), 192.*

ed on a charge of selling impure literature and taken to court, where Judge George Anderson declared that he would not interfere with Mencken's constitutional right to "raise hell" in Boston.

Other trials followed in which Hays exposed the complex process by which the Watch and Ward Society had censored the press in Boston. Hays happily noted that "Massachusetts became the Tennessee of the North," which both states took as an insult to their honor. The Watch and Ward Society was laughed into oblivion. But the battle continued. The Post Office banned the *American Mercury* from the mails, and more

trials followed in federal courts. After the Watch and Ward Society went out of business in Boston, the Boston Police and district attorneys became even more active than before, even attempting to ban Theodore Dreiser's *American Tragedy,* Sinclair Lewis's *Elmer Gantry,* and many works by Upton Sinclair. Hays arranged another media circus. Upton Sinclair appeared on the streets of Boston, hawking a special edition of his book *Oil!,* in which passages that offended the police were replaced by typographical fig leaves. Once again, humor was his most effective weapon.[63]

Page 203 from the Fig Leaf Edition of Upton Sinclair's novel Oil!. *Houghton Library, Harvard University.*

Hays took so many cases that his practice became a history of civil liberties in the 1920s. He defended Sacco and Vanzetti in New England. Just before their execution he helped organize a demonstration at Boston's State House by the beautiful poet Edna St. Vincent Millay and Ellen Hayes, seventy-six years old, a professor of astronomy and math at Wellesley College, a striking figure in white hair, a straight-cut gray jacket, and square-toed shoes. Both women were arrested by burly policemen and hauled into court for "sauntering" and "loitering." They responded that they were neither sauntering nor loitering but engaged in "the most serious business of their life." A Boston judge found them guilty, much to the satisfaction of Hays, who then demanded a jury trial and won a triumphant acquittal. It was a victory for free expression, petition, and assembly.[64]

Hays defended the civil liberties of Communist John Strachey, the Fascist German American Bund, and Puerto Rican nationalists.[65] He fought tirelessly for civil liberties of workers and union organizers. In other cases he defended William Randolph Hearst when his private telegrams were subpoenaed, and Henry Ford on a free speech issue. Some of his most courageous stands were to bring freedom and liberty to squalid company towns and rural counties. Hays took his life in his hands and went to the company town of Vintondale, Pennsylvania, which was brutally run by coal and iron police. He also went to Logan County, West Virginia, and challenged the tyranny of Sheriff "Two Gun" Don Chafin.

The poet Edna St. Vincent Millay picketing the Massachusetts State House, April 1927, in support of civil liberties and Sacco and Vanzetti. From Arthur Hays, Let Freedom Ring.

His object was to get arrested and to start processes of law.[66]

Hays was very careful to keep civil liberties in the American mainstream. He and Clarence Darrow assisted in the defense of the Scottsboro defendants in Georgia, but he broke decisively with American Communists who tried (with some success) to get control of the case and turn it to their own purposes.[67] His most enduring legacy was the American Civil Liberties Union, in which he took a leading role. He helped make it an organization that was narrow in its devotion to civil liberties but broad in its inclusion of people of many different views and its devotion "to the protection of the unpopular."[68]

Hays summarized his vision of liberty and freedom in a document that he called his "Ten Commandments for Civil Rights."

1. the right to speak, and hear, and print, and read
2. the right to be arrested, which set the due process of law in motion, and protected against the worst abuses of police and vigilantes
3. the right to associate, and to refuse to associate
4. the right to personal prejudices, and not to like or employ Protestants, Catholics, Jews, Negroes, Communists, or Nazis
5. the right to privacy
6. the right to persuade and refuse to be persuaded; the right to be a nuisance, other fellow has a right to refuse to associate with you
7. the right to bargain, in every activity of life
8. the right to obey your conscience as to oaths, flags, soldiering
9. the right to be provocative and to be protected from mobs
10. the right to assert your own idea of Americanism

This vision of civil liberties in the 1920s differed from others that came afterward. For example, Hays believed that everyone had a right to "personal prejudice." Later generations rejected that idea and condemned private as well as public discrimination. Hays also gave much attention to problems that faded in later periods: the right to be protected from mobs and vigilantes, for example. But overall, his thinking was very spacious and large-spirited. He defined civil liberties to include everyone and cast them not in terms of constitutional doctrines but of everyday activities. Mostly he meant to create the greatest possible autonomy for the cantankerous individuals who made up his beloved society of porcupines.[69]

In his own time, Arthur Garfield Hays sometimes made himself as unpopular as many of his clients. His tactics were aggressive, his manner was abrasive, and his speech was painfully assertive. But by the late 1920s, Americans who did not admire Hays or his clients began to awaken to the importance of the cause that he so passionately defended. More than anyone, he made the "protection of the unpopular" into a popular movement. He created a new vision of civil liberties as a democratic cause.

LIVING FREE

Visions of Personal Liberation and Existential Freedom

I believe in only one thing: Liberty.

—ERNEST HEMINGWAY, 1935

WHILE Arthur Garfield Hays led his lifelong campaign for civil liberties, many Americans were expanding liberty and freedom in another direction. In the 1920s, American artists and literati invented new visions of personal liberation in their works and lives. Part of this movement overlapped Hays's idea of civil liberties. A great literary battle centered on the distribution of James Joyce's novel *Ulysses,* one of the great transforming works of modern fiction. The United States Customs Service decreed that it was just another dirty book and prohibited its entry into the country. That attempt at censorship greatly stimulated interest in Joyce's work, and the battle was joined. Literate Americans were outraged by an invasion of what Hays called "the right to read." The American Civil Liberties Union and other groups fought the question in court. In 1933, after a long struggle, they won an epic victory for *Ulysses* in the Federal District Court of New York.

At the same time, writers and artists had another purpose. They sought to live free. In the process they developed a very powerful vision of liberty as emancipation from the constraints of conventional morality, and freedom as a communion of free spirits. Much of this movement was about gender and sex, both as an expression and an instrument of personal liberation. The literature of the 1920s developed an idea of sexuality as central to the human condition and fundamental to both liberty and freedom. Sexual liberation was seen as vital to spiritual release from the tyranny of society and also an instrument of union with other free spirits.

Ernest Hemingway's Vision of Liberty

In the 1920s and 1930s, two American writers made themselves into symbols of these ideas. The most prominent was Ernest Hemingway, who became a popular icon of existential freedom and personal liberation. A graphic example of this vision is Hirschfeld's high-spirited caricature of Hemingway, dressed in a shocking chartreuse jacket, sitting happily in the Stork Club, smiling from ear to ear, stubbing a cigarette with one hand, reading a forbidden copy of *Ulysses* with the other, and taking physical delight in the intoxication of all his highly stimulated senses. Hirschfeld's Hemingway appeared as an exaggerated symbol of emancipated masculinity, with a chest like a bear, a neck like a bull, and two massive hands that were accustomed to take whatever they pleased.[70]

Hemingway was a product of middle America. He was born in middle-class Oak Park, Illinois; raised in sturdy Middle West values of individual independence; and taught by his father to hunt and shoot and live free on the middle border. He liked to say that he learned to write in the city room of the *Kansas City Star*, where he mastered his plain style of short sentences, active verbs, and simple language, "the best rules I ever learned for the business of writing," he said. Hemingway remained a reporter all his life, and in the twenties he discovered a rare talent for writing popular fiction that was instantly recognized as great literature. Novels such as *The Sun Also Rises* and *A Farewell to Arms* became enduring classics.

In his own time, Hemingway was known as much for his life as for his art. He pushed his way to the center of great events. In the First World War he was rejected by the Army for weak eyes but volunteered as an

Al Hirschfeld, "Ernest Hemingway reading James Joyce's Ulysses," in the Stork Club, New York City, gouache on paper, ca. 1950. Courtesy of Louise Hirschfeld. Iconography Collection, Harry Ransom Humanities Research Center, University of Texas, Austin.

ambulance driver and came home a war hero, decorated for saving men under fire though gravely wounded himself. After the war Hemingway married a woman of wealth, lived in Paris, and moved in the circles of Joyce and Picasso. As a journalist he covered the great events of the twenties and thirties, and was involved in the Spanish Civil War. During World War II, he hunted submarines in the Caribbean, flew bombing raids over Germany, landed in Normandy, claimed to liberate Paris (or at least the bar of the Ritz), and fought alongside American infantry on the frontiers of Germany. Between events, he met and married four extraordinary women, lived well in Key West and Sun Valley, and hunted and fished throughout the world. In 1954, he was nearly killed in an African plane crash and escaped only by using his head as a battering ram to break through the burning wreckage. He never recovered from his injuries, found work difficult, and fell prey to severe depression. Psychiatrists administered a sequence of shock treatments that destroyed his memory and ended his writing. Unable to live and work as he wished, Ernest Hemingway chose to die by his own hand. Early on the morning of July 2, 1961, he shot himself in the head with his shotgun. He was sixty-one years old.

In this extraordinary life, so crowded with experience and achievement, Hemingway made himself into a highly cultivated image of a man who lived as he chose, went where he wished, and did what he pleased. He also created for himself a career in which inspiration made its own rules and genius transcended them. The artist's life became his greatest work of art, and a symbol of spiritual liberation.

In 1935, Hemingway wrote, "I believe in only one thing: Liberty." He despised Republican presidents in the twenties and hated New Deal Democrats in the thirties. "All the state has ever meant to me is unjust taxation," he wrote. "I believe in the absolute minimum of government." Hemingway thought that a writer "owes no allegiance to any government. If he is a good writer he will never like the government he lives under. His hand should be against it and its hand will always be against him." The only presidential candidate he really liked was Eugene Debs, less for his socialism than because he was "an honest man and in jail."[71]

Hemingway's politics were not ideological in any conventional sense. He hated Fascism with a passion, despised liberalism and conservatism, wrote with respect of some Communists but disliked Communism. To John Dos Passos he wrote, "I suppose I am an anarchist—but it takes a while to figure out.... I don't believe and can't believe in too much government—no matter what good is the end. To hell with the Church when it becomes a State, and the hell with the State when it becomes a Church."[72]

Every major Hemingway novel was a vision of liberty and a personal declaration of independence from government, authority, and systems of social convention. Hemingway's life was a demonstration that this dream could be a reality, because he made it so. His vision had strong appeal in a modern world that was increasingly organized, institutionalized, bureaucratized, rationalized, routinized, and regulated.

But this idea of liberty as personal autonomy was only one part of Hemingway's vision. Another was an idea of a communion with other free spirits in the world. Some were writers and journalists such as himself; others were African hunters, Cuban fishermen, Key West roustabouts, Spanish matadors, Paris intellectuals, and soldiers of fortune. All his life he loved other free spirits with what Dorothy Parker described as an "immense, ill-advised, and indiscriminate tenderness."[73]

Yet another element was the old idea of living free through discipline. On the surface Hemingway lived a life of extreme self-indulgence. At the same time, he lived by a code of personal discipline that was as rigorous as a New England Puritan's. Dorothy Parker was amazed to discover that "he works like hell, and through it." Always he followed the discipline of work and also cultivated a discipline in life. Another example was his idea of courage—not merely to do brave deeds but to live bravely. It was Hemingway who spoke of courage as "grace under pressure," which became a discipline as demanding as any in the world. These three things were one in Hemingway's vision of living free: liberty as independence, freedom to become one with other liberated spirits, and a discipline of work and life.

Edna St. Vincent Millay's Dream of Liberation

Other American writers in the twenties also became symbols of liberty and freedom. A heroine for many in that age was the lyric poet Edna St. Vincent Millay (1892–1950). She was born on the coast of Maine and raised in genteel poverty by a strong-willed mother who banished her husband for "bitter abuse" and devoted herself to the education of her three daughters, all bright and beautiful. They lived in a ramshackle four-room house, but one room was a music room, and it held one of the largest libraries in their small town. The Millay sisters were relentlessly encouraged to perfect their talents for free expression in painting, music, drama, and especially poetry. All became poets. One was touched by genius.[74]

At an early age it was apparent that there was something extraordinary about Edna St. Vincent Millay's mind. She wrote, "I can remember everything I ever did, every place I was ever in, every face I ever saw. My mind is a labyrinthine picture gallery, in which every painting is a scene from my life." More than that, she wrote that "I feel intensely every little thing... every emotion, that is, the motions that I have not physically felt I have imagined so vividly as to make them real to me." As a child, she read insatiably, studied the world around her, wrote obsessively in diaries, and dashed off snatches of verse that were so good her teachers could not believe she had written them.[75]

Much of her poetry was about liberty and freedom. The long poem that made her reputation was called "Renascence" (1912). It began with a sense of confinement, became a story of spiritual death and rebirth, and ended with a triumphant ode to liberation of the soul. On publication, it was instantly recognized as a major work.

Even more remarkable was its impact when the poet herself recited it. Millay was very small and very slight, with fine-boned features, ivory skin, green-gold eyes, and bright red hair. People who knew her said that no photograph captured her beauty. They remembered her voice as "sibylline," "magical," even "mesmerizing." When she first recited "Renascence" at the White Hall Inn, which still stands in Camden, Maine, two women in the audience were so taken by her that one offered to send her to Vassar and the other to Smith. It turned out to be Barnard for a year, then Vassar, and the literary scene in New York.[76]

Millay moved to Greenwich Village, a community of free spirits— women and men such as John Reed, who boasted: "We are free who live in Washington Square. We dare to think as Uptown wouldn't dare." Much of that idea of living free was about sexual liberation. Millay cultivated freedom of speech in a way that Madison and Jefferson could never have imagined. When her sister came to stay, Edna made her practice speaking obscenities while they sat darning stockings together, chanting softly, "Needle in, Shit. Needle out, Piss. Needle in, Fuck. Needle out, Cunt. Until we were easy with the words."[77]

Edna St. Vincent Millay in 1913, photograph by Arnold Genthe at the Kennerley estate, Mamaroneck, N.Y. Library of Congress.

She had a series of love affairs

with women and men and plunged headlong into what she called the "whirlpool of eros." The first affair appears to have been in 1912, with a woman in Maine. In ten years, there would be more than one hundred affairs, sometimes five or six at once. She took delight in her own body:

> *A small body*
> *Unexclamatory,*
> *But which,*
> *Were it the fashion to wear no clothes,*
> *Would be as well-dressed as any.*

Often she had herself photographed in the nude, sometimes alone or with a lover or a group. Some of the photographs survive in the Library of Congress, where they are restricted until the year 2010.[78] Many lovers fell hopelessly in love with this extraordinary young woman who seemed so "wild and elusive." One of them was Edmund Wilson, who wrote, "She was one of those women whose features are not perfect, and who in their moments of dimness may not seem even pretty, but who, excited by the blood or the spirit, becomes almost supernaturally beautiful."[79]

The passion of these relations became a vital part of her poetry. A little book called *A Few Figs from Thistles* (1920) was best remembered for "First Fig":

> *My candle burns at both ends;*
> *It will not last the night;*
> *But ah, my foes, and oh, my friends—*
> *It gives a lovely light.*

That simple stanza has been called the anthem of her age. Other books followed rapidly: *Second April* in 1921, and *The Harp-Weaver,* which won the Pulitzer Prize, in 1923. Her reputation spread rapidly, both for her work and for her life of sexual liberation. Ross Wetzsteon writes, "Though regarded as the poet of sexual freedom, she actually celebrated spiritual independence—which meant not only the freedom to love, but the freedom to forsake love for a higher calling."[80]

As with Hemingway, Millay's first love was always her work. Her poetry was highly disciplined and deadly serious in its celebration of spiritual emancipation. A growing public also loved its lyric beauty. She was one of the first poets to reach a large public by radio, and her readings became cultural events. When she appeared at Dartmouth in 1924, Richard Eberhart, then an undergraduate, remembered that he "followed

THE LIBERTY BELLE—(She's cracked!)

"Liberty Belle; Down with Inhibitions, Liberate the Libido," cartoon from Judge, February 6, 1926. Library of Congress.

her back to the inn, lagging a hundred feet behind her, anonymous, afraid to go up and say hello or touch her. I was not only enraptured but afraid of the greatness of poetry. I worshipped Millay as a possessor of immortality. She was too beautiful to live among mortals. She symbolized Platonic beauty."[81]

In 1923, Millay married a rich and self-effacing Dutch businessman. They exchanged "vows of unpossessive love," and he devoted his life to her "absolute freedom to create poetry." The affairs continued, and so also did her productivity, in a great flow of poetry and drama. She embraced many public causes, but the center of her life lay elsewhere, in her own idea of liberty and freedom.[82]

In middle age Millay began to lose her beauty and her sexual energy, and the deep well of her creativity slowly ran dry. She kept working, but the spirit drained out of her poetry, and she sank into a sad decline, with much alcohol and morphine to dull the pain. Her devoted husband held her together. After he died she was gone within a year, perhaps by her own hand. She wrote her epitaph in *The Harp-Weaver:*

> *What lips my lips have kissed, and where, and why,*
> *I have forgotten, and what arms have lain*
> *Under my head till morning; but the rain*
> *Is full of ghosts tonight that tap and sigh*
> *Upon the glass and listen for reply.*
> *And in my heart there stirs a quiet pain*
> *For unremembered lads that not again*
> *Will turn to me at midnight with a cry.*
> *Thus in the winter stands a lonely tree,*
> *Nor knows what birds have vanished one by one,*
> *Yet know its boughs more silent than before:*
> *I cannot say what loves have come and gone,*
> *I only know that summer sang in me*
> *A little while, that in me sings no more.*[83]

CORNUCOPIA AMERICANA

Edward Filene's Vision of the Department Store as "A School of Freedom"

> It was in Progressive America that the promise of mass consumption became the foundation for a new definition of freedom to supplant the now obsolete ideal of economic autonomy.
>
> —ERIC FONER

WHILE SOME Americans followed Hemingway and Millay in search of spiritual emancipation, millions more thought of liberation in material terms. The result was yet another expansive vision of liberty and freedom in the 1920s. It combined a modern ideology with an ancient myth.

The Greeks had a wonderful story about their great god Zeus. They believed that he was suckled by the goat Amalthea, a magical creature with a curved horn that filled to overflowing with all the material things that one could possibly desire. The Romans called the goat's horn *cornu copiae*, the horn of plenty. European artists used it as an image of abundance in the sculpture of the Renaissance and the painting of the Enlightenment.

Americans gave the legend of the cornucopia another meaning in the early republic. They developed the idea that material abundance was an artifact of liberty and freedom. In the process, they also invented a new meaning of freedom itself and changed it from a spiritual idea to a material condition. This vision appeared early in the new republic, when a common motif was an image of Miss Liberty with an American flag in one hand and a cornucopia in the other. In the 1920s it became a major theme, even a central theme, in American culture.[84]

A leading apostle of this idea was Edward Albert Filene (1860–1937), one of the great American characters of the 1920s. Born in Massachusetts

Edward Filene. Filene Papers, Boston Public Library.

on the eve of the Civil War, he went to work at his family's clothing store in Boston. After his father's death he became president of William Filene's Sons and made it one of the most enlightened and successful ventures in American business.

Filene specialized in women's fashions and developed his parents' clothing shop into the largest specialty store in the world. Its success flowed from new methods of "segmented marketing," which were designed to give women more choices in the selection of clothing. Filene offered a shopper many levels of possibility in cost, quality, and selection. A shopper could visit the up-market main floors or descend into the depths of Filene's Basement (opened in 1902), which was a bargain hunter's paradise. By the early twenties, a customer could consult Filene's Clothing Information Bureau, which was designed to help shoppers understand the fashion choices before them. By 1924, the store offered women systematic advice on the choice of colors that were harmonious and becoming. Filene's published a "colorscope," which was not

Filene's Department Store, Boston, cutaway drawing. Filene Papers, Boston Public Library.

meant to tell women what they should choose but how they should educate their choices.

Edward Filene engaged his female employees in this new method of retailing by treating them as colleagues. He favored a minimum wage and maximum hours, eight-hour days and five-day weeks, profit sharing and an employee credit union, fringe benefits, collective bargaining, and compulsory arbitration. To serve the spirit of these reforms, he also founded the United States Chamber of Commerce and the Twentieth Century Fund. All his life he worked tirelessly for enlightened business practices and civic reform.

Filene's speeches and books reached a very broad public. He was a fervent believer in capitalism and democracy and the prophet of a new American order. He wrote at length on mass production, mass marketing, and mass consumption. In many publications he argued that a modern retail store was a "school of freedom." The growing abundance of goods opened new possibilities for individual choice, and created a new dimension of freedom.[85]

Other American businessmen took up the same ideas. Eric Foner has observed that American advertising during the 1920s overflowed with this new image of liberty and freedom. In 1928, a chain of 2,800 self-service markets called Piggly Wiggly Stores published a full-page advertisement in the *Saturday Evening Post*. It offered shoppers open shelves with "no clerks to wait for." It promised "the woman of today" that "she may be entirely free to choose for herself."[86]

In New York City, Macy's Department Store created another set of images on Thanksgiving Day in 1924, when it sponsored the first Macy's Christmas Parade. In the words of a trade journal, Macy's offered a "great mechanical showing of Christmas Toys," in time for children to ask for them as Christmas presents. It developed from an invented tradition among immigrants in New York, where poor children paraded on Thanksgiv-

The department store as a vision of freedom in its choices for shoppers at Filene's. Filene Papers, Boston Public Library.

A dissenting view of the department store as the enemy of liberty and freedom, and life itself: "The Commercial Vampire," chromolithograph by Leon Barritt, from VIM, *1898. Chicago Historical Society.*

ing Day and begged contributions from spectators. William Leach reports that Macy's retailers took over this folk custom and made it into a marketing device. So also were its Christmas window displays. Other retailers were quick to follow. They began to address children as incipient consumers and tried to educate their free choices just as Filene's had done in women's fashion.[87]

The cornucopia of the expanding American economy was thought to enlarge the meaning of freedom even for children, in several ways at once. Material abundance promised freedom from the tyranny of poverty. It also meant freedom of choice. It created a new sense of social urgency in 1929, when the market crashed and the economy fell into the depths of a great depression. The collapse of the economy was perceived not only as an economic crisis but as a fundamental threat to liberty and freedom.

THE FARMERS OF PRIMGHAR

Depression Images of Liberty, Freedom, and Justice

> General Prosperity had been a great ally in the election of 1928. General Depression was a major enemy in 1932.
>
> —HERBERT HOOVER, MEMOIRS

I N T H E E A R L Y S P R I N G of 1933, times were hard for the farmers of Primghar, Iowa. The market for their crops had collapsed, even as Americans were starving in the cities. Many farmers had large mortgages and no money to make payments. The Depression threatened them with disaster.

In April, when the planting time came nigh, disaster duly arrived in the form of a lawyer with court orders that authorized him to foreclose on the mortgages and drive the families off the land. The lawyer was escorted by sheriffs and deputies with clubs in their hands.

The farmers of Primghar thought of themselves as a peaceable people, but this was too much to bear. They rose in fury against the lawyer, and there was a fight. The sheriff was soundly thrashed, and the deputies were reduced to begging for their lives. The farmers let them go, on two conditions. The lawyer was asked to accept token payments on the mortgages with a promise of more money when times improved. He was quick to agree. The farmers then added their second demand, that the sheriff and his deputies and even the lawyer should fall on their knees in front of the courthouse and kiss the American flag, as a symbol of liberty and freedom and justice. They did that too. Then they fled the town in mortal fear, and the farmers of Primghar went back to planting.[88]

Similar scenes were enacted in many American towns during the Great Depression. In these domestic struggles, two ideas of liberty and freedom met in violent collision. On one side were the creditors, lawyers, judges, and sheriffs who insisted that government should actively intervene to protect the sanctity of private property and the security of the possessing classes, by enforcing contracts and preserving order. This, they believed, was a matter of constitutional liberty.

On the other side were the debtors and farmers who rose in righteous rebellion. For them, liberty and freedom meant a natural right not to be oppressed by creditors and lawyers and sheriffs, not to lose their homes and farms for debts that nobody could pay and circumstances that nobody could control, and not to forfeit the freedom of their community for the gain of a few.

This was the way that the lines had been drawn in America for many generations. It had been so in the Tenants' Rebellions and Backcountry Regulations of the colonial era. It was the same again in Shays's Rebellion, the Anti-Rent War, and the Helderberg War in the mid-nineteenth century, and in rural risings and the Populist movement of the late nineteenth century.

Most of these rural protests won a few victories but were suppressed by forces of order and law, in the name of constitutional liberty. It was so from the seventeenth century to the early twentieth century. But in the 1930s, something fundamental changed in America. Another vision of liberty and freedom became more prominent than ever before. It was an idea that people had a right to be protected from the tyranny of circumstance and that a democratic government should be their protector. It held that farmers had a right to keep their fields, and families to be secure in their homes, and this was a birthright of liberty and freedom. Further, it insisted workers had a right to a job, and families to food and shelter, and everyone to the means of life itself. Most Americans who thought this way in the thirties did not talk of equality. They spoke of freedom, and liberty, and rights.

Some Americans had said these things many times before, but in 1933 for the first time in American history the president of the United States was saying them, and Congress was listening. Some of these ideas began to be enacted into law, which gave courts and lawyers and sheriffs new roles to play. But none of this happened without a fight. In the thirties, American politics became a pitched battle between different visions of freedom and liberty.

"GREATER FREEDOM, GREATER SECURITY"

Franklin Roosevelt's Vision of a New Deal for Americans

> *May Craig:* I would like your opinion on which way you are going.
>
> *President:* I am going down the whole line a little left of center.
>
> —FRANKLIN ROOSEVELT, DECEMBER 19, 1944

URING THE DECADE of the 1930s, fresh ideas of liberty and freedom developed in a running controversy over the New Deal, which added many images and icons to American culture. Its leading symbol in 1933 was President Franklin Delano Roosevelt himself, who became a vision of hope and confidence for the future. In a dark and painful time, the nation responded to his spirit and style. Few Americans at the time knew how much it cost him to create that image. Crippled by polio, he could no longer walk. But he trained himself to stand upright and even to move by shifting his frozen legs in their heavy steel braces and corsets while he supported himself on the strong arm of his son. At his inauguration in 1933, he gave the appearance of walking effortlessly to a podium, even though he could not walk at all. To watch the old newsreels of Franklin Roosevelt on his first inauguration and to know the agony of every step is to be deeply moved, not only by what he did that day, but by the spirit in which it was done.

To his contemporaries Franklin Roosevelt became an image of complete confidence in the free institutions of the republic. He learned to laugh in the face of his affliction, with his chin held high, head thrown back, cigarette holder at a jaunty angle, and a smile that radiated strength and optimism. The nation instantly responded to his infectious example. His painfully invented image of easy grace changed the tone of the

The New Deal: Franklin Roosevelt as a Living Symbol of his "broader definition of liberty" and "a greater freedom, a greater security." New Yorker cover, March 4, 1933. Peter Arno/Courtesy of The New Yorker, *Condé Nast Publications, Inc.*

American presidency, and his idea of an open society turned the course of American history.

For President Franklin Roosevelt himself, these invented images became a new vision of liberty and freedom. In his second Fireside Chat in 1934, the president discussed those ideas. He told the American people that he rejected "a return to that definition of liberty under which for many years a free people were being gradually regimented into the service of the privileged few." He added, "I prefer and I am sure you prefer that broader definition of liberty under which we are moving forward to a greater freedom, a greater security for the average man than he has ever known in the history of America."[89]

Sometimes he called this new idea liberty. Part of it was built upon the old Roman idea of *libertas* as emancipation from bondage, but it went farther in its understanding of bondage as poverty, hunger, illness, degradation, and despair. Another part of Roosevelt's "broader definition" developed from old ideas of liberty as a set of individual rights, but he expanded the idea of rights to include the right to be treated with decency and respect, the right to work, the right to life itself, the right to the means of subsistence, the right to food and shelter, and the right to be safe and secure from the depredations by other human beings. Further, these ideas were understood not only as rights but as entitlements that reached beyond any earlier vision of liberty in American history.

Sometimes Franklin Roosevelt spoke of his "broader definition" as freedom, and it became an idea of membership in a community of free people. In that sense it descended from ancient folkways of *Freiheit* for the members of a tribe, but it was no longer a tribal idea. This was freedom-as-belonging as a universal idea for all Americans, even all humanity. The New Deal went farther in that direction than any earlier reform movement.

Often Franklin Roosevelt spoke of freedom and liberty together, and the deepest meaning of these ideas came from the way that he combined them. His "broader definition of liberty" encompassed many things, but in itself it was one thing, and something new in the world. Most measures of the New Deal were a series of experiments in mixed enterprise, all designed to serve this larger idea of liberty and freedom. Franklin Roosevelt and his administration attempted to stimulate America's capitalist system, in which the president deeply believed. But he also greatly expanded the role of public agency and government regulation, in sectors where he believed that private enterprise could not promote the human rights of individual Americans.

These purposes appeared in the first New Deal measure, the Emergency Banking Relief Act, which passed the House of Representatives by unanimous vote and ended a monetary panic by stabilizing private banks. This and other measures such as the Glass-Steagall Act increased federal regulation of the banking industry and protected private depositors by a system of federal banking insurance.

A similar combination of public stimulus and private enterprise appeared in the National Industrial Recovery Act, an ill-considered experiment that began to fail even before the Supreme Court found it unconstitutional. The same approach was written into the Agricultural Adjustment Act and the Farm Credit Act. For transportation, it was developed in the Emergency Railroad Transportation Act. All of these reforms were experiments in mixed enterprise, public and private together.

In a nation where one worker in four was unemployed in 1933, the legislation of the Hundred Days also recognized the right of workers to a job, and it tried to get people working again. One of its many measures, the Civilian Conservation Corps Reforestation Relief Act, created jobs for two million Americans. The National Employment System Act encouraged public agencies on every level to help people find jobs in the private sector.

The Federal Emergency Relief Act added something else to this vision: a national responsibility for the right to life and a duty to help Americans achieve individual economic independence. It gave money to cities and states for the relief of suffering in the Depression. Part of the Agricultural Adjustment Act was designed to refinance farm mortgages and to help family farms stay afloat. The Home Owners Refinancing Act helped families keep their homes.

These measures were undertaken in an experimental spirit that was

An iconography of the New Deal: Blue Eagle pierced appliqué and embroidered quilt, 1934. Franklin D. Roosevelt Presidential Library, Hyde Park, N.Y. The American eagle holds an industrial gear and a lightning bolt, with the motto "U.S. We Do Our Part." The quilt is embroidered with gold dollar signs and edged with prairie points. A commentator notes that "the tassels made of grocery string are certainly appropriate, for every store of the period displayed NRA posters or window stickers." The NRA was declared unconstitutional, but its emblematic blue eagle remained a symbol of the New Deal.

central to the early New Deal. They differed in substance and method, but all of them shared the same central purpose and spirit. They were designed to serve Franklin Roosevelt's "broader definition of liberty" and his vision of "greater freedom, greater security" by strengthening a capitalist and democratic system through the method of mixed enterprise. The New Deal generated its own distinctive iconography of these ideas. One familiar emblem of the New Deal was the Blue Eagle, an art deco abstraction of the national bird, with wings outstretched. It was introduced as part of the National Industrial Recovery Act (1933). Every merchant in compliance with its many provisions could display the Blue Eagle.

The New Deal gave employment to many American artists and put them to work creating murals and sculptures in federal buildings. Many of these works centered on large-spirited visions of liberty and freedom. But the leading image of these ideas was always President Franklin Roosevelt himself, with his jaunty air of confidence and unquenchable optimism.[90]

Yet another round of legislation in 1934 and 1935 made Franklin Roosevelt's definition of liberty and freedom larger still. One of the most important parts of the New Deal was its strong support for the rights of labor. A landmark was the National Labor Relations Act of July 5, 1935, better known as the Wagner Act. It is often called Labor's Bill of Rights. The Wagner Act guaranteed the right of workers to join labor unions, and to engage in collective bargaining, as fundamental human rights. Like so many New Deal measures, this one increased freedom in its literal meaning—freedom as a right of association among workers. The Supreme Court declared it constitutional in 1937, and it was followed by many state Wagner Acts.

The labor movement also laid claim to another kind of liberty and freedom: as an entitlement to a living wage, a five-day week, an eight-hour day, an end to child labor, and security in old age. An iconography for these ideas emerged in the 1930s. An example was a campaign poster in the election of 1936. It came from the American Labor Party and the Dressmakers Union, and urged workers to vote for Franklin Roosevelt and Democratic Senator Robert Lehman. In the foreground it displayed the iconic emblem of the labor movement: clasped hands of solidarity, set within the circle of an industrial gear.[91]

This American iconography was very different from the symbols of the European labor parties. It showed little sense of class consciousness and less of class conflict. Six figures, male and female, held picket signs that proclaimed the rights of labor. All were dressed in the manner of the broad American middle class. Behind them was the skyline of Manhattan. There was no sense of alienation from American institutions. The American labor movement thought of itself as all the people. Like the New Deal itself, it swam in the mainstream.

One of the most enduring measures of the New Deal was the Social Security Act of 1935, which created national systems of unemployment insurance, old-age insurance for most Americans, federal aid for destitute children, and support for the blind and crippled and others who could not hold a job. It also established federal aid for maternity care, vocational

The Rights of Labor: The New York State American Labor Party for Roosevelt and Lehman. Issued by the Joint Board, Dressmaker's Union. Collection of David J. and Janice L. Frent.

training, and much more. It was the most sweeping social measure in American history.

Hostile critics have called the Social Security Act an incoherent mix of many approaches to welfare. In fact it was highly coherent. Though furiously denounced from both the right and the left, its purpose was to use the power and resources of the national government to help Americans prepare for their own needs and to model a public program on systems of private insurance.

In company with many Americans, President Franklin Roosevelt did not like welfare for the poor. "The Federal Government must and shall quit this business of relief," he said. "I am not willing that the vitality of our people be further sapped by the giving of cash. . . . We must preserve not only the bodies of the unemployed from destitution, but also their self-respect, their self-reliance." Social Security was meant to be an instrument of liberty and freedom for Americans. Most received it in that spirit.[92]

Other New Deal measures brought electricity to the homes of the rural poor, helped families resettle themselves, provided for protection of the environment and the managed use of natural resources, and required utility holding companies to make themselves useful and efficient or be dissolved. Where private enterprise was unable to manage large undertakings, the New Deal authorized public sector projects such as the Tennessee Valley Authority, which greatly stimulated the capitalist economy of an entire region.

The American Way: Liberty and Justice for All: "Balance the Scales of Justice," children's game, ca. 1940. Collection of Gerald E. Czulewicz, Senior.

Some of these New Deal acts were declared unconstitutional by a conservative Supreme Court. Others were experiments that failed. Through it all, the Great Depression was very slow to end. But the New Deal succeeded in another way. It made Franklin Roosevelt's "broader definition" of liberty and freedom a permanent part of the American system. It also transformed the function of the federal government in America and made it responsible for promoting Franklin Roosevelt's vision of mixed enterprise, liberty, and freedom. It has maintained that role ever since, despite repeated attempts by conservatives to change it.

During the 1930s, this linkage of liberty and freedom to social justice appeared in the rhetoric of the president himself and permeated American life. A small but telling example was a children's game of a sort that flourished in the 1930s. It was a cheap tin box with a glass top. Inside were small chrome-plated steel balls and a set of pockets. The object of the game was to shake the balls into the pockets. One of these games was called "The American Way." It showed a map of the United States, with an image of Uncle Sam on one side and the Statue of Liberty on the other. In the center were the scales of justice. At the top was written "Liberty and Justice for All." At the bottom were the instructions: "Balance the Scales of Justice." A child played the game by trying to distribute the steel balls in a way that promoted liberty and justice for everyone. Here was Franklin Roosevelt's "broader definition" at work, as a problem that even American children were invited to solve.[93]

THE LIBERTY LEAGUE

Conservative Visions of Constitutional Liberty

The Constitution, Fortress of Liberty

—MOTTO OF THE AMERICAN
LIBERTY LEAGUE, 1936

O N A STEAMY summer day in 1934, Washington reporters were called to a news conference at the law office of Jouett Shouse, a genial gentleman farmer from Kansas who was chairman of the Democratic National Committee. He had rebuilt the Democratic Party after the shattering defeat of Al Smith in 1928 and helped lead it to victory in 1932. The reporters turned out, even in Washington's August heat, for Jouett Shouse was always good copy.

Shouse began by announcing that he was about to take a job as head of a new group called the American Liberty League. Its purpose was to uphold the Constitution, defend rights of property, and oppose new "legislation that appeared dangerous" in Congress. The wilted reporters suddenly sat upright. The head of the Democratic Party was telling them that he was going to lead a movement against Franklin Roosevelt's New Deal.[94]

In less than two years, President Roosevelt had made himself the best-loved and worst-hated man in the country. In the Congressional elections of 1934 his party won 72 percent of the Senate and 74 percent of the House, a victory unequaled since Reconstruction. At the same time, he was opposed by 80 percent of the press and a similar proportion of American leaders in business, law, medicine, and the armed forces.[95]

Most American publishers were strenuously hostile to Franklin Roosevelt and the New Deal. Their newspapers kept up a daily drumbeat of invective against "that man" and all his works. Much of this abuse appeared in images. Some were colorful and amusing. A lively example in a Condé-Nast publication of 1935 was a cheerful watercolor that looked to be a cross between Breughel and Raoul Dufy. It showed Uncle Sam as Gulliver, deprived of his liberty by hordes of Lilliputian bureacrats who tied him to the earth with New Deal regulations. In the foreground were the Lilliputian leaders, recognizable as Franklin Roosevelt, Frances Perkins, Henry Morgenthau, and other eminent New Dealers. In the background were mobs of dark proletarian masses descending on Washington. Overhead was a flight of Blue Eagles who looked more like a flock of vultures.[96]

A hostile vision of the New Deal: Uncle Sam as Gulliver, New Dealers as Lilliputians. William Gropper/Vanity Fair, July 1, 1935 © 1935 Condé Nast Publications, Inc.

Most attacks on Roosevelt were not as good-humored as this genial satire. Many were angry and venomous. The result was one of the most bitter political battles in American history, fought mainly over competing visions of liberty and freedom. The many enemies of the New Deal were motivated both by material interest and moral principle, a potent combination in politics, and they included many people of great power and influence.

In 1934, opponents of the New Deal observed President Roosevelt's rising popularity with dismay and wondered how they could stop him. Part of the problem was their own diversity. Most were deeply conservative, but they wished to conserve different things. Some were corporate leaders, lawyers, and financiers, who felt that the new regime was dangerous to their property. More than that, they believed that the New Deal would sap the vital energy of free enterprise in America. Prominent among them were three du Pont brothers, Irénée, Lammot, and Pierre. Working with them were many top business leaders: Alfred Sloan Jr. of General Motors, Sewell Avery of Montgomery Ward, Howard Pew of the Sun Oil Company, and many more. Most were staunch Republicans, but as Franklin Roosevelt went from strength to strength, they doubted that the Republican Party would be able to stop him.

Other enemies of the New Deal were conservative Democrats who wanted their old party back: the party of Jefferson and Jackson. Among them were John W. Davis and Al Smith, Democratic candidates for president in 1924 and 1928, and former party chairman John J. Raskob. They felt that Franklin Roosevelt had removed them from power, broken the promises of the Democratic platform in 1932, and betrayed the founding principles of their party. In 1934, they met in Detroit and organized themselves as the National Jeffersonian Democrats. They resolved to fight the New Deal but also agreed that no self-respecting Democrat could ever vote Republican or organize a third party. They searched for a way to defeat a Democratic president without disrupting the Democratic Party, no easy task.[97]

A third group lived below the Mason-Dixon line and called themselves the Southern Committee to Uphold the Constitution. Their ideas of "constitution" and "upholding" were ones that Jefferson Davis would have approved. The leader was John Henry Kirby, an unreconstructed Texas oilman who regarded the New Deal as a fundamental threat to southern ways. He revived the old rhetoric of Southern Liberty.

Yet another conservative cause was the anti-tax movement. Its leading organization was the old American Taxpayers League, which had fought Woodrow Wilson's New Freedom and now turned against Franklin Roosevelt's New Deal. It worked hard against taxes on personal incomes, corporations, gifts, and estates. At the same time it promoted state sales taxes with high success. The anti-tax movement was strong in the Midwest. It was more egalitarian in manner than eastern Republicans but more conservative in attitudes toward government.

Another conservative image of the New Deal as the enemy of Liberty: "Uncle Sam at the Crossroads" appeared on the cover of Country Gentleman, *October 1936. Curtis Publishing Company.*

In 1934, Democratic business leader John Raskob suggested a bipartisan national coalition against the New Deal that might unite these various conservative movements. He found strong support from Irénée du Pont, a Republican who to his eternal regret had voted for Franklin Roosevelt in 1932, much in the way that some Federalists voted for Andrew Jackson in 1828, two spectacular cases of mistaken identity.

Raskob and du Pont organized private meetings in the offices of Al Smith, the boardroom of General Motors, and the gentlemen's clubs of New York City. The result was a new organization called the American Liberty League. Its purposes were clear: to unite American conservatives in defense of liberty, to stop the New Deal in its tracks, and to defeat Franklin Roosevelt in the election of 1936. The businessmen put up the money, $1.2 million, a mighty war chest in 1934. Two-thirds of the cash came from thirty men. Nearly one-third came from the du Pont family.[98]

Conservative Democrats contributed oratory and an air of bipartisanship. Al Smith started the campaign in January 1936 with a keynote speech at a bipartisan banquet in Washington's Mayflower Hotel. Reporters unkindly called it "dinner with the du Ponts." Al Smith's speech was strong stuff. He insisted that there was no middle ground between old-fashioned American liberty and the new evil of Communism. At the climax he declared, "There can be only the clear pure fresh air of free America or the foul breath of Communistic Russia." Al Smith accused the New Deal and his hated rival Franklin Roosevelt of incipient Bolshevism. It was a big mistake. The rhetoric was so extreme that the press and the country turned against Smith. New Dealers jeered that he had swapped his brown derby for a top hat. He was booed in the streets, and his reputation never recovered. Al Smith's Mayflower Speech destroyed what little was left of his shattered political career.[99]

Undaunted by this disaster, the Liberty League moved quickly to establish organizations in twenty states and enrolled 125,000 members. Most of its money went into a public campaign against the New Deal. Much of it was a presentation of speeches and pamphlets with titles such as "The Constitution, the Fortress of Liberty." Two words recurred: constitution and liberty. The central question was always the same as the title of one of its leading pamphlets: "Shall we have constitutional liberty or dictatorship?"[100]

Some of this rhetoric was addressed to American elites. An example was a speech by President George Cutten of Colgate University, who deployed the arguments of Social Darwinism and asserted that the New Deal was overturning the order of nature. Cutten said, "Nothing could threaten the race as seriously as this. It is begging the fit to be more unfit."[101]

Another campaign was aimed at a larger public. It made much use of modern advertising methods, with short slogans and simple images. The leading symbol was the Liberty Bell. It was used as both a link to older ideas of liberty in the American past and as an alarm bell, warning of dictatorship in America's future.

Cartoons made the point that the New Deal was threatening to destroy the foundations of American Liberty. In 1935, a cartoon by Carey Orr called "The Trojan Horse at Our Gate" represented the American republic as the citadel of Troy, with the Stars and Stripes flying above the ramparts, and a heavy gate marked "Constitution of the United States." In front of the gate was a wooden horse labeled "New Deal Tyranny." The same charge was leveled in more personal terms against Franklin Roosevelt himself. In 1936, stickers distributed by the National Republican Council showed a jaunty president lighting his cigarette with a burning copy of the Constitution.[102]

The same businessmen who backed the Liberty League also supported the Southern Committee to uphold the Constitution, which used different approaches in its own region. Most notorious were the so-called Nigger Pictures, which showed Eleanor Roosevelt in the company of two handsome black ROTC officers from Howard University.[103]

Supporters of the New Deal were quick to reply, and President Roosevelt himself was first off the mark. Two days after the Liberty League was announced, he held a press conference. In a jovial style that maddened Republicans even more than the substance of his ideas, he observed that the Liberty League was like an organization founded "to uphold two of the Ten Commandments." The President said that the Liberty League was very attentive to the rights of property, but it forgot about the rights of people who had lost their jobs and were in danger of losing their homes. Most of all, he said, it forgot the commandment to "love thy neighbor as thyself."

In Congress, Hugo Black led a formal investigation, which documented the heavy flow of contributions from a small handful of rich businessmen and especially the du Pont family, to many anti–New Deal organizations: the Liberty League, the Southern Committee, the Taxpayers League, and more. Other Congressional investigators heard sensational testimony from Marine General Smedley Butler, two-time winner of the Medal of Honor. Butler swore under oath that he had been asked to become a "man on a white horse" and to lead an army of veterans from the American Legion in a revolution that would overthrow the Constitution and remove the Roosevelt administration by force of arms. General

Butler specifically named members of the Liberty League as co-conspirators. Scholars are still debating the truth of Butler's testimony. This historian believes that he was correct about a few individuals, but many leaders of the Liberty League were as sincere in defending their idea of constitutional liberty as were New Dealers on the other side. Both sides deeply believed in their own cause, and each accused the other of wishing to establish a dictatorship.

As the election of 1936 approached, Roosevelt and his advisors decided to make the Liberty League their major campaign issue. James Farley wrote that "the Democratic National Committee's first 'battle order' was to ignore the Republican Party and to concentrate fire on the Liberty League."[104] Democratic leader Edward L. Roddan was appointed to coordinate the attack. "It was simple," Roddan said, "all we did was parade their directorate before the people." He labeled the Liberty League "the Millionaire's Union" and mocked its lofty appeals to the Constitution as "dupontifical."[105]

Franklin Roosevelt himself developed the central theme at the Democratic National Convention in 1936. The president, a published historian of the American Revolution, appealed to the example of that earlier struggle for liberty. His central idea was that the American people had defeated the political tyranny of George III in the War of Independence and now it was time to destroy economic tyranny. The president summarized his thought in a sentence: "The royalists of the economic order have conceded that political freedom was the business of government, but they have maintained that economic slavery was nobody's business." His references to "economic royalists" appealed to the heritage of the Revolution.[106]

Opponents of the New Deal believed that they were the true defenders of old-fashioned American liberty against Franklin Roosevelt's vision of "a greater freedom, a greater security." This conservative idea appeared in campaign badges for Republican candidates Alfred M. Landon in 1936 and Wendell L. Willkie in 1940. Collection of David J. and Janice L. Frent.

Roosevelt concluded by saying, "To some generations much is given. Of others much is expected. This generation of Americans has a rendezvous with destiny." These phrases echoed through the campaign of 1936: "rendezvous with destiny" and "economic royalists." His leading examples of economic royalism were the board of directors of the American Liberty League. The du Pont family became exhibit A. The election of 1936 ended in triumph for the Democrats. Liberty Leaguers watched in horror and disbelief as "that man in the White House" defeated Republican candidate Alfred Landon by 523 electoral votes to 8. Al Smith remarked in his corrupt and cynical way, "You can't beat Santa Claus," but it was more than that. Of all the visions of liberty and freedom that were deployed in the election of 1936, Roosevelt's "broader definition" proved the most persuasive to most Americans.

Roosevelt's opponents failed to convince others, but they deeply believed in their idea of liberty. The du Ponts continued to support the Liberty League for another four years. After 1936, nearly all of its resources came from them. Finally, in 1940, the League disbanded. But their work was not in vain. In the bitter battles of the Roosevelt era, conservative and liberal images of liberty and freedom both gained strong followings. The contest between them would continue to shape political discourse in the United States for many years to come.

LIBERTY AND FREEDOM ON THE FRINGE

American Fascists, Communists, and Populists

Communism is Twentieth Century Americanism.

—BANNER AT A RALLY IN BOSTON GARDEN,
1939, WHERE EARL BROWDER SPOKE ON HIS
DOCTRINE OF AMERICAN EXCEPTIONALISM

SINCLAIR LEWIS, America's first Nobel Laureate for Literature, published a political novel in 1935 called *It Can't Happen Here*.[107] His subject was Fascism, and his argument was that it *can* happen here. Many Americans were aware that it was happening in the United States when he wrote his book. In 1934, small bands of Fascists were multiplying rapidly on the outer fringe of American politics. Most were inspired by the success of Mussolini's Black Shirts and Hitler's Brown Shirts. Prominent among them were the American Silver Shirts of William Dudley Pelley, a California cultist who claimed that he had passed into eternity for seven minutes and returned to earth on a divine mission to deliver America from Franklin Roosevelt by persuasion if possible, and force if necessary. To that end he founded a college in North Carolina, churches throughout the country, and a military training camp in Oklahoma City.

Another group was known as the White Shirts, or Crusaders for Economic Liberty. A larger organization was called the Blue Shirts and claimed the title of American Minutemen. A ragged band of Khaki Shirts grew out of the Bonus March. There were also the Gray Shirts of the American Home Protective Association, the American Black Shirts, who were strong in the South, and the inevitable Brown Shirts who recruited German Americans and imported their uniforms directly from the *Vaterland*.

The uniforms of these many groups, with their cavalry britches, leather boots, Sam Browne belts, and riding crops, symbolized a set of values that were common to Fascists throughout the world. All were hypernationalist, intensely racist, virulently anti-Semitic, authoritarian, and infatuated with violence. They made much of the Führer principle and conceived a bitter hatred for democracy and the rule of law.

But in other ways American Fascists were different from European groups. Mussolini and Hitler had incorporated elements of socialism in their ideology. American Fascists went another way. They combined nationalism, racism, and the Führer principle with a vision of liberty and freedom. White Shirts favored an idea of "economic liberty." Blue Shirts cherished the memory of the American Revolution. The Silver Shirts published their anti-Semitism in a newspaper called *Liberation*, which celebrated an idea of liberty for the master race. Nearly all American Fascists claimed to be the defenders of liberty against the "communistic New Deal" and the dictatorship of "that Jew Roosevelt."

Many of these images appeared at a mass meeting of the German-American Bund in New York's Madison Square Garden, on February 20, 1939. Its leader, Fritz Kuhn, called it a "pro-American celebration of George Washington's Birthday." A color guard of pathetic specimens of the master race stood together in postures that appeared to be burlesques of military bearing. Their flags and banners linked symbols of a free

American Fascists claimed symbols of American liberty in this celebration of George Washington's Birthday by the German-American Bund at Madison Square Garden, New York City, February 20, 1939. Image donated by Corbis/ Bettmann.

American republic with emblems of German Fascism. Towering above them was a huge backlighted painting of Washington as an American Führer, looking down upon these supermen with a baleful expression. New Yorkers were so outraged by this spectacle that 4,700 policemen were needed to protect these Nazis from the wrath of the people.

Deep-rooted traditions of liberty and freedom in the United States created a difficult problem for American

Fascists. To attack liberty and freedom head on, as German Fascists and Japanese militarists did, was to banish their movement to the margins of American culture. But to embrace these ideas was to destroy the authenticity of their cause. In the end, both things happened. American Fascists were impaled on both horns of the same dilemma.[108]

Fascism continues in America even to our own time, but as a marginal movement that communicates in cryptic symbols such as 88 for HH, the eighth letter of the alphabet (Heil Hitler). When it takes a public stance in America it struggles with the problem of a fundamental contradiction between its beliefs and those of a free society.[109]

American Communist Images of Liberty and Freedom

On the far left, there was always a litany of complaint against the New Deal. Some leading American artists were Communists or fellow travelers. They created an iconography of Marxist rage against Franklin Roosevelt and his cause. A prominent example was William Gropper, a painter of radical principles. In 1934, Gropper did a pen-and-ink drawing of Franklin Roosevelt as Mae West saying, "Come Up and See Me Sometime." Gropper's Roosevelt wears a Blue Eagle necklace and stands before a picture of J .P. Morgan signed, "With love, Wall Street." On a table beside the picture are love letters from William Green, president of the American Federation of Labor, and Senator Robert Wagner of New York, author of the Wagner Act. Gropper was discharged by the conservative *New York Tribune* for his radical politics. Ironically, he was commissioned by New Deal Democrats to do a mural for the U.S. Department of the Interior in Washington.[110]

From William Gropper's perspective, almost every prominent American politician was the enemy. The leaders of Capital, Labor, and Government all appeared to be part of a cunning conspiracy against the proletariat, assisted by the "false consciousness" of 99.6 percent of the American electorate. Even in the depth of the Great Depression, all Socialist and Communist candidates combined won less than four-tenths of 1 percent of the vote in the United States.[111]

In 1935, Communist parties throughout the Western democracies changed their tactics. They received orders from the Soviet Union to join with socialists and liberals in "Popular Fronts." In the United States, Communist leaders adopted the language of liberty and freedom, especially in the years from 1935 to 1939. The head of the party, Earl Browder, developed the Marxist doctrine that he called "American exceptionalism."

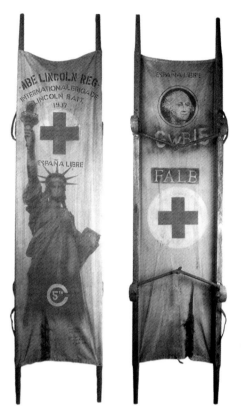

American Communists insisted that they were the guardians of American liberty in these emblems printed on stretchers for the Abraham Lincoln Brigade in the Spanish Civil War. Early American History Auctions, Inc.

It held that the dialectical process of feudalism, capitalism, and socialism did not operate in American history and that Communism could be combined with American traditions of a free and open society. This became an egalitarian vision of liberty and freedom. It had strong appeal to a small number of radicals and intellectuals in the United States, but most Americans regarded it as a contradiction in terms.

Even so, the American Communist Party during the 1930s claimed the mantle of Jefferson and Jackson, especially Abraham Lincoln, and even George Washington. In 1937, the Young Communist League in the United States sponsored a celebration of Paul Revere's ride and scolded the Daughters of the American Revolution for not joining them.[112] Many examples of this imagery appeared among American volunteers who joined Communist-organized units during the Spanish Civil War. Their formations took the names of Abraham Lincoln and George Washington. Their equipment bore liberty symbols. A canvas stretcher, one of 150 made for the Abraham Lincoln Brigade by the Goldmedal Company in Wisconsin, was stenciled "Abe Lincoln Reg., International Brigade, Lincoln Batt." It displayed an image of the Statue of Liberty, with the inscription España Libre." Only after the collapse of the Soviet Union did firm evidence emerge from Kremlin archives that the Abraham Lincoln Brigade was rigidly controlled by Stalinists in Moscow.[113]

The Popular Fronts collapsed in 1939, after the Molotov-Ribbentrop Pact. The alliance between Stalin and Hitler dealt a heavy blow to the Communist Party in the United States, but the Marxist vision of American exceptionalism persisted among many scholars and journalists who have no memory of its origin.[114]

Populist Visions

More successful than Fascists and Communists were the many American populists who flourished in the Depression. Some were charismatic leaders who combined radical promises to share the wealth with down-home appeals to conservative values. They attracted millions of followers, especially in 1934 and 1935. After the election of 1936, they began to fade away, but for a brief period they had a major impact on the New Deal and were an important presence in American history.

The most appealing of these populist leaders was Francis Townsend, "Father Townsend" as millions knew him, an elderly California physician who worked in the Long Beach Health Department during the Great Depression and was overwhelmed by the tide of human misery that rose around him. Some of the worst suffering was among elderly Californians who lost their savings in the Crash and their jobs in the Depression. In 1933, Townsend lost his job, too, at the age of sixty-seven, and he could not get another. "I had little else to do," he wrote, so he started sending letters to the newspapers, arguing that a remedy for the Depression would be an old-age pension of $150 a month for everyone over sixty, on condition that they "spend the money as they get it," to revive the economy.[115]

The idea caught on. Californians loved the idea of spending their way to the salvation of the republic. Townsend skillfully used the methods of modern advertising to attract a large following in his state. He told the elderly that they were the "civil veterans of the republic," and their happy duty was to save it by becoming "circulators of money" and "distributor custodians of the nation's wealth." In 1934, his followers were strong enough to elect their own congressman from Long Beach, who introduced a bill to enact the Townsend Plan. It lost, but petitions poured in.

This populist vision of a free America appeared in the imagery of the Townsend movement, which promised "financial freedom" to Americans in 1936. Metal license plate. Virginia Historical Society.

Townsend himself claimed a following of 3.5 million voters, and probably had them.[116] A large part of Townsend's purpose was liberty and freedom for elderly Americans, so that they could escape the tyranny of fear and hunger and continue as full members of a free society through their lives. Politicians were quick to take notice, and the Social Security Act was in part a response to the Townsend movement.[117]

A very different breed of populist was Michigan's Catholic "radio priest," Father Charles Coughlin. He began his media career by broadcasting church services to shut-in parishioners during the 1920s. After the Great Crash his radio message became more political, and in 1935 he organized a National Union for Social Justice. Coughlin gained a following by attacking the New Deal for not going far enough to help those in need. He accused Franklin Roosevelt of being in collusion with Wall Street and corporate leaders. He put heavy pressure on the New Deal to move further in the direction of social programs.[118]

Increasingly Father Coughlin also became anti-Semitic, and he picked up many Fascist themes even after the beginning of the Second World War. As he became more extreme, his followers turned away, and in 1942 the Roman Catholic hierarchy silenced him. But in the mid-1930s he was a major presence in American politics.[119]

The most successful of these populist leaders was Huey Long, the "Kingfish." He started as a traveling salesman, became a poor man's lawyer, and entered politics in Louisiana, campaigning against big corporations and the Democratic machine in New Orleans. Elected governor in 1928, he launched a vast program of state spending on roads and schools, narrowly escaped conviction for corruption, and made himself virtual dictator of Louisiana. He ended autonomous local government and ruled with an iron hand, in secret alliance with the same machine politicians and corporate leaders whom he publicly attacked.[120]

While continuing as governor, Long became a U.S. senator in 1930. He turned against Roosevelt and won a national following for his "Share the Wealth Society," which promised to make "every man a king," with a homestead allowance of $6,000 and a guaranteed minimum annual income of $2,500. He was preparing to run for president when he was assassinated by his son-in-law, Dr. Carl Weiss, in 1935.[121]

In 1936, the leadership of Huey Long's movement passed to Gerald L. K. Smith, who saw a possibility of victory for a populist alliance that brought together the followers of Father Coughlin in the Northeast and Midwest, Dr. Townsend in California, and Huey Long in the South. In 1936, he succeeded in forming a coalition that hopefully called itself the

Union Party, but it was so disjointed that the only motto it could agree upon was "anybody but Roosevelt." The leaders persevered, and at a convention in Cleveland they nominated William Lemke, a populist congressman from North Dakota and a follower of Father Coughlin. Lemke disliked both the liberal New Deal and the conservative Liberty League. He promised Americans a new vision of freedom through farm relief, the confiscation of all estates over $500,000, and an economic nostrum called "Lemke Money," which proposed to repeal Gresham's Law and much of classical economics. This vision of a free America attracted nearly a million voters in the election of 1936, even though Lemke got on the ballot in only thirty-five states. The populists failed in their own purposes, but they succeeded in making Franklin Roosevelt's new vision of liberty and freedom a little larger than it might have been without them.[122]

REINFORCING THE CENTER

Sol Bloom and the "Cult of the Constitution"

> Our celebration was very timely. It emphasized the
> contrast between our own kind of free government and
> the despotism that threatened to envelop all of
> Europe.
>
> —SOL BLOOM

IN THE ELECTION OF 1936, Franklin Roosevelt's vision of "a greater
security, a greater freedom" was supported by the great majority of
the American people. But on another major issue even his closest
supporters turned against him. It concerned the Constitution and the
Supreme Court.

Much to the fury of the president, conservative justices on the Court
struck down large parts of his New Deal program. They overturned major
parts of the Agricultural Adjustment Act, the National Industrial Recovery Act, the Sugar Act, the Farm Bankruptcy Act, the Railroad Retirement Act, the Coal Conservation Act, and much more. In 1936, they even
declared state minimum wage laws unconstitutional. A deeply conservative majority on the Court invoked the principle of "liberty of contract"
between workers and employers against the new vision of economic regulation for "a greater freedom, a greater security."[123]

The Court's decision caused deep concern in the country. Franklin
Roosevelt was outraged by it. He proposed to break the conservative
"Four Horsemen" on the Federal bench by expanding the Supreme Court
from nine to fifteen seats and appointing justices who were more sympathetic to his purposes. This "Court-packing plan," as it came to be
known, caused a national debate. Some of Roosevelt's strongest supporters stood against him, just as Jefferson had been opposed by many in his
own party when he had attacked the judiciary. Many Americans who

deeply disliked the conservatism of the Supreme Court also believed in the sanctity of the Constitution and an independent judiciary as a bulwark of liberty. Roosevelt suffered a sharp defeat in Congress and a heavy blow to his public standing. His attack on the Court seemed to confirm conservative charges against him, and his reputation never fully recovered.

But even before the fight was over, the Supreme Court shifted its ground. It reversed itself overnight on the question of the constitutionality of state minimum wage laws, which had brought on the crisis. Within a few years, Roosevelt was able to replace most of his opponents on the Court, and New Deal legislation began to be found constitutional.[124]

All this had major consequences for the republic. The failure of Roosevelt's Court-packing plan reinforced the idea that the New Deal's vision of freedom must operate within a constitutional framework. The transformation of the Court on substantive questions also established that it could do so effectively. The result was to strengthen the doctrine of judicial review, which ironically does not appear in the Constitution itself. It created a new vision of the Constitution as the foundation of American democracy, and the Supreme Court as the guardian of both. One of Roosevelt's liberal appointees, Justice William O. Douglas, declared that "the Supreme Court *is* the Constitution."

Not everyone shared that sentiment, but most Americans from the far right to ultra left became more mindful of the Constitution and the rule of the law in the 1930s, when many nations were moving in the opposite direction. In 1938, even the Communist Party in the United States endorsed the Federal Constitution. It drew up a constitution of its own, which pledged to "defend the United States Constitution against its reactionary enemies who would destroy democracy." Similar sentiments were also expressed by leaders of both the Democratic and Republican parties. Liberals, conservatives, radicals, and reactionaries all agreed. In the 1930s, Americans learned to think of the Federal Constitution as something more than a legal document. It was a popular symbol, and the text itself became a sacred icon of freedom and liberty. This was something new.[125]

During the nineteenth century, the Constitution had passed through a long period of comparative neglect. For many years the Declaration of Independence was more prominent and more widely reproduced as an icon of American liberty and freedom. The Constitution received less attention, and the document itself was much neglected. In the Jeffersonian era it was stored in a brick building at 17th and G streets in Washington. During the War of 1812, when a British force attacked the capital, the

Constitution was put in a linen bag and carried to a gristmill in Virginia, then taken deep into the countryside and hidden in an abandoned house. After the war it was brought back to Washington and stored at the Treasury Department until 1866. Then it was moved again, appropriately to the Washington Orphan Asylum, where it remained until 1875, when it was transferred to the State Department.[126]

In 1882, the American historian J. Franklin Jameson made a search for the original copy of the Constitution. He went to the State Department and was told that it was on display in the library. In the central room, he was led to a majestic document, "mounted in all elegance," and discovered that it was the Declaration of Independence. Jameson asked again and was taken to a dark closet in the basement. Inside, he found the original copy of the Constitution, "folded up in a little tin box in the lower part of a closet, while the Declaration of Independence . . . was exposed to the view of all."[127]

A few years later, Jameson returned to the closet and the Constitution was gone. He was told that it was being mounted for public display beside the Declaration of Independence, because the public had recently begun to express "a more general desire to see it." In 1895, the Constitution was photographed for the first time, for display at the Cotton States Exposition in Atlanta, Georgia. After the photograph was made, the Constitution went back to the closet.[128]

There it remained until 1921, when Warren Harding became president of the United States. Harding was an amiable man, sometimes confused in thought and speech but clear in his love of liberty and faith in the Constitution. In 1913, he was outraged when Charles Beard published his *Economic Interpretation of the Constitution,* arguing that it was the work of "four groups of personal interests . . . money, public securities, manufactures, and trade and shipping." Warren Harding's small-town Ohio paper, the *Marion Star,* covered Beard's book as a crime story with the headline, "Scavengers, Hyena-like, Desecrate the Graves of the Dead Patriots."[129]

In 1921, one of Warren Harding's first acts as president was to issue an executive order that the Constitution and the Declaration of Independence should be moved to the Library of Congress and put on permanent display. The Washington bureaucracy moved so slowly that Harding was in his grave before the work was done. Finally, in 1924, the two great documents were brought together as icons of American freedom. President Calvin Coolidge dedicated a shrine for them in the Library of Congress. Facsimile copies were widely displayed in classrooms and public places.

In the thirties, a movement that historian Michael Kammen calls the "cult of the Constitution" developed rapidly. It was helped along by the sesquicentennial of the framing of the Constitution in 1937. Congress appointed a committee to honor the occasion, and many groups joined in. It was an odd alliance. Conservative Republicans, corporate lawyers, and eminent jurists gave strong support, but the leader was a staunch New Deal Democrat named Sol Bloom, one of the more improbable figures in the history of the American republic. In the somber world of Washington lawyers, judges, and legislators, Sol Bloom dressed in bright-colored clothes, with a pair of black-ribboned pince-nez spectacles perched precariously on the tip of his nose. Barely five feet six inches high, he dominated the space around him by his energy and invincible enthusiasm.

Sol Bloom, leader of the Constitutional Celebrations in 1937. Library of Congress.

The son of Jewish immigrants, Sol Bloom made his own way in the world as hustler, dreamer, promoter, fixer, and entrepreneur. At an early age he found a job selling music. Soon he was the owner of a chain of music stores, the national distributor of Victor talking machines, and inventor of the hootchy-kootchy dance, which he turned into a national craze. Sol Bloom made a fortune in the music business, lost it, and made another fortune in Manhattan real estate. In 1920, he decided to retire from business and do "something noble" for his nation. At the age of fifty he ran for Congress as a liberal Democrat. He was a great success with his constituents and served from 1923 until his death in 1949. Bloom became a strong supporter of the New Deal. At the same time, he was a fierce patriot and a believer in the sanctity of the Constitution.

In 1932, Sol Bloom organized a huge national celebration of George Washington's bicentennial birthday. Five years later he was appointed to organize the sesquicentennial for the Federal Constitution and given a generous budget. Sol Bloom outdid himself. He created an organization that resembled a New Deal agency, with an historical division, a legal division, a library division, a woman's division, and an education division.

The actual celebrations began in Philadelphia on May 14, 1937, when

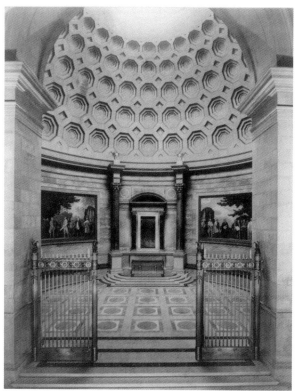

The Shrine of the Constitution in the National Archives, 1937. Library of Congress.

the mayor struck the Liberty Bell thirteen times with a hammer made of a dogwood tree from Valley Forge. Then came speeches, a reenactment of the Constitutional Convention, a military parade, a pontifical mass in Philadelphia Stadium for a hundred thousand Catholics, a regatta on the Schuykill River, a Mummers Parade, and dancing in the streets. Other cities tried to outreach Philadelphia. Bloom estimated that Constitution celebrations were held in fifty thousand American communities. There was music, dancing, pageants, plays, films, pamphlets, books, and memorabilia of many kinds. Sol Bloom sold the Constitution with the same entrepreneurial spirit with which he had promoted Victor's talking machines and the hootchy-kootchy dance.

Many in Congress began to wonder if the primary purpose was to promote Sol Bloom, and in 1938 Republicans demanded an investigation. No wrongdoing was found, but funds were cut off a year earlier than Congress had originally intended. Sol Bloom continued to speak and act around the nation and pronounced the event a success in creating a "new constitution consciousness."[130]

In the 1930s, the Constitution and the Declaration of Independence also moved into a new home. Two large temples of constitutional liberty and freedom rose in Washington. One of them was Cass Gilbert's new Supreme Court Building. Another was the National Archives, which became both an archive and a shrine with much official iconography. Murals were painted in the National Archives by Harry Faulkner in 1936. A new painting was done for the Capitol by Howard Chandler Christie. He called it *The Signing of the Constitution*. It showed the Founding Fathers hard at work. Above them hovered a much larger figure of a modern Miss Liberty, with a choir of angels and a stern figure of Justice who extended a forbidding hand—in the general direction of Franklin Roosevelt.

REDISCOVERING THE BILL OF RIGHTS

Visions of a System of Individual Freedom and Liberty

> When I refer to political freedom, I am concerned
> with those liberties guaranteed by the Bill of Rights.
>
> —ARTHUR GARFIELD HAYS, 1939

Y ET ANOTHER ICON was added a few years later, in what
Michael Kammen has called the "discovery of the Bill of Rights." It
happened more suddenly than the rediscovery of the Constitution,
and after a longer period of neglect. For many years after the first ten
amendments to the Constitution were ratified on December 15, 1791,
Americans showed remarkably little interest in the Bill of Rights. Through
a period of 130 years, the courts rarely enforced them. Six generations of
jurists generally agreed that the Federal Bill of Rights had nothing to do
with the internal affairs of the states. On rare occasions when the Supreme
Court dealt with the Bill of Rights, its decisions tended to shrink their
protections, and in some cases to define them out of existence.[131]

Even the physical documents themselves were forgotten. In 1924,
when the Constitution and the Declaration of Independence were moved
to the Library of Congress, original drafts of the Bill of Rights in its various legislative stages remained in storage, locked in the basement of the
State Department.[132]

A change came in the late 1930s. As dark clouds of tyranny gathered in
a distant sky, Americans began to discover how rare and precious were
their special gifts of freedom, democracy, and the rule of law. They also
began to realize that their free institutions were very much in danger. For
many, this discovery came in 1940–41, when free governments were top-
pling in Europe.

These years brought a sudden surge of interest in the Bill of Rights. A leading figure was the impresario of civil liberties, Arthur Garfield Hays. With the same energy that he had brought to the defense of individual cases in the twenties and early thirties, Hays worked tirelessly to promote general recognition of the Bill of Rights in speeches, essays, and a book called *Democracy Works* (1939). Its angle of vision appeared on the dedication page: "Dedicated to my radical friends who regard me as a conservative, to my conservative friends who regard me as a radical, but chiefly to that increasing number of Americans who, like myself, are 'just liberals.'"[133]

Democracy Works was a lawyer's brief in defense of the Bill of Rights, not by appeals to abstract principle or the wisdom of the Founding Fathers or a political ideology. It made a different argument that a free and democratic society was more efficient than a Fascist tyranny, more equitable than a Communist dictatorship, and more creative than any other system, because it was more open to new ideas. It was also a celebration of "the deep-seated idealism of the average American that he will fight so fiercely for hopelessly lost causes."[134]

Hays played a major role in the revival of interest in the Bill of Rights and was widely publicized in the periodical press. Americans to the left and right were strongly supportive. In 1940, the American Bar Association's Bill of Rights Committee began to publish a new *Bill of Rights Review*. The American Legion organized public meetings to "arouse interest in support of the Bill of Rights."

An important catalyst was the sesquicentennial anniversary of the ratification of the Bill of Rights in 1941. It began in the way of sesquicentennials, with oratory, parades, and public ceremonies. Franklin Roosevelt proclaimed December 15 (when the first ten amendments to the Constitution took effect in 1791) as Bill of Rights Day throughout the nation. It was to be a day for speeches, celebrations, and study, a time for Americans to remember their rights and their responsibilities for maintaining them. Several states, including New York

The revival of interest in the Bill of Rights appeared the popularity of facsimiles such as this. Facsimile No. 1, United States Archives, Washington, D.C.

and California, created an entire Bill of Rights Week.[135] These events continued through the 1940s and 50s. The Bill of Rights rapidly acquired an iconic status which, surprisingly, it had never possessed before.

At the same time, the idea of rights changed, and so also did the process of their enforcement. Not the least of the legacies of the New Deal was a transformation in the relationship between power and right. In the 1920s, many believed that civil liberties must be protected against abusive governments. By the 1930s, government became the protector of civil liberties. In 1939, Attorney General Frank Murphy organized a permanent Civil Liberties Unit in the Criminal Division of the Justice Department. He informed President Roosevelt that "for the first time in our history, the full weight of the Department will be thrown behind the effort to preserve in this country the blessings of liberty." He used the Bill of Rights, the Reconstruction Statutes, and the Thirteenth, Fourteenth, and Fifteenth amendments to prosecute violations of individual rights, and was upheld by the Supreme Court in 1941.[136]

The American people increasingly sued for their rights in ways that greatly expanded their range. Gradually the courts ruled that the state and local governments were bound by the provisions in the Bill of Rights, a process that began in the 1920s and continued for many years. Other cases expanded the meaning of rights to include educational opportunities. As early as 1938, the Supreme Court ruled in limited decisions that separate facilities for blacks were not equal and were a violation of the Fourteenth Amendment's equal protection clause.

Others expanded the idea of constitutional rights to include many social and economic entitlements. New Dealers took the lead, in agencies such as the National Resources Planning Board, which proposed a "new bill of rights" that would include educational opportunity, adequate health care, decent housing, a good job that paid a living wage, and social security. Franklin Roosevelt took up the idea of an economic bill of rights in 1943 and insisted that they were for all Americans, without limits of race or class. The idea continued to grow and was later adopted by conservative Republicans such as Ronald Reagan, who also spoke of an economic bill of rights.[137]

It is common to center the expansion of the Bill of Rights on the Supreme Court, but this was a much larger process, and it had a different set of drivers. For every decision handed down by a high court, many cases were filed by Americans who believed that the Bill of Rights applied to them. And many legal proceedings rose from social movements. The Supreme Court functioned mainly to ratify a process that

In the 1930s, Hollywood promoted a vision of liberty and freedom as sensual gratification. One symbol was Mae West as Miss Liberty in Belle of the Nineties, *a film released by Paramount Pictures in 1934. Universal Studios.*

flowed from the American people, who shared a new consciousness of liberty and freedom as an expanding web of individual rights.

To all this, other visions were added of individual liberty as a right to privacy and the pursuit of pleasure.

Altogether, the decade of the 1930s was a time of interlocking trends in the history of liberty and freedom. In the crisis of the great depression, Franklin Roosevelt and the New Deal created a larger definition of liberty and freedom, which included an idea of entitlement to individual rights for all Americans. It also developed the idea of a democratic government as the guarantor of those rights. At the same time, Roosevelt's opponents in the Liberty League defended another idea of rights as the protection of private property from public authority. These visions were fundamentally opposed, but not beyond the possibility of compromise and reconciliation.

Even as Americans divided on these questions, they came together in other ways. A national consensus developed in the 1930s on the sanctity of the Constitution and the Bill of Rights. That vision of collective agreement on the importance of individual rights persisted even in the face of deep divisions. [138]

Men such as Sol Bloom and Arthur Garfield Hays deliberately promoted this constitutional movement as a way of bringing the nation together They turned the nation's fundamental documents into icons, with that end in mind. Once again the centrifugal tendencies in America's tradition of liberty were balanced by stronger centripetal forces in its heritage of freedom.

AMERICA IN THE SECOND WORLD WAR

Learned Hand's Skeptical Spirit of Liberty and Freedom

> What then is the spirit of liberty? I cannot define it;
> I can only tell you my own faith. The spirit of liberty is
> the spirit which is not too sure that it is right; the spirit
> of liberty is the spirit which seeks to understand the
> minds of other men and women.
>
> —JUDGE LEARNED HAND, 1944[139]

THE SECOND WORLD WAR began with a catastrophe for liberty and freedom. In 1933, twenty-five free governments had existed in Europe. By 1941, only two remained: Sweden and Switzerland. Both had made their separate peace with Fascism and even supported it. Britain and the Commonwealth nations stood alone against Nazi Germany as the last lonely defender of liberty and freedom in the Western World.

Americans watched these events with dismay, but also with detachment. In 1939, most people in the United States wished not to become involved in European troubles. Some thought that isolation was the best hope for liberty and freedom at home. More than a few prominent Americans such as Joseph Kennedy and Charles Lindbergh believed that Fascism was the way of the future.

Japanese militarists and German Fascists made clear their contempt for open societies and their hatred of liberty and freedom. Both had watched as their own nations adopted democratic governments during the 1920s and then fell apart in the Great Depression. Fascists judged the free nations of the West by the confusion and disorder in their own countries when they first introduced free institutions. They formed their impressions of America from Hollywood films, modern fiction, and the writings of alienated intellectuals. From that evidence, Fascists concluded that the Western democracies were fatally weakened by liberty and freedom. On January 22, 1933, when Hitler was coming to power as Chancellor of Germany, fifteen thousand brown-shirted Nazi storm troopers marched through Berlin chanting, "We shit on freedom! We shit on the Jew Republic!"[140]

Slowly, very slowly, Americans awakened to a sense that their own free society was threatened by these distant events. It was a discovery by degrees: Germany in 1933, Ethiopia in 1935, Spain in 1936, China in 1937, Czechoslovakia in 1938, Poland in 1939, western Europe in 1940, the Balkans, the Soviet Union, and Indo-China in 1941. Nation after nation was overrun with incredible speed: France in four weeks, the Netherlands in five days, Denmark in eight hours. Almost everywhere the armed forces of Germany and Japan were invincible, and democratic nations seemed powerless to defend themselves. By 1941, Americans were consumed by anxiety for the future of liberty and freedom, but they could not agree on what to do about it. Many still wished to stand apart.

Then came the Japanese attack on Pearl Harbor. Americans instantly put aside their differences and went to war, united as never before in their history. The source of their unity was not merely the treachery of Japan's attack on Pearl Harbor, or the mad hubris of Hitler's declaration of war on the United States four days later. The deepest root of unity was a growing sense that the rulers of Germany and Japan were bitter enemies of free societies everywhere and were dedicated to their destruction.

The America First Committee labored to keep the United States out of World War II. Its members shared a vision of liberty and freedom in one country, separate from the world; their attitudes and acts appeared in this collage of images from Stan Cohen, V for Victory: America's Home Front during World War II (Missoula, Mont., 1991), 125.

Among the rulers of the Axis powers, this attitude of contempt and hatred for freedom and liberty grew stronger as the war continued and was demonstrated in many strange ways. A small event, symbolic of that hostility, happened in the Pacific Ocean on March 28, 1944. The American battleship *Iowa* was bombarding the small Japanese-held island of Mili in the Marshall Islands when a Japanese coast-defense battery returned fire and scored several hits on the American vessel. After the battle, *Iowa*'s crew found a fragment from a Japanese shell. The after-action report described it as "a small twisted piece of a US buffalo nickel, bearing the first three letters of the word 'Liberty.'"[141]

On the American side, new visions of liberty and freedom appeared in the course of this great conflict. The tone of the Second World War was very different from the that of the First. It was less authoritarian and more democratic, less coercive and more tolerant of others, less dogmatic and more skeptical.

An eloquent statement of this new attitude appeared in 1944, when Judge Learned Hand gave a speech in New York City's Central Park to newly admitted citizens of the United States. His chosen theme was the "The Spirit of Liberty." He began by saying that this idea was not to be found in courts or laws or constitutions. "Liberty lies in the hearts of men and women; when it dies there, no constitution, no law, no court can even do much to save it. While it lies there, it needs no constitution, no law, no court to save it."[142]

Learned Hand went on to explain his vision of liberty. "What then is the spirit of liberty?" he asked. "I cannot define it," he answered. "I can only tell you my own faith. The spirit of liberty is the spirit that is not too sure that it is right; the spirit of liberty is the spirit which seeks to understand the minds of other men and women; the spirit of liberty is the spirit which weighs their interests alongside its own without bias; the spirit of liberty remembers that not even a sparrow falls to earth unheeded; the spirit of liberty is the spirit of Him who, nearly two thousand years ago, taught mankind that lesson it has never quite learned, but has never quite forgotten; that there may be a kingdom where the least shall be heard and considered side by side with the greatest."[143]

He spoke only for himself, but Learned Hand's vision was widely shared by the generation of the Second World War. It was very different from attitudes in Woodrow Wilson's generation and other generations to come.

REMEMBERING PEARL HARBOR
Liberty and Freedom as Eternal Vigilance

Ammunition beats persuasion if you are looking for freedom.

—WILL ROGERS

THE GREAT AWAKENING came with the attack on Pearl Harbor. Soon after that event on December 7, 1941, a poster showed a tattered American flag flying in Hawaii against a dark background of dense black smoke. Behind the smoke one could see in the distance a bright blue sky with fair-weather clouds. Emerging from the smoke was a passage from Abraham Lincoln's Gettysburg Address: "We here highly resolve that these dead shall not have died in vain." Below in big red letters was the inscription: "Remember Pearl Harbor!"

Those words were taken up by the press and echoed across the United States. In the earlier years of the war, "Remember Pearl Harbor" was embroidered on pillows, embossed on license tags, crudely stamped on pencils and rulers, and engraved on elegant brooches with a single mnemonic white pearl. Business firms printed the words on advertisements and letterheads, with such frequency that sometimes they were abbreviated as "Remember PH," or merely "RPH." American households displayed them on wall plaques and small devotional statues in the manner of a religious icon. Americans wore them on neckties, hats, and even underwear. The new mood was captured early in the war by patriotic women's panties that bore the inscription "Remember Pearl Harbor. Don't get caught with your pants down." An irreverent generation took the lesson to heart with a self-deprecating laugh, a scorn for high-blown oratory, a taste for low humor, and deadly seriousness about the task at hand.[144]

514

The coinage of the phrase is credited to an American newspaper, the *Portland Oregonian*, immediately after the event. It grew from the short Pearl Harbor Speech that President Franklin Roosevelt delivered to the Congress and the nation on December 8, 1941. It introduced the theme of memory in its immortal opening phrase ("a date which will live in infamy") and returned to it in the climax ("always will our whole nation remember").[145]

Americans had often used such words before. On April 21, 1836, Texans went into the battle of San Jacinto shouting, "Remember the Alamo!" In the Civil War, U.S. Colored Volunteers cried, "Remember Fort Pillow." In 1898, the rallying cry was "Remember the Maine!" But this time, "Remember Pearl Harbor" had a different intensity and another meaning.

It was not as if any American of that embattled generation could have forgotten Pearl Harbor. More than sixty years after the event, Americans who were alive on December 7, 1941, still vividly recall where they were and what they were doing when the news of Pearl Harbor reached them. Every memoir of World War II describes that moment in painful detail. Every year while the war went on, Pearl Harbor Day was observed as a national holiday.

That memory was reinforced by films, radio programs, and popular songs. A clue to its meaning appeared in a song by Don Reid and Sammy Kaye called "Remember Pearl Harbor," which raced to the top of the hit parade in 1942:

> *We will always remember*
> *How they died for Liberty*
> *Let's REMEMBER PEARL HARBOR*
> *And go on to victory.*[146]

The repetition of this ritual phrase was meant not merely to keep alive the memory of the event but also to link it to other themes, of which the most important were liberty and freedom. A wooden plaque, mass-produced by the Syroco Wood Products Company, imposed the slogan "Remember Pearl Harbor" on a torch of freedom and an image of the Liberty Bell. A window sticker showed the same words with an image of the Statue of Liberty and the inscription "America and Freedom."[147]

These images connected Pearl Harbor to a particular idea of freedom and liberty. The memory of that event gave new meaning to an old truth, variously attributed to Patrick Henry, Thomas Jefferson, and Irish Radical writer John Philpot Curran: "The price of liberty is eternal vigilance."

The American response to the Japanese attack on Pearl Harbor appeared in artifacts that linked liberty and freedom to themes of national unity and service. This mood often appeared in the darkest moments of American history. These examples are from Martin Jacobs, World War II Collectibles *(Iola, Iowa, 2000), 21-23.*

Franklin Roosevelt made that theme clear in his Pearl Harbor Speech on December 8, 1941: "We will not only defend ourselves to the uttermost, but will make it very certain that this form of treachery shall never endanger us again."[148]

It was that sudden dawning consciousness that made Pearl Harbor a pivotal moment in modern American history. Before December 7, 1941, many Americans believed that their freedom was safe and secure in the New World, far from the tyrannies of Asia and Europe. After the Japanese attack, American attitudes were never the same again. A determined enemy, deeply hostile to a free society, had projected his power across the widest ocean in the world and struck a heavy blow without warning. The lesson was very clear. Friends of liberty and freedom must always be alert, and stronger than their enemies.

Here was a new mood in the American history of liberty and freedom. After Pearl Harbor, habits of the heart took on a harder edge. In 1943, a visiting British scholar observed the change in America. "No one fresh from London could fail to be overwhelmed by the contrast," H. G. Nicholas wrote. "The moment which crystallized the contrast...occurred in flight over the plains of Nebraska. Here if anywhere was normality— hundreds of miles of it and not a sight or a sound to remind one that this was a country at war. And then my stewardess deposited my lunch tray in front of me and there suddenly was my Mene Mene Tekel Upharsin. As I reached avidly to attack my butter pat there, neatly inscribed on it, was the injunction REMEMBER PEARL HARBOR. It needed the butter to remind one of the guns."[149]

The idea of eternal vigilance was everywhere in America after Pearl Harbor. Americans who were alive during the Second World War kept it always in their minds. A bizarre example, typical of that generation, was reported from Japan immediately after the war. During the American occupation a U.S. Army dentist named E. J. "Jack" Mallory was ordered to make a set of dentures for General Hideki Tojo, head of the government that attacked Pearl Harbor, now a prisoner of war. The American dentist was a ham radio operator with a knowledge of Morse code. He engraved the words "Remember Pearl Harbor" in dots and dashes on Tojo's false teeth. "It wasn't done in anger," Dr. Mallory explained. "It's just that not many people had a chance to get those words into his mouth."[150]

But in all of these antics, some fundamental had changed in the way that Americans thought. There was a new wariness in their vision of the world. It led to a fundamental transformation in the way that they thought about their free society.

**THIS IS AMERICA
—for this we fight**

Eternal Vigilance Is the Price of Liberty

Pearl Harbor inspired a grim vision of liberty and freedom as requiring eternal vigilance, an idea that had sometimes appeared in earlier periods of American history. After December 7, 1941, it was never far from American thoughts. World War II poster. National Archives.

A DEMOCRACY GOES TO WAR

Archibald MacLeish and the Strategy of Truth

> The motion picture must remain free. . . . I want no censorship.
>
> —LOWELL MELLETT, FOR THE OFFICE OF FACTS AND FIGURES

As the war expanded in 1942, all the Allied and Axis powers mobilized their populations for total war, but in different ways. Fascist Germany and Imperial Japan resorted to brutal coercion. By 1944, their economies rested largely on slave labor. At least ten million people worked as slaves in Germany, and many more in occupied Europe. The Japanese Empire also ran on forced labor. On the island of Java alone, two million Indonesians were compelled to work for the "Greater East Asia Co-Prosperity Sphere." Japanese masters employed many millions of slaves in Korea, Manchuria, China, Thailand, Malaysia, Burma, the Philippines, and the Pacific islands. After 1942, Germany and Japan also increasingly imposed systems of forced labor on their own people.[151]

The Soviet Union made even heavier use of forced labor. Communist leaders enslaved millions of prisoners of war and larger numbers of their own citizens. From 1938 to 1953, the Soviet Gulags grew into a gigantic labor system that employed more than eighteen million people as penal slaves. Many were not criminals, or even "politicals," but ordinary people who were swept up in mass arrests for their labor. Another fifteen million people were subject to forced labor in other forms. The largest and cruelest expansion of this Soviet system happened during the Second World War.[152]

In China during the Second World War, millions of peasants were compelled to work by Nationalists, Communists, and warlords alike. The same thing happened in India and Africa. The nations of the British Commonwealth also conscripted labor on a large scale in World War II, even in Britain itself. Potential workers, both male and female, were required to register for national labor service in the United Kingdom, Australia, and New Zealand. Many British subjects, men and women alike, were forced to work at jobs they did not want, in places where they did not wish to be.[153]

Only one major power did not resort to forced civilian labor during the Second World War. The United States used coercion in other forms: military conscription, rationing, and price controls. But it left civilians free to work in the war effort, or not to work if they preferred, or to change jobs as they pleased. The president and Congress made a policy decision to maintain a free labor market during the war. They believed that free labor was more efficient than forced labor. They also agreed that a free society was what they were fighting to preserve, and that freedom itself was one of the greatest assets of the Allied cause. Alone among the great powers, President Roosevelt and other American leaders chose to mobilize American workers by persuasion rather than compulsion.[154]

The question was how to persuade so large and diverse a nation to join a common cause. Here President Roosevelt made another decision not to follow American practices in the First World War. Roosevelt wanted no Office of Propaganda in his administration, and he refused to create one until 1941, when his wife, Eleanor, and Fiorello La Guardia convinced him to set up a very different sort of agency, which was carefully called the Office of Facts and Figures. It was run by upright liberals whom Secretary of War Henry Stimson contemptuously called "the cherubs."

The head cherub was Archibald MacLeish, one of America's most distinguished poets and the Librarian of Congress. With the president's approval, MacLeish staked out a new approach to a campaign of persuasion. He called it the "strategy of truth." The Office of Facts and Figures took the high road of honesty, candor, and appeals to principle. It made a special point of not appealing to fear, hatred, or national prejudice. It went out of its way to reveal any flaw or failure in the American war effort, sometimes in excruciating detail. This noble experiment won no respect from American journalists, who protested that they were overwhelmed by dreary facts and could not get the colorful stories that they needed to sell their newspapers. Other complaints came from academic social scientists such as Harold Lasswell, who argued that a "strategy of truth" required "tactics of clarity and vividness."[155]

In 1942, Roosevelt responded to a growing chorus of criticism by setting up a new Office of War Information. To run it he appointed three able and highly honorable men: publisher Gardner Cowles Jr. (for domestic affairs), playwright Robert Sherwood (foreign affairs), and radio journalist Elmer Davis (in charge of the entire agency). MacLeish remained, and so did his strategy of truth, but Lasswell's "tactics of clarity and vividness" received more attention.[156]

At the same time, the Roosevelt administration adopted a policy of free expression and used it as yet another instrument of war mobilization. It urged everyone to speak out freely in a collective effort to persuade American workers to support the war effort. Industrial corporations that had been Roosevelt's severest critics were offered tax exemptions for public service messages. Many became very active in that way. The advertising industry was heavily recruited, and in 1942 the War Advertising Council was founded by private initiative to support the war effort. Industry leader James Young told his colleagues, "We have within our hands the greatest aggregate means of mass education and persuasion the world has ever seen—namely the channels of advertising communication. . . . Why not use it?"[157]

The entertainment industry was brought into the campaign of persuasion. The Roosevelt administration encouraged Hollywood to make films without heavy censorship, unlike Woodrow Wilson's Justice Department, which had actively policed the motion picture industry in World War I. In turn, Hollywood and Broadway were urged to join voluntarily in the war effort, which they did in their own way. Their approach was to make the mobilization in itself a form of entertainment. As early as October 1941, leading figures in show business organized a rally called "Fight for Freedom" at New York's Madison Square Garden. Walt Disney designed a program that showed Mickey Mouse, Donald Duck, and Pluto

Hollywood's hedonistic vision of living free appeared in Walt Disney's image "It's Fun to be Free," which appeared on a program cover for a Fight for Freedom Rally at Madison Square Garden, New York City, October 1941. Courtesy of Eric Foner and Freedom House.

marching for freedom with flag, fife, and drum. Over their heads was the title: "It's fun to be free."[158]

Many branches of the government joined the campaign. The Treasury Department under Secretary Henry Morgenthau was very active in its promotion of savings bonds. The War Department gave growing attention to public information. It used old images of liberty and freedom, but in a fresh light. Once again another American generation gave new meanings to old ideas.

At the same time, the old emblems were put to work in a new spirit. Uncle Sam, Miss Liberty, and the Minuteman all enlisted in the war effort, joining "for the duration," as people said at the time. These national symbols had often gone to war before, but this time they served in a different way.

Uncle Sam was a case in point. In World War I he had been a stern authority figure, the leader of the nation-state. Some of these images were recycled in the early years of the Second World War. The old Kitchener poster was put to work once more. But after Pearl Harbor, Uncle Sam presented another image that was more congenial to a new generation and very different from what it was in the First World War, increasingly so as the second war progressed.

In World War II Uncle Sam became a representative of the people— unassuming, down to earth, folksy, no different from anybody else. He took off his coat and vest, opened his collar, rolled up his sleeves, and went to work with everyone else. One factory poster showed him not giving orders, as in 1917, but asking for suggestions about how the war effort might be managed more efficiently. On another poster in 1942, Uncle Sam's high hat was replaced by a GI helmet. He was a militant figure, ready for a fight, but no longer the authority figure of James Montgomery Flagg's memorable "I Want You" poster in 1916. He continued to be an

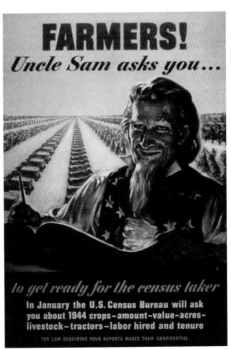

The American mood in World War II was different from the tone of the First World War. Symbols of liberty and freedom were more democratic, more irreverent, and less authoritarian. An example was this new image for Uncle Sam, a folksy figure far from the spirit of James Montgomery Flagg, as depicted on this war poster: "Farmers! Uncle Sam asks you . . ." National Archives.

The democratic spirit of World War II also appeared in new images of Miss Liberty. An example was Remington Schuyler's poster for the Boy Scouts, in which Liberty appeared as the girl next door, not much older than the Scouts themselves. She carries the Bill of Rights and represents a new interest in that document. Library of Congress.

icon of liberty and freedom but in a new way that was more closely associated with equality and democracy.

These new elements appeared very widely in the iconography of World War II. They expressed a stronger linkage between freedom and equality, in a distinctively American meaning. American equality never meant equal shares of wealth or material condition. It meant equality of opportunity, equality of rights, equality of manners, and most of all equality of esteem. It was the equality of the Yankee farmer who told his son to remember that he was just as good as everybody else—and no better. This American ideal was very distant from American realities in 1941, but the ideal itself became a reality in its own right during the Second World War and an important engine of change.

A new image of Miss Liberty communicated that vision without elaborate statements of ideology, which ran against the grain of this American generation. These new symbols were deliberately created as a contribution to the war effort. Miss Liberty became not merely the symbol of freedom but also its instrument, in a very different way than in the last war.

The Liberty Bell made a perfect symbol. It had begun as the expression of the Quaker idea of liberty and freedom that was both unitary and universal. As we have seen, the antislavery movement had adopted it as an emblem of its cause. In the Civil War it grew into a national symbol. During the Second World War it expanded yet again and became an emblem of liberty and freedom that belonged to all the world. This historian remembers hearing the Liberty Bell rung, or rather sounded, on D-Day, June 6, 1944. Its sound was carried around the world by Armed Forces Radio to mark the impending liberation of western Europe.

Another national icon, the Statue of Liberty, also gained a new image during the war. It appeared in grainy black-and-white newsreels of troop transports outward bound past Bedloe's Island with millions of Americans in khaki and blue.[159] Every generation that honored these old symbols also changed them. In the process of defending these ideas during the Second World War, people transformed them more than anyone intended when the war began.

Another face of Miss Liberty appeared in Norman Rockwell's "The Home Front," for the cover of the Saturday Evening Post, *September 4, 1943. Courtesy of the Norman Rockwell Family Agency.*

V FOR VICTORY—AND FREEDOM

Victor de Laveleye's Symbol of Resistance and Triumph

> V is the first letter of the words *"Victoire"* in French,
> and *"Vrijheid"* in Flemish, two things that go together.
>
> —VICTOR DE LAVELEYE

WHILE THE OLD IMAGES changed, new emblems of liberty and freedom appeared during the Second World War. They tended to have a distinct character, different from American symbols in other conflicts. Most were very simple and highly accessible and were designed for frequent repetition in sight and sound. They tended to be less nationalist than in the First World War. A major purpose was to unite people throughout the world in a common cause.

In January 1941, a leader of the Belgian resistance movement searched for such a symbol to rally his own nation. Belgium had been invaded and conquered yet again by the German army. It was divided by culture and language, Flemish and Francophone, and the task of bringing the Belgian people together in a common cause was not an easy one.

The resistance leader was Victor de Laveleye, a lawyer and secretary of the Belgian Liberal Party. After the German conquest in 1940, Laveleye went to London, joined the Resistance movement there, and made short-wave broadcasts on a new station called Radio België/Radio Belgique.[160] On January 14, 1941, Victor de Laveleye made a suggestion to the Belgian people. He said, "I propose to you as a rallying emblem the letter *V*, because *V* is the first letter of the words 'Victoire' in French, and 'Vrijheid' [freedom] in Flemish: two things that go together, as Walloons and Flemings are at the moment marching hand in hand, two things which are the consequence one of the other, the Victory which will give us back our freedom, the Victory of our good friends the English. Their word for victory also begins with *V*. As you see, things fit all round."[161]

It was a brilliant idea, a small gesture of resistance that anyone could make, a simple sign that gained strength from repetition. It did so most of all in the hearts of those who made it, and also in the minds of its enemies. Laveleye told his countrymen, "The occupier, by seeing this sign, always the same, infinitely repeated, would understand that he is surrounded, encircled by an immense crowd of citizens eagerly awaiting his first moment of weakness."[162]

It instantly caught on. V-signs began to blossom on Belgian walls, houses, streets, barracks, and even the weapons of the despised German conquerers. The Flemish broadcasts of Radio België were also heard in the Netherlands, and the French programs of Radio Belgique reached a large audience in France. The British Broadcasting Corporation decided on June 27, 1941, to begin all of its European broadcasts with the letter *V* in international Morse code (..._) followed by the first four notes of Beethoven's Fifth Symphony, which repeated the same rhythm. The next day, the BBC added a stirring Morse *V* as a drumbeat. It became the station identification and also its interval signal.

BBC broadcasts urged people throughout Europe to repeat the Morse code V-signal in the clap of a teacher's hands, the tap of a blacksmith's hammer, the ring of a church bell, and the knock on a door. The people of Paris staged a "knocking campaign" throughout their occupied city. By mid-July 1941, even Stalinist Authorities of Radio Moscow adopted

The V-symbol was invented by Belgian lawyer Victor de Levelaye, who explained that it stood for "victoire" in French and "vrijheid" (freedom) in Flemish. In that spirit, it was taken up by Winston Churchill, Franklin Roosevelt, and millions of people everywhere. From the collection of Martin Jacobs.

Everybody did it: American GIs shaving their heads for victory and freedom, ca. 1945, and Hollywood stars waving to their fans, ca. 1942 (see opposite page). Photographs from Hulton Archive/Getty Images.

the V for Victory and Freedom from the German invader—if not yet from the tyrant Josef Stalin.

In the darkest days of the war this buoyant symbol captured the imagination of people throughout the world. It was so through the grim winter of 1941 and spring of 1942, when the Allied cause suffered what Winston Churchill called a "cataract of disaster" in every theater. Throughout Asia and the Pacific, Japanese forces indulged themselves in six months of savage conquest. In Africa, Rommel captured a British army in Tobruk and drove another into Egypt. On the eastern front, German invaders advanced deep into the Soviet Union, even to the River Don. In the Atlantic, German U-boats sank a large part of America's tanker fleet within sight of its own coast. But even as the newsreels reported these defeats, they also showed Prime Minister Winston Churchill with a look of fierce determination on his John Bull face, raising two pudgy fingers in a defiant V for Victory, and Franklin Roosevelt in a military haircut, making the same symbol.

After Pearl Harbor, the V-sign spread swiftly through the United States. Americans wore Victory Buttons, sold Victory Stamps, flew Victory Flags, planted Victory Gardens, and built thousands of Liberty Ships and Victory Ships. Savings bonds were sold in V-campaigns. Children in classrooms lined up to form a letter *V.* Women who played professional baseball during the war formed the letter *V* while the national anthem was played.[163]

As this emblem traveled through the world, the two simple strokes of the V-sign acquired different shades of meaning. In occupied Europe the chalked letters were a symbol of resistance. In Britain the two splayed fingers of Winston Churchill became a gesture of defiance. In the United States, the V-sign meant a nation's resolve to fight for nothing less than total victory.[164]

Franklin Roosevelt gave that idea of total victory a concrete meaning by adopting the policy of nothing less than the unconditional surrender by the Axis powers and the total destruction of Fascism. He did so as early as May 1942. On December 2, 1942, he told Polish General Wladislaw Sikorski that "we have no intention of concluding this war with any kind of armistice or treaty. Germany must surrender unconditionally." In 1943, he asked for a meeting with Winston Churchill, partly to advance this idea. Churchill was not happy about it. "I would not myself have used those words," he later wrote. The American secretary of state, Cordell Hull, also opposed the idea. But Roosevelt insisted, and his policy prevailed. In a joint press conference "unconditional surrender" became the official Anglo-American policy. It was driven by the will of one leader, but it also represented the wishes of the American people, who were determined to destroy utterly the Fascist regimes that had attacked them.[165]

"Unconditional surrender" became an iconic phrase—ritual words, repeated by Roosevelt, accepted by Churchill, secured by a sense of moral obligation, and widely supported by the American people. German and Japanese leaders and many European conservatives were (and still are) appalled by this way of thinking. After the war, revisionist historians argued that demands for unconditional surrender prolonged

V symbols were explicitly linked to liberty and freedom, as in these examples from the collections of Martin Jacobs and Stan Clark, AP/WideWorld Photos.

"V for Victory" quilt made during World War II, by Mrs. W. B. Lathouse, Warren, Ohio. America Hurrah Antiques; collection of Joel Kopp.

the war by stiffening resistance in Japan and Germany, which was not the case. They have trouble understanding that for the American people, unconditional surrender was the object of the war. It rested upon a belief that free societies could never be safe in a world where fascism continued to exist.

When Franklin Roosevelt framed his policy of total victory, he was also thinking of postwar policy. He said, "Victory in this war is the first and greatest goal before us. Victory in the peace is next." Conservative writers in the United States argued after 1945 that unconditional surrender lost the Cold War by destroying the possibility for a common front between Fascists and Democrats against Communism—an idea that quietly disappeared in 1989. Unconditional surrender was critical to the total

destruction of Fascism and decisive in the outcome of the Cold War. It meant that the
United States and its allies did not have to
fight an ideological war on two fronts, which
they might well have lost. For American liberals, this was the meaning of the V-sign.[166]

Americans of African descent gave the V-
sign yet another meaning. In February 1942,
the *Pittsburgh Courier*, an Afro-American
newspaper, invented the "Double V," for victory abroad against Fascism, victory at home
against racism. This idea was taken up during
the war, more as an iconic phrase than image.
It reverberated through the rhetoric of Afro-
American speakers during the war years and
helped to crystallize a new concern for freedom at home.[167]

A striking image of the Double V was a
small fringed banner, like so many that were
hanging in American homes during the war.

*African Americans adopted the Double V, victory against fascism
and victory for civil rights. Cloth banner, ca. 1944. New York
State Museum.*

This one showed an American soldier, half black and half white. His
combat boots were still in chains, but his arms were raised high. In one
hand he held the American flag. In the other he clutched the Bill of
Rights with an eagle perched above it. The motto made its meaning dou-
ble-clear: "Black America Wants Civil Rights Now!"

All of these allied meanings were variations on a common theme.
Everywhere, the V-sign linked ideas of freedom and victory and also
became an emblem of unity in the common cause. In 1944, as Allied
troops entered Rome, Paris, Brussels, and Manila, they were greeted
everywhere with V-signs by cheering crowds. To make the V-sign was to
express one's solidarity with freedom-loving people everywhere.

The V-sign also carried yet another layer of meaning. It was an image
not merely of the struggle for freedom but also of its inevitable triumph. In
the midst of cruelty and destruction and evil on a scale that the world had
never known before, it was an emblem of hope and exaltation in the human
spirit. It became an idea of history as the inevitable progress of liberty and
freedom. This time the end of total war would be total victory. A world
struggle would not end in another armistice between the warring powers,
but in the entire destruction of Fascism, and the triumph of freedom.

CIVIL LIBERTIES IN TIME OF WAR

Francis Biddle's Vision: A Government of Rights

> We must be free not because we claim freedom, but because we practice it.
>
> —WILLIAM FAULKNER

IN THE SECOND WORLD WAR, Franklin Roosevelt kept a portrait of Woodrow Wilson in the Cabinet Room. He explained to friends that he did so as a reminder not to make the same mistakes twice. Among Wilson's errors, in Roosevelt's judgment, were the armistice, the heavy-handed propaganda of his Committee on Public Information, the authoritarian tone of the American effort in the First World War, and especially the restraints on civil liberties. This time the war would be run in another way. Here was a new vision of leadership in a free society during a great war.[168]

In regard to civil liberties, the central figure was Francis Biddle (1886–1968), a patrician Democrat, born in Paris, schooled at Groton and Harvard, private secretary to Oliver Wendell Holmes, and an eminent Philadelphia lawyer. In 1935, Franklin Roosevelt asked him to serve as chairman of the National Labor Relations Board, the first of many tough assignments that Biddle handled with much success. He became attorney general in 1941 and served through the war.[169]

Much in Biddle's background made him a strong supporter of civil liberties: his Quaker ancestry, his schooling at Groton by Endicott Peabody, his service with Holmes in the period of the great dissents, and his experience of the New Deal. Biddle was a member of the American Civil Liberties Union and later its national chairman. He wrote a stage play that celebrated William Penn. In his vision of an open society, he believed that the government should be most active in defending civil liberties at moments when they were most in peril.[170]

Franklin Roosevelt and Francis Biddle were haunted by the failures of Woodrow Wilson in the First World War and were determined not to repeat his errors. Before Pearl Harbor, Roosevelt declared that "free speech and a free press are still in the possession of the people of the United States and it is important that it should remain there." This would be the administration's policy throughout the war, but its practice was sometimes different. The president, a supreme political pragmatist, has been called "somewhat of a fair weather civil libertarian."[171] When the newspaper of his bitter enemy Colonel Robert McCormick announced to the world after the battle of Midway that the U.S. Navy was reading Japanese codes, Roosevelt was so angry that he wanted to send Marines to the office of the *Chicago Tribune,* arrest Colonel McCormick, and try him for high treason. But Attorney General Biddle persuaded him to desist, and even the *Chicago Tribune* remained free to publish its daily hate against the president and all his works with impunity.[172] In general Biddle succeeded in protecting freedom of speech and press through the war. He ordered federal attorneys throughout the country not to prosecute for sedition without his permission, and complaints brought to him were dismissed, with instructions that "free speech as such ought not to be restricted."[173]

Biddle did not hesitate to restrain overt acts that threatened the war effort. Under his direction, the Justice Department prosecuted Communists in the Teamsters Union, and the Socialist Workers Party in Minneapolis, for "conspiring to effect insubordination in the armed forces."[174]

At the same time, Biddle moved against conservative business leaders who broke the law. One of them was Montgomery Ward's president, Sewell Avery, who refused to honor his contractual agreements with the federal government, which required a minimum wage, recognition of unions, and acceptance of collective bargaining. Avery believed that he was released from these obligations by a higher law of liberty and staged a sit-down strike in his own office chair. When all else failed, Biddle arrived with a military detachment sufficient to overawe Montgomery Ward's company police. As cameras clicked, U.S. troops in helmets and combat gear picked up Avery and his executive chair and carried them both into the street. As they passed the attorney general, Avery shouted the worst insult he could imagine: "You! you . . . New Dealer!" he said.

The incident and the photograph became front-page news throughout the country. Conservatives saw it as an image of New Deal tyranny

Freedom as the rule of law: Sewell Avery, president of Montgomery Ward, who refused to keep Federal labor agreements his company had made. He staged a sit-down strike in his office and was removed by troops in combat gear for disrupting the war effort, Chicago, 1944. Americans took this iconic image to mean that nobody was above the law in a free society. Image donated by Corbis/Bettmann.

over the sovereign liberty of a businessman to hire and fire his workers at will and pay them whatever he pleased. Liberals, and most Americans in the center, saw it differently, as the just and necessary act of a democratic government to protect the rule of justice and the rights of American workers against a tyrannical business leader who believed that he was above the law.[175]

Overall, the federal government under Franklin Roosevelt and Francis Biddle compiled an excellent record for the protection of civil liberties, very different than in World War I, the Civil War, and the American Revolution. But there was one great and glaring exception: the forced internment of Japanese American citizens in California, Oregon, and Washington.

It deeply divided American leaders during the war. Some demanded it. Far-right journalist Westbrook Pegler wrote. "To hell with the habeas corpus until the danger is over." Walter Lippmann took a similar view. Pacific Coast politicians including California's attorney general, Earl Warren, wanted it. Within the Roosevelt administration, the strongest voices in favor were those of Assistant Secretary of War John McCloy, Secretary of War Henry Stimson, and Secretary of the Navy Frank

Knox.[176] The leading opponent of internment was Attorney General Biddle, along with J. Edgar Hoover, who reported that most Japanese Americans were not threats to security. Military Intelligence officers and Republican Senator Robert Taft also did not favor mass internment.[177]

The climax came in a cabinet meeting on February 19, 1942. Stimson demanded internment, Biddle protested, and President Roosevelt said, "This must be a military decision." He issued Executive Order 9066, authorizing military commanders to remove "any or all persons and to provide transportation, food and shelter." No mention was made of Japanese Americans. The president left the decision to military officers in the nation's defense commands.

They went different ways. In the Western Defense Command on the Pacific slope, General John DeWitt strongly supported internment after initially opposing it. DeWitt ordered the removal of all people of Japanese ancestry from California, Oregon, and Washington to the interior of the country. "A Jap's a Jap," the general said. ". . . It makes no difference whether he is an American citizen or not. I don't want any of them." On his orders 120,000 Japanese Americans were relocated. Many were at first confined in horse stalls at the Santa Anita race track. Later most were moved to ten big internment camps in the interior.[178]

In the Hawaiian Defense Command, Air Corps General Delos Emmons decided differently for a much larger population of Japanese

Civil liberties in time of war: Ansel Adams took this iconic photograph of Japanese internment, the greatest failure of civil liberties during the Second World War. Manzanar Relocation Center, California, 1943. Library of Congress.

Americans. Nearly 2,000 aliens and citizens were arrested for cause in Hawaii, but Emmons ordered that nearly 175,000 Issei and Nisei should remain free. Emmons used many arguments, among them that the labor of Japanese Americans was necessary for the economy of the island and important to the war effort. He also spoke of civil liberties, decency, and fair play. As a consequence, a majority of Japanese Americans in the United States and the territories were not interned—a story that has yet to find its historian. It was an act of courage and conscience by Emmons. He defied the United States Navy, top leaders in the War Department, and many western politicians, at heavy cost to his career. We remember the story of 120,000 Japanese Americans from four western states who were cruelly confined during the war. But we have forgotten the story of a larger number of 175,000 Japanese Americans who remained free. Mainly these decisions came down to two men. General John DeWitt yielded to panic and hysteria on the West Coast. General Delos Emmons found the courage and wisdom to go another way in Hawaii.

The internment camps were run by Milton Eisenhower, brother of Dwight. He tried to make them as humane as possible, but they were very grim, and they became an indelible image of injustice and the denial of human rights to American citizens because of their ethnicity. The Supreme Court upheld the constitutionality of internment in 1943, but issued a split decision in the *Korematsu* case (1944). The next day the administration ordered that "full rights be restored." After the war, many administrations tried to make amends. In 1948, reparations of ten cents on the dollar were offered for property losses, and in 1988, the Civil Liberties Act awarded all internees $20,000. In 1998, Bill Clinton offered an apology and a symbolic Medal of Freedom to one internee.

Some Americans continued to justify Japanese internment, long after the fact. Assistant Secretary of War John J. McCloy was unrepentant and outspoken to the end. Others went the opposite way and used the issue of internment as a general indictment of American institutions. An example was the Smithsonian Institution, which came down with an extreme case of political correctness in the 1990s. It mounted a standing exhibition on the United States in the Second World War, on the upper floor of the Museum of American History. Half the space was given to a reconstruction of an American internment camp. Most Americans reject both of these views. They carry in their mind's eye an image of the Japanese internment camps as gross injustice and an American aberration.

ROSIE THE RIVETER

Rose Monroe & Mary Doyle as Feminine Symbols of Freedom

> The more women at work the sooner we win!
>
> —WAR POSTER FOR THE U.S.
> EMPLOYMENT SERVICE

WOMEN WERE GIVEN new roles in many nations during the Second World War, but in different ways. In Adolf Hitler's Germany, married women of what Nazis called Aryan descent were encouraged to stay at home and raise large families of little Aryans, in keeping with fascist ideology and the German tradition of *Kinder, Kirche, Kuchen*—children, church, and kitchen. Non-Aryan women in German-occupied Europe were compelled to work as captives and slaves in factories, fields, and concentration camps, where millions died of starvation and brutality and worse. In the Soviet Union, women were conscripted for war labor in many jobs. Great Britain and some nations of the British Commonwealth required women to register for war work, and many were compelled to work against their will. The United States Congress rejected the conscription of women and refused even to enact a system of registration. Throughout the war, American women worked as volunteers. Millions freely did so, joining the war effort as an act of choice.

An elaborate campaign was organized to recruit them. Part of that promotional effort was a song called "Rosie the Riveter." One version was written by Redd Evans and John Jacob Loeb in 1942 and widely performed by the Vagabonds in 1943. Another was popularized by bandleader Kay Kyser, who celebrated Rosie the Riveter in his concerts. Kay Kyser's Rosie was said to be inspired by a woman named Rosalind Walter who worked in an assembly line on Long Island.

"We Can Do It!" This image of women in war work became a symbol of rights and empowerment in this war poster by J. Howard Miller for the Westinghouse Corporation. National Museum of American History, Smithsonian Institution.

In 1943, that song was ringing in the ears of American film actor Walter Pidgeon when he visited a huge aircraft factory in Ypsilanti, Michigan, to a make a film for the war effort. On the factory floor, Pidgeon discovered a real-life Rosie and put her in his movie. She became a symbol of women in defense work and an emblem of an egalitarian spirit that united all Americans in a common effort without distinction of age or gender or class.

The story of Walter Pidgeon's real-life Rosie the Riveter was even more interesting than her image. Her name was Rose Monroe. She was twenty-three years old, a beautiful, charming, and fiercely independent young woman. Before the war she grew up in Somerset, Kentucky. Her husband died in a car crash, and she moved north and took a factory job near Detroit. Rose Monroe was a free spirit in more senses than one, and her idea of freedom was different from that of the academic ideologists who later claimed Rosie the Riveter as a symbol of radical feminism and proletarian socialism. Her daughter remembered, "My mother was the type of person who never believed in government assistance." Rose Monroe thought that people should make their own way. After the war, she took her earnings from the factory in Ypsilanti and went into business for herself. She ran a beauty shop, then founded a company called the Rose Builders and constructed luxury homes in the postwar building boom. At the same time she raised a family of eight children, nine grandchildren, and thirteen great grandchildren. In spare moments she learned to fly; she became a member of the local aero club and was an active pilot. In 1997, Rose Will Monroe died at the age of seventy-seven, of injuries sustained in a plane crash. In her full life and fierce independence, this real Rosie the Riveter personified the freedom that she and many women helped defend during the war. Her daughter said, "They couldn't find a better role model, to be honest. Everything she does, she does well. She makes it very tough for the rest of us to follow in her footsteps."[179]

The most popular image of Rosie the Riveter was another model, painted by Norman Rockwell for the cover of the *Saturday Evening Post* on May 29, 1943. It showed a muscular and free-spirited young woman with bright red hair, white skin, and blue overalls. She was sitting at her lunch break, with a rivet gun in her lap. Her foot rested firmly on a crushed copy of Hitler's *Mein Kampf.* Under her arm was a lunchbox, and across the bib of her overalls she wore a row of buttons and badges, her decorations for war service. Rockwell's Rosie wore a Red Cross button as a blood donor, a white "V for Victory" button for buying war bonds, and a Blue Star button for supporting a serviceman overseas. She displayed a presidential *E* badge for excellence in her work, two bronze awards for faithful service, and her own personal identity disc. Rosie's badges and buttons were emblems of individual effort and voluntary action.

A model for these images was a real-life Rosie the Riveter, Rose Will Monroe, ca. mid-1940s, who lived the idea of liberty and freedom that the image represented. Associated Press. AP/WideWorld Photos.

Altogether, Norman Rockwell's Rosie became the new face of Miss Liberty in the Second World War: not a Roman goddess, republican matron, or domestic female, but a woman working in what had been a man's job, building ships and tanks and aircraft. She was a figure of strength and self-reliance but also of devotion to the common cause. In that sense she was a figure of freedom and liberty together.

Norman Rockwell's model was Mary Doyle, nineteen years old. She was not actually a riveter but a telephone operator in Arlington, Vermont. She was shocked to see what Rockwell had done to her figure, and remembers that the artist called to apologize. Most American women had jobs that were more like Mary's than Rosie's. The number of American women employed outside the home rose from 12 million in 1940 to 18 million in 1944. Of that number, only 2.7 million were factory workers. Most worked in clerical jobs or service occupations. Many millions more did not appear in labor statistics but worked just as hard on family farms, at home, and in voluntary service. Whatever they did, many of these

The classic image of Rosie, with a complex iconography and a pose modeled on Michelangelo's Isaiah, was Norman Rockwell's "Rosie the Riveter," a cover painting for the Saturday Evening Post, May 29, 1943. *Courtesy of the Norman Rockwell Family Agency.*

women also became iconic symbols of freedom—a new image of Miss Liberty as a heroine for the people and a shining example that was indeed "hard for us to follow."

Norman Rockwell's Rosie brilliantly caught this spirit of popular heroism in the cause of liberty and freedom. In a hilarious combination of iconic elements that was much noticed at the time, he posed Rosie on the heroic model of Michelangelo's Isaiah in the Sistine Chapel. The prophet's book was replaced by a battered rivet gun. A ham sandwich was improbably added in the heroine's left hand, and a halo appeared above her head.

After the painting appeared on the cover of the *Saturday Evening Post*, many Americans were quick to remark on the resemblance between Rockwell's Rosie and Michelangelo's Isaiah, which added to the mood of national delight in the work. Rockwell's *Rosie* was a major change in the artist's style. It captured the mood of an American generation—irreverent, good-humored, casual, egalitarian, and at the same time confident, strong, and deadly serious in its cause of liberty and freedom.[180]

"WE ARE AMERICANS TOO!"

Jesse Owens, Joe Louis, Philip Randolph

Free from Want! Free from Fear! Free from Jim Crow!

—THE NEGRO AMERICAN MARCH, 1941

A MERICAN HISTORIES give growing attention to problems of race during the Second World War, sometimes more than to the war itself. These accounts stress American failures in race relations, of which there were many: race riots in Detroit and Chicago, "zoot suit riots" in Los Angeles, racial violence near military bases in the South, and segregation everywhere. The refusal of the armed forces to make full use of African Americans was a moral failure and a material weakness in the American war effort.

But there is also another story to be told about race and a free society in the Second World War. It is about a change of mind and a change of direction. For two centuries, racism had been growing in America and the world. In the United States it had hardened into laws and institutions that diminished liberty for African Americans and denied them freedom to share the rights of citizenship in American society. Mostly it was about freedom in that sense.

Racist attitudes began to move in a new direction in the era of the Second World War, largely because of that great struggle against Fascism. A large part of the cause was Fascism itself, a movement that carried racism and tyranny to such an extreme of horror and cruelty that it shocked the conscience of humanity into new ways of thinking. Another major factor in the United States rose from individual achievements of African Americans themselves, who began to triumph over prejudice and discrimination in highly visible ways. The early successes were mostly symbolic, but symbols have the power to move people and to change their minds. That is what happened, a moment of deep change when one dynamic change-regime yielded to another in the American history of race and freedom.

That story begins on the eve of World War II, when African Americans began to win personal victories over race prejudice, discrimination, and even Fascism itself, in ways that gained the respect and admiration of the nation and the world. Some of the most important victories happened at the Berlin Olympics in 1936. Germany's Fascist regime meant the games to be a showcase for "Aryan" supremacy. They became a triumph for African American athletes instead.

Americans rejoiced when an Alabama sharecropper's son, Jesse Owens, won four gold medals, and Ralph Metcalfe gained two more. They cheered when Cornelius Johnson and David Albritton took gold and silver medals in pole vault. They celebrated John Woodruff's brilliant victory in the 800-meter run, which became a parable of race prejudice. Boxed in by a strong field, Woodruff slowed down and let every other runner pass. Then he moved to the outside, ran an extra fifty meters around the entire field, and won the gold medal.

Hitler was enraged. He openly snubbed Johnson and Albritton and turned his back on Jesse Owens. Americans were thrilled by the victories of the black athletes in Berlin, appalled by the vicious manners of Adolf Hitler, and inspired by the grace and good sportsmanship of a German athlete who behaved very differently from the Führer. Luz Long was a blond Nordic giant, the leading rival of Jesse Owens in the long jump. Owens was nearly eliminated in the qualifying rounds for repeated foot faults. Luz Long intervened on the American's final round and showed him a way to qualify safely. Then they went into the finals together, and Jesse Owens set a record that stood for twenty-five years. Luz Long won the silver medal. After the event, the blue-eyed German hero was the first to congratulate the son of a black sharecropper for his victory. The two men forged a bond of friendship that was an example to the world until Luz Long was killed fighting for his country at the battle of San Pietro in 1943.

The African American victors in the Berlin Olympics became national heroes in the United States. Jesse Owens was honored with ticker tape parades in New York and went on to a long career in the public eye. One of his friends described him as "a professional good example." He became an icon of racial justice, a standing reproach to Jim Crow in America, and a living vision of freedom for the world.

A similar career was in store for another black athlete in the 1930s and 1940s. Joe Louis was a heavyweight boxer, known to the nation as "the Brown Bomber." In 1936, he was knocked out by the German Max Schmeling in a match that Fascist writers proclaimed as a victory for the "Aryan race." Two years later, Joe Louis knocked out Schmeling. The Fascist press fell silent, and the Brown Bomber was much admired not only for his prowess in the ring but also for his quiet modesty, dignity, and grace. In World War II, his nickname was used as an American password by white infantrymen in the Battle of the Bulge.

The Battle of the Bulge itself marked a milestone in race relations and in freedom as full citizenship for black Americans. Infantry divisions in the U.S. Army took heavy losses in the winter of 1944–45, and the supply of replacements ran dry. Commanders in desperation sent black soldiers to combat units, and the Army began to be integrated at its cutting edge. It was not done for principle or policy. The integration of infantry battalions, even to the platoon and squad level, was introduced because of necessity, and continued because it worked. De facto integration continued to the end of the war. The War Department reported that black infantry as "fighting men [were] no less courageous or aggressive than their white comrades."[181]

On the home front, black leaders became more outspoken and more effective. One of the most successful was Asa Philip Randolph (1889–1979), head of the Brotherhood of Sleeping Car Porters and Maids, an all-black union for men and women who worked on Pullman cars. Randolph, trained as a Shakespearean actor, was a man of great dignity and presence who combined the manners of a southern gentleman with a militant moral purpose. He moved north from Florida to join the Harlem Renaissance, fought against segregation in World War I, and was arrested by Woodrow Wilson's attorney general Mitchell Palmer, who called him the most dangerous Negro in the country. In 1925, he was invited to head the Sleeping Car Union because he

A. Philip Randolph, a Shakespearean actor who became head of the Brotherhood of Sleeping Car Porters. He was one of the most effective leaders for freedom in American history, and in his own time a symbol of that movement. Library of Congress.

was not a porter and could not be fired by the Pullman company. He accepted and served for more than forty years.

As the nation prepared for war, Randolph persuaded black leaders to join in a movement against racial discrimination in the armed forces and defense industries. Student of drama that he was, he proposed to call attention to the cause by a march on Washington and suggested that ten thousand people might turn out. Black leaders responded with enthusiasm. The NAACP committed its resources, and the black churches pitched in. The scale of the proposed march grew to one hundred thousand. White liberals and New Dealers supported it, among them Harold Ickes, Harry Hopkins, and Eleanor Roosevelt.

Franklin Roosevelt was appalled by the idea. He feared that it would divide the country at the moment when he was attempting to unite it. The president summoned Philip Randolph to a meeting in the White House and asked him to call it off. Randolph refused. The president asked what he wanted. Randolph said an executive order prohibiting racial discrimination in defense plants. A deal was struck. The march was called off, and on June 25, 1941, Franklin Roosevelt issued Executive Order 8802, forbidding discrimination by race, creed, color, or national origin in defense plants with federal contracts. He also created a new agency to enforce it, the Fair Employment Practices Committee.[182]

It proved to be a major event in the history of race relations. The result was the largest expansion of economic opportunity for African Americans since the Emancipation Proclamation. African Americans left southern farms and streamed north and west in large numbers. The results included a massive redistribution of African Americans in the country, a rise in income for black families, the growth of a black middle class, and revolution of rising expectations. There was also a white backlash, a surge of racial violence in Los Angeles, Detroit, Chicago, New York, and Mobile. The riots were suppressed as dangerous to the war effort, and employment opportunities continued to grow.

Another result was a rise of black militancy. Other marches and mass meetings were organized, and Afro-Americans demanded their fair share of the liberty and freedom for which the country was fighting. A broadside in the spring of 1943 summarized their purposes in a single sheet. Below a photograph of a mass meeting was the caption: "Millions of Negro Americans All Over This Great Land Claim the Right to Be Free!" It was a vision of freedom that drew upon Franklin Roosevelt's larger definition: "Free from Want! Free from Fear! Free from Jim Crow!" This was an idea of freedom as belonging. Its motto was "We are Ameri-

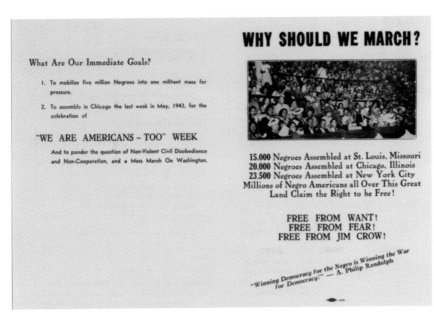

What Are Our Immediate Goals?

1. To mobilize five million Negroes into one militant mass for pressure.

2. To assemble in Chicago the last week in May, 1943, for the celebration of

"WE ARE AMERICANS – TOO" WEEK

And to ponder the question of Non-Violent Civil Disobedience and Non-Cooperation, and a Mass March On Washington.

15.000 Negroes Assembled at St. Louis, Missouri
20.000 Negroes Assembled at Chicago, Illinois
23.500 Negroes Assembled at New York City
Millions of Negro Americans all Over This Great
Land Claim the Right to be Free!

FREE FROM WANT!
FREE FROM FEAR!
FREE FROM JIM CROW!

"Winning Democracy for the Negro is Winning the War for Democracy." — A. Philip Randolph

"Free from Want! Free from Fear! Free from Jim Crow!" The Second World War brought a new consciousness of rights and freedom among African Americans. Flier, 1941. A. Philip Randolph Papers, Manuscript Division, Library of Congress.

cans too." The same flier proposed new ways to achieve these ends, including "Nonviolent Civil Disobedience and Non-Cooperation."[183]

The racial conscience of the nation was awakened by the war—partly by the efforts of black Americans, partly by the unspeakable atrocities that were committed in the name of race by Germans and Japanese, partly and most of all by the logic of the Allied cause. A nation embarked on a world struggle against the evil of Fascism discovered that it had problems of its own.

This change of attitude became evident in the iconography of freedom during the war itself. Most early war art portrayed Americans as white only. By the end of the war a new spirit emerged. In 1945, Norman Rockwell did a painting called *The Long Shadow of Lincoln*. It showed a disabled veteran in his uniform. In the foreground of the painting was a cross with dog tags and an empty GI helmet to represent the cost of the war. Grouped around the central figure was a tight circle of Americans, of every creed and color—black and white together. By 1961, Norman Rockwell did another iconographic painting called *The Golden Rule*. Once again it showed humanity as a great circle, but this time African Americans moved to the center. Here was an indicator of how the world was changing—slowly and unsteadily, but changing nonetheless. The victories of the 1940s would lead to greater gains in years ahead.

NOSE ART, PATCH ART, AND GI GRAFFITI
Irreverent Visions of a Free World

> I couldn't find the four freedoms among the dead men.
>
> —ERNIE PYLE, 1943

A MONG MEN IN UNIFORM, the Second World War had a different tone from earlier American conflicts. During the Civil War, soldiers on both sides sent home passionate letters about ideas of liberty and freedom. In the Second World War, American servicemen cultivated a different style. They rarely wrote about war aims, large principles, or ethical abstractions of any kind. From the start they tried to appear tough-minded, hard-boiled, irreverent, and profane. Americans in uniform had little taste for the high-blown rhetoric that had appeared in earlier American wars. As the war went on, attitudes changed, mainly becoming more pronounced. In 1943, Ernie Pyle observed that the "basic language has changed from mere profanity to obscenity." The tone of this great struggle appeared in the gritty prose of Pyle himself and in the black humor of Bill Mauldin.[184]

If GIs did not talk much of war aims or politics or ideology, it was partly because they did not have to search far for an answer to those questions. In North Africa, Ernie Pyle described the attitude he found among American infantrymen in the front lines during the desperate days of 1942. "I can't quite put it in words," he wrote. "It isn't any theatrical proclamation that the enemy must be destroyed in the name of freedom; it's just a vague but growing individual acceptance of the bitter fact that we must win the war or else."[185]

Unlike other wars, the moral necessity of this great struggle was not in doubt for most Americans, at least not until a later generation of academic revisionists began to write about it long after the war had been safely won. Most American soldiers in World War II, behind their facade of irreverence, were like Cromwell's russet-coated captain who knew what he fought for and loved what he knew. They had little use for lofty phrases, but their tacit understanding of what they fought for had much to do with liberty and freedom. Americans in uniform improvised an iconography that was unprecedented in the history of war. Popular signs and symbols appeared in the squadron patches that pilots wore on their leather flight jackets. Many of these emblems were designed by Walt Disney's artists as a contribution to the war effort, and they made heavy use of Disney characters. American airmen were the first warriors in world history who went into battle bearing images of Mickey Mouse, Donald Duck, Goofy, Snow White, and the Seven Dwarfs.

American fliers also invented another genre of images, which they painted on the fuselages of their aircraft and called nose art. Admiral Ernest King sternly prohibited the practice in the U.S. Navy and Marine Air Wings, but it flourished in the Army Air Corps. Nose art ran to big emblems and bright colors, which tended to get bigger and brighter as the war went on. It was created by servicemen themselves, designed by the crews of each aircraft and painted by amateur artists in the field. Their technique was often crude, but nose art was good-humored and high-spirited, and it captured the self-deprecating manner of citizen soldiers who had very little of the military-madness that was so pronounced in Germany and Japan.

American nose art centered on naked women, cartoon characters, and outhouse humor and often combined these elements with symbols of freedom and liberty. GI artists used old emblems in ways that their forebears had never imagined. One example was a B-29 Superfortress in the Seventy-third Bomb Wing that flew from the Marianas against Japan in 1945. The crew named their plane *Mrs. Tittymouse* and adorned its nose with a full-length portrait of the lady herself as a reincarnation of the Statue of Liberty. Mrs. Tittymouse still carried a torch, but she had put down her book, stripped off her classical robe, and wore nothing but a happy smile of freedom.[186]

Southerners used other symbols of liberty and freedom that combined regional traditions with the culture of their own generation. An example in the 490th Bomb Group in England was a B-17 named *Carolina Moon*. She displayed a proud old Carolina emblem, the liberty crescent that had flown over Charleston's forts in the Revolution and the Civil War. To that

GI images of liberty and freedom testified to the unique spirit of that irreverent generation. An example was this World War II nose art on American aircraft. A B-29 in the 73rd Bomb Wing carried the image of Mrs. Tittymouse, a new incarnation of the Statue of Liberty. From Jeffrey L. Ethell, World War II Nose Art in Color (Osceola, Wisc., 1993).

ancient symbol, the crew of *Carolina Moon* added a leggy blonde, reclining on a crescent in a languorous manner that was far removed from the iconic style of Colonel William Moultrie or Robert Barnwell Rhett.[187]

Yet another symbol of freedom appeared on the nose of a C-47 of the 433rd Troop Carrier Group, attached to Fifth Army in Italy. The aircraft was called *Texas Hellcat*. Her emblem was a Texas woman who wore nothing except a ten-gallon hat, cowboy boots, a lone star of Texas liberty, and a pair of artfully arranged six-guns. Here were three traditional images of liberty and freedom, all used in a new spirit by the American generation of World War II.[188]

Carolina Moon, a B-17 in 490th Bomb Group, used the old Carolina crescent of liberty in a way that Colonel Moultrie never imagined. Jeffrey L. Ethell, World War II Nose Art in Color (Osceola, Wisc., 1993).

Patch Art

Other examples of American iconography appeared in the shoulder patches that identified individual units and were among the few touches of color on uniforms of khaki, forest green, and olive drab. Many shoulder patches were official insignia, formally authorized by the War Department. Others were self-created designs, invented by the men who wore them, manufactured overseas, and worn without official sanction.

Most American shoulder patches made no formal reference to traditional values. But as the war went on, emblems of liberty and freedom began to appear in military insignia, and in ways that symbolized the expansion of these ideas. A case in point was a series of shoulder patches for the 442nd Regimental Combat Team, a formation of 2,600 soldiers of Japanese ancestry who fought the Germans in Italy and France and won more combat decorations than any unit of comparable size in the U.S. Army.

The first shoulder patch of the 442nd was designed by some mindless factotum in the War Department and was a monument to bureaucratic insensitivity. It showed a red, white, and blue bomb burst, crossed by a strong bright yellow arm that was meant to represent the race of the soldiers in the unit. That design was deeply resented by the men who were ordered to wear it. Some refused to sew it on their uniforms. Six months later it was replaced by another patch that showed the upraised arm and torch of the Statue of Liberty on a red, white, and blue background. The men of the 442nd wore this one with pride—a modern emblem of universal freedom and an indicator of how that idea was expanding in the war.

Other liberty motifs were adopted by the Second Marine Division, the Seventy-seventh Infantry Division, the Indiana State Guard, and many other units. The Liberty Bell was used by the Army recruiting service. Spread eagles and screaming eagles became increasingly popular. Most of these emblems combined the theme of universal freedom with streamlined designs in keeping with modern sensibilities. They gave the old images a new identity.

Japanese American soldiers in the 442d Regimental Combat Team refused to wear their first shoulder patch (top), with its insensitive emphasis on race. The result was a second patch, which centered on a symbol of universal liberty and freedom. Photographs from Barry Jacob Stein.

The Beech Trees of Wallendorf: GI Graffiti

In the summer of 1944, Allied armies advanced so rapidly across Europe
that they outran their supplies and came to a halt very near the western
frontier of Germany. The weather turned wet and cold, and American
troops of the Fifth Armored Division went to ground in a forest of beech
trees near the village of Wallendorf in Luxembourg. The beech forest was
a strong position, on a high plateau above the junction of the Sauer and
Our rivers, overlooking the west wall of Germany. While they waited for
the next fight, the men of the Fifth Armored Division amused themselves by carving graffiti on the trees.

As the fall turned into winter, the Fifth Armored Division moved out
and other American units replaced them. They also left their graffiti on
the beeches. Then the Germans attacked in the Battle of the Bulge, captured the forest, and added their carvings. In bitter cold and heavy fighting, American troops drove them out once more. Early in 1945, men of
the 771st Tank Destroyer Battalion were in the forest and added yet more
graffiti to the beech trees before they were ordered into Germany, on the
final advance that brought the war to an end.

Fifty years later all the young soldiers were gone, but the beech trees
were still standing. Luxembourg historian Roland Gaul visited the forest
with his camera and discovered the graffiti, still visible as deep black scars
on the smooth gray bark. The letters and symbols that the soldiers carved
into the trees were as clear as on the day when they were put there, half a
century before.[189]

The American graffiti shared one element in common. Much of it
included a date or at least the year. The soldiers who made these carvings
were very conscious of time. In 1944, their prospects for survival were
uncertain at best, and they wanted to leave an enduring mark of their
moment in time, so that someone would remember them. This was the
most common impulse. Otherwise, no two inscriptions were quite the
same. One American GI wished to be remembered by his name, home,
and unit: "Paul Zuhlki, 51 11th Avenue, Chicago." Underneath he proudly
carved the triangular shoulder patch of the Fifth Armored Division. Others left only their name and hometown, and nothing more. But many
added a word or symbol that was a clue to why they were there, far from
home, and deep in a Luxembourg forest during the bitter winter of 1944.
The most common symbols were of nationhood: the letters USA, or an
American flag waving proudly in an imaginary breeze. In the U.S. Army,
more than any other in the world, men from many states soldiered

together in the same unit, and their diversity of origins reinforced a sense of national identity.

A few had a strong sense of regional belonging. One soldier carved the lone star of liberty and added next to it the word "Texas." These marks were more than mere addresses. Several of the national emblems had hearts carved next to them. Roland Gaul remarked of the soldier who carved one of them that he "immortalized his love for his country."[190]

There was absolutely no sense of alienation in these symbols—no hint of the despair that appeared in soldiers' writings during the First World War, or the alienation and anomie that marked in the helmet art of Vietnam. Conditions were miserable in the Ardennes during the bitter winter of 1944, much worse than even the worst of Vietnam. GIs in World War II had no rotation policy like that in Southeast Asia. Combat soldiers stayed with their units until they were wounded or dead. But the generation of World War II showed remarkably little of the indulgent narcissism and self-pity that appeared too often among some (not all) Vietnam veterans. The men of World War II knew the horror of total war more intimately than those who served in later conflicts, but they also knew what they were fighting for. They did not know if they would survive, but they shared a certainty that their cause was just and it would triumph. The beech trees of Wallendorf still stand as testimony to their vision of freedom.

NOW ALL TOGETHER!

Freedom and Unity in the War Effort

United We Stand; Land of the Free; Together We
Win; What Price Freedom

—HOME FRONT HOMILIES

MORE THAN ANY other event in American history, the Second World War inspired an extraordinary sense of collective effort in a common cause. A nation that had been deeply divided by region, race, class, region, and ethnicity came together as never before.

A striking and very colorful example appeared on July 4, in 1942. Paul MacNamara, a public relations man for Hearst magazines, proposed that every magazine in the United States should display an American flag on its cover that week, with images of its own special character. The National Publishers Association endorsed the idea, as did Treasury Secretary Henry Morgenthau Jr. Hundreds of American magazines responded with colorful covers in which the flag was the central motif, with the motto "United We Stand," but each magazine did so in its own way. *Screenland* magazine showed the flag with Veronica Lake in a red, white, and blue bathing suit. *Family Circle* featured a mother, father, and children holding small American flags as a military color guard passed by. *Ring* magazine put Joe Louis in uniform, saluting the flag. *Vogue* had an elegant model in a flowing white gown, doing her bit between two American flags. *Negroes and the War* had a regiment of black soldiers standing proudly to attention behind the national colors. *WNYF*, the magazine of the New York Fire Department, featured a fire boat flying the national ensign with the Statue of Liberty in the background. *Time*'s issue for July 4 displayed the

Freedom and unity were commonly linked in the iconography of the Second World War. Implicit in these images was a vision of freedom as rights and responsibilities of belonging for all Americans. An example was this simple poster with its very strong theme: "Together We Win! Get Behind Your Labor-Management Committee!" National Archives.

"Now All Together!" was one of strongest images of unity in the cause of freedom. This poster derived from a photograph by Joe Rosenthal, taken on Iwo Jima, February 23, 1945. It was deeply moving to Americans of that generation, who had counted the cost. National Archives.

Stars and Stripes with a painting of small-town America, with the caption "Land of the Free, What Price Freedom." Its cover combined themes of freedom with unity in a nation of great diversity.[191]

That idea inspired an American iconography during the war. A striking example was a war poster that showed three hands in mutual support. One was the hand of labor, another of management, and the third of Uncle Sam. The theme was captured in three words: "Together We Win!"

The most powerful image of this idea was a combat photograph shot on Iwo Jima by Associated Press photographer Joe Rosenthal, of five Marines and a Navy hospital corpsman raising a small American flag on a heavy pole above the crest of Mount Suribachi. The men appeared to be locked together in a common effort, their legs and arms moving so closely in unison that they seemed to become one. Above them fluttered a symbol of nationality and freedom.

Joe Rosenthal took the photograph on February 23, 1945. Within two days it was on the front page of newspapers throughout the United States. The image deeply moved a generation of Americans, all the more so because three of the six men in the photograph were killed in the fighting on Iwo Jima. The image was reproduced in many forms.

After the war it took on many different meanings. For some it was a symbol of patriotism. For others it represented an ideal of courage and an emblem of the United States Marine Corps. Like all great American icons, it was also attacked by debunkers and iconoclasts in the 1960s. But to the generation of World War II it carried another message that appeared on war posters with the caption, "Now All Together!" Here was a symbol of unity in a common cause of freedom.[192]

THE FOUR FREEDOMS

Norman Rockwell's Vision of Roosevelt's "Essential Ideas"

> Words like Freedom and Liberty draw close to us only
> when we break them down into the homely fragments
> of daily life.
>
> —ADVERTISEMENT, LIFE, OCTOBER 13, 1942

THE MOST MEMORABLE IMAGES of American freedom in
the Second World War came not from men in uniform or public
agencies but from a private citizen in a small New England town.
They were the work of Norman Rockwell, with much help from many
friends and neighbors in Arlington, Vermont.

Norman Rockwell was a man of high complexity, very different from
what his paintings suggest. He was a successful commercial artist who
specialized in sentimental scenes of small-town life, but he himself was a
sophisticated city slicker. Born and raised in Manhattan, he was trained at
the National Academy and the Art Students League. His paintings sold
briskly, and during the 1920s and 1930s Rockwell lived the fashionable
metropolitan life—a high-paying job and a suburban house, cocktails and
social climbing, a private bootlegger and Brooks Brothers suits, a modern
marriage and a messy divorce, remarriage and a growing restlessness of
spirit. In the Depression decade, Norman Rockwell made a million dollars from his folksy cover art, but he felt that something was not right in
his life.[193]

In 1938, Rockwell and his wife Mary were driving through the New
England countryside and found themselves by chance in the small town
of Arlington, Vermont. They stayed the night at the Colonial Inn and
after dinner sat together on the lawn, "watching the dusk gather beneath
the huge elms which lined the street." Overhead the stars appeared in a

deep blue sky above the green mountains. They listened to the wind in
the trees, and Norman Rockwell began to have a feeling that he had come
home.[194]

A few months later they moved to Arlington, and Norman Rockwell
began to live the small-town life that he had painted. His new neighbors
were friendly and welcoming. Rockwell himself was as tall and lean as a
stereotypical Yankee Vermonter. His plain speech and simple manners fit
comfortably into the rhythm of small-town life. A snapshot of Norman
Rockwell's family in front of their new house looked remarkably like a
Rockwell painting.

Then came Pearl Harbor. Rockwell had joined the army in the First
World War and was too old to enlist. He decided that the best way he
could serve was by painting posters for the war effort. "They didn't satisfy
me," he wrote. "I wanted to do something bigger than a war poster, make
some statement about why the country was fighting the war."[195]

He searched for a suitable theme and found it in a speech that President Franklin Roosevelt had given in 1941, before the United States
entered the war. The occasion was the president's campaign to win support for Lend-Lease from a reluctant Congress that was still strong for
neutrality. How could he persuade them? Roosevelt had pondered the
problem in his swivel chair, surrounded by several aides and a stenographer. One remembered that there was "a long pause, so long that it began
to become uncomfortable." Then suddenly the president spun in his chair
and dictated six quick sentences in a burst of thought:

> In the future days, which we seek to make secure, we look forward to a
> world founded upon four essential freedoms. The first is freedom of
> speech and expression—everywhere in the world. The second is freedom
> of every person to worship God in his own way—everywhere in the
> world. The third is freedom from want—which translated into world
> terms, means economic understandings which will secure to every nation
> a healthy peacetime life for its inhabitants. The fourth is freedom from
> fear. . . . This is no vision of a distant millennium. It is a definite basis for a
> kind of world attainable in our own time and generation.[196]

The Four Freedoms might be understood as the final distillation of Roosevelt's "broader definition of liberty" and his idea of "a greater freedom, a
greater security" that had been growing in his mind since the Great
Crash. They were also connected to the idea of his economic bill of
rights, this time not for America alone but the world.

Rockwell studied the president's words, and their echo in the Atlantic Charter, and wondered if he could paint them. Many American writers and artists were working with the same idea. In the Office of War Information, Archibald MacLeish did a pamphlet called *The United Nations Fight for the Four Freedoms* in August 1942, and his Washington staff encouraged an active group called Artists for Victory to sponsor a competition to illustrate the Four Freedoms. The best hundred works were selected for an exhibition. Photographers did collages; painters produced murals; printmakers did many smaller works. The artists were able and highly trained, but they had great difficulty creating a successful image of Franklin Roosevelt's idea.[197]

Rockwell struggled at length with the same problem. "The language was so noble, platitudinous really, that it stuck in my throat.... I tried this and that," he remembered. "Nothing worked.... It was so darned high blown. Somehow I just couldn't get my mind around it."

One night he was tossing in his bed, "rejecting one idea after another, and getting more and more discouraged." Then suddenly he remembered a recent town meeting. A neighbor named Jim Edgerton stood up and spoke against an idea that everyone else was for. Nobody agreed with him, but the town listened. Rockwell sat bolt upright in bed. "My gosh, I thought, that's it. There it is. Freedom of Speech. I'll illustrate the Four Freedoms using my Vermont neighbors as models. I'll express the ideas in simple, everyday scenes."[198]

By five o'clock that morning Rockwell was at his easel, working frantically on quick charcoal sketches. He bundled them into a portfolio and took a train to Washington. He went to the Office of War Information with his sketches under his arm and showed them to the people who were running the agency. To his amazement, nobody was interested. An arrogant official said, "The last war

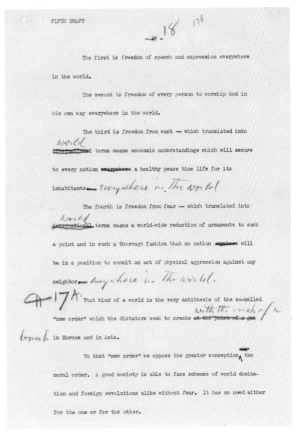

Franklin Roosevelt's Four Freedoms: his speech to Congress in 1941 on Lend Lease; fifth typed draft, with changes in his own hand. Franklin D. Roosevelt Library, Hyde Park, N.Y.

you illustrators did the posters. This war we're going to use fine arts men, real artists." Another suggested that maybe Rockwell could do a few drawings to illustrate a Marine Corps manual on calisthenics.[199]

Rockwell was crushed. He departed for Vermont but decided on impulse to stop at Philadelphia and consult with Ben Hibbs, his friend and editor at the *Saturday Evening Post*. Rockwell showed him the sketches and explained what had happened. Hibbs instantly saw their potential. "Norman," he said, "you've got to do them for us. . . . Drop everything else."

Still, the hard work remained to be done. Rockwell's seminal image of freedom of speech worked well, but only on the third try. Freedom from want became an image of Thanksgiving dinner in his own dining room, around a family table. Freedom from fear was represented by two small children, tucked safely in their American beds by their father while he held a newspaper with headlines about the horrors of war in Europe. The hardest was freedom of worship, which didn't work as a genre scene. Rockwell turned it into something different, a gathering of heads and hands in prayer, by people throughout the world.

Rockwell's models for all of these paintings were his neighbors. His image of free speech was Carl Hess, who ran a gas station in West Arlington. "My neighbors are always my best critics," Rockwell wrote. "Whenever I'm having trouble with a picture I ask their advice." They gave it freely, and the paintings weren't complete until they passed muster in the neighborhood.

Finally the work was done, and Rockwell sent the paintings to the *Saturday Evening Post* in Philadelphia. Hibbs thought them an "inspiration . . . in the same way that the clock tower of old Independence Hall, which I can see from my office window, inspires me." He published them in four weekly issues, with short essays by leading American writers.[200]

The paintings caused a sensation. Requests for copies poured in. The *Saturday Evening Post* permitted reprints without charge. The Office of War Information awakened to what Rockwell had done and distributed four million copies around the world. Treasury Secretary Henry Morgenthau organized a Four Freedoms Show that traveled to major department stores throughout the country, along with Rockwell's original models from Arlington.

The artist received more than sixty thousand letters about the paintings. A few people were not pleased. A Republican Congresswoman from Massachusetts, Edith Nourse Rogers, complained that Rockwell should have done a fifth painting on "freedom of private enterprise." Another

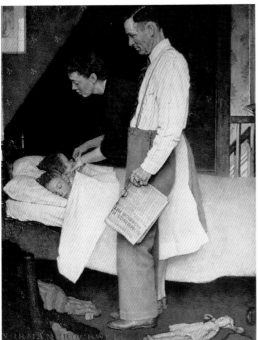

Norman Rockwell's Four Freedoms: freedom of speech, freedom from want, freedom from fear, freedom of worship. Copies of these images were distributed in posters such these examples without charge by the Curtis Publishing Company, the U.S. Treasury Department, and the Office of War Information. Courtesy of the Virginia Historical Society.

conservative wrote that Mr. Rockwell should have confined himself to the Bill of Rights. "Why don't you make pictures of the American freedoms instead of the New Deal freedoms?" he asked.[201]

Others expressed approval in unexpected ways. The Pioneer Suspender Company wrote that it specially liked "Freedom from Fear." It observed that Norman Rockwell had meticulously painted the father in a clearly recognizable pair of Pioneer suspenders, which gave another reason for freedom from fear, as his trousers were firmly secured by their reliable product.[202]

Most Americans were thrilled by the paintings. Some said that for the first time they understood what the war was about. Many wrote that Norman Rockwell's images truly defined the purposes of the war. Rockwell's paintings also did something else. They changed American ways of thinking about freedom in a fundamental way.

Great ideas live by change. They change in many different ways: by the entailment of their internal logic, by the pressure of external force, by the play of contingent events, and from time to time by a process of intellectual crystallization that converts a plastic process of thinking into hard structures of thought. In all of those ways the meaning of liberty and freedom changed profoundly during the Second World War. When the United States and its allies began their struggle against Fascism, they were clear about what they were fighting against, but only as the war approached its end did many Americans begin to consider what they were fighting for. As in the Revolution and the Civil War, they discovered new depths of meaning in their old values and beliefs. The speeches and Fireside Chats of Franklin Roosevelt did much to inspire new ideas of liberty and freedom. The paintings of Norman Rockwell converted the vision of a great and controversial Democratic leader into images that everyone could understand.

A PEOPLE AMONG OTHERS
Global Visions of Liberty and Freedom, 1945–2004

Freedom Marchers, August 28, 1963, the first large integrated protest march in Washington. Photograph by Flip Schulke.

V-J DAY AND THE GI BILL

Visions of Liberation and Entitlement

> We have accepted, so to speak, a Second Bill of Rights.
> ... Among these are the right to a useful and remuner-
> ative job ... adequate food and clothing and recreation
> ... a decent home ... adequate medical care ... pro-
> tection from the economic fears of old age, sickness,
> accident and unemployment ... the right to a good
> education.
>
> —FRANKLIN D. ROOSEVELT'S MESSAGE
> TO THE CONGRESS, JANUARY 11, 1944

ON AUGUST 14, 1945, at precisely 7:00 P.M. Eastern War Time, President Harry Truman studied his watch, walked to a microphone, and in his matter-of-fact Missouri way announced the unconditional surrender of Japan. The nation responded with an explosion of joy. In every American town, people took to the streets in what David Behrens described as "one great back-slapping, jitterbugging, hugging-and-kissing reunion." That night, two million people gathered in the streets around Times Square. The party continued the next day, and the day after that.[1]

Cameraman Alfred Eisenstaedt captured the moment in a photograph of a sailor and a nurse kissing in Times Square. The nurse was bright in her white uniform; the sailor dark in his dress blues. Their bodies were bent together in the arc of a close embrace, "like a piece of sculpture," Eisenstaedt said, a "one in a million composition." His photograph was widely reenacted, painted, sculpted, and mass-produced in small statuettes. It became the nation's favorite image of V-J Day.[2]

Many years later the nurse was identified as Edith Shain, who recalled that "it was a good kiss, it went on for a long time." A large part of the United States Navy claimed the honor of having kissed her. Bill Swicegood, a sailor from Kansas City, Missouri, was one. He remembered happily, "I must have kissed a thousand girls that day."[3]

The mood was much the same throughout the nation. On main

"The Kiss," photograph by Alfred Eisenstaedt, New York City, August 15, 1945; this iconic American image became a symbol of personal liberation on V-J Day. It inspired small statuettes and replicas. Photograph from Time Life Pictures/Getty Images; statuette from Martin S. Jacobs, V for Victory Collectibles.

streets in most American cities, caravans of flag-decked cars drove slowly through dancing crowds.[4] A soldier in Tennessee remembered that "it seemed like all the insane asylums in the country opened their doors to Memphis. Everywhere people acted like lunatics."[5] The wildest parties were on the West Coast, where American troops had been embarking for the invasion of Japan. In San Diego, men and women embraced in the city's flowing fountains.[6] In Los Angeles, hardened veterans who thought they had seen everything remembered with awe Hollywood's "three-day celebration of V-J Day."[7] In San Francisco the revels were so enthusiastic that thirteen people died celebrating.[8]

In the general jubilation of V-J Day, Americans celebrated many things. Part of it was about victory, but reporters noted with surprise that most people did not speak in those terms. A journalist in Chicago observed, "everybody talked of 'the end of the war,' not 'victory.'"⁹ Mainly, Americans rejoiced that the killing was over. More than sixty million people had died in World War II. The United States was more fortunate in that respect than other countries, but even in America four hundred thousand homes were entitled to display the small red and white banners with a gold star that signified a death in military service. Another seven hundred thousand Americans had been wounded, maimed, or mutilated.

Most of these losses came in the last twelve months of the war, when the carnage seemed without end. On April 13, 1945, Harry Truman's first day in the White House, his military commanders had told him "it would take six months to finish Germany, and another year and a half to defeat Japan." In June and July, battle-weary American troops were preparing for the invasion of the Japanese home islands, which everyone expected to be the bloodiest campaign in American history.¹⁰

Then the atomic bombs fell on Hiroshima and Nagasaki, and the Soviet army attacked Japan, and millions of young Americans suddenly awakened to the discovery that they were going to survive the war. Jack Russell, a sailor in Times Square on V-J Day, remembered, "It suddenly hit me that our ship wouldn't be going to Japan and the whole terrible thing was ending." A San Diego cameraman caught the feeling in a photograph of two Marines with battle stars on their campaign ribbons and broad smiles on their faces. Together they held up a newspaper that said it all in a single word: PEACE!¹¹

That was the central theme of the celebrations, but they were also about something else. On August 14, 1945, individual Americans rejoiced in their own personal liberation from the war. They were celebrating a private vision of liberty and freedom that was different from the lofty thoughts of Franklin Roosevelt or the heroic cadences of Winston Churchill. For twelve million Americans in military service, V-J Day meant an end to uniforms, orders, drill, discipline, and all the tedium and terror of war. To civilians on the home

V-J Day in New York City: huge crowds gathered at Times Square in front of a large replica of the Statue of Liberty. Image donated by Corbis/Bettmann.

front, it promised a release from painful separations, cruel uncertainties, double shifts, and doing without for "the duration."

More than that, V-J Day meant a fresh start. It was about coming home, buying a car, building a house, having a family, and getting on with life. Here was a very powerful vision of personal liberty. For many Americans, it was also an idea of freedom. It was about gaining the rights of citizenship in a free society and a fair share of the opportunities that had been denied to them before the war.

That spirit of personal liberation found material support in a new public program that was framed explicitly in terms of liberty and freedom. Its foundation was the Servicemen's Readjustment Act of 1944, which most Americans called the GI Bill of Rights. This remarkable law was one of the most large-spirited pieces of social legislation in American history, and also one of the most successful. It was very surprising in its political origins.

In many ways the GI Bill of Rights in 1944 resembled Franklin Roosevelt's economic bill of rights. An early version was proposed by New Dealer Samuel Rosenman. It incorporated specific New Deal proposals for housing and mortgage guarantees. More than that, it was the product of the general New Deal philosophy that active and highly flexible intervention by the federal government could promote individual enterprise in a free society and help millions of Americans to realize their own dreams.

But this was only part of the story. A version of the final bill was written by Harry Colmery, a conservative Republican from the Midwest who worked as a lobbyist for the American Legion. Colmery wrote out a draft in longhand in Room 570 of Washington's Mayflower Hotel. It was put through Congress by an unusual coalition of the left and right. A strong supporter was Edith Nourse Rogers, the rock-ribbed New England Republican who had scolded Norman Rockwell for omitting property rights from the Four Freedoms. Another sponsor was John Rankin, a racist demagogue from Mississippi who reviled Franklin Roosevelt and Black Republicans. Midwestern isolationists such as Bennett Clark backed it, as did the newspapers of William Randolph Hearst. These unlikely allies joined the president and leading New Dealers to support the GI Bill.[12]

As finally enacted, it gave veterans the full cost of four years' tuition at any college or training program and also paid a living allowance while they went back to school. It helped them buy a home without a down payment, or get a farm, or start a business. It assisted them in finding jobs and paid unemployment benefits for up to a year while they were looking.

Congress insisted that the money must be spent for serious purposes of training, education and investment. It was not to be a dole on the model of the Civil War pension system. In that sense the GI Bill was very much a New Deal measure. It invested public resources to promote private initiative, for individual profit and the common good.

Among the few who opposed it were college administrators such as Robert Hutchins at the University of Chicago, who complained that "colleges and universities will find themselves converted into educational hobo jungles." The arrogance of Hutchins was very useful to backers of the bill. They used it to win broad support in Congress, and it passed in both houses by unanimous votes. Franklin Roosevelt signed it into law on June 22, 1944, looking very pleased with himself and his newfound allies who crowded around him.[13]

In the decade after V-J Day, the GI Bill paid for the education of 7.8 million veterans, more than half of all Americans who served in uniform during the Second World War. Among its beneficiaries were George H. W. Bush, who went back to Yale, and Henry Kissinger, who attended Harvard. Throughout the country it helped veterans of every region, class, and ethnic background.[14] Later acts extended the program to another ten million veterans of the Cold War and millions more in the Gulf War and the War on Terror.[15]

The GI Bill of Rights: President Franklin Roosevelt signing the legislation on June 22, 1944, surrounded by an uncomfortable alliance of New Dealers, conservative Republicans, and southern Democrats. In collaboration, if not in harmony, they enacted one of the most liberating social laws in American history. Image donated by Corbis/Bettmann.

The GI Bill of Rights, as its name implied, represented a new vision of liberty and freedom. For veterans it recognized an entitlement to equal opportunity as a matter of right. Americans had talked of equality of opportunity since the mid-nineteenth century, mainly as an idea that a society or government should not get in the way of individual achievement. But this was something more than that. It was an idea that government should help to create opportunity and that all veterans had an equal right to assistance that way. This was a novel idea, not highly developed in other societies. When James B. Conant became U.S. High Commissioner in Germany and tried to speak of these things in central Europe, he was amazed to discover that there was at that time no equivalent phrase in German for "equality of opportunity."[16]

In that spirit, the GI Bill made a difference in millions of American lives. Many veterans who had lived in deep poverty during the Depression were given the means to move into the middle class, and they brought their families with them. Except for a few revisionists who are still as uncomprehending as Robert Hutchins, most people rightly remember the GI Bill as one of the most successful pieces of social legislation in American history. This generous vision of liberty and freedom as mixed public and private enterprise helped millions of Americans to realize the dream of V-J Day.[17]

FREEDOM TRAIN!

William Coblenz's Vision of National Unity and Civic Responsibility

> I am an American. A free American. . . .
> Free to stand for what I think right.
> Free to oppose what I think wrong.
>
> —FREEDOM PLEDGE, 1947

AMERICANS who were children after the Second World War share another vivid memory. It centers on the image of a gleaming railroad train with a streamlined locomotive and seven sleek modern coaches. The engine and the cars were painted glossy white, with stripes of red, white, and blue from head to tail, and a name in gold letters three feet high: FREEDOM TRAIN.[18]

It began as an idea in the mind of William Coblenz, a government worker in Washington. On a spring day in 1946, Coblenz took a lunch break from his desk job in the Justice Department's Public Information Division and visited the National Archives. Two sets of documents were on display. One was a special collection of captured Nazi materials that revealed the inner workings of Fascism in horrible detail. The other was a permanent exhibit of America's charters of liberty and freedom, which had just returned from storage during the war.

Coblenz was deeply moved by the contrast and wished that every American could see it. He went to his boss, division chief William McInery, and suggested that the Justice Department might sponsor a small traveling exhibition of German and American documents, which could tour the nation in a railroad car. McInery liked the idea and took it to Attorney General Tom Clark, who thought it was just what the country needed. Clark was a New Dealer from Dallas who believed passionately in liberty, the rule of law, and what he called "the American brand of democracy." He worried that young Americans were losing touch with the founding principles of liberty and freedom, at a moment of a great test by "fascism, communism, or the various degrees of socialism."[19]

Tom Clark had the Texas habit of thinking big. He thought to himself, if the American people could not come to Washington and read the charters of their rights, then the documents should go to the people—all of the great documents, for all the people. The attorney general went to see President Harry Truman, who warmed to the idea and gave it his "strongest endorsement." A traveling exhibition, said the president, should "make it possible for every man, woman and child in America to enrich their pride in the institutions that have made us great."

The president told Tom Clark to make it happen. The result was another classic example of mixed enterprise, which that generation of the Second World War did so well. In Washington, Clark rallied strong support from liberal Democrats and conservative Republicans. He went to the private sector and asked Barney Balaban, president of Paramount Studios, to recruit top figures in the entertainment industry.[20] He approached Thomas D'Arcy Brophy, head of the Advertising Council that had been founded to support the war effort, and asked him to enlist

The Freedom Train leaving Philadelphia, where it was dedicated on September 17, 1947. In the background is Philadelphia's City Hall, with its colossal statue of William Penn, another iconic image of liberty and freedom. Schenectady County Public Library, with thanks to Robert Sullivan.

the leaders of the advertising industry in a national campaign "to sell America to Americans."[21]

All responded with enthusiasm. Clark, Brophy, and Balaban (Protestant, Catholic, and Jew) founded the American Heritage Foundation to raise the money. Winthrop Aldrich of the Chase National Bank agreed to serve as president, and the captains of corporate America joined the board. The nation's top labor leaders, Charles Murray of the CIO and William Green of the AFL, became vice presidents. All worked together with the same spirit of cooperation, and the same sense of urgency that Americans had brought to the war effort.[22]

They agreed that the project should center on ideas that most Americans supported. The Nazi materials disappeared. Every effort was made to avoid controversy and build consensus. Barney Balaban thought that the purpose should be to demonstrate "the essential unity of the American system." Thomas Brophy wanted documents that were "universally accepted": the great charters of political liberty and religious freedom, the texts of the American Revolution and the Declaration of Independence, the Federal Constitution and the Bill of Rights, the Second World War and the United Nations. The Four Freedoms were omitted because business leaders thought that Franklin Roosevelt was a divisive figure. Some wanted to include the Wagner Act as labor's great charter of freedom. Others believed that the Taft-Hartley Act was a charter of individual economic liberty. Both were rejected as controversial.[23]

The name of the project was also changed with the same purpose in mind. William Coblenz had originally called it the Bill of Rights Exhibit. That name was thought to be too constraining. It was changed to the Liberty Train, and in February 1947 it became the Freedom Train. Tom Clark said that the object was "to restablish the common ground of all Americans" and "to blend our various groups into one American family." Here was a vision of freedom as rights of membership in a free society for everyone in the United States.[24]

The more Tom Clark thought about the project, the bigger it grew. The single railroad car became an entire train, specially built for the occasion in a crash construction program. The staff of the National Archives put together a unique collection of 126 documents on the theme of freedom, from a fourteenth-century copy of England's Magna Carta to the Charter of the United Nations that had been signed only the year before. American texts included the original Mayflower Compact, Thomas Jefferson's draft of the Declaration of Independence with corrections by John Adams and Benjamin Franklin, George Washington's copy of the Federal Constitution, James Madison's draft of the Bill of Rights, Abraham

Lincoln's text of the Emancipation Proclamation, and a manuscript copy of the Gettysburg Address.

Twelve documents came from movements of American "revolt and protest" for liberty and freedom, mostly in the distant past. A large part of the collection was about World War II. Physical artifacts included an ensign that had flown on the Perry expedition to Japan, a flag that had been raised at Iwo Jima, and another flag that had flown from the battleship *Missouri* in Tokyo Bay.

Elaborate precautions were taken to safeguard these treasures by an American generation who knew how dangerous the world could be. The exhibition cars were protected by heavy armor plate, and the documents were encased in inch-thick bulletproof glass. The temperature of the train was held at a steady seventy-five degrees by a primitive system of air-conditioning that consumed thirty-two thousand pounds of ice every twelve hours. The Marine Corps supplied a detachment of twenty-seven chosen men to guard the train.

The work was completed in a few months of frantic work, and on September 17, 1947, the Freedom Train was dedicated in Philadelphia. Its tour began in the northeastern states. Then it traveled south and west and back again to journey's end in the nation's capital in January 1949. Altogether, the Freedom Train visited every state and 326 cities and towns. It was the longest train trip in American history.

Children aboard the Freedom Train, studying the documents and artifacts with the same reverence and rapt concentration that millions of Americans brought to this event in 1947–49. Time Life Pictures/Getty Images.

At every stop, the train opened to visitors at ten o'clock in the morning. Long lines of parents and children had begun to form before sunrise. At Grand Central Station in New York, the line stretched four abreast for fifteen city blocks. Everywhere, people waited patiently for their turn to see the documents, sometimes in driving rain and heavy snow. The millionth visitor was a sixteen-year-old girl in Oklahoma who traveled sixty miles through a blizzard.[25]

Improbable as it may seem today, American teenagers in 1947 celebrated the Freedom Train with an enthusiasm that later generations of adolescents would reserve for sex queens and rock musicians. In Brooklyn, Marine guards were baffled by the sudden disappearance of the white stripe from the side of the Freedom Train. They discovered that a high school girl had kissed the engine of the train and left a smear of bright red lipstick. Four thousand other high school girls followed her example, until the white stripe became a scarlet ribbon of adolescent affection.[26]

This historian remembers visiting the Freedom Train in Baltimore. We drove to a large railroad yard and waited in long lines with thousands of others. Baltimore in 1947 had the air of a small town, and we had the illusion that we knew everybody in it. But standing in line with us were Baltimoreans we had never seen before. Some were immigrants from eastern Europe. Others were Appalachian mountain folk who had moved north to work in the war plants. Large numbers were Marylanders of African descent. In 1947, Baltimore was a Jim Crow town. There were not many public places in Maryland where blacks and whites stood together on a footing of equality.

In the Deep South, other communities were even more rigidly segregated. People had wondered what would happen when the Freedom Train arrived. Langston Hughes wrote a poem about it.[27]

> *I seen folks talkin' about the*
> *Freedom Train*
> *Lord, I been a-waitin for the*
> *Freedom Train! . . .*
>
> *I hope there ain't no Jim Crow on the Freedom Train*
> *No back door entrance to the Freedom Train.*
> *No signs FOR COLORED on the Freedom Train,*
> *No WHITE FOLKS ONLY on the Freedom Train.*
>
> *I'm gonna check up on this*
> *Freedom Train.*[28]

The sponsors considered that question and decided that there would be no Jim Crow on a Freedom Train. In 1947, most Americans agreed. Nearly all southern towns accepted the integration of the Freedom Train, and black and white families visited it together as they did in Baltimore.

A small number of southern leaders stubbornly refused to agree. In Memphis, city boss Ed Crump insisted that the Freedom Train must be segregated when it stopped in his town. Birmingham's chief of police,

Eugene Theophilus "Bull" Connor, did the same thing in Alabama. The managers of the Freedom Train responded by removing Memphis and Birmingham from the train's itinerary, much to the approval of many people in the South. In the elections of 1948, Boss Crump's Memphis machine was defeated, partly as a result of his attempt to impose Jim Crow on the Freedom Train. Bull Connor survived in Birmingham to play an iconic role of high importance as the arch-demon of racist tyranny in the national drama of the civil rights movement.

Other critics of the Freedom Train appeared on the far left. The American Communist Paul Robeson denounced it and dropped lower in the national esteem. The effect of the Freedom Train was to marginalize its opponents on the left and right. It made them appear to be enemies of freedom, and it reinforced the broad American center.

In that respect the Freedom Train itself was only a small part of a larger educational project, which centered on a vision of freedom as civic responsibility. Its sponsors mounted a national advertising campaign, one of the biggest on record. Irving Berlin composed a special song and recorded it with Bing Crosby and the Andrews Sisters. A movie called *Our American Heritage* was produced by Dore Schary and narrated by Joseph Cotten. Historians compiled two books for the occasion. One of them, Frank Monaghan's *Our Heritage of Freedom*, reproduced a set of documents that Eric Goldman called "a semi-official definition of American liberty." Another book, called *The Good Citizen*, centered on questions of civic responsibility.[29]

Local programs were coordinated with the schedule of the Freedom Train. Advance men visited each town before the train arrived. Advertisements and feature stories saturated the local press and radio stations. Each community was urged to observe an entire "rededication week," with individual days devoted to particular groups: a Women's Day, a Labor and Industry Day, a Religion Day, and a Veterans Day.

These programs reached a larger public than the train itself. Altogether, about 3.5 million people went aboard the Freedom Train. More than 10 million saw the train. Approximately 50 million Americans participated in related events. Virtually the entire population of 144 million was reached by the public campaign in one way or another. The Freedom Train and its traveling icons helped to persuade a generation of young Americans that the nation's heritage was something that belonged to all of them. Its purpose was to mobilize the entire country in a common effort of civic engagement. The motto was "freedom is everybody's job."

Inside the Freedom Train, interior passages were dimly lighted, and the documents were bright and legible, glowing in their glass windows. Parents and children gathered in tight circles around the great charters of freedom, and their faces reflected the light. They took their time, often ignoring the efforts of Marine guards to move them along. Many read aloud, quietly and carefully, studying the documents and whispering together in low voices. There was a tone of awe and even reverence, as if in a cathedral or a shrine.

After the visitors left the train, they were invited to take a Freedom Pledge and to sign a Freedom Scroll. In Burlington, Vermont, half the population signed. A later generation would have laughed cynically, but in 1947 Americans were a nation of believers. They had just been through a war for liberty and freedom. The words of the Freedom Pledge had meaning to them, for their generation had counted the cost.

THE FREEDOM PLEDGE

I am an American. A free American.
Free to speak—without fear
Free to worship God in my own way
Free to stand for what I think right
Free to oppose what I think wrong
Free to choose those who govern my country
This heritage of freedom I pledge to uphold
For myself and all mankind.

This was not a pledge of allegiance or a loyalty oath. It proclaimed the autonomy of individual citizens to stand for their idea of the right and to fight what they thought wrong. It was not about "my country, right or wrong," but the very opposite. The American generation that emerged from the Second World War had a larger idea of their country and themselves. Most of all, they were invited to unite in an idea of freedom as civic responsibility.

The Freedom Train combined that large vision with other meanings. The train itself and its streamlined cars were emblems of modernity, and its big locomotive (number 1776) was a symbol of American power. By contrast, the documents seemed old and fragile. They were symbols not of power but of right, and their condition made clear their need to be protected in a dangerous world. Altogether the Freedom Train expressed the material strength and moral resolve of a united people. For those of an impressionable age, that vision still lingers in the mind.

THE COLD WAR

Harry Truman, George Marshall, and the "Wise Men"

Liberty is a long distance race.

—ALBERT CAMUS

Freedom is never free.

—AMERICAN PROVERB

AS THE FREEDOM TRAIN toured the nation, Americans were appalled to find themselves in yet another world conflict, larger than World War II and infinitely more dangerous. This time the challenge came not from Fascism on the far right but from totalitarian Communism on the extreme left. It became a bitter struggle that continued forty-five years, included more than a hundred wars throughout the world, and threatened a nuclear apocalypse that could extinguish life on the planet. But mainly it was a different kind of conflict, which Bernard Baruch (or his publicist Herbert Bayard Swope) may have been the first to call the Cold War. It tried the moral stamina of the American republic as never before and severely tested American traditions of liberty and freedom.

The Cold War started in 1945. Americans watched in dismay as the rulers of the Soviet Union conquered every nation in eastern Europe and imposed new tyrannies on countries that had just escaped from Fascism.[30] These Communist regimes claimed to govern in the name of the people, but none was elected to office. All seized power by force and maintained it by a reign of Communist terror that was brutal beyond imagining—more cruel even than Fascism. In 1997, a careful study by a team of European scholars, mostly of the left, found evidence that Communist governments killed 106 million of their own people, mostly in the years from 1945 to 1989, a number so large that it is beyond imagining.

The human toll of Communism was nearly twice as large as that of Fascism, enormous as that had been. This great and terrible crime of the left was another holocaust, on a scale without equal in modern history.[31]

It was also a mortal threat to liberty and freedom. Communist leaders expressed bitter hatred of "bourgeois democracy" and dedicated themselves to the destruction of what Josef Stalin contemptuously called "Anglo-Saxon Liberty." Wherever they were firmly in power, they moved quickly to destroy fundamental human rights. Lenin made a joke of it. He said, "It is true that liberty is precious, so precious that it must be rationed."[32]

Early in 1945, Americans hoped for peace through coexistence and international cooperation. The Four Freedoms were to be protected by Franklin Roosevelt's idea of "the Four Policemen." But it was not to be. Before his death Roosevelt concluded sadly, "We can't do business with Stalin. He has broken every one of the promises he made at Yalta."[33]

Most of these shattered agreements were about liberty and freedom. Soviet leaders gave guarantees of safe conduct for Polish leaders, but when those men flew to Warsaw in American and British aircraft, they were imprisoned by Soviet officials and many were never seen again. Communist leaders promised free elections and human rights in eastern Europe, then broke their promises everywhere.

The Soviet Union deliberately disrupted international agreements for free trade, monetary problems, open communications, nuclear arms control, occupation policies, and the United Nations. While the United States reduced its armed forces from 12 million to 1.5 million, the Red Army remained largely intact, and Soviet security troops, Gulag guards, and secret police multiplied by millions. More ominous was the pattern of their deployment. While the Western allies were bringing their forces home, Soviet forces were sent abroad in great strength to eastern Europe, the Baltic nations, the Balkans, Iran, and Manchuria. Evidence mounted of attempts at Communist subversion in western Europe and North America.

In 1945, reports of this activity streamed into Washington from refugees, diplomats, radio intelligence, and Americans with relatives in eastern Europe. But what could be done? The problem was more difficult than Fascism had ever been. Europe was a ruin. Asia was in turmoil. Only the United States could lead the free world, but it was dismantling its armed forces, and its citizens wanted to get on with their lives.

Americans also had a sense that the republic lacked a leader in 1945, and the new president did not seem up to the job. The man at the center was Harry Truman. In 1945, nobody could understand why Franklin Roosevelt had made him vice president. It wasn't for his early achievements. Truman came from a family of Missouri slaveholders who had fallen on hard times and were too poor to give him an education. He was the only president in the twentieth century who never went to college. In his youth he failed at farming, zinc mining, oil drilling, and half a dozen other jobs. During the First World War he did well in difficult circumstances as an artillery officer in France. But then he failed again in the haberdashery business and went into politics with the backing of the corrupt Pendergast machine. In 1922, he was elected county judge and chief executive of Johnson County, Missouri. Truman had a difficult start in that office, but he slowly built a reputation for honesty and ability. In the hard times of the Great Depression he did an excellent job, and Pendergast got him elected to the U.S. Senate in 1934. Again the rhythm of his career repeated itself. Truman was slow to win acceptance in Washington, but after Pearl Harbor he was appointed chairman of a watchdog committee on the war effort and surprised everyone by his leadership and judgment. By 1944, he was a respected leader in the Senate.

Like Franklin Roosevelt, Truman described himself as a little left of center. The operative word was center. He strongly backed New Deal legislation but detested New Deal "bureaucrats." He supported organized labor but opposed John L. Lewis. He had an equal horror of Fascism and Communism and wrote in 1941 that Soviet leaders were a ring of gangsters "as untrustworthy as Hitler and Al Capone." In all of these attitudes he was far removed from Henry Wallace, whom he replaced as vice president, and he was closer to what Roosevelt in his centrist way thought that the country needed.[34]

Then suddenly Harry Truman was president. Once again, as so often in his life, he started slowly. He was utterly unprepared for the office and surrounded himself with old friends he could trust. The staff work was terrible. He stood by while two cabinet members, James Byrnes and Henry Wallace, pursued diametrically opposite foreign policies and even appeared to back them both. The new president

The Coming of the Cold War: Herblock's cartoon of Harry Truman as a small figure, ringing a large global Liberty Bell. Courtesy of Herb Block Foundation.

seemed confused, indecisive, and often mistaken. So many things went wrong that people made a joke of it: "To err is Truman," they said.

But slowly, as he had done so often before, the new president began to find his way. He gathered a team of very able men, always the acid test of leadership. George Marshall and Averill Harriman replaced Byrnes and Wallace in the cabinet. The president began to listen to a group that McGeorge Bundy later called the "Wise Men." An excellent book has portrayed them as an American "establishment," but that British phrase has never accurately described the pluralism of American elites.[35]

Harry Truman put together a team who represented many styles of leadership. One group came from the Army. Their model was George Marshall, a Virginian who inherited the stoic tradition of Washington and Lee, a soldier-statesman of deep Christian faith and high integrity. Another circle were New Yorkers and New Englanders who came from Groton and Yale, Wall Street and State Street: progressive Republicans such as Robert Lovett and patrician Democrats such as Averill Harriman and Dean Acheson. A third circle were dour Scots-Irish Presbyterians, often Princeton educated: George Kennan in Democratic administrations and the Dulles brothers among Republicans. A fourth group were Harry Truman's poker-playing, bourbon-drinking backcountry buddies from Missouri, Kentucky, and the Southwest: Charles Ross, Fred Vinson, Clinton Anderson, and Tom Clark, all rough diamonds but highly skilled at democratic politics.

These American elites were open to talent. They reached out to able men such as John J. McCloy and James Forrestal, both sons of Irish Catholic immigrants. They promoted Benjamin Cohen and David Lilienthal, who were of Jewish families, and African Americans such as Ralph Bunche. These men gave the republic the leadership it needed in a moment of crisis. They also developed a new vision of a free world.

Visions of the Wise Men

Harry Truman's team shared a dream of liberty and freedom. For all their differences, they had much in common that way. They were of the same historical generation, with a unique combination of experience. Most of them were born between 1880 and 1905 and raised to the moral purposes of the high Victorian era. Harriman and Acheson and Lovett met that Victorian ethic in a great teacher, Endicott Peabody at Groton. Kennan learned it from the Christian humanism of Presbyterian Princeton: George Marshall acquired it in a southern Stoic form at Lexington, Virginia, in the shadow of Lee and Washington. Truman himself and his southwestern friends acquired it in a different way from their families and churches. These traditions gave them a strong idea of freedom as civic responsibility. They also shared a conviction that the United States must exercise moral leadership in the world. They were flexible about many things, but never about that. George Marshall wrote, "Let us raise a standard to which the wise and honest may repair."[36] No American of his generation laughed cynically at that thought.

After their Victorian youth, this generation came of age in the twentieth century. Many served in the First World War; Truman and Marshall witnessed the slaughter at first hand. After the war they held jobs of high responsibility in politics, diplomacy, law, finance, and the Army during the difficult years of the twenties and thirties. They were national leaders in the Second World War, and even the youngest of them (McCloy and Forrestal) worked directly with Franklin Roosevelt.

Their experience of crisis and war gave them no hope for human perfectibility, but it reinforced their moral purposes. In particular it strengthened their belief in the urgent necessity of democracy and the rule of law, precisely because of the evils that they had seen. They believed that all nations must be free to govern themselves in a democratic way, because no nation or class or race was fit to govern others. They also believed in a system of regulated capitalism, mainly because every other economic system had failed in their own time. Most of all, they believed in liberty and freedom, because they had seen what happened when those values were lost.

Their unique combination of a moral education in the late nineteenth century, and an experience of horrors in the twentieth century, gave this American generation a distinctive vision of democracy, capitalism, liberty, and freedom. From active engagement in international affairs during two world wars they learned to think globally. Their role in great events also taught them to think historically, about choice and contingency. They knew that individual acts could make a difference in the world. Practical experience also led them to be highly experimental and flexible in their own acts, within the frame of large purposes.

These habits of thought shaped their vision of a free world. They worked for what George Marshall called "democratic processes in many countries." The events of the twentieth century also taught them that moral processes must have a material base, and open societies must have military strength to defend themselves in a hostile world.[37] They believed that the only practical hope for world peace was the extension of rights to all humanity and "institutions upon which human liberty and individual freedom have depended."

These men were confident that they could succeed. Most had been highly successful in their own lives. They were Whiggish in their memory of the past and full of optimism for the future, more so than any American generation since the Civil War. But they were also aware of the terrible consequences of failure, in a world that was divided into warring camps and armed with nuclear weapons.

The Critical Moment, February 9, 1946

This vision inspired a new foreign policy, which emerged very suddenly from the Soviet challenge. The critical moment came on February 9, 1946, when Josef Stalin gave a speech to a gathering of Communist leaders at the Bolshoi theater in Moscow. He declared at length that Communism and capitalism could never coexist and that the Soviet people must prepare

for a new war. American leaders were shocked by the depth of Stalin's hatred of the West and appalled by his paranoia. Even men of the left such as William Douglas received Stalin's speech as a "declaration of World War III" against the United States. It was a pivotal moment.[38]

Urgent inquiries on Soviet intentions went from Washington to George Kennan, American chargé d'affaires in Moscow. On February 22, 1946, Kennan replied with his "Long Telegram," a vital document in American history. In five thousand words he defined a vision for a free world and framed a new foreign policy. Most important, he found the arguments that persuaded American leaders to accept it.

Kennan wrote that Soviet militancy derived from "traditional Russian insecurity," compounded by Marxist ideas of world struggle and "capitalist encirclement." He predicted that the leaders of the Soviet Union would work relentlessly

George Kennan, in his long telegram of February 22, 1946, defined a vision of a free world that guided American policy for many years. On November 11, 1952, Kennan, the U.S. ambassador to Moscow, posed with wife and children on their return home after he was declared "persona non grata" and expelled from the Soviet Union. Image donated by Corbis/Bettmann.

to build their military strength, expand their police state, isolate the Russian people, and extend Soviet power, first in Iran, Turkey, and the Mediterranean, and then in other parts of the world.

But Kennan also reported that the Soviet Union was weaker than it appeared, much weaker than Western states. He observed that Soviet power "does not take unnecessary risks" and "is highly sensitive to the use of force." He recommended that the United States should maintain "sufficient force" and be ready to use it, and he predicted that the Soviet leaders would retreat on particular points rather than risk a general war. Kennan also believed that Soviet policy "does not represent natural outlook of Russian people" and that Soviet power "bears within itself the seeds of its own decay." In another essay he wrote that the United States could succeed by "long term, patient but firm . . . containment of Russian expansive tendencies."[39]

Kennan's papers circulated widely in Washington, and they were impressively confirmed by events that followed. On March 2, 1946, the Soviet Union broke another solemn promise to withdraw forces from Iran, as Britain and the United States had withdrawn theirs. American diplomats reported heavy Soviet troop movements into that country and to the borders of Turkey, as well as growing Soviet aid for Communists in Greece. At the same time, Canadian authorities uncovered a large Soviet nuclear spy ring and made many arrests.

On March 12, 1947, President Truman delivered an urgent speech to Congress. He observed that every nation faced a choice between "alternative ways of life." One choice led to "free institutions, representative government, individual liberty, freedom of speech and religion, and freedom from oppression." The other brought "terror and oppression" and "the suppression of personal freedom." Truman declared, "I believe that it must be the policy of the United States to support free peoples who are resisting attempted subjugation by armed minorities or outside pressures . . . primarily through economic and financial aid."

This "Truman Doctrine" won bipartisan support from two-thirds of the Senate. Economic and military assistance was rushed to Greece and Turkey. A powerful naval force was sent to the Mediterranean, the beginning of a presence that would continue to the twenty-first century. The Soviet Union was told to remove its troops from Iran or face a war. By May it did so. It also backed away from Turkey and abandoned the Communist movement in Greece, which was defeated. George Kennan's policy of containment worked just as he predicted. Its vision of a free world became the foundation of American policy for many years.

The new policy of containment met with mixed results. In 1947, Dean Acheson and Secretary of State George Marshall announced the Marshall Plan. It sent many billions of dollars to help European nations build a material foundation for free institutions, which was done with high success. Communism was defeated in western Europe, a critical victory for the free world. Middle Europe was a different story. In 1948, Czechoslovakia was lost to yet another Communist coup, and the Soviet Union carried the Cold War to a new stage by imposing a military blockade of Berlin, in the hope of expelling the Western powers.

Communist leaders were confident that the "bourgeois democracies" would yield to threats. But with Kennan's policy and Truman's leadership, the United States and its allies sent an aerial armada to Germany and supplied two million Berliners by a massive airlift. Its strategy required the Soviets to fire the first shot if they wished to stop it, which would have united America and the world against them. Further, President Truman sent strategic bombers to Europe in a clear demonstration of his determination to meet force with force, even nuclear force. Soviet leaders retreated, and America's allies also got a message. In 1949, twelve Western nations created the North Atlantic Treaty Organization and began to rearm. For the first time, the United States joined a formal peacetime military alliance in Europe.[40]

Success in Europe was followed by shattering defeat in Asia. China's Nationalist dictatorship of Chiang Kai-shek collapsed in 1949. A Communist regime seized control of the most populous nation in the world and held it by terror and mass murder. In 1950, the Communist Army of North Korea invaded the Republic of Korea, and came close to victory. To the amazement of the Soviet leaders, Harry Truman resolved to fight. The American people supported him and went grimly to war again, with a heavy heart but a clear sense of its necessity. President Truman called it a police action, but it became a world conflict that involved every major power in the free world and the Communist bloc. On the plains of central Europe, even larger military forces prepared to fight a third world war. At the same time, the nuclear arms race accelerated. The Soviet Union had acquired its first atomic bomb in 1949. Within four years, both sides tested hydrogen bombs of terrible destructive power. Americans began to build bomb shelters and prepared for nuclear war. Never before had the United States been more powerful and less secure.

But so strong was the vision of Truman's leaders that even these challenges did not shake their resolve to secure a free world by the containment of Communism. Some Americans did not agree. A few deluded critics on the left, such as Henry Wallace, believed that the United States had started the Cold War and that the Soviet Union was on the side of social justice. Many others on the right demanded a policy not of containment but of liberation. But most American presidents adopted George Kennan's centrist policy of containment, "long term, patient but firm." The American people supported it. In a struggle of forty years, it succeeded in stopping the expansion of Communism and building open societies in Japan, Germany, and western Europe.

Anti-Communist Images of a Free World

In this long war against Communist tyranny, Americans developed new visions of liberty and freedom. George Kennan's Long Telegram urged that the United States should "put forward to other nations a much more positive and constructive picture of the sort of world we would like to see." Every American statement of policy defined the Cold War as a world struggle for freedom and liberty, in ways that differed from the fight against Fascism in the Second World War. A new set of anti-Communist values began to form: democracy as free elections and the rule of law, capitalism as free enterprise, liberty as national independence and individual rights, and freedom as civil rights for all.

During the Cold War, American history began to be rewritten around these themes. Before 1945, the leading survey of American history was written by Charles and Mary Beard, who stressed Progressive themes of revolutionary ferment, social conflict, democracy, and equal rights. In the 1950s, that interpretation passed rapidly out of fashion. A new literature stressed themes of "consensus and continuity" in American history rather than models of conflict and change. New work by constitutional historians put heavy stress on the rule of law. New interpretations of American history by Richard Hofstadter centered on ideas of free enterprise and entrepreneurial liberty. A large literature celebrated both Hamilton and Jefferson as architects of a free society, which was understood in terms of capitalism, democracy, and individual rights.

In Boston this vision inspired journalist William Schofield and churchworker Bob Winn to propose in 1947 a "Freedom Trail" that might link the historic sites in that city to a new sense of American values. Their idea caught on. A Freedom Trail Foundation was founded, and the trail was quickly built. Visitors walked a narrow line of red bricks that ran two and a half miles through downtown Boston. It began on Boston Common, ascended Beacon Hill to the Massachusetts State House, then came down the hill again to Park Street Church, the Old Granary Burying Ground, King's Chapel, and the Old South Meetinghouse, where the Tea Party began. It moved on past the Old State House to Fanueil Hall, where town meetings were held, then to the Paul Revere House and across the Charles River to Bunker Hill and the USS *Constitution*. The sequence of sites told a story of John Adams's "first American Revolution" in the "hearts and minds" of a people who were determined to be free, of their resistance to British tyranny, of the crisis in 1775 and the War of Independence.

Most sites on Boston's Freedom Trail had some association with Paul Revere, who became its most vivid historical figure. His image made a perfect symbol for anti-Communist ideas of freedom and liberty during the Cold War. Paul Revere came to be remembered as a man of the people who helped to rally the farmers of Middlesex County to the common cause of liberty and self-government. He was also a successful man of business and represented the linkage of democracy and capitalism with liberty and freedom.[41]

Another Cold War theme was freedom through strength and vigilance. At the same time that the Freedom Trail was created, another group of New Englanders founded Minuteman National Historic Park, which followed the line of the Battle Road from Lexington to Concord and commemorated the events of April 18–19, 1775. Here another iconic figure became more prominent: the Minuteman who defended his town in the American Revolution. His monuments at Lexington Green and Concord Bridge were already familiar to Americans. Much use had been made of them in both world wars. During the 1950s, the Minuteman embarked on a new career as a Cold Warrior. In anxious days of that era, the image of the Minuteman became a symbol of steadfast courage in the face of danger, a reassuring emblem of a common resolve to resist tyranny, and a sign of the nation's readiness to fight for liberty and freedom at a moment's warning.[42]

A third iconic theme centered on global visions of a free world. In 1948, a cartoonist did a sketch of President Harry Truman as a small figure ringing a very large Liberty Bell for all the world.[43] In 1949, a new version of the Liberty Bell was created for the Cold War. The National Committee for a Free Europe raised the money for the a World Liberty Bell, which had the same shape as the old Philadelphia bell but a larger size and a different message. It weighed ten tons. In place of the Quaker inscription, it was decorated with a wreath of peace and five figures representing the races of humanity passing the torch of freedom from one to

A World Liberty Bell modeled on the old Quaker Bell, with inscriptions embracing all humanity. In free Berlin, it became a symbol of a "crusade for freedom" against communist tyranny. Photograph by Allyn Baum, October 25, 1950. Image donated by Corbis/Bettmann.

another. This World Bell was installed in Berlin as the symbol of a free world and global liberation.[44]

The National Committee for a Free Europe was a private group with public funding. It sponsored a Crusade for Freedom and Radio Free Europe, broadcasting to eastern Europe from studios in West Germany. In 1953, it added programs in Russian, with readings of Pasternak, Solzhenitsyn, Sakharov, and Djilas. Other broadcasts were targeted at ethnic minorities in the Soviet Union. Within ten minutes of the first transmission, the Soviet Union responded with massive jamming of radio signals. Communist agents assassinated employees of Radio Free Europe and in 1981 blew up its headquarters in Munich.

The purpose of Radio Free Europe was not containment but liberation. It was opposed by American liberals such as William Fulbright, who thought that it made promises the United States government was not prepared to keep. But it was strongly supported by east European liberals such as Lech Walesa and Vaclav Havel, who testified to its impact in their countries.

A REPUBLIC IN ARMS

Freedom as Civil Control over Military Institutions

> The supremacy of the civil over military authority I
> deem the essential principles of our Government.
>
> —THOMAS JEFFERSON, 1801

T HE LONG STRUGGLE against Communism created new dangers for liberty and freedom in the United States. A hostile power
pledged to the total defeat of American values and institutions
possessed nuclear weapons that could destroy the United States as completely as Rome had destroyed Carthage, and with only a few moments'
warning. For the first time since independence, the American people faced
the problem of extreme military insecurity as a permanent condition.

As a consequence, the Great Republic was compelled to maintain
large military forces in time of peace for the first time in its history. It was
compelled to create secret agencies with extraordinary powers of surveillance. The United States also organized a permanent armaments industry,
which Dwight Eisenhower called the "military-industrial complex."[45] As
President Eisenhower himself observed in his Farewell Address, it posed
a fundamental danger to liberty and freedom. Many ancient and modern
republics had been destroyed by their own armies and generals. It had
happened in the Greek city-states, the Roman republic, the republics of
the Italian Renaissance, the English and French Revolutions, and many
nations during the twentieth century.

From the beginning of the Cold War, civilian and military leaders in
the United States were deeply aware of this danger. They worked hard at
reviving an old Anglo-American vision of liberty and freedom as civil
supremacy over military affairs. This idea had developed as early as the

seventeenth century. Its early elements included legislative oversight of the armed services, civilian leaders of military institutions, and close civil control over military appropriations.

These traditions had long been so strong in the military that officers as civic-minded as George Marshall and Dwight Eisenhower believed that it was unprofessional for them even to vote in elections or to join in any sort of partisan activity as long as they were on active duty. That attitude ended in the Cold War, but other traditions of civil supremacy were carefully nourished. A massive effort was made to reinforce the tradition of civil supremacy in the education of officers in the armed services. Cadets and midshipmen in service academies and ROTC programs were required to take courses in the history of military affairs. The primary purpose was to indoctrinate officers in the customs and values of a free society.[46]

But traditions of freedom and liberty have never been established by rote or rule. They develop through historical precedents, iconic events, and symbolic examples. One such event happened in the early years of the Cold War, when one of the highest-ranking officers in the U.S. Army directly challenged the national tradition of civil supremacy. He was General Douglas MacArthur, a leader of extraordinary ability and achievement. He was a cultural product of the American backcountry, raised to a border idea of liberty as personal independence, and had long been a law unto himself in a brilliant and turbulent career. MacArthur was first in his class at West Point, but his career almost ended in his first assignment because of insubordination to his commanding officer. After outstanding service in the First World War, he rose rapidly to become chief of staff, but he ran afoul of Franklin Roosevelt over military appropriations and in 1935 was openly insubordinate to his commander-in-chief. The president called him one of the "two most dangerous men" in the republic (the other being Huey Long), encouraged his retirement from active duty, and helped arrange a job for him in the Philippine Islands, twelve thousand miles from Washington. In the Second World War, MacArthur became a national hero (more for his image than his acts), but once again he had major conflicts with civil leaders and military superiors in Australia and the United States. After the war he served as head of occupation forces in Japan, made himself the virtual ruler of that nation, and governed with wisdom and moderation.

When the Korean War began, Douglas MacArthur became the commander of United Nations forces. He broke the North Korean army in a brilliant campaign but suffered a heavy defeat when Communist China entered the war in great force. MacArthur wanted a full-scale escalation

President Harry Truman and General Douglas MacArthur meeting on Wake Island, October 15, 1950. The collision of these two leaders defined an American tradition of civil control over the military, fundamental to liberty and freedom in the United States. Image donated by Corbis/Bettmann.

of the war against China, even to the use of nuclear weapons. President Truman and the Joint Chiefs chose a different policy of containment, massive commitment of strength in Europe, and a carefully limited war in Asia. Once again MacArthur became openly insubordinate to his superiors and was ordered not to speak without Washington's approval. He defied that order, and the Joint Chiefs failed to rein him in. Air Force General Hoyt Vandenberg said, "What good would that do. He wouldn't obey the orders. What can we do?"

When General MacArthur learned that President Truman had decided to end the Korean War by a negotiated peace, he deliberately disrupted that policy by proposing his own negotiations and threatening to invade China. He continued to speak defiantly against his country's foreign policy. After much discussion, and with great reluctance, Truman made a decision that amazed the country. He removed MacArthur from command, not because of policy differences but because the general had put himself above the president, the Constitution, and his own military superiors. MacArthur had broken the rule of civil control over military affairs.

Harry Truman believed that tradition to be fundamental to the preservation of American liberty and freedom. Most American leaders agreed with him: the joint chiefs of the armed services, the chief justice, the vice president, the speaker of the House, and many in both political parties. But conservative newspapers were highly critical, and the American people took the other side; 69 percent supported MacArthur, and he was received as a hero in the country. Truman's approval ratings sank to 26 percent, but he remained steadfast in his decision. It was the darkest hour of his political career and a great act of civic responsibility in a free society. Fifty years later, the American people came to understand him that way and ranked him near the top of American presidents. The American tradition of civil supremacy gained new strength from Douglas MacArthur's failed challenge, and from Harry Truman's leadership during the Cold War.[47]

THE GREAT FEAR

Cold War and Civil Liberties

> We cannot defend freedom abroad by deserting it
> at home.
>
> —Edward R. Murrow

G EORGE KENNAN'S Long Telegram had also dealt at length
with domestic dangers to liberty and freedom in the United
States. He warned that Communist parties, "directed in
Moscow," were working to disrupt American institutions and to subvert
"our traditional way of life" so that Soviet power would be secure. Kennan urged that the United States should restrain this activity, but at the
same time he argued that it must "remain true to our own values of a free
society." He added, "Much depends on the health and vigor of our own
society."

Here was another Cold War dilemma. Kennan warned that the America way was threatened both by Communist subversion of a free society
from without and by anti-Communist suppression of liberties from
within. His Long Telegram urged his countrymen to work on both problems at the same time.

This part of Kennan's advice was followed by the Truman administration. It proved to be more difficult than foreign policy or military affairs,
and it tested the nation in yet another way. One of the first tasks was to
deal with Soviet agents in the United States. Left-leaning historians have
written about the prosecution of Alger Hiss and the execution of the
Rosenbergs as a "witchhunt" and "redbaiting," as it is still called in academe. But much evidence from Soviet sources and American intercepts
released after the end of the Cold War have established that Alger Hiss

and Rosenberg were guilty of spying for the Soviet Union. Communist espionage and subversion were genuine problems during the Cold War.

After the discovery in 1946 of a large Soviet espionage ring in Canada, Truman moved quickly but with respect for due process. In 1946–47, he created a Federal Loyalty and Security Program. In five years, three million federal workers were cleared for service, and 212 were dismissed. The Justice Department also prosecuted twelve leaders of the American Communist Party and won convictions against them for attempting to overthrow the American republic. These measures were much criticized from the left, but constitutional historian Paul Murphy carefully observes that from 1946 to 1949 "on the whole the administration moved with regard for justice and civil rights."[48]

After 1948, the politics of the loyalty program changed fundamentally when right-wing Republicans and conservative Democrats attempted to seize control of it in Congress and tried to use it as a weapon against not only Communists but also against liberal Democrats. Congressmen Richard Nixon of California and Karl Mundt of South Dakota undertook to expand the House Un-American Activities Committee, and they attempted to create a congressional machinery of internal security. Some Republican leaders supported them, but they were strongly opposed by Thomas Dewey, Republican candidate for the presidency in 1948, and held in check for a time.

But the national mood changed in 1949, after China fell under Communist control and conservatives gained strong majorities in Congress. Legislative committees began to investigate Communist subversion throughout the United States. The result was a great repression that did heavy damage to civil liberties. The most reckless attacks were made by Senator Joseph McCarthy, who alleged in February 1950 that he had a list of 305 Communists who were working in the State Department. Under scrutiny, the list began to shrink. In the end McCarthy was unable to identify a single Communist in the State Department, though he named a few people of liberal or radical opinions. His accusations were investigated by a congressional committee and found to be without substance.

Undaunted, McCarthy continued his campaign. After 1953, he became chairman of a Senate Permanent Investigations Subcommittee and began to center his efforts on Communist sympathizers throughout the federal government. Senator William Jenner's Senate Internal Security Subcommittee searched for treason in educational institutions. Representative Harold H. Velde, chair of the House Un-American Activities Committee, investigated the entertainment industry. The result was an epidemic of persecution. The House Un-American Activities Committee began to attack the civil liberties of Americans who had nothing to do with Communism or the Soviet Union. The cause of anti-Communism was used by conservative Republicans to settle scores against New Dealers. Southern businessmen used it as a tool to break labor unions. The American Medical Association invoked it to stop national health insurance, all in the name of liberty and freedom. The major Hollywood studios moved to blacklist writers who refused to testify against friends or took the Fifth Amendment. Universities fired faculty for associations with the left. One of the worst records was that of Harvard University, which discharged Professor Ray Ginger after demanding that his wife take an oath that she was not a member of the Communist Party. Other American institutions were more respectful of civil liberties. Ginger was hired and promoted by Brandeis University, whose president, Abram Sachar, was a fierce defender of civil liberties. The diversity of American society proved to be its saving grace. But many lives were ruined by false and reckless persecutions in a Great Fear that overspread the country.[49]

The Great Fear began to have another effect. Its excesses inspired a great revival of civil liberties in the United States during the Cold War. An awakening came in response to Senator Joseph McCarthy. At first he attracted a following of Republican colleagues, conservative publishers, and American voters who shared his resentment of liberal leaders and institutions. But McCarthy became increasingly reckless in his attacks on the presidencies of Franklin Roosevelt and Harry Truman as "twenty years of treason." He even accused General George Marshall of betraying the country and proclaimed that Communists had infiltrated the Army. These excesses inspired a countermovement of great power. Leading newspapers and television commentators turned against him. American writers attacked him in works such as Arthur Miller's *Crucible*. These polemics took aim not merely at the man himself but at his cause. Highly effective were the

"YOU MEAN I'M SUPPOSED TO STAND ON THAT?"

The Cold War had a double impact on civil liberties. It caused an abridgment of American rights by Senator Joseph McCarthy and others like him and, at the same time, inspired the largest expansion of civil liberties in American history. This Herblock cartoon, which invented the word McCarthyism, captured both of these movements in a single image, March 29, 1950. Courtesy of Herb Block Foundation. Herblock Collection, Library of Congress.

cartoons in the *Washington Post* by Herbert Block, known to a large public as Herblock. In 1949, he drew a sketch of McCarthy's supporters in
the U.S. Senate, pushing and pulling an unhappy Republican elephant
toward a pile of tar barrels labeled "McCarthyism," a word of Herblock's
invention. The term instantly caught on, and the senator from Wisconsin
became a byword for the reckless destruction of civil liberties.

McCarthy's attacks on the army brought strong reactions, even from
the right. His hearings began to be televised, and millions of Americans
observed his methods at first hand. In 1953, Eisenhower at last turned
against him, and McCarthy added the Republican president to his list of
traitors. The Senate launched a new investigation, this time of McCarthy
himself, and the result was a resolution of censure on December 2, 1954.
In 1955, evidence became known that his associate, Assistant U.S. Attorney Roy Cohn, had encouraged witnesses to perjure themselves. The
destructive career of Joseph McCarthy gave civil liberties a good name.[50]

Many Americans remember the Cold War as a time when things went
wrong, but to study this struggle in the larger context of liberty and freedom is to see it in a different light. While the excesses of Senator
McCarthy played on television, deeper currents were stirring in America.
The result was a growing movement for rights that had been denied to
people within the United States and another great expansion of liberty
and freedom.[51]

The largest extension of civil liberties in American history occurred in
the middle years of the Cold War, from as early as 1950 to early 1973 and
mainly in the 1960s. First Amendment rights of free expression were
greatly enlarged in *New York Times v. Sullivan* (1964). So were legal protections in the Bill of Rights, in *Gideon v. Wainwright* (1963), *Escobedo v.
Illinois* (1964), and *Miranda v. Arizona* (1966). The equal protection clause
of the Fourteenth Amendment was given a broad political application in
Baker v. Carr (1962). Other rights nowhere mentioned in the Constitution became an accepted part of American life: the expanded right of privacy in cases such as *Griswold v. Connecticut* (1965) on the sale of
contraceptives, and many other cases.

Earl Warren and the Supreme Court were a central part of this revolution in civil liberties, but this was a much larger story, embracing state
courts, legislatures, the Congress, the Justice Department, the press, the
American Civil Liberties Union, and many individual Americans who
brought the landmark cases to the courts. Conservatives were bitterly
unhappy but slowly made their peace with this revolution in civil liberties.
The Miranda ruling, for example, was angrily opposed by police and by

conservative politicians such as Richard Nixon. But public order did not collapse as they predicted. Miranda himself was convicted after his confession was thrown out. The ruling worked its way into the fabric of American life, and *Miranda* became a general noun, an adjective, and even a verb: to mirandize. It was gradually accepted by most police forces, and the revolution in civil liberties slowly became a part of American culture.

All of this happened during the Cold War, and in large part because of it. An important theme in the 1950s and 1960s was the need to strengthen a free society in its world struggle against Communism. Every great war has had that effect in American history. The War of Independence began with the persecution of Tories and Quakers. It ended by stimulating a new birth of civil liberty in the federal and state Bills of Rights. The Civil War started with acts of extreme repression by federal authorities. It led to another revolutionary expansion of civil rights in the congressional statutes and constitutional amendments from 1863 to 1876. The First World War and the Bolshevik Revolution caused a cruel persecution of aliens and dissenters by the Wilson administration and still more by state and local authorities, but it also led to a great surge of civil liberties in the 1920s. Each of these movements for civil liberties in turn inspired a conservative reaction, which limited the new ideas in some ways but also anchored them in the American system.

Exactly the same thing happened during the Cold War. That great struggle began by diminishing civil liberties in the United States and ended by expanding them. A similar trend appeared in civil rights. In general it might be said that civil rights are to freedom as civil liberties are to liberty and autonomy. The impact of the Cold War on rights and liberties was its most important legacy for American domestic life.

Civil rights are to civil liberties as freedom is to liberty. The impact of the Cold War on civil rights appeared in this poster, with the words of Shirley Chisholm. Collection of Mary Haskell.

The poster reads: UNLESS WE START TO FIGHT and defeat the enemies of poverty & racism in our own country and make our talk of equality and opportunity ring true, we are exposed as hypocrites in the eyes of the world when we talk about making other people free.

FREEDOM NOW!

The Cold War and the Revolution in Civil Rights

> We are exposed as hypocrites in the eyes of the world
> when we talk about making other people free.
>
> —SHIRLEY CHISHOLM, 1969

THE SECOND WORLD WAR and the Cold War quickened the conscience of the nation about what Gunnar Myrdal in 1944 called "the American Dilemma." The problem of race, which had long been invisible to many white Americans before the war, suddenly became apparent in a new way. In the city of Baltimore, when people came home from a war for freedom, they found the same battered old signs at bathing beaches that openly proclaimed WHITES ONLY. Restrooms bore labels that said COLORED and WHITE. Many places of "public accommodation" were rigidly segregated by race. In Baltimore, African Americans had their own city within a city, with segregated schools, churches, colleges, and even their own main street, Pennsylvania Avenue, where whites rarely ventured.

This was merely one of several systems of separation in Baltimore. Other bathing beaches in this city had signs that read WHITE GENTILES ONLY. In the city's most desirable neighborhoods, restrictive covenants forbade the sale of real estate to Jews and required them to live apart in a suburban ghetto that was ironically called Liberty Heights.[52]

It was much the same in other American cities, and they were places of enlightenment by comparison with rural America. Similar patterns of discrimination existed for blacks in the South, Asians on the Pacific slope, Indians in the Dakotas, Jews in eastern cities, Latin Americans in the Southwest, French Canadians and Irish Catholics in New England.

594

From the end of Reconstruction to the beginning of the Second World War, these systems of discrimination were sanctioned by the Supreme Court, enforced by state and local governments, and widely accepted by white Protestant Americans.

After 1945, things began to change, slowly at first but with growing momentum. The struggle against Fascism and Communism led Americans to ask if ideas of liberty and freedom were for export only. The result was a series of countervailing movements that began to accelerate very rapidly in the 1950s. On the one side were people of every creed and color and region who demanded their American birthrights, in the cause of freedom. On the other side were Americans, mostly white and southern but of every class and region, who resisted these ideas, and demanded the right to live apart from others, in the name of liberty.[53] One of America's great poets, Langston Hughes, wrote about this great collision between liberty and freedom, in a poem called "Refugee in America":

> *There are words like Freedom*
> *Sweet and wonderful to say.*
> *On my heart-strings freedom sings*
> *All day everyday.*
>
> *There are words like Liberty*
> *That almost make me cry.*
> *If you had known what I know*
> *You would know why.*[54]

The center of concern was the denial of rights of citizenship to African Americans in the South. Race prejudice was still very strong in the United States after the Second World War. Even President Harry Truman shared the racial prejudices of his time and place and often expressed them in his early life. But after 1945, his attitudes changed, with much encouragement from others around him. Part of it was about politics. Truman needed the votes of African Americans. Another part was about the Cold War. Soviet propaganda made very effective use of Jim Crow. But mostly it was a genuine change of heart that was happening very widely in America after World War II. In 1947, Harry Truman gave a speech at the Lincoln Memorial. He wrote to his sister, "Momma won't like what I say because I wind up quoting old Abe. But I believe what I say and I'm hopeful we may implement it."[55]

Truman created a Civil Rights Committee, which in 1947 issued a major document called *To Secure These Rights*. It proposed a sweeping program of reform: desegregation of the armed forces, a Civil Rights Division in the Department of Justice, a U.S. Commission on Civil Rights, tough federal laws against lynching, an end to poll taxes, and new statutes that restored voting rights to African Americans and other minorities.[56]

While northern Republicans and conservative southern Democrats controlled Congress, no legislation was possible on these questions. Truman took action anyway, by executive order. In 1948, as Truman was introducing the military draft for the Cold War, he faced a major challenge from Philip Randolph, who organized a Committee Against Jim Crow in Military Service. On March 28, 1948, Randolph met with the president and threatened demonstrations against the draft unless segregation ended in the armed forces. Four months later, on July 26, Truman issued an executive order calling for integration of the armed forces. By 1950, the Air Force was the first of the services to abolish the color line. The Army followed quickly and found in the Korean War that integrated combat units were more effective than segregated units. The Navy lagged behind, but Truman succeeded in integrating these major American institutions with high success.

As early as December 1947, President Truman also authorized the Justice Department to support a major civil rights case against restrictive covenants in real estate. The result was the Supreme Court decision in *Shelly v. Kraemer* (1948), which ruled that restrictive covenants were unconstitutional. Many other cases followed. *Henderson v. U.S.* led to a Supreme Court decision against Jim Crow in railroad dining cars. In 1952, Truman's Justice Department filed the most important briefs in the case of *Bolling v. Sharpe,* on segegration in the District of Columbia. It also strongly supported many cases on Jim Crow in the schools that reached the Supreme Court. The result was the great decision of *Brown v. Board of Education,* handed down on May 17, 1954, which reversed the "separate but equal" doctrine of *Plessy v. Ferguson* (1896), and struck a heavy blow against de jure segregation throughout the country.

In the 1990s, it became an academic fashion for revisionists to condemn the *Brown* decision, partly because de facto segregation stubbornly persisted in the inner cities. This was true, but the *Brown* decision had a profound importance in another way. It inspired a new hope and vision of a world without Jim Crow. For many years the NAACP distributed posters that reminded Americans to "Remember May 17." In the 1950s, many Americans of African descent did not have to be reminded about the meaning of that day. At the critical moment it had a major impact on the growth of a civil rights movement in the United States.[57]

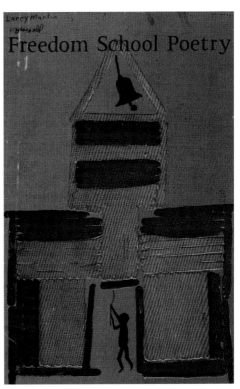

"Remember May 17th": African Americans long remembered the day in 1954 when the Supreme Court handed down its decision in Brown v. Board of Education. *For many people it was a pivotal moment in American history. This poster was distributed by The National Association for the Advancement of Colored People (NAACP). Virginia Historical Society.*

The struggle over education inspired new visions of freedom as a school, without prejudice or discrimination. This book called Freedom School Poetry *was published in Mississippi by African American children. One child created this image, a freedom school with an open door and a bell that rings for all children everywhere. Collection of Mary Haskell.*

Many things began to happen after the *Brown* decision. President Dwight Eisenhower was less supportive of civil rights than Harry Truman had been, but he sent federal troops to Arkansas in support of integration, and a Democratic Congress in 1957 passed a Civil Rights Act, the first since Reconstruction. The Civil Rights Commission and the Civil Rights Division of the Justice Department actively intervened in the cause of freedom.[58]

On the other side were the Hearst newspapers, the Luce publications, and conservative politicians on the right who strongly opposed civil rights on different grounds. Southern demagogue Strom Thurmond tried to stop the Civil Rights Act of 1957 by a personal filibuster that lasted more than twenty-four hours, the longest on record. He failed, in part because many young Americans had begun to act in a grassroots movement for freedom that spread rapidly through the South.

"I JUST WANTED TO BE FREE"

Rosa Parks's Vision of Freedom as Dignity and Justice

> It was about dignity.
>
> —Rosa Parks

T HE LAST PLACE where one might have expected the civil rights movement to flourish was the city of Montgomery, Alabama, first capital of the Confederacy and a citadel of southern racism. But that was where it happened, and in an extraordinary way. The day was Thursday, December 1, 1955. At Court Square, about 5:30 in the afternoon, a quiet middle-aged black woman in a cloth coat and glasses climbed aboard a city bus and sat down in the first row of the colored seats, beside a black man and two black women.[59]

It was the rush hour, and the white seats at the front of the bus filled rapidly. Then another white man got on, and there was no place for him to sit. When that happened, the rules of the bus company and the ordinances of the city required that black passengers in the first row of the colored section must get up and surrender their seats. The bus driver intervened. He was a poor white named Jimmy Blake who didn't like black people.

"All right, you folks," he shouted, "I want those two seats."

Nobody moved. The driver was angry now, and his voice rose to a scream. "Y'all better make it light on yourselves, and let me have those seats." Three black people got up and moved to the back of the bus. The quiet woman in glasses stayed where she was.

"Look, woman," said Jimmy Blake, "are you going to stand up?"

"No," she said, "I'm tired of being treated like a second-class citizen."

The driver called the police, and they took her to the station. She asked for a drink of water and was told that the drinking fountain was for whites only. The police didn't want to deal with this difficult woman, but the bus driver insisted on pressing charges. The police wrote down her name, age, and occupation: Rosa Parks, forty-two, tailor's assistant. Four days later, she went to trial and was found guilty of disorderly conduct and fined ten dollars plus four dollars for costs. It was a routine event in the Deep South.[60]

Then something happened that was not routine. On the day that Rosa Parks went to trial, crudely lettered signs appeared at bus stops in Montgomery. One said, "Don't ride the bus today." Another added, "Don't ride for freedom." All through the city of Montgomery, black people stayed off the buses, even though some had to walk miles to work. That night a meeting at Holt Street Baptist Church resolved to keep the boycott going. The white community of Montgomery tried to stop it. Employers threatened to fire black workers. Police arrested black drivers who gave people a lift. The bus company was sure the boycott would fail, but the African American people of Montgomery kept it going for more than a year. They also sued in federal court, and to everybody's surprise they won. A federal court ruled that segregation of public transportation violated the Fourteenth Amendment to the Constitution, which forbade any state to deprive any person of "life, liberty or property, without due process of law" or "the equal protection of the laws." It ordered that the buses of Montgomery must be integrated, 385 days after Rosa Parks refused to give up her seat to a white man who was standing in the aisle. It was exactly the result that she and her friends had planned.[61]

The story of Rosa Parks was a saga of courage, resolve, and victory, and it got better with the telling. Americans love a hero who fights alone against great odds and wins a famous victory. Winning is important in America. Rosa Parks became a hero that way and was celebrated as a "simple seamstress" who took on the lily-white, Jim Crow, Negro-hating, racist South all by herself. One sculpture showed her as a solitary figure, sitting alone on a bus seat, wrapped in her long coat, eyes hidden behind glasses, entirely self-contained. Through the years she was celebrated in those terms. When Mount Holyoke College gave her an honorary degree, the citation read, "When you led, you had no way of knowing if anyone would follow."[62]

What actually happened was very different from that erroneous understanding of this event, and an even better story. The real Rosa Parks was not a "simple seamstress" or a solitary figure. Her greatest achievement was not merely to sit alone in a segregated seat but to mobilize others in a common cause. Most of Rosa Parks's life had been a preparation for that act. Born at Tuskegee, Alabama, in 1913, she grew up on her grandparents' farm in Pine Level, Alabama, surrounded by the terror that was part of life for African Americans in the Deep South during those dark years. Rosa Parks remembered "hearing the Klan ride at night," and "hearing the sounds of a lynching," and being afraid that the house would burn down. All her life she lived with fear, but her family taught her not to give way to it and never to despair.[63]

Her mother was a teacher and had faith in education. Rosa was sent to the Montgomery Industrial School for Girls, which taught bright young black women to believe in themselves. She went on to college, married Raymond Parks, and settled in Montgomery. Her husband was a barber, and Rosa was a "tailor's assistant" in a Montgomery department store, but their true calling was something else. Their deepest interest was fighting Jim Crow in the South.

Rosa Parks, portrait sculpture (painted wood) by Marshall D. Rumbaugh, 1983. The artist represents Rosa Parks as a small three-dimensional figure, against her larger but less powerful captors who are more nearly in two dimensions. National Portrait Gallery, Smithsonian Institution.

In 1943, Rosa Parks joined the NAACP and worked closely with E. D. Nixon, a former Pullman porter who was said to be "the most powerful black man in town." Nixon became the head of the NAACP in Montgomery, and Rosa Parks became secretary of the organization. Later they held the same positions in the state conference of the NAACP. Together they organized voter registration campaigns and a protest march on the registrar's office in 1944. Rosa Parks attended Ella Baker's leadership conferences, which had a great impact on African Americans in the South. She went to the Highlander School in Tennessee, which trained many leaders of the civil rights movement.[64]

As early as the 1940s, Rosa Parks had refused to obey Jim Crow rules on Montgomery buses. It was said that "some bus drivers recognized her on sight and simply refused to stop for her." By the early 1950s, she was one of many African Americans throughout the South who were fighting Jim Crow in a systematic way. In 1954, the Supreme Court's unanimous decision against school segregation came as a great encouragement to Rosa Parks. More than that, it was an inspiration. Rosa and two friends, E. D. Nixon and Jo Ann Robinson, a faculty member at Alabama State College, decided to mount a formal challenge against the segregated buses in Montgomery.[65]

First they tried to reason with white leaders in the city. E. D. Nixon warned the mayor to expect a boycott of the buses if Jim Crow continued. The mayor did nothing. Individual black riders began to challenge Jim Crow seating. Three of these incidents happened in 1955. Nixon and Robinson carefully considered each of them but decided that they weren't quite right. Then came the arrest of Rosa Parks, a quiet, middle-aged, respectable woman, for refusing to give up her seat to an able-bodied white man when another white man was screaming at her. It was a perfect case for a protest movement in the Old South. From jail, Rosa Parks called Nixon and told him what had happened. In less than a day they had convened meetings of black leaders; in four days they had a boycott organized throughout the city.

Rosa Parks also served in another role as a symbol of the movement, and the symbolism was also carefully managed. In the news, she appeared as a "simple seamstress" who acted alone. She herself encouraged that understanding and wrote, "It was not pre-arranged. It just happened that the driver made a demand and I just didn't feel like obeying. . . . I was quite tired after spending a full day working." All that was true, but there was more to it. This was not a spontaneous response or a solitary action. It was an organized campaign that had been many years in the making. Rosa Parks was one of its organizers.

Rosa Parks made many contributions to the civil rights movement, but mainly she served it as a symbol. Her image was intended to mobilize people throughout the country to fight for their rights. It was meant to show that one person could make a difference, and it succeeded beyond anyone's expectations. Rosa Parks became a marked woman in the South. Violent racists in Alabama were consumed by blind rage against any "nigra" who stood up (or sat down) against them. Threats were made against her life. Rosa's friends feared for her safety, and she moved to Detroit, where she joined the staff of Congressman John Conyers.

She rapidly became an iconic figure for the civil rights movement, and her example inspired others to follow where she had led. She also set an example in the character of her acts. When asked for an explanation she said, "It was about dignity." Her most revealing book carried the simple title *Quiet Strength*. That is the way she still appears in our memory of this event, sitting strong and quiet in her bus seat, hands folded on her lap and head held high in freedom.[66]

Others were inspired by the quiet example of Rosa Parks. Young people took up the cause of civil rights in public accommodations wherever Jim Crow existed. Many were college students. On February 1, 1960, four African American freshmen from North Carolina College in Greensboro went to the Woolworth's store and sat down at the lunch counter that was for whites only. They did not get served but stayed until the manager closed the store. The next day twenty-four students showed up, and sit-ins began to spread through the South.

The students were in most cases models of restraint and nonviolence, but the reactions of southern whites were unspeakably brutal. At a "freedom sit-in" at a lunch counter in Jackson, Mississippi, on May 28, 1963, three young people were assaulted by a jeering mob. Photographer Fred Blackwell caught it with his camera, and the result was an iconic photograph that awakened the conscience of the world.

Freedom Sit-In: Tougaloo college students in sit-in at a Woolworth's lunch counter in Jackson, Miss., May 28, 1963. This photograph by Fred Blackwell became an iconic image that drew much of the world to the support of civil rights. AP/Wide World Photos.

"FREE AT LAST!"

Martin Luther King's Dream of Freedom as Truth and Love

> We will reach the goal of freedom, because the goal of America is freedom.
>
> —MARTIN LUTHER KING JR., 1963

THE MOVEMENT for civil rights had many leaders. In every part of the South, men and women came forward with high courage, often at extreme risk. When they were beaten, or run out of town, or murdered in the night, others took their place. The civil rights movement was strong because it was broad and deep. Among those many leaders, one man became preeminent. In the few years that were given to him, Martin Luther King Jr. stamped his image on this great cause. Others were more important as organizers, but he became the spiritual leader of the civil rights movement and a symbol of its values. He also turned it in a new direction.[67]

Many histories might be written about Martin Luther King Jr. One of them centers on a story of contingency. When E. D. Nixon, Jo Ann Robinson, and Rosa Parks were organizing the Montgomery bus boycott, they needed a figure who could unite their community and represent them to the public. By chance a new minister had just come to town and taken his first job at the Dexter Street Baptist Church. He had a freshly minted doctorate from a Yankee university (a doubtful asset in deepest Alabama), but he came of good family, and his father was one of the most respected ministers in the South. Martin Luther King Jr. hadn't been in Montgomery long enough to have made enemies. He happened to be the right man in the right place at exactly the right time.

Another history might also be written about this extraordinary man.

No man is free until all men are free.

Martin Luther King's vision of freedom as dignity and universal rights appeared in this poster, which summarized his movement in a single sentence: "No man is free until all men are free." Collection of Mary Haskell.

It is a story of long preparation and large purpose. His early life, like that of Rosa Parks, was pointed to this moment by his early experience of injustice in the South, the example of his father, his Christian upbringing, and a long intellectual journey. He studied Marxism and rejected it, mainly because of its materialism, its "ethical relativism," its ruthless exploitation of individual people, and its rejection of liberty and freedom. "To deprive man of freedom," he wrote, "is to relegate him to the status of the thing."

He read Nietzsche and was utterly repelled by his "glorification of power," his "contempt for ordinary mortals," and his attack on "the whole of the Hebraic-Christian morality." He read Bentham and Mill, Hobbes and Rousseau, all in vain, and remembered the moments when he "despaired of the power of love in solving social problems" and thought that "the only way we could solve our problem of segregation was an armed revolt."[68]

Then he heard a sermon by Dr. Mordecai Johnson, president of Howard University, who had just returned from a visit to India and talked about the work of Gandhi. King remembered the "electrifying" moment when he first learned of Gandhi's idea of *satyagraha* (truth and love as force). He saw it as a way of linking the teachings of Jesus to the task of fighting for the rights of the dispossessed. In that revelation, Martin Luther King found his way forward to a new idea of freedom and a new way of attaining it.[69]

Early on the morning of December 2, 1955, Martin Luther King was working in his Montgomery parsonage when the telephone rang. It was E. D. Nixon, who told him about Rosa Parks's arrest the night before, and the boycott, and a meeting of Afro-American leaders. King was asked to be president of a new association and to make a speech on the boycott at the Holt Street Baptist church.[70] The Afro-American citizens of Montgomery turned out in such numbers that they filled the streets for five blocks around the church. Martin Luther King had twenty minutes to collect his thoughts and no time to write them out. He wrote later that it was "the most decisive speech of my life."

It was a long speech, rich in the rhetorical cadences of black preaching in the South but also addressed to the nation and the world. Martin Luther King told the story of Rosa Parks, and he picked up her chosen theme. "There comes a time," he said, "when people get tired of being trampled over by the iron feet of oppression. There comes a time, my friends, when people get tired of being plunged across the abyss of humiliation. . . . There comes a time when people get tired."

He talked about the boycott as part of a larger cause. "We, the disinherited of this land," he said, "we who have been oppressed so long, are tired of going through the long night of captivity. And now we are reaching out for the daybreak of freedom." He spoke of freedom and justice and love. Most of all he talked about the importance of doing the right thing in the right way. "Let us be Christian in all of our actions."

There was an air of optimism and certainty in his message. "We are not wrong!" he said. "We are not wrong in what we are doing. If we are wrong, the Supreme Court of this nation is wrong. If we are wrong, the Constitution of the United States is wrong. If we are wrong, God almighty is wrong. If we are wrong, Jesus of Nazareth was merely a utopian dreamer that came down to earth. And we are determined here in Montgomery to work and fight until justice runs down like water and righteousness like a mighty stream."[71]

When he finished there was a long silence. Martin Luther King sat down, thinking he had failed. Then all those thousands of people rose to their feet and began to applaud, and kept on applauding. "I had never seen such enthusiasm for freedom," King remembered, "and yet this enthusiasm was tempered by amazing self-discipline." He led his new congregation in a spirit that combined unyielding resolve with discipline, restraint, dignity and calm.[72]

Martin Luther King gave the civil rights movement many gifts. One was his gift of serious thought, which framed the movement in a new way, and shaped its meaning. Another was his passion for nonviolence and the rule of Christian love and "beloved community" that sought to bring whites and black together. A third was a depth of caring for others, the old Christian *caritas*, which Martin Luther King communicated by acts as well as words. A young civil rights worker, John Lewis, remembered such a moment on the march to Selma, Alabama: "I had been hurt, had received a concussion, and we were walking along in the rain, and he took off a brown cap from his head and told me, 'John, you need to wear this cap, you've been hurt.' It was a small thing, but it meant so much to me."[73]

The most important gift was Martin Luther King's vision of freedom. His civil rights movement always appealed primarily to principles of freedom. He made the word itself into a weapon. One march was led by a young African American woman, dressed with dignity and pride, holding a simple sign that bore a single word in handwritten letters: "Freedom." In other signs it was not just freedom but "Freedom Now." But always it was freedom as the ancient idea of the rights of belonging, a principle that brought free people together in love and understanding.

Martin Luther King sometimes talked of equality, too; racial equality. He embraced the old American ideas of equal rights, equality of esteem, equal protection, and equality of opportunity. His notion of equality was a positive idea of leveling up, mainly by leveling the playing field. But mostly he talked about freedom. In his "I Have a Dream" speech, the dream was freedom. His heavy stress on freedom was different from other groups in the civil rights movement, such as the Congress of Racial Equality. Martin Luther King understood an old truth in American politics. Equality divides Americans; freedom unites them.[74]

Martin Luther King's contribution was also to give these ideas an image that spread round the world. He was a master of the modern media. Articulate and telegenic, he himself became a symbol of the civil rights movement. The media centered its coverage on him. *Time* and *Newsweek* were positive in their coverage of King, and represented him as the statesman of the civil rights movement. The more conservative *U. S. News and World Report* was negative and represented him as a "dangerous demagogue" until the day he died, and then began to use his memory as a way of reproaching other Afro-American leaders who were still alive.[75]

The more Martin Luther King was loved in the world, the more he was hated in the South. Racists reacted in their immemorial way and tried to reduce him to a condition of equality with themselves by blowing out his brains. While decent people watched in silence, they made assassination and terror an instrument of power. Among the most savage were a band of Klansmen in Natchez, Mississippi, who gloried in the name of the Cottonmouth Moccasin Gang. They invoked the image of the snake yet again in the southern backcountry. In 1966, they resolved to murder a black man (any black man) with one purpose in mind: to draw Martin Luther King onto their ground so that they could assassinate him. In cold blood they killed an elderly black caretaker named Ben Chester White who was not active in the civil rights movement. They merely used him as bait, shot him in cold blood, and threw his body in a creek. The Cottonmouth Moccasin Gang failed in their larger object, but others in the South kept trying. In 1968, at the age of thirty-nine, Martin Luther King was caught in another trap and murdered in Memphis, Tennessee, where he had come to support a strike of garbage collectors.[76]

The murder of Martin Luther King was only the beginning of his career as a symbol of freedom such as Americans had never known before. People everywhere rallied to his cause. Every American state but one made a holiday of Martin Luther King's birthday, and Congress made it a national holiday as well. His image became an icon of freedom for all the world. It inspired other movements and changed the meaning of freedom itself. He linked it to all the people, especially the poor and disinherited. At the same time, he gave it dignity and grace. Most of all, he connected freedom to an idea of Christian love for all people who are not free, even for their oppressors, and he joined it to an old tradition of Christian responsibility in the world.[77]

MASSIVE RESISTANCE

White Citizens Councils and Visions of Southern Liberty

> States Rights and Southern Liberty
> Impeach Earl Warren
>
> —SOUTHERN BUMPERSTICKERS

IN THE DEEP SOUTH, many whites turned strongly against civil rights. The result was a fierce collision between two social movements. Once again, as so often before in America, each side passionately believed that it was the true defender of liberty and freedom. The conservative reaction began to grow immediately after the Supreme Court's desegregation decision in 1954. It kept on growing through the late 1950s and accelerated in the 1960s and 1970s. Moderate politicians fell silent. Even Presidents Dwight Eisenhower and John Kennedy kept very quiet and failed to give the country the leadership it needed in a critical moment. Eisenhower reluctantly enforced integration decisions but told his friends that the appointment of Earl Warren as chief justice was the greatest mistake of his career. Kennedy was appalled by the violence of white southerners against the first Freedom Riders in 1961 and sent six hundred federal marshals to Alabama after southern leaders refused to restore order. But he also tried to shut down the Freedom Marches and sent a peremptory order to his civil rights advisor, Harris Wofford. "Call it off!" President Kennedy demanded. "Stop them! Get your friends off those buses." Kennedy felt that the Freedom Rides were "embarrassing" before his Summit meeting with Soviet leader Nikita Khrushchev. In another episode, African diplomats on the road between Washington and New York complained of Jim Crow in restaurants along Maryland highways. President Kennedy replied, "Tell them to fly!"[78]

With those attitudes in the Oval Office during the presidencies of Eisenhower and Kennedy, and with open encouragement for massive resistance from southern governors such as Orval Faubus in Arkansas, Ross Barnett in Mississippi, and George Wallace in Alabama, smoldering pockets of southern racism suddenly burst into flame. White supremacy organizations multiplied below the Mason-Dixon line. The Ku Klux Klan became active again. These groups turned to terror and violence as a tool for crippling the civil rights movement. Arsonists burned black churches and Jewish synagogues. Assassins murdered civil rights leaders. Bombs killed and maimed black children in schools and homes. This violence was done with strong support from some wealthy and powerful people throughout the southern states.

The ideology of the southern conservative movement was cast in libertarian terms: liberty from the hated federal government and especially the Supreme Court; liberty from "outside agitators and "nigger equality"; liberty for "states' rights" and "southern rights." Its rhetoric reached back to the iconography of southern independence in the Civil War. So also did its symbols. A modern revision of the old Confederate battle flag became the leading emblem of white supremacy and massive resistance. It claimed a kinship with Robert E. Lee, but this was not the old four-square "stainless banner" that had been carried with honor by the Army of Northern Virginia in the Civil War. This was something different, a twentieth-century polyester Jim Crow flag with rectangular proportions

The struggle for civil rights created a countermovement for southern autonomy, white supremacy, states' rights, and the liberty of one race to rule another. An example was this painting of the Ku Klux Klan, which celebrates a connection between the Klan and the police in the South. Print from a painting by grand dragon Marshall Kornegay, 1966. Virginia Historical Society.

that were ironically closer to the Stars and Stripes than to the old Confederate battle flags. The southern flag of massive resistance was a new image, invented for a second civil war and quickly adopted by racist movements in many parts of the world.

The iconography of massive resistance was complex. An example appeared in a photograph by Cecil Williams of a run-down rural gas station at Sandy Run in Calhoun County, South Carolina. It served whites only; in some parts of the Deep South even gas pumps were segregated by race. The windows of the battered building bore many images: a devotional portrait of Jesus, a modern Jim Crow flag of massive resistance, angry bumper stickers for white supremacist candidates, and defiant racist slogans.[79]

In the twentieth century, these symbols inspired a new civil war within the South. On one side were angry southern whites who used extreme violence as an instrument of repression. The beatings and bombings and murders were mostly the work of downtrodden poor whites whose only claim to distinction was that they were not black. They were funded and protected by southern leaders of wealth and power.

On the other side were southern blacks and white liberals who chose the weapons of nonviolence during the 1950s and early 1960s, at a heavy cost but with ultimate success. These contending groups were very different in many ways, but the two warring southern movements for civil rights and white supremacy shared a common heritage. Both were strongly Christian and evangelical and quoted the same Bible. Both had deep roots in American history and shared a strong sense of rights and entitlements. Both were very southern in speech and manner. But in other ways, the contrast could not have been more complete. Here was a collision of rage against reason, hatred against love, brutality against humanity, force against nonviolence. It was also a conflict of separation against integration, hierarchy against equality, and liberty against freedom.

FREEDOM IN THE CAMERA'S EYE

Photo-Icons of the Civil Rights Struggle

> With the exception of those involved at the time, no
> one knows how important the effective use of the news
> media was to our safety, and even our lives.
>
> —MARTIN LUTHER KING JR.

THE CIVIL RIGHTS MOVEMENT brilliantly used the camera to advance its cause. Photographic iconography was not new, but a developing technology of compact equipment, automated cameras, and fast film created many opportunities. A new expertise with this equipment had developed in news photography, mass advertising, television journalism, and sports coverage. The result was a gritty, grainy genre, at once highly spontaneous and elaborately studied. The camera's eye captured extraordinary acts by ordinary people and combined the powerful appeal of authenticity with the immediacy and intimacy of an unposed photograph. The camera froze fleeting moments into immortal images and enlarged them into visions of a great cause.

The leaders of the civil rights movement understood these things and deliberately used photographic images with high effect. One of their most powerful icons was a photograph by James Karales of the Selma March in 1965. It shows a long column of freedom marchers, seen in silhouette against a lowering southern sky. In the van is an American flag. Behind the flag, the column stretches as far as the camera's eye can see. The image of this event created a sense of drama, dignity, peace, courage, and resolve, combined with a sense of righteousness, justice, and irresistible moral strength.

Photographic icons were used to simplify the central issue of the movement. The most common images were snapshots of earnest and

Martin Luther King led the Great Selma March of 600 demonstrators 56 miles from Selma to Mont-gomery, Alabama, on March 7, 1965, a day remembered as Bloody Sunday. It gave rise to a rain of violence by mobs and Alabama police armed with clubs, guns, bull-whips, gas, and even rub-ber truncheons tightly wrapped with barbed wire. It also produced one of the most powerful and enduring images of the civil rights movement, in this Pulitzer Prize–winning photograph by James Karales. © Estate of James Karales, with special thanks to Monica Karales.

attractive young women and men, holding signs and symbols of freedom. These photographs linked that idea to themes of justice, dignity, strength, and peace. They were highly effective devices for associating one cause with another. One freedom marcher in Orangeburg, South Carolina, was photographed in 1963 with a sign that said simply, "My Brother's in Berlin. He's a Freedom Fighter."[80]

Among the camera's greatest gifts to the civil rights movement were indelible images of its opponents. Southern white supremacists made an open spectacle of violence and delighted in displays of brutality. It was a cultural style in dark corners of the Deep South, where sadistic savagery was a form of entertainment and barbarity became a badge of honor. A man who did the Devil's work was celebrated as a "hell-of-a-fella," in the expression of W. J. Cash.

A case in point was Commissioner Theophilus "Bull" Connor of Birmingham, Alabama, the same official who had tried to impose racial segregation on the Freedom Train in 1947. In the civil rights demonstra-tions of the 1950s and 1960s, Bull Connor and his men became favorite images for photojournalists. They were frequently in the public eye: Birmingham firemen turning high-pressure hoses on elderly women and small children; Birmingham policemen using attack dogs to rip the cloth-ing and rend the flesh of nonviolent student demonstrators; sheriffs' deputies attacking peaceful marchers with clubs, truncheons, and electric

The movement for civil rights was greatly aided by its enemies. A leading example was Theophilus "Bull" Connor, who ruled the streets of Birmingham, Alabama, with the ironic title of "Commissioner of Public Safety." When civil rights workers marched bravely onto his turf on May 3, 1963, Connor told his men, "I want 'em to see the dogs work. Look at those niggers run." Photographer Bill Hudson recorded the scene of dogs biting and tearing the clothing and flesh of demonstrators. AP/Wide World Photos.

On July 15, 1963, Bill Hudson photographed burly Birmingham firemen who used high-pressure hoses to inflict severe injuries on nonviolent women and children. Such scenes of tyranny and brutality explained the meaning of freedom in the civil rights movement, and also its heavy cost. They gave the civil rights vision a power far greater than its oppressors. AP/Wide World Photos.

cattle prods; and crowds of southern white girls in summer frocks jeering from the sidelines. Photographers caught their faces, twisted with hatred and violence. More than anything else, more than the violence itself, these images shocked the conscience of decent people and awakened strong sympathy for the American civil rights movement throughout the world.

The cameras also added another element. The Grand Dragons and Imperial Wizards of the Ku Klux Klan in their hoods and sheets became visible in a new way. Images that had inspired terror in the dark shadows of a southern night looked very different in the glare of television cameras. In bright light, the Ku Klux Klan appeared farcical, comical, even absurd. This, too, had a major impact on events. Many white leaders of the New South hated the civil rights movement, but they were embarrassed by camera images of white supremacy and appalled by the disgrace it brought to their beloved region. It was also bad for business. Southern elites of wealth and power who had acquiesced in the violence of massive resistance (and even encouraged it) began to have second thoughts.

THE FEMININE MYSTIQUE

Betty Friedan's Vision of Psychological Liberation
and Social Engagement

> The feminine mystique has succeeded in burying millions of American women alive.
>
> Men weren't really the enemy—they were fellow victims suffering from an outmoded masculine mystique that made them feel unnecessarily inadequate when there were no bears to kill.
>
> —BETTY FRIEDAN

THE MOVEMENT for civil rights inspired other struggles for freedom and liberty. Among the most important was a new feminism, which sprang to life during the decade of the 1960s.[81] It rose among American women, who possessed many human rights, more than most men in the world. By 1963, women in the United States received more formal education than men. They had the right to vote and hold property. They shared many civil liberties and were active in social causes and cultural organizations.

But in the 1950s, highly educated American women became increasingly conscious that they were also victims of prejudice and discrimination. It was difficult to find a career for which their schooling had prepared them. Women who worked outside the home tended to hold jobs of lower rank than men. Even in the same jobs, they received less pay and had fewer prospects for advancement. From 1950 to 1968, the median wage of working women in the United States actually declined as a percentage of men's pay. The home became a gilded cage for middle-class women who found themselves narrowly confined within a domestic role, sometimes much against their will and inclination.[82]

All this gave rise to a new feminism in the United States and other nations. The movement began to grow after the Second World War, partly because of it. A major event was the publication of Simone de Beauvoir's scholarly treatise *The Second Sex* (1952), a restrained but powerful indictment of discrimination by gender. Other events of importance were in a series of careful quantitative studies by private foundations and public agencies. One of the first was the Ford Foundation's *Womanpower* (1957). Another came from the Kennedy administration's Commission on the Status of Women, which published a report in 1963. These inquiries measured the magnitude of discrimination by gender and concluded that it was damaging not only to women but to the entire society.

The first chairman of the Commission was Eleanor Roosevelt. In the years of her maturity, she became the leader of American feminism and brought that cause a dignity, intelligence, seriousness, and gravitas that had great weight with all but the most rabid Roosevelt-haters. She also had direct access to four presidents and used it actively in her cause.

The success of the civil rights movement and the progress of civil liberties in the courts during the Cold War gave great encouragement to the new feminism and created a climate for change. Important legislation was enacted in Congress. An Equal Pay Act passed with strong support in 1963. More important was the Federal Civil Rights Act of 1964. Southern conservatives tried to defeat the entire measure by adding a section that forbade discrimination by gender as well as race. To their horror it passed. The new statute gave rise to a growing body of case law in support of women's rights. Commissions on Women were appointed in many states and met annually in Washington. These meetings increasingly expressed growing frustration with laws that were not enforced, reports that were not read, recommendations that were ignored.

The struggle for civil rights inspired a new feminist movement. A pivotal figure was Betty Friedan. Her book, The Feminine Mystique *(1963) created a new vision of liberty and freedom and invented a new method of consciousness-raising. It was inspired by the experience of Jewish suffering in the Second World War and informed by the work of psychologists and social scientists. Photograph, August 26, 1970, New York City. Corbis/Bettmann.*

A new tone appeared in 1963, when Betty Friedan published a pivotal book called *The Feminine Mystique*. The author was an American housewife, middle class and middle aged, forty-two years old with three children. She wrote for other women such as herself, about what she called "the problem that has no name." Betty Friedan asserted that women were the silent victims of a "feminine mystique" that deprived them of "personal identity and achievement" apart from their home and family roles as wife and mother.[83]

The rhetoric of the book was very strong. Friedan argued that the home had become a domestic "concentration camp," which "infantilized" women. That phrase was more than a metaphor. It derived from a psychological model that drew heavily on the work of psychologists and psychiatrists such as Bruno Bettelheim, Olga Lengyel, and Eugen Kogon, who had been prisoners in Dachau, Buchenwald, and Auschwitz and described their experience of psychological enslavement. Their writings had a great impact on Betty Friedan and led her to a new vision of liberty and freedom as a process of psychological liberation.[84]

Friedan's book inspired an awakening that called itself by many names: women's liberation, the women's movement, or simply feminism. It sought to improve the social and material condition of women, but mainly it attempted to "raise consciousness," to elevate a woman's sense of self-esteem, and to transform her way of thinking about herself.

This large purpose inspired a new group called the National Organization for Women (NOW) in 1966, which came together in Betty Friedan's hotel room at a National Conference of State Commissions on Women. The primary goal was to increase pressure in Washington and to "raise consciousness." It met with spectacular success. Friedan herself wrote that "the absolute necessity for a civil rights movement for women had reached such a point of subterranean urgency by 1966, that it took only a few of us to get together to ignite the spark—and it spread like a nuclear chain reaction."[85]

The most important achievement of the new feminist movement was the explosive growth of a new consciousness of freedom for women, and it moved at lightning speed through America and the world. At the same time, the new feminism changed the meaning of freedom itself. The movement took many forms. Some centered their thinking on an idea of equality. But in America, most of it was about issues of freedom and liberty. In its early years, American feminists spoke of their goal as "women's liberation" from what Gerda Lerner summarized as "the suffering of discrimination, inferior rights, indignities, economic exploitation."[86]

In some ways it was similar to older ideas. As early as 1794, William Blake had written in his *Songs of Experience:*

> *In the cry of every man,*
> *In every infant's cry of fear,*

In every voice, in every ban,
The mind-forg'd manacles I hear.

But Betty Friedan's feminism broke new ground in its idea of psychological liberation and "consciousness raising." It was a modern movement for emancipation from "mind-forg'd manacles," grounded in a depth of psychological insight that had developed in the twentieth century.

After Friedan's book appeared, other feminists carried her consciousness raising in different directions. Some were exclusively interested in the condition of women. Others wished to raise the consciousness of men as well. Some were liberal and radical. Sara Evans remembers that among her friends on the far left of the women's movement, "models for consciousness raising ranged from the earliest SNCC meetings, to SDS's 'Guatemala Guerrilla' organizing approach, to the practice of speaking bitterness in the Chinese Revolution."[87]

Others gravitated toward the center or the right. But altogether the new feminists, more than any other movement, worked in highly original ways to liberate women from the shackles of the mind, by collective instruments of consciousness raising. In their means and ends, they created a new vision of liberty and freedom, by developing more fully than ever before the psychological dimension of liberation. They created a model that would be followed by other movements for liberty and freedom in the years to come.

A colorful emblem of feminist consciousness-raising was this image of Ms. Liberty, discarding her brassiere as an emblem of self-inflicted oppression. It appeared on the back cover of Mad *magazine in June 1975. Art by Mutz, idea by Al Jaffee.*

A MURDERED PRESIDENT

Iconic Events in American History

> It seemed then that life changed at that moment.
>
> —ELAINE WETHINGTON, REMEMBERING
> THE MURDER OF JOHN F. KENNEDY

A CRITICAL MOMENT in American history occurred on the afternoon of November 22, 1963. The events of that day might be understood as an historical analogue to what chemists call a change of phase. It happened suddenly, as changes of phase are apt to do, and at a moment when it was least expected.

In most parts of the United States, the afternoon of November 22, 1963, was a warm and sunny day in a season of prosperity and peace. The world economy was flourishing. After a period of severe strain, relations between the United States and the Soviet Union appeared to be improving. A Nuclear Test Ban Treaty had been signed by the great powers in August, ratified by the Senate in September, and accepted by ninety-nine nations when it went into effect on October 10. A problem was growing in Vietnam, where fighting had been going on for nearly twenty years, but in September the president said that it was "their war," and Americans breathed a sigh of relief. The future seemed very bright.

Then, on the afternoon of November 22, 1963, President John F. Kennedy was murdered on a public street in Dallas, Texas. Every American who was then alive remembers the shock of that event. It is a cliché of contemporary history that we all recall exactly where we were and what we were doing when we heard the news from Dallas. Some events have a strange mnemonic power that way. The Japanese attack on Pearl Harbor had that effect. People remembered where they were when the news of that event reached them on December 7, 1941, and they preserved that memory. It was the same for the Lexington Alarm in 1775, and the attack on Fort Sumter in 1861, and the assault on the World Trade Center in 2001.

One might ask why. Part of the answer is that these events caught us by surprise. More than that, they were not only unexpected but unimagined, even unimaginable, before they happened. They were also dramatic events and contingent events, which flowed from individual choices and particular circumstances. Most important, they were instrumental events and transforming events. They changed the course of things, but they did so in different ways.

Some were important as crystallizing events. When people learned of them, the past and future took on new meanings with great clarity. Diaries and letters show that in 1941, during the weeks and months before Pearl Harbor, many Americans came to believe that war was highly probable, and even inevitable, but a cloud of uncertainty loomed over events. Then the war came, in a way that scarcely anyone had anticipated, and many things became clear.

Other events are important in a different way. They are shattering catastrophes that disrupt our understanding of the world and create a

One of the great iconic events in American history was the assassination of President John F. Kennedy on November 22, 1963. The shock of that event was reinforced by other assassinations that followed: the murder of Robert Kennedy, Martin Luther King, and many other civil rights leaders. The victims of this violence became martyrs to liberty and freedom. This textile was dedicated to the memory of Robert F. Kennedy, Martin Luther King, and John F. Kennedy. Virginia Historical Society.

deep sense of confusion and uncertainty. The assassination of John F. Kennedy had that effect. The first moment of shock and horror was followed by a dawning discovery that something had gone profoundly wrong in America, something even more terrible than the event itself.

The more Americans reflected about the assassination of President Kennedy, the greater was that feeling of uncertainty and loss. Nobody was sure who had done it. The right accused the left, and the left suspected the right. Was it the work of one man alone, or a small circle, or a larger group? Was it the KGB or CIA, Cubans or Texans, the Establishment or the Mob? Each of these theories found a following. Even Vice President Lyndon Johnson was thought to have done it in some circles. The more Americans learned about the event, the more they began to doubt their leaders, institutions, ideals, and even themselves.

The scene of the assassination itself and its aftermath was caught on film and lingered in the mind's eye, reinforced by constant repetition. It became an indelible image, and the image became a symbol, and the symbol became an instrument of thought. In all of these ways, this shattering event changed the way that Americans understood their free institutions and how they felt about their world.

For more than twenty years, from Pearl Harbor through much of the Cold War, Americans had been coming together, gravitating toward the political center. After 1963, they began to move apart. The murder of President Kennedy was not the cause, but it was one of a series of polarizing events that turned Americans away from the center, dividing to the left and right. Other divisions appeared in terms of class, race, gender, and age.

Once begun, this dividing time continued through the 1960s and 1970s. So deep were its divisions that Americans are still divided in how they remember it. Some who came of age around the year 1968 remember the period from about 1963 to 1975 (often inaccurately called the sixties) as the best of times, bright with the promise of better things to come. They still think of it as Wordsworth thought of his youth in the era of the French Revolution: "Bliss was it in that dawn to be alive, But to be young was very heaven."[88]

Others of an older generation remember the period from 1963 to 1975 as America's Dark Age, even the nadir of its national existence, when the people of the great republic were riven by age, gender, class, race, and ideology. Some of the deepest divisions were between different visions of liberty and freedom. Once again, as in the painful years of the mid-nineteenth century, freedom and liberty were opposed, in a great struggle that continued many years.

In the reaction to President Kennedy's assassination, liberal causes became more successful than ever before in American history. The five years from 1963 to 1968 were a period of sweeping reform, with new legislation in civil rights, voting rights, social welfare, and environmental movements. Drives for voter registration enfranchised large numbers of African and Hispanic Americans, as well the poor and the young and women, all of whom tended to support liberal causes in greater proportion than older affluent men. The mood of these reform movements was dark, and so was their vision of America. The tone appeared in an image for a registration drive: an American eagle with a tear in its eye.

VOTE, a 1971 record cover, showed the American eagle with a tear in its eye. That image captured the complex mood of the country after the assassinations of the 1960s. The suffering gave rise to a distinct American iconography and inspired new achievements in civil rights and civil liberties. But it also created a dark mood of deep distress, and doubt about the possibilities of change in America. National Museum of American History, Smithsonian Institution.

THE RADICAL RIGHT
Libertarian Visions of Friedrich Hayek & Barry Goldwater

Extremism in defense of liberty is no vice!

—BARRY GOLDWATER, ACCEPTING THE
REPUBLICAN NOMINATION IN 1964

My God! He's going to run as Barry Goldwater!

—AN AMAZED REPORTER

IN REACTION TO expansive movements for liberal reform (Roosevelt's New Deal, Truman's Fair Deal, Kennedy's Great Frontier, Lyndon Johnson's Great Society), a countermovement developed on the American right during the late fifties and early sixties. It was the revival of conservatism as yet another vision of liberty and freedom.

From 1932 to 1952, liberal Democrats held the political initiative for an entire generation. Often their liberal program was strongly opposed. Many members of Congress, both Democrats and Republicans, were deeply conservative. But after the debacle of the Liberty League, Franklin Roosevelt's "broader definition of liberty" and his vision of "a greater freedom, a greater security" dominated political debate. From Wendell Willkie to Dwight Eisenhower, the leaders of the Republican Party were unable to offer a convincing alternative.

This trend was noted by an Austrian-born British economist of strong neoclassical views. Friedrich Hayek expressed amazement that American conservatives had allowed the left to claim the idea of liberty, and he decided to do something about it. In 1944, Hayek published a book called *The Road to Serfdom,* which argued that the new welfare-state liberalism was profoundly dangerous to liberty itself. He argued a simple thesis: that liberty is the right to be "free from coercion" and that economic planning by governments is its greatest enemy in the modern world. Hayek lumped together Fascism, Communism, socialism, and welfare-state liberalism.

He insisted that their different ends mattered less than their common means, which he believed to be profoundly dangerous to a free society.[89]

Hayek had two complaints against government planning of the economy. He insisted that it did not work as efficiently as a free market. He also believed that even well-meaning social programs contained the seeds of a new tyranny that would make people into serfs of a welfare state. Hayek's work was a vision of liberty as independence from big government and economic planning. It was also an idea of freedom as the right of every individual to participate without restraint in a free-market economy and an open society.

The thinking of this European intellectual had its greatest impact in America. *The Road to Serfdom* became a bestseller in the United States and found its most avid readers on the far right. Hayek insisted that he was not a conservative but a classical liberal. He also strongly supported a regulatory role for government to protect liberty and a free market by antitrust actions, by regulation of minimum wages and maximum hours, and by programs that guaranteed the necessities of life for all people. These passages disappeared from some American editions of his book. Friedrich Hayek found in classical liberalism the new vision that American conservatives had long been seeking.[90]

In the United States many conservative movements began to revive during the 1950s and 1960s, at first with small impact on American politics. Part of the problem was that their conservative goals were not the same. At least four major movements appeared on the right. They might be called libertarian conservatism, religious conservatism, racial conservatism, and militant conservatism. They shared a deep commitment to an idea of liberty, intense anti-Communism, antipathy to big government, hostility to what they regarded as America's liberal establishment, and, ironically, a desire for radical change in the American system.[91]

Within this common frame, there were many different conservative ideologies in America. Their agendas overlapped in detail, but each had its own distinct center. The most influential on public policy was libertarian conservatism. In America it went far beyond Hayek in demanding absolute freedom for capitalism, free markets, private ownership, minimal government, and very low taxes. In the 1960s, this way of thinking began to make converts among economists, who shifted from Keynesian models to neoclassical theory. A major center was the University of Chicago. Some of the more dogmatic neoclassical economists demanded privatization of national parks and the armed forces, abolition of Social Security and health care, the end of the income tax, corporate taxes, estate taxes, and similar measures. Few business leaders and no conservative politicians were as relentlessly dogmatic and libertarian as academic economists of the Chicago School.[92]

Another group with a very different set of goals were religious conservatives, who attracted strong popular support from evangelical Protestants, Roman Catholics, and Orthodox Jews, groups that were growing more rapidly than the general population. In some ways their purposes were opposed to libertarian conservatism. They demanded active government intervention to support their ideas of religion and morality. They wanted laws that regulated sexual behavior, forbade abortions, stopped the spread of contraception, and punished homosexuality as a crime. Some wanted prohibition of teaching about evolution, active government funding of churches and church schools, and religious education in public schools.[93]

A third group were racial conservatives. Most of the conservative intelligentsia disowned this idea, but it had strong popular appeal as a reaction against the civil rights movement. This was especially the case throughout the South, where Ulrich Phillips had written that the "central theme of southern history" was a determination that the South should always remain a "white man's country." Racial conservatism attracted large numbers of southern Democrats and was the leading factor in the growth of the Republican Party in the South. It also spread to the northern cities.[94]

Another movement might be called militant conservatism. It centered on the right to keep and bear arms as a protection against criminals and even against government itself. It also valued the martial virtues of courage, honor, discipline, and service to the nation. Some of the most militant groups were small and very extreme, but a larger constituency of hunters and gun collectors strongly sympathized with these ideas and supported conservative candidates. Militant conservatism found strong support among millions of military veterans. Leaders included retired military officers and even some on active duty, such as General Edwin A. Walker.[95]

Many smaller and more extreme conservative groups appeared, some of them intensely racist, anti-Semitic, anti-Catholic, and potentially destructive of conservatism as a whole. The problem was how to organize this movement into a common vision of American conservatism. Part of this work was done by conservative writers, especially William Buckley, who founded *The National Review,* tried to reinforce the central tendencies, and worked to banish fringe groups from the movement. Buckley

helped to found Young Americans for Freedom, a student organization
formed in 1960 at Buckley's home in Connecticut.[96]

A major purpose of these men was to wrest control of the Republican
Party from moderate conservatives who had made their peace with the
New Deal. The critical moment was the election of 1964, and the leader
was Barry Goldwater. He lost the presidential election in that year, but
his supporters gained control of the Republican Party. They developed a
common conservative vision of liberty (more than freedom): free enterprise and minimal government in economics; active regulation on moral
issues; and strict enforcement of law and order. They also gave strong
support to religions of many denominations. [97]

Their tone was radical and utterly uncompromising. In the election of
1964, the emblems of radical conservatism included a striking image of
Barry Goldwater and his slogan: "Extremism in the Defense of Liberty Is
No Vice; Moderation in the Pursuit of Justice Is No Virtue." Other
Goldwater badges proclaimed, "I Am a Right Wing Extremist," "I'm an
Extremist; I Love Liberty," "What's Wrong with Being Right," "Victory
over Communism," and "Goldwater or Socialism." This radical conservatism broke fundamentally with the centrist conventions of American
politics.

A major thrust of Goldwater conservatism was to separate individual
American citizens from their own American government, and especially
from the federal government. It returned to the Ninth and Tenth
Amendments, strict construction of the Constitution, and ideas of small

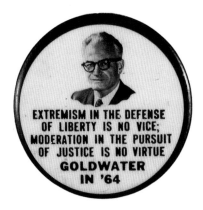

*In the election of 1964, the leaders of the new conservatism gained control of the Republican Party. They
were defeated by Democratic incumbent Lyndon Johnson, but they built a coalition of white southerners,
antigovernment westerners, blue-collar conservatives, and evangelical Christians. Its passion appeared in
Barry Goldwater's campaign buttons. Collection of David J. and Janice L. Frent.*

The new conservatism of the 1960s was in large measure a youth movement. College-age members of Young Americans for Freedom and contributors to the National Review *became leaders of American conservatism and the Republican Party for many years. Time Life Pictures/Getty Images.*

government, even minimal government. The idea of government itself became a great evil. So strong did this habit of thought become that this historian heard President George Bush senior refer to the federal government and his own administration as "Them," even while he lived in the White House.

Radical conservatism generated an array of images and symbols drawn from American history. Favorite historical figures personified a conservative idea of American individualism. Some of these figures, from Daniel Boone to Charles Lindbergh and the first astronauts, were remembered (very inaccurately) as heroic loners. In the twentieth century a favorite icon of conservative liberty was film actor John Wayne, who often played the part of the heroic loner and also appeared in that role at Conservative rallies. Here was another theme: the linkage of conservative libertarianism to American individualism.

At the same time that the new conservatives preached their gospel of liberty as material independence from the government, they also demanded moral restraints to preserve the fabric of a free republic. Goldwater conservatives were strong for "law and order." They wanted moral censorship of the mass media and moral restraints by the government on forms of sexual behavior that they did not approve. They favored restriction of abortion to protect the "right to life" and the "rights of the unborn" but strongly favored a return to capital punishment.

The Democrats in 1964 responded by shifting in a different direction, away from any idea of liberty or freedom. They used advertising techniques to associate Barry Goldwater with nuclear war and mushroom clouds: "Barry G and World War III." Lyndon Johnson made much of his Texas origins and claimed the legacy of the welfare programs of the New Deal, but in the elections of 1964 he and his party made remarkably little reference to liberty or freedom and moved away from those iconic ideas. The Republicans were happy to claim liberty and freedom (mostly liberty) as their own. Democrats allowed them to do so by default, a disastrous error of political judgment from which the Democratic Party would be very slow to recover.

A major factor in American politics is possession of the imagery of liberty and freedom, which has shifted many times from one party to the other. In that respect, a consistent pattern appears throughout American history. The party that has the strongest and most compelling vision of liberty and freedom wins. The party that loses touch with these great principles always falls from power and remains in the wilderness until it returns to the founding principles of the republic. It happened to the Federalists in 1799, Whigs in 1852, Democrats in 1860, Republicans in 1932. In that respect, the election of 1964 was a pivotal moment in American history.

THE NEW LEFT IN THE UNIVERSITIES
SDS and the Free Speech Movement

> We regard men as infinitely precious and possessed of unfulfilled capacities for reason, freedom and love. In affirming these principles we are aware of countering perhaps the dominant conceptions of man in the twentieth century, that he is a thing to be manipulated.
>
> —PORT HURON STATEMENT, JUNE 15, 1962

O N T H E L E F T, other movements multiplied in America during the 1960s and 1970s. One of the most important groups came together at the University of Michigan in 1962. It was a small group of about sixty students who were deeply interested in democratic socialism. With encouragement from labor unions and the old League of Industrial Democracy, they founded their own voluntary association and called themselves Students for a Democratic Society, or SDS.

Their manifesto was a document written by Tom Hayden and called the Port Huron Statement, after the place where they met. Its vision of a free America was very much in the American grain. This was to be a New Left, devoted to the ideal of a just society that respected the independence of individuals. Tom Hayden summarized the central idea in a sentence. He wrote, "We seek the establishment of a democracy of individual participation, governed by two central aims—that the individual share in those social decisions determining the quality and direction of his life; that society be organized to encourage independence in men and to provide the media for their common participation."[98]

The Port Huron Statement was distributed in many thousands of mimeographed copies to colleges throughout the country. The members of SDS undertook community organizing in northern industrial cities, with funding from Walter Reuther and the United Auto Workers. But mainly it remained a small, cerebral academic movement, with a serious

New Left groups multiplied rapidly on college campuses; especially important was the Free Speech Movement at Berkeley in 1964. Collection of Mary Haskell.

interest in solving intellectual problems. Members of SDS were trying to invent a New Left out of American materials and within a tradition of liberty and freedom.

Many New Left movements followed on their example. The Free Speech Movement at Berkeley developed in 1964, fighting censorship within its own university in the name of liberty and freedom. By the mid-1960s, most American colleges had their own array of New Left organizations. In the late 1960s, they grew into larger campus movements, and in 1968 they engaged in strikes and academic insurrections that attacked the universities that sheltered them. One of the largest disturbances was at Columbia University, led by a student named Mark Rudd.

It was a disaster for the New Left. An elder statesman of the old left, John Roche, observed in dismay that the student radicals of 1968 were the first army in history who began their campaign by destroying their own base. Some went farther and advocated the use of violence and terror against other institutions of American society. Students for a Democratic Society came apart in angry disputes over means and ends. One militant group led by Mark Rudd broke away from SDS, called themselves Weathermen after a song by Bob Dylan, and went underground in New

York City. In 1969, they started attacks on police and a terrorist campaign. The only casualties were three of their own members, killed in 1970 while making bombs in Greenwich Village. The Weathermen went to war against the institutions of a free society and suffered the inevitable fate of every American group that has set itself against the central values of American culture.

Others on the American left tried to go a different way. In 1975, a strike in Worthington, Massachusetts, inspired a radical group in the college town of Amherst to engage the American tradition of liberty and freedom in their movement. They called themselves the Amherst Political Workers Collective and claimed a New England heritage of radical action. A poster called "The Liberty Tree" developed their theme of "Old Roots New Roots in Rebellion," from the colonial era and the American Revolution to the twentieth century, all in the cause of a free society. But this was the road not taken by the New Left.

In New England universities, some groups in the New Left built their movement on regional traditions. An example in the Connecticut Valley was the Amherst Political Workers Collective, who drew upon a New England heritage of three centuries. This vision appeared in a poster called The Liberty Tree that supported a strike in Worthington, Massachusetts, in 1975. Collection of Mary Haskell.

DO IT!

The Beat Movement as a Vision of Freedom and Liberty

> Whither goest thou, America, in thy shiny car in
> the night?
>
> —JACK KEROUAC

AS THE RADICAL RIGHT and New Left gained strength, other Americans were on the road, traveling in a different direction. This was mainly a movement of the young, who did not "dig" the ways of their parents. They moved out of the mainstream of middle America and called themselves the "counterculture," but, like every great reform movement in the United States, they shared the national obsession with liberty and freedom and gave these old ideas yet another set of meanings.[99]

The first stirrings of this impulse appeared in the early 1950s in a literature of youthful alienation. J. D. Salinger's *Catcher in the Rye* (1951) had a vogue among highly privileged students in private colleges and preparatory schools. They were taught to believe in liberty and freedom, and yet they felt profoundly unfree. They were raised to think and act as individuals, but they complained of conformity, hypocrisy, censorship. They were the most affluent generation in American history, but they attacked materialism and the tyranny of material things. They were raised to the promise of freedom from fear, but the world seemed more dangerous than ever, with the constant alarms of the Cold War and the growing threat of nuclear annihilation. Some of them began to act on these feelings by living apart from the conventions of the world, and then by thinking and writing and singing about a new vision of liberty and freedom.

At the center was a small circle who found one another in New York

City during the 1950s. In some ways they could not have been more diverse. Jack Kerouac was born Jean Kérouac to poor French Canadian immigrants in the mill city of Lowell, Massachusetts, and raised a devout Catholic, which he always remained. He had many gifts, loved to write, and started a novel in junior high school called *Jack Kerouac Explores the Merrimack,* in the tradition of Thoreau. He was also a superb athlete, a hero in his school and town, and went to Columbia on a football scholarship.[100]

At Columbia, Jack Kerouac met Allen Ginsberg, son of an English professor and a mad housewife, raised in a household full of books and love of learning, but much at odds with the world around him. He was Jewish in a Christian culture, radical in a liberal republic, homosexual in a heterosexual world. In New York City, Ginsberg and Kerouac met William Burroughs, nine years older, raised in wealth, schooled at Harvard, a tall man with a patrician air, but inwardly a dark character who had an obsession with extreme experiences, a compulsion to break every rule, and a genius for expression.[101]

The three of them were working-class Catholic, middle-class Jewish, and upper-class Protestant. They were appalled by American materialism and conformity and inspired by what Ginsberg called the "wild America" and "historic America" of Whitman and Thoreau. All were excited by American idioms of jazz, with its spontaneous flow of creativity. They were fascinated by the New York underworld of criminals, street people, and Broadway "hipsters." Their heroes and models included an existential car thief named Neil Cassady and a charming murderer named Lucien Carr. All were seekers after liberty and freedom, in a world that could never be free enough for them. Neil's long-suffering wife Carolyn Cassady, who mothered them all, wrote, "As far as I could see, they all believed that the purpose of life was spontaneous 'experience,' so at least they had that."[102]

Jack Kerouac called his friends "beats," a word of many meanings. He used it to mean "poor, down and out, deadbeat, on the bum, sleeping in subways." It also meant "beatific" from his Catholic boyhood. At the same time, it meant in his words "a kind of beatness. . . a weariness with all the forms, all the conventions of the world." He told his friend John Clellon Holmes, "You might say we're a beat generation," and Holmes wrote an article in 1952 called "This Is the Beat Generation."[103]

The beats traveled back and forth across America, experimented with drugs and drink, talked of Buddhism and William Blake, and began to write compulsively, mostly about their own experiences. In 1951, Jack

Yet another American vision of liberty and freedom emerged from the "beat generation" in the 1950s and 1960s. Their prophet was Jack Kerouac, a gifted, prolific and highly disciplined writer, here gazing at his own reflection in a storefront window in Manhattan during the autumn of 1953, which Allen Ginsberg remembered as the "time of Subterranean writing." Photograph by Allen Ginsberg. Corbis.

Kerouac resolved to do a series of books about himself and his friends, a "continuous narrative" of their adventures. He retreated to a loft in New York, writing frantically with a pile of benzedrine tablets by his side. In three weeks he wrote a novel on a roll of teletype paper, which a friend described as "a single-spaced unbroken paragraph 120 feet long." Published as *On the Road* in 1957, it was instantly praised as a major work, reviled by the New Critics, and celebrated as a bestseller. Among the young it gained a large and devoted following.[104]

His friend and biographer Ann Charters observed that young people read *On the Road* "not as literature but as an adventure." They "recognized that Kerouac was on their side, the side of youth and freedom, riding with Cassady over American highways chasing after the great American adventure—freedom and open spaces, the chance to be yourself, to be free." She understood it as a special "vision of freedom, a return to the solipsistic world of childhood, to an irresponsibility so complete that no other world could ever intrude for long."[105]

That was part of it, but Kerouac combined his drive to be a free with a remarkable discipline. In the ten years after *On the Road* he wrote fifteen novels, which required discipline, *Sitzfleisch,* and serious labor. The editor of his papers was amazed to find that "his study was a meticulously preserved literary archive, as carefully organized as archives I used . . . at

Columbia," with annotated copies of his correspondence. He also brought another kind of discipline to his work. Jack Kerouac's novels were meant to be a history of the beats. Close students have found that he was very accurate, kept "detailed journal notes," and "omitted facts rather than invent them."[106]

Jack Kerouac sought liberty on the open road but also freedom in his communion with other free spirits. This other side of the movement appeared when his beat friends found a home in San Francisco. The pivotal moment came on the evening of October 13, 1955, in the Six Gallery, a former automobile repair shop on San Francisco's Fillmore Street, where Kenneth Rexroth, "father of the Frisco poetry scene," invited five young poets to present their work. Together they represented the diversity of this movement and what Ginsberg called their "revolutionary individuality." One of them was Michael McClure, who read his mystic-ecological poems "Point Lobos" and "For the Death of 100 Whales." Philip Whalen recited "mystical-anarchic" verse. Philip Lamantia was a surrealist poet who celebrated a friend who had died of drugs. Gary Snyder read "The Berry Feast," about tribal rituals of communal belonging. The climax was Allen Ginsberg's poem "Howl," which began with a lament: "I saw the best minds of my generation destroyed by madness." Ginsberg raged against their destroyer, the monstrous "Moloch" of American society. He ended by celebrating "angel-headed hipsters" who found another path and a creed that promised deliverance: "Everything is holy! everybody's holy! everywhere is holy! everyday is eternity."[107]

Ginsberg chanted his lines like a Jewish cantor, while Jack Kerouac sat on the stage, pounding on an empty wine jug and shouting, "Go go go." The crowd took up the cry, and the evening ended in tears of exaltation. These young fugitives believed that they invented a new world of freedom. Others thought they had outraged decency and broken the law. Ginsberg's "Howl" was banned as obscene, which greatly increased its

Another leader of the Beat Generation was Allen Ginsberg, here reading to a crowd in New York's Washington Square Park, August 28, 1966, after a state court decision that allowed poets to read freely in public parks without censorship. Ginsberg joined that idea of liberty of expression to a vision of freedom as the right to commune with others. AP/Wide World Photos.

impact. Its author fought many battles for "liberty of speech" against a crumbling regime of censorship.[108]

Allen Ginsberg also had a vision of freedom, which appeared in a personal Declaration of Independence on July 4, 1959. It was another howl against "an America gone mad with materialism, a police-state America, a sexless and soulless America." It also celebrated "the wild and beautiful America" and "historic America" of Whitman and Thoreau. It glorified the "few individuals, poets," who "have had the luck and courage and fate to glimpse something new." This was a vision of "spiritual independence" where "each individual was an America," and the universe was "more huge and awesome than all the abstract bureaucracies and authoritative official-doms of the world combined."

Ginsberg's personal Declaration of Independence was also about freedom to use "opiates and junk" and any "vision-producing agent." It was the freedom of all people "to loaf, think, rest in visions, act beautifully on their own, speak truthfully in public, inspired by democracy." It was freedom to publish without censorship, "to determine our mode of consciousness," to experience "our sexual enjoyments." Most of all it was freedom to enter "the world of the spirit."

All this was similar in some respects to the writings of William Burroughs, of whom it was said that "the primary theme running through both his life and his work was resistance to all threats against personal liberty." His writings were described as "instruction on how to frustrate the mechanisms of control that rob us of freedom."[109]

Jack Kerouac, as always, went his own way. As most of the beats moved to the left, Kerouac appalled his many admirers by rebelling against the revolution and becoming an enthusiastic admirer of the squarest man in America, neoconservative William Buckley. Kerouac explained, "I'm pro-American and the radical political involvements seem to tend elsewhere." His biographer added, "Kerouac couldn't join forces with the anarchist radicals or the Liberal Left, and he wouldn't attend the conservatives' fundraising dinners. . . . There was only one solution, to drop out in the great American tradition of Thoreau, Mark Twain and Daniel Boone." Jack Kerouac retreated to a dark room in St. Petersburg, Florida, and drank himself to death in 1969. He was forty-seven years old.[110]

STONE FREE

Hippie Dreams: Individual Liberation & Communal Freedom

> Selected Hippie names in order of popularity: Rainbow, Sky, Dharma, Moonbeam, Harmony, Hope, Love, Free, Freedom, Joy, Lily, Peace, Earth, Kharma, Lennon, Dylan, Janis.
>
> —WWW.HIPPY.COM/HIPPYNAMES

IN THE SIXTIES, Allen Ginsberg's "angel-headed hipsters" grew into the hippie movement. Many hippie heroes remembered Kerouac's *On the Road* and Ginsberg's "Howl" as formative experiences in their early youth. They shared some of the same impulses, but they were another American generation. Born in the 1940s or 1950s, the hippies came of age in the troubled times of Vietnam. Where the beats had reacted against American conformity and consensus in the postwar years, the hippies emerged in a country that seemed to be coming apart. They thought of themselves as constructing a "counterculture," with a distinctive "lifestyle" that was an alternative to a society that wasn't working very well. To that end, hippies created their own visions of liberty and freedom.

These new visions combined several strong themes. One of them was an emancipation of the spirit. It sought a new kind of liberty in the intoxication of the senses, through hallucinogenic drugs, rock music, and sexual experiment. These visions were expressed in new genres of psychedelic art, with floating forms and intense acrylic colors. They inspired new symbols of spiritual liberation and new uses for old symbols. A favorite image was the freedom bird, which combined the middle European tradition of *Vogelfreiheit* and the Afro-Indian motifs of a West Indian folk song, with such success that it was instantly co-opted by the corporate executives of an American airline.[111]

Part of the movement was intensely individualist. It encouraged every

The beat writers inspired a larger hippie movement, which created psychedelic images of inner liberty and outward freedom in communes and happenings. One of its emblems was a psychedelic freedom bird that is also a bird of peace. Those two causes appeared together in a hippie poster, ca. 1970. Collection of Mary Haskell.

person to "do your own thing." A popular slogan was "Turn on, tune in, drop out." Expressions of individual autonomy flourished in bizarre and creative forms of dress, manners, speech, art, music, furniture, and housing. Here was an idea of liberty as autonomy.[112]

Another part was strongly communitarian. The hippie movement invited others to "get on the bus," in Ken Kesey's phrase, and sought harmony of the spirit through unity with others. Hippies invented new forms of group consciousness. They created utopias, communes, love-ins, be-ins, and gatherings of kindred souls. This was a new version of freedom as belonging to a community and even a communion of free spirits.[113] An important element of the hippie movement was about "networking," which linked individuals and groups in a great web of communication. Hippies began with bulletin boards and underground newspapers that spread the word. They moved quickly into the Internet; some of them helped to invent it.[114]

A major hippie theme in an age of trouble and violence was heartfelt yearning for peace: nuclear peace, peace in Vietnam, peace between nations, peace among families, and peace within the soul. The favorite hippie salutation was the simple greeting, "Peace." The rallying cries of the movement were "Peace and Freedom," "Peace and Love."

Hippies thought of themselves as a revolutionary movement. Some of their "straight" contemporaries were frightened by their wild appearance, but this was not a revolution through violence. It was to be a revolution through love and togetherness. Hippies believed that sex and nudity were more subversive of the establishment than guns and bombs. They fought against war by organizing the Bare Breasts for Peace Brigade. The Shiva Fellowship in San Francisco practiced "immediate nudity as resistance to hostile cops at public demonstrations."[115] One hippie wrote in 1968, "If I have any liberty at all, I have the liberty to be naked. . . . If the state shall deny me this right, then it may deny me any other right it sees fit."

Nudity also became an idea of freedom, as a way of removing obstacles to communication among free spirits, and achieving "communion with all of God's creations."[116]

The hippie movement was deeply spiritual and religious. It embraced Christ as a teacher and example. Eastern religions were a prominent part of it. So was astrology and the idea of a New Age of Aquarius; so were all manner of pantheistic dreams. Much of its iconography consisted of spiritual and religious symbols as instruments of escape from the troubles of the world.

All of these visions were one in an expanding idea of "togetherness." The movement itself became its own largest symbol in huge spontaneous gatherings. One of them happened at San Francisco's Golden Gate Park in January 1967, where a large crowd celebrated the drug cult of psychologist Timothy Leary and chemist Augustus Owsley Stanley III. The largest of these iconic events was the Woodstock Festival on August 15–17, 1969, when four hundred thousand young people gathered on a dairy farm in Bethel, New York, for three days and nights of music and "togetherness." The promoters who organized the event lost control of it and were overwhelmed by vast crowds who jammed the roads for miles around with battered Volvos, ancient pickups, bright painted Volkswagens, and psychedelic buses.[117]

It was a gathering of all the hippie tribes: peaceniks with love beads and Vietnam vets in khaki, black nationalists and racist rednecks, gays and straights, urban communards and rural utopians, acid droppers and eco-hippies, potheads and purity freaks. The music they came to hear was another indicator of how the movement had expanded from the small circle of the beats. The Woodstock crowds heard folksingers Joan Baez and Arlo Guthrie. They listened to the sitar music of great Indian artist Ravi Shankar; the soft rock of Crosby, Stills, and Nash; the hard rock of the Grateful Dead and the Who; the blues of Janis Joplin and the guitar of Jimi Hendrix. Most of the Woodstock performers had urgent messages about liberty and freedom, and two especially: Janis Joplin and Jimi Hendrix.

In 1969, Janis Joplin was the high priestess of hip. Born and raised in Port Arthur, Texas, she grew up hard and tough, moved in and out of colleges and communes, and stayed briefly at the University of Texas in Austin, where she drank heavily, dealt drugs, and got herself elected the ugliest man on campus. Somewhere along the way she read an article in *Time* magazine about Jack Kerouac and the beats, and she went on the road to San Francisco.[118] Her passion was music, especially the blues, most of all the blues of Odetta and Bessie Smith, and she found a calling in their example. She invented a unique style of shrieks and wails and

A living symbol of the hippie movement was the great blues singer Janis Joplin, who sang its new anthem of freedom in the Kris Kristofferson ballad "Me and Bobby McGee": "Freedom's just another word for nothin' left to lose." Corbis.

Ginsbergian howls that had an apparent spontaneity but were in fact the product of careful study and controlled discipline. Janis Joplin deliberately set out to make herself a great blues singer in the idiom of her own generation, and she reached her goal. Success came suddenly at the Monterey Festival in 1967.[119]

Janis Joplin made herself into a hippie symbol and was renowned for her appearance and lifestyle. She hid herself behind big hair, enormous dark glasses, layers of colorful extravagant clothing, big bell bottoms, and body tattoos. She lost herself in casual sex, drugs, and drink and was often stoned in her performances. Always she insisted that she was not a hippie but a beat. She explained, "Beatniks believe things aren't going to get any better and say the hell with it, stay stoned, and have a good time." She studied her art and lived for the moment. "Get it while you can." she said. "You can destroy your now, by worrying about tomorrow."[120]

This dark vision of freedom was the theme of her best-known song, Kris Kristofferson's "Me and Bobby McGee." Many others sang it, but Janis made it her own, and one line in particular: "Freedom's just another word for nothin' left to lose." The composer was asked what it meant. Kristofferson answered, "I was writing about the irony of personal freedom. It's like a two edged sword. The freer you are the lonelier you are. But it's something that I need." It was the story of Janis Joplin's life. She said, "Onstage I make love to twenty-five thousand people, then I go home alone." In 1970, Janis Joplin died in a Hollywood motel from an overdose of heroin. She was twenty-seven years old.[121]

If Janis Joplin was the hippie queen, the king was Jimi Hendrix, who also sang a song of freedom. His friend Curtis Knight wrote that Jimi Hendrix was "sent from another time and place to give us a message of love, peace and freedom." He was born in the Pacific Northwest, joined the Army, became a paratrooper, hurt his leg in a jump and was honorably discharged, then made a career of music. He was a guitarist of extraordinary talent, who loved every kind of music from Bach to rock and back again and was highly inventive in his performances. Always he was a restless soul, and his life was a whirl of cities, costumes, drugs, and

Another hippie symbol was Jimi Hendrix, who sang a song of freedom: "Stone Free." He lived by that vision, in which stone freedom became a compulsion that destroyed the dream he espoused. Photograph of Hendrix and friends, Toronto, 1969. Image donated by Corbis/Bettmann.

many women. One of his lovers, Kathy Etchingham, said, "Jimi was totally free like the wind. To have tried to possess him would have been like putting a wild bird in a cage."[122]

He wrote a visionary song about his way of life, called "Stone Free." It was a celebration of absolute liberty to do whatever he pleased, to go where he wished, and to keep moving—as free as the wind. There was a strange compulsion in this life of stone freedom, and it came to an end in a London hotel room, where Jimi Hendrix died of asphyxiation, with a heavy overdose of barbiturates in his body.[123]

An epitaph for Janis Joplin and Jimi Hendrix was written by Jerry Rubin, who remarked that "politics is how you live your life." To the many on the right, beats and hippies and the New Left seemed anarchic, irresponsible, self-destructive, and profoundly un-American, even anti-American. But they were quintessentially American in their obsession with liberty and freedom, and they made a difference in the world. Allen Ginsberg once observed, "Artists, to my mind, are the real architects of change." So it was for their generation and ours as well. Millions of Americans who did not turn on, tune in, or "drop out" lived their own lives differently as a consequence, and America itself became a little more open and free.[124]

THE VIETNAM WAR & THE PEACE MOVEMENT
Freedom and Liberty as a Flower and a Flag

> This is not a jungle war, but a struggle for freedom on every front.
>
> —LYNDON JOHNSON, 1964

> Peace and Freedom.
>
> —HIPPIE RALLYING CRY

I N 1965, a civil war in Vietnam exploded into a world conflict between world powers, in which China, the Soviet Union, and most of all the United States became deeply involved. Americans were amazed to find themselves in yet another major struggle on the Asian mainland. It grew from a dilemma of containment and a cascading failure of American leadership, after the retirement of the Wise Men. Part of it was the incompetence of an American ambassador in Saigon and other officials who recklessly involved their nation in a military coup that was illegal, immoral, and disastrous in its consequences. Another part of this disaster was a failure of military leaders who misjudged the war and then mismanaged it. The largest failure was that of President Lyndon Johnson, the weakest American war leader since the War of 1812. During his tenure, the war in Vietnam went careening out of control.

At the same time, the economy also went wrong. Price inflation began to accelerate throughout the world as early as 1962, and in the United States from 1965. Neoclassical economists profoundly misunderstood its cause. Working within narrow econometric models, they erroneously believed that inflation was the result of American monetary policy, public spending on the Vietnam War, and economic expansion in the United States. In fact, the long inflation rose from a global surge in aggregate demand, caused by a world population explosion and by new standards of freedom and social justice, which recognized that even the poor had a

642

right to the necessities of life. As a result of this economic misunder-standing, the Treasury Department and the Federal Reserve Board responded by "cooling the economy," which made things worse. They did not slow inflation, which had a different cause and kept accelerating in sharp surges until rates of population growth began to decline. But America's economic leaders succeeded in driving their economy into a long decline that combined the worst of both worlds: inflation and reces-sion. The cost of living and unemployment increased rapidly; and social tensions began to grow.[125]

These troubles reached a peak in 1968, which was by any standard one of the most troubled moments in American history. The year began with the seizure of USS *Pueblo* by North Korea on January 23 and the Tet Offensive in Vietnam on January 31. North Vietnamese and Viet Cong forces suffered heavy tactical defeats, but the event persuaded many Americans that the war in southeast Asia could not be won, except by an effort that the Johnson administration was unable to make.

Then came the assassination of Martin Luther King on April 4, 1968, and the murder of Robert Kennedy on June 5. The spring brought a wave of student rebellions in American colleges. The summer saw the worst urban rioting in American history and unprecedented political violence outside the Democratic National Convention in Chicago, in which radical groups rioted against the police and then the police rioted against the radicals. It was a global crisis in many nations but especially severe in the United States. In 1968, the nation reeled under one blow after another. One of the more gen-tle cartoons from this unhappy era showed Uncle Sam and Miss Lib-erty as pathetic and bewildered figures, dodging a barrage of abuse that was hurled at them from every direction.[126]

These troubles grew partly from the corrosive effect of the Cold War on the United States. By 1968, this

"Freedom and Peace," painting on paper by He Qi, ca. 2000. Courtesy of the artist.

great struggle had continued more than twenty years. The American policy of containment had largely succeeded in stopping the spread of totalitarian Communism, but at heavy cost. In 1968, Americans under the age of forty had known nothing in their lives but war and the threat of war. A peace movement began to organize against the war in Vietnam. Two symbolic images defined it. One was a crowd of antiwar protesters, facing a line of soldiers in Washington with weapons at the ready. The protesters placed flowers in the muzzles of the rifles.

The other image appeared on April 15, 1967, when a large rally of young students was organized against the Vietnam War in New York's Central Park. It reached its climax in the ritual burning of an American flag. An infuriated Congress responded in 1968 with a new flag law, which required that anyone who "knowingly casts contempt upon any flag of the United States by publicly mutilating, defacing, defiling, burning or trampling" could be jailed for a year or fined a thousand dollars or both. The predictable result was a great wave of flag-burnings, followed by more than a thousand flag prosecutions, mostly under state law. Icons of freedom and liberty that had long been treated with reverence were now reviled and burned and desecrated, not only by foreign mobs but by young Americans.[127]

The nation watched these scenes on its television sets and found itself divided in a new way. On one side were militant and increasingly radical young people who thought of themselves as heralds of a new age. On the

A Peace March on the Pentagon in 1967 produced this indelible image of a disciplined military formation with weapons at the ready. A solitary demonstrator came forward and placed a flower in the muzzle of each weapon, and a harried lieutenant removed the flowers, one by one. It was a vision of freedom and peace in the demonstrator, and of respect for civil liberty in an establishment that allowed its critics an extraordinary liberty to protest as they pleased. Photograph by Bernie Boston, October 21, 1967. Washington Star/ Washington Post.

other were veterans of earlier wars who thought of the young as spoiled children who demanded all of the privileges of a free society but accepted none of its responsibilities. On both sides it was a period of high creativity for images of liberty and freedom.[128]

In the peace movement, one of the most eloquent voices belonged to Robert Zimmerman. He was born in 1941 and raised in the iron-range town of Hibbing, Minnesota. With many others of his generation he was deeply influenced by beat writers and popular music, especially American folk music. In 1961, he dropped out of the University of Minnesota after one semester, changed his name to Bob Dylan (after the poet Dylan Thomas and western television hero Matt Dillon), and traveled east to visit his hero Woody Guthrie and to become a songwriter and folksinger. His first album in 1962 was an act of homage to Guthrie and American folk music. The second, *Freewheelin' Bob Dylan* in 1963, consisted of his own songs. They were all about freedom. Dylan explained that his purpose was "not protest for protest's sake, but always in the struggle for freedom, individual and otherwise. I hate oppression."

Bob Dylan's songs were both testimony and argument. They argued that the only hope for humanity was a new generation of liberated youth. He told the young generation that they could save the planet by doing their thing.[130] One of his admirers, Todd Gitlin, explained what their message meant to him. For Gitlin it was a "lilt of absolute liberty in an infinite present time severed from the past; this was the transcendent fan-

Hardhats for War were less tolerant of the peace movement than was the Pentagon or the Johnson administration. Throughout the Vietnam War, polls showed that a silent majority of most Americans supported the war, and believed that it was necessary to their idea of a free world. New York City, May 1970. Image donated by Corbis/Bettmann.

tasy of the wholly abstractly free individual, . . . liberated to the embrace of nature and the wonder of essential things, in an America capable of starting the world again."[131]

Nobody had a greater impact on young people in the 1960s than Bob Dylan. The Woodstock Census asked a large sample of that generation who they "most admired and were influenced by." At the top of a long list were the Beatles (76 percent) and Bob Dylan (72 percent), followed by Martin Luther King (62 percent). Near the bottom were Lyndon Johnson (5 percent) and Richard Nixon and Nelson Rockefeller, who were tied with Lieutenant William Calley of My Lai (3 percent).[132] Young Americans copied Dylan's rumpled blue jeans, leather motorcycle jacket, boots, and laborer's cap. They imitated his strange idea of proletarian speech. Todd Gitlin recalled, "We followed his career as if he were singing our song; we got in the habit of asking where he was taking us next."[133]

BLACK POWER, WHITE BACKLASH

Freedom as a Clenched Fist

> There is a place in Mississippi called Liberty
> There is a department in Washington called Justice
>
> —SIGN IN SNCC OFFICE,
> JACKSON, MISSISSIPPI, 1963

IN THE SPRING OF 1961, two hundred young black leaders met in Raleigh, North Carolina, to talk about a strategy for civil rights. They heard Dr. Martin Luther King Jr. invite them to join his non-violent movement and get themselves arrested. His strategy was to force a choice upon the South: either fill its jails to overflowing with its own youth or give way on Jim Crow. Then two militant leaders, Ella Baker and James Lawson, said that the ministers and NAACP were not radical enough. They urged an independent student movement.

The result was the Student Non-Violent Coordinating Committee, always spoken of as "the SNCC" and pronounced Snick. Its members worked tirelessly throughout the South, organizing voter drives and marches for integration. They were arrested so many times that they lost count and were brutally assaulted as they stood or sat together, chanting, "Free-dom, Free-dom," over and over again.

They were different from Martin Luther King. The SNCC put heavy emphasis on equality, more so than other civil rights groups. At its rallies, two different visions appeared in its imagery. One black demonstrator wore a hard hat labeled "Freedom." A white demonstrator appeared with a mathematical equality sign written on his forehead. These were the two faces of the SNCC.[134]

Some members of the SNCC also found the path of nonviolence very difficult, even impossible. An argument developed about that between

Growing divisions disrupted the civil rights movement after 1963. One face of the movement was an African American demonstrator in a hard hat blazoned with Martin Luther King's rallying cry: freedom. Another face was a white worker in the new Congress of Racial Equality, his ideology written on his forehead in the mathematical symbol for equality. Photographs by Flip Schulke.

two leaders of the SNCC. One of them was John Lewis, chairman of the SNCC in 1963. He was born in Alabama, raised to southern manners, a strong Christian, and a veteran of many sit-ins and freedom rides. He was severely beaten by southern mobs but remained a strong believer in nonviolence, integration, and liberal reform.

The other leader was Stokely Carmichael, born in Trinidad, raised in Harlem and the East Bronx, a student of Darwin and Marx, secular and

In 1966, Stokely Carmichael grew weary of nonviolence after his 27th arrest and many beatings. He rallied young radicals to a new vision of freedom through Black Power and violence against violence. He also became an outspoken Marxist and an angry critic of American institutions. Many of his generation raised hands in his support. Los Angeles, November 26, 1966. Image donated by Corbis/Bettmann.

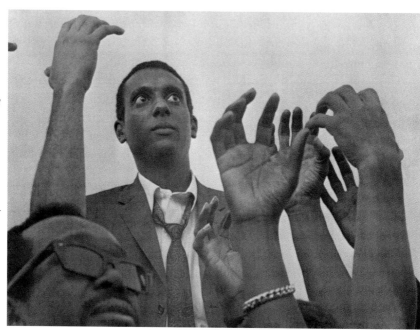

very militant. He also was on the freedom rides and went to jail in Mississippi's infamous Parchman Prison. In a Mississippi voter drive he organized the Lowndes County Freedom Party. Required by state law to have a symbol on the ballot, he chose a black panther.

In 1966 Stokely Carmichael was arrested yet again in Greenwood, Mississippi, roughed up, and then released. Before a crowd of three thousand people he spoke angrily of his arrest: "This is the twenty-seventh time. I ain't going to jail no more. We've been saying 'Freedom' for six years. What we are going to start saying now is 'Black Power.'" The crowd instantly took up the phrase and began to chant it, and it grew into a great roar: "Black Power! Black Power!" Stokely Carmichael was not the first to use that phrase. Black editors such as John Mitchell of the *Richmond Planet* had employed it as early as 1907. But Stokely Carmichael made it the mantra of a new movement, and it reverberated through the country.[135]

Carl Louis's vision of free America received less attention than those of Black Power and black separatists. But one very powerful image was created by photographer Ron Borowski in 1968. It showed a middle-class African American, in a button-down shirt, suit, and tie. One side of his face was painted as an American flag with colors reversed. Above was the Pledge of Allegiance, ending with its words "liberty and justice for all." It is an image of civic ambivalence—of two identities, both strongly held.

The meaning of Black Power was complex and ambiguous in many ways, sometimes deliberately so. Stokely Carmichael always spoke of it as another path to freedom. He told a group of high school students, "Nobody gives anybody their freedom. People can only deny somebody their freedom. ... They don't give us anything! You've got to get that clear in your mind."[136]

I pledge allegiance to the flag of the United States of America and to the republic for which it stands, indivisible, with liberty and justice for all.

Most African Americans went a different way. They also were weary of the racism and violence but chose to work within the system. It was a difficult position, full of deep ambivalence. An image was this poster inspired by a Ron Borowski's photograph in 1965. The poster was called "I Pledge Allegiance," and it showed a middle-class African American in a business suit, with half of his face painted in the colors of the American flag. Above his head were the words "with liberty and justice for all." Collection of Mary Haskell.

Black Power also meant the "coming together of black people to fight for their liberation by any means necessary." Black Power meant inner strength, a pride in blackness, and black culture.

Always it meant violence against violence. Carmichael said, 'Yeah, I'm violent. Somebody touch me, I'll break their arm." It meant "hitting back white people when they hit you." Often it was a revolutionary idea: "Law and order without justice ain't nothing but fascism." Sometimes Black Power became black racism. Carmichael told huge crowds, "The honkies don't have love, can't spell nonviolence, don't know what religion is all about, and you know they ain't got rhythm. But they have power, that's what they have. Power over our lives! So we got to get it clear; the thing we need is power."[137]

Carmichael was elected chairman of the SNCC and put his idea of Black Power to work. He insisted that whites must leave the organization and refused even to talk to white reporters. John Lewis remembered, "That statement on the part of Stokely Carmichael was not a wise one. I opposed that, but I lost out. And that was one of the reasons I was elected and deelected as president of the SNCC. The early days of the student movement, we made a commitment to integration, to the idea of the beloved community. I took a position then, and I take it today."

Lewis followed his vision of freedom to a different goal: integration, reform within the system, voter education projects, cooperation with Jimmy Carter, a seat on the Atlanta City Council and election to the U.S. Congress, where he became a national leader for integration and civil rights and liberal reform.[138]

Carmichael's Black Power deeply divided the movement. Martin Luther King gently called it "an unfortunate choice of words." Civil rights leaders condemned it as racism in reverse. But many young African Americans were strongly drawn to the ideas of Black Power, black nationalism, and black separatism. They wore combat fatigues, jump boots, and black berets, and carried unloaded weapons as symbols of their cause. They followed Stokely Carmichael, but it was hard to keep up with him. In 1967, he traveled abroad to Communist countries, urged American blacks to become "urban guerrillas" and ready themselves for a "fight to the death." He was asked to leave the SNCC and joined the Black Panthers, then broke with them as well. In 1969, he moved to Guinea, a Marxist dictatorship, changed his name to Kwame Ture, went deep into Marxist-Leninism, and died at the age of fifty-seven.[139]

Stokely Carmichael's vision of Black Power intersected with other trends in American cities. On August 11, 1965, a white policeman in Los

Angeles arrested a young black man for a traffic violation. It happened in the sprawling black ghetto of Watts, and an angry crowd began to gather. Tempers flared, and some in the crowd attacked the policeman. The fight grew into a riot, which exploded into a firestorm of violence. Enraged black mobs set fire to their own neighborhood, shouting "Burn, whitey, burn!" A week later thirty-four people (mostly black) were dead, four thousand were arrested, and much of Watts was in ruins.[140]

Another movement of black militancy was led by Malcolm Little. While in prison for robbery, he converted to Islam and took the name of Malcolm X. His road to freedom was black nationalism and separatism. He was moving toward another and more inclusive idea when he was assassinated in Harlem in 1965. New York City, August 6, 1963. AP/Wide World Photos.

In the next three years similar scenes occurred in most American cities. Mobs shouting for Black Power set fire to stores, public buildings, even their own homes. In 1966, an insurrection in Chicago was in some ways worse than that in Los Angeles. In 1967, a rising in Detroit was bigger than both combined and could be controlled only by the intervention of the U.S. Army. The worst violence followed the assassination of Martin Luther King in 1968, when riots broke out in 129 American cities.

As divisive as these acts of collective violence may have been, solitary acts of symbolic action captured the attention of the media. In 1968, the Olympic Games were held in Mexico City. Prominent on a strong American team were two black sprinters, Tommie Smith and John Carlos. Both were members of a group called the Olympic Protest for Human Rights. In the 200-meter dash, Tommie Smith won the gold medal with a new world record and John Carlos took the bronze. In the medal ceremony, both men mounted the dais in bare feet, wearing the badges of the civil rights movement. When "The Star-Spangled Banner" was played, Smith and Carlos bowed their heads, and each raised one hand in a black glove, with the fist clenched in the Black Power salute. Later they told reporters that their bare feet were a symbol of black poverty in America,

The open hands of Stokely Carmichael's followers became the clenched fists of these black athletes, Tommie Smith and John Carlos, at the Olympic Games in 1968. They were expelled from the games. The world press supported them; Americans were bitterly divided. Freedom became a clenched fist on every side of the question. Mexico City, October 16, 1968. Image donated by Corbis/Bettmann.

and the clenched fist was an emblem of black unity and strength. They explained that they bowed their heads during the national anthem because America was free for whites only.[141]

Many people supported them. Australian runner Greg Norman, who finished second in the same event, wore a Black Power badge as a token of sympathy. The world press was generally positive. But the Olympic Committees were outraged by what they saw as an intrusion of politics on the Games (the intrusion of conservative politics had never bothered them). The two black athletes were suspended from international competition and given forty-eight hours to leave Mexico.[142]

In the United States, reactions were deeply divided. Smith and Carlos became heroes in black ghettos, but white journalists made them pariah figures, and they were pilloried in the press. One sportswriter called them "black-skinned storm troopers." Their careers were ruined, and for many years they were unable to find good jobs in athletics. They became symbols and victims of racial conflict and media tyranny in America.[143]

Other events severely damaged what little remained of racial comity in America. A small group of black radicals persuaded themselves that a campaign of destruction against the most beloved icons of American liberty and freedom would promote their cause. In 1965, leaders of the Black Liberation Front planned to attack the Statue of Liberty with bombs. Their purpose was to blow up the head and torch of the "old bitch," as they called her.[144] They did not succeed and were condemned by most black leaders. But moderate mainstream civil rights leaders also turned away from the old American icons. Atlanta's mayor Andrew Young remarked, "No one in the black community is really excited about the Statue of Liberty. We came here on slave ships, not via Ellis Island." These statements caused white liberals to despair and conservative racists to rejoice. They contributed to an angry backlash that turned many moderate Americans to the right.[145]

Backlash: Liberty from Busing and Freedom for White Neighborhoods

In the North, a white backlash began to spread very rapidly, especially after the reformers adopted compulsory busing as a way of integrating neighborhood schools. Some of the worst scenes happened in Boston, when a federal judge who lived in the lace-curtain suburb of Wellesley ordered the integration of Boston's inner-city schools by forced busing of children over long distances through the city.[146]

On the morning of April 5, 1976, an angry crowd of high school students from Irish Catholic neighborhoods of South Boston and Charlestown marched on Boston's City Hall. One of the demonstrators was a student named Joseph Rakes, who lived with his large family in a South Boston tenement. Life was not easy for them. The collapse of the American economy had fallen hard on their neighborhood. Joseph Rakes's father was hard-pressed to put food on the table. Many people turned to crime simply to survive. Joseph Rakes's brother went to jail for armed robbery.[147]

In a conversation with *Boston Globe* reporter Thomas Farragher, who reconstructed the story twenty-five years later, Rakes remembered, "I was too angry with everybody. I didn't like anybody. I didn't care for anybody. I took care of my family, I watched out for my brothers and sisters and my relatives and my friends. We all watched out for each other." His brother Robert remembered that their father was strong against busing, as were most in South Boston. "My parents kind of raised us to be pit bulls," he explained to Farragher. "People in Southie sent their kids out there and said, 'go get 'em.'"[148]

Young Joseph Rakes led the march on City Hall, carrying a big American flag, which stood for their liberty not to be bul-

Artist Tomi Ungerer created a commentary on these conflicts in a poster called "Black Power/White Power," which showed the defenders of both ideas devouring one another. It is reproduced with the kind permission of the owner, Mary Haskell, and Diogenes Verlag AG, Zurich.

lied or bused. It also was about their freedom to belong to the tight-knit community of South Boston. At City Hall the students met City Council President Louise Day Hicks, an outspoken enemy of busing. She invited the students into the Council Chamber. While Joseph Rakes held the flag, the students recited the Pledge of Allegiance and repeated its promise of freedom and justice for all. They left more angry than ever, outraged that their rights had been trampled by a federal judge from out of town.

The students left the building and walked into the new City Hall Plaza, a barren concrete wasteland of brutal modern architecture. A group of counterdemonstrators heckled them. Then a black man appeared in their path. He looked prosperous, middle class, and well dressed in a three-piece suit. His name was Theodore Landsmark, he was twenty-nine, and his life had been transformed by busing and affirmative action. The son of a subway conductor in New York City, he had been raised by his grandmother, was bused from Harlem to a mostly white school, and went on to St. Paul's School and Yale. He got a job as executive director of an affirmative action program that sought business for minority contractors, which had brought him to City Hall Plaza. The students from Southie knew none of this, but they recognized Landsmark as a symbol of what they were against. The kids from South Boston shouted, "Get the nigger!" They swarmed around the black man, knocked off his glasses, and broke his nose in a flurry of fists. One held him while Joseph Rakes turned his flagstaff into a weapon and charged. Landmark remembered, "I could see the flag coming. It was a big flag. But the flag bearer was swinging it.... In fact he swung it at me and I was able to lean back just enough that it didn't actually hit me, thank God."

Photographer Stanley Forman from the *Boston Herald* snapped a picture of Joseph Rakes, who appeared to be trying to impale Theodore Landsmark with his American flag. It was not exactly what happened, but it made a scene of startling power, an "iconographic moment," as the *Boston Globe* called it. The photograph won Forman a Pulitzer Prize. Rakes was arrested, pleaded guilty to assault and battery, and received a two-year suspended sentence.[149]

Twenty-five years later, when *Globe* reporter Thomas Farragher did an anniversary story on the event, he found that Theodore Landsmark had kept moving up and had become president of the Boston Architectural Center. Joseph Rakes went another way. His teachers remembered that before the incident "Joe was a good athlete and basically a good kid," rarely in trouble. Afterward he was "the flag guy" and the "kid from City

The civil rights movement spread to the north in campaigns for affirmative action and school busing. The result was a strong backlash. In Boston, white high school students used the American flag as a weapon in their cause of "liberty from busing" against an African American who represented the cause of freedom through affirmative action. Photographer Stanley Forman caught the scene in a Pulitzer Prize–winning photo called "The Soiling of Old Glory." It is reproduced with the permission of Stanley Forman, and the help of the Boston Herald, where it appeared on April 6, 1976.

Hall Plaza," and he was often in trouble. More fights followed. In 1983, he was arraigned for the murder of a man who had allegedly mistreated his sister, and was a fugitive for five years. Later he gave himself up, and the case was not prosecuted for lack of evidence. He pulled his life together, married the woman he loved, raised a family, moved to a coastal town north of Boston, and held a job on the Big Dig. He kept the flag and still believes in liberty from busing and freedom for South Boston.

WOMEN'S LIBERATION, WOMEN'S RIGHTS

Grassroots Feminism, Liberal Feminism, and Radical Feminism

All MEN are created equal;
What about US?

—Feminist motto, ca. 1970

I N T H E M I D - T W E N T I E T H C E N T U R Y, a revolution occurred in the lives of American women. The prime mover was a change in patterns of employment. Women, especially married women, began to work outside the home in growing numbers. From 1900 to 1930, the proportion of females over sixteen in the labor force fluctuated at about 20 percent. After the beginning of the Second World War, employment outside the home rose very rapidly, and except for a reversal after the war, it kept on rising at a remarkably steady pace: 30 percent in 1941, 40 percent in 1960, 50 percent in 1980, 60 percent in 2000. At the same time, the proportion of adult men in the work force fell from 90 percent in the Second World War to 70 percent in 2000. By the start of the twenty-first century, patterns of employment for men and women were converging.[150]

Most married women did not work because they wanted to. They needed the money to help pay the mortgage and put the children through college. In an economy of high inflation, falling real wages, and frequent layoffs, the only way that most American families could get ahead was for both the husband and the wife to bring home a paycheck.

This economic trend brought a change of attitudes and relationships. In 1962, a Gallup Poll found that one-third of American women felt they suffered from gender discrimination. By 1970, that proportion had risen to two-thirds. Their consciousness had been raised by the civil rights movement, by growing attention to civil liberties in American society, and by powerful polemics such as the work of Betty Friedan. Whatever the cause, the results were very clear. In the decade of the 1960s a majority of American women came to feel that they were objects of "sexism" in their homes and the workplace, and they shared a growing sense that something had to be done. The result was not one movement but many, with different visions of women's rights.[151]

Grassroots Feminism: A Vision of Cultural Fairness

The largest and most important movement happened at the grass roots. It developed in the 1960s and 1970s among many millions of American women who did not think of themselves as feminists. Survey researchers in this period found that only a small proportion of women in the United States called themselves by that name. But most shared a growing discontent about gender discrimination.[152]

This grassroots movement grew mainly from an idea that women had a right to fair treatment in their individual lives, and they had not been treated fairly. With the inspiration of Betty Friedan and encouragement from one another, they began to do something about it. These women were not much for marching, carrying signs, going to court, or abusing men in general. They wanted better relations with men and fairness for themselves, for their friends, and, especially, for their daughters.

To that end, the grassroots movement changed many things. First, it sought what Confucius called a rectification of terms. Women became highly sensitive to gender discrimination in words, and they worked at a transformation of language. No longer were men allowed to speak of humanity as mankind, or human rights as the rights of man. Women worked relentlessly at their husbands' pro-

The main thrust of American feminism in the 1960s and 1970s was a grass roots movement that engaged millions of supporters and sought to change the cultural condition of women. Its spirit appeared in a wonderful quilt by Carol Wagner, called "Freedom to Dream to Be Me," Roseville, Minn., 1985–86. It is reproduced with permission of Carol Wagner and the Minnesota Historical Society.

nouns, as a way of challenging unconscious biases that were embedded in ordinary thought. Slowly this effort began to work. By the 1990s, the speech and attitudes of even the most recalcitrant males had been transformed.

Another change at the grass roots happened in the routine of family life. When women began to work outside the home in larger numbers, they were expected by their husbands to keep running the home and raising the children. Now fathers became more actively engaged in child rearing. Sons pitched in with jobs that had been reserved for daughters. Husbands increasingly helped with the cooking and cleaning. This transformation started slowly, but by the end of the twentieth century most households were caught up in it.

American women also changed the way they dressed. Through this period one finds the eternal whirl of fashion, but also a deeper trend. Women's clothing became less confining than in any period since the age of the French Revolution. Girdles, corsets, and brassieres went out of fashion. Rituals of radical feminism often included the burning of these articles. A classic of image of women's liberation was the Statue of Liberty holding up her discarded bra.

At the same time, women's dress became more eclectic than ever before. Women could wear miniskirts or maxiskirts, granny gowns or muumuus, blue jeans or almost anything they pleased. They could iron their hair, cut it short, pile it on top of their heads, or put it in braids. They could wear flats, heels, spikes, sandals, or go-go boots, or they could go barefoot if they wished. Once started, this eclecticism began to expand. It allowed women increasingly to dress in ways that pleased themselves and to think and act as individuals.

Sexual relationships also changed very rapidly. A large part of the sexual revolution of the 1960s consisted in women's demands for equality of sexual condition as a matter of right. No longer were they willing to be passive "sex objects." They expected lovers to be more attentive to their feelings, and they became more active in their sexual relationships. Sexual surveys in the 1960s documented this transformation in detail. In the Woodstock Census, a young male reported in the language of that age, "I finally got a chance to score the foxiest chick I knew. When the big moment came, I jumped on her and pumped a few times, got off and jumped off. She called me an asshole, set out to teach me how she wanted her sex. I received 'oral instructions' and have never forgotten them. I'd like to thank her again."[153]

Another male reported, "Three aggressive women sexually attacked me at a commune in Madison, Wisconsin, simultaneously getting me off and explaining feminist dialectic." The editors commented, "Women agree that the freedom to make their own choices, even the freedom to lecture men on feminist dialectic, was what the sexual revolution was all about."[154]

This grassroots movement for women's rights had enormous impact on American society. It built on Betty Friedan's vision of liberty as consciousness raising and as emancipation from the many constraints on women's lives. It was also an idea of freedom as rights of full membership in American society. It transformed lives, thoughts, relationships and ordinary experiences. Most American lives, female and male, were changed by it.

Liberal Feminism: A Vision of Constitutional Rights

At the same time that the women's movement expanded, it also divided. In the mid-1960s, another variety of feminism appeared. It was mainly an institutional movement of large voluntary associations, academic programs, and women's groups that multiplied rapidly. The largest was the National Organization for Women (NOW), which in the beginning was very much in the mainstream of American reform. NOW was founded on June 30, 1966. Its founder and first president was Betty Friedan, who wrote a proposal for the new organization on a napkin. The primary purpose was to seek enforcement of Title VII of the Civil Rights Act of 1964, which prohibited discrimination by gender. The trigger was a decision by the Equal Employment Opportunity Commission to concentrate its efforts on racial discrimination and not to act on cases of gender discrimination.

The National Organization for Women began as a small organization of highly educated middle-class American women who sought legal remedies for discrimination. One of

Another movement was a highly organized liberal feminist movement that built upon a long tradition of collective effort and on new associations such as the National Organization of Women (NOW), which sought to work within the system. An image was a quilt called "Mother of Exiles." It represented feminism as a sequence of organized efforts by Anne Hutchinson, Betsy Ross, Harriet Tubman, Susan B. Anthony, Emma Lazarus. and Eleanor Roosevelt, all supporting a feminine symbol of liberty. It is reproduced here with the permission of the artist, Rebekka Seigel, of Owenton, Ky.

its first acts was to draw up a Bill of Rights for women, which demanded rights of equal opportunity in education, liberty from discrimination in employment, equal pay for equal work, the legalization of abortion, recognition of a woman's reproductive rights, and a right to child care. NOW also worked as a lobbying group in Washington. It began to have an impact on Congress and, especially, the courts. In 1970, NOW added a legal defense fund and began to use litigation as an instrument of liberty and freedom. It also sought an Equal Rights Amendment to the Constitution and sponsored a march that brought a hundred thousand women to Washington in 1978.

By 2002, the National Organization for Women claimed 500,000 "contributing members" in 550 chapters in all fifty states and most cities. Together with other organizations such as the Women's Equity Action League, Federally Employed Women, and Human Rights for Women, it was highly effective in changing institutions and laws.

Radical Feminism: A Vision of Revolutionary Violence

Other feminists went a different way. Some became more combative and confrontational. Many had served in the civil rights movement and the peace movement and were raised in the hard school of ethnic politics during the 1960s. They were accustomed to the sound and fury of that troubled era, when the decibels rose so high that sometimes only a scream could be heard. The result was a growth of small and very radical women's groups who adopted a new style of in-your-face feminism in the late 1960s and early 1970s. Their leaders were Bella Abzug, Ti-Grace Atkinson, Shulamith Firestone, Robin Morgan, and Kate Millett. Their organizations called themselves New York Radical Women (New York, 1967), WITCH (New York, 1968), The Feminists (New York, 1968), Cell 16 (Boston, 1968), DC Women's Liberation (1968), Redstockings (New York, 1969), the Stanton-Anthony Brigade (New York, 1969), Bread and Roses (Boston, 1969), the Furies (Washington, 1971).

Many of these groups were small and short-lived. They had only a few hundred members, some only a few dozen. They did not represent the feminist movement as a whole. By comparison with the big mainstream movements, in-your-face feminists were less instrumental and more expressive. They were always in the news, which was their purpose. Their marches and demonstrations were designed to capture the front pages and did so with success. In the period from 1968 to 1975, they shaped the public image of the women's movement out of all proportion to their numbers.

These groups cultivated many different public images. Cell 16 was the most militant. Its members wore khaki, took a pledge of celibacy, learned karate, studied Chairman Mao, quoted Che Guevara, and talked of armed guerrilla warfare against the male establishment. WITCH (Women's International Terrorist Conspiracy from Hell) dressed in black, carried brooms, and held Sabbaths and special meetings on Halloween. An organization called SCUM (Society for Cutting Up Men) had only a single member, Valerie Solanas, who shot and nearly killed Andy Warhol in June 1968. Other radical feminists defended her and tried to make her a martyr of their movement.[155]

Radical feminists engaged in what they called "zap actions," designed primarily to "shock and offend." One of the largest zap actions was a protest against the Miss America Contest in 1968. In a Rabelaisian scene, a sheep was anointed Miss America. Brassieres, girdles, and false eyelashes were ripped off and hurled into a "Freedom Trash Can." Another zap action became the Women's Strike for Equality on August 26, 1970, which organized marches in many cities. Radical women carried signs that read "Don't Cook Dinner—Starve a Rat Today" and "End Human Sacrifice! Don't Get Married!!"

In-your-face feminism delighted in outraging the bourgeois sensibilities of a middle-class nation. It went out of its way to attack capitalism in an economy where most Americans firmly supported free enterprise and private property. It picketed marriage license bureaus in a society that believed deeply in marriage and the family. It attacked journalists in a culture of mass communications. It was intensely hostile to men in general and argued for the biological inferiority of males while complaining bitterly of sexism. Some radical feminist groups forbade members even to speak to a man on pain of excommunication. They began by declaring half of the electorate to be their enemy and wondered why they lost elections.

Much of the energy in this movement was absorbed by furious internal bat-

In a protest against Miss America contests in 1968, a prominent figure was Florika and her Amerika Dollie with chains around both their bodies. "Voice of the Woman's Liberation Movement," September 7, 1968, with thanks to Redstockings Archives.

tles over "feminist theory" and issues of ideological purity. Jealousy among leaders was also a problem. In 1969, Marilyn Webb was expelled from the coordinating committee of DC Women's Liberation "on the grounds that she permitted the press to single her out as a leader."[156] Even as the numbers of radical feminists remained very small, they dominated the public image of the women's movement.

The feminist movement for an Equal Rights Amendment inspired this poster from a group called Montana Liberty in 1984. The Democratic candidates, Walter Mondale and Geraldine Ferraro, appear as revolutionaries in the spirit of Delacroix's 1830 painting "Liberty Leading the People." Art by Kip Overton; published by Montana Citizens for Liberty. Virginia Historical Society.

Success and Failure in the Feminist Movement

Radical feminists also had an impact on larger mainstream movements such as the National Organization for Women. In that group founders such as Betty Friedan were replaced by new leaders who changed their tactics and goals. They became more interested in militant protest and mass demonstrations. Abortion rights became a leading cause. In 1992, NOW organized a march that brought 750,000 women to Washington in defense of abortion rights. This question deeply divided American women and gave rise to an opposing right-to-life movement, which was a major blow to the feminist movement and limited its reach among Roman Catholics and Protestant fundamentalists, two very large groups who might have been strong supporters of women's rights if the right-to-life issue had not developed.

Feminist ideas changed too. Betty Friedan had centered her efforts on liberal ideas such as a Feminine Bill of Rights. Radical feminists and the new leaders of NOW instead shifted from freedom and liberty to equality as their central goal. The Bill of Rights disappeared from the Web site of the National Organization of Women. In its place was a Declaration of Sentiments, which began with a demand for "women's equality and women's empowerment." It insisted on nothing less than "equal representation" of women in "all decision-making structures of Americans society" and summarized its goal as "full equality for women in truly equal partnership with men."[157]

The campaign for an Equal Rights Amendment was more about equality than rights. The result was a hard-fought struggle and a narrow defeat for feminism. The Equal Rights Amendment was approved by Congress in 1972, but the campaign for ratification by the states continued for many years and in the end fell short by three states. It was a defeat that did not have to happen. Feminist leaders made the fatal error of shifting their movement from appeals to liberty and freedom to arguments for radical equality. As Martin Luther King Jr. clearly understood, centrist appeals to liberty and freedom tend to unite Americans, even in support of sweeping change. Arguments to radical equality always divide them, even when the substantive reforms are very limited. Nearly all of the purposes of the feminist movement could have been recast in terms that attracted broader support without any substantive loss.

Further, as feminist organizations competed with one another, their rhetoric became more stridently anti-male and alienated potential supporters. Polls in the early stages of the campaign over the Equal Rights

Radical feminism brought the inevitable backlash. One man took to the streets in the cause of male liberation and created yet another American image of liberty and freedom. Photograph by Morton Beebe in New York. Corbis.

Amendment found more support among northern men than southern women. These male allies were attacked and reviled, when small numbers of supporters on the margin spelled the difference between success and failure. In the process, feminist leaders split their own base, alienated potential supporters, and missed a major opportunity by the narrowest of margins. The result was a textbook example of how not to lead a reform movement in a free society. It is also an example of the difference that a vision can make in the outcome of a political movement.[158]

At the same time that radical feminism lost ground, grassroots feminism continued to have more positive results. This great movement transformed attitudes toward gender, family life, and opportunities for women. Even as radical feminists suffered a heavy defeat on the Equal Rights Amendment, the popular movement for women's rights continued to expand. It won a sweeping victory for the rights of individuals and for its vision of a free society.

SINGLE LIBERTIES, SPECIAL FREEDOMS

A Proliferation of Particular Causes

> Freedom arises from a multiplicity of sects.
>
> —JAMES MADISON

AT A SOUTHERN GUN SHOW in the year 2000, a T-shirt was for
sale. It proclaimed, "The 2nd Amendment Makes All The Others Possible." Here was another expanding theme in the American history of liberty and freedom: a highly organized movement that
centered on a single issue.

Many such movements flourished in America during the late twentieth century and drew strong support from particular constituencies on the
left, right, and center. Some were devoted to a particular right that
appeared in the U.S. Constitution or the Bill of Rights. A leading example was the Second Amendment to the Constitution, with its guarantee
of the right to keep and bear arms. Another was the First Amendment

*Two movements contested the meaning of the second amendment to the Constitution. One
side enlarged the idea of liberty to keep and bear arms. The other had a vision of freedom and
community in a nation where guns were strictly regulated, and even "gun free." This pro-gun
T-shirt is in the Virginia Historical Society. The anti-gun image appeared on a Web site.*

right to free expression in general, and to various forms of free expression in particular.

Other single-issue groups took up individual rights that were in the Declaration of Independence, with its promise of a right to life, liberty and the pursuit of happiness. Two movements centered on "the right to life." On the conservative side, a movement for the "rights of the unborn" strongly opposed abortion, but many of its supporters strongly favored capital punishment. On the left, another right-to-life movement opposed capital punishment, but many of its adherents strongly favored rights of abortion, contraception, and "a woman's right to choose." Both groups defended the same large idea of an inalienable right to life itself, in ways that were not only different but opposed.

Others enlarged established ideas of civil rights and civil liberties for groups that had not been protected by them. The leading example was the movement for gay rights. As late as the 1960s, homosexuality was widely diagnosed by psychiatrists as a perversion, punished as a crime by the courts, condemned as a sin by the churches, and suppressed as a threat to national security by the armed forces. Even so, every large city had a homosexual underground. Many people were arrested for homosexual activities, and more were attacked by angry mobs.

Attitudes began to change very rapidly in the 1960s. In a more permissive climate, homosexuals began to "come out" and openly proclaim that they were "gay." The first response was an increase in repression and open resistance by homosexuals. A pivotal event was the "Stonewall Rebellion"

Other movements took opposite sides on the question of abortion, and both defended liberty and freedom. One side demanded the right to life for the unborn. The other defended a woman's right to choose. Poster from Collection of Mary Haskell.

in June 1969, which grew from a raid by New York City police on a gay bar called the Stonewall Inn. Militant homosexuals fought the police for four days in Greenwich Village. The Stonewall Rebellion inspired the creation of many gay rights organizations. In 1969–70, Gay Liberation Fronts brought together male and female homosexuals who demonstrated for "gay rights" and "gay pride." In communities such as San Francisco, Provincetown, and Key West, homosexual groups were large enough to have a major impact on local elections.

In the late twentieth century, the movement for gay rights began to win court cases. Some states enacted laws for the extension of civil rights to same-sex marriages and to protection against discrimination in employment and access to public accommodations. Public attitudes toward homosexuality changed very rapidly. Here again a new vision of liberty and freedom developed mainly through the transformation of attitudes and beliefs. Courts and legislatures ratified these changes in the minds of many Americans.

Other single-issue groups expanded ideas of liberty and freedom in many directions. Environmental organizations linked their purposes to liberty and freedom in a vision of a right to live free of pollution and environmental destruction. Others extended rights to animals and strongly opposed vivisection and other experiments on animals, and cruelty to animals in many forms. Early expressions of the animal rights movement appeared among Quakers in the seventeenth and eighteenth centuries. Early Quakers believed in the reincarnation of souls. When

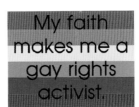

In the late 1960s, movements for gay rights developed on the model of civil rights and feminism. The result was yet another unique iconography of liberty and freedom in badges, buttons, signs, and Web sites.

FREEDOM

Animal rights found many adherents. One of the most striking visual images was Jennifer Howard's appeal for the rights of greyhounds in the name of freedom. © Jennifer Howard.

John Woodman saw a man beating his horse he warned him that in the next life he might be a horse.

Hundreds of these movements flourished in the United States, and many had deep roots in the American past. Protestant sects and denominations were a fertile breeding ground for these causes, which often rose from a religious imperative. Early reformers also gave them much encouragement in the nineteenth century. But the great era of single-rights movements was the late twentieth century, when they multiplied at a rapid rate, became more elaborately organized, and used the latest technology of electronic communications to mobilize support and reach a large public.

Each of these movements had its own history, but they tended to share qualities in common. They believed that some rights are more urgent than others, and often that one right is the most urgent of all. The result is continuing ferment of thought and judgment on the question of balancing one right against another. This eternal contest is at the very heart of a free society.

MR. NIXON AND THE KITCHEN DEBATE

Liberty and Freedom as Material Dreams

> If you think the United States has stood still, who built
> the largest shopping center in the world?
>
> —RICHARD NIXON

THE PRESIDENTIAL ELECTION OF 1968 was a pivotal event in American history. It shattered the New Deal coalition of rural South and ethnic North and ended thirty-five years of national rule by liberal Democrats and moderate Republicans. President Richard Nixon represented yet another new conservatism, highly flexible and pragmatic in its politics, secular and materialist in moral values, devoted mainly to the pursuit of wealth and power, increasingly authoritarian and secretive, and not overscrupulous about means. It had been developing for many years among both Republicans and Democrats. Attitudes and political styles changed in Washington, in a slow shift from the idealism of the Second World War to more materialist ways of thinking. It was associated with the gradual growth of what Arthur Schlesinger called the imperial presidency, in which the Democratic administrations of Kennedy and Johnson were in some ways closer to the Republican Nixon than they had been to Franklin Roosevelt or Harry Truman.

Increasingly, Nixon Republicans regarded the Cold War not as a clash of creeds and values but as a rivalry between competing superpowers and economic systems. Within the United States, images of American freedom and liberty were redefined in material terms. Richard Nixon himself played a leading role in that process.

An iconic event happened in the summer of 1959, when Nixon was vice president. The United States and the Soviet Union agreed to a series

669

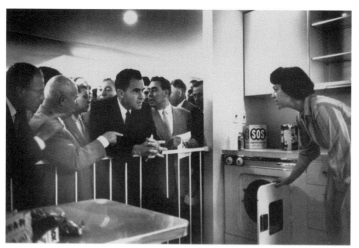

Yet another American vision of liberty and freedom appeared in a debate between Richard Nixon and Soviet leader Nikita Khrushchev. Mr. Nixon argued that American liberty and freedom rose mainly from an abundance of material possessions and labor-saving devices. Photograph by Howard Sochurek, July 1, 1959, Moscow. Time Life Pictures/ Getty Images.

of highly publicized cultural exchanges. An American National Exhibition was allowed to open in Moscow, and Vice President Nixon spoke at the inaugural ceremony. Americans who lived in the Soviet Union strongly advised Nixon to put heavy emphasis on the contrast between American idealism and Soviet materialism. He decided to go another way. Nixon chose the theme of "what freedom means to us." To the surprise of his audience, he spoke mainly of material things. His defense of freedom put heavy emphasis on material abundance in the United States. He argued that capitalism delivered very high levels of income to American families and that this improvement in living standards was the source and substance of American freedom.[159]

Afterward, Nixon and Nikita Khrushchev walked together through the United States exhibition. It included a full-scale American suburban ranch house, complete with a "miracle kitchen," which was meant to be a symbol of high living standards, the strength of a free enterprise, and the "American way of life." A spontaneous debate developed between the Soviet premier and the American vice president. They were standing together at the kitchen with its many appliances, including a robot that swept the floor. Nixon attempted a joke. He pointed to the robotic floor cleaner and said (to the horror of his handlers). "You don't even need a wife."

As they talked by the kitchen, Nixon returned to the theme of his speech, the linkage of freedom to material abundance. Incredibly, it was left for Khrushchev to speak of freedom as a cultural idealism, while Nixon appeared to be thinking in more material terms than the historical materialist he was debating. Both sides declared a victory in the Great Kitchen Debate, which brought to mind a favorite parable of Abraham Lincoln, about two political rivals who had a wrestling match in frontier Illinois, and managed wrestle themselves into each other's coats.[160]

WATERGATE AND CONSTITUTIONAL RIGHTS

Richard Nixon as an Image of Tyranny and Corruption:
Watergate as a Symbol of a Free Republic

> Watergate showed more strengths in our system than
> weaknesses.
>
> —ARCHIBALD COX

I N WASHINGTON, the Nixon administration lost the moral compass
that had guided the Truman and Eisenhower administrations in the
early years of the Cold War. Part of the problem was the continuing
war in Southeast Asia. In February 1969, Communist forces launched a
new offensive, which American and South Vietnamese troops contained
at heavy cost. The newly inaugurated president responded by "vietnamiz-
ing" the war. Richard Nixon began to withdraw American troops from
their peak strength of 541,500 in March 1969 to 24,000 in 1972.

Nixon tried to buy time for "vietnamization" by broadening the war.
He secretly authorized the bombing of Cambodia in 1969 and ordered
another Cambodian "incursion" by ground forces in 1970. This was followed by a massive invasion of Laos in 1971 and heavy bombing of North
Vietnam in 1972 and 1973, all in hope of breaking the will of the enemy
and forcing them to the conference table.

But it was the will of American leaders that had already broken.
Morale plummeted among U.S. troops who remained in Vietnam. Without trust in leaders or faith in their cause, the U.S. Army, which entered
the war as a first-class fighting force, suffered the worst collapse of discipline in its history. Combat units had growing problems with drugs,
gangs, "fragging" of officers, and atrocities against civilians.

While American troops began to pack up and go home, the bravest
units in the South Vietnamese army suffered heavy casualties, as did mil-

lions of civilians in Vietnam, Cambodia, and Laos under a rain of American bombs. Many Americans, even those who had supported the war, regarded the Vietnam policy of President Nixon as unlawful, immoral, and ineffectual. Secretary of State Henry Kissinger introduced a European style of *Realpolitik* and broke fundamentally with moral traditions of American diplomacy that had dominated the conduct of foreign affairs from Washington and Jefferson to Wilson, Roosevelt, Truman, and Eisenhower. It was a policy that failed miserably. The men of the Nixon administration exalted American power even as they weakened it, and darkened a defeat by adding the stain of national dishonor.

American troops in Vietnam created their own political symbols and drew them on their helmet covers. Soldiers in every American war had made much use of emblems and symbols, from the decorated powder horns of the Revolutionary War to the iconic soldiers' envelopes of the Civil War and the graffiti of World War II. But the helmet art in the last years of the war in Vietnam was without precedent in American history. This was an iconography of deep alienation from the war, the Army, and American leaders. One of the most common emblems was the peace symbol, which appeared on many helmets. It signified not only peace itself but hostility to the war by conscripts who had been compelled to fight while privileged middle-class youths were able to gain exemptions from military service. The American soldiers who wore peace symbols on their uniforms after 1968 had little interest in the liberation of Vietnam from the thrall of Communism. They counted the days until they were free from Vietnam and a war in which they did not believe.

At home, demonstrations against the war reached a peak of intensity and violence after the American invasion of Cambodia in the spring of 1970. Students were killed at Kent State University in Ohio. News photographs from Kent State became icons of the peace movement, much as in the civil rights struggle. Opposition to the war increased rapidly in the universities after the American invasion of Laos in 1971.

Most Americans did not share these antiwar attitudes. Public opinion polls showed that a majority of American adults supported the Vietnam War to the very end. While demonstrators for peace gathered in Washington, construction workers rallied for the war in New York City. On one side, the old emblems of patriotism became more popular than ever; on the other, they were bitterly attacked and reviled. The strife continued until the war ended in a shattering defeat for the United States.

Domestic troubles in Washington soon eclipsed the disaster in Vietnam. Scandals began to erupt in the national capital on an unprecedented scale. One of them centered on a failed burglary at the Watergate offices of the Democratic Party on June 17, 1972. The *Washington Post* began an inquiry and kept it going long after other newspapers lost interest. It found evidence that President Nixon's staff were deeply involved.

Reporters for the *Washington Post* uncovered evidence that the FBI, CIA, and military intelligence services had repeatedly violated the civil liberties of American citizens. Other scandals began to multiply in the Nixon administration. By the measure of criminal indictments and convictions of cabinet officers and senior White House staff, the Nixon presidency was the most corrupt in American history. A congressional inquiry followed, and a special prosecutor was appointed in 1973. President Nixon obstructed the investigations and on October 20, 1973, ordered the dismissal of Special Prosecutor Archibald Cox. To the amazement of Washington, the American people responded with a wave of anger so strong and sudden that observers compared it to a political firestorm. Few leaders realized the depth of feeling that had been growing in the country. Americans suddenly awakened to a discovery that President Nixon's actions were a fundamental threat to constitutional liberty and freedom.

Congress heard from its constituents, and the pace of the investigations picked up. Five members of President Nixon's cabinet and many other officials were found guilty of criminal acts. The president himself was implicated. As the scandals multiplied, his conduct became increasingly bizarre, and even his supporters turned against him. On July 27, 1974, after a national agony of many months, the House Judiciary Committee voted articles of impeachment, which described a pattern of criminal misconduct without equal in the history of the American presidency. Richard Nixon was accused of obstruction of justice in the Watergate burglary and "other covert activities." He was charged with repeated violations of the Constitution and with criminal acts against the "rights of citizens." Other articles of impeachment, not voted for tactical reasons, accused him of violating the Constitution in his secret bombing of Cambodia and many instances of bribery, extortion, tax evasion, and personal corruption.

Faced with the certainty of conviction if he were tried in the Senate, President Nixon announced his resignation on August 8, 1974. He was succeeded by Vice President Gerald Ford, who quickly granted Nixon an unconditional pardon in advance of criminal prosecution. Many presidents had left office in a cloud of public scandal, but the fall of Richard Nixon was something new in American history, far beyond the scandals that dogged the administrations of James Monroe, James Buchanan, Ulysses Grant, and Warren Harding.

In his disgrace, and the dishonor that he brought to the presidency, Richard Nixon became an American symbol of tyranny and corruption. Negative symbols of that sort had long been an important part of American visions of liberty and freedom. In early America the most common negative symbol was the Devil himself. As we have seen, an image of the Devil was hung on Boston's Liberty Tree and was prominent in the political iconography of the American Revolution. British leaders such as Bute, Grenville, and Mansfield became classic examples of negative symbols and were used reflexively in political art. Demonic figures often appeared in prints and drawings and in works of political theater.

Other negative symbols of tyranny, corruption, and oppression were prominent in every period of American history. Each political party had its own favorite images, but some figures transcended partisanship and united the republic against them. Benedict Arnold played that role in the War of Independence, and Aaron Burr in the early republic. Boss Tweed was a negative symbol in the Gilded Age, and the robber barons in the Progressive era, and Al Capone in the twenties. As the Watergate affair grew into a constitutional crisis, Richard Nixon began to play this role. A leading historian of American political art finds that many political figures have been stigmatized in one way or another, but only two men have been "stigmatized sufficiently to gain immortality as a generic figure for the ages." One was Boss Tweed of Tammany Hall, who became an enduring figure of infamy in the cartoons of Thomas Nast. The other was President Richard Nixon. He was made to appear as a figure hostile to American republicanism. Edward Sorel drew him as Milhous I, in the manner of Louis XIV.[161]

The Watergate affair and the collapse of the Nixon administration caused a crisis in the United States. Revelations of wrongdoing by President Nixon and high officials in the government created new symbols of tyranny and oppression. One example was Edward Sorel's image of Richard Nixon as the absolute monarch Louis XIV, "Milhous I, Lord of San Clemente, Duke of Key Biscayne, Captain of Watergate," March 14, 1974. Reproduced by permission of Edward Sorel. Library of Congress.

After Watergate, Nixon began to appear in cartoons and political caricatures not merely as a doer of evil deeds but as a symbol of evil incarnate. Roger Fischer, an historian of political art, called it the "Lucifer legacy." He collected many examples of Nixon as the personification of all that was dangerous to liberty and freedom. Even staunch Republicans began to see Richard Nixon in that light. At a grid-iron dinner in Washington, conservative Republican Senator Bob Dole saw former Presidents Ford, Carter, and Nixon sitting on the speaker's platform. "Look," said Dole, "See No Evil...Hear No Evil...and Evil!" [162]

For many years, Nixon's image echoed in American iconography as a generic symbol of wrongdoing. In 1980, when cartoonist Pat Oliphant wanted to accuse Jimmy Carter of demagoguery, he drew an image of the president as a Jekyll and Hyde character, slowly morphing into Richard Nixon. When Israeli leader Menachem Begin was accused of ordering the murder of Lebanese refugees, cartoonist Paul Conrad showed Nixon on the phone, saying, "Menachem, you should have burned the bodies." When supporters of Ronald Reagan stole a Carter briefing book, cartoonist Steve Lindstrom showed Nixon as the Devil whispering to Ronald Reagan, "Deny everything, erase the evidence, tell them you are not a crook."

It went on that way for many years. After the execution of demonstrators in China, a cartoon by Draper Hill showed Nixon, in a tub of rotten fish, raising his glass to Deng Xiaoping, who was sitting in a tub of blood; Nixon said, "To America's short memory, the triumph of expediency over evil, and your eventual return to respectability." When the "Irangate" scandal erupted in the administrations of Presidents Reagan and Bush, the negative icons of the Nixon years were used yet again. In 1998, President Clinton was accused of telling Monica Lewinsky, "Deny, deny, deny," and the specter of Richard Nixon returned yet again to the White House.[163]

These negative images were symbols of what liberty and freedom were not. They played an important role in the Watergate crisis and the collapse of the Nixon presidency. In that process they also helped to reaffirm constitutional liberty in America and were part of a process that revived the vital principle that nobody in America is above the law. The negative example of secrecy, tyranny, and corruption in the Nixon administration inspired many reforms by Congress. The War Powers Act (1973) set a limit on the use of troops abroad without congressional authority. A Campaign Finance Law (1974) required strict public disclosure of sources and uses of political contributions, and became the foundation for other reforms to follow. A Freedom of Information Act (1974) greatly expanded an earlier and largely ineffective law of the same name. Congressional investigations of the FBI and CIA led to many reforms of intelligence agencies. Executive orders prohibited unlawful acts in the conduct of American foreign policy, such as assassinations, bribery, and covert criminal acts. Integrity was restored to the civil service system after a concerted effort by the Nixon administration to destroy it, a story that went largely unreported in the American press.

In the armed forces, a heroic and highly successful effort was made to purge the Army and Navy of drug gangs who constituted a profound threat to a free republic and the peace of the world. The leaders in that effort were small groups of sergeants, junior officers, and senior officers of high integrity. The story of that military reform movement was not reported by the press and has yet to find its historian.[164]

Most of these reforms happened during the much maligned presidencies of Gerald Ford and Jimmy Carter, who both did much to restore an ideal of decency, honesty, and integrity to government. These administrations also revived an old-fashioned vision of a free republic as an open system of responsible government under the rule of law. The free institutions of the United States were stronger at the end of the Watergate crisis than they had been at its beginning. In that sense, the response to the misconduct of Richard Nixon and the men around him enlarged the meaning of liberty and freedom in the United States.

THE AGE OF THE ICONOCLASTS

Images of Alienation in America's Dark Age, 1973-79

Live Free or Die

—MOTTO ON ALL NEW HAMPSHIRE
LICENSE PLATES

DEAD

—PERSONALIZED LICENSE PLATE
ON ONE NEW HAMPSHIRE CAR

I N 1980, the *Chicago Tribune*'s gifted artist Jeff MacNelly observed that "many cartoonists would be hired assassins if they couldn't draw."[165] That tendency became more pronounced in the aftermath of Watergate and Vietnam, which was one of the most painful periods in American history. Opinion polls in 1979 found that the proportion of Americans who said they were satisfied with the state of the nation had fallen to 11 percent, the lowest since national polling began.[166] A large part of the problem was the state of the economy, which suffered the highest annual rates of peacetime inflation in American history (13.5 percent in 1980) and the largest drop in real wages. To restrain inflation, the Federal Reserve Board and the Treasury Department adopted severely repressive economic policies, which sent the American economy into another steep decline. Unemployment surged. Some of the social consequences were worse than the Great Depression. The period from 1972 to 1981 was marked by the highest rates of violent crime, the highest levels of drug use, and the worst problems of family disruption that modern America had ever experienced.[167]

Those problems were compounded by other trends. Watergate and Vietnam changed the tone of public discourse in the United States. Ten years of leadership by Lyndon Johnson and Richard Nixon from 1963 to 1973 created an attitude of profound distrust for political leaders and public institutions. The press became increasingly hostile to the government.

677

This attitude overflowed in editorial cartoons on Presidents Gerald Ford and Jimmy Carter, which were very unfair. Both were decent and honorable men who worked faithfully to restore integrity to government. They occupied the nation's highest office, which most Americans had long held in high respect even when they did not approve of the incumbent. But after Watergate and Vietnam a different tone appeared. The successes of the Ford and Carter presidencies passed largely unnoticed by the press. Their failures became the center of attention. Both presidents were cruelly mocked by the media, in ways that also made a mockery of American images of liberty and freedom. One cartoon showed Jimmy Carter as the Statue of Liberty himself, with a toothy Carter grin. He held the torch of human rights in one hand and a neutron bomb in the other. Gerald Ford was shown as the Statue of Liberty in rags, holding a tin cup instead of a torch.[168]

While cartoonists attacked American leaders and institutions, artists and literati gave expression to an even deeper spirit of alienation. Some began to attack American values, even liberty and freedom. Leading examples were images of the Statue of Liberty, always a sensitive indicator of cultural trends. One artist represented American liberty as Fascism, with the Statue of Liberty in a Nazi uniform.

Another artist made her a symbol of decay and pollution, with an X-ray of blackened lungs. Some attacked liberty as materialism and self-indulgence. John Heinly did an ink drawing of a beleaguered Miss Liberty and Uncle Sam dodging a barrage of tomatoes. Many embraced an idea of liberty as the pursuit of pleasure, without regard to any altruistic principle. This self-indulgent vision of hedonistic liberty became a popular theme in the 1970s and 1980s.

Others expressed a different spirit of uncertainty without equal in any earlier period of American history. Hudson Talbott was inspired by Manet's *Déjeuner sur l'Herbe* to paint the Statue of Liberty as a bemused and bewildered young woman sitting naked in Central Park, with two surrealist companions offering her what appears to be marijuana.

Haruo Miyauchi "Liberty," acrylic, 1972. Collection of the artist.

Another theme in this period was a loss of certainty. It appears in Hudson Talbott's whimsical 1982 painting of the Statue of Liberty, inspired by Manet's "Luncheon on the Grass." Used by permission of Hudson Talbott.

The republic had seen similar moods before. In every American generation, dark undercurrents of uncertainty, alienation, cynicism, and self-indulgence flowed against the mainstream, and in turbulent times they sometimes rose to the surface. Examples included the popular Pyrrhonism of Benjamin Franklin in the mid-eighteenth century, the skepticism of Mark Twain and the cynicism of Ambrose Bierce after the Civil War, and the rise of the Debunkers after the First World War (the word *debunk* was coined in 1923).

After Vietnam and Watergate, that old impulse took a new form. This was an age of American iconoclasts, who were very different from their predecessors. The Debunkers of the 1920s had tended to be white Protestant Anglo-Saxon males whose politics were to the right of center. Chief among them were Henry Ford, Charles Francis Adams, and H. L. Mencken. They delighted in mocking the pomposity of professional patriots and satirized the tyranny of self-appointed censors. They attacked the cruelty of literary bullies and mocked the dogmatism of religious bigots with great relish. By and large the debunkers made fun of American democracy, but they were believers in the Great Republic. Much of their work was an appeal for tolerance. Most of it was a vision of greater liberty

Another emerging theme in the late 20th century was a hedonist vision of liberty and freedom as the pursuit of pleasure. An image of this idea was James L. Stanfield's photograph "Chocolate Liberty." It showed baker José Balcells Pallares with his creation, a life-sized chocolate Statue of Liberty. The creator stood beside it with a happy smile, licking his chocolate-covered fingers. Courtesy of the National Geographic Society; © 1984, James L. Stanfield.

and freedom. Mencken, Adams, and Ford all thought of themselves as working to make American society more open and more true to its founding principles, in which they deeply believed.

The American iconoclasts of the late twentieth century were different. Their politics were mostly of the left, even the far left. Most came of age in the 1960s. They hoped and believed that America was on the edge of social revolution in 1968. More than a few began to call themselves American Marxists in the late twentieth century. They watched in horror as their revolution failed and socialist governments began to collapse throughout the world. Some remained faithful to their own dreams, but others became unbelievers. When their own light failed, they could see nothing but darkness. More than a few Marxists became extreme relativists. They set about the work of smashing the idols of other causes in a mood of relentless fury.[169]

Some of these angry iconoclasts undertook to revise American history. Their favorite targets were white male Anglo-Saxon heroes of American history. Many prominent figures in American history received the same treatment. Puritans made easy marks, so easy that there was scarcely much satisfaction in attacking them. The iconoclasts preferred to go after the great liberal heroes. Thomas Jefferson, Andrew Jackson, Abraham Lincoln, Woodrow Wilson, and Franklin Roosevelt all became favorite targets. At the same time, American iconoclasts celebrated other American figures who had long been condemned as enemies of liberty and freedom. Benedict Arnold, Aaron Burr, Jefferson Davis, Boss Tweed, and Al Capone all received sympathetic biographies by American historians in the late twentieth century. Some iconoclastic works combined a strong spirit of historical and ethical relativism with a revulsion against the values of American society, even values of liberty and freedom. This was not typical of historical writing as a whole, but it was a strong theme in a difficult period.

MORNING IN AMERICA

The Reagan Revolution and the Revival of Liberty and Freedom

Dream no small dreams, for they have no power to move the hearts of men.

—RONALD REAGAN BUMPERSTICKER
(AFTER VICTOR HUGO)

IN A DARK MOMENT of economic decline and cultural despair, a new spirit began to stir in America, as so often before in times of trouble. In 1932, this great revival had come from the left and centered on the leadership of Franklin Roosevelt. In 1860 it rose from the center and was led by Abraham Lincoln. In 1980, the revival came from the right and found its leader and symbol in Ronald Reagan.

Few American presidents have been as much maligned by hostile critics as was Ronald Reagan, and even fewer have made themselves as much loved by the American people. None was more skillful in the mobilization of visual symbols of liberty and freedom. Ronald Reagan's experience as screen actor, television host, and manager of public relations for business corporations prepared him well for modern media campaigns, more so than an orthodox political career might have done.

Ronald Reagan began his political life as a New Deal Democrat. As president of the Screen Actors Guild he was an outspoken liberal and trade unionist, the only officer of a labor union ever to be elected president. But after bruising fights with Communists and fellow travelers in the screen guilds during the early years of the Cold War, he turned sharply to the right. In 1962, he became a Republican and strongly supported Barry Goldwater's militant conservatism.

Ronald Reagan brought an evangelical enthusiasm to his new cause, along with a distinctive style of popular rhetoric. He also had an unrivaled mastery of the modern media. It was said that "Ronald Reagan thinks like Barry Goldwater but sounds like FDR," whom he always greatly admired. His strength as a campaigner won him the governorship of California in 1966 and 1970 and the presidency of the United States in 1980 and 1984.[170]

Opponents always underestimated him. Learned observers judged Ronald Reagan's campaigns and speeches by conventional standards of academic discourse and found them "lacking in substance," "primitive," "vague," "empty," and an "ideological vacuum." Nothing could have been farther from the fact. Ronald Reagan's campaigns were highly sophisticated and substantive in a way that his critics did not understand. Many rivals to the left and right were buried beneath Reagan landslides and never understood what hit them.

In substantive terms, Ronald Reagan's speeches made frequent reference to freedom and liberty—never at great length but with great force and impact. He gave those ideas an explicit meaning, which was nationalist, libertarian, and antigovernment. "Freedom and liberty" to Ronald Reagan was something that belonged specially to America. It was a national idea. It also meant a minimum of government interference in private affairs. Government was the enemy in Reagan's imagery, even the American government when he was running it. He promised to reduce taxes and did so. But at the same time, he was also careful not to reduce government spending for Social Security, Medicare, or most other existing government services. The result was a surge in the national debt. Reagan's administration added more to the national debt than all prior presidencies combined.

Ronald Reagan firmly believed that the triumph of freedom was inevitable in the world. He had a distinct philosophy of history, which scholars call the "Whig interpretation": an idea that history is a teleological process, moving onward and upward toward the inevitable triumph of freedom and democracy. After a prolonged time of troubles in America, Ronald Reagan assured the nation that everything would be all right. No president had talked that way for many years. The American people were used to dire warnings and exhortations to sacrifice.

The substance of Ronald Reagan's politics and the secret of his success as "the Great Communicator" were not to be found in issues, programs, or policies. His speeches and images consisted mainly in the manipulation of simple metaphors, dramatic examples, graphic symbols, and powerful icons. Every political campaign had used these devices before. Ronald Reagan used them in a new way.

In the Reagan era, American iconographers labored under a new difficulty. For many generations, political images in America derived their power from a common heritage of symbols in the King James Bible, classical myths, the plays of Shakespeare, the novels of Dickens, historical events, and inherited folkways of America itself. By the late twentieth century, many of these symbols had become very faint in American culture. Others had disappeared entirely. An historian of political graphics in America observed a major change that way. He noted that the great cartoonists of the nineteenth and early twentieth centuries all relied heavily on that common cultural heritage. This was the case with Thomas Nast in *Harper's Weekly,* Joseph Keppler in *Puck,* and Bernhard and Victor Gillam in *Judge.* By the late twentieth century, Roger Fischer writes, "This common cultural matrix had waned to the point of extinction." He found that "scripture, classical mythology, Shakespeare and the like have given way to the more familiar, instantly recognized icons of contemporary television, Tinseltown, the top forty, the comic strips, and other manifestations of popular culture." These new "icons" of American culture tended to be highly ephemeral. The images of "contemporary television" were those of the past few seasons. Popular songs after a few years became "golden oldies," and those of greater age were forgotten, or at least no longer shared in common.[171]

The same trend appeared in political symbols. Cartoonists of the nineteenth century had a rich vocabulary of political symbols at their disposal: Magna Carta and King John, Roundheads and Cavaliers, Whigs and Tories, Federalists and Jeffersonians. In the late twentieth century, these political references had become meaningless to many Americans. Many Americans today have never heard of King John or Magna Carta, Cavaliers or Roundheads, or even Whigs and Tories.

This was the problem that Ronald Reagan faced in California, where many residents had moved away from their roots and cultural institutions were not strong. To communicate with his electorate Reagan developed an iconography that required very little in the way of cultural memory. To understand a speech by President Reagan, no prior knowledge was required. He rarely referred to facts, theories, or complex ideas. A Reagan speech used other means.

In his public appearances, Ronald Reagan became his own political icon. A close student of his rhetoric wrote, "Reagan is a communicator whose body, voice, and smile do the necessary emotional embellishing." He had a unique way of representing himself in public. He would begin quietly, looking down at the ground, speaking hesitantly as if public appearances were entirely strange to him. One observer, Mark Crispin Miller, noted these characteristics of a Reagan appearance and added, "He often punctuates his statements with a folksy little waggle of his head and shoulders so that we shouldn't take his speechifying too seriously." As he warmed to his subject, he began to exude an air of confidence, clarity, optimism, and complete sincerity. Reagan talked with an easy-going middle western twang. He affected a self-deprecatory gee-whiz, aw-shucks manner and liked to use plain words and simple down-home metaphors. His speeches made heavy use of repetition and emphasis and little of rhetorical embellishment. This was not merely a personal style. It was elaborately studied by a large and expert staff who cultivated the common touch. One of his army of speechwriters, Adam Bakshian Jr., said that "speechwriting is to writing as Muzak is to music." Behind that facade lay one of the most complex and sophisticated public relations machines in American history.[172]

People loved it. Ronald Reagan's manner and appearance won over voters who were bored by facts, repelled by reasoned arguments, and alienated by complex thoughts. He reached voters who demanded quick and easy solutions to complicated problems. People on the right liked him for his substantive positions. Americans in the center liked him for his manner.

It was a style that did not succeed everywhere. New Englanders were not attracted to it, and university audiences ran the other way. But in the broad middle reaches of the American republic, this new style of political iconography worked brilliantly. When a cabdriver was asked in 1980 why he voted for Ronald Reagan and the Republicans, he answered, "He's the only politician I can understand."[173]

Many politicians who came after Ronald Reagan tried to emulate him. George Bush did his best with an acquired Texas twang, but his Yankee heart wasn't in it, and he had a special problem with what he called the "vision thing" that came so easily to the Great Communicator. Mr. Bush's vice president, Dan Quayle, had another problem. On the subject of freedom, Mr. Quayle once observed, "We are on an irreversible trend toward more freedom and democracy. But that could change."[174]

Ronald Reagan was *sui generis*. His style was so personal and idiosyncratic that it could not be imitated by others. The public relations machine that ran so smoothly behind him faltered and failed when it no longer had Ronald Reagan up front. People talked of a "Reagan Revolution" in governance. It is not clear that there was such a thing in substantive terms. Big government grew bigger in Ronald Reagan's presidency.

During his administration, it was business as usual in the Congress and most parts of the federal government. But there was clearly a Reagan Revolution in the tone of American politics and the manipulation of public imagery.

An example in the election of 1980 was Ronald Reagan's television commercial called "Morning in America." It offered little in the way of ideas or issues, but by the manipulation of familiar images it created a warm haze of hope and confidence. It encouraged people to feel that everything would be all right again, with Ronald Reagan in the White House. Experts observed that it worked brilliantly.

Part of it was the infectious optimism of Mr. Reagan, who, as George Will remarked, had a "talent for happiness." Part of it was a change in the economy, which began to improve in the 1980s, in a long boom that continued through the 1990s. Social conditions changed for the better as inflation declined from its peak in 1979–80, employment increased, real income rose, and social problems such as violent crime and drug use diminished.

A deep change also occurred in international affairs. Socialist systems labored under increasing difficulty, while free societies suddenly began to revive and flourish. The material stresses of the 1970s and early 1980s that had been a crisis for free-market systems were a catastrophe for Communist command economies. By the early 1980s, it was clear that they had suffered a heavy blow. Scarcely anyone realized that it was a mortal blow,

The Reagan Revolution, with its theme of revival and its message of "morning in America," often referred to liberty and freedom. This image of President and Mrs. Reagan with the Statue of Liberty in the background captured the spirit of this political movement. Photograph by Diane Walker, 1986; Getty Images.

but the United States and its allies were clearly doing better in world affairs, and the Communist bloc was less menacing than before. These powerful trends predated the Reagan presidency, but he was quick to make the most of them.

A major part of Ronald Reagan's appeal was his close identification with liberty and freedom, in terms so general that they appealed to followers of Barry Goldwater and Franklin Roosevelt. He was carefully photographed with icons of liberty and freedom in the background, linking him to these ideas without specifying their meaning. This was an omnibus vision of liberty and freedom that was often asserted but never defined. It had an impact not only on electoral choices but on the way that Americans thought about their country.

By the mid-1980s, Americans were feeling better about themselves and their free institutions. Survey researchers asked Americans how they felt about the American Dream of progress and prosperity, and they mapped the results on a county base—red for optimism and blue for despair. The country appeared as a sea of red, with two exceptions. The inner cities showed a bluish tinge, and university towns were deep, deep blue. Except for the pessimism of academic subcultures and the misery that persisted in urban ghettos throughout the country, Americans were increasingly optimistic about the future and more confident of their free institutions.

The old symbols of a free society revived during the Reagan presidency, with much encouragement from the Great Communicator. The Liberty Trees returned and were given a new meaning. At the end of the nineteenth century America had more than a hundred million elm trees, many of great age. They had been planted a century before, on town greens, college campuses, city parks, country roads, public lands, and private estates. They grew from the roots of the republic and represented the memory of a nation. Then in 1930 a Cleveland furniture maker imported a piece of wood from Europe that contained a colony of beetles that escaped into the city and began to bore into its many elms. They caused a disease that destroyed the circulatory systems of the trees. In the era when the republic itself slipped into the depths of the Great Depression, America's beloved elm trees began to die. The disease spread inexorably, and nobody could stop it. By the 1970s, American elms were dying everywhere. Most were lost in the era of Vietnam and Watergate. In 1980, more than 90 percent of American elm trees were gone. It seemed that the elm would go the way of the chestnut. Its extinction seemed only a matter of time.

In 1985, a New England Yankee named John P. Hansel observed that Americans were fighting fiercely to save the California redwoods, but "practically nothing was done about the fatal disease in the trees over our heads." Hensel founded the Elm Research Institute of America and ran it from an abandoned factory building in Harrisville, New Hampshire. A fungicide was found to have a 96 percent success rate if injected in a tree before its foliage began to flag. At the University of Wisconsin, two faculty members developed a disease-resistant American elm by breeding a few trees that survived and called it the American Liberty elm. John Hensel's Elm Institute gave away half a million seedlings, and Boy Scouts began to plant them from one end of the republic to another. Dan Erickson, seventeen, of Manchester, New Hampshire, looked up from his elm seedlings and told an amazed reporter, "We take so much and give so little that it's neat to think that with a little shoveling and pruning, you can give your community something that might be around two centuries from now."[175]

Dan Erickson and other Scouts of his generation planted liberty seedlings along the entire reach of U.S. Route 1, 2,909 miles from northern Maine to south Florida. The Liberty Trees increased and multiplied, as the older generation looked on astonishment. In an age of renewal, America was beginning to recover faith in its founding principles, and even the Liberty Elm was back again, thanks largely to the labors of the coming generation.

At the same time, the Statue of Liberty was elaborately restored at great expense. In 1981, President Reagan created the Statue of Liberty–Ellis Island Commission. Its head was business executive Lee Iacocca, working closely with the National Park Service and engineers in America and France. In 1983, a huge free-standing aluminum scaffold, the tallest ever built, rose around the entire monument.

A symbol of the Reagan revival was the restoration of the Statue of Liberty, here surrounded by scaffolding that iconoclasts interpreted as a cage. But she emerged from that confinement as a brighter and stronger symbol. Critics scoffed, but something was happening in America as so often before, a return to first principles and recovery of American values and institutions. Courtesy of Jeffrey Dozik, Statue of Liberty National Monument.

The most powerful evidence of this American revival in the late 20th century came from individuals. A remarkable example of the return of confidence in American values of liberty and freedom was this a quilt by Yvonne Wells, an African American artist in Tuscaloosa, Alabama. She called it "Being in Total Control of Herself," 1985–86. Thanks to Yvonne Wells and the International Quilt Study Center, University of Nebraska.

It looked like a prison cage, and iconoclasts had a field day. Then a large team of highly skilled restorers went to work, American and French together. The entire system of iron armatures that supported the monument was found to be severely weakened by rust and corrosion. All were replicated in stainless steel. The copper skin was badly damaged in many places. It was carefully repaired and cleaned by a method that preserved its handsome and functional green patina. The upraised arm was found to be very shaky. Bob Hope said at a fund-raiser, "I knew she was in trouble when I waved at her and she waved back." The torch and flame were removed and replaced, with a brightly gilded flame as its builders had originally intended. The cost of the entire project, with many improvements, was nearly a quarter of a billion dollars. The work was completed in three years, and the monument was rededicated by Ronald Reagan in 1986. It inspired a revival of interest in symbols of liberty and freedom throughout the country.[176]

The new mood had many individual expressions. In 1990, Yvonne Wells of Tuscaloosa, Alabama, made herself a quilt. She called it "Being

A similar mood appeared in this quilt by Charlotte Warr Anderson of Kearns, Utah. She called it "Spacious Skies." It combined many symbols of American liberty and freedom with a revival of faith in American values. It also connected the American past to its present and future. American Folk Art Museum.

in Total Control of Herself." It was the celebration of American freedom by a black woman in the Old South. Yvonne Wells used bright colors and strong motifs to represent the old icons of American freedom in a new way. Her image of the Statue of Liberty held a black baby in one hand and a bundle of money in the other. In the background were the American flag, the Liberty Bell, and a map of the United States. After many years of racial strife in Alabama, Yvonne Wells made peace with America, and on her own terms. The quilt celebrated her pride of race, gender, nation, and, most of all, self. It also expressed a new sense of confidence in American values and institutions. Here was yet another dynamic vision of freedom and liberty, independence and belonging.[177]

OF MELTING POTS AND GORGEOUS MOSAICS

Liberty as Diversity; Freedom as Multiculturalism

> Since the Second World War, the national unity of
> Americans has been tied to a strong civic culture that
> . . . protects their freedom—including their right to
> be ethnic.
>
> —LAWRENCE FUCHS, 1990

WHILE OLD EMBLEMS of liberty and freedom revived in the late twentieth century, new ones were created. Among the most important were images of American liberty and freedom as multicultural ideas.

Multiculturalism was a term that entered general usage in Canada during the Trudeau ministry, as a counterweight to bicultural conflicts between Anglophones and Francophones. For Pierre Trudeau and his followers, multiculturalism was a way of holding Canada together. The idea spread quickly to the United States. Americans had long been conscious of their country as a diverse society, but their images of that idea changed through time.

For many years, ideas of diversity were linked to images of assimilation. Herman Melville wrote that America's "blood is as the blood of the Amazon, made up of a thousand noble currents all pouring into one. We are not a nation so much as a world." He thought of it as a place where "all tribes and people are forming into one federated whole."[178]

Ralph Waldo Emerson introduced another metaphor of America as a "smelting pot." Emerson predicted that "all the European tribes, and the Africans and Polynesians, will construct a new race, a new religion, a new state, and a new literature, which will be as vigorous as the new Europe that came out of the smelting pot of the Dark Ages."[179]

In the twentieth century. Emerson's idea was taken over by Jewish

690

immigrant Israel Zangwill in his American metaphor of "God's crucible, the great melting pot." Zangwill wrote, "What is the glory of Rome and Jerusalem where all nations and races come to worship and look back, compared with the glory of America, where all nations and races come to labor and look forward." These metaphors of smelting pots and melting pots all centered on an idea of people of many different origins becoming one in their common allegiance to liberty and freedom.

There were always strenuous dissenters from this melting-pot model, even in the generations of Melville, Emerson, and Zangwill. Walt Whitman had a very different vision of America and was comfortable with diversity. He heard America singing in many voices, not even in the same key, and he delighted in cacophony. That attitude became more widely shared in the twentieth century. An example was the work of Horace Kallen, a Jewish scholar who became an active critic of the melting-pot model and assimilation metaphors. In sixty years of publishing Kallen developed an idea that he may have been the first to call "cultural pluralism."[180] Something similar appeared in the work of the Jesuit scholar R. J. Henle, who developed a model of "cultural diversity." A third scholar, Stewart G. Cole, began to use the phrase "multi-culture America" as early as 1956. He stressed the "integrity of transmitted cultures from the old world, the right of ethnic people to be different, and the obligation of the government of the United States to respect and protect multiple-group ways of living." Here was another idea of liberty and freedom, as the liberty to be different and the freedom to belong to "multiple-groups" with their own cultures.[181]

In the 1980s and 1990s, these images developed into a formal ideology of multiculturalism. It was expressed in metaphors and images, which appeared in great variety. In Boston, a political movement headed by Afro-American

This colorful image of multicultural America as a rainbow coalition appeared in the presidential campaign of Jesse Jackson (1984). National Museum of American History, Smithsonian Institution.

leader Mel King developed the idea of a "rainbow coalition." That image
became very popular throughout the United States. It envisioned a multicultural society as a set of color bands—solid, separate and distinct, existing side by side in a single spectrum of diversity.

Another multicultural image was America as a tapestry, an image as old
as Randolph Bourne, who wrote that "America is coming to be not a
nationality but a transnationality, a weaving back and forth, with other
lands, of many threads of all sizes and colors." Here was a more interactive
image of multiculturalism than the American rainbow. Other multicultural images began to be invented in great profusion. Mayor David Dinkins of New York described his city and nation as a "gorgeous mosaic." A
fourth image, less elegant but similar in substance, was of American society as a "salad bowl" where oil and vinegar mix without merging.[182]

Some people thought that these images were too static. Brandeis
scholar Lawrence Fuchs complained that "the ingredients of a salad bowl
are mixed but do not change." Fuchs himself searched for a kinetic vision
of American multiculturalism. In 1990, he borrowed Mayor Dinkins's
"beautiful mosaic" and changed it to an "American kaleidoscope," which
was a mosaic in motion, endlessly rearranging itself in new patterns. Similar to this idea was James Baldwin's idea of America as a "color wheel."[183]

Here were many visions of a free society as a multicultural system: a
rainbow and a tapestry, a salad bowl and a beautiful mosaic, a kaleidoscope and a color wheel. Some were assimilationist and others not, but
they shared qualities in common. All of them thought of Americans

Many ethnic groups created their own multicultural images of liberty and freedom; among them was this wonderful image of a Liberty
Hanukkah lamp or menorah called "Mother of Exiles," by Mae Rockland Tupa, 1995. Collection of Marie L. and Robert J. Cotton.

mainly in terms of ethnicity and race. They were cast in a calculus that referred not to individuals but to groups. They combined an idea of cultural heterogeneity in the nation with an assumption of cultural homogeneity within ethnic and gender groups. These models of multiculturalism became popular in America because they were useful. They made sense for leaders of ethnic groups who wished to create a sense of group solidarity within a context of national diversity. In academe they were also much favored by faculty who were fighting for the autonomy of ethnic programs and gender studies.

But these multicultural visions had a major weakness. They were fundamentally mistaken as models of how American society actually worked in the 1980s and 1990s. Evidence of voting patterns in American politics showed that pluralism was alive and well in American culture, but not the simple pluralism of the rainbow or the mosaic, or even the kaleieoscope and color wheel.

In the local elections of 1993, for example, several leading candidates ran explicitly on a multicultural platform. They did not do well. One was Mayor Dinkins of New York City, who made the gorgeous mosaic into a campaign slogan. A second was Governor Jim Florio in New Jersey. A third was gubernatorial candidate Mary Sue Terry in Virginia. Others included three mayoral candidates in Boston who failed to survive the primary—one was Afro-American, another was a strong feminist.

At the same time, pluralism was flourishing in other ways. In that year, Boston elected Thomas Menino, the first Italian mayor in its history. His inauguration ended sixty-three years of Irish incumbents since James Michael Curley in 1930. Menino ran well in South Boston and Charlestown, two traditional citadels of Irish Boston, and carried some of the most strongly Irish neighborhoods in the city against an Irish challenger. The *Boston Globe* noted that the voting patterns "cut across ethnic neighborhood lines."[184]

Something similar happened in other cities. African American mayors were elected in two large cities that had exceptionally small African American populations. Sharon Sayles Belton won in Minneapolis, where nearly 80 percent of the city was white. Norman Rich was elected mayor of Seattle by a landslide in a city that was 75 percent white. On the other side, the city of Hartford, which was heavily black, elected a white mayor, and Miami's predominantly Hispanic voters chose an Anglo-Saxon.[185]

The same tendency appeared in regard to gender. In New Jersey's gubernatorial election of 1993, Republican Christine Whitman won male voters by 55 to 45 percent, and Democrat Jim Florio attracted the support of women, by 53 to 47 percent. The same thing had happened when Whitman ran against Senator Bill Bradley in 1990. Clearly, voters were not casting their ballots by ethnicity or gender in solid blocs. Other factors were more powerful in shaping their choices.[186]

How do we interpret these results? A reporter for the *New York Times* observed in 1993 that "a notable feature of mayoral elections around the country was how secondary a role race and ethnicity played." Its headline writer went even farther and proclaimed, "Results hint at new indifference toward race.... A new generation emerges into a more pragmatic political climate." This was not correct. Americans were far from indifferent to race and ethnicity, but they were increasingly concerned with other things.[187]

Most of these elections showed that voters were making their choices in ways that did not conform to simple, solid visions of beautiful mosaics

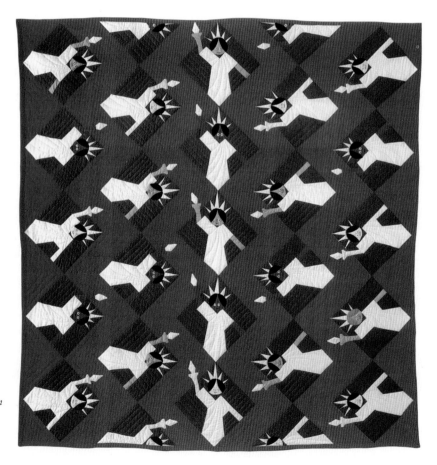

An individuated image of multiculturalism was this quilt by Julia K. Swan, "The Many Faces," made in Cambridge, Ohio, 1985–86. With thanks to the artist.

or rainbow coalitions. Pluralism worked most powerfully in a way that transcended the old ethnic and racial blocs that were the units of the rainbow coalition.

The problem here was that ethnic leaders had a strong interest in ethnic blocs. In their hands, multiculturalism became a new form of interest-group politics. But the progress of diversity outstripped their thinking. Marriage patterns are an example. Marriage across ethnic lines increased so rapidly in America that by the 1990s more than 90 percent of Polish Americans married spouses who were not Polish. In a majority of marriages involving Jews, one spouse was not Jewish. Here again, we find patterns of pluralism that are reaching beyond images of multiculturalism.

The images and icons of melting pots and pluralism and multiculturalism are images of a free society and visions of how liberty and freedom works in America. So strongly held are the ideas that have called them into being that the models and metaphors have themselves became icons of freedom and liberty. Fierce battles are being waged between the friends and enemies of these varying ideas, in wars about what is called "political correctness."

But what is most interesting here is that the images and icons of multiculturalism have lagged behind the pattern of historical change in contemporary American culture. The progress of pluralism is operating today as a solvent of rainbow coalitions, beautiful mosaics, American kaleidoscopes, and color wheels. It opens new possibilities for autonomy and community in a free society. Such is the power of our multicultural visions of liberty and freedom. Our world has changed more rapidly than our thoughts about it. The dawn of this new consciousness was yet another Morning in America, far removed from Ronald Reagan's thinking.

BOOMERS: BILL CLINTON & GEORGE W. BUSH

Visions of Freedom and Liberty for a New Generation

> I issue a call to action . . . for peace, freedom and pros-
> perity. And above all, action to build a more perfect
> union at home.
>
> —BILL CLINTON, 1997

> The enemies of liberty and our country should make
> no mistake. . . . We will defend our interests. . . .
> America at its best is a place where personal responsi-
> bility is valued and respected.
>
> —GEORGE W. BUSH, 2001

FOR SIXTY YEARS, from 1933 to 1993, the American republic was led by the generation of World War II. On the day of Pearl Harbor their ages ranged from seventeen to fifty-nine, and their rank in service varied from midshipman to commander-in-chief. In politics and personality they were very diverse, but every chief executive from Franklin Roosevelt to the elder George Bush shared the common experience of a great event that defined their moment in time.[188]

In 1993, the presidency passed to another postwar generation who called themselves boomers, after the postwar baby boom in which they were born. The first to reach the White House were William Jefferson Clinton and George W. Bush. These two men were born barely six weeks apart: Bush on July 6, 1946; Clinton on August 19, 1946. Both were raised in the American Southwest: Bush in the booming Texas cities of Midland and Houston; Clinton in the Arkansas towns of Hope and Hot Springs. They went away to eastern colleges, both as members of the star-crossed class of 1968. A formative experience in their lives was the war in Vietnam, where many of their generation were killed and wounded. Bill Clinton and George Bush escaped the draft, but even that experience left scars deeper than the wounds of battle.

Their generation was tested severely by events, more so than the generation of World War II, and in a different way. As young adults they were caught up in the troubled culture of the boomer generation. They shared its music and language, its experiments with drugs and sex, its bright hopes and deep despair, its narcissism, alienation, and anomie.

After college they went to professional schools at Yale and Harvard, made false starts in law and business, and found a calling in politics. Both suffered early defeats that made Clinton less liberal and Bush more conservative than perhaps they wished to be. But they were good at working with the mass media, brilliant at "retail politics," and highly successful at the sordid business of campaign finance. They climbed the greasy pole with lightning speed and made national reputations as state governors. Bill Clinton was elected governor of Arkansas four times; in 1991, his peers voted him the most effective governor in the nation. George W. Bush defeated a strong and popular Democratic governor in Texas, was reelected by a landslide, and earned 80 percent approval ratings in his state. Those successes took them to the White House, as the first American presidents of the boomer generation.

Within those shared experiences, Bill Clinton and George Bush were as different as two presidents of the same generation have ever been. Clinton was the posthumous son of a traveling salesman, born into a poor and broken family, and raised with a stepfather who was an abusive alcoholic. He grew up in a world where opportunities were fleeting and success was hard to achieve and even harder to maintain. But he was very bright, did well in school, graduated near the top of his class, and won a Rhodes scholarship. He never had a scholar's *Sitzfleisch* and failed to take his degree at Oxford, but he always took a scholar's delight in the life of the mind.

George Bush was the son of a president, born to an American dynasty, raised in a world of privilege where the doors of opportunity opened easily on well-oiled hinges. He got off to a slow start, did badly in school, was treated with appalling cruelty by some of his teachers, rebelled against them, graduated closer to the bottom than the top of his class, and made a shambles of his young life. But he was smarter and tougher than he appeared: a quick study and good at working with people. He also had strength of character and managed by strong effort to pull himself together, with much help from family and friends. Success followed swiftly.

The political principles of these two men were shaped by their origins and experiences. Both made frequent reference to liberty and freedom, but they gave those ideas different and even opposite meanings. To study their words and acts is to discover two very distinct visions of a free America.

Bill Clinton's Vision of Freedom: A Community of Free People

Bill Clinton was a lifelong Democrat, raised to the liberal virtues of sharing and caring for others. The struggles of his early life taught him that people needed help and that government could make a positive difference in their lives. Many different American liberal traditions became part of his life. He grew up among poor people who voted for Franklin Roosevelt and the liberal programs of the New Deal. In 1963, he met his hero President John F. Kennedy at the White House and was impressed by the cool, hip, tough-minded liberalism of the Kennedy circle. His mentor was Arkansas Senator William Fulbright, a southern liberal of another stripe, a strong internationalist, and a man of high principle.

Bill Clinton's greatest inspiration was the civil rights movement. He memorized Martin Luther King's "I Have a Dream" speech and startled his college friends by reciting it in entirety. He supported the peace movement at an early date and made many friends on the left at Oxford and Yale. From these sources, Bill Clinton absorbed much from America's many diverse liberal traditions. He was also influenced by the collapse of socialism and communism, by the power of conservative politics in the American Southwest, and still more by the revival of neoclassical free-market ideas. All of these elements came together in his "New Democratic" thinking, a powerful and creative approach to public questions.

Bill Clinton's inaugural addresses celebrated the "blessings of liberty" in phrases from the past and spoke also of the "bright flame of freedom spreading throughout all the world." A clue to his vision appeared in one of his most successful speeches, delivered in the Irish town of Dundalk before an enthusiastic audience of sixty thousand people. "The story of the United States," Clinton told them, ". . . is largely about three things: love of liberty, belief in progress, struggle for community. The last has given us the most trouble, and troubles us still."[189]

Many of Bill Clinton's campaign materials expressed a vision of freedom as a community of rights. Author's collection.

That linkage was a strong and steady theme in his presidency. Much of his rhetoric centered on an idea of bringing free people together, as in a speech called "Shared Values and Soaring Spirit," which was a "celebration of the American spirit in every community" and a vindication of "our common culture" in a multicultural age.[190]

The same ideas appeared in his commencement speech at the University of California at San Diego in 1997, which centered on a vision of "One America in the 21st Century." It celebrated the idea of a society that gave "freedom and a fair chance" to everyone and rejected images of individual autonomy. "Living in islands of isolation—some splendid and some sordid—is not the American way," he said. "We have torn down the barriers in our laws. Now we must break down the barriers in our lives, our minds and hearts."

American political theory is often a chapter of autobiography, and so it was with Bill Clinton. He said, "I grew up in the shadows of a divided America, but I have seen glimpses of one America." He lived through the divisions of the 1970s and dreamed of leading "one nation at peace with itself, bound together by shared values and aspirations and opportunities and a real respect for our differences."[191]

Here was a vision of freedom in its aboriginal sense of kinship and belonging to other free people, and a sharing of rights. It was an old idea, renewed in its vision of a multicultural community that respected the diversity of its members. This idea of "coming together" appeared not only in Bill Clinton's rhetoric but in his policies and personality. It was closely linked to both his virtues and his vices. A weakness was his obsession with the approval of others, both in general and individual terms. He rarely acted without taking polls, even in one case before he made a choice of a vacation. A strength was his empathy for others, which manifested itself in acts and words and overflowed in tears and bear hugs.

All this had great appeal to Americans of the boomer generation. People warmed to Bill Clinton without entirely trusting him. Even before the troubles of his second term, a cartoonist represented him in an affectionate way as "The Flim Flam Man." But people responded to him with the same affection that he showed to others. Women strongly supported him, even after the scandals began to break. Erica Jong wrote, "Women hated what Bill Clinton did, but we just couldn't seem to hate Mr. Clinton. He was just such a good communicator. He talked to us. He listened to us. He was in touch with our feelings."[192]

Black Americans also responded to his inclusive vision of America and to the warmth of his manner. At Yale Law School, a classmate remembered that "he found a seat for himself at the black table, a place rarely visited by other whites . . . Clinton broke the self-imposed color barrier

Joyous photographs such as this one of Bill Clinton in Harlem, July 30, 2001, and his decision to place his office there after leaving the White House, showed the character of his vision of freedom as a sharing of rights. Corbis/Bettmann.

simply by sitting down and talking . . . he soon won them over." His friend Bill Coleman remembered of the black students, "They feel some part of the soul that touches each other. . . . Bill had it."[193]

Most of Clinton's presidential acts were attempts to build a community of free people on the basis of universal rights and mutual respect. A leading example was his National Service Plan and the Americorps, which opened opportunities for American youth (at first strongly resisted by Republicans in the 1990s). Others included an ill-fated attempt to create a national health program that would guarantee care for all Americans (defeated in the Congress), the opening of the military to homosexuals (bitterly attacked by conservatives), a very large expansion of national parks and protected lands (fought tooth and nail by western business groups), and more rigorous environmental controls (resisted by corporations).

In foreign affairs Bill Clinton favored international agreements to promote human rights throughout the world and played a major role in seeking peace in the Middle East, Asia, the Balkans, and Northern Ireland. One of his greatest successes was his economic policy, which combined liberal policies with fiscal conservatism and free-market economics—a powerful and popular combination but deeply disliked by unions and corporations in need of protection. As governor and president, Bill Clinton led his party to the center. With Secretary of the Treasury Robert Rubin he pursued a rigorous policy of fiscal restraint, a balanced budget, and higher taxes that gave conservative Republicans an issue they used with great effect in congressional elections, especially in the South and West. His economic policy was unpopular in the region of his birth, but it was a successful attempt to stimulate growth and stability in the economy.

In other ways, Bill Clinton did badly as president. Areas of persistent weakness were military affairs and international security. He had no knowledge of military problems, alienated the armed services, failed miserably as a military leader in Somalia, and was one of the least successful commanders-in-chief in American history. Even so, Bill Clinton's vision of freedom had strong appeal to the American people. His personal approval ratings were high for most of his presidency and he won reelection by a comfortable margin—the only Democratic president to win two national elections since the New Deal.

His idea of freedom as full membership for all people in a free society was seen from the right as profoundly hostile to liberty as individual independence and responsibility. Among conservatives, he became the most hated liberal president since Franklin Roosevelt. Bill Clinton outraged the right when he raised taxes, regulated business, spent money on schools and social services, protected homosexuals in the military, defended a woman's right to have an abortion, and supported affirmative action for racial minorities.

He was caught in a personal scandal that ended in impeachment, crippled his administration, and gravely weakened his moral authority. In opinion polls, a majority of Americans continued to support him, but conservative opponents became even more hostile than before. Ironically, a president who tried to bring Americans together ended by dividing the nation. He opened the way for the election of George W. Bush, who had a very different vision of America and the world.

George W. Bush's Vision of Liberty as Individual Responsibility

George W. Bush was born into a family of conservative New England Republicans with a strong sense of civic responsibility. In Midland and Houston he absorbed the raw entrepreneurial conservatism of the oil patch and the antigovernment lone star conservatism of the Texas backcountry. Through family and friends, he associated with corporate conservatives who deeply believed that what was good for big business was best for everyone. He also acquired the libertarian conservatism of the Republican intelligentsia, embraced the Christian conservatism of Billy Graham, and shared the militant conservatism of his hunting and shooting friends. At least six of America's many conservative traditions came together in his life. Together they made him the most conservative president in American history, well to the right of Ronald Reagan, Calvin Coolidge, and even his very conservative father.

But this mix of conservative values also made him different from others on the far right. His relentless Texas liberal critic Molly Ivins wrote from long observation that "George W. Bush is not stupid, and he is not mean." He was good at remembering names because he took an interest in people. The folkways of West Texas gave him what he called his "populist streak." But it was a streak on a very conservative animal. Most of all he was steeped in the conservative virtues of loyalty, fidelity, and individual responsibility.[194]

In the election of 2000, George Bush insisted that he "had a clear vision of where I want to lead America." Liberal journalists showed no interest in his ideas and cruelly mocked his language, but as Molly Ivins wrote, "You can usually tell what he meant to say." George Bush often talked of liberty and freedom. Much of his electioneering imagery in the election of 2000 centered on those ideas. A favorite campaign button showed Bush with the Statue of Liberty on one side and the Liberty Bell on the other. Underneath was the double slogan "Liberty and Freedom." Another campaign badge showed him with the Liberty Bell and the words "Liberty" and "Bush."[195]

The campaign emblems of George W. Bush showed a strong consciousness of liberty and freedom and both ideas together. They also communicated a deep belief of individual rights. Author's collection.

George Bush had a vision of liberty that centered on an idea of individual responsibility. Like Bill Clinton, his political thought was a chapter of autobiography, but with a different theme. "Because I come from the baby-boomer generation," he said, "we've got to usher in an era of responsible behavior."[196]

That idea often recurred in his thinking and was informed by two books, Myron Magnet's *The Dream and the Nightmare: The Sixties Legacy to the Underclass* and Peter Collier and David Horowitz's *Destructive Generation: Second Thoughts about the Sixties.* Both books argued that individual responsibility in the boomer generation had been destroyed by the entitlements of the liberal welfare state.[197]

George Bush believed deeply in an idea of liberty as individual autonomy and responsibility, and of "big government" as its enemy. As governor of Texas he cut taxes so deeply that the state did not have funds for social programs. As president he did exactly the same thing and succeeded in reducing Federal taxes so severely that a huge federal surplus that had been painfully accumulated over the past decade vanished in less than a year.

At the same time, George W. Bush reduced the regulatory role of government in the economy. Once he said, "Entrepreneurship equals freedom." By entrepreneurship he meant the autonomy of an entrepreneur in private business. "I understand small business growth," he said. "I was one." As governor and president, he worked to reduce regulations for environmental protection, product safety, and public health.

George Bush subscribed to the American business creed, which held that private business was the soul of the American system and the source of its material strength. He had no objection to government activity in support of private enterprise and believed in an alliance between government and people of wealth. At the Al Smith Dinner in New York he made a joke of it. "This is an impressive crowd, the haves and the have mores," he said. "Some people call you the elite. I call you my base."[198]

The lion's share of George W. Bush's tax cuts went to people of wealth, mostly to people of great wealth. He favored government subsidies for private corporations in many forms: free access to public lands for private profit; free use of public resources by private elites. As the head of a professional sports franchise called the Texas Rangers, he

George W. Bush at Crawford, Texas, August 10, 2002. Mr. Bush's home on the open range of west Texas, his western boots and cowboy hat, and his T-shirt with emblems of lone star Texas liberty all communicated a strong sense of liberty as autonomy and individual responsibility. Photograph by Eric Draper, Associated Press/The White House via AP/Wide World Photo.

did not hesitate to use public powers of eminent domain to take private land from small property holders for a highly profitable sports and media corporation, even as he argued for minimal government and the sanctity of private property.[199]

Mr. Bush's ecological proposals reduced environmentalists to apoplexy. He relaxed pollution controls and opened conservation lands to economic exploitation, all in the name of liberty. He put forward various programs for privatization of welfare, health, and education. The arguments of Marvin Olasky's *Tragedy of American Compassion* persuaded him to try to shift social services from government to private "faith-based" religious institutions. He was the first president of either party to attempt a fundamental change in the Social Security program, by privatizing its trust funds.[200]

His deeply conservative foreign policy also broke with the policy of every American administration in the previous seventy years. Since the Second World War, every Democratic and Republican president had favored international alliances and agreements to promote peace, democracy, human rights, and free markets. Even Warren Harding and Calvin Coolidge had supported international arms control, and Herbert Hoover was a strong internationalist. George W. Bush went a different way. In the first year of his administration he refused to join international efforts to protect the environment, promote human rights, restrict bacteriological and chemical warfare, stop illegal arms sales, and limit the deployment of new ballistic missiles. In many of these instances, the United States was alone in refusing to participate. The Bush administration also became less involved in the pursuit of peace for Ireland, eastern Europe, Israel/Palestine, and, for a time, Korea. His vision of liberty in foreign affairs meant an idea of lone star diplomacy that set him apart from every president in fifty years.

George W. Bush also favored a shift in defense policy. He began his administration by abandoning the rule of maintaining conventional forces sufficient to fight two wars at the same time, a cornerstone of American military policy for many years, and he pushed deployment of long distance weapons that could be used directly from Fortress America. The twin ideas of what might be called lone star diplomacy and longhorn military strategy were grounded in a conservative vision of American liberty as autonomy and separation from others. He also adopted a policy of preemptive war, breaking fundamentally with one of America's longest traditions.

In economic policy, the Bush administration became less active in support of other national economies throughout the world and less successful in stimulating the domestic economy, a major shift from the Clinton administration. The center of its economic policy was a faith in business leaders and the "invisible hand" of the free market to put things right.

But he was not much for civil liberties or civil rights. He appointed an attorney general, John Ashcroft, and Defense Secretary Donald Rumsfeld, whose records on civil liberties were worse than A. Mitchell Palmer's. In the election of 2000, Bush repeatedly sent signals to southern supporters that he had no interest in helping racial minorities. A Bush campaign button displayed the Confederate flag, not the four-square "stainless banner" of the Civil War but the rectangular flag of massive resistance against integration and civil rights in the 1960s. Nearly 90 percent of African Americans voted against George W. Bush.

Clinton had led his party to the center. Bush took his party to the right. Midway through his first year, moderate Republican Senator Jim Jeffords of Vermont grew so unhappy with the libertarian conservatism of the Bush administration that he left the Republican party, giving control of the Senate to the Democrats. Throughout the world, America's friends were increasingly hostile to his foreign policy. The uniformed chiefs of armed services opposed his military policy. Scientists criticized his intervention on stem cell research as hostile to the progress of science.

By the summer of 2001, the country appeared to have settled into a new routine. George W. Bush retreated to the isolation of his ranch in Crawford, Texas, and to golfing and hunting resorts favored by corporate leaders. At the same time, former President Bill Clinton opened his own retirement office in the center of Harlem and continued to practice the symbolic politics of community-in-diversity.

In 2001, partisanship increased rapidly in the administration, Congress, and the mass media. American politics were deeply corrupted by campaign contributions of special interest groups to both political parties. The economy slipped into decline. It was not the republic's finest moment.

Then suddenly an event intervened. As so many times before, a single incident changed the course of American history. It also changed the president and the presidency, and the way that Americans thought about themselves. Most of all, it transformed their ideas of liberty and freedom.

AMERICA ATTACKED

Freedom, Liberty, and Responsibility in a World of Terror

> Freedom and Responsibility are like Siamese twins. They die if they are parted.
>
> —Lillian Smith

> If the people will lead, eventually the leaders will follow.
>
> —Florence Robinson

Most Americans remember what they were doing on the morning of Tuesday, September 11, 2001. In the strange ways of modern memory, they vividly recall small ironies in the way the day began. New Yorkers remember the weather. It was a perfect September morning. The air above the city was very clear, and the tall buildings were sharply etched against a bright blue sky. At about 8:45 A.M., a pilot was admiring the view from a south window in a midtown skyscraper. He was amazed to see a big airliner flying straight down Manhattan Island, very low and very fast. Before his eyes, the plane veered toward the World Trade Center and crashed directly into the North Tower. A bright orange fireball billowed above the tower, and the shattered building began to burn fiercely.[201]

Film crews arrived within minutes. A little after nine o'clock, their cameras picked up another large airliner approaching from the southwest. Millions of Americans were now watching on television as it flew directly into the South Tower, and another great building became a pyre of blazing fuel and black smoke. People throughout the world were watching as a scene of unimagined horror unfolded before their eyes. From the tops of burning towers, men and women leaped to their deaths in a desperate effort to escape the flames. In the streets below, thousands ran from the shattered buildings as firemen and police rushed inside to help the victims.

At 9:50 the entire South Tower gave a strange shudder and suddenly collapsed, straight down like the descent of an elevator, into a huge pile of burning rubble. Forty minutes later the North Tower went down in the same way with the force of an earthquake. Six other buildings were destroyed by the collapse of the towers, and many were severely damaged. Reports arrived that a third aircraft crashed into the Pentagon, and a fourth plane had come down in rural Pennsylvania.[202]

Throughout America, most people thought that the first crash was a bizarre accident. Then came the second crash, and everyone knew that America was under attack. That discovery triggered all the emotions that terrorists hope to create. The first emotion was disbelief and even denial. Then came shock and horror. After the shock came fear, and after the fear was anger that any human being could be so evil as to turn hundreds of innocent people into human bombs and use them to kill thousands more.

Some demanded quick revenge, and a few lashed out at anyone who vaguely resembled a Middle Eastern terrorist. But most Americans responded differently. They were quick to understand that fear and rage are terror's friends. Courage and resolve are its mortal enemies. Many began to act in this spirit. They did so on their own initiative in a manner that is unique to a free society and rooted in American traditions of liberty, freedom, and responsibility.

This remarkable response appeared in the first moments of the attack. As in other surprise events in American history, the nation's top leaders were not in a position to lead. It wasn't their fault. President Bush was in Florida when the attacks came. He had stayed overnight in a golfing resort and was having a photo opportunity in an elementary school when the attack came. The first concern of his staff was for his safety. He was rushed to Air Force One, which took off in much confusion. It flew away from Washington and New York to a "secure facility" at a remote Air Force base in Louisiana, then farther to another base in Nebraska. The president disappeared into an underground bunker and remained there for much of the day. Even the extreme conservative William Bennett commented in dismay, "This is not 1812. It cannot look as if the president has run off."[203]

In Washington, there was panic at the White House. Secret Service agents ran into the office of Vice President Richard Cheney, "grabbing his arms, his shoulders and his belt," and "all but carried him" to a bunker deep underground. In the Executive Office Building, security officers went "racing through the offices," "screaming" at the presidential staff,

"Get out! Get out! This is real!" News photographs showed White House workers fleeing for their lives across Lafayette Park.[204]

These scenes brought to mind earlier crises in American history. On April 19, 1775, the day of Lexington and Concord, the two top New England leaders of the Revolution were thought to be in mortal danger. Samuel Adams and John Hancock were led away from Lexington and spent the day as fugitives in safe houses. On August 24, 1814, when the British burned Washington, President James Madison was taken into the countryside, away from the action, for the same reason. In a moment of danger these men were thought to be more important as symbols than as leaders, and they were rushed to a place of safety, much against their inclination.[205]

On the morning of September 11, the most interesting thing is what happened next. Other Americans began to act on their own initiative. Among them were air traffic controllers and their boss, Federal Aviation Administrator Jane Garvey, a former schoolteacher from Massachusetts. Immediately after the second attack, duty officers in the air traffic control system took it upon themselves to shut down the entire aviation system. Planes in the air were ordered to land. Jane Garvey and Transportation Secretary Norman Mineta supported them and made a series of unprecedented decisions to hold all American aircraft at departure gates. At about 9:40 Jane Garvey and others ordered all civil aircraft to land immediately at the nearest feasible airport. Such a decision had never been made before. It may have saved many lives. Credible evidence later revealed that other large aircraft also had teams of terrorists on board.[206]

In the Justice Department, "barely minutes" after the planes crashed into the World Trade Center, FBI agents moved quickly to obtain authorization for surveillance of telephone calls by suspected terrorists. Authority was speedily granted by a special court, and the Justice Department began to intercept calls from terrorists, who were arrested. It is believed that these decisions also prevented other terrorist acts.[207]

On American Flight 11, which crashed into the North Tower, flight attendant Madeline Sweeney called her airline as the hijacking began and reported what had happened, and the news was quickly passed to other agencies. "She was very calm, almost eerily calm," a source said. Passengers and crew on other flights did the same thing. Aboard the fourth hijacked aircraft, between nine and ten o'clock, passengers learned by cell phone what was happening. On their own initiative, they rose against the terrorists and stopped them. At the cost of their lives, they saved many others.[208]

In New York City, many people in the burning buildings helped oth-

ers to get out. Witnesses reported that there was remarkably little panic. Nearly three thousand people died that day, but as many as twelve thousand escaped from the burning buildings, with much aid from others. New York's beleaguered Mayor Rudolph Giuliani rose to the occasion with a strong and calming presence that was a model of spontaneous leadership. Many New Yorkers acted in the same spirit. Firemen, police, rescue workers, and strangers in the streets rushed to help the victims, and many sacrificed their lives for others.

Some of the most courageous acts happened in the upper stories of the burning towers, where hundreds of men and women were trapped above the fires and knew that they would soon be dead. Many thought first of helping others and called on cell phones or regular telephones or e-mail to offer consolation and support to their loved ones. These examples continued through that terrible day, which might have been even worse had it not been for spontaneous acts of initiative and leadership by many individuals.[209]

Throughout the country, millions of Americans thought of others before themselves. They acted as their ancestors had done before them in difficult times. As early as 1776, Benjamin Rush thought that it was a tendency of people in republics to behave better when times are worse. "Our republics cannot long exist in prosperity," he wrote in the dark days of the American Revolution. "We require adversity and appear to possess most of the republican spirit when most depressed."[210]

This response inspired an iconography of helping and caring for others, which was central to the ancient spirit of freedom—an awareness that rights of belonging brought responsibility and obligations in a time of desperate urgency. A new symbol of this old idea was an American flag made for the people of New York by children in the first grade in Centerville, Virginia. It was not the usual pattern of stars and stripes. Instead the children made a design of hearts and hands, reaching others in need.

Terror and the Traditions of a Free Society

These reactions were remarkably similar to responses to other catastrophic events in American history. People knew what to do on September 11 without having to be told. In a long and bloody history Americans had been attacked many times before, often on their own soil, sometimes in their own homes. In 2001, few Americans remembered the earliest attacks. Nobody spoke of Jamestown in 1622, or New England in 1675, or Deerfield in 1704, or the day of Lexington and Concord in 1775, when a sudden attack by British Regulars killed more Americans in proportion to the total population of the colonies than did the terror attacks of 2001.[211]

In 2001, those distant events were forgotten, but they had created an historical tradition that was remembered in a uniquely American way.

The crisis of 9/11 revived a vision of liberty and independence that hearkened back to the American Revolution. In 2002 the United States Navy brought back the old rattlesnake flag that Americans had flown in 1776. Every warship was ordered to fly it as a warning to the world: "Don't Tread on Me!" This tattered flag was flown by amphibious vessels in Assault Craft Unit 2, while carrying troops of the 24th Marine Expeditionary Unit during Operation Iraqi Freedom in 2003. Courtesy of the U.S. Navy.

Other traditions in Europe and Asia work through long memories and elaborate rituals of remembrance. American traditions function differently. After the assault on the World Trade Center, Americans remembered the surprise attack on Pearl Harbor, and they talked of it as a precedent and a model. In the same way, Americans in 1941 recalled the Civil War, and people in 1861 recalled the American Revolution, and the generation of 1775 was keenly aware of the colonial wars.

This is the way that American traditions work. They are a long chain with short links that span sixteen generations of historical experience. On the morning of September 11, 2001, that tradition made a difference. Americans responded in exactly the same way as their forebears had done many times before. They also reacted in a way that is unique to people in free societies everywhere, with extraordinary initiative, energy, and autonomy. Free people are accustomed to acting on their own initiative. It is the way they live their lives. And in a community of freedom, they are experienced in the ways of acting together and improvising voluntary efforts that are both individual and collective.

Terror Perceived as an Attack on Liberty and Freedom

While Americans acted in these ways, they were gathering their thoughts about the event. One can follow the flow of their thinking on the Internet, in the electronic "threads" of chat-room conversations that were spun out through the day. Throughout the country, responses were remarkably alike. Without much guidance from top leaders, American attitudes and thoughts began to crystallize within hours of the attack.

Americans were quick to perceive the terrorist assault as an organized attack on their values and their way of life. Many believed that the target of the terrorists was not America but a free society, even liberty and freedom itself. This idea, more than any other, came instantly to many minds. Americans were keenly aware that an open society was highly vulnerable to such an attack. Not only was it freedom in the United States that made them so, but the expansion of freedom throughout the world. As people and ideas and goods and money could move more freely, criminals could operate in ways not possible before. Freedom was perceived to be an instrument of terror as well as its target.

In chat-rooms, Americans often expressed two thoughts on that subject. The first was that the nation's first purpose must be the defense of freedom and liberty. The second thought was that it was necessary to find a new balance between civil liberties and security. Within hours of the attack, Americans were weighing that balance in their thoughts. Most Americans favored granting the government larger powers of surveillance and detention. Many favored some restraints on freedom of movement. But it was interesting to see that many people also agreed on the importance of maintaining civil liberties where possible in a time when they were at risk.

The press was filled with debates. On the editorial page of the *Wall Street Journal,* a conservative writer insisted that "security comes before liberty" and recited a list of doubtful precedents: the Alien and Sedition Acts during the Quasi-War with France in 1798, the suspension of habeas corpus in the Civil War, the Espionage and Sedition Acts of 1918, and the imprisonment of Americans of Japanese descent in three Pacific states during the early years of World War II. But as the debate developed one could see that ideas of civil liberties were beginning to grow larger as they were challenged, which also had happened in most American wars. The result was legislation that abridged many liberties, but also a strong countermovement that sought to enlarge them.[212]

Others began to think that the new balance was between civil liberties and freedom from fear. A chat-room participant on September 11 who took the name of Sikander wrote, "Freedom means nothing if fear is attached to it." He added, "For each person who believes in true liberty, there is another who fears liberty enough to try to take it away from others. This is what a terrorist does—preys on our fears, our prejudices and ignorance."[213]

Sikander argued that one must find a balance between civil liberties

Among the most moving responses to 9/11 were those of Islamic Americans. One young woman represented herself in Islamic dress with the colors of the American flag. She combined elements of liberty as a consciousness of individual cultural identity with a strong claim to the rights of belonging in a free republic. Courtesy of Martha Cooper, the photographer.

and freedom from fear. Much began to be said and written by Americans on the subject of freedom and fear. In the *New York Times,* Deborah Solomon contributed a piece that centered on Norman Rockwell's painting *Freedom from Fear.* She wrote, "To see the painting today is to see six decades slip away. We know now what it means to crave freedom from fear, the freedom to walk kids to school and toss a baseball in a park without feeling a shadow of trepidation darken the face of American democracy."[214]

The *New York Times* itself ran a full-page reprint of Norman Rockwell's *Freedom from Fear* with one change—the newspaper in the father's hand was changed to the *Times* on September 12, with the headline "U.S. Attacked" and a photograph of the World Trade Center in flames.[215] For Americans it was suddenly clear that a free society required yet another sort of balance between freedom from fear and civil liberties. They went in search of it in both collective effort and individual action.[216]

Americans also rediscovered the old truth that in a moment of mortal danger, a free society must be sustained by the unity of its people. Closely linked to that idea was another: that freedom itself was a form of belonging in a united community of free people. Suddenly American flags appeared everywhere. In Kent, Connecticut, Kevin Sabia painted the entire front of his house to resemble an American flag. In New York City, a fashion designer wrapped his office building in an enormous mesh flag. At a baseball game in Los Angeles, players unrolled a flag so large that it covered the entire outfield. Teenage girls painted their lips and nails red, white, and blue.[217]

Mottos and slogans of unity blossomed spontaneously on message boards throughout the United States. On Maine's Route 3 in Ellsworth, every church and mall and motel and roadside merchant posted messages of unity, mostly drawn from patriotic songs and poems: "God Bless America," "United We Stand," "Home of the Brave," "Land of the Free." Many of these expressions of unity were combined with symbols of liberty and freedom. On the Connecticut Turnpike and the New York Thruway, huge billboards displayed the favorite slogan "United We Stand" with an image of the Statue of Liberty.

Watching from abroad, Cornel Nistorescu, managing editor of the Rumanian newspaper *Evenimentul Zilei,* wrote, "Why are Americans so united? They don't resemble one another even if you paint them! They speak all the languages of the world. . . . Still, the American tragedy turned three hundred million people into a hand put on the heart." He asked why: "What on earth can unite the Americans in such a way? Their land? Their galloping history? Their economic power? Money? I tried for hours to find an answer. . . . I thought things over, but I reached inevitably one conclusion. Only freedom can work such miracles."[218]

Other events were quick to follow. A war in Afghanistan further united Americans, but then another war in Iraq deeply divided them. In a whirl of great events, the collision of contested visions of liberty and freedom continued, stronger and more intense than ever before.

CONCLUSION

The View from Tocqueville's Terrace

> In America, free *moeurs* have made free political insti-
> tutions; in France it is for free political institutions to
> make free *moeurs*.
>
> —ALEXIS DE TOCQUEVILLE

W HAT HAVE WE LEARNED from this inquiry? How are we
to understand the history of liberty and freedom in America?
With every answer, new questions continue to multiply. What
have been the main lines of change, and major patterns of cause and consequence? How does the American experience compare with other cultures in the world today? What does the record of the past have to teach
us for the present and future?

A good way to approach these problems is in the company of Alexis
de Tocqueville: not the brilliant young author of *Democracy in America*,
who is widely read in the United States, but Tocqueville in the wisdom of
his maturity, who is better known in Europe. The time and place to have
explored the subject with him would have been at Sorrento, in the south
of Italy, during the winter of 1850. Tocqueville had gone there to repair his
ruined health and to plan his next writing project. One day he had a visit
from his young friend Jean Jacques Ampère. The two men walked
together on the terrace of Tocqueville's mountain villa and admired one of
the finest views in Italy. The terrace looked over a landscape of feudal
estates, ancient villages, and medieval churches. Ampère recalled that "it
was a magical prospect. The eye plunged into valleys filled with orange
trees whose fruit sparkled in the sun. From their midst rose domes, bell
towers, white villas."[1]

The view from Tocqueville's terrace was a panorama of Europe's old regime, which was still flourishing in 1850 after three generations of revolution. That paradox of persistence and change was deeply interesting to Tocqueville. He resolved to make it the subject of his next work, a multivolume history that would be the capstone of his career. Its theme was to be the history of liberty in the modern world, and the first volume would be called *The Old Regime and the Revolution*.[2]

Tocqueville spoke of his plan to his friend. "What fine subtle lofty things I heard him say on that terrace," Ampère remembered. The two men talked of old regimes and revolutions, and the progress of liberty in the modern world. Ampère was about to visit the United States and had just read *Democracy in America*. He was full of praise for the work, but Tocqueville felt that something important had eluded him. *Democracy in America* had much to say about equality in the New World but remarkably little about liberty.[3]

Tocqueville was puzzled by the history of liberty, and baffled by the task of explaining its meaning to others. "Love of liberty defies analysis," he wrote in his draft of *The Old Regime*. "Do not ask me to analyze this sublime sentiment. It is something one must feel, and logic has no part in it. It enters of itself into the noble hearts that God has prepared to receive it. It fills them, and enraptures them. We cannot explain it to souls who have never felt it."[4]

At Sorrento in 1850, Tocqueville was just beginning to collect his thoughts on that subject in a systematic way, but after a lifetime of reflection some things were clear to him. He was convinced that liberty and equality were different in their histories. Equality, he thought, was something new in the world. Liberty was older, deeply rooted in Europe's *ancien régime* even as it became a revolutionary rallying cry.[5]

Tocqueville believed that ideas of equality and liberty also differed in the way that people thought about them. The modern idea of equality existed as a philosophical abstraction, a social doctrine, and a political ideology that strongly attracted some people and repelled others. Liberty was all of those things, but mainly it was something else. In nations such as the United States, Tocqueville believed that a habitual love of liberty was rooted in what he called *moeurs*, by which he meant a fabric of inherited customs, traditions, folkways, and *habitudes*.[6]

In that respect Tocqueville observed a difference between the Old World and the New. In English-speaking America, he believed, the *moeurs* of liberty had always been very strong and kept growing stronger. In Europe, they had been strong in the distant past but had grown weak in the modern era. The result was a profound difference between the

American and French revolutions. "In America," Tocqueville wrote, "free *moeurs* have made free political institutions; in France it is for free political institutions to make free *moeurs*."[7]

Tocqueville planned to develop these ideas in his next work. Unhappily, he was not able to complete it. His health did not improve, and after a long illness he died in 1859, at the age of fifty-three. Only the first volume of his great project was drafted. That small fragment was instantly recognized as a classic, but Tocqueville's great history of liberty remained unwritten. No other scholar has followed his line of thought. Nobody has attempted to write a history of liberty and freedom as "habits of the heart."[8]

Toward a History of Liberty and Freedom

This work has attempted that task. Rather than studying the history of these great ideas primarily as a sequence of formal texts, philosophical abstractions, learned discourses, and ideological controversies, we have approached them as a set of customs, traditions, and folk beliefs. In America they are very old, but constantly renewed, and radically transformed in complex processes of persistence and change.

We have studied these folk beliefs about liberty and freedom as a sequence of visions that are seen in the mind's eye, and revealed in many forms of evidence. Most accessible is the evidence of language: that is, the history of the words themselves, and patterns of ordinary speech. Even more revealing are the signs and symbols that people have used to communicate their visions to others. Also very helpful are supporting documents, which help us to understand the meaning of these visions to people who created them and put them to work.

This inquiry began with words: a chance discovery about the origins and ancient meanings of *liberty* and *freedom*. Among the tribes of Europe and the Middle East, *freedom* derived from an Indo-European root that meant beloved. It had the same root as *friend* and described a vision of belonging to a community of free people. A free person was connected to other free people by ties of kinship or affection, and in that way unlike a slave.

Libertas and *eleutheria* in ancient Mediterranean civilizations had a different root. They derived from words for separation and meant a condition of being independent from another's will, and in that way unlike a slave. Most people in the Western world inherited one or another of these traditions: either *Freiheit* or *liberté*. English-speaking people inherited them both. The result was a dynamic tension between liberty-as-separation and freedom-as-belonging to a community of free people that is unique to the English-speaking world.

In this inquiry, the two words *liberty* and *freedom* have been used in their original and literal meanings. *Liberty* refers mainly to ideas of independence, separation, and autonomy for an individual or a group. *Freedom* means the rights of belonging within a community of free people. The phrase "liberty and freedom" refers to the combined heritage of English-speaking people and to the entire range of beliefs that have developed from their interaction. Most modern visions of these ideas bring together elements of liberty and freedom but in very different proportions.

To the archaeology of words and speech, we added the evidence of historical ethnography, mainly by drawing on a related inquiry published in *Albion's Seed.* That study finds evidence that very different visions of liberty and freedom were carried to America by English-speaking colonists during the seventeenth and early eighteenth centuries. In the New World, these ideas became folk traditions, deeply embedded in the emerging regional cultures of British America, which had their centers in New England, the Delaware Valley, the Chesapeake Bay, and the southern backcountry. Each had its own traditions of order, power, freedom, and liberty.

Other evidence of images and artifacts in this inquiry revealed many more visions of liberty and freedom in early America, and an extraordinary fertility of thought. Some of these ideas were close to classical ideas of liberty, and others to ancient visions of freedom, but most attempted to combine both liberty and freedom. Before 1776, these visions appeared in a great variety of emblems, symbols, and icons of liberty and freedom. They had developed as customs and traditions for five generations before the American Revolution. The result was a complex and dynamic culture in early America, which embraced many living traditions of freedom and liberty, all as "habits of the heart."

Consensus and Continuity:
The Centrality of Liberty and Freedom in American Thought

The American Revolution set in motion a new historical process, which combined strong elements of change and continuity. A fundamental element in any study of change is an understanding of patterns of persistence. Through four centuries, problems of liberty and freedom have always remained near the center of American thought. They have been urgently important to every American generation, even obsessively so.

More than that, they are the values that have validated other beliefs in America. From the arrival of the first English-speaking settlers to our own time, liberty and freedom have retained their central place through sixteen generations of American history.

Every now and then, these ideas have faded a little. But events intervened to make them strong again. In moments of crisis, Americans have always returned to their first principles and then moved forward to new understandings of their meaning in a changing world. In the late twentieth century, for example, moralists complained that Americans of Generations X and Y and Z had lost touch with the founding purposes of the republic. Then came the attack on the World Trade Center. In that great and terrible event, American ideas of liberty and freedom (especially freedom as rights of belonging) instantly returned to the center of American thought and became stronger than ever before.

These recurrent patterns reveal deep and highly persistent structures of value and belief. They also expose what might be called the dynamics of persistence, in the profound importance of contingent events and individual choices that reinforce those structures, and reshape them in unexpected ways.

Not every American has supported this broad tradition of liberty and freedom. In every generation some dissenters have turned against these ideas. After Jefferson's victory in 1800, a few extreme Federalists attacked an idea of "infant liberty nursed by mother mob," but younger members of that party went a different way and learned to play the game of democratic politics in an increasingly free and open system. In the Deep South, some defenders of slavery turned against liberty and freedom, but most slaveholders justified their peculiar institution in terms of liberty to enslave others. At the end of the twentieth century, some writers on the academic left lost interest in liberty and freedom. A few turned against these ideals, and tried to suppress free expression in the universities by imposing "speech codes" and a repressive regime of "political correctness" (an old Marxist term).

But American courts intervened to remind these internal exiles from an open society that they were part of a larger world. And some of the most able historians on the academic left have been trying to persuade their colleagues that to lose touch with liberty and freedom is to condemn themselves to complete irrelevance in America and the world. That is a theme of Eric Foner's excellent *Story of American Freedom,* and it is also a purpose of this work. One hopes that others on the left will respond. The intellectual failures of the academic left and leaders of the Democratic Party have severely weakened their own causes and done grave injury to public discourse and civic spirit in the United States. For three centuries, American movements that lost interest in liberty and freedom succeeded only in removing themselves from the main currents of American life.

Conflict and Change: Contested Meanings of Liberty and Freedom

Other patterns also emerged from this inquiry. In every generation many different visions of liberty and freedom have flourished in America. This was so from the beginning of British settlement. In early America we found a broad diversity of established ideas, each with its own strong cultural base, and many with a regional hegemony. There were profound differences among these cultures, but few contests between them. The most important conflicts occurred within them, as aliens and dissenters challenged dominant regional folkways.

After 1750, the most important collisions were between these provincial cultures and the British Empire. A small imperial elite with large ambitions and its own visions of liberty and freedom mounted a major challenge to every provincial culture in the American colonies. In the face of a common threat, many Anglo-American cultures came together in a Continental cause, but they retained their different traditions of liberty and freedom.

In the War of Independence that followed, Americans searched for visions of liberty and freedom that could unite them in a common cause. That search inspired new ideas of liberty and freedom: unitary and pluralist, national and sectional, republican and democratic, traditional and modern. This diversity of common visions rapidly became a contest of ideas in the party battles of the new republic and in the sectional tensions of the new nation.

In the mid-nineteenth century, other conflicts began to grow from new currents of social reform. One result was a collision between the world's strongest system of slavery and largest antislavery movement. It grew into a sectional conflict between liberty and freedom that led to the Civil War. On one side was a vision of southern independence, of liberty to keep a slave, and the right of one race to rule another. On the other was a vision of free labor, free soil, free speech, and rights of belonging for all. The Civil War was fought between competing visions of southern liberty and northern freedom.

In the end freedom triumphed, but liberty endured, and the conflicts continued through the era of Reconstruction and beyond. After Reconstruction, ideas of universal freedom were taken up by persecuted minorities in American life: new immigrants in the North, former slaves in the South, and Indians in the West.

In the 1870s, there was also a great revival of liberty as a social and economic principle, and a new concern for order. These trends collided in new conflicts in politics, economics, religion, and cultural life. These contests were complex struggles over liberty, freedom, and order. The attempt to resolve these problems led to a creative period of thought about free society in the reform movements of Populism, the labor movement, and Progressivism.

In the twentieth century, American traditions of liberty and freedom were severely tested by challenges from abroad. The result was a series of four world wars against militarism, Fascism, Communism, and terrorism, all mortal enemies of a free society. Each of these great struggles began by restricting liberty, freedom, and human rights but ended by enlarging these ideas in new contests over liberty and freedom. In intervals of peace between these world conflicts, other contests developed at home over the divisive issues of the 1920s, the Great Depression, the struggle for civil liberties and civil rights in the 1950s and 1960s, the cultural clashes of the 1970s, and a multitude of causes in the late twentieth century.

In these many contests, some ideas of liberty and freedom have been stronger than others. It is interesting to study the history of political parties in that connection. From time to time some political parties have succeeded in developing very powerful visions of liberty and freedom, which were the keys to their success and to long periods of political hegemony. The leading examples were the Jeffersonian Democrats from 1800 to 1824, the Republican Party from 1860 to 1884, liberal Democrats from 1932 to 1952, and conservative Republicans in the late twentieth century. In American politics, victory always went to the parties and leaders with the strongest and clearest visions of liberty and freedom, sometimes on the left and in other periods on the right.

Other political parties drifted away from ideas of liberty and freedom and allowed their opponents to take possession of these ideas. This happened to the Federalists in the late 1790s, Democrats in the late 1850s, Republicans in the mid-twentieth century, and Democrats at the end of the twentieth century, when one of the many mistakes of the left was to allow the right to claim the mantle of liberty and freedom. This error has often happened in American history. It has always been fatal for parties and presidents who made it.

Growth and Development: Toward a Whig History of Liberty and Freedom

These many differences over the meaning of liberty and freedom have been drivers of change in American history. Every major conflict inspired new visions of those old ideas. Most enlarged the meaning of liberty and freedom by combining them in highly inventive ways. The result was a long process of change and growth. Every American generation without exception has expanded the meaning of liberty and freedom. There have been occasional moments of stagnation and even reversal. Eric Foner reminds us that sometimes revolutions can move backward. But these retreats have been short-lived and insubstantial. The central theme of American history is about the growth of liberty and freedom.

That process of growth was stronger in some periods than others. It was strong in the era of the American Revolution, when people with different visions of liberty and freedom found themselves working together against a common enemy. The search for common visions inspired larger meanings for liberty and freedom. Other enlargements followed in the new republic, when Americans invented visions of liberty and freedom as national, republican, and democratic ideas. Another change also occurred. Values that had been understood as ancient and timeless principles began to be understood as ever-changing modern ideas that derived their meaning from their relevance to the present and their promise for the future.

Yet another long period of growth followed in the mid-nineteenth century. The great reform movements created expansive visions of liberty and freedom as social and moral principles that reached into new areas of life and culture. The antislavery movement was especially important in developing a very large vision of liberty as emancipation from bondage and freedom as full rights of citizenship for the emancipated.

After the Civil War, many groups who had been excluded from the American republic took a leading part in developing ideas of universal freedom as rights of citizenship. The leaders were former slaves in the South, Indians in the West, and new immigrants in northeastern cities. All kept the idea of universal freedom growing in a period when other groups were moving in a different direction. At the same time, other Americans enlarged the meaning of liberty as autonomy for individuals and groups. This expansion happened in many sectors of American life. It took the form of entrepreneurial liberty, religious liberty, political liberty, and many forms of cultural liberty.

The most expansive period in the long history of liberty and freedom was the twentieth century. Four world struggles against the enemies of a free society inspired new visions of liberty and freedom. The First World War against European old regimes and the repressions of the Wilson administration led to a movement for liberty and democracy. The Second World War against Fascism inspired more attention to individual liberties in the Bill of Rights and more egalitarian visions of freedom. The Cold War against Communism reinforced visions of free enterprise, civil liberties, and civil rights. The War on Terror, and the secrecy and repression of the Bush administration, may (or may not) lead to a countermovement for the opening of secret institutions in government, business, and the Catholic church.

These contests had the effect of expanding liberty and freedom in several dimensions at once. The ideas became larger in their own substantive meaning. They came to embrace a greater part of the American population. They encompassed a broader range of rights and liberties.

Many of these enlargements of liberty and freedom inspired strong resistance and even reaction, which carried in the opposite direction. But most of these countertendencies were responses to the central trend. In short, the history of liberty and freedom clearly fits a Whig model of American history. That idea became unfashionable in America during the late twentieth century, but the evidence is very clear. Through the span of four centuries, every American generation without exception has become more free and has enlarged the meaning of liberty and freedom in one way or another.

Cause and Consequence: Diversity as the Great Driver

We might ask why this is so. One conclusion emerges from this inquiry. What keeps America free is the diversity of its traditions of liberty and freedom. The tensions and contradictions in this heritage have inspired new visions of liberty and freedom and a great fertility of thought. The strength of this open system is its infinite variety. The gravest dangers to our free society are born-again apostles of one particular liberty and freedom who are incapable of imagining any way except their own. The greatest hope is that we have so many of these people, and their beliefs are so diverse.

If a free society is ever destroyed in America, it will be done in the name of one particular vision of liberty and freedom. Many single-minded apostles of a narrow idea of a free society have become tyrants in their turn. We have seen it happen in Woodrow Wilson's attorney general Mitchell Palmer. It is happening again as this book goes to press with other high officeholders. These men are passionate in their defense of a free society, but America's tradition of liberty and freedom is broader than their thoughts about it.

Liberty and Freedom in the Contemporary World: Three Models of Our Future

What is the future of freedom and liberty in the world? This was a question of great interest to Tocqueville. It has been increasingly on American minds after the attacks on the World Trade Center and the beginning of a new world war against yet more enemies of liberty and freedom. What lies ahead for us in this great struggle?

Three answers have come to mind. The first might be called the model of Americanization. Some believe that for better and for worse, the culture of the United States represents the future of the world. Many American leaders have shared this view. They think that the central theme of contemporary history is the spread of liberty and freedom, and they understand those ideas entirely in American terms. Since the end of the Cold War, American foreign policy has centered on the construction of constitutional democracies, free-market economies, and open societies very much on the American model. This vision of the future is shared even by people who oppose it. Many writers in the United States and abroad complain bitterly against the Americanization of the world.

A second prophecy, and a very dark one, is a catastrophic model of mortal conflict among irreconcilable civilizations, leading to a global apocalypse. That was the warning of a gloomy book called *The Clash of Civilizations* (1996), which predicted conflicts among eight civilizations: Sinic, Japanese, Hindu, Islamic, Orthodox Russian, African, Latin American, and the West (which includes western Europe and the English-speaking nations). The putative cause was the spread of Western culture through the world and a sense of threat and danger in other civilizations. This idea was much discussed after the terrorist attack on the United States in 2001. Some saw that event as the first of a series of world wars among civilizations that could destroy life on this planet. It is always possible that such a thing could happen. It has happened many times before on a smaller scale. But other evidence strongly suggests that our world is moving in a different direction.

If we apply the methods of this inquiry to the study of liberty and freedom throughout the world, we find a third model of the future. To study the modern history of other cultures is to discover that liberty and freedom are growing in many nations but never twice in the same way. As these ideas travel through the world, they change profoundly. Every nation (without exception) has created new visions of liberty and freedom, often by combining them with old customs and traditions. That process is similar in its dynamics to what we have observed in American history but different in its substance and scale. A few examples might make it clear.

The Goddess of Tiananmen Square: Chinese Visions of Freedom

During the spring of 1989, a new spirit of liberty and freedom blossomed in the cities and universities of China. Students marched in the streets, challenging their Communist rulers to liberate a captive nation. In Shanghai, on May 25, 1989, they formed a procession and carried a small replica of the American Statue of Liberty as a symbol of their cause. A few days later, the Federation of Beijing University Students organized a larger demonstration in Tiananmen Square. They invited students at the Central Academy of Fine Arts to create a sculpture and suggested that a large copy of the Statue of Liberty would do well. The art students were given three days to complete the task, and 8,000 yuan ($2,000 U.S.) to pay for materials.

The art students accepted the assignment but did not agree that a replica of the Statue of Liberty would be right for the occasion. They embraced the movement for a free China but did not like the idea of a symbol from another country and condemned the idea of replication itself as hostile to their creative responsibilities as artists.

The students searched for an inspiration in Chinese art but found, in the words of sculptor Tsao Hsingyuan, that "there is no tradition in China for sculpture that expresses a political concept, apart from Communist revolutionary sculptures, which would not have been appropriate." They decided to create a new image by combining elements from three sources and made a maquette to bring their themes together. They began with a piece of statuary that had been used in their art classes, a teaching model of a young male Chinese athlete holding an upraised pole in two hands. They removed the male athlete's head and replaced it with the features of a Russian woman, copied from Vera Mukhina's heroic sculpture *Worker and Collective Farm Woman*, a popular expression of equality and revolutionary realism that had been made for the Soviet Pavilion at the

1937 Paris World's Fair. The art students completed the figure by adding a third element of American inspiration. They cut off the athlete's pole and converted it to a torch inspired by the Statue of Liberty but held aloft in two upraised hands. The students combined Chinese, Russian, and American elements to create a new symbol that combined their own revolutionary vision of freedom, equality, and democracy with the two-handed Confucian and Daoist values of ancient China.

When the maquette was complete, they worked in frantic haste to build a larger version, thirty-nine feet high, of Styrofoam and plaster. In the night they carried it in bicycle carts to Tiananmen Square and erected it on the central axis of the square directly between a huge portrait of Mao Tse-tung and the ancient entrance to the Forbidden City. The work was done by dawn on the morning of May 30, 1989.

The students called it the Goddess of Democracy, and they clearly understood what would happen next. Their sculpture was built to be destroyed, which was also part of its symbolism. One of them wrote, "The statue of the Goddess of Democracy is made of plaster, and of course cannot stand here forever. But as the symbol of the people's hearts, she is divine and inviolate. Let those who sully her beware: the people will not permit this! We believe strongly that this darkness will pass, that the dawn must come. On the day when real democracy and freedom come to China, we must erect another Goddess of Democracy here in the square, monumental, towering, and permanent.... Long live the people! Long live freedom! Long live democracy!"[9]

This was a piece of performance art, in which the Communist rulers of China were summoned to play their inexorable part. The first evening, the students' plan nearly went awry when the statue was buffeted by a heavy storm, but it stood firm the next morning, dominating the huge space of Tiananmen Square. The Communist leaders seemed not to know what to do about it. They allowed it to remain four days, while Western journalists swarmed around the square and the Goddess of Tiananmen Square became a global image.

On the fifth day, its end came in symbolic scenes of high drama that the students had expected and even intended. The Communist authorities ordered a heavy Soviet tank to topple the Goddess of Democracy and crush it beneath its treads. Even as the statue was shattered into pieces, it was reborn in electronic images that flashed throughout the world. In China, popular uprisings increased from 1993 to 2003 (42,000 in that year alone).

As the image of the Goddess of Tiananmen Square spread to other

The Goddess of Tiananmen Square, erected in Beijing on May 30, 1989, was not an imperfect copy of the Statue of Liberty, as many Americans believed, but a different vision that combined an American symbol of universal freedom with European ideas of social justice and elements of Chinese culture in a new vision of a free and open society. Photograph by Peter Turnley; Corbis/Bettmann.

nations, people understood it in different ways. American journalists and politicians mistook it for a crude replica of the Statue of Liberty. Even many years after the event this interpretation is widely shared in the United States. But what seemed in American eyes to be a clumsy copy of their own icon was in fact a highly sophisticated representation of another idea, and one that was executed with skill and success.

The Chinese Goddess of Democracy was a paradigm of a new iconography that developed rapidly in the last decade of the twentieth century. As ideas of freedom and liberty spread to many cultures around the world, they grew and changed in unexpected ways. The same thing was happening in America itself. Even after many millennia of striving, the history of liberty and freedom had barely begun.

Ambedkar's Dream: The Old New Way of Indian Freedom

On August 15, 1997, the people of India celebrated the fiftieth anniversary of their national independence. The event was called a Festival of Freedom: freedom from the British Raj, the success of free institutions in South Asia, and the progress of a free society against caste and bondage. The idea of freedom was everywhere. The founders of the nation were called freedom fighters. A billboard in Hyderabad City proclaimed, "India—the new word for Freedom."[10] In fifty years of independence, visions of freedom had become profoundly important to Indians. "Every living soul yearns for freedom," wrote Kanchan Banerjee in that year, "and freedom is the first condition for any individual or nation to achieve their fullest potential."[11]

The idea of freedom was much discussed by Indians in 1997, as it had been in 1947 at the birth of the nation. When India became a free and independent nation precisely at the stroke of midnight on the night of August 14–15, 1947, the National Assembly was in session, and Pandit Nehru gave a speech called "Awake to Freedom," which is still remembered. Nehru told the assembly, "At the stroke of midnight hour, when the world sleeps, India will awake to life and freedom." He urged his country not to think of freedom as merely independence from another power. Indian freedom, he said, was something more than that. It was a moment "when the soul of a nation, long suppressed, finds utterance."[12]

Nehru's language was similar in some respects to speeches about freedom in America and Europe, and his thinking incorporated Western ideas. In the struggle against British rule, Indian leaders spoke often of freedom of speech and press, freedom of religion, economic freedom, and inalienable rights of self-government and national independence.

At the same time, Indian freedom meant something more and other than these Western ideas. The people of India have a word for free: *bindaas*. It has a double meaning. An Indian writer defines *bindaas* as "unshackled and free to be." He quotes a young Indian girl who says, "I am just happy to be *bindaas* in this great free country." The people of India joined Western conceptions of freedom to this idea of *bindaas*. They created a new meaning for freedom by grafting modern ideas on the ancient roots of Indian civilization.[13]

An early version of this Indian vision came in the writings of Swami Vivekananda in the late nineteenth century. He traveled widely in the world, spent four years in the United States, admired its open institutions, and regularly celebrated the Fourth of July in the Vale of Kashmir, even commissioning an Indian tailor to make an American flag for the occasion.

At the same time, Vivekananda joined Western ideas of freedom to his own Hindu faith. "Where is true independence?" Vivekananda asked.

He answered, "It is not freedom *of* the senses; it is freedom *from* the senses." He added, "He is free, he is great, who turns his back upon this world, who has renounced everything, who has controlled his passion, and who thirsts for peace. One may gain political independence, but if one is a slave to one's passions and desires, one cannot feel the joy of real freedom." One of his followers wrote, "His conception of freedom came from his immersion in the ideas and ideals of the Upanishads and the *Bhagavad Gita*. He knew and tried to convey to us that men would never be content with a partial and temporary image of freedom."[14] Vivekananda's freedom was also an idea of growth. Repeating a long line of Indian holy men, he said, "What you think you are, you become. Think constantly of the spirit and spirit you become, for freedom and bondage are of the mind."[15]

Within this broad frame, Indian freedom had many meanings, which were contested as strongly as American visions had been. India's Communist leader E.M.S. Namboodiripad observed in a speech at Nehru University, "For the Hindus freedom meant the revival of the golden Maurya Gupta period, for the Muslims it meant the revival of the dead Sultanate, and for the Sikhs freedom meant the rule of Maharajah Ranjit Singh. The freedom struggle thus expressed itself in different forms."[16]

But in these different programs of liberation, one finds a common vision that united many people in South Asia and distinguished them from others in the world. One finds it in the poet Rabindranath Tagore, in his "Song of Free India," as an idea of liberty as emancipation from British rule and freedom as unity with the spirit of the universe itself.[17]

One of the most remarkable visions of Indian freedom came from a Hindu turned Buddhist, Dr. B. R. Ambedkar. He was born an untouchable, in a caste so low that he could not sit with others or drink at the same well. As a child he was treated worse than an animal by other Hindus. British officials and the maharajah of Baroda founded a school for untouchables, and Ambedkar attended it. He did so well that he was sent to Columbia University in New York, where he earned a Ph.D. in economics. Then he became a barrister in London and returned to India to work for the rights of untouchables.[18]

Ambedkar became a leader in the movement for Indian independence. He and Gandhi have been compared to Frederick Douglass and Abraham Lincoln in the United States. When India became a nation, he was its first minister of law and framed the Indian constitution. But he found himself increasingly at odds with the ruling Congress Party. Most of all, Ambedkar felt that the Indian people were losing their way in the modern world and losing touch with their own values. He found himself increasingly drawn to Buddhism, a religion of high importance in India's past but with few followers in his own time.[19]

Ambedkar searched for a way to correct problems that flowed from Hindu belief in a rigid caste system, inevitable karma, and fixed hierarchy without denying the integrity of Indian values. He found a solution in Buddhism, which had deep roots in Indian culture and a strong belief in the equality of all living things. He wrote to a friend, "There is an onslaught of ideas on our people from different countries from the four corners of the world. In this flood our people may be confused. There are strong attempts to separate the people struggling hard from the main lifestream of this country, and attract them towards other countries. Even some of my colleagues who are disgusted with 'untouchability,' poverty and inequality are ready to be washed away by this flood. I must show them the way. At the same time we have to make some changes in the economic and political life. That is why I have decided to follow Buddhism."[20]

On October 14, 1956, Ambedkar became a Buddhist. So large was his following that by the end of the next day half a million Indians converted to Buddhism, and three million in the next few years, and many more thereafter. The center of this movement was Maharashta in western India, which is rich in ancient Buddhist shrines that became the center of a living faith.

Ambedkar died in December 1956, and he himself became a Buddhist icon. In parts of western India where Buddhism is strong, one sees by the roadsides sacred images of Buddha and Ambedkar side by side. Buddha appears in his saffron robe. Ambedkar wears a blue business suit with a white shirt and red tie. He wears reading glasses and has an American fountain pen in his pocket. In one hand he carries a law book, which is labeled *Bharat* (India).[21] Ambedkar has become a national icon in India. A bronze statue was erected in front of the Parliament Buildings in New

A living symbol of liberty and freedom in India was Dr. B. R. Ambedkar, a Hindu Untouchable who attended British schools and earned a doctorate from Columbia University. He combined Western ideas of liberty, freedom, and democracy with ancient Hindu and Buddhist values. In India today one finds Buddhist shrines to Ambedkar in Western dress, sometimes next to Buddha in his robes. He inspired a uniquely Indian vision of a free and open society in harmony with its ancient Hindu and Buddhist faiths. Photograph from Alistair McMillan, Nuffield College, Oxford.

Delhi and the Secretariat in Bombay.[22] But other images represent him in a different way, as a Buddhist saint in Indian dress, absorbed in deep contemplation, and in the study of values very different from those of the Western world.

Ambedkar is remembered and understood for many contributions to his nation. He played a major role in the design of India's national flag, which he conceived as a symbol of freedom. It grew from Gandhi's chakra flag, adopted by the All India Congress Committee in 1931, which displayed a simple domestic spinning wheel called the chakra, a symbol of freedom through self-reliance. It reminded the people of India that they could be free only by spinning their own thread and growing their own food. Gandhi's chakra was set on three horizontal bands of color: saffron for Hindu, green for Moslem, and white for harmony. In 1947, the Assembly adopted the flag with one change. Ambedkar proposed that Gandhi's spinning wheel or chakra should become the dharmachakra, the Buddhist wheel, taken from an ancient Sarnath Lion Capital. In Buddhist iconography it had many meanings. It was the wheel of law. At the same time, it was also an image of the cosmos itself, a circle and not a line. Something of Gandhi's spinning wheel was preserved in another way. Today all true Indian flags are made of khadi, or homespun cloth. For daily use they are made of cotton khadi, and for ceremony silk khadi. But always a proper Indian flag is made of threads spun on Gandhi's simple domestic chakra. Here is an emblem that Hindus, Moslems, Sikhs, and Buddhists could share as a dream of freedom. The Indian Communist leader Namboodiripad wrote that Marxism never appealed to the majority of the Indian people, in large part because it turned away from the idea of freedom itself, which was the strongest principle of unity in a pluralist nation. A leading architect of that distinctively Indian idea of unity and freedom was Ambedkar.[23]

Slota Wolnusc: Poland's Golden Freedom in a New Age

Yet another vision of freedom appeared in eastern Europe. It appeared on Sunday, June 4, 1989, when the people of Poland went to church in such numbers that the congregations overflowed into the streets. Then they went to vote in the first free elections that most of them had ever known. It was a quiet day, without violence or even demonstrations, but it was also a day of revolution, such as the world had never seen. A brutal Communist regime allowed itself to be voted out of power by a rising of the Polish people.

In the months that followed, ten other Communist regimes collapsed in eastern Europe. The world watched this event in amazement and wondered how it could have happened. Americans saw it as the triumph of their struggle for freedom in the Cold War. Russians thought it was the result of glasnost and perestroika. The princes of the Catholic Church believed that it flowed from their acts. Academic writers who were unable to predict it were quick to explain it as the inevitable result of historical determinants. But it was the people of eastern Europe who did the work. Mary Kaldor urges us to remember the importance of "agency," which she understands as "the actions and behavior and thinking of the actors who actually carried out the revolutions in the period immediately preceding 1989."[24]

For centuries, Poland had suffered more from tyranny than any other nation in the world. It had an ancient memory of *slota wolnusc,* golden freedom, a Polish tradition that flourished in the fifteenth and sixteenth centuries and was defined by its history. For the Polish people, *slota wolnusc* meant an independent country that governed itself with an elective king and a diet called the *sjem,* an assembly of autonomous nobles who were a large part of the population (much larger than in western Europe). Poland's *slota wolnusc* was also an idea of comity, and *civitas.* It included a spirit of tolerance that embraced Czechs, Byelorussians, Germans, and millions of Jews who increased and multiplied in Poland more than anywhere else in the world.

This system of *slota wolnusc* flourished in the early modern era, but it had a fatal weakness. Poland was surrounded by predatory rulers, and its open institutions were unable to stand against them. In the eighteenth century, at the time when the United States was winning its independence, Poland was conquered by the rulers of Prussia, Austria, and Russia, who reduced the Polish people to a condition of misery and bondage. It was an event that gave liberty and freedom a bad name in central Europe. Many thought that Poland's open institutions were the cause of its misfortunes. The English traveler William Coxe wrote in 1792, "Polish liberty may be considered as the source of Polish wretchedness."[25]

Poles remember their history in a different way, as a never-ending struggle for liberty and freedom. Every Polish generation fought for this idea in the revolutions of 1794, 1830, 1848, 1863. Every revolution failed, but the idea of freedom persisted, and Poland's struggle continued for many generations. They created a national culture without a nation-state, and a culture of freedom that flourished in the face of tyranny.

In the modern era, the great plains of Poland became a battleground for the powers of central Europe. The wars of the eighteenth century took a heavy toll. So did the wars of Napoleon. In the First World War, Poland suffered terribly. Its young men were conscripted by both Russia and Germany, and millions died in the fighting that moved back and forth across Polish soil.

In 1918 independence was restored to Poland, largely by the intervention of American President Woodrow Wilson. Armistice Day, November 11, is still celebrated as Liberation Day in Poland. After 1918, Polish armies under Marshal Josef Pilsudski defeated both Russian and German forces in heavy fighting, and Poland remained free for twenty years. But its institutions were unstable, and its neighbors were more predatory than ever. In 1939, German Fascists joined with Russian Communists to conquer Poland, and once again it disappeared from the map of Europe. Seven million Poles died in the Second World War, more than 20 percent of the nation, a larger proportion than in any other country. There is a saying: Squeeze the soil of Poland, and blood flows.

After the Second World War, Poland became nominally independent, but a Communist terror was fastened on the Polish people by the Red Army, and the struggle for freedom continued. Stalin complained that to build Communism in Poland was like trying to saddle a cow—but this was not a nation of cattle. Polish freedom fighters attacked Soviet tanks in Poznan in 1956. They took to the streets in 1968 and again two years later, in 1970, when they set fire to police buildings and Communist Party headquarters throughout the country. The results of armed resistance were always the same: brutal defeat and bloody repression.

Then something remarkable happened. A new generation of Polish leaders decided to continue the struggle for freedom in a different way. Many Poles were part of this great effort. Prominent among them was journalist Adam Michnik. During the 1950s and 1960s he was active in clandestine associations such as the Club of the Crooked Circle and the Flying Universities, which kept alive the idea of freedom in the darkest years. Michnik spent six years in prison and was lucky to come out alive. In his cell, he reflected on Poland's special tradition of freedom and the failure of its many revolutions.

The result was a collection called *Letters from Prison* (1978) and an essay called "The New Evolutionism," which proposed another method of resistance. A major part of this method was nonviolence. Michnik wrote in his *Letters from Prison*, "Our knowledge about the mechanisms of the Bolshevik dictatorship led us to reject violence as a way of fighting for freedom." He concluded that violent revolution would either "be doomed to fail" or, if it succeeded, "freedom would not win."

Michnik called for another method of resistance—a revolution not to seize power by brute force but to change the relationship between society and the state. He proposed to break down the totalitarian system by nurturing "institutions of parallel society" and creating an idea of what he called "civil society." Its object was to pry open a closed society by creating internal spaces within a totalitarian system. It was also to wear down a tyranny by constant erosion, like water dripping on stone.[26]

Michnik argued that this "parallel society" already existed in Polish institutions that stood apart from the Communist system. Some were created by intellectuals such as Michnik himself in their secret clubs and clandestine universities, in the mass media that were called "the second circulation," in the stubborn independence of Polish farmers, and in the Catholic Church, which for generations had been "the only independent institution in our conquered country." For its defense of Polish freedom the Catholic Church won massive support. At mass the priests prayed, "O Lord, please return us to our free fatherland."

Other elements were the Polish labor unions. In 1976, worker protests in Radom and Ursus led to the creation of the Committee for the Defense of the Workers, which Adam Michnik called one of the "first institutions of the parallel society." Then at the Lenin Shipyard in Gdansk, a new leader emerged, Lech Walesa (Valensa), an electrician who had been born in a mud hut during the German occupation, never received much formal education, and boasted that he never read a serious book in his life. He was a brilliant organizer and instantly understood Michnik's idea of a parallel society. Walesa urged his fellow workers, "Instead of burning Communist committee buildings down, create your own committees."[27]

In 1980, the workers, the Church, and the intellectuals began to work together in a movement called Solidarity, a loose federation with many centers and millions of sympathizers throughout the country. In the spring of 1989, walls and kiosks displayed its vivid emblem: the simple word *Solidarnosc*, in bright red letters against a white background—the colors of Polish freedom and independence. When one looked closer, the letters of *Solidarnosc* became a procession of Polish people, moving freely together in a common cause. Here was a symbol of Adam Michnik's idea of a civil society, Lech Walesa's Solidarity, and Poland's ancient dream of golden freedom.

Westerners were very slow to understand what was happening. French historian François Furet wrote, "With all the fuss and noise, not a single new idea has come out of eastern Europe in 1989." A German scholar named Jurgen Häbermas missed it entirely and wrote contemptuously of "a peculiar characteristic of this revolution, namely its total lack of ideas that are either innovative or oriented towards the future." Western intellectuals could not understand that freedom and liberty flourish best as customs, traditions, and folk beliefs, not as doctrines or ideologies. So creative were Polish leaders within the frame of their own tradition that French and German intellectuals found their thinking incomprehensible.[28]

Americans misunderstood in another way. It was easy for them to make that mistake. One of the most famous Polish posters summoned people to vote with an individual figure of the Gary Cooper of *High Noon*, in his sheriff's clothing, with a six-gun on his hip and a Solidarity badge on his vest. When Solidarity succeeded, American presidents descended on Poland and proclaimed that the Polish Revolution was an extension of America ideas. On July 5, 1992, George Bush senior declared that Polish freedom was mainly about "free government and free enterprise." Other American leaders have shared that misconception. They looked at new images of free society in Poland and mistakenly saw it as a mirror of their own American society.

**W SAMO POŁUDNIE
4 CZERWCA 1989**

This poster summoned the people of Poland to vote at noon on June 4, 1989, their first free elections in more than fifty years. Americans saw an image of Gary Cooper in the film High Noon *and believed that their ideas of liberty and freedom were spreading to eastern Europe. But something else was happening here: Gary Cooper was wearing the badge of Poland's Solidarnosc (Solidarity) Party. It was striving for another new idea of a free society that combined an American visions of living free with Adam Michnik's ideas of civic society and deep Polish traditions of* slota wolnusc *(golden freedom). Poster in the collection of the author.*

In 1989, we were invited to visit Poland and to observe the first free elections. We talked with Polish leaders of Solidarity and with academic colleagues. In these conversations, most Polish leaders were deeply devoted to ideas of liberty and freedom, for they had experienced life without them. But their visions of these ideals were far from American ways of thinking. Lech Walesa observed that "capitalism is not the best way of running things."[29] The Pope addressed the Polish parliament on June 11, 1999, and urged that there could be "no freedom without solidarity" and expressed strong belief in "the moral lessons of Solidarnosc" and the memory of a "Polish tradition" that offered values distinct both from Russian communism and American capitalism.[30]

Poland has its own idea of living free. Its

In the end we come to a quilt called "Hope" by the American artist Barbara Barber of Westerly, R.I., 1985. It derives from an old photograph of an immigrant family gazing at the Statue of Liberty, and the words of Emma Lazarus are stitched around the border. The dress of the family is changed to clothing that is worn throughout the world in our own time. The image is a memory of the past and a vision of the future bright with the promise of liberty and freedom. Courtesy of Barbara Barber.

memory of *slota wolnusc,* its dream of *solidarnosc,* and its understanding of Adam Michnik's ideal of civic society all came together in a dream of liberty and freedom that is unique to the experience of this nation, and an original contribution to the world history of these "habits of the heart."

In China, India, and eastern Europe, these old and yet very new visions of liberty and freedom touch the lives of half the people in the world. Other new chapters in this contemporary history are being written in countries around the world. Not all of them are success stories. But for every nation that is struggling to find its own way, many more are creating new visions of freedom and liberty by joining these expansive ideas to their own cultures. As freedom and liberty travel through the world, they change and grow in unexpected ways, mainly by the interplay of new ideas and old folkways.

All of them draw on ancient beliefs in liberty and freedom that rose three millennia ago. Each creates new versions of these principles, in ways that nobody could have predicted or even imagined. That is the very nature of freedom and liberty. Their history is as open as the ideas themselves. This free and open process is the source of their strength in the world today, and it is bright with the promise of a better world to come.

ABBREVIATIONS

AA4 and *AA5*   Peter Force, ed., *American Archives,* 4th ser., 6 vols., March 7, 1774, to
Aug. 21, 1776, and 5th ser., 3 vols., May 3, 1776, to Dec. 31, 1776
(Washington, 1837–53)

AHR   *American Historical Review*

AL   *Collected Works of Abraham Lincoln,* ed. Roy P. Basler, 8 vols. (New
Brunswick, 1953)

APS   American Philosophical Society

BL   British Library

BM   British Museum

CSMP   *Colonial Society of Massachusetts Publications*

CTHSC   *Connecticut Historical Society Collections*

EIHC   *Essex Institute Historical Collections*

GW   *The Papers of George Washington, Revolutionary War Series,* ed. W. W.
Abbott, Dorothy Twohig, Philander D. Chase, and Beverly H.
Runge (Charlottesville, 1983+)

HSD   Historical Society of Delaware

HSDP   *Historical Society of Delaware Papers*

HSP   Historical Society of Pennsylvania

JP   *The Papers of Thomas Jefferson,* ed. Julian Boyd (Princeton, 1950–)

JW/F   *The Writings of Thomas Jefferson,* ed. Paul L. Ford, 10 vols. (New
York, 1892–99)

JW/L&B	*The Writings of Thomas Jefferson,* ed. A. A. Lipscomb and A. E. Bergh, 20 vols. (Washington, 1903)
LC	Library of Congress
MDHM	*Maryland Historical Magazine*
MDHS	Maryland Historical Society
MHS	Massachusetts Historical Society
MHSP	*Massachusetts Historical Society Proceedings*
NA	National Archives
NCHR	*North Carolina Historical Review*
NDAR	William Bell Clark, ed., *Naval Documents of the American Revolution,* vol. I (Washington, 1964)
NEQ	*New England Quarterly*
NJH	*New Jersey History*
NJHSP	*New Jersey Historical Society Proceedings*
NYHS	New-York Historical Society
NYHSQ	*New-York Historical Society Quarterly*
NYH	*New York History*
PMHB	*Pennsylvania Magazine of History and Biography*
PRO	Public Record Office, Kew
SCHS	South Carolina Historical Society
VHS	Virginia Historical Society
VMHB	*Virginia Magazine of History and Biography*
WMQ3	*William and Mary Quarterly,* 3d series

NOTES

Introduction

1. The historian was Mellen Chamberlain (1821–1900), a jurist and antiquarian of high probity. The interview took place when Chamberlain was twenty-one and Preston was ninety-one.

    The young scholar may have asked Captain Preston what he meant by "always . . . free," for two versions of the interview survive. In one account, Captain Preston answers, "We always had been free. . . ." In the other he says, "We always had governed ourselves and we always meant to. They didn't mean we should." It is possible that one of these answers led to another. In any case, the question remains. What did Captain Preston mean by "always . . . free" and "governing ourselves"?

    For the two versions of the interview see "Why Captain Levi Preston Fought: An Interview with One of the Survivors of the Revolution by Hon. Mellen Chamberlain of Chelsea," *Danvers Historical Collections* 8 (1920), 68–70; John S. Pancake, *1777, the Year of the Hangman* (University, Ala., 1977), 7; and a note in David Hackett Fischer, *Paul Revere's Ride* (New York and Oxford, 1994), 163, 397.

2. On the classical heritage see Orlando Patterson, *Freedom,* vol. 1, *Freedom in the Making of Western Culture* (New York, 1991); Paul A. Rahe, *Republics, Ancient and Modern* (Chapel Hill, 1992); Richard M. Gummere, *The American Colonial Mind and the Classical Tradition: Essays in Comparative Culture* (Cambridge, 1963); on the Judeo-Christian tradition, Henning Graf Reventlow, *The Authority of the Bible and the Rise of the Modern World,* tr. John Bowden (Philadelphia, 1985); on medieval thought, A. P. D'Entrèves, *The Medieval Contribution to Political Thought* (New York, 1959); on the Renaissance, J.G.A. Pocock, *The Machiavellian Moment: Florentine Political Thought and the Atlantic Republican Tradition* (Prince-

ton, 1975); on the Reformation and liberty, Ralph Barton Perry, *Puritanism and Democracy* (New York, 1944, 1964); on seventeenth-century English thought, G. P. Gooch, *English Democratic Ideas in the Seventeenth Century,* ed. H. J. Laski (London, 1898, 1927, 1955); A.S.P. Woodhouse, ed., *Puritanism and Liberty* (London, 1951); Caroline Robbins, *The Eighteenth-Century Commonwealthman: Studies in the Transmission, Development, and Circumstances of English Liberal Thought from the Restoration of Charles II Until the War with the Thirteen Colonies* (Cambridge, 1959); on English opposition ideology, Bernard Bailyn, *Ideological Origins of the American Revolution* (Cambridge, 1967); on the natural rights tradition see Morton White, *The Philosophy of the American Revolution* (New York, 1978); on the Enlightenment, Peter Gay, *The Enlightenment: An Interpretation,* 2 vols. (New York, 1966, 1969); on the Scottish Enlightenment, Garry Wills, *Inventing America: Jefferson's Declaration of Independence* (New York, 1978); on Irish writers, R. B. McDowell, *Irish Public Opinion, 1750–1800* (London, 1944); on eighteenth-century political thought, R. R. Palmer, *Age of the Democratic Revolution: A Political History of Europe and America, 1760–1800,* 2 vols. (Princeton, 1959, 1964); Jacques Godechot, *Les Révolutions, 1770–1799* (Paris, 1963); on classical liberalism, Joyce Appleby, *Liberalism and Republicanism in the Historical Imagination* (Cambridge, 1992).

3. A similar approach is to organize the history of liberty and freedom around a series of these contexts. Many examples come to mind. One of them is Benjamin Constant's distinction between what he inaccurately called "liberties of the ancients" (rights of participation in a Greek city-state) and "liberties of moderns" (rights of conscience and liberty of expression). Others include analytic disjunctions between Lockean liberty and Rousseau's liberty, or between the ideas of Locke and Harrington, which have been used *a priori* as framing devices, so that the historical question becomes, was some particular thinker or thought essentially Lockean, or Harringtonian, or Rousseauian? Suffice to say that these analytic tools are too brittle for historical use; they shatter at the first application. For various attempts, cf. Benjamin Constant, "Liberty of the Ancients Compared with That of the Moderns," in Benjamin Constant, *Political Writings,* tr. Biancamaria Fontana (New York and Cambridge, 1988); John Rawls, *Justice as Fairness: A Restatement* (Cambridge, 2001), 2; John Brooke, *The Heart of the Commonwealth* (Cambridge, 1989).

4. Michael Kammen, *Spheres of Liberty: Changing Perceptions of Liberty in American Culture* (Madison, 1986).

5. Isaiah Berlin, "Two Concepts of Liberty," in *Four Essays on Liberty* (New York, 1969), 118–72; in a very large literature see John Gray, "On Positive and Negative Liberty," *Political Studies* 28 (1980).

6. One can understand how Berlin came to this idea. His thinking was embedded in a German cultural context, which routinely distinguishes between *Freiheit von* and *Freiheit zu.* It also was part of a Jewish tradition of freedom that developed in response to many centuries of persecution in Christian Europe and centered on ideas of "noninterference with my own activity" and "being one's own master." Ideas of liberty and freedom in hegemonic cultures of Britain and the United States have always been very different. The disjunctive structure of the work was

also a response to the Bolshevik Revolution, the Cold War, and acts of cruelty in the cause of Communism that Berlin had actually witnessed in his youth.

For expanded texts, a full discussion, and a review of critical literature, see Isaiah Berlin, *Liberty: Incorporating Four Essays on Liberty,* ed. Henry Hardy (Oxford, 2002). This work includes an essay by Ian Harris on Berlin and his critics among philosophers but misses criticism by historians and historical perspectives on Berlin's work. Cf. Eric Foner, *The Story of American Freedom* (New York, 1998), xviii, passim.

7. Foner, *Story of American Freedom;* W. B. Gallie, "Essentially Contested Concepts," *Proceedings of the Aristotelian Society* 56 (1955–56), 167–98.

8. When one attempts to do so, the first discovery is the vast complexity of the subject. One historian has identified more than two hundred definitions of *liberty* or *freedom* in English usage. Others have found an even greater variety of specific rights. The subject becomes more manageable if we center it on liberty and freedom as general principles for the organization of a free society. The question is, how have these larger ideas changed through time and varied from one person to another? Cf. Mortimer J. Adler, *The Idea of Freedom* (New York, 1958); James M. McPherson, *Abraham Lincoln and the Second American Revolution* (New York, 1991), 45; Daniel T. Rodgers, *Contested Truths: Keywords in American Politics Since Independence* (New York, 1987).

9. Tocqueville wrote, "J'entends ici l'expression de *moeurs* dans le sens qu'attachaient les anciens au mot *mores;* non seulement je l'applique aux moeurs proprement dites, qu'on pourrait appeler les habitudes du coeur, mais aux différentes notions que possèdent les hommes, aux diverses opinions qui ont cours au mileu d'eux, et à l'ensemble des idées dont se forment les habitudes de l'esprit." Alexis de Tocqueville, *De La Démocratie en Amerique,* 2 vols. (Paris, 1835; ed. J. P. Mayer [Paris, 1961]), 1:300; also idem, *Voyages en Sicile et aux États-Unis,* in *Oeuvres Complètes,* ed. J. P. Mayer (Paris, 1957), 1:179. See also the English text of *Democracy in America,* ed. J. P. Mayer and Max Lerner (New York, 1966), 264. All this has nothing but four words in common with Robert Bellah et al., *Habits of the Heart: Individualism and Commitment in American Life* (Berkeley, 1985), a sociological polemic against individualism that has a different subject, problem, method, discipline, theme, and purpose.

10. All of this draws heavily on the epistemology of Robin Collingwood, and also on the methods of empiricism. Each method alone leads us into error. Both together are the only way forward. The empirical part of this process, much neglected and even despised in much of American academe today, is the only way to make historical inquiry an honest game. As Dostoevski reminds us, the worst lies that we tell are the lies we tell ourselves. For an attempt to find an adductive method that might mediate between these ideas, see David Hackett Fischer, *Historians' Fallacies* (New York, 1970) and the preface to *Albion's Seed* (New York, 1989).

11. Orlando Patterson, *Freedom* (New York, 1991).

12. J. B. Pritchard, ed., *Ancient Near Eastern Texts Relating to the Old Testament* (Princeton, 1969), texts 160–80; Martin Ostwald, "Freedom and the Greeks," in R. W. Davis, ed., *The Origins of Modern Freedom in the West* (Stanford, 1995), 42–43.

13. Aeschylus, *Prometheus Bound,* tr. Herbert Weir Smith, in *Aeschylus,* 2 vols., Loeb Classical Library (Cambridge and London, 1988), 1:219, l. 50.

14. The very large literature on liberty and freedom gives remarkably little attention to the relationship between these two words and ideas. The only exceptions I have found are a very interesting passage in C. S. Lewis, *Studies in Words* (Cambridge, 1981), 111–17, 124–25; a brief and badly tangled discussion of liberation and freedom in Hannah Arendt, *On Revolution* (New York, 1963), 22–26, 236; and a more extended essay by Hannah Fenichel Pitkin, "Are Freedom and Liberty Twins?" *Political Theory* 16 (1988), 523–52.

15. Several different origins of *eleutheros* have been suggested. Some scholars think that both the Latin *liber* and the Greek *eleutheros* descend from the Venetic root *leudheros.* See Dieter Nestle, *Eleutheria: Die Griechen* (Tübingen, 1967); Pitkin, "Are Freedom and Liberty Twins?" 529. Others believe that *eleutheros* derived from the Greek verb for unrestricted movement, as in the idiom *eleutherin hopos ero,* I go where I will; see Max Pohlenz, *Freedom in Greek Life and Thought* (New York, 1966); T. G. Tucker, *Etymological Dictionary of Latin* (Chicago, 1976).

    Eleutheria was carried into English during the early modern era, though it is rarely used today. In 1647, a group of English colonists who founded a libertarian utopia in the Bahamas called it Eleutheria Island. For Eleutheria Island see Henry C. Wilkinson, *The Adventurers of Bermuda* (London, 1933); J. H. Lefroy, *Memorials of the Bermudas* (London, 1877–79); W. Hubert Miller, "The Colonization of the Bahamas, 1647–1670," *WMQ* 3 (1945), 33–46; Michael Craton and Gail Saunders, *Islanders in the Stream: A History of the Bahamian People* (Athens, 1992), 74–91.

16. During the fifth and fourth centuries before Christ, and specially in the context of the Persian and Peloponnesian wars, these ideas of *eleutheria* were enlarged into a soaring vision of the human spirit. Plato and Aristotle, who lived by the light of reason, both believed in their different ways that only a person who possessed *eleutheria* was truly capable of reasoning at all. In that sense, the *eleutheria* of the ancient Greeks meant both "liberty from" and "liberty to." But like Roman *libertas,* it always implied separation or independence.

17. For the etymology and modern derivatives see the *Oxford English Dictionary,* which offers many related terms in use from the seventeenth to the nineteenth centuries: *eleutherian, eleutherism, eleutheromania, eleutheromaniac, eleutheriarch.* For more general discussions of freedom in ancient Greece see Martin Ostwald, "Freedom and the Greeks," in Davis, *Origins of Modern Freedom in the West,* 35–63.

18. The Indo-European roots are *pri* and *priyos.* See Emile Benveniste, *Indo-European Language and Society* (Coral Gables, Fla., 1973), 266–67. In Old English, where *frei* became *freoh,* the same word gave rise to cognate terms such as *freond,* kinsman, or *freodohtor,* legitimate daughter. Similar cognates appeared in Norse and Germanic languages.

    The semantic origins of *freedom* and its cognates may be followed in the *Oxford English Dictionary;* Joseph Bosworth, *Anglo-Saxon Dictionary* (Oxford, 1898); Thomas Northcote Toller, *Supplement to an Anglo-Saxon Dictionary . . .* (Oxford, 1921); Alistair Campbell, *Enlarged Addenda and Corrigenda . . .* (Oxford, 1972); Richard L. Venezky and Antoinette di Paolo Healey, *A Microfiche Concor-*

dance to Old English (Toronto, 1980). For a learned discussion of the terminology of freedom and servitude in Old English see David A. E. Pelteret, *Slavery in Early Medieval England, from the Reign of Alfred to the Twelfth Century* (Woodbridge, Suffolk, 1995), 41–49, 261–330.

19. The noun *ama-ar-gi* has been translated as release from slavery, debt, taxation, and punishment. It was also used as a legal term for manumission or emancipation or freedom. A discussion is in Ake W. Sjoberg, ed., *The Sumerian Dictionary of the University of Pennsylvania Museum* (Philadelphia, 1998), vol. 1A, pt. 3, 208–10, 200–201; thanks to my friend and colleague Professor Tzvi Abusch for his expert advice.

    This Sumerian word is thought to be the oldest recorded expression for something like our ideas of freedom and liberty. It has become the logo of Liberty Fund, Inc., and its Library of Economics and Liberty. It is also worn as a tattoo by libertarian conservatives. But its meaning appears to have been closer to freedom than to *libertas* or *eleutheria*, which are akin to modern libertarian thinking. *Amagi* has also been used by radical feminists. The correct form is *ama-ar-gi*.

20. Ch. Wirszubski, *Libertas as a Political Idea at Rome During the Late Republic and Early Principate* (Cambridge, 1950, 1968), 3.

21. Johannes Brondsted, *The Vikings* (Harmondsworth and Baltimore, 1960, 1967), 55. These customs were described in ancient Germany by Tacitus, *Germania*, bks. 11–13, Loeb Classical Library (Cambridge and London, 1914, 1980) 1:147–52.

22. Jesse L. Byock, *Medieval Iceland: Society, Sagas, and Power* (Berkeley, 1988), 51–71, passim; Adam of Bremen, *Gesta Hammburgensis Ecclesiae Pontificum* (1072–76), tr. *History of the Archbishops of Hamburg-Bremen* (New York, 1959); primary sources include Ari Thorgillson "the Learned," *Islendingabók*, a short survey of Iceland's history from 1870 to 1120. It appears in Jakob Benediktsson, *Islenzk Fornit* (Reykjavik, 1968).

23. Many descriptive passages appear in the Icelandic sagas, in particular *Njal's Saga*, tr. Magnus Magnusson and Hermann Pálsson (1960; Harmondsworth, 1980), 40, 108, 110, 137–38, 144, 153, 240, 248, 251, 254; *The Vinland Sagas*, tr. Magnus Magnusson and Hermann Pálsson (1965; Harmondsworth, 1975), 76–77; *Egil's Saga*, tr. Hermann Pálsson and Paul Edwards (1976; Harmondsworth, 1980) 136–69; also Richard F. Tomasson, *Iceland: The First New Society* (Minneapolis, 1980), 15–16.

24. On the decline of slavery in Iceland see Byock, *Medieval Iceland*, 23, 99. For Norway see P. H. Sawyer, *Kings and Vikings* (London, 1982), 42.

25. Wirszubski, *Libertas as a Political Idea at Rome*, 3.

26. Examples of these other ranks were widespread in Europe, from the Lombard *aldius*, or half-free person, to the Norse *halffre peowe*, a semiemancipated slave who was allowed personal freedom but could not marry, alienate property, or share equally in rights of succession. For Lombards see Katherine Fischer Drew, *The Lombard Laws* (Philadelphia, 1973), 257; for the Norse, K. von Maurer, "Die Freigelassenen nach altnorwegischem Rechte," *Sitzungsberichte der philosophisch-philologischen unde historischen Classe der königlich bayerische Akademie der Wissenschaften, 1878* (Munich, 1878), 21–87.

27. For *fulborn* and *foulcfree* see Drew, *Lombard Laws*, 259.

28. Sir Frederick Pollock and Frederic William Maitland, *The History of English Law*

Before the Time of Edward I, 2 vols. (1895; Cambridge, 1968), 1:412; see also Maitland, *A Historical Sketch of Liberty and Equality* (1875, 1911; Indianapolis, 2000), mostly on philosophical models from the seventeenth century.

29. Wirszubski, *Libertas as a Political Idea at Rome,* 18–19.

30. Roman ideas of *artes liberales* and *homo liberaliter educatio* were the fruit of that condition and the means of its attainment. They survive in modern notions of the liberal arts and liberal education.

31. Epictetus, *Discourses, Book 4,* "On Freedom [*Eleutherias*]", in vol. 2 of *Epictetus,* Greek text with English tr. by W. A. Oldfather, Loeb Classical Library (Cambridge, 1928, 1985), bk. 4, ch. 1; bk. 3, ch. 24; passim. Marcus Aurelius, *Meditations,* in *Marcus Aurelius,* Greek text with English tr. by C. R. Haines (Cambridge, 1916, 1979), esp. bks. 1, 2, 3, 6.

32. Laws of Anglo-Saxon kings: Æthelberht, 560–616; Hlothhære and Eadric, 673–86; Wihtræd, 690–725; Alfred, 871–901; Edward the Elder, 901–24; Athelstan, 924–39; Edmund I, 939–46; Edgar, 959–75; also North People's Law, Mercian Law; all in *Internet Medieval Sourcebook: The Anglo-Saxon Dooms, 560–975,* http://www.fordham.edu/halsall/source/560-975dooms.html (1988). For discussions see Ernest Percival Rhys, *The Growth of Political Liberty* (London, 1921).

33. Michael Ventris and J. Chadwick, *Documents in Mycenean Greek* (Cambridge, 1973), 198–300, 469; Ostwald, "Freedom and the Greeks," 36.

34. Wirszubski, *Libertas as a Political Idea at Rome,* 7.

35. Jonathan Wylie, *The Faeroe Islands* (Lexington, Ky., 1987), 90.

36. John 8:32–36.

37. 1 Corinthians 9:1.

38. Martin Luther, *An den Christlichen Adel Deutscher Nation: Von der Freiheit eines Christenmenschen; Sendbrief vom Dolmetschen,* ed. Ernst Kähler (Stuttgart, 1958); tr. W. A. Lambert in Martin Luther, *Three Treatises* (Philadelphia, 1982); also in Jaroslav Pelikan et al., eds., *Luther's Works,* 54 vols. (Philadelphia, 1957), vol. 44.

39. Klaus Schwarzwaller and Dennis D. Bleifeldt, eds., *Freiheit als Liebe bei Martin Luther* (Freedom as Love in Martin Luther) (Frankfurt am Main, 1995).

40. Pitkin, "Are Freedom and Liberty Twins?" 523. The tensions between liberty and freedom appear in Magna Carta (1215), a document that modern students invariably read with a feeling of disappointment. Magna Carta seems very limited to a modern reader. It is a long list of hierarchic privileges, granted to particular groups of nobles, freemen, clergy, and burgesses. This is the classical, hierarchical tradition of liberty. But if we look more closely, we discover that some of its provisions include North European ideas of freedom as a birthright of all free men. An example is the famous thirty-ninth clause: "No free man shall be taken, imprisoned, disseised, banished or in any way destroyed, nor shall we go upon him or send upon him, except by the lawful judgment of his peers or the law of the land." Here in one great document were two traditions of freedom and liberty, in uneasy coexistence. See William S. McKechnie, *Magna Carta* (Glasgow, 1914), 375–95; W. L. Warren, *King John* (London, 1961).

  In modern German, the word *Libertät* is occasionally used in formal writing but rarely appears in common usage. See Leonard Krieger, *The German Idea of Freedom: The History of a Tradition from the Reformation to 1871* (Chicago, 1960), 3.

41. *Julius Caesar,* III.i.79.

42. A.S.P. Woodhouse, ed., *Puritan and Liberty: Being the Army Debates (1647–9) from the Clarke Manuscripts with Supplementary Documents* (London, 1951), 53, 68.

43. Thomas Hobbes, *Leviathan* (1651), ed. Michael Oakeshott (1946; Oxford, 1955), pt. 2, ch. 21, pp. 136–37. For Royalists and liberty, see David Underdown, *A Freeborn People* (Oxford, 1996), 89.

44. Ethan Allen, *A Narrative of Colonel Ethan Allen's Captivity* (1779), ed. Brooke Hindle (New York, 1961), 9.

45. David Hackett Fischer, *Albion's Seed: Four British Folkways in America* (New York and Oxford, 1989), esp. 199–205, 410–18, 595–603, 777–82.

46. Ivan Turgenev, *Fathers and Sons* (1862), tr. Bernard Gureney, Modern Library (New York, 1961), 113 (ch. 16).

Early America

1. Samuel Adams to Arthur Lee, 4 March 1775; Committee of Correspondence of Boston to Committee of Correspondence in Littleton, 31 March 1775; both in Harry A. Cushing, ed., *The Writings of Samuel Adams,* 4 vols. (New York, 1907), 3:15, 195.

2. James Pike's powder horn is on permanent exhibit in the Chicago Historical Society. A discussion of its doubtful provenance and biographical material appears in Alfred F. Young and Terry Fife, with Mary E. Janzen, *We the People: Voices and Images of the New Nation* (Philadelphia, 1993), xvii–xix, 64–65, 221, 224.

   A Revolutionary pension application and narrative of service of James Pike is available on microfilm at the New England Branch of the National Archives, Waltham, Massachusetts. He appears to have been born in Plaistow, New Hampshire, lived in several towns on both sides of the border between Massachusetts and New Hampshire, was wounded at Bunker Hill, was discharged in January 1776, and reenlisted in the militia of Haverhill, Massachusetts, during the summer of 1776. This James Pike is thought to be the maker, but at least twelve other James Pikes also appear in Revolutionary pension records for Massachusetts.

   For studies of horn carving in early America see Rufus A. Grider, "Powder Horns and Their Use," *NYHSQ* 15 (1931), 3–24; Stephen V. Grancsay, *American Engraved Powder Horns* (New York, 1946); William H. Guthman, *Drums A'beating, Trumpets Sounding: Artistically Carved Powder Horns in the Provincial Manner, 1746–1781* (Hartford, 1793), with an excellent bibliography.

3. Samuel Gardner Drake, *The History and Antiquities of Boston* (Boston, 1856), 812; Samuel Adams Drake, *Old Landmarks and Historic Personages of Boston* (1872; rev. ed., Boston, 1906, rpt. 1986), 331–59 passim. For modern studies see Arthur M. Schlesinger, "The Liberty Tree: A Genealogy," *NEQ* 25 (1952), 435–58; Robert P. Hay, "The Liberty Tree: A Symbol for American Patriots," *Quarterly Journal of Speech* 55 (1969), 414–24.

4. *Boston Gazette,* 19 and 26 Aug. 1765; *Boston Evening Post,* 19 Aug. 1765; Thomas Hutchinson, *History of the Colony and Province of Massachusetts Bay* (1764–1828),

ed. Lawrence Shaw Mayo, 3 vols. (Cambridge, 1936), 3:84–89; and a separate volume of *Additions to Thomas Hutchinson's "History of Massachusetts Bay,"* ed. Catherine Barton Mayo (Worcester, 1949), 3:87, 101. For a discussion of the construction of eighteenth-century effigies, which included very realistic likenesses, see Kenneth Silverman, *A Cultural History of the American Revolution* (New York, 1976), 75–77.

For Oliver see Clifford Shipton, "Andrew Oliver," in *Sibley's Harvard Graduates* (Boston, 1945), 7:393–400; Peter Oliver, *Origin and Progress of the American Rebellion,* ed. Douglass Adair and John A. Schutz (Stanford, 1961), 111–12, 140. Pauline Maier, *From Resistance to Revolution* (New York, 1974), 58, 85–87, 307.

5.   John Rowe, *Letters and Diary of John Rowe, Boston Merchant,* ed. Anne Rowe Cunningham (Boston, 1903), 88–89 (14 Aug. 1765). The published text of this passage is inaccurate and should be compared with the manuscript in the Massachusetts Historical Society. In fact, Bute voted against the Stamp Act in the House of Lords and was the rival of George Grenville. But the colonists believed that he was generally responsible for the new imperial policy that the Stamp Act represented.

See also Catherine L. Albanese, *Sons of the Fathers: The Civil Religion of the American Revolution* (Philadelphia, 1976). These events inspired many others in the colonies that used many of the same iconic elements, but sometimes in ways that made Boston's Loyal Nine seem restrained. Compare the effigies in Norwich, Connecticut, explicitly designed on the Boston model; and another in Lebanon, Connecticut, where the Devil "turned up his breech and discharged fire, brimstone and tar" in the face of an effigy of Jared Ingersoll, Connecticut's stampmaster. Cf. Silverman, *Cultural History of the American Revolution,* 77–81.

6.   Jonathan Mayhew to Thomas Hollis, *MHSP* 69:174–75. On the Green Ribbon Club see Maurice Ashley, *England in the Seventeenth Century* (Baltimore, 1952), 146. Some of New England's oldest flags had been green. In 1684, the colors of Captain Thomas Noyes's Company of Foot were ordered to be "green, with a red cross with a white field in the angle, according to the antient customs of our own English nation." Joshua Coffin, *A Sketch of the History of Newbury . . .* (Boston, 1845).

7.   John Adams attended a meeting in January 1766, and found those nine men present. See John Adams, *Diary and Autobiography,* ed. L. H. Butterfield, 4 vols. (Boston, 1961), 1:294 (15 Jan. 1766). Other lists omit Field (who may have been a guest like Adams) and add Henry Welles. See also Maier, *From Resistance to Revolution,* 85, 307.

The ancestors of John Avery came from Hampshire in the great Puritan migration and were in Boston before 1643. Henry Bass's family had been in Roxbury, Watertown, and Boston since 1630. Stephen Cleverly's ancestors had been in Boston and members of the First Congregational Church since at least the mid-seventeenth century. Thomas Crafts's forebears arrived with the Winthrop fleet in 1630 and settled in Roxbury and Boston. The Edes family came a little later; they were in Charlestown and Boston since 1674. George Trott's progenitors were in Dorchester by 1640 and Boston by 1655. Of the doubtful members, John Adams was descended from Henry Adams, a shoemaker who migrated from East Anglia to Massachusetts ca. 1632–35. The ancestors of Thomas Chase and Joseph Field had been in New England for many generations, but the family lines are tangled. John Smith's genealogy cannot be followed through so many New England Smiths. James Savage, *Genealogical Dictionary of the First Settlers of New England,* 4 vols. (Boston, 1860–62).

8. J. Adams, *Diary and Autobiography* 1:294 (15 Jan. 1766).

9. 5 George III c. 12; Danby Pickering, ed., *The Statutes at Large* (Cambridge, 1762–1869), 26:179–87, 201–4; rpt. in Edmund S. Morgan, ed., *Prologue to Revolution: Sources and Documents on the Stamp Act Crisis, 1764–1766* (Chapel Hill, 1959), 35–43.

10. John Rowe, Diary, 14 Aug. 1766, MHS.

11. Peter Shaw, *American Patriots and the Rituals of Revolution* (Cambridge, 1981), 10.

12. For "publick" liberty (sometimes liberties) see *Writings of Samuel Adams* 3:15, 194–95; for personal liberties, ibid. 1:65 passim.

13. Sources include Gov. Francis Bernard to Halifax, 16 Aug. 1765, House of Lords Manuscripts for 14 Jan. 1766, transcript in LC, in Morgan, ed, *Prologue to Revolution,* 106–7; John Rowe, Diary, 14 Aug. 1765, MHS; *Boston Gazette,* 19 Aug. 1765; George P. Anderson, "Ebenezer Mackintosh, Stamp Act Rioter and Patriot" and "A Note on Ebenezer Mackintosh," *CSMP* 26 (1927), 15–64, 348–61.

14. *Boston Gazette,* 16 Sept. 1765; for an announcement that summoned the Sons of Liberty to "assemble at Liberty Hall under the Liberty Tree" see Boston Records, 312. The Sons of Liberty took their name from a speech in Parliament by English Whig Isaac Barré in answer to Charles Townshend, who had referred to the Americans as "Children planted by our care, and nourished up by our indulgence … and protected by our Arms." Barré replied that the children were "sons of Liberty." "Planted by your care? No! your Oppressions planted 'em in America. … Nourished by *your* indulgence? they grew by your neglect of 'em." The city of Wilkes-Barre, Pennsylvania, bears his name. See *CTHSC* 18 (1920), 322–23.

15. *Boston Chronicle,* 22 May 1769. When William Billings published his *New England Psalm-Singer* in 1770, he noted on the title page that the book could be had from "Deacon Elliott, under the Liberty Tree." Silverman, *Cultural History of the American Revolution,* 200.

16. J. Adams, *Diary and Autobiography,* 1:311–12 (4 May 1766).

17. Schlesinger, "Liberty Tree," 448, 452; *New England Magazine* (1895), 503.

18. (Charleston) *South Carolina Gazette,* 3 Oct. 1768; Richard Walsh, *Charleston's Sons of Liberty: A Study of the Artisans, 1763–1789* (Columbia, S.C., 1959), 31, 32, 40, 46, 48, 50, 87, 98, 116; Edward McCrady, *The History of South Carolina Under the Royal Government, 1719–1776* (New York, 1899), 589–91, 604, 652–53, 664–71, 679–80; idem, *South Carolina in the Revolution, 1775–1780,* 2 vols. (New York, 1901), 1:40.

19. Hutchinson, *History of Massachusetts Bay* 3:136; Samuel Eliot Morison, *Three Centuries of Harvard, 1636–1936* (Cambridge, 1936, 1963), 133.

20. In 1953, when elms still stood in many American towns, a New Englander observed, "Every tree has a character of its own, but our native American elm seems to unite in itself, either in the different stages of its growth, or in some single noble specimen, all the distinguishing beauties of other trees, while it has some peculiar to itself. It combines the grandeur of the oak, the stateliness of the

linden, the symmetry of the maple, with the delicate grace of the young weeping willow." Michael Kammen, "The Old House and Elm Trees," in *Meadows of Memory: Images of Time and Tradition in American Art* (Austin, Tex., 1992),145.

21. Ibid., 133–181, offers many examples.

22. Ibid., 136; Bernard Bailyn, *Voyagers to the West* (New York, 1986), 538.

23. Bernard to Hillsborough, 18 June 1768, in S. A. Drake, *Old Landmarks and Historic Personages of Boston* (1872; Rutland, 1971), 398. For Cade's Rebellion see James Gairdner, ed., *Three Fifteenth-Century Chronicles, with Historical Memoranda by John Stowe,* Camden Society n.s., vol. 28 (London, 1880), 94. For the Norfolk Rising see S. Bindoff, *Ket's Rebellion* (London, 1949, 1968).

24. The elm trees at Deacon Elliott's corner were said to have been planted by Garrett Bourne, who owned the property in 1646. Susan Wilson, *The Liberty Tree* (Boston, 2000).

25. For the New England shillings, see Sydney P. Noe, *The Silver Coinage of Massachusetts* (Lawrence, Mass., 1973). The tale of Sir William Temple and the King is from George H. Preble, *Origin and History of the American Flag,* rev. ed., 2 vols. (Philadelphia, 1917), 1:190. The story of the Royal Oak has been told in many versions. The most authentic is the account that the king dictated to Samuel Pepys. It appears in William Matthews, ed., *Charles II's Escape from Worcester* (London, 1967), and is discussed in Richard Ollard, *The Escape of Charles II* (London, 1966).

26. An engraving of a "pavillon de Nouvelle Angleterre en Amerique" appeared in an early European flag book, *La Connaissance de pavilons ou bannières que la plupart des nations arborent en mer* (The Hague, 1737); it is reproduced in Preble, *Origin and History of the American Flag* 1:189. At least one of these flags replaced the cross with a red and white English rose, to show loyalty without idolatry (ibid., 180).

27. Harriet S. Tapley, *Salem Imprints, 1768–1825* (Salem, 1927), 14, qtd. in Schlesinger, "Liberty Tree," 444.

28. *Boston Gazette,* 24 Feb. 1766, *Boston Evening Post,* 24 Feb. 1766, *Boston News-Letter,* 20 Feb. 1766; Dirk Hoerder, *Crowd Action in Revolutionary Massachusetts, 1765–1780* (New York, 1977), 130.

29. Silverman, *Cultural History of the American Revolution,* 96.

30. D. H. Watson, "Joseph Harrison and the *Liberty* Incident," *WMQ3* 20 (1963), 589; John Philip Reid, *In a Rebellious Spirit: The Argument of Facts, the* Liberty *Riot, and the Coming of the American Revolution* (University Park, 1979), 95; crowd estimates from Gov. Francis Bernard to Hillsborough, 16 June 1768, in *Letters to the Ministry from Governor Bernard, General Gage, and Commodore Hood* (Boston, 1769), 33; *Boston Gazette,* 20 June 1768; on the red flag, Preble, *Origin and History of the American Flag* 1:195.

31. For the flags on the Liberty Tree as signals, see [Samuel Adams], *An Appeal to the World, or a Vindication of the Town of Boston. , , ,* (Boston, 1769), in *Writings of Samuel Adams* 3:418.

32. J. Adams, *Diary and Autobiography* 1:341–42; *Boston Gazette,* 21 Aug. 1769; a list of the Sons of Liberty who dined at Dorchester is in *MSHP* 1st ser., 11 (1869–70), 140. Other Liberty Tree Feasts are recorded in John Rowe, Diary: 14 Aug. 1767, "This day the Colours were displayed on the Tree of Liberty & about sixty people

Sons of Liberty met at one o'clock & drank the King's health." 15 Aug. 1768, "Dined at Greatons with a Number of gentlemen about One Hundred—who were very jovial and pleasant and in the forenoon a great number of people were at Liberty Hall where there was a great variety of Good Musick exhibited & Great Joy appeared in every countenance, being the Anniversary Day of the Sons of Liberty." 14 Aug. 1769, "The Sons of Liberty met at Liberty Tree & dined at Robinson's at Dorchester—they contained 139 Carriages on their return. Mr. Hancock preceded the company and Mr. Otis brought up the rear." 14 Aug. 1770, "A large party of the Sons of Liberty dined this day at the House of Thomas Carnes at Dorchester." 14 Aug. 1773, "This day the Sons of Liberty held their annual feast at Roxbury in the Training Field by John Williams—there were upwards of four hundred that dined there." The published transcription of this diary contains many errors. The original is in MHS.

33. Peter Oliver, "Origin and Progress of the American Rebellion to the Year 1776," Gay Transcripts, MHS; Schlesinger, "Liberty Tree," 438.

34. Hutchinson, *History of Massachusetts Bay* 3:100–102.

35. *New York Mercury,* 7 April 1766; Robert J. Christen, *King Sears: Politician and Patriot in a Decade of Revolution* (New York, 1982), 92.

36. Tories responded in kind. A party of British Regulars tarred and feathered a Yankee peddler who had offered to buy their muskets and carried him to the Liberty Tree. Joan D. Dolmetsch, *Rebellion and Reconciliation: Satirical Prints on the Revolution at Williamsburg* (Charlottesville, 1976), 66–69.

37. *New England Chronicle,* 24–31 Aug. 1775.

38. Hoerder, *Crowd Action,* 209.

39. For other Liberty Trees on powder horns see the Jonathan Gardner horn, inscribed "Liberty Property or Death," Roxbury, Mass., 1776; the Elijah Case horn, Roxbury, Mass., 7 Nov. 1775, inscribed, "Great britton Please to Condescend, Our Liberty Once More Defend"; and the Jabez Arnold horn, Roxbury, Mass., Oct. 1775, in Guthman, *Drums A'beating,* 202, 170, 161.

40. British Lieutenant John Clarke believed that no flags were on the field. Clarke wrote, "Nor did I see any colours to their regiments the day of the action." A committee of flag experts was convened to study the question and concluded that there was a good deal of the fog of war between Lt. Clarke and the American redoubt. Another American flag describes a blue flag with a Liberty Tree. Cf. Emmet V. Mittlebeeler and Dorothy Claybourne, "What Flag Flew at Bunker Hill?" *Flag Bulletin* 17 (1978).

41. An unnamed privateer was captured off the coast of Massachusetts in late 1775 by ships of the Royal Navy, which carried home her flag. It was described as "a pale green palm-tree upon a white field, with the motto, 'We Appeal to Heaven.'" Another privateer, *Yankee Hero,* was captured flying a Liberty Tree Flag as late as June 1776. For this and many materials about Liberty Tree Flags on floating batteries in the siege of Boston, see Preble, *Origin and History of the American Flag* 1:200–204, 227, 229.

42. Philip S. Foner, ed., *Complete Writings of Thomas Paine,* 2 vols. (New York, 1969), 2:1091–92.

43. Hell, *Suite de notes sur les arbres de la liberté* (Paris, n.d.), and Abbé H. Grégoire,

Essai historique et patriotique sur les arbres de la liberté (Paris, year II), qtd. in Mona Ozouf, *Festivals and the French Revolution* (Cambridge, 1988), 244–45; J. David Harden, "Liberty Caps and Liberty Trees," *Past & Present* 146 (1965), 90n. At first their name followed the English form, *arbre-liberté* or *arbre de liberté*. Later it became *arbre de la liberté,* and their character was transformed. The same trends appeared throughout Europe.

44. The *mai sauvage* represented this process as a painful and violent event. French maypoles were sometimes cut to resemble a gibbet, which threatened destruction to the enemies of the people. This association of maypoles with Liberty Trees did not exist in Massachusetts, where "frisking" around a maypole had been condemned as idolatry from the beginning of Puritan settlement. Joel Barlow drafted "A Genealogy of the Tree of Liberty," in which he linked it to phallic emblems in the ancient world; ms. notebook, Houghton Library, Harvard; Schlesinger, "Liberty Tree," 436n; Ozouf, *Festivals and the French Revolution,* 252.

45. *AA5* 2:244; a drawing appears in Edward W. Richardson, *Standards and Colors of the American Revolution* (Philadelphia, 1982), 204. Many symbols of these ideas appeared on New England powder horns. One common motif was an image of a close-built New England town as a free community, which appeared on many powder horns in 1775. Another associated liberty with a living heart. Several powder horns featured liberty hearts as a symbol of attachment and organic unity. For liberty hearts see the powder horns of John Noyes and Edward Sherburne in Guthman, *Drums A'beating,* 54, 91, 93, 183, 185, plate 15. On town symbols for New England: New Haven, Roxbury, and Charlestown appear on powder horns in ibid., 148, 162, 164, 175 (all from New England, 1775 and early 1776).

46. Richardson, *Standards and Colors,* 97.

47. The Bedford flag was said to have been carried by Cornet Nathaniel Page of the Bedford militia and given by the Page family to the town. By one account it was made in England in 1659. Several seventeenth-century writers have challenged its authenticity, but the provenance is well established, and supporting documentation exists in British sources.

49. This emblem was engraved on Connecticut's paper money.

50. Charles Botta, *History of the War of the Independence of the United States of America,* 2 vols. (Boston, 1837, 1845; rpt. 1970), 1:206. A month after Bunker Hill, Connecticut and Massachusetts troops under General Israel Putnam held a review in Cambridge. They raised a New England Union Flag "bearing on one side this motto, 'An Appeal to Heaven,' and on the other, 'Qui Transtulit Sustinet.'" So lusty were the cheers that according to a local newspaper "the Philistines on Bunker's Hill heard the shout of the Israelites, and, being very fearful, paraded themselves in battle array" (*New England Chronicle,* 21 July 1775). Emblems of liberty and freedom are more difficult to find in early New Hampshire, and they had a different texture. Some of the founders of that colony were refugees from the Puritan commonwealth. From the start, others moved there to escape higher taxes and land prices in Massachusetts. Emblems of liberty and freedom in New Hampshire have tended to be cast more in terms of individual rights, and especially rights of property. A New Hampshire protest against the Stamp Act carried a flag that read, "Liberty, Property, and No Stamps." In memory of that move-

ment, Portsmouth's Swing Bridge was named Liberty Bridge (Preble, *Origin and History of the American Flag* 1:192). In that vision of liberty, there is a remarkable continuity from the seventeenth- and eighteenth-century settlements in this colony to the extremely tax-averse New Hampshire conservatives in the twenty-first century.

51. Richard Montagu, *The Acts and Monuments of the Church Before Christ Incarnate* (London, 1642), 62; Admiral William Henry Smyth, *The Sailor's Word Book: An Alphabetical Digest of Nautical Terms* (London, 1867).

52. For the adoption of the anchor in 1647, with a sketch, see John Russell Bartlett, ed., *Records of the Colony of the Rhode Island and Providence Plantations*, 10 vols. (Providence, 1856; rpt. 1968), 1:151. The heart motif appears on Rhode Island paper money as early as 16 Aug. 1710; see Eric P. Newman, *The Early Paper Money of America*, 4th ed. (Iola, Wisc., 1997), 368–400. A drawing of the black battalion of the Rhode Island Regiment appears in Jean-Baptiste Antoine De Verger, *American Foot Soldiers, Yorktown Campaign*, watercolor (1781), Brown University Library; Sidney and Emma Kaplan, *The Black Presence in the Era of the American Revolution* (Amherst, 1989), 34–35, 64–65.

53. For seventeenth-century English models of these New England emblems, see "The Devises, Motto's &c used by the Parliamentary Officers on Standards, banners &c in the late Civil wars, taken from an original manuscript done at ye time now in ye hands of Benjan. Cole of oxford," broadside, "published at ye Desire of divers Gentlemen to be bound up wh ye lord Clarendon's History," n.d., BL.

54. John Winthrop, "Speech to the General Court," 3 July 1645; John Cotton, *An Exposition upon the 13th Chapter of Revelation* (London, 1656), 71–73; Roger Williams, *The Bloudy Tenant of Persecution* (London, 1643); idem, *The Bloudy Tenant Yet More Blody* (London, 1651).

55. John Wise [1652–1725], *A Vindication of the Government of New-England Churches* (Boston, 1717).

56. They also had no idea of universal equality, and yet they believed in equal rights among themselves. John Wise called it "the Equality of our Race." He wrote, "Other states there are, composed of different Blood, and of unequal Lines.... The Parity of our Descent incline us to keep the like Parity by our Laws, and to yield precedency to nothing but Superiour Vertue, and Wisdom" (ibid.).

57. Oliver A. Rink, *Holland on the Hudson: An Economic and Social History of Dutch New York* (Ithaca, 1986); Peter O. Wacker, "The Dutch Culture Area in the Northeast, 1609–1800," *NJH* 104 (1986), 1–21; David Cohen, "How Dutch Were the Dutch of New Netherland?" *NYH* 62 (1981), 43–60; Charles T. Gehring, "The Survival of the Dutch Language in New York and New Jersey," *De Haeve Maen* 3 (1984), 7–9; Gerald F. De Jong, *The Dutch Reformed Church in the American Colonies* (Grand Rapids, 1978). One colorful continuity runs from the cartmen of Old Amsterdam to those of New Amsterdam and on to the cabbies of New York City; see Graham Hodges, *New York City Cartmen, 1667–1850* (New York, 1986).

58. William Livingston, *The Independent Reflector*, ed. Milton M. Klein (New York, 1752–53; Cambridge, 1963), esp. 171–214; Bernard Bailyn, *Pamphlets of the American Revolution* (Cambridge, 1965), 1:152–53.

59. Livingston, *Independent Reflector*, 74.

60. G. D. Scull, ed., *The Montresor Journals*, pub. in *NYHS Collections for the Year 1881* (New York, 1882), 368.

61. Ibid., 370; cf. Schlesinger, "Liberty Tree," 441, who is mistaken in his date of 4 June 1766, having missed Montresor's first entry on 21 May, an error repeated in other works.

62. "A pine post where they daily exercised, called by them the Tree of Liberty," *Montresor Journals*, 382 (11 Aug. 1766). From an early date most observers described it as a pole; see, e.g., Gage in *Letters to the Ministry from . . . Bernard, . . . Gage, . . . and Hood.*

63. Isaac Leake, *Memoir of the Life and Times of General John Lamb* (Albany, 1857; rpt. 1970), 9–11; Isaac Sears, John Lamb, et al. to Nicholas Ray, 10 Oct. 1766, Lamb Papers, NYHS.

64. Alexander McDougall, Diary, 1 May–13 July 1770, NYHS.

65. Leading primary sources are the Lamb Papers and McDougall Papers in NYHS; *Montresor Journals*, 349–70 passim; and the newspapers of the period. Biographical studies include Donald A. Grinde Jr., "Joseph Allicocke, African-American Leader of the Sons of Liberty," *Afro-American Life and History* (Summer 1990); Leake, *Memoir of . . . General John Lamb;* Christen, *King Sears.*

66. Johann Joachim Winckelmann, *Versuch einer Allegorie (Dresden 1766) and "De L'Allegorie (Paris, an VII [1799]),* ed. Stephen Orgel (New York, 1976). A French edition appeared in 1766. See Harden, "Liberty Caps and Liberty Trees," 9n. For representations of the wand and pileus in British and American art during the period 1766–1770 see Dolmetsch, *Rebellion and Reconciliation,* 42, 46, 53, 74; and Clarence S. Brigham *Paul Revere's Engravings* (Worcester, 1954), 22f.

67. *Nederlands Dank-Offer,* in Adrianus Valerius, *NederLantsche Gedenck-Clanck* [Netherlands Commemorative Anthem] (Haarlem, 1626); Simon Schama, *The Embarrassment of Riches* (New York, 1987), 99; F. G. Stephens and M. Dorothy George, *Catalogue of Prints and Drawings in the British Museums: Division I, Political and Personal Satires,* 11 vols. (London, 1870–1954), 1:1176; Harden, "Liberty Caps and Liberty Trees," 74.

68. A wooden pileus from a New York Liberty Pole is in the collection of the New York State Museum.

69. A historian of this event writes, "Mariners played a vital and persistent role in the Golden Hill riot; they probably built the liberty pole, which was constructed like a ship's mast; they were the first civilians to attack the soldiers. . . . The sailors hated the working soldiers." Lee R. Boyer, "Lobster Backs, Liberty Boys, and Laborers in the Streets: New York's Golden Hill and Nassau Street Riots," *NYHSQ* 57 (1973), 306–7.

70. For the Liberty Pole as a ship's mast, see Christen, *King Sears,* 96.

71. Preble, *Origin and History of the American Flag* 1:193.

72. John Shy, *Toward Lexington: The Role of the British Army in the Coming of the American Revolution* (Princeton, 1965), 382, passim.

73. General Thomas Gage to Duke of Richmond, 26 Aug. 1766, I, *The Correspondence of General Thomas Gage,* ed. Clarence E. Carter, 2 vols. (New Haven, 1933; rpt. 1969), 1:103–4; *Pennsylvania Journal,* 28 Aug 1766; (Williamsburg) *Virginia Gazette* 5 Sept., 13 Nov., 4 Dec. 1766; Shy, *Toward Lexington,* 279, 382.

74. Shy, *Toward Lexington,* 388.

75. Gage to Lt. Col. William Dalrymple, 8 Jan. 1770, Gage Papers, Clements Library, 89.

76. (Williamsburg) *Virginia Gazette,* 22 Feb 1770; Boyer, "Lobster Backs, Liberty Boys, and Laborers."

77. For the erection of this Liberty Pole, see "To the Sons of Liberty in this City, Feb. 3, 1770," NYHS.

78. Thomas Jefferson Wertenbaker, *Father Knickerbocker Rebels* (New York, 1948), 21.

79. *Newport Mercury,* 3 Oct. 1774, qtd. in Schlesinger, "Liberty Tree," 450; *Holt's Journal,* 6 April 1775.

80. This estimate is from a quantitative search of 78,000 sites mentioning Liberty Poles on the Web, 13–17 Dec. 2001. Another concentration of Liberty Poles after the Revolution appeared in Wisconsin, the prairie states, and new settlements in the West during the nineteenth century. Comparatively few were to be found in the southern states.

81. Bernard to Hillsborough, 18 June 1768, in S. A. Drake, *Old Landmarks,* 398. The Tories of Boston appointed among themselves a Demolition of Liberty Pole Committee.

82. Schlesinger, "Liberty Tree," 444.

83. Wesley Frank Craven, *The Legend of the Founding Fathers* (New York, 1956), 38.

84. Lee Newcomer, *The Embattled Farmers* (New York, 1953), 41; R. S. Longley, "Mob Activities in Revolutionary Massachusetts," *NEQ* 6 (1933), 98–130.

85. Richardson, *Standards and Colors,*108

86. Ibid., 122.

87. The Liberty Pole also became a leading symbol in Savannah, Georgia, where it was the rallying point for the Whigs in the town and a place where the Declaration of Independence was read in 1776. Cf. Pauline Maier, *American Scripture* (New York, 1997), 157.

88. In the 1980s, publications distributed by the National Park Service minimized the role of dead white colonial males in its invention, in an effort to make a stronger connection to antislavery, civil rights, multiculturalism, and political correctness. The Liberty Bell has many associations. One need not diminish one to demonstrate the other. For examples see David Kimball's *The Story of the Liberty Bell* (1989; Philadelphia, 1997), and other publications and Web site materials distributed by the National Park Service.

89. James Allen, "Diary," *PMHB* 9 (1885), 185.

90. Still very helpful is Isaac Sharpless, *Political Leaders of Provincial Pennsylvania* (New York, 1919).

91. Isaac Norris I to Isaac Norris II, 10 April 1722, Norris Letterbook, HSP.

92. Isaac Norris I to Daniel Zachary, 3 Oct. 1701, Norris Letterbook, HSP.

93. "The Charter of Privileges," in Richard S. Dunn et al., eds., *The Papers of William Penn* (Philadelphia, 1987), 4:104–10.

94. Isaac Norris I to Daniel Zachary, 3 Oct. 1701, Norris Letterbook, HSP.

95. Isaac Norris II to Robert Charles, 7 Oct. 1754, Norris Letterbook, HSP, qtd. in Frederick B. Tolles, *Meeting House and Counting House: The Quaker Merchants of Colonial Philadelphia* (New York, 1948), 25.

96. Richard Ryerson, "The Quaker Elite in the Pennsylvania Assembly," in Bruce Daniels, ed., *Power and Status: Officeholding in Colonial America* (Middletown, Conn., 1986), 106–35; Ryerson's results are exactly confirmed by Alan Tully in *William Penn's Legacy: Politics and Social Structure in Provincial Pennsylvania, 1726–1755* (Baltimore, 1977), 170–73.

97. David Hackett Fischer, *Albion's Seed* (New York, 1989), 601, passim.

98. Jean R. Soderlund, *Quakers and Slavery* (Princeton, 1985), 137.

99. Fischer, *Albion's Seed,* part 3.

100. Several recent works have tried to debunk this part of the bell's history, in the iconoclastic spirit of so much American historiography in the late twentieth century.

The leading example is David Kimball, *The Story of the Liberty Bell* (1989; Philadelphia, 1997), a book commissioned by Kathy Dilonardo, chief of the National Park Service's Division of Interpretation and Visitor Services. Kimball begins by stating frankly that "the author did no original research." He attempts to debunk the linkage between the bell and the Charter of Privileges, and also between the Norris family and William Penn.

The National Park Service has done the same thing in its "Liberty Bell Timeline." It has only two scraps of evidence. One of them is that Norris ordered the bell with a date of 1752, not 1751, and therefore it could not have been a commemoration of the Charter of Privileges. The bell was actually agreed on in 1751.

It also suggests that the fact that the colony's name is spelled "Pensylvania" in Norris's instructions is evidence that Norris and others wished to avoid reference to William Penn. This is not so; variations of spelling were routine in the eighteenth century.

Kimball adds an argument that "Norris's ancestors had helped extort the Charter from William Penn," and "Norris [II] was himself an antiproprietary leader," and that all this "makes less likely the inference that the bell was meant to commemorate the Charter of Liberties." There are many errors here. The charter was not extorted from Penn; Norris I and Penn produced it together and generally agreed except on the Council; Norris II was deeply concerned about defending the colony's Charter of Privileges in 1751.

Kimball argues that historians who claim a connection between the bell and the charter "have spent too much time reading between the lines." In fact they have read the lines themselves.

101. Whitechapel Bell Foundry, "500 Years of History," http://www.whitechapelbell foundry.co.uk.

102. Victor Rosewater, *The Liberty Bell: Its History and Significance* (New York, 1926), 10.

103. The British makers offered to supply another bell at the same price, deducting £17 for the scrap metal. A sister bell was acquired, and was destined to have many adventures in the New World. It ended its career in the Roman Catholic Church of St. Augustine at Fourth and Vine streets, where it was destroyed in a nativist riot that deliberately burned the church in 1844.

More than two centuries later, in 1976, a group of American "demonstrators" who called themselves the Procrastinators Society of America picketed the

British bell foundry with signs that read "We Got a Lemon" and "What About the Warranty?" The foundry replied that it would be happy to replace the bell, "as long as it was returned to us in the original packaging." Whitechapel Bell Foundry, "Story of the Liberty Bell," http://www.whitechapelbellfoundry.co.uk.

104. For the sound of the Liberty Bell, see Henry C. Watson, *The Old Bell of Independence, at Philadelphia in 1776* (Philadelphia, 1851).

105. *Pennsylvania Packet,* 8 May 1754.

106. Rosewater, *Liberty Bell,* 34.

107. The first Fourth of July celebration happened in Philadelphia during the following year. The city staged a great festival, and the State House Bell was heard, while the town enjoyed an excellent Hessian band that had been captured at the battle of Trenton.

108. John Baer Stoudt, *The Liberty Bell in Allentown and Allentown's Liberty Bell* (Allentown, Pa., n.d., ca. 1927); idem, *The Liberty Bells of Pennsylvania* (Philadelphia, 1930).

109. Walter Klinefelter, *York's Liberty Bell* (La Crosse, Wisc., 1975).

110. Interview of Emmanuel Rauch, *New York Times,* 16 July 1911; Craven, *Legend of the Founding Fathers,* 107.

111. *Philadelphia PublicLedger,* 26 Feb. 1846.

112. Rosewater, *Liberty Bell,* 194; in 1854, Joel Headly repeated the myth of the bell rung on the Fourth of July 1776 in his "Life of George Washington," *Graham's Magazine* (1854), 123.

113. William Cabell Bruce, *John Randolph of Roanoke,* 2 vols. (New York, 1922), 2:203.

114. Edmund Burke, "Speech on Conciliation with the Colonies," 22 March 1775, in *Speeches and Letters on American Affairs* (London, 1908), 94.

115. *Proceedings of the Convention of Delegates . . . in the Colony of Virginia* (1776; Richmond, 1816), 85–86; in this edition of the journal the date appears as July 5, 1776.

116. Ibid.

117. The leading study is still Edward S. Evans, "The Seals of Virginia," Virginia State Library *Report* (1909–10).

118. The source for the Virginians' image of Virtus and Libertas appears in a letter from John Page, who wrote to Jefferson, on July 20, 1776, "The Workman Engraver . . . may also be at a loss for a Virtus and Libertas, but you may refer him to Spence's Polymetis which must be in some library in Philadelphia" (*JP* 1:469–70). This was Joseph Spence, *Polymetis; or, An Inquiry concerning the Agreement between the Works of Roman Poets, and the Remains of the Antient Artists* (London, 1747).

119. Cf. Edmund Morgan, *American Slavery, American Freedom* (New York, 1975).

120. Samuel Johnson, *Taxation No Tyranny: An Answer to the Resolutions and Address of the American Congress* (London, 1775).

121. Burke, "Speech on Conciliation with the Colonies."

122. John Page wrote, "We are very much at a loss here for an Engraver to make our seal." Page to Thomas Jefferson, 20 July 1776, *JP* 1:469–70.

123. Jefferson to John Page, 30 July 1776, *JP* 1:482.

124. Jefferson employed Pierre Eugène Du Simitiére, who recorded in his notebooks an entry, "August [1776] a drawing in indian ink for the great Seal of the State of

Virginia in two sides 4 1/2 inches diameter. See Ev. Post July 18." Du Simitiére Notebooks, 1774–83, LC; *JP* 1:485. The seal is described in the *Pennsylvania Evening Post*, 18 July 1776.

125. Evans, "The Seals of Virginia," 37.

126. Bruce, *John Randolph of Roanoke* 2:203; Robert Dawidoff, *The Education of John Randolph of Roanoke* (New York, 1979), 32.

127. Silverman, *Cultural History of the American Revolution*, 264.

128. William Moultrie, *Memoirs of the American Revolution*, 2 vols. (New York, 1802), 1:90–91.

129. The main lines of the flag's design are clear in Moultrie's *Memoirs*, but one point is in dispute: the prominence of the word *Liberty*. That the word *Liberty* appeared on the flag is accepted by most historians. It was the motto of the Second South Carolina Regiment, and a passage in Drayton's *Memoirs* indicates that it was probably on the flag. But was it set on the blue field or on the crescent itself? In the nineteenth century the irrefragable flag historian Admiral George Preble concluded that the word *Liberty* was set on the blue field, and he published an illustration that has been widely followed in other works. But a South Carolinian has unkindly observed that Admiral Preble was a "New England writer" and that the word *Liberty* may have been set much smaller on the crescent. On the other hand, many flags in the early months of the Revolution displayed the word *Liberty* in large letters, and this design was explicitly urged by Continental General Charles Lee. On this ground, I conclude that Preble probably got it right, Yankee though he may have been.

    For the Liberty Flags see below, 153–54. On the Moultrie flag see also Wylma A. Wates, *A Flag Worthy of Your State and People: The History of the South Carolina State Flag*, 2d ed. rev (Columbia, S.C., 1996); Moultrie, *Memoirs;* John Drayton, *Memoirs of the American Revolution . . . ,* 2 vols. (Charleston, 1821); Alexander S. Salley Jr., *The Flag of the State of South Carolina* (Columbia, S.C., 1915); Barnard Elliott, "Diary of Captain Barnard Elliott," *Charleston Yearbook, 1889,* ca. 194–222; and Terry W. Lipscomb's excellent *The Carolina Lowcountry, April 1775–June 1776, and the Battle of Fort Moultrie* (Columbia, S.C., 1944).

130. St. Julian Ravenel, *Charleston: The Place and the People* (New York, 1906), 357; Terry W. Lipscomb, *South Carolina in 1791: George Washington's Southern Tour* (Columbia, S.C., 1993), 42–43.

131. Moultrie, *Memoirs* 1:90–91.

132. Richardson, *Standards and Colors*, 132; John Mollo, *Uniforms of the American Revolution* (New York, 1975), plates 187–88, p. 213.

133. Drayton, *Memoirs,* 1:45.

134. From contemporary drawings of the Queen's Rangers, made by Captain James Murray in 1780, now in the Toronto Central Library; a modern rendering appears in Mollo, *Uniforms of the American Revolution*, plates 179, 183–85, pp. 211–13.

135. Richardson, *Standards and Colors*, 131.

136. Edward McCrady, *History of South Carolina in the Revolution, 1775–1780,* 2 vols. (New York, 1902), 1:158; Drayton, *Memoirs* 2:303

137. Benson J. Lossing, *Pictorial Field-Book of the Revolution,* 2 vols. (New York, 1851; rpt., ed. Terence Barrow, Rutland, Vt., 1972), 2:532, 551.

138. Preble, *Origin and History of the American Flag* 1:211; an 1883 photograph of the Charleston monument is in Lipscomb, *Carolina Lowcountry*, 41.

139. The battalion appeared as the fifty-second on a roster of fifty-three Pennsylvania Battalions of Associators in 1775. The combat record of the men who served in it was described by Margaret Craig, daughter of an officer in the battalion; Ash Swamp was a fight at Plainfield, New Jersey, in the winter of 1777. The original flag survives in remarkably good condition. It was preserved in the family of General Samuel Craig, who had been the colorbearer in the battalion, and its provenance is established in detail. In 1880, Preble described the flag in great detail and discussed it with Margaret Craig. In 1907, Davis found it in the hands of Miss Jane Craig of New Alexandria, Pennsylvania. In 1914, it passed to the state of Pennsylvania and was put in the Harrisburg museum, where Richardson studied. See Preble, *Origin and History of the American Flag* 1:205–6; Gherardi Davis, *Regimental Colors of the War of the Revolution* (New York, 1907); Richardson, *Standards and Colors*, 115–6; cf. John B. B. Trussell, *The Pennsylvania Line: Regimental Organization and Operations, 1775–1783* (Harrisburg, 1977, 1983).

140. Lawrence M. Glauber, *Rattlesnakes*, 2d ed., 2 vols. (Berkeley, 1997), 1:531–33, 1240–43; John Behler, *Field Guide to North American Reptiles and Amphibians* (New York, 1979), 688, 619, 653; William R. Furlong, Byron McCandless, and Harold D. Langley, *So Proudly We Hail: The History of the United States Flag* (Washington, 1981), 71–73.

141. Richardson, *Standards and Colors*, 117; Trussell, *Pennsylvania Line*, 164.

142. The history of this unit is complex. It began as the Pennsylvania State Rifle Regiment and was consolidated with the Pennsylvania State Battalion of Musketry to create the Pennsylvania State Regiment in 1777, numbered the Thirteenth Pennsylvania Regiment in that year. It came to an end after the battle of Monmouth; many personnel served in the Second Pennsylvania Regiment. See Trussell, *Pennsylvania Line*, 164–87. The Peale painting is in a private collection. It was studied, discussed, and reproduced by Richardson, *Standards and Colors*, 118–19. The rattlesnake is very clear, but the motto is illegible. Richardson believes from close examination of the original that it was "Don't Tread on Me."

143. Captain Philip Slaughter, in Rev. Philip Slaughter, *A History of St. Mark's Parish, Culpeper County, Virginia* (Baltimore, 1877; rpt. 1994, 1998), 106–8.

144. The evidence for this flag is doubtful. It first appeared as a drawing in Lossing, *Pictorial Field-Book of the Revolution* 2:299. His source is thought to have been a memoir and diary by Captain Philip Slaughter, which were destroyed in the Civil War. Excerpts from the memoir are published in Slaughter, *History of St. Mark's Parish*, 106–8. They include a description of the hunting shirts, but the published passages do not describe the colors. The present members of the Culpeper Minutemen accept the authenticity of Lossing's drawing, with Culpeper spelled with three *p*'s.

145. For the Massachusetts rattlesnake see William G. Anderson, *The Price of Liberty: The Public Debt of the American Revolution* (Charlottesville, 1983), 130–34. It does not appear in Brigham, *Paul Revere's Engravings*, probably because the author thought it was engraved by Nathaniel Hurd.

146. The major documents on Gadsden flag, as it is commonly called, appear in *AA4*

4:468–69 and *NDAR,* Bradford's Pennsylvania Journal, 27 Dec. 1775; Albert Matthews, "The Snake Devices, 1754–1776, and the Constitutional Courant, 1765," *CSMP* 11 (1910), 409–53; Richardson, *Standards and Colors,* 115–16; Furlong et al., *So Proudly We Hail,* 72–73.

147. Nicholas Verien, *Livre curieux* (Paris, 1685?); idem, *Recueil d'emblêmes, dévices, médailles et figures hieroglyphiques* (Paris, 1696, 1724); Lester C. Olson, *Emblems of American Community in the Revolutionary Era* (Washington, 1991), 13, 25.

148. *Pennsylvania Gazette,* 9 May 1754; Mathews, "Snake Devices, 1754–1776."

149. Mathews, "Snake Devices, 1754–1776."

150. Brigham, *Paul Revere's Engravings,* plate 70.

151. Silverman, *Cultural History of the American Revolution,* 253, 307.

152. *Pennsylvania Journal,* 27 Dec. 1775 .

153. Fischer, *Albion's Seed,* pt. 4.

154. John Sullivan, a New Hampshire general who adopted the rattlesnake emblem for his standard, was the Scots-Irish son of two immigrants from Protestant Ireland. The Sullivan Standard, as it is sometimes called, survives in the Rhode Island Historical Society and is thought to have been carried by Sullivan's Life Guard in his expedition against the Iroquois in 1779. The provenance of the flag is doubtful, and nothing appears to have been recorded until the twentieth century. Cf. Richardson, *Standards and Colors,* 19–20, plate 20. For Sullivan see Charles P. Whittemore, *A General of the Revolution: John Sullivan of New Hampshire* (New York, 1961).

155. Qtd. in V. V. McNitt, *Chain of Error and the Mecklenburg Declarations of Independence* (New York, 1960), 30–31. The authenticity of the Mecklenberg Declaration of Independence has been much debated. It is clear that later texts of what purports to be a version of the Mecklenberg Declaration were written after Jefferson's Declaration and copied passages from his text. But McNitt summarizes strong evidence for the event itself at an earlier date. The problem of the Mecklenberg Declaration can be solved by separating the event from the text.

156. McNitt, *Chain of Error,* 24; Legette Blythe and Charles R. Brockmann, *Hornet's Nest: The Story of Charlotte and Mecklenberg County* (Charlotte, 1961), 88, 398.

157. These images appear today on Charlotte's Great Seal and many other emblems.

158. "Steve's Civil War Relics," relicpro@att.net.

159. Guthman, *Drums A'beating,* 196.

160. Richardson, *Standards and Colors,* 19, 139; Olson, *Emblems of American Community,* fig. 7.

161. *Before Freedom Came: African American Life in the Antebellum South* (Richmond, 1991), 126, for two surviving examples, one of which is reproduced.

162. John K. Thornton, "African Dimensions of the Stono Rebellion," *AHR* 96 (1991), 1101-13.

163. Douglas R. Egerton, *Gabriel's Rebellion: The Virginia Slave Conspiracies of 1800 and 1802* (Chapel Hill, 1993), 51.

164. Sidney Kaplan and Emma Nogrady Kaplan, *The Black Presence in the Era of the American Revolution,* rev. ed. (Amherst, Mass., 1989), 230; C. Malcolm Watkins, "A Plantation of Difference—People from Everywhere," Peter C. Marzio, ed., *A Nation of Nations* (New York, 1976), 55.

165. Hector St. John Crèvecoeur, *Sketches of Eighteenth-Century America*, ed. H. L. Bourdin et al. (New Haven, 1925), 310.

166. "Yankee Doodle; or, The Negroes Farewell to America," VHS.

167. Alice Hinkle, *Prince Estabrook, Slave and Soldier* (Wilmington, Mass., 2001)

168. David Hackett Fischer, *Ebony Tree*, forthcoming.

169. William C. Nell, *The Colored Patriots of the American Revolution* (Boston, 1855); a puzzle about this unit is that nothing has been found as yet in military records of the Revolution.

170. The flag was purchased from the family of the ensign who had received it from John Hancock, and presented to the Massachusetts Historical Society, which still owns it.

171. Kaplan and Kaplan, *Black Presence*, 65–66.

172. Benjamin Quarles, *The Negro in the American Revolution* (Chapel Hill, 1961), 76.

173. U.S. Bureau of the Census, *1990 Census of Population, Supplementary Reports: Detailed Ancestry Groups* (Washington, 1991).

174. For a general work, mainly on German Lutherans in the eighteenth century but with some attention to Swiss Reformed and other Germanic groups, see A. G. Roeber, *Palatines, Liberty, and Property: German Lutherans in Colonial America* (Baltimore, 1993). It puts heavy emphasis on liberty and property. Another work, with a very different interpretation, is Leonard Krieger, *The German Idea of Freedom: The History of a Tradition from the Reformation to 1871* (Chicago, 1960).

175. Isaac Zane, fireback, Bucks County {Pennsylvania] Historical Society.

176. "America, Freiheit," broadside, Philadelphia, 1766, in Silverman, *Cultural History of the American Revolution*, 96.

177. Morrison H. Heckscher and Leslie Greene Bowman, *American Rococo, 1750–1775: Elegance in Ornament* (New York, 1992), 203, 207, 208.

178. Four finial busts of John Locke appear in Robert C. Smith, "Finial Busts on Eighteenth-Century Philadelphia Furniture," *Magazine Antiques* 100 (1971), 900–905. A fifth bust of Locke, at Stratford in Virginia, is noted in Heckscher and Bowman, *American Rococo*, 253n. A Locke bust also appears on a chest-on-chest at Cliveden in Pennsylvania. It was long thought to be a Philadelphia piece, but Michael Kammen tells me that it is now believed to be of British origin (Kammen, communication, 25 March 2002). Others are turning up, perhaps as many as a dozen altogether by the estimate of Wendell Garrett in "Garrett's Attic," http://www.artnet.com/magazine, 11 Aug. 1999. Another example of a Locke finial appears in an eighteenth-century Philadelphia scroll-top desk and bookcase from the collection of Mr. and Mrs. Lammot du Pont Copeland, auctioned by Sotheby's, 19 Jan. 2002.

179. Another pediment bust has also been found, of an unidentified young man in simple but very handsome eighteenth-century dress. I wonder if it might be a youthful John Dickinson, in the role of the Pennsylvania Farmer. Cf. Hecksher and Bowman, *American Rococo*, 203–8.

180. Two Milton busts appear in Heckscher and Bowman, *American Rococo*, 253n, and *Magazine Antiques* 126 (1984), 1031.

181. This famous piece of furniture, known as the Pompadour Highboy, is in the collections of the Metropolitan Museum of Art. It was made in Philadelphia

between 1762 and 1775. The carvings of the swans and serpents are copied from an emblem book, Thomas Johnson, *A New Book of Ornaments* (London, 1762). Some authorities believe that the carver of the Pompadour bust was Hercules Courtnay, an artisan who moved from London to Philadelphia in 1765. See Hecksher and Bowman, *American Rococo*, 202–3; Wendell Garrett in "Garrett's Attic," http://www.artnet.com/magazine, 11 Aug. 1999.

182. [Charles Willson Peale], *A Description of the Picture and Mezzotinto of Mr. Pitt, done by Charles Willson Peale, of Maryland*, broadside (London, 1767).

183. Ibid.

184. Ibid.

185. Schlesinger, "Liberty Tree," 441; Charles Warren, *Jacobin and Junto* (Cambridge, 1931), 33–34.

186. Robert B. Hanson, *The Diary of Dr. Nathaniel Ames of Dedham, Massachusetts, 1758–1822*, 2 vols. (Camden, Me., 1998), 1: 139; Mabel M. Swan, "Simeon Skillin, Senior, America's First Sculptor," *Antiques* 46 (1944), 21.

187. Hanson, *Diary of Nathaniel Ames* 1:139.

188. *Boston Gazette*, 19 May 1766; (Boston) *Massachusetts Gazette*, 22 May 1766.

189. Brigham, *Paul Revere's Engravings*, 21–25; Lucius M. Sargent, *Dealings with the Dead* (Boston, 1856), 145; E. H. Goss, *The Life of Colonel Paul Revere*, 2 vols. (Boston, 1891), 1:40.

190. I have found no surviving example of the Sons of Liberty medal. A contemporary verbal description by James Kimball appears in *EIHC* 12:204; see also Goss, *Life of Colonel Paul Revere* 1:113.

191. Oft-repeated quotations attributed to Adams that one-third of the American people were for, one-third against, and one-third neutral are in error. They come from two sources, often misinterpreted in secondary and tertiary literature. One is a letter to James Lloyd in which Adams used almost exactly those words, but he was referring to American attitudes toward the French Revolution!

In another source, Adams wrote that the Continental Congress in early 1776 was equally divided three ways on the question of independence: those who were opposed, those who were too timid to take a stand, and those who were "true blue." This referred only to opinion within the Congress at a particular moment in time, and Adams's idea of "timidity" was another man's "Whiggery." David McCullough, *John Adams* (New York, 2001), 90.

On the larger question of attitudes toward the Revolution among the American people in general, he had a correspondence with Thomas McKean in which he estimated that two-thirds were for and one-third against. The original is in the McKean Papers, HSP.

192. The earliest American use of *Tory* as a political term is in a work of New England literature, which in 1634 referred to "King Charles his tories." See William Wood, *New England's Prospect*, ed. Alden Vaughan (1634; Amherst, Mass., 1977), pt. 2, ch. 18, p. 110. *Whig* appears in North Carolina as early as 1711 (*North Carolina Colonial Records* 1:768).

193. See Loyalist verses of Jonathan Odell, Joseph Stansbury, Myles Cooper, and James Rivington in Silverman, *Cultural History of the American Revolution*, 269, 308–9, passim.

194. Douglass Adair and John A. Schutz, eds., *Peter Oliver's Origin and Progress of the American Rebellion* (Palo Alto, 1961, 1969), 3–9.

195. E.g., "Britain's Rights Maintained: Or French Ambition Dismantled," 1755, in Dolmetsch, *Rebellion and Reconciliation*, 18.

196. *Rivington's New-York Gazetteer*, 10 June 1780; Claude Halstead Van Tyne, *The Loyalists in the American Revolution* (1902, Gloucester, 1959), 265.

197. "Second Guidon of the King's American Dragoons," n.d., after the regiment's royal warrant of 1768, New Brunswick Museum, Nova Scotia; in Robert S. Allen, ed., *The Loyal American: The Military Role of the Loyalist Provincial Corps and Their Settlement in British North America, 1775–1784* (Ottawa, 1983), 38. This is an excellent catalogue of a traveling exhibition by the Canadian War Museum in association with the New Brunswick Museum.

198. See *Rivington's New-York Gazetteer*, 19 Jan. 1775, for a discussion of mastheads.

199. Richardson, *Standards and Colors*, 122.

200. David L. Jacobson, ed., *The English Libertarian Heritage: From the Writings of John Trenchard and Thomas Gordon* (Indianapolis, 1965) 106.

201. Charles Le Roux, Andrew Hamilton Freedom Box, HSP. The motto: *Demersa leges timefacta libertas haec tandem emerguit.*

202. Eliza Farmer to Jack Halroyd, 28 June 1775, Eliza Farmer Letter Book, HSP, qtd. in David John Mays, *Edmund Pendleton*, 2 vols. (Cambridge, 1952), 1:23.

203. Michael Kammen, *Spheres of Liberty* (Madison, 1986), 26.

204. James Kelly, "Aera Fireback," curatorial notes, VHS.

205. Patrick Henry in the Virginia Convention, 23 March 1775.

206. Lord Percy to General Harvey, 20 April 1775, in Charles Knowles Bolton, *Letters of Hugh Lord Percy* (Boston, 1902), 53.

207. Eliza Farmer to Jack Halroyd, 28 June 1775, Eliza Farmer Letter Book HSP, qtd. in Mays, *Edmund Pendleton* 1:23.

208. Silverman, *Cultural History of the American Revolution*, 112–18, with many examples; see also Frank Moore, *Songs and Ballads of the American Revolution* (New York, 1856).

209. R. R. Palmer, *The Age of Democratic Revolution* (Princeton, 1959), 1:243.

210. *Gazetya Warszawskieya*, 5, 8, 12, 22 July 1775, Harvard University.

211. Adolph Benson, *Sweden and the American Revolution* (New Haven, 1976), 11.

212. Palmer, *Age of Democratic Revolution* 1:258, citing "Considérations sur la Révolution de l'Amérique" (1784), in G. K. van Hogendorp, *Grieven en Gedenkshriften* (The Hague, 1866), 1:407.

213. Samuel Shaw, *The Journals of Major Samuel Shaw, the First American Consul at Canton, with a Life of the Author by Josiah Quincy* (Boston, 1847; rpt. 1970), 234n.

A Republic United

1. Robert Frost, "The Black Cottage," in *North of Boston* (1914).

2. Still very useful is John H. Hazelton, *The Declaration of Independence: Its History* (New York, 1906), 156–283; Jay Fliegelman, *Declaring Independence: Jefferson, Natural Language, and the Culture of Performance* (Stanford, 1993).

3. It is probable that a draft or even several drafts were printed for the use of the Congress and gathered up and destroyed except for a fragment in HSP. See Wilfred J. Ritz, "From the *Here* of Jefferson's Handwritten Rough Draft of the Declaration of Independence to the *There* of the Printed Dunlap Broadside," *PMHB* 116 (1992), 499–512. See also Julian Boyd, *Declaration of Independence: Evolution of the Text*, rev. ed. (Lebanon, N.H., 1999); Hazelton, *Declaration of Independence*, 476–559; Pauline Maier, *American Scripture* (New York, 1997), 273–74.

4. Cedric Lawson, "Patriotism in Carmine: 162 Years of July 4th Oratory," *Quarterly Journal of Speech* 26 (1940), 12–25; Fletcher M. Green, "Listen to the Eagle Scream: One Hundred Years of the Fourth of July in North Carolina," in *Democracy in the Old South and Other Essays* (Nashville, 1969), 111–56; A. V. Huff, "The Eagle and the Vulture: Changing Attitudes Toward Nationalism in Fourth of July Orations in Charleston, 1788–1860," *South Atlantic Quarterly* 73 (1974), 10–22.

5. Thomas Dring, *Recollections of the Jersey Prison Ship* (1829; rpt. New York, 1961).

6. Philip F. Detweiler, "The Changing Reputation of the Declaration of Independence: The First Fifty Years," *WMQ3* 19 (1962), 557–74; Jacob Hiltzheimer, *Extracts from the Diary of Jacob Hiltzheimer, of Philadelphia, 1765–1798,* 4 July 1791, (Philadelphia, 1893), 170. Note that Independence Day was firmly established before the party battles of the 1790s, which have been identified erroneously as the beginning of this custom.

   On Charles Janson see Charles William Janson, *The Stranger in America, 1793–1806* (New York, 1935), and Len Travers, *Celebrating the Fourth* (Amherst, Mass., 1997), 1–3, a full and helpful study of Independence Day. The oration as printed was very different from what Janson heard. Cf. John Quincy Adams, *An Oration Pronounced July 4th., 1793, at the Request of the Inhabitants of the Town of Boston; in Commemoration of the Anniversary of American Independence* (Boston, 1793).

7. (Worcester) *Massachusetts Spy,* 24 July 1776.

8. Hazelton, *Declaration of Independence,* 560–61, 570 n87; Maier, *American Scripture,* 159.

9. Lafayette, *Mémoires et correspondance du général La Fayette,* 6 vols. (Paris, 1857–58), 3:197, qtd. in Carl L. Becker, *The Declaration of Independence* (New York, 1922), 231.

10. Becker, *Declaration of Independence;* Morton White, *The Philosophy of the American Revolution* (New York, 1978); Garry Wills, *Inventing America: Jefferson's Declaration of Independence* (Garden City, N.Y., 1978).

11. Jefferson to James Madison, 30 Aug. 1823, and Jefferson to Henry Lee, 8 May 1825, in *JW/F* 10:266–69, 342–43; Jefferson to James Mease, 26 Sept. 1825, in *JW/L&B* 16:122–23.

12. In Britain many writers argued with it. The *Scots Magazine* 38 (Aug. 1776), 433, reprinted the Declaration of Independence with a footnote on equality: "Are all men created equal? Certainly not in size, strength, understanding, figure, moral or civic virtue. . . . Every ploughman knows that they are not created equal in any of those."

   For a discussion of Dr. Ames see Charles Warren, Jacobin and Junto (Cambridge, 1931), and Robert B. Hanson's excellent edition of *The Diary of Dr. Nathaniel Ames . . . ,* 2 vols. (Camden, Me., 1998).

13. *Ordinances Passed at General Convention . . .* (Williamsburg, 1776), 100–103.

14. Patrick Henry, "Instructions to George Rogers Clark Esqr Colonel & Commander in Chief of Virginia Troops in the County of Illinois," Dec. 1778. This remarkable document was included in the pension file of James Meriwether and turned up in the records of the Veterans Administration, NA. A transcript is published in Frank Monaghan, ed., *Heritage of Freedom* (Princeton, 1947), 100–101.

15. [Thomas Paine], "Address to the People of Pennsylvania," *Pennsylvania Packet,* 1 Dec. 1778, in Philip S. Foner, ed., *Complete Writings of Thomas Paine,* 2 vols., New York, 1969), 2:287.

16. For a discussion see George Peek, ed., *Adams: His Political Writings* (Indianapolis, 1954), 94–96.

17. John Mollo, *Uniforms of the American Revolution* (New York, 1975); Charles M. Lefferts, *Uniforms of the American, British, French, and German Armies in the War of the American Revolution* (New York, 1926; rpt. 1971).

18. Charles Lee, "Mr. Lee's Plan," in Worthington Chauncey Ford, ed., *Correspondence and Journals of Samuel Blachley Webb,* 3 vols. (New York, 1893), 1:85–87. Webb published this document with a letter from Lee to Silas Deane, 20 July 1775. But the document itself has no date, and the letter makes no reference to it, or to its subject.

19. Edward W. Richardson, *Standards and Colors of the American Revolution* (Philadelphia, 1982), 13.

20. Bernhard A. Uhlendorf, ed., *Revolution in America: Confidential Letters and Journals of Adjutant General Major Baurmeister of the Hessian Forces* (New Brunswick, 1956), 41, 56.

21. E. J. Lowell, *The Hessians* (1884), 65; G. F. Scheer and H. F. Rankin eds., *Rebels and Redcoats* (New York, 1957), 187.

22. Richardson, *Standards and Colors of the American Revolution,* 15.

23. George H. Preble, *History of the Flag of the United States* (Boston, 1880), 246.

24. Richardson, *Standards and Colors,* 21, 62.

25. *Commodore Hopkins, Commander in Chief of the American Fleet,* 22 Aug. 22, 1776, portrait by John Martin. The original is in the Pennsylvania Maritime Museum. A mezzotint was published by Thomas Hart and is in LC; it is reproduced in Lester C. Olson, *Emblems of American Community in the Revolutionary Era* (Washington, 1991), fig. 11; the later French engraving is reproduced in Richardson, *Standards and Colors,* 62.

26. *Journal of the Proceedings of the Congress, Held at Philadelphia, September 5, 1774* (Philadelphia, 1774; John Norman, *A Collection of Designs in Architecture* (Philadelphia, 1775).

27. John Adams to Abigail Adams, 14 Aug. 1776, Adams Papers, MHS.

28. "Report on a Seal for the United States and Related Papers," [20 Aug. 1776], in *JP* 1:494–97, with the proposals by Franklin, Jefferson, and Du Simitière, but not Adams, together with the final report. For Du Simitière see Joel J. Orosz, *The Eagle That Is Forgotten: Pierre Eugène Du Simitière, Founding Father of American Numismatics* (Wolfeborough, N.H., 1988); and Paul G. Sifton, "Pierre Eugène du Simitière (1737–1784): Collector in Revolutionary America" (Ph.D. diss., University of Pennsylvania, 1960). His manuscripts are in HSP, the Library Company of Philadelphia, and APS.

29. A pencil sketch in Du Simitière's hand survives in the Jefferson Papers, LC. It is crudely reproduced in *JP* 1:550.

30. For a learned disquisition on the classical origins of the phrase see M. E. Deutsch, "E Pluribus Unum," *Classical Journal* 18 (1922–23), 387–407. Jefferson's idea for a national motto appears in his account book for 1774 and *JP* 1:495n.

31. "American Independence, Declared July 4th, 1776," Boston, 1776, Winterthur Museum, reproduced in Alvin M. Josephy, *The American Heritage History of the Congress of the United States* (New York, 1975), 33.

32. Eric P. Newman, "Benjamin Franklin and the Chain Design," *Numismatist* (Nov. 1983); idem, *The Early Paper Money of America,* 4th ed. (Iola, Wisc., 1997), 40, 74, 146–47, 123, 286, 431.

33. James Wilkinson, *Memoirs of My Own Times,* 3 vols. (Philadelphia, 1816; rpt. 1973), 1:150–51.

34. *History of First Troop, Philadelphia City Cavalry, 1774–1874* (Philadelphia, 1874).

35. The bills for the flag from John Folwell on 16 Sept. 1775, who charged £1.15 for the design, and James Claypoole on 8 Sept. 1775, who asked £8 for painting, are reproduced in facsimile in George H. Preble, *Origin and History of the American Flag,* 2 vols. (Philadelphia, 1917), 1:257.

36. Milo M. Quaife, Melvin J. Weig, and Roy E. Appleman, *The History of the United States Flag* (New York, 1961), plate 2. A detail of the knot appears in Preble, *Origin and History of the American Flag* 1:253.

37. William S. Appleton, *Augustin Dupré and His Work for America* (Cambridge, 1890).

38. Carl Zigrosser, "The Medallic Sketches of Augustin Dupré in American Collections," *APSP* 101 (1957), 535–50.

39. Winfried Schleiner, "The Infant Hercules: Franklin's Design for a Medal Commemorating American Liberty," *Eighteenth-Century Studies* 10 (1976–77), 235–44; Olson, *Emblems of American Community,* 189–91.

40. Benjamin Franklin to R. R. Livingston, 4 March 1782, 15 April 1783.

41. Claypoole's *American Daily Advertiser,* 18 March 1793.

42. Olson, *Emblems of American Community,* 189–91; see also Appleton, *Augustin Dupré and his Work for America.*

43. For general works see E. McClung Fleming, "The American Image as Indian Princess, 1765–1783," *Winterthur Portfolio* 2 (1965), 65–84; "From Indian Princess to Greek Goddess: The American Image, 1783–1815," ibid. 3 (1967), 37–66; and "Symbols of the United States: From Indian Queen to Uncle Sam," in Ray Browne et al., *Frontiers of American Culture* (Muncie, Ind., 1968), 1–24; Alan Leander MacGregor, "Tammany: The Indian as Rhetorical Surrogate," *American Quarterly* 35 (1983), 391–407.

44. An example was a British print in 1755, which represented the colonies as an Indian child who was under the protection of Britannia.

45. "The Able Doctor, or America Swallowing the Bitter Draught," *London Magazine* 43 (April 1774), facing 185; copy by Paul Revere, *Royal American Magazine,* June 1774.

46. "Bunker's Hill, or the Blessed Effects of Family Quarrels," 1775, BL; "The Female Combatants," 26 Jan. 1776, John Carter Brown Library; "The Reconcilia-

tion Between Britannia and her Daughter America," Colonial Williamsburg Foundation.

47. "Liberty Triumphant No. 1 or the Downfall of Oppression," Colonial Williamsburg Foundation; "L'Angleterre suppliante" (1780), Bibliothèque Nationale; "The General P—s, or Peace" (1783), LC.

48. For Saint Tammany see John Leacock, *The Fall of British Tyranny, or American Liberty Triumphant* (Philadelphia, 1776), an American play by a Philadelphia goldsmith who was a member of the Sons of Liberty.

49. "The Curious Zebra. Alive from America! Walk in Gem'men and Ladies, Walk in," in Olsen, *Emblems of American Community*, 202, 212, fig. 41.

50. "Amusement for John Bull and His Cousin Paddy, or the Gambols of the American Buffalo," in Olsen, *Emblems of American Community,* 250.

51. For buckskins see Kenneth Silverman, *A Cultural History of the American Revolution* (New York, 1976), 55, and David Hackett Fischer, "John Beale Bordley...," *Journal of Southern History* 28 (1962), 327–42; for Pennsylvania bucktails in the Revolution see Preble, *Origin and History of the American Flag* 1:252.

52. Robert Beverley, *The History and Present State of Virginia* (1715; Chapel Hill, 1947), 311–12.

53. Preble, *Origin and History of the American Flag* 1:192, 197. Later, the state of Wisconsin made the beaver its symbol.

54. Marquis de Chastellux, *Travels in North America in the Years 1780, 1781, and 1782,* ed. Howard C. Rice Jr., 2 vols. (Chapel Hill, 1962), 1:126, 291–92; Henry Phillips, *Historical Sketches of Paper Currency of the American Colonies,* 2 vols. (Roxbury, Mass., 1865–66); Benson Lossing, "Continental Money," *Harper's New Monthly Magazine* 26 (1863), 433–47; George Everett Hastings, *The Life and Works of Francis Hopkinson* (Chicago, 1926).

55. Olson, *Emblems of American Community,* 202.

56. For the history of the national seal, see Quaife et al., *History of the United States Flag,* 115–23; Preble, *Origin and History of the American Flag* 2:683–97.

57. For a general discussion see Philip M. Isaacson, *The American Eagle* (Boston, 1975).

58. Benjamin Franklin to Sarah Bache, 26 Jan. 1784, in *Writings of Benjamin Franklin,* ed. A. H. Smyth, 10 vols. (New York, 1905–7), 9:161–66.

59. Marquis de Chastellux, "The Progress of the Arts and Sciences in America, in the Form of a Letter to the Reverend James Madison, President of the College of William and Mary," Jan. 1783, first printed as an appendix in *Voyages dans l'Amérique septentrionale* (Paris, 1786), tr. Rice, *Travels in North America* 1:529.

60. Elinor Lander Horwitz, *The Bird, the Banner, and Uncle Sam: Images of America in Folk and Popular Art* (Philadelphia, 1976), 40.

61. *OED;* Raymond Williams, *Keywords: A Vocabulary of Culture and Society* (New York, 1976), 178–80.

62. Isaiah 40:31.

63. The painting is in CHS.

64. Albert K. Weinberg, *Manifest Destiny* (Baltimore, 1935).

65. Yvonne Brault Smith, *John Haley Bellamy, Carver of Eagles* (Portsmouth, N.H., 1982); Wendy Lavitt, *Animals in American Folk Art* (New York, 1990), 29–32.

66. See illustrations of Miss Liberty, below.

67. General works include Preble, *Origin and History of the American Flag;* Quaife et al., *History of the United States Flag;* Boleslaw Mastai and Marie-Louise D'O-trange Mastai, *The Stars and the Stripes: The American Flag as Art and as History from the Birth of the Republic to the Present* (New York, 1973); Whitney Smith, *The Flag Book of the United States* (New York, 1970, 1975).

68. In a very large literature, the most informative works are still Preble, *Origin and History of the American Flag* (2 vols., 1872, 1880, Philadelphia 1917); Quaife et al., *History of the United States Flag* (New York, 1961); and W. Smith, *Flag Book of the United States.*

69. "We have just received the following intelligence from Taunton—that on Friday last a Liberty Pole 112 feet long was raised there on which a vane, and a Union flag flying with the words Liberty and Union thereon." *Boston Evening Post,* 24 Oct. 1774.

70. (Boston) *Massachusetts Spy,* 7 July 1774; Clarence S. Brigham, *Paul Revere's Engravings* (Worcester, 1954), 136ff. For an early image of a flag with vertical stripes and a serpent see "The Taking of Miss Mud Island, October, 1777," engraved by W. Faden, Charing Cross, 1778, in Richardson, *Standards and Colors,* 13, 14; see also Mastai and Mastai, *The Stars and the Stripes.*

71. Whitney Smith, "The Forster Flag: The First American Flag Ever Made," *Flag Bulletin* 205 (May–June 2002), 82–118.

72. Many models have been identified for the Union Flag as it has variously been called. Some think it descended from the British Red Duster or "meteor flag." Quaife writes that "it had been created by adding six white stripes to the field of England's Meteor banner." Preble and many others pointed out that it closely resembled the flag of the British East India Company, which had as few as nine and as many as thirteen stripes and was in use from as early as 1704 to as late as 1834. A "View of Philadelphia; taken by George Heap," published in 1754, shows a ship in the foreground flying an ensign very much like the Grand Union Flag.

   An eighteenth-century flag book (1737) shows many striped flags of similar design flown by Scottish ships (eleven red and white stripes with a white canton and red cross); also the flags of Rotterdam (green and white stripes) and North Holland (thirteen red and yellow stripes). None have been linked conclusively to the Grand Union Flag.

   Cf. Quaife et al., *History of the United States Flag,* 26–27; Alfred M. Cutler, *The Continental "Great Union" Flag* (Somerville, 1929); *La Connaissance des pavillons ou bannières que la plupart des nations* (The Hague, 1737); George H. Preble, "The Grand Union or Continental Flag of the United Colonies," in Preble, *Origin and History of the American Flag* 1:223–47, also 217–21; communication from Dr. Whitney Smith, executive director, Flag Research Center, Winchester, Mass.

73. Washington to Reed, 4 Jan. 1776 *GW* 3:23–27.

74. Captain John Chapman, Royal Navy, report to Admiral Young, 29 July 1776, and log of HMS *Shark,* ADM 51/895, 5/125, PRO; *AA5* 7:609, 706, 8:323; Robert C. Alberts, *The Golden Voyage: The Life and Times of William Bingham, 1752–1804* (Boston, 1969), 28–29; William Bell Clark, *Lambert Wickes: Sea Raider and Diplomat* (New Haven, 1932).

The Grand Union Flag appeared on North Carolina currency issued in April 1776 and was flown at the Virginia Convention in May 1776. It was also worn by the Continental ship *Alfred* (Captain John Paul Jones), perhaps as early as late December 1775 or early January 1776, and used by Commodore Esek Hopkins's fleet at the capture of New Providence on 17 March 1776, and by Benedict Arnold's ships on Lake Champlain in the summer of 1776. It was still in use at Fort Schuyler as late as 1777. See Preble, *Origin and History of the American Flag* 1:23–34; Quaife et al., *History of the United States Flag,* 25–28; Cutler, *Continental "Great Union" Flag,* 26–28, passim.

75. The ensign of the East India Company appears flying from the high stern of a heavily armed East Indiaman in George Heap's "View of Philadelphia" in 1754. Richardson, *Standards and Colors,* 16.

76. Ibid., 21–36.

77. Ibid., plates 18–19, passim.

78. Several copies of this painting survive. One of them (34 by 24 inches) is in the Firestone Library at Princeton. Another is owned by the Historical Society of Pennsylvania. Both came out of the atelier of the Peales. The Philadelphia copy was painted by the apprentice William Mercer. The Princeton copy is unsigned and attributed to James Peale, but it is much more crude than the work he was doing at the same time and is more likely to be another painting by Mercer. Dates are also in doubt. The Princeton painting is dated 1779, and the Philadelphia painting 1784. Others are at West Point, the Smithsonian, the National Gallery, and Winterthur.

79. Peale's son Titian wrote of this flag in the Washington portrait, "I don't know that I ever heard my father speak of that flag, but the trophies at Washington's feet I know he painted from the flags then captured, and which were left with him for the purpose. He was always very particular in matters of historic record in his pictures."

80. The original painting is in the Pennsylvania Academy of Fine Arts. Copies are at Colonial Williamsburg, Yale, Mt. Vernon, Princeton, New York's Metropolitan Museum of Art (2). Others change the background to Yorktown and are at the Maryland State House in Annapolis and the Château Rochambeau at Vendôme. Another copy by Samuel Smith is in Independence Hall. See Richardson, *Standards and Colors,* 25; Samuel Stelle Smith, *The Battle of Trenton* (Monmouth Beach, N.J., 1965); Charles Coleman Sellers, *Portraits and Miniatures by Charles Willson Peale* (Philadelphia, 1952) and *Supplement* (1969); idem, *Charles Willson Peale: A Biography* (New York, 1969).

81. Edward Richardson believes that it was created "sometime after the flag resolution of June 14, 1777"; *Standards and Colors of the American Revolution,* 19. Whitney Smith thinks that Washington's "personal command flag" might have become first, and describes the hypothesis of its "possible influence" on the Flag Resolution as one of several "plausible theories"; *Flags Through the Ages and Around the World* (New York, 1975), 193. Donald W. Holst has suggested that this standard might have been an artillery standard and is shown in contemporary images near the guns. He read the evidence of the Mercer and the Peale paintings differently. In the former, the standard is close to Washington and far from the nearest guns.

In the latter, the guns are trophies, taken from the Hessians. See Holst, "Notes on Continental Artillery Flags and Flag Guns," *Military Collector and Historian* 46 (1994), 122–28, 171–74.

82. For the founding of the headquarters guard see General Orders, 11 March 1776, in *GW* 3:449–49. For the guard in combat see Joseph Plumb Martin, *Private Yankee Doodle* (Boston, 1962), 120. For a general history see Carlos E. Godfrey, *Commander-in-Chief's Guard: Revolutionary War* (Washington, 1904), and Robert K. Wright Jr., *The Continental Army* (Washington, 1989), 88. Douglas Southall Freeman's assertion that the guard was recruited from Virginia regiments is not correct. Its commander was a New Englander, Captain Caleb Gibbs, and his lieutenant was George Lewis, Washington's nephew. Other men in the unit were drawn from many regiments in the army.

83. For his displeasure with the Grand Union Flag see Washington to Joseph Reed, 4 Jan. 1776; his views that the military colors should "bear some kind of similitude to the uniform" are in General Orders, 5 Jan. 1776; his sense of urgency about colors and standards is in Washington to Israel Putnam, 28 May 1776, all in *GW* 3:23–26, 4:400–401. Washington also had another headquarters standard, an elaborate painted motif. But this was much later, from the years of his presidency.

84. Richardson, *Standards and Colors,* 57, 250–64. Richardson examined the standard and concluded it has "the original homespun linen heading. The heading material appears to be the same as that of Washington's marquee" (57). The marquee is discussed in George Washington to Samuel Washington, 30 Sept. 1775, in *GW* 2:72.

85. Older works that strongly support the legend include William J. Canby, "The History of the Flag of the United States," unpublished paper, 14 March 1870, Huntington Library, copies in HSP and on the Betsy Ross Home Page, http://www.ushistory.org/betsy/more/canby.htm; idem, *The First American Flag and the Family History of Betsy Ross* (Philadelphia, 1882); Lloyd Balderston, *The Evolution of the American Flag from Materials Collected by the Late George Canby* (Philadelphia, 1909); Edwin S. Parry, *Betsy Ross, Quaker Rebel* (Philadelphia, 1930); "Memorial to Betsy Ross," U.S. Congress, 74th Cong., 2d sess., House Report 2265 (1936); and the Betsy Ross Home Page (http://www.ushistory.org/betsy).

Strongly critical are Hugh F. Rankin, "The Naval Flag of the American Revolution," *WMQ3* 11 (1954), 339, 346–47; Theodore Gottlieb, *The Origin and Evolution of the Betsy Ross Flag: Legend or Tradition?* (n.p., 1938); "The American Flag," *NJHSP* 57 (1939), 178; Quaife et al., *History of the United States Flag* (New York, 1961), 94–96, 184.

Tertiary expressions of academic skepticism include Elizabeth Cometti, "Betsy Ross," in Edward T. James, ed., *Notable American Women: A Biographical Dictionary,* 3 vols. (Cambridge, 1971), 3:198–99; Betty Wood, "Betsy Ross," in Jack P. Greene and J. R. Pole, *The Blackwell Encyclopedia of American History* (Oxford, 1991), 774.

Careful works of primary research include Roy Thompson, *Betsy Ross: Last of Philadelphia's Free Quakers* (Fort Washington, 1971); Edward Richardson, "Betsy Ross," in *Standards and Colors,* 265–74; which in general support the family traditions.

86. William D. Timmins and Robert W. Yarrington, *Betsy Ross: The Griscom Legacy* (Woodstown, N.J., 1981), 128; Robert Morris, *The Truth About the Betsy Ross Story* (Beach Haven, N.J., 1982), 6–18.

87. Church records confirm that they did in fact sit in adjacent pews, with a column between. Morris, *Truth About the Betsy Ross Story,* 23–24; Christ Church in Philadelphia, *The Story of Christ Church* (Philadelphia, 1959), 12. An American flag stands perpetually by their pews.

88. Thompson, *Last of the Free Quakers.*

89. The paper was not published (see n. 85 above), but the gist of it appears in letters from William Canby to George Preble, 29 March 1870 and 9 Nov. 1871, in Preble, *Origin and History of the American Flag* 1:266. When Canby presented his paper, at least three of Betsy Ross's daughters were still alive and confirmed its accuracy, as did other friends and relations.

90. Affidavit of Rachel Fletcher, daughter of Elizabeth Claypoole [Betsy Ross], affirmed on 27 May 1870, reproduced on Betsy Ross Home Page, http://www.ushis tory.org/betsy/flagaffs.html.

91. Ibid.

92. There is a large literature in mathematics and origami on this method of folding a paper so as to produce a five-pointed star with a single snip. The result is called the "Betsy Ross star." Instructions appear at http://www.ushistory .org/betsy/flagstar.html.

93. Affidavits of Rachel Fletcher (daughter), 31 July 1871, Sophia B. Hildebrant (granddaughter), 27 May 1870, and Margaret Donaldson Boggs (niece), 3 June 1870, http://www.ushistory.org/betsy/flagaffs/html.

94. This is Louis-Nicolas Van Blarenerghe, *The Surrender at Yorktown,* in a private collection in France, reproduced with enlargements in color in Richardson, *Standards and Colors,* 228–31.

95. See above, 155.

96. On the meeting itself, the affidavits of the Ross family are consistent with Washington's presence in Philadelphia and with his concern for the design of standards and colors in his army, and they are also highly accurate in their description of Washington's standard (square shape, six-pointed stars, pattern, etc.). The Ross family could have had no other way of knowing about that flag in the mid-nineteenth century, other than from Betsy Ross's description, and did know what they were describing, all of which strongly suggests that such a meeting did actually take place.

    On the other hand, it is not correct that the men who visited Betsy Ross were a Congressional committee. Two of the three were not then members of Congress. Congress did not appoint a flag committee at that time and did not approve the Stars and Stripes until a year later. Some have suggested that they might have done these things secretly, but what is the point of a secret flag? There is no supporting evidence that the Stars and Stripes flew anywhere in the spring of 1776.

97. Pennsylvania Navy Board, Minutes, 29 May 1777, which authorized payment of £14.12s.2d for "ships colors"; *PA* 2d ser., 1:164; John W. Jackson, *The Pennsylvania Navy, 1775–1781* (New Brunswick, 1974), 17, 408–9n. The going price appears to

have been £1.2s.10d for a single flag. A receipted bill from Elizabeth Claypoole to Caesar A. Rodney, $27. for a "large ensign," is dated 28 May 1813; Rodney Collection, HSD; Timmins and Yarrington, *Betsy Ross*, 156.

98.   The Membership Book and Statement of Principles of the Free Quakers is owned by APS; a facsimile appears in Morris, *Truth About the Betsy Ross Story*, 110–13.

99.   *Pennsylvania Colonial Records* (Harrisburg, 1837–53), 11:212, 3 June 1777; Preble, *Origin and History of the American Flag* 1:267; Rankin, "Naval Flag of the American Revolution," 345n.

100.   Newman, *Early Paper Money of America*, 66.

101.   George Hastings, *The Life and Works of Francis Hopkinson* (Chicago, 1926), 240–44; Scot M. Guenter, *The American Flag, 1777–1924: Cultural Shifts from Creation to Codification* (Rutherford, N.J., 1990).

102.   Grace Rogers Cooper, *Thirteen-Star Flags: Keys to Identification*, Smithsonian Studies in History and Technology 21 (Washington, 1973).

103.   The Bennington flag survives at the Bennington Battle Monument and Historical Society, Bennington, Vermont. It is often said to have been flown at the battle of Bennington. But its size (5 1/2 by 10 feet) would have made it very difficult to carry into action; some experts have wondered if it was a camp flag. Its authenticity has been challenged by a textile expert who studied it through its glass frame and concluded that the fabric was woven on a power loom and the flag may have dated from the nineteenth century; the question remains in doubt. The fragment of another Bennington flag survived in the family of General John Stark. It had a green field, with thirteen gold stars in rows (3,2,3,2,3) painted on a blue canton. William Lea Furlong and Byron McCandless, *So Proudly We Hail: The History of the United States Flag* (Washington, 1907), 105–8.

104.   Preble, *Origin and History of the American Flag* 1:263.

105.   Also added to this version of the Stars and Stripes were, included among the stars, "a ship, a plough and three sheaves of wheat, the crest an eagle volant; the supporters two white horses." A description and a sketch appear in Ezra Stiles, Diary, 24 April 1783, Yale.

106.   For general works see Oscar Sonneck, *The Star Spangled Banner* (Washington, 1914); George J. Svejda, *History of the Star Spangled Banner from 1814 to the Present* (Washington, 1969); Lonn Taylor, *The Star-Spangled Banner: The Flag that Inspired the National Anthem* (New York, 2000); Irvin Molotsky, *The Flag, the Poet, and the Song: The Story of the Star-Spangled Banner* (New York, 2001). A comprehensive collection of manuscripts, books, newspapers, sheet music, drawings, and other primary materials is in P. W. Filby and Edward G. Howard, *Star-Spangled Books* (Baltimore, 1972).

107.   Francis Scott Key Smith, *Francis Scott Key, Author of the Star Spangled Banner* (1911); Edward S. Delaplaine, *Francis Scott Key: Life and Times* (Brooklyn, 1937); Sam Meyer, *Paradoxes of Fame: The Francis Scott Key Story* (Annapolis, 1995).

108.   *Poems of the Late Francis Scott Key, Esq., with an Introductory Letter by Chief Justice Taney* (New York, 1857).

109.   David Hackett Fischer, *The Revolution of American Conservatism* (New York, 1965), 162, 363.

110. James H. Broussard, *The Southern Federalists, 1800–1816* (Baton Rouge, 1978), 154–56.

111. Francis Scott Key to John Randolph of Roanoke, 5 Oct. 1814, Howard Papers, MDHS.

112. Molotsky, *The Flag, the Poet, and the Song*, 74–82.

113. Donald E. Graves, *Sir William Congreve and the Rocket's Red Glare* (Alexandria Bay, N.Y., 1989); Neil Swanson, *The Perilous Fight* (New York, 1945), 459–67.

114. Primary accounts by John S. Skinner in *Baltimore Sun*, 29 May 1849; also Roger B. Taney to Charles Howard, 12 March 1856, in Samuel Tyler, *Memoir of Roger B. Taney* (Baltimore, 1872), 109–19.

115. George Armistead to Secretary of War, 24 Sept. 1814, in John Brannan, ed., *Official Letters of the Military and Naval Officers of the United States During the War with Great Britain in the Years 1812, 13, 14, & 15 . . .* (Washington, 1823), 439–41; Anthony S. Pitch, *The Burning of Washington: The British Invasion of 1814* (Annapolis, 1998), 189–217; George R. Gleig, *A Subaltern in America: Comprising His Narrative of the Campaigns of the British Army at Baltimore, Washington, etc., during the Late War* (Baltimore, 1833), 90–102.

116. R.J.B. [Robert J. Barrett], "Naval Recollections of the Late American War," *United Service Journal and Naval and Military Magazine*, pt. 1 (April 1841), 455–67; pt. 2 (May 1841), 13–23.

117. Pitch, *Burning of Washington*, 218–22; Filby and Howard, *Star-Spangled Books*, 51–59.

118. The texts of the song follow the earliest extant manuscript of the song in the hand of Francis Scott Key, MDHS, and reproduced in Filby and Howard, *Star Spangled Books*, M7. Later copies by Key himself vary in small details, as does the official version that is commonly sung today.

119. Delaplaine, *Francis Scott Key*, 374–82.

120. C[harles] D[urang] in *Historical Magazine* 8 (1864), 347–48; reproduced in Sonneck, *Star Spangled Banner*, 72; cf. Filby and Howard, *Star-Spangled Books*, 60.

121. For the printing history see Sonneck, *Star Spangled Banner*, 83.

122. *OED*, s.v "nationalism," "nation."

123. "A Grand Chorus, to Be Sung on the Fourth of June," broadside, Philadelphia, 1766, in Silverman, *Cultural History of the American Revolution*, 98.

124. (Philadelphia) *Pennsylvania Chronicle*, 17 Sept. 1770, and *Boston Gazette*, 10 Sept. 1770, in Silverman, *Cultural History of the American Revolution*, 148–49.

125. A. J. Wall, "The Statues of George III and the Honorable William Pitt Erected in New York City, 1770," *NYHSQ* 4 (1920), 36–57; Frank Moore, *Diary of the American Revolution*, 2 vols. (New York, 1860), 1:271, 284; Silverman, *Cultural History of the American Revolution*, 324.

126. C. H. Hart, "Patience Wright, Modeller in Wax," *Connoisseur* 19 (1907), 18–22; Silverman, *Cultural History of the American Revolution*, 383, 455.

127. For general studies of the iconic Washington see Marcus Cunliffe, *George Washington, Man and Monument* (Boston, 1958); M. E. Thistlethwait, *The Image of George Washington* (Philadelphia, 1977); Barry Schwartz, *George Washington: The Making of an American Symbol* (Ithaca, 1987); Barbara J. Mitnick, *The Changing Image of George Washington* (New York, 1989); idem et al., *George Washington,*

American Symbol (Stony Brook, N.Y., 1999). For biographies see Paul K. Long-more, *The Invention of George Washington* (Berkeley, 1988), an excellent study of his early life; Edmund Morgan, *The Genius of George Washington* (New York, 1980); Richard Brookhiser, *Founding Father: Rediscovering George Washington* (New York, 1996); Douglas Southall Freeman et al., *George Washington,* 7 vols. (New York, 1948–57); James Thomas Flexner, *George Washington,* 4 vols. (Boston, 1965–72).

128.   At least four scarves are known to survive: one in the New-York Historical Society, another in the collections of John R. Monsky, and two at the Winterthur Museum. For its origin, see an account by the maker's daughter, Sarah Hewson Alcock, *A Brief History of the Revolution with a Sketch of Captain John Hewson* (Philadelphia, 1943), 9; and John R. Monsky, "From the Collection: Finding America in Its First Political Textile," *Winterthur Portfolio* 37 (2002), 239–64.

129.   Mark E. Lender, Barbara J. Mitnick, et al., *George Washington and the Battle of Trenton: The Evolution of an American Image* (Trenton, 2001).

130.   Garry Wills, *Cincinnatus: George Washington and the Enlightenment* (New York, 1984).

131.   For Weems stories that had a foundation in fact see Freeman, *Washington* 1:64n, 146n, passim; see also Paul L. Ford and Emily Ford Skeel, *Mason Locke Weems: His Works and Ways,* 3 vols. (New York, 1929); Jay Fliegelman, *Prodigals and Puritans* (Cambridge, 1982); Wills, "Weems and the Cherry Tree," in *Cincinnatus,* 39–53.

132.   Noble E. Cunningham Jr., *Popular Images of the Presidency from Washington to Lincoln* (Columbia, Mo., 1991), 2–12.

133.   (Boston) *New England Palladium,* 3 May 1814.

134.   Nian-Sheng Huang, *Benjamin Franklin in American Thought and Culture, 1790–1990* (Philadelphia, 1994); Charles C. Sellers, ed., *Benjamin Franklin in Portraiture* (New Haven, 1962); A. O. Aldridge, *Franklin and His French Contemporaries* (New York, 1957); Claude-Ann Lopez, *Mon Cher Papa: Franklin and the Ladies of Paris* (New Haven, 1966). For biographies see Carl Van Doren, *Benjamin Franklin* (New York, 1938); Esmond Wright, *Franklin of Philadelphia* (Cambridge, 1986).

135.   Benjamin Franklin, *Poor Richard, an Almanack . . .* (Philadelphia, 1732–50), in Leonard W. Labaree et al., eds., *The Papers of Benjamin Franklin* (New Haven, 1959+), 1:357, 353 (1734); 2:141 (1736); 2:192 (1738); 2:219 (1739); 3:5 (1745); cf. Ralph Ketchum, ed., *The Political Thought of Benjamin Franklin* (Indianapolis, 1965); Gerald Stourzh, "Reason and Power in Benjamin Franklin's Political Thought," *American Political Science Review* 47 (1953), 1092–115; Paul W. Conner, *Poor Richard's Politicks: Benjamin Franklin and His New American Order* (New York, 1965)

136.   I. Bernard Cohen, *Franklin and Newton* (Philadelphia, 1956); idem, *Benjamin Franklin's Experiments* (Cambridge, 1941).

137.   Esmond Wright, *Franklin of Philadelphia* (Cambridge, 1986), 269; Durand Echeverria, *Mirage in the West: A History of the French Image of American Society to 1815* (Princeton, 1957), 15–17, 85.

138.   Johann Martin Will, after a drawing by Charles Nicolas Cochin, *Benjamin Franklin,* 1778? mezzotint (13 by 9.25 inches).

139.   Jean Honoré Fragonard, *Eripuit Coelo Fulmen Sceptrumque Tyrannis, in Roger Por-*

talis, Honoré Fragonard, sa vie et son oeuvre (Paris, 1889), 141–42; Aldridge, *Franklin and His French Contemporaries,* 124–27; for the chamber pot, Lopez, *Mon Cher Papa,* 184; the source is Henriette de Campan, *Mémoires sur le vie de Marie-Antoinette* (Paris, 1858).

140. Joseph Duplessis, *Benjamin Franklin,* 1778, oil on canvas (oval 23 by 28.5 inches), Metropolitan Museum of Art, New York.

141. "The Apotheosis of George Washington and Benjamin Franklin," printed textile, n.d., ca. 1785–90, Winterthur Museum.

142. Page Smith, *John Adams,* 2 vols. (Westport, Conn., 1969), 2:802.

143. Franklin, Codicil, 23 June 1789, in Carl Van Doren, *Benjamin Franklin* (New York, 1938), 762; Lopez, *Mon Cher Papa,* 189; Smyth, *Writings of Franklin,* 10:493–501. After Washington's death, the walking stick was said to have passed to the federal government and to have been acquired by the Smithsonian Institution, but from early descriptions it appears not to be the same as the walking stick that is exhibited in the Smithsonian's permanent collections.

144. "HOPE: A Rhapsody," broadside, New York, July 1774, qtd. in Silverman, *Cultural History of the American Revolution,* 263; *Virginia Gazette,* 1 Sept. 1774; and Francis Hopkinson, *A Pretty Story* (Philadelphia, 1774); idem, *Miscellaneous Essays and Occasional Writings,* 3 vols. (Philadelphia, 1792); George E. Hastings, *Life and Works of Francis Hopkinson* (Chicago, 1926).

145. Artifacts on http://www.acpweb.net/ACPweb/SalazarMosley/Original.htm.

146. Maier, *American Scripture,* 150.

147. The first small painting included forty-eight figures; the second one for the Capitol omitted Thomas Nelson Jr. Missing signers include William Thornton, Button Gwinnett, Lyman Hall, John Penn, Thomas Stone, Caesar Rodney, Francis Lightfoot Lee, John Morton, John Smith, and John Hart. Nonsigners present are George Clinton, a leading member of Congress, who was away on "state business"; Thomas Willing and John Dickinson, who were very prominent in the Congress but did not at that moment support independence; and Charles Thomson, who was the secretary of Congress. Theodore Sizer, *The Works of Colonel John Trumbull: Artist of the American Revolution,* rev. ed. (New Haven, 1967), fig. 159, includes a key to the painting and reproduces many of Trumbull's life studies. See also Irma B. Jaffe, *Trumbull: The Declaration of Independence* (New York, 1976). Trumbull himself wrote about the painting in a reply to "Detector" in *Port Folio,* 1819, reproduced in Charles Sanford, ed., *Quest for America, 1810–1824* (New York, 1964), 155–62. Other discussions appear in Maier, *American Scripture,* 181–83, 278; and Wills, *Inventing America,* 345–48.

148. Among others in this tradition, see Sidney Mead, *The Lively Experiment* (New York, 1963).

149. The names were chosen by Timothy Pickering "after conversation with gentlemen on the subject" and submitted to President Washington with five others (*Defender, Fortitude, Perseverance, Protector,* and *Liberty*). The president merely underlined the first five. See Tyrone G. Martin, *A Most Fortunate Ship: A Narrative History of Old Ironsides* (Annapolis, 1997), 11, 375.

150. David Waldstreicher, *In the Midst of Perpetual Fetes* (Chapel Hill, 1997), 93, with copious illustrations.

151. Banner of the Society of Pewterers, NYHS.

152. "Order of Procession," broadside, New York, 1788; "Ode for the Federal Procession," broadside, New York, 1788; Whitfield J. Bell, "The Federal Processions of 1788," *NYHSQ* 46 (Jan. 1962), 5–39; Sarah H. J. Simpson, "The Federal Procession in the City of New York," *NYHSQ* 9 (July 1925), 39–57; Silverman, *Cultural History of the American Revolution,* 585–87.

153. Fischer, *Revolution of American Conservatism,* ch. 7, app. 3.

154. Thomas Jefferson, First Inaugural Address, 4 March 1801.

155. (Washington, Pa.) *Herald of Liberty,* 18 March 1799, in Alfred F. Young, Terry J. Fife, and Mary E. Janzen, *We the People: Voices and Images of the New Nation* (Philadelphia, 1993), 131.

156. All this from Fischer, *Revolution of American Conservatism,* 129–49.

157. Roger A. Fischer, *Tippecanoe and Trinkets Too: The Material Culture of American Presidential Campaigns, 1828–1984* (Urbana, 1988), 4, 7.

158. Eugene Perry Link, *Democratic-Republican Societies, 1790–1800* (New York, 1965).

159. "See Porcupine in Colours Just Portray'd," 1797, HSP, reproduced in William Murrell, *A History of American Graphic Humor,* 2 vols. (New York, 1933), vol. 1, fig. 34.

160. "Infant Liberty Nursed by Mother Mob," drawn by Elkaneh Tisdale, a Federalist artist from Lebanon, Conn. (b. 1771), and engraved by British artisan William S. Leney; Murrell, *History of American Graphic Humor,* vol. 1, fig. 50.

161. Fletcher M. Green, "Listen to the Eagle Scream: One Hundred Years of the Fourth of July in North Carolina," *NCHR* (July 1954), 304.

162. Maier, *American Scripture;* Jaffe, *Trumbull;* John C. Fitzpatrick, *The Spirit of the Revolution* (Boston, 1924).

163. Shakespeare, *Richard III,* V.iii; David Claypoole Johnson, "Richard III," reproduced in James G. Barber, *Andrew Jackson: A Portrait Study* (Nashville and Washington, 1991), 162; originals in AAS, NYHS; John Ashton, *English Caricature and Satire on Napoleon I* (New York, 1868), 358.

164. Stephen Hess and Milton Kaplan, *The Ungentlemanly Art: A History of Political Cartoons* (New York, 1968), 202.

165. Edward Clay Williams, "King Andrew the First," 1834, Tennessee Historical Society.

166. R. Fischer, *Tippecanoe and Trinkets Too,* 21.

167. Tennessee Museum, Nashville; from Jim Kelly.

168. The earliest mention of "Old Hickory" in print appears in *The Reviewers Reviewed; or, British Falsehoods Detected by American Truths* (New York, 1815), 67.

169. R. Fischer, *Tippecanoe and Trinkets Too,* 15–18.

170. Michel Chevalier, *Society, Manners, and Politics in the United States* (1840; Ithaca, 1961), 306.

171. Arthur M. Schlesinger, "The Liberty Tree: A Genealogy," *NEQ* 25 (1952), 457.

172. David Hackett Fischer, *Paul Revere's Ride* (New York, 1994), 44–45.

173. J. R. Pole, *The Pursuit of Equality in American History* (Berkeley, 1979).

174. Everything about this question is controversial. The evidence for Shuckburgh's paternity consists of testimony from three people, all recorded in the nineteenth century, long after the event. The first was an account published in *Farmer and Moore's Collections* 3 (July 1824), 217–18. It reported a family tradition that the song

was written in 1755, in a camp on the land of the Van Rensselaer family a little south of Albany on the east bank of the Hudson River: "Among a club of wits that belonged to the British army there was a physician attached to the staff by the name of Doctor Shuckburgh, who combined with the science of the surgeon, the skill and talents of the musician. To please brother Jonathan he composed a tune, and with much gravity recommended it to the officers.... Brother Jonathan exclaimed it was nation fine, and in a few days nothing was heard in the provincial camp but the air of Yankee Doodle."

Another account came separately from a member of the Van Rensselaer family who wrote in the nineteenth century, "The story of 'Yankee Doodle' is an authentic tradition in my family. My grandfather, Brigadier General Robert Van Rensselaer, born in the Green Bush Manor House, was a boy of seventeen at the time when Doctor Shuckburgh, the writer of the verses, and General Abercrombie were guests of his father, Col. Johannes Van Rensselaer, in June 1758. We have a picture of the old well, with the high stone curb and well-sweep, which has always been associated with the lines written while the British surgeon sat upon the curb." A third account, similar in substance but different in detail, appeared in *Magazine of American History* 11 (1884), 176.

Learned critiques appear in Oscar G. T. Sonneck, *Report on "The Star Spangled Banner," "Hail Columbia," "America," "Yankee Doodle"* (Washington, 1909), 79–156; S. Foster Damon, *Yankee Doodle* (Providence, 1959); and J. A. Leo Lemay, "The American Origins of 'Yankee Doodle,'" *WMQ3* 33 (1976), 435–64.

Sonneck concluded that Shuckburgh's authorship was doubtful, but less so than any other hypothesis. Damon was strongly hostile to the Shuckburgh thesis, mainly because he believed from internal evidence that the song must have been written by an American with an intimate knowledge of colonial culture. Lemay concludes that parts of the song "*could* [*sic*] have been written by Shuckburgh," but he believes that "Yankee Doodle" itself was of New England origin as early as the 1740s. Part of Damon's and Lemay's evidence is a verse:

> *Aminadab is just come home,*
> *His eyes all greased with bacon.*
> *And all the news that he cou'd tell*
> *Is Cape Breton is taken.*

The fortress of Louisbourg on Cape Breton was captured by New England troops in 1745. Lemay and Damon also find evidence of an early date of origin in other "cornshucking" verses that refer to corn huskings, frolics, and other Yankee folkways.

A major problem here is that Louisbourg was taken twice: June 16, 1745, and again on 26 July 1758, after it had been returned to France. Another difficulty is that the "cornshucking" verses refer to customs that were kept in New England through the eighteenth and early nineteenth centuries, and the verses in question first appeared in a later version of "Yankee Doodle" called "Yankee Song," which did not appear until after 1810. A third problem is that "Yankee Doodle" was not recorded in any source until just after the French and Indian War. From 1767 on, the references come thick and fast.

On the other side of the question, the three accounts of Shuckburgh's author-ship are inconsistent in dates and inaccurate in detail. Was it 1755 or 1758? Shirley or Abercrombie? Further, if "Yankee Doodle" was written no later than June in 1758, the Cape Breton verse could not have referred to the second conquest of Louisbourg, which happened in late July.

Another interpretation should be considered. British and provincial troops camped near Albany in the Amherst expeditions of 1759 and 1760, as well as the Shirley campaign of 1755 and the Abercrombie campaign of 1758. It is possible that Shuckburgh wrote "Yankee Doodle" in 1759 or even 1760. Grandfather's tales often become corrupted in points of fact, even as they are truthful in their main lines.

The author of the song must have been someone who knew the colonies well, was well acquainted with the whirl of London fashion, and also had the wit and temperament for good-natured comic humor. All of these characteristics closely match what is known about Doctor Shuckburgh. Lemay believes (453), that the early verses of "Yankee Doodle" "would never have been written as a satire on the Americans—not because they are so knowledgeable about Americans but because they are so good natured." But their good nature is perfectly consistent with what is known about Shuckburgh's attitudes and temperament.

We have three interlocking sets of evidence to support this hypothesis. First there are the three accounts from the nineteenth century, flawed in detail but pos-sibly correct in their substance; all testify that Shuckburgh was the author during the French and Indian War.

Second, early references in the song can be assigned dates that converge on the period 1758–60. They include the reference to the taking of Cape Breton (1758), the use of the folk melody about Kitty Fisher, who was at the peak of her short-lived notoriety in 1759, and London slang such as *macaroni*, which was coming into fashion circa 1760.

Third, we have evidence of the character and temperament of Dr. Shuckburgh himself. These three sets of evidence are mutually reinforcing. No other hypothe-sis can be supported, and the timing of published versions of "Yankee Doodle," which began to multiply rapidly from 1767, is more consistent with the Shuck-burgh hypothesis than with any other. I conclude on this basis that Shuckburgh probably created "Yankee Doodle" in an Anglo-American camp near Albany dur-ing the French and Indian War.

175.   *Rivington's New-York Gazetteer,* 26 Aug. 1773.

176.   Dr. Richard Shuckburgh to Sir William Johnson, 18 April 1763, qtd. in Sonneck, *Report,* 152.

177.   The date is in doubt. One source asserts that it happened in 1755, when William Shirley's expedition marched on Canada and won a victory at Lake George. Two other accounts dated it in 1758, when a British and colonial force commanded by General Abercrombie marched north to defeat at Ticonderoga. More likely it happened in 1759 or 1760, when large armies commanded by Lord Jeffrey Amherst took possession of Ticonderoga and Crown Point. In 1758, 1759, and 1760, large forces camped near Albany and passed close to Green Bush Manor. Cf. Sonneck, *Report,* 150–58, and Lemay, "American Origins," 441–45. On the

Amherst expeditions of 1759 and 1760 see J. C. Long, *Lord Jeffrey Amherst: A Soldier of the King* (New York, 1933), 86–143.

178. The expression appeared as early as 1711 as *maccherone* in Addison's *Spectator.*

179. For evidence of the existence of this nursery rhyme, and inaccuracies in earlier discussions see Sonneck, *Report,* 114–19, and *Notes and Queries* 8 (1865), 155; for Kitty Fisher see Nicholas Penny, *Reynolds* (London, 1986), 94, 95, passim.

180. Lemay, "American Origins," 442.

181. (Philadelphia) *Pennsylvania Journal,* 24 May 1775, qtd. in Alton Ketchum, *Uncle Sam: The Man and the Legend* (New York, 1959), 25.

182. Royall Tyler, *The Contrast* (1787). The song appeared in many versions and under many titles: "The Procession, with the Standard of Faction" (New York, John Vardill, 1770), MHS, NYHS; "The Yankey's Return From Camp" (n.p., n.d., 1775?), AAS; "The Lexington March" (London: "C——," 1775), Huntington Library; "A New Song, to the Tune *Yankey Doodle,*" *Bath Chronicle,* 21 Nov. 1776, in Opie and Opie, *Oxford Dictionary of Nursery Rhymes,* 440; "Yankee Doodle," in Arnold's opera *Two for One,* 1782, in Sonneck, *Report,* 119; "Yankee Doodle," in James Aird, *Selection of Scotch, English, Irish, and Foreign Airs* (Glasgow, 1782); "The Lexington March," (London, "Sk" [Skillern], ca. 1783–94?); "The Farmer and his Son's return from a visit to the CAMP . . ." (n.p., n.d., ca. 1786?); "General Wayne's New March . . ." (Philadelphia, 1794); "Yankee Song" (Windsor, Vt., Jessie Cochran, ca. 1810+).

183. C. A. Browne, *The Story of Our National Ballads* (New York, 1919), 22.

184. Ibid.

185. John Trumbull, *M'Fingal* (London, 1792), 43n, qtd. in Lemay, "American Origins," 464.

186. Preble, *Origin and History of the American Flag* 2:748.

187. Much careful scholarship has been done on the subject. The leading work in a very large literature is Winifred Morgan, *An American Icon: Brother Jonathan and American Identity* (Newark, Del., 1988). Other studies include Albert Matthews, "Brother Jonathan," *Col. Soc. of Mass. Transactions* 7 (1900–2), 94–122; idem, "Brother Jonathan Once More," ibid. 32 (1935), 374–86; idem, *Brother Jonathan* (Cambridge, 1902); Marston Balch, "Jonathan the First," *Modern Language Notes* 46 (1931), 281–88; Constance Rourke, *American Humor* (New York, 1931), 1–32, Cameron C. Nickels, *New England Humor, from the Revolutionary War to the Civil War* (Knoxville, 1993), 35, 39–40, 141–44, passim; Ketchum, *Uncle Sam,* 27–33.

188. Albert Matthews pointed out many years ago that the earliest written version of this tale was recorded by a journalist in 1846, from the memory of an octogenarian long after Washington and Trumbull were in their graves. Historians have found no evidence to support it, and strong sources for another origin. Matthews, "Brother Jonathan."

189. Ibid.; Morgan, *American Icon,* 201n.

190. Ezra Stiles, *Literary Diary,* 3 vols. (New York, 1901), 2:2 (21 March 1776).

191. "Yankee Doodles Intrenchments near Boston," 1776, BM, reproduced in Morgan, *American Icon,* 65.

192. In Vietnam, "Charlie" derived from the military phonetics "Victor Charlie" for *VC* or Viet Cong.

193. (New York) *Royal Gazette,* 27 May 1780.

194. Matthew Darly, "The English and American Discovery, Brother, Brother, We Are Both in the Wrong," 1778, John Carter Brown Library, reproduced in Morgan, *American Icon,* 67.

195. The iconic image of John Bull first appeared in 1757, as a symbol of the British people. See Dorothy George, *English Political Caricature to 1792* (Oxford, 1959), 1:116–18.

196. Horwitz, *The Bird, the Banner, and Uncle Sam,* 934.

197. *The Contrast* was first performed in April 1787; it was the first American comedy produced by a professional company. Atkinson's *A Match for a Widow* is from 1788.

198. James K. Paulding, *The Diverting History of John Bull and Brother Jonathan* (New York, 1812; illus. in 3d ed., 1827).

199. Nickels, *New England Humor,* 60.

200. Qtd. in ibid., 58–59.

201. "The Spoilt Child," *Punch,* 1856, reproduced in Ketchum, *Uncle Sam,* 74.

202. "Imprudence du Petit Jonathan l'Américain," cartoon in the collections of *American Heritage,* used as a cover for *American Heritage* 18, no. 4 (June 1967).

203. *Exeter News Letter,* 15 June 1841.

204. Frank Moore, ed., *Rebellion Record, 1861–1865* (New York, 1867), 4:69; qtd. in Ketchum, *Uncle Sam,* 32–33.

205. The family name was originally spelled Willson, later Wilson. Samuel Willson himself had it both ways.

206. (Troy) *Northern Budget* [after 31 July 1854], qtd. in Ketchum, *Uncle Sam,* 57.

207. Ketchum, *Uncle Sam,* 54–55.

208. Albert Matthews in *AAS Proceedings,* n.s. 19 (1908), 21–65.

209. William Faux, *Memorable Days in America* (London, 1823), 126, 140, 162, 188, 215, qtd. in Ketchum, *Uncle Sam,* 132n.

210. *New York World-Telegram,* 20 March 1937, qtd. in Ketchum, *Uncle Sam,* 133n.

211. Frank H. T. Bellow, "Uncle Sam, you have been overeating . . . ," dated 1852 but probably earlier; in Ketchum, *Uncle Sam,* 62.

212. Ketchum, *Uncle Sam,* 132–33.

213. Arthur Henkel and Albrecht Schoene, *Emblemata* (Stuttgart, 1967).

214. In Rome, emancipated slaves received the *pileus libertatis* as an emblem of manumission, and servants were allowed to wear it on the Saturnalia, a much loved Roman holiday on the seventeenth of December, when masters and servants reversed roles for a day. The word *pileus* became a word for liberty itself, as in Livy's *servos ad pileum vocare,* "to call the slaves to liberty."
    The wand and pileus together represented the Roman ceremony of manumission, in which a master tapped the slave with the wand and gave him a felt cap.
    In other representations, the goddess of liberty carried the pileus on the tip of a pikestaff. This image was associated with Salturnius, who conquered Rome in 263 B.C. and carried a pileus on the tip of a pikestaff as a sign that slaves who rallied to him would be free. Nancy Jo Fox, *Liberties with Liberty* (New York, 1986), 4.

215. Addison, *Tatler* 161 (1710); Cesare Ripa, *Iconologia*; Silverman, *Cultural History of the American Revolution,* 85–86, for many other examples.

216. Edward Savage, *Liberty in the Form of the Goddess of Youth, Giving Support to the Bald Eagle,* steel engraving, 1796; New York State Historical Association, Cooper-

stown; Abijah Canfield, *Liberty in the Form of the Goddess of Youth, Giving Support to the Bald Eagle,* from an engraving by E. Savage, n.d., ca. 1800, Greenfield Village and Henry Ford Museum, Dearborn, Mich.; artist unknown, *Liberty,* n.d., Edgar William and Bernice Chrysler Garbisch Coll., National Gallery of Art, Washington; artist unknown, *Liberty in the Form of the Goddess of Youth, Giving Support to the Bald Eagle,* painting on velvet, 1800–30, Abby Aldrich Rockefeller Folk Art Center; Betsey B. Lathrop, *Liberty in the Form of the Goddess of Youth, Giving Support to the Bald Eagle,* watercolor on silk, ca. 1810, collection of Sybil and Arthur Kern. See Fox, *Liberties with Liberty,* 9–11.

217. Anna Rawle to Mrs. Samuel Shoemaker, 4 Nov. 1780, *PMHB* 35 (1911), 398; Nabby Adams to John Quincy Adams, 13, 16 Feb. 1786, Adams Family Papers, microfilm ed., reel 367; Robert C. Alberts, *The Golden Voyage: The Life and Times of William Bingham, 1752–1804* (Boston, 1969), 154, 120, 96, 154.

218. Abigail Adams to Nabby Adams, 26 Dec. 1791, in C. F. Adams, ed., *Letters of Mrs. John Adams, Wife of John Adams,* 2 vols. (Boston, 1848), 1:351; Caroline De Windt, ed., *Journal and Correspondence of Miss Adams, Daughter of John Adams, Second President of the United States* (Boston, 1841), 1:59; 145, 147, 212; Anne Willing Bingham to Thomas Jefferson, 1 June 1787, reproduced in Alberts, *Golden Voyage,* app. 3; Rufus Wilmot Griswold, *The Republican Court; or, American Society in the Days of Washington* (New York, 1855), 253–54; Joshua Fisher, *Recollections* (Boston, 1929), 200–202, Albert, *Golden Voyage,* 147, 151, 213, 214, 217.

219. Anne Willing Bingham to Thomas Jefferson, 1 June 1787, reprinted in Alberts, *Golden Voyage,* app. 3; Abigail Adams to Mary Smith Cranch, 30 Sept. 1785, qtd. in ibid., 150–51.

220. Alexander Pope, Iliad, bk. 3, l. 208; Alberts, *Golden Voyage,* 153, 155.

221. Alberts, *Golden Voyage,* 212.

222. Walter Breen, *Walter Breen's Complete Encyclopedia of U.S. and Colonial Coins* (New York, 1988); R. S. Yeoman, *A Guide Book to U.S. Coins* (Racine, Wisc., 2000); Cornelius Vermeule, *Numismatic Art in America* (Cambridge, 1971); Al C. Overton, *Early Half Dollar Die Varieties, 1794–1836,* 3d ed. (Escondido, Calif., 1990); Jules Reiver, *The United States Early Silver Dollars, 1794 to 1803* (Iola, Wisc., 1998); Don Taxay, *The U.S. Mint and Coinage* (New York, 1966).

223. Norman Rockwell, *Miss Liberty,* 1943, painting for a *Saturday Evening Post* cover, collection of Laurence Cutler and Judy Goffman; Suzanne C. Ryan, "The Illustrated Mansion," *Boston Globe,* 2 June 2001.

224. "Bob Mackie's Lady Liberty Barbie," FAO Schwarz Web page.

225. Jock Macdonald, *American Girl,* 1990, black-and-white photograph (13 by 12 inches), in Kit Hinrichs, Delphine Hirasuna, and Terry Hefferman, eds., *Long May She Wave: A Graphic History of the American Flag* (Berkeley and Toronto, 2001), 84.

226. *Fourth of July Picnic on Weymouth Landing,* ca. 1853, watercolor, Chicago Art Institute; reproduced on the cover of Diana Karter Applebaum, *The Glorious Fourth* (New York, 1989), 13.

227. *New York Tribune,* 16 Nov. 1859.

228. These examples come mostly from Michael Kammen, *The Mystic Chords of Memory* (New York, 1991).

229. Browne, *Story of Our National Ballads,* 75.

A Nation Divided

1. Ralph Waldo Emerson in *The Dial,* July 1843, in *Complete Works,* 12 vols. (Boston, 1903–4), 10:352.

2. Alice Felt Tyler, *Freedom's Ferment* (Minneapolis, 1944), is a Whig history of American reform, and still one of the best surveys of the subject. Ronald Walters, *American Reformers, 1815–1860* (New York, 1978), is a general overview, with a perspective from the left after the civil rights movement.

    David Brion Davis, ed., *Ante-Bellum Reform* (New York, 1967), collects many essays and interpretations, including John L. Thomas, "Romantic Reform in America, 1815–1865," *American Quarterly* 17 (1965), 656–81, which sets the reformers within the romantic movement. Whitney Cross, *The Burned Over District: The Social and Intellectual History of Enthusiastic Religion in Western New York, 1800–1850* (Ithaca, 1950).

    Another school of interpretation in the 1960s and '70s was strongly anti-Whiggish, iconoclastic, and unsympathetic to the reformers. Most of it argues that reformers were driven by ulterior motives to control others or to exalt themselves. Much insists that reformers were the captives of their own fears and anxieties. Some of this work tends to deny the possibility of a genuine and disinterested altruism. Leading works include Joseph Gusfield, *Symbolic Crusade: Status Politics and the American Temperance Movement* (Urbana, 1966); David J. Rothman. *The Discovery of the Asylum: Social Order and Disorder in the New Republic* (Boston, 1971); and Michael Katz, *The Irony of Early School Reform* (Boston, 1968).

    The historiography of antebellum reform received less attention in the period from 1980 to 2000, when the reform impulse was weaker in the United States. As the spirit of reform is reviving in the twenty-first century, it is time for a fresh look at this old subject.

3. Len Gougeon, "Thoreau and Reform," in Joel Myerson, ed., *The Cambridge Companion to Thoreau* (Cambridge, 1985), 199.

4. David Donald, "Toward a Reconsideration of the Abolitionists," *Lincoln Reconsidered* (New York, 1956), 19–36; James McPherson, "Origins of Abolitionists and Entrepreneurs," in *Ordeal by Fire* (1982; 2d ed., New York, 1992), 48; Lawrence J. Friedman, *Gregarious Saints: Self and Community in American Abolitionism, 1830–1870* (Cambridge, 1982); Edward Magdol, *The Abolitionist Rank and File: A Social Profile of the Abolitionists' Constituency* (Westport, Conn., 1986).

5. Elwood P. Cubberley, *Public Education in the United States,* rev. ed. (Cambridge, 1934), 183.

6. David Wood, personal communication.

7. Among the best introductions are two anthologies of primary materials: Joel Myerson, ed., *Transcendentalism: A Reader* (Oxford, 2000); and Perry Miller, ed., *The American Transcendentalists: Their Prose and Poetry* (New York, 1957).

8. Bronson Alcott, Journal, 8 May 1846, in Odell Shephard, ed., *The Journals of Bronson Alcott* (Boston, 1938), 180.

9. Convers Francis, Diary, Aug. 1862, qtd. in E. H. Cady and Louis J. Budd, eds., *On Emerson; The Best from American Literature* (Durham, 1988), 196–215, 214 qtd.; see also in Joel Myerson, "Convers Francis and Emerson," *American Literature* 50 (1978), 17–36.

10. Emerson, *Nature*, sec. 1, par. 4, in *Selected Writings*, ed. Brooks Atkinson (New York, 1940, 1950), 6.

11. Theodore Parker, "Emerson," in H. S. Commager, ed., *Theodore Parker: An Anthology* (Boston, 1960), 195–206, 199 qtd. Emerson in turn called Parker "the standard-bearer of liberty" (ibid., 196).

12. Emerson, Journals, April 1840, in William H. Gilman, et al., eds., *Journals and Miscellaneous Notebooks of Ralph Waldo Emerson*, 16 vols. (Cambridge, 1960–82), 7:342; Emerson, "Self Reliance," par. 3, in *Selected Writings*, 146–47.

13. Thoreau, Journal, 10 Oct. 1851 (Princeton ed. 4:137).

14. Phyllis Cole, *Mary Moody Emerson and the Origins of Transcendentalism: A Family History* (New York, 1998).

15. Emerson, *Journals and Miscellaneous Notebooks* 8:249; Wesley T. Mott, "The Age of the First Person Singular: Emerson and Individualism," in Joel Myerson ed., *A Historical Guide to Ralph Waldo Emerson* (Oxford, 2000), 61–100, 79; P. Miller, *American Transcendentalists*, 6.

16. Emerson, *Journals and Miscellaneous Notebooks* 8:249.

17. Emerson, *Essays*, "Compensation," in *Selected Writings*, 179, 182; Myerson, *Historical Guide*, 74.

18. Emerson, *Essays*, "Self-Reliance," in *Selected Writings*, 161, 166.

19. Mott, "Age of the First Person Singular," 64.

20. Carlos Baker, *Emerson Among the Eccentrics: A Group Portrait* (New York, 1996, a posthumous publication); Cole, *Mary Moody Emerson and the Origins of Transcendentalism;* Len Gougeon, *Virtue's Hero: Emerson, Antislavery, and Reform* (Athens, 1990); Myerson, *Historical Guide;* Robert D. Richardson, *Emerson: The Mind on Fire* (Berkeley, 1995).

21. Robert D. Richardson Jr., "Thoreau and Concord," in Joel Myerson, ed., *The Cambridge Companion to Thoreau* (Cambridge, 1995), 12–24, 16; Joel Porte, *Emerson and Thoreau: Transcendentalists in Conflict* (Middletown, Conn., 1966).

22. *Walden and On the Duty of Civil Disobedience*, ed. Charles R. Anderson (New York, 1962), 107, 237; Myerson, *Cambridge Companion to Thoreau*, 14.

23. Thoreau, Journal, 15 Feb. 1851, in Bradford Torrey and Francis H. Allen, eds., *The Journal of Henry David Thoreau*, 14 vols. (Boston, 1906), 2:162.

24. Ibid., 162–63.

25. Thoreau, *Walden* (ed. Anderson), 18, 51.

26. Thoreau, Journal, 21 July 1851 (Torrey and Allen 2:352).

27. Thoreau, "Walking," in Miller, *American Transcendentalists*, 143–48 and online at www.bartleby.com.

28. Thoreau, *Walden* (ed. Anderson), 116–17, 228.

29. Thoreau, *Civil Disobedience* (ed. Anderson), 243.

30. Thoreau, Journal, 18 June 1854 (Torrey and Allen 6:370).

31. Gougeon, "Thoreau and Reform," 196.

32. Thoreau, "Walking," par. 31.

33. David Hackett Fischer, *Albion's Seed* (New York, 1989), 286–97; David D. Hall, ed., *The Antinomian Controversy, 1636–1638* (Middletown, Conn., 1968); Julia Cherry Spruill, "Mistress Margaret Brent," *MDHM* (1934), 259–69.

34. Constantia, "On the Equality of the Sexes," *Massachusetts Magazine* (Spring 1790); Mary Wollstonecraft, *A Vindication of the Rights of Woman* (London, 1792;

rpt. Boston and Philadelphia, 1792, Dublin, 1793), ed. Charles W. Hagelman (New York, 1967). John Singleton Copley's appealing portrait of Judith Sargent Murray has become an icon of feminism for her posterity.

35. Charles Capper, *Margaret Fuller: An American Romantic Life; The Private Years* (New York, 1992); Mason Wade, *Margaret Fuller, Whetstone of Genius* (New York, 1940); Joan von Mehren, *Minerva and Muse: A Life of Margaret Fuller* (Amherst, Mass., 1994).

Two of the introductions and studies of her work are anthologies: Perry Miller, ed., *Margaret Fuller, American Romantic: A Selection from Her Writings and Correspondence* (Garden City, N.Y., 1963); Ball Gale Chevigny, ed, *The Woman and the Myth: Margaret Fuller's Life and Writings* (Old Westbury, N.Y., 1976). Another collection is Mason Wade, *The Writings of Margaret Fuller* (New York, 1941).

A modern edition of her correspondence is Robert Hudspeth, ed., *The Letters of Margaret Fuller,* 6 vols. (Ithaca, 1983–94). Also, Judith Mattson Bean and Joel Myerson, eds., *Margaret Fuller, Critic: Writings from the New York Tribune, 1844–46* (New York, 2002, with CD-ROM).

Memoirs by those who knew her include Ralph Waldo Emerson, James Freeman Clarke and William Henry Channing, *Memoirs of Margaret Fuller Ossoli,* 2 vols. (Boston, 1852); and Thomas Wentworth Higginson, *Margaret Fuller Ossoli* (Cambridge, 1884).

36. Wade, *Margaret Fuller,* 16; she appears to have suffered from scoliosis and curvature of the spine. See Caleb Crane, "A Star Is Born," *New York Review of Books,* 23 May 2002.

37. Emerson et al., *Memoirs of Margaret Fuller Ossoli* 1:204, 216.

38. Emerson, *Journals and Miscellaneous Notebooks* 11:463. It was even stronger in his source, *quae divum incedo regina,* "who move as queen of the Gods."

39. P. Miller, *American Transcendentalists,* 101; Baker, *Emerson Among the Eccentrics,* 63.

40. Qtd. in Wade, *Margaret Fuller,* 17.

41. Margaret Fuller, "The Great Lawsuit. Man versus Men. Woman versus Women," first published in *The Dial,* July 1843, and enlarged as *Woman in the Nineteenth Century* (1844; ed. Larry J. Reynolds, New York, 1998).

42. Wade, *Margaret Fuller,* 721.

43. [Caroline Sturgis?], "A Transcendental Conversation," 22 March 1841, in Emerson et al., *Memoirs of Margaret Fuller Ossoli* (Boston, 1852), as rpt. in P. Miller, *American Transcendentalists,* 101–3.

44. Odell Shepard, ed., *Writings of Margaret Fuller* (New York, 1941), 109, 113, 117, 118, 130, 142, 151, 213.

45. P. Miller, *American Transcendentalists,* 330.

46. Child was moving this way as early as 1833, when she published *An Appeal in Favor of That Class of Americans Called Africans.*

47. Elizabeth Cady Stanton, *Eighty Years and More, Reminiscences, 1815–1897* (New York, 1971); Ellen Dubois, ed., *Elizabeth Cady Stanton, Susan B. Anthony: Correspondence, Writings, Speeches* (New York, 1981). On Seneca Falls see *Proceedings of the Woman's Rights Conventions, Held at Seneca Falls & Rochester, N.Y., July & August, 1848* (New York, 1970); Bradford Miller, *Returning to Seneca Falls: The*

First Woman's Rights Convention and Its Meaning for Men and Women Today (Hudson, N.Y., 1995).

48. Elizabeth Cady Stanton, "The Solitude of Self," speech at the Annual Meeting of the National American Woman Suffrage Association (Washington, 1892).

49. The total number of Calvinist churches (Congregational, Separatist, Presbyterian, Dutch Reformed, German Reformed, French Reformed, Calvinist-Baptist, and smaller denominations) was approximately 62 percent of all the churches throughout the United States in 1780. Further, these Calvinist congregations were larger and more active than non-Calvinist churches. Computed from data in Edwin S. Gaustad et al., *New Historical Atlas of Religion in America,* 3d ed. (New York, 2001).

50. Stephen J. Stein, *The Shaker Experience in America* (New Haven, 1992), 12–15, 27, 60, 101; Stephen A. Marini, *The Radical Sects of Revolutionary New England* (Cambridge, 1982).

51. Priscilla J. Brewer, *Shaker Communities, Shaker Lives* (Hanover, 1986), 2; Stein, *Shaker Experience,* 89.

52. *Joseph Brackett's "Simple Gifts," Evolution of a Shaker Dance Song* (Stoughton, Mass., 1997).

53. Roger Hall, "Religion in Song: The Craftsmanship of Shaker Music," *Shaker Journal,* June 1999, http://home.att.net/~shakercrafts/docs/hall.html.

54. Edward Deming Andrews, *The People Called Shakers* (New York, 1963), 142–43; Brewer, *Shaker Communities, Shaker Lives;* Stein, *Shaker Experience,* 69.

55. Stein, *Shaker Experience,* 190.

56. Martha Graham, *Blood Memory* (New York, 1991); Howard Pollack, *Aaron Copland: The Life and Work of an Uncommon Man* (New York, 1999); Lijntje A. Zandee, "Martha Graham and Modern American Dance," http://www.let.uu.nl/hist/ams/xroads/dancehtm.

57. David Crumm, "150 Years of Simple Gifts," *Detroit Free Press,* 11 Nov. 1998.

58. Ibid.

59. The Census of 1860 enumerated 385,000 masters and 3,954,000 slaves, in a southern population of 12,302,000 people. All of these numbers were undercounts. See *A Century of Population Growth from the First Census of the United States to the Twelfth, 1790–1900* (Washington, 1909); and *Negro Population in the United States, 1790–1915* (Washington, 1918).

60. Arthur P. Newton, *The Colonizing Activities of the English Puritans* (New Haven, 1914), 149; Karen Ordahl Kupperman, *Providence Island, 1630–1641: The Other Puritan Colony* (Cambridge, 1993), 46–49, 74, 168–69, 177, 243; John Russell Bartlett, ed., *Records of the Colony of Rhode Island and Providence Plantations,* 10 vols. (Providence, 1856–65), 1:243. The law ordered that "no black mankinde or white" could be held more than ten years "from the time of their cominge within the liberties of this Collonie." The law appears not to have been enforced. For Sewall's *Selling of Joseph,* see Milton Halsey Thomas, ed., *The Diary of Samuel Sewall,* 2 vols. (New York, 1973), 2:1117–23.

61. Josiah Wedgwood, "Am I Not a Man and a Brother?" ceramic medallion, basalt on jasper, 1787, reproduced in Sidney Kaplan and Emma Nogrady Kaplan, *The Black Presence in the Era of the American Revolution,* rev. ed. (Amherst, Mass., 1989), 273; "Am I Not a Man and a Brother?" engraving, Prints Division, LC.

62. Arthur Zilversmit, *The First Emancipation: The Abolition of Slavery in the North* (Chicago, 1967). Still useful is George Livermore, *An Historical Research Respecting the Opinions of the Founders of the Republic on Negroes as Slaves, as Citizens, and as Soldiers* (1863; rpt. New York, 1970). An excellent general work is David Brion Davis, *The Problem of Slavery in the Age of Revolution* (Ithaca, 1975); on the imagery of this movement see Kaplan and Kaplan, *Black Presence.*

63. Elizabeth Langhorne, "Edward Coles, Thomas Jefferson, and the Rights of Man," *Virginia Cavalcade* 23 (1973–74), 30–37; Ralph L. Ketcham, "The Dictates of Conscience: Edward Coles and Slavery," *Virginia Quarterly Review* 36 (1960), 47–60; David Hackett Fischer and James Kelly, *Away, I'm Bound Away* (Richmond, 1993), 242.

64. On colonization, the manuscript holdings of the Maryland Historical Society are very full, especially the papers of the Maryland Colonization Society and the papers of Robert Goodloe Harper. The fullest account is still P. J. Staudenraus, *The African Colonization Movement, 1816–1865* (New York, 1961). An example of pejorative literature is Lawrence Friedman, "Purifying the White Man's Country: The American Colonization Society Reconsidered," *Societas* 6 (1976), 1–24, which insists that the rhetoric of the movement was more important than its reality and compares African colonization to defecation. Attempts at balance and understanding appear in David H. Fischer, "Robert Goodloe Harper" (senior thesis, Princeton, 1958); Eric Robert Papenfuse's excellent *The Evils of Necessity: Robert Goodloe Harper and the Moral Dilemma of Slavery* (Philadelphia, 1997); and Douglas Egerton, *Charles Fenton Mercer* (Jackson, 1989). On black colonizers see Lamont Thomas, *Rise to Be a People: A Biography of Paul Cuffe* (Urbana, 1986).

65. Theodore Dwight Weld, *Slavery as It Is: Testimony of a Thousand Witnesses* (New York, 1839); Benjamin P. Thomas, *Theodore Weld, Crusader for Freedom* (New Brunswick, 1950).

66. John L. Thomas, *The Liberator: William Lloyd Garrison* (Boston, 1963), 387.

67. On Garrison, the best source is the file of *The Liberator,* now widely available. His correspondence is collected in Walter M. Merrill and Louis Ruchames, eds., *The Letters of William Lloyd Garrison,* 6 vols. (Cambridge, 1971–78). Leading biographies include Thomas, *Liberator;* and Walter M. Merrill, *Against Wind and Tide: A Biography of William Lloyd Garrison* (Cambridge, 1963).

68. On political antislavery, the leading work is Richard H. Sewell, *Ballots for Freedom: Antislavery Politics in the United States, 1837–1860* (Oxford, 1976).

69. William Lee Miller, *Arguing About Slavery: The Great Battle in the United States Congress* (New York, 1996); Russell Nye, *Fettered Freedom: Civil Liberties and the Slavery Controversy, 1830–1860* (East Lansing, 1949); Gag Rule Petitions, Massachusetts Archives, Boston.

70. Edward Beecher, *Narrative of the Riots at Alton* (N.Y., 1838; rpt. with an introduction by Robert Merideth, New York, 1965), the leading account by an eyewitness; also important is Joseph and Owen Lovejoy, *Memoir of the Rev. Elijah P. Lovejoy, Who Was Murdered in Defence of the Liberty of the Press, at Alton, Illinois, November 7, 1837* (New York, 1838).

71. Jean Fagan Yellin, *Women and Sisters: The Antislavery Feminists in American Culture* (New Haven, 1989), discusses this iconography.

72. Albert J. Von Frank, *The Trials of Anthony Burns: Freedom and Slavery in Emerson's Boston* (Cambridge, 1998); Charles Emery Stevens, *Anthony Burns: A History* (1856; rpt. Williamstown, 1973), a participant-historian; Austin Bearse, *Reminiscences of Fugitive-Slave Days in Boston* (Boston, 1880), an account of the Vigilance Committee; Paul Finkleman, ed., *Fugitive Slaves and American Courts: The Pamphlet Literature,* 4 vols. (New York, 1988).

73. C. Vann Woodward, ed., *Mary Chesnut's Civil War* (New Haven, 1981), 168.

74. *Narrative of the Life of Henry Box Brown, Written by Himself* (1845; rpt. Oxford, 2002); the fullest survey of this literature is Marion Wilson Starling, *The Slave Narrative: Its Place in American History* (Washington, 1988).

75. Douglass dolls, 1852, New Bedford Whaling Museum, New Bedford, Mass.

76. Solomon Northup, *Twelve Years a Slave: Narrative of Solomon Northrup a Citizen of New York, Kidnapped in Washington City in 1841, and Rescued in 1853, from a Cotton Plantation near the Red River, in Louisiana,* ed. with a preface and an appendix of supporting documents by David Wilson (Auburn, Buffalo, and London, 1853), ch. 19. The editor claims that the text is "a faithful history of Solomon Northup's as he received it from his lips," but the language appears to have been changed for publication. For a modern edition with much supporting documentation of Bass and Epps from the sources see Sue Eakin and Joseph Logsdon, eds., *Twelve Years a Slave* (Baton Rouge, 1968). For discussions see Charles Davis and Henry Louis Gates Jr., eds., *The Slave's Narrative* (New York, 1991), 161–63, 232–37; Marion Wilson Starling, *The Slave Narrative: Its Place in American History* (Washington, 1988), 173; other documentation appears in *Liberator,* 22 Aug. 1856.

77. James Henry Hammond, *Two Letters on Slavery in the United States, Addressed to Thomas Clarkson, Esq.* (Columbia, S.C., 1845), rpt. as "Letter to an English Abolitionist," in Drew Faust, ed., *The Ideology of Slavery: Proslavery Thought in the Ante-Bellum South, 1830–1860,* 171.

78. For differences within the South see George M. Fredrickson, *The Black Image in the White Mind* (New York, 1971), 58–64; see also J. William Harris, *Plain Folk and Gentry in a Slave Society: White Liberty and Black Slavery in Augusta's Hinterlands* (Middletown, Conn., 1985); Joseph P. Reidy, *From Slavery to Agrarian Capitalism in the Cotton Plantation South: Central Georgia, 1800–1880* (Chapel Hill, 1992); William W. Freehling, *The South vs. The South* (New York, 2001).

79. *Liberator,* 26 Oct. 1860, qtd. in Fredrickson, *Black Image in the White Mind,* 61.

80. William Jenkins, *Pro-Slavery Thought in the Old South* (Gloucester, 1959), 190; Fredrickson, *Black Image in the White Mind,* 62.

81. J.D.B. DeBow, *The Interest in Slavery of the Southern Nonslaveholder . . .* (Charleston, 1860), 3–12.

82. Rollin G. Osterweis, *Romanticism in the Old South* (New Haven, 1949), 94.

83. Pierre L. van den Berghe, *Race and Racism: A Comparative Perspective* (New York, 1967), 17.

84. Hammond, *Two Letters on Slavery,* in Faust, *Ideology of Slavery,* 176; William Harper, *Anniversary Oration, South Carolina Society for the Advancement of Learning* (Washington, 1836), rpt. as *Memoir of Slavery* (Charleston, 1838) and in Faust, *Ideology of Slavery,* 86; John C. Calhoun, *Disquisition on Government,* first pub. in R. K. Crallé, ed., *The Works of John C. Calhoun* (New York, 1854), 1:59.

85. Harper, *Anniversary Oration,* in Faust, *Ideology of Slavery,* 110.

86. George Fitzhugh, *Cannibals All! or Slaves Without Masters,* ed. C. Vann Woodward (1857; Cambridge, 1959), 77.

87. Zephaniah Kingsley, *Treatise on the Patriarchal or Co-operative System of Society* (1828, with additions, 1829, 1833, 1834), rpt. in Daniel W. Stowell, ed., *Balancing Evils Judiciously: The Proslavery Writings of Zephaniah Kingsley* (Gainesville, 2000).

88. Eugene D. Genovese, *The Southern Tradition: The Achievement and Limitations of an American Conservatism* (Cambridge, 1994), 1:35–40.

89. *National Era,* 19 Aug. 1858, qtd. in Clement Eaton, *The Freedom-of-Thought Struggle in the Old South* (Durham, 1940; rpt. 1964), 155.

90. Ibid.; William Gienapp, *The Origins of the Republican Party* (New York, 1987), 360.

91. Eaton, *Freedom-of-Thought Struggle,* 191, 347, 349.

92. William H. Williams, *Slavery and Freedom in Delaware, 1639–1865* (Wilmington, 1996), 142–43.

93. Moses Austin to Maria Brown, 25 Jan. 1785, and Stephen F. Austin, 9 April 1836, Texas Memorial Museum, facsimile in Fischer and Kelly, *Away, I'm Bound Away,* 212–14; Eugene C. Barker, *Stephen Austin, Founder of Texas, 1793–1836* (New York, 1968); for Sam Houston see John Hoyt Williams, *Sam Houston: A Biography of the Father of Texas* (New York, 1993).

94. Marshall De Bruhl, *Sword of San Jacinto* (New York, 1993); for the flag see Charles E. Gilbert Jr., "San Jacinto Flag," in *Flags of Texas* (1964; rpt. Gretna, La., 1989), 70.

95. Ibid.

96. Geoffrey C. Ward, *The West: An Illustrated History* (New York, 1998).

97. Charles E. Gilbert Jr., *A Concise History of Early Texas, as Told by Its 30 Historic Flags* (Houston, 1964, 1972).

98. Ibid.

99. On the history of the Texas Goddess of liberty see Texas State Preservation Board, "Goddess," http://www.tspb.state.tx.us/tspb.htm.

100. Roger Fischer, *Tippecanoe and Trinkets Too* (Urbana, 1988), 60–67.

101. Robert W. Johannsen, *Stephen A. Douglas* (New York, 1973), 451.

102. Abraham Lincoln, "Address Before the Wisconsin State Agricultural Society," 30 Sept. 1859, in *AL* 3:478.

103. C. E. Fairman, *Art and Artists of the Capitol of the U.S.A.,* 69th Cong., 1st sess., Senate Document 95.

104. Robert L. Gales, *Thomas Crawford, American Sculptor* (Pittsburgh, 1964).

105. The story that follows is told in Vivien Green Fryd, *Art and Empire: The Politics of Ethnicity in the United States Capitol, 1815–1860* (New Haven, 1992), whose account I follow.

106. Meigs to Crawford, 27 April 1854, qtd. in ibid., 189–90.

107. Ibid., 190–200.

108. Eric Foner, *The Story of American Freedom* (New York, 1998), 94.

109. *New York Tribune,* 10 Dec, 1863, qtd. in Fryd, *Art and Empire,* 199.

110. R. M. Johnston and W. W. Browne, *Life of Alexander H. Stephens* (Philadelphia,

1878), 355–56; Allen Nevins, *The Emergence of Lincoln,* 2 vols. (New York, 1951), 2:262.

111. William B. Hesseltine, ed., *Three Against Lincoln: Murat Halstead Reports the Caucuses of 1860* (Baton Rouge, 1860), is a leading source, by a Cincinnati newspaperman who attended all the nominating conventions of 1860.

112. Ibid., 122.

113. Kirk Harold Porter and Donald Bruce Johnson, comps., *National Party Platforms, 1840–1956* (Urbana, Ill., 1956), 30.

114. Salomon de Rothschild to Nathaniel Rothschild, 30 March 1860, in Jacob R. Marcus, ed., *Memoirs of American Jews, 1775–1865* (Philadelphia, 1956), 3:81–82.

115. Qtd. in William C. Davis, *Breckinridge: Statesman, Soldier, Symbol* (Baton Rouge, 1974), 514.

116. Ibid., 208–9, 223, 228, 231.

117. Nevins, *Emergence of Lincoln* 2:287, 308.

118. Stephen Douglas to Julius N. Granger, 21 Sept. 1834, and Douglas to Caleb Cushing, 4 Feb. 1852, in Robert W. Johannsen, ed., *The Letters of Stephen A. Douglas* (Urbana, Ill., 1961), 9, 237.

119. Douglas to Granger, 22 Feb. 1835, ibid., 11

120. Ibid., xxvi; Harry Haffa, *Crisis of the House Divided* (Chicago, 1955), 47.

121. H. S. Lehr, "A Weaver's Spool Boy," Heterick Memorial Library, Ohio Northern University.

122. Johannsen, *Letters of Douglas,* xxv.

123. "Notes for Speeches at Cincinnati and Columbus, Ohio," 16 Sept. 1859, in *AL* 3:430; also 3:444, 469, 486, 500; 4:4, 10, 16, 19, 169; and in many other public statements.

124. *AL* 4:3.

125. Marginal note on an issue of the *Missouri Democrat,* 17 May 1860, in *AL* 3:50, 432.

126. For a contemporary image from *Harper's Weekly* see Arthur M. Schlesinger, Fred L. Israel, and David J. Frent, eds., *Running for President: The Candidates and Their Images, 1789–1896* (New York, 1994), 249.

127. *Charleston Mercury,* 11 Oct. 1861.

128. Wylma A. Wates, *A Flag Worthy of Your State and People: The History of the South Carolina State Flag* (Columbia, S.C., 1996), 5.

129. Charles H. Lesser, *Relic of the Lost Cause: The Story of South Carolina's Ordinance of Secession,* 2d. ed. rev. (Columbia., S.C., 1996). The banner survives and is on display at the SCHS in Charleston. It was painted by Isaac Alexander, an immigrant to South Carolina.

130. Wates, *A Flag Worthy of Your State,* 6, 7.

131. Lincoln, "Address at Sanitary Fair," Baltimore, 18 April 1864, in *AL* 7:301–3.

132. Lee, Special Orders, 9 Sept. 1861, in Clifford Dowdey and Louis H. Manarin, *The Wartime Papers of Robert E. Lee* (Boston, 1961), 73.

133. Alexander H. Stephens, "Speech," Savannah, 21 March 1861, in Henry Cleveland, *Alexander H. Stephens in Public and Private* (Philadelphia, 1866), 721.

134. Whitney Smith, *The Flag Book of the United States* (New York, 1970; rev. ed. 1975), 84, 124.

135. Ibid., 77, 108, 140, 212.

136. Lincoln "Address at Sanitary Fair," Baltimore, 18 April 1864, in *AL* 7:301–3.

137. Devereux D. Cannon Jr., *The Flags of the Confederacy* (Gretna, La., 1994), 38.

138. Ibid., 44–45, fig. 41.

139. Booth's letter qtd. in James W. Clarke, *American Assassins: The Darker Side of Politics* (Princeton, 1982), 30, and Michael Kammen, *Spheres of Liberty* (Madison, 1986), 137.

140. Among them is the peculiar Texas variant on the American folk custom of "topping out" new buildings. When new buildings are raised in the United States, the highest part of the structure is decorated with an evergreen tree and an American flag. This custom is observed everywhere except Texas. There buildings are topped out with a Lone Star Flag.

141. Nevins, *Emergence of Lincoln* 2:318.

142. Cannon, *Flags of the Confederacy*, 31–33, Irwin Silber, *Songs of the Civil War* (New York, 1960), 52–54.

143. Ruth Painter Randall, *Colonel Elmer Ellsworth* (Boston, 1960); Charles A. Ingraham, *Elmer E. Ellsworth and the Zouaves of '61* (Chicago, 1925), a work that must be used with caution.

144. Cannon, *Flags of the Confederacy*, 51–65.

145. Bell Wiley, *Life of Johnny Reb* (Indianapolis, 1943), 22.

146. Ibid., 82.

147. Robert Justin Goldstein, *Saving "Old Glory": The History of the Flag Desecration Controversy* (Boulder, Colo., 1995).

148. The flag is now in the Smithsonian Institution. John Bartlett, *Familiar Quotations* (Boston, 1942), 601b; s.v. "Driver, William."

149. George Pope Morris, "The Flag of Our Union" (New York, 1851).

150. Qtd. in Bell Irvin Wiley, *The Life of Billy Yank* (Indianapolis, 1952), 29.

151. Bruce Catton, "'Old Abe,' the Battle Eagle," *American Heritage* 14 (Oct. 1963), 32–33, 106–7.

152. Wiley, *Life of Billy Yank*, 80; David McLain, "The Story of Old Abe," *Wisconsin Magazine of History* 8 (1925), 410–11; J. H. Greene, *Reminiscences of the War: Extracts from Letters Written Home from 1861 to 1865* (Medina, Ohio, 1886), 20.

153. Catton, "'Old Abe.'"

154. McLain, "Story of Old Abe"; J. H. Greene, *Reminiscences of the War: Extracts from Letters Written Home from 1861 to 1865* (Medina, Ohio, 1886), 20; Bruce "'Old Abe,'"; John M. Williams[?], *The Eagle Regiment* (1890); Wiley, *Life of Billy Yank*, 80.

155. C. F. Morse, "Yankee Volunteers Marching to Dixie," in Alton Ketchum, *Uncle Sam: The Man and the Legend* (New York, 1959), 84.

156. "Why He Cannot Sleep," in Morton Keller, *The Art and Politics of Thomas Nast* (Oxford, 1968), 21; Thomas Nast, self-portrait with Uncle Sam, "Watch and Pray," in Ketchum, *Uncle Sam*, fig. 90, p. 90.

157. Francis Bicknell Carpenter, *Six Months at the White House with Abraham Lincoln* (New York, 1866), 208.

158. A leading work is Irwin Silber, *Songs of the Civil War* (New York, 1960).

159. Ibid., 8.

160. Harry McCarthy, "The Bonnie Blue Flag," sheet music by A. E. Blackmar (New Orleans, 1861); Silber, *Songs of the Civil War*, 65.

161. James Ryder Randall, "Maryland, My Maryland," sheet music by A. E. Blackmar (New Orleans, 1862); Randall, *Maryland, My Maryland and Other Poems* (Baltimore, 1908); Randall to Kate Hammond, 16 Oct. 1863, Southern Historical Collection, University of North Carolina; Daniel Aaron, *The Unwritten War* (New York, 1973), 239; Silber, *Songs of the Civil War,* 70–72.

162. Francis James Child, *War Songs for Freemen* (Boston, 1863); Silber, *Songs of the Civil War,* 15–16, 41–42.

163. George F. Root, *The Story of a Musical Life: An Autobiography* (Cincinnati, 1891); idem et al., *War Songs* (Boston, 1890); The rallying song first appeared in print as "Battle Cry of Freedom," sheet music by Root and Cady (Chicago, 1862); the battle song appeared as "Battle Cry of Freedom," sheet music by Root and Cady (Chicago, 1863).

164. Silber, *Songs of the Civil War,* 8–9, 121.

165. Boyd B. Stutler, "John Brown's Body," *Civil War History* 4 (1958), 251–60.

166. Edmund Wilson, *Patriotic Gore* (New York, 1962), 92.

167. Isaiah 63:1–6. This text had also had inspired a Puritan song that Cromwell's soldiers sang after the battle of Naseby in the English Civil War.

> Oh! Wherefore come ye forth, in triumph from the North,
> With your hands, and your feet, and your raiment all red?
> And wherefore doth your rout send forth a joyous shout?
> And whence be the grapes of the wine-press which ye tread?
>
> Oh, evil was the root, and bitter was the fruit,
> And crimson was the juice of the vintage that we trod;
> For we trampled on the throng of the haughty and the strong,
> Who sat in the high places, and slew the saints of God.

This song had been published by Macaulay, and Julia Ward Howe may have known it from that source.

168. John Hope Franklin, *The Emancipation Proclamation* (Garden City, N.Y., 1963); Hans L. Trefousse, ed., *Lincoln's Decision for Emancipation* (1975); Michael Vorenberg, *Final Freedom: The Civil War, the Abolition of Slavery, and the Thirteenth Amendment* (Cambridge, 2001).

169. David Homer Bates, *Lincoln in the Telegraph Office* (1907; ed. James A. Rawley, Lincoln, Neb., 1995), 138–42; Franklin, *Emancipation Proclamation,* 20–54; Carpenter, *Six Months at the White House,* 67, passim; *Diary and Correspondence of Salmon P. Chase* (Washington, 1903), 48ff.; Gideon Welles, "The History of Emancipation," *Galaxy* 14 (1872), 842–43.

170. "The Abolition Catastrophe, or the November Smash-Up" (New York, 1864), Lincoln Memorial University, in Harold Holzer, *Washington and Lincoln Portrayed: National Icons in Popular Prints* (Jefferson, N.C., 1993), 146.

171. William B. Hesseltine, *Lincoln and the War Governors* (New York, 1948); V. Jacque Voegeli, *Free but Not Equal: The Midwest and the Negro During the Civil War* (Chicago, 1969).

172. David Gilmore (var. Gilmour), Blythe, "President Lincoln Writing the Proclamation of Freedom," LC; B. W. Chambers, *The World of David Gilmore Blythe,*

1815–1865 (Washington, 1980); Elizabeth Johns, *American Genre Painting: The Politics of Everyday Life* (New Haven, 1992).

173. Adalbert Volck, "Writing the Emancipation Proclamation," Karolik Collection, Boston Museum of Fine Arts; also George McCullough Anderson, *The Work of Adalbert Johann Volck, 1828–1912, who chose for his name the Anagram V. Blada, 1861–1865* (Baltimore, 1970).

174. The many drafts of the Emancipation Proclamation include: "First Draft," 22 July 1862, Lincoln Papers, LC; "Preliminary Emancipation Proclamation," autograph draft signed in the New York State Library; engrossed copy, 22 Sept. 1862, NA; *AL* 5:336–337, 433–36; "Preliminary Draft of Final Emancipation Proclamation," 30 Dec. 1862, Lincoln Papers, LC; "Final Emancipation Proclamation," 1 Jan. 1863, photograph, Lincoln Papers, LC; engrossed copy, NA. Members of the cabinet also had their own draft copies. See Charles Eberstadt, "Lincoln's Emancipation Proclamation," *New Colophon* (1950), 312–56.

175. The artist tells his story in Carpenter, *Six Months in the White House.*

176. A Brady photograph for the painting is reproduced in Philip B. Kunhardt Jr. et al., *Lincoln: An Illustrated Biography* (New York, 1972), 274.

177. Thomas Ball, *Emancipation Group*, 1865, cast 1873, bronze, Montclair Art Museum; Thomas Ball, *My Threescore Years and Ten: An Autobiography* (Boston, 1892).

178. John Quincy Adams Ward, *Freedman*, 1863, bronze, 19 1/2 inches, American Academy of Arts and Letters, New York; Adeline Adams, *John Quincy Adams Ward* (New York, 1912)

179. John Rogers, *The Fugitive's Story*, 1869, painted plaster, 21 3/4 inches, NYHS; David H. Wallace, *John Rogers: The People's Sculptor* (Middletown, Conn., 1967); Dorothy C. Barck, "Rogers Groups in the Museum of the New-York Historical Society," *NYHSQ* 16 (1932), 67–86.

180. Augustus Saint-Gaudens, *Robert Gould Shaw Memorial*, 1884–97, bronze, 11 by 14 feet, Boston Common, Beacon Hill, Boston; idem, *Heads of Black Soldiers,* 1884–97, cast bronze, 1964–65, Augustus Saint-Gaudens National Historic Site, Cornish, N.H.

181. Ira Berlin, Barbara Jeanne Fields, Steve F. Miller, Joseph Reidy and Leslie Rowland, eds., *Freedom: A Documentary History of Emancipation*, 4 vols. to date (Cambridge, 1982–).

182. R. C. McCormick, qtd. in James D. Horan, *Mathew Brady: Historian with a Camera* (New York, 1955), 31.

183. Lincoln, "Campaign Speech, Springfield, Illinois," 17 July 1858, in *AL* 2:504–21; also Holzer, *Washington and Lincoln Portrayed*, 80.

184. William S. Walsh, ed., *Abraham Lincoln and the London "Punch"* (New York, 1909), 100.

185. Photographs survive of John Quincy Adams, Andrew Jackson, Martin Van Buren, John Tyler, James Knox Polk, Zachary Taylor, Millard Fillmore, Franklin Pierce, and James Buchanan. The first four were photographed after they left office.

186. David Donald, *Lincoln* (New York, 1995), 238.

187. Kunhardt et al., *Lincoln*, 100; Holzer, *Washington and Lincoln Portrayed*, 86–87.

188. Lincoln to James F. Babcock, 13 Sept. 1860, in *AL* 4:114.

189. Holzer, *Washington and Lincoln Portrayed,* 87.

190. Donald, *Lincoln,* 238.

191. Horan, *Mathew Brady,* 32; James Mellon, *The Face of Lincoln* (New York, 1979); Charles Hamilton and Lloyd Ostendorf, *Lincoln in Photographs: An Album of Every Known Pose* (Dayton, Ohio, 1985); Lincoln, "Address at Cooper Institute," 27 Feb. 1860, in *AL* 3:522–50.

192. Harold G. Villard and Oswald Garrison Villard, eds., *Lincoln on the Eve of '61: A Journalist's Story* (New York, 1941), 91–95; Harold Holzer, Gabor S. Boritt, and Mark Neely Jr., *Changing the Lincoln Image* (Fort Wayne, Ind., 1985), 13–14.

193. Kunhardt et al., *Lincoln,* 143–44.

194. For the photographs with McClellan and Pinkerton, see Kunhardt et al., *Lincoln,* 170–71, 10–11; an intermediate height might have appeared in a photograph with Quartermaster General Montgomery Meigs on May 19, 1862, but the authenticity of this photograph is doubtful.

195. Kunhardt et al., *Lincoln,* 252.

196. Carpenter, *Six Months at the White House,* 30.

197. Alexander Gardner, 8 Nov. 1863, LC; Kunhardt et al., *Lincoln,* 222.

198. Lincoln, photograph by Alexander Gardner, 15 Feb. 1865, LC; Kuhnhardt et al., *Lincoln,* 222, 403.

199. Ronald C. White Jr., *Lincoln's Greatest Speech: The Second Inaugural* (New York, 2002).

200. *Lincoln's Second Inaugural,* Alexander Gardner, 4 March 1865, LC, Lincoln portrait on ribbon, White, *Lincoln's Greatest Speech,* plate 11, from *The Railsplitter.*

201. Mark E. Neely Jr., Harold Holzer, and Gabor S. Boritt, *The Confederate Image: Prints of the Lost Cause* (Chapel Hill, 1987), 55.

202. Long had been Lee's military secretary through much of the war from 1861 to 1863. After the war, Long became blind and worked in darkness for twenty years, writing his huge book on a blackboard, word by painful word. Cf. Armistead Long, *Memoirs of Robert E. Lee* (London, 1886), 84, 88–89. For Lee's own words about slavery see Lee to Mary Lee, 27 Dec. 1856, Lee Family Papers, VHS; Robert E. Lee, Deed of Emancipation, 29 Dec. 1862, Emory Thomas, *Robert E. Lee: A Biography* (New York, 1995), 178, 273–74.

203. Lee, General Order 75, 7 July 1862, in *Wartime Papers,* 210–11.

204. He repeatedly professed his attachment to the old Union: "I am willing to sacrifice everything but honor for its preservation." But, he added, "a Union that can only be maintained by swords and bayonets, and which strife and civil war are to take the place of brotherly love and kindness, has no charm for me." Lee to Mary Lee, 27 Dec. 1856, Lee Family Papers, VHS; Thomas *Robert E. Lee,* 178.

205. Lee to May, 9 July 1866, in Alan T. Nolan, *Lee Considered: General Robert E. Lee and Civil War History* (Chapel Hill, 1991), 57; J. William Jones, *Personal Reminiscences of Gen. Robert E. Lee* (New York, 1875); idem, *Life and Letters of Robert E. Lee, Soldier and Man* (Washington, 1906; rpt. Harrisonburg, Va., 1986), 391.

206. Thomas L. Connelly, *The Marble Man: Robert E. Lee and His Image in American Society* (Baton Rouge, 1977), 171; Douglas Southall Freeman, *R. E. Lee: A Biography,* 4 vols. (New York, 1934–35), 3:236.

207. Epictetus, *The Discourses* (London and Cambridge, 1925), bk. 4, ch. 1, p. 245.

208. Thomas, *Robert E. Lee,* 19.

209. Connelly, *Marble Man,* 198; Michael Fellman, *The Making of Robert E. Lee* (New York, 2000).

210. Connelly, *Marble Man,* 204

211. Ibid., 189.

212. Thomas, *Robert E. Lee,* 19, 34, 45–46.

213. Others judged him differently, including some of the Custis slaves. After seeking guidance from the probate court, Lee decided to restore the estate to solvency, pay off the debts, and then to free the slaves. Amazingly he succeeded, but it took him the full five years, and the slaves were not happy. Several ran away, were caught, and were whipped by the county constable. On the ownership of slaves, Thomas believes that he "continued to own black people until at least 1846," and again in the 1850s, and probably until the emancipation of the Custis slaves in 1862–63 (*Lee,* 71, 173, 184, 273). On Lee and the Custis slaves see Wesley Norris, communication, *National Anti-Slavery Standard,* 14 April 1866, rpt. in John Blassingame, ed., *Slave Testimony* (Baton Rouge, 1977), 467–68; also Lee to Mary Lee, 27 Dec. 1856, Lee Papers, VHS; Freeman, *Lee* 1:371–73.

214. Marshall Fishwick, *Lee After the War* (New York, 1963), 228.

215. William C. McDonald, "The True Gentleman: On Robert E. Lee's Definition of a Gentleman," *Civil War History* 32 (1986), 119–38.

216. Lee himself had thought to write his own history of the Army of Northern Virginia, in which his men would be exemplars of this tradition. See Allen W. Moger, "General Lee's Unwritten 'History of the Army of Northern Virginia,'" *VMHB* 71 (1963), 341–63. His men took over the task and shifted the center to Lee himself. Among many works were Edward Pollard, *Lee and His Lieutenants* (New York, 1867); Jubal Early, *The Campaigns of Robert E. Lee* (Baltimore, 1872).

217. J. William Jones, *Personal Reminiscences of General Robert E. Lee* (rpt. Baton Rouge, 1994); Fitzhugh Lee, *General Lee* (rpt. New York, 1994); Robert E. Lee, *Recollections and Letters of General Robert E. Lee* (New York, 1905; rpt. 1988); Roy Meredith, *The Face of Robert E. Lee in Life and Legend* (1947, New York, 1947; rpt. 1981).

218. Norris in Blassingame, *Slave Testimony,* 467–68.

219. Michael Paul Williams, "John Mitchell Jr.," *Richmond Times Dispatch,* 1 Feb. 2002.

220. Douglas Southall Freeman, *R. E. Lee: A Biography,* 4 vols. (New York, 1934–35), and *Lee's Lieutenants: A Study in Command;* Eisenhower qtd. in McDonald, "True Gentleman," 122.

221. Connelly, *Marble Man;* Gaines M. Foster, *Ghosts of the Confederacy: Defeat, the Lost Cause, and the Emergence of the New South* (New York, 1987); Alan T. Nolan, *Lee Considered: General Robert E. Lee and Civil War History* (Chapel Hill, 1991); and Michael Fellman, *The Making of Robert E. Lee* (New York, 2000).

222. *Washington Post,* 18 Jan. 1999, 19 Jan. 2000; *Talk Richmond,* 30 June 2002; *Richmond Times-Dispatch,* 19-20 Jan. 2000, 10 May 2002; *Winchester Star,* 12 Jan. 2001.

223. Thomas, *Robert E. Lee;* Gary Gallagher ed., *Lee and His Generals in War and Memory* (Baton Rouge, 1998); idem, ed., *Lee and His Army in Confederate History* (Chapel Hill, 2001); and Joseph Harsh's trilogy, which began with *Confederate Tide Rising: Robert E. Lee and the Making of Southern Strategy* (Kent, Ohio, 1998).

224. Horatio Bateman, "Reconstruction," lithograph, New York, 1967.

225. Edward A. Pollard, *The Lost Cause: A New Southern History of the War of the Confederates* (New York, 1866); for general studies see Thomas J. Pressly, *Americans Interpret Their Civil War* (Princeton, 1954; rev. ed., New York, 1962); Gaines M. Foster, *Ghosts of the Confederacy.*

226. Neely, Holzer, and Boritt, *Confederate Image,* 105.

227. Major Innes Randolph, CSA, "The Good Old Rebel"; Silber, *Songs of the Civil War,* 350, 356.

228. Alfred Waud, "The First Vote," *Harper's Weekly,* 16 Nov. 1867.

229. Thomas Kelly, "The Fifteenth Amendment," chromolithograph, New York, 1870.

230. Sachse and Company, "The Shackle Broken by the Genius of Freedom," chromolithograph, Baltimore, 1875.

231. Deposit Book, Freedman's Savings and Trust Company, n.d. [ca. 1870?], in Eric Foner and Olivia Mahoney, *America's Reconstruction: People and Politics After the Civil War* (New York, 1995), 61.

232. A. Zenneck, "Murder of Louisiana," 1873, in ibid., 113.

233. Charlotte Perkins Gilman, *The Living of Charlotte Perkins Gilman* (New York, 1975), 16–17, qtd. in William S. McFeely, *Grant: A Biography* (New York, 1981), 281.

234. Mary Lewis, "Forever Free," in Foner and Mahoney, *America's Reconstruction,* 17.

235. McFeeley, *Grant,* 285; Svend Petersen, *A Statistical History of the American Presidential Elections* (New York, 1963), 41.

236. George M. Fredrickson, *The Inner Civil War: Northern Intellectuals and The Crisis of the Union* (New York, 1965).

237. Elinor Lander-Horwitz, *The Bird, the Banner, and Uncle Sam* (Philadelphia, 1976).

238. Qtd. in Victor Rosewater, *The Liberty Bell: Its History and Significance* (New York, 1926), 137, from Richard Henry Stoddard, *A Century After: Picturesque Glimpses of Philadelphia . . .* (Philadelphia, 1876), 14.

239. Rosewater, *Liberty Bell,* 173.

240. The story of the dinner party was told by F. A. Bartholdi in *The Statue of Liberty Enlightening the World, Described by the Sculptor Bartholdi,* ed. A.T. Rice (New York, 1885); for Laboulaye see Jean Claude Lamberti, "Laboulaye and the Common Law of Free Peoples," in Pierre Provoyeur and June Hargrove, eds., *Liberty: The French-American Statue in Art and History* (New York, 1986), 20–26. Among Laboulaye's major works were *La Liberté religieuse* (Paris, 1858); *Etudes morales et politiques* (Paris, 1862); *L'Etat et ses Limites* (Paris, 1864); *Histoire des Etats-Unis,* 3 vols. (Paris, 1855–66, 3d ed., 1868); and *Le parti libéral* (Paris, 1871). For studies of his work, Walter D. Gray, *Interpreting American Democracy in France: The Career of Edouard Laboulaye, 1811–1883* (Newark, Del., 1994); also Daniel Coit Gilman, *Bluntschli, Lieber, and Laboulaye* (Baltimore, 1884).

241. Gray, *Interpreting American Democracy in France,* 76, 31.

242. "Lincoln, honnête homme, abolit l'esclavage, rétablit l'union, sauva la République, sans voiler la statue de la liberté." Hertha Pauli and E. B. Ashton, *I Lift My Lamp: The Way of a Symbol* (New York, 1948), 7–38; Marvin Trachtenberg, *The Statue of Liberty* (New York, 1976), 28.

243. Jacques Betz, *Bartholdi* (Paris, 1954); J. M. Schmitt, *Bartholdi, une certaine idée de la liberté* (Paris, 1985).

244. Bartholdi to Laboulaye, 15 July 1871, qtd. in Janet Headley, "Voyage of Discovery: Bartholdi's First American Visit (1871)," in Provoyeur and Hargrove, *Liberty*, 100–05.

245. Laboulaye, "Speech at the Opera of Paris, 25 April, 1876"; Christian Blanchet, "The Universal Appeal of the Statue of Liberty," in W. S. Dillon and N. G. Kotler, eds., *The Statue of Liberty Revisited* (Washington, 1994), 35. For *architecture parlante* see Jean-Marie Pérouse de Montclos, *Etienne Louis Boullé, 1728–1799: Theoretician of Revolutionary Architecture* (New York, 1974); Trachtenberg, *Statue of Liberty*, 156.

246. Agénor Bardoux, *Journal des débats*, 10 June 1883; Gray, *Interpreting American Democracy in France*, 134–35.

247. Pauli and Ashton, *I Lift My Lamp*, 139.

248. Trachtenberg, *Statue of Liberty*, 108, 117.

249. Richard Seth Hayden and Thierry W. Despont, *Restoring the Statue of Liberty: Sculpture, Structure, Symbol* (New York, 1986); Bertrand Lemoine, *Gustave Eiffel* (Paris, 1980); Henri Loyette, *Gustave Eiffel* (New York, 1985).

250. Gray, *Interpreting American Democracy in France*, 132.

251. On Stone see *Dictionary of American Biography* 9:72; and Mark M. Boatner III, *Civil War Dictionary*, rev. ed. (New York, 1959, 1988), 800.

252. A. Geschaedler, *True Light on the Statue of Liberty and Its Creator* (Narbeth, Pa., 1966), 137; Trachtenberg, *Statue of Liberty*, 216.

253. Rudolph J. Vecoli, "The Lady and the Huddled Masses," in Dillon and Kotler, *Statue of Liberty Revisited*, 39–70, 62n, from Doris Brown, "Lazarus and the Promised Land(s)" *Moment* (1985), 49–52.

254. Vecoli, "The Lady and the Huddled Masses"; for Catholic criticism see "Our Great Goddess and Her Coming Idol," *American Catholic Quarterly Review* 5 (1880), 593.

255. Cori and Steiner qtd. in Vecoli, "The Lady and the Huddled Masses," 41.

256. Jewish History Pageant in Milwaukee, with Golda Meir as the Statue of Liberty, 1919, State Historical Society of Wisconsin.

257. Thomas Bailey Aldrich, *Poems*, 2 vols. (Boston, 1907), 2:72, Vernon Louis Parrington, *Main Currents in American Thought*, vol. 3, *The Beginnings of Critical Realism in America, 1860–1920* (New York, 1930), 58.

258. Qtd. in Vecoli, "The Lady and the Huddled Masses," 45.

259. Ibid., 62n.

260. Glenda Gilmore, *Gender and Jim Crow* (Chapel Hill, 1990), xv.

261. General Gideon Granger, General Order 3, Ashton Villa, Tex., 19 June 1865.

262. Writings on Juneteenth include Francis E. Abernethy, Alan Govenar, and Patrick B. Mullen, eds., *Juneteenth Texas: Essays in African American Folklore*, Publications of the Texas Folklore Society, no. 54, (Denton, Tex., 1996); Douglas DeNatale, ed., *Jubilation! African American Celebrations in the Southeast* (Columbia, S.C., 1994); William H. Wiggins Jr., *Oh, Freedom!: Afro-American Emancipation Celebrations* (Nashville, 1987, 1990); Charles Taylor, "The Black Church and Juneteenth," http://www.actom.com/njclchistory.htm; Ralph Ellison, *Juneteenth: A Novel* (New York, 1999, a posthumous publication); James M. Smallwood, *Time of Hope, Time of Despair: Black Texans During Reconstruction* (Port Washington, N.Y., 1981); Robert Selim, *Juneteenth: Celebrating Emancipation* (Washington, 1985).

263. Taylor, "The Black Church and Juneteenth."

264. Charles M. Payne, *I've Got the Light of Freedom: The Organizing Tradition and the Mississippi Freedom Struggle* (Berkeley, 1995), 1.

265. Gilmore, *Gender and Jim Crow*, xv.

266. George Fronval and Daniel Dubois, *Indian Signals and Sign Language* (1978; New York, 1994), 63.

267. Virginia Irving Armstrong, ed., *I Have Spoken: American History Through the Voices of the Indians* (Chicago, 1971), 65–66; Roger L. Nichols, *Black Hawk and the Warrior's Path* (Arlington Heights, Ill., 1992).

268. Chief Joseph, "An Indian's Views," *North American Review* 128 (April 1879), 412–33, qtd. in Alvin M. Josephy, *The Indian Heritage of America* (New York, 1968), 329–30; idem, *The Nez Perce Indians and the Opening of the Northwest* (New Haven, 1965); M. Gidley, *With One Sky Above Us* (New York, 1979).

269. Thomas Henry Tibbles, *Standing Bear and the Ponca Chiefs* (Lincoln, Neb., 1995); idem., *Buckskin and Blanket Days* (Lincoln, Neb., 1957).

270. *U.S. ex rel. Standing Bear vs. George Crook* (1879); transcript in *Omaha Herald*, 13 May 1879.

271. *Omaha Herald*, 18 May 1879.

272. "Standing Bear's Farewell . . . One of the Most Remarkable Indian Speeches on Record," *Omaha Herald*, 20 May 1879.

273. Plateau Indian bag, late nineteenth century; Lakota horse mask, late nineteenth or early twentieth century; both from collection of Joel Kopp, New York State Historical Association; in Toby Herbst and Joel Kopp, *The Flag in American Indian Art* (Cooperstown, N.Y., 1993), 116.

274. Ibid.

275. Ibid.

276. U.S. Congress, 90th Cong., 1st sess., Senate Committee on Labor and Public Welfare, Special Subcommittee on Indian Education, 1–15 Dec. 1969, pt. 1, 221–22, qtd. in Armstrong, *I Have Spoken*, 157.

277. Mary Remington, in *Philadelphia Evening Star*, 2 Sept. 1872, italics in orig.; qtd. in Eric Goldman, *Rendezvous with Destiny* (New York, 1952), 17.

278. R. Fischer, *Tippecanoe and Trinkets Too*.

279. Charles Austin Beard, *The Rise of American Civilization* (New York, 1930) 2:35.

280. Goldstein, *Saving "Old Glory,"* 10.

281. Thomas Nast, "Get Thee Behind Me, (Mrs.) Satan," *Harper's*, 17 Feb. 1872.

282. Eric Goldman found this passage in Parrington's ms. autobiography (Goldman, *Rendezvous with Destiny*, 37–38); see also Richard Hofstadter, *The Progressive Historians* (New York, 1969), 357–62; also Parrington, *Main Currents in American Thought* 3:259–66.

283. Jackson Turner Main, *Social Structure of Revolutionary America* (Princeton, 1965), 67; *Historical Statistics of the United States, Colonial Times to 1970*, D75–77.

284. On Cyclone Davis see Henry Demarest Lloyd, "The Populists at St. Louis," *Review of Reviews* 14 (1896), 278–83; on Watson, C. Vann Woodward, *Tom Watson, Agrarian Rebel* (1938).

285. The pioneer historian John D. Hicks (*The Populist Revolt* [Minneapolis, 1931]) knew the Populists and their world and was strongly sympathetic. Richard Hofstadter and Oscar Handlin knew them not and condemned them from a distance as

ignorant savages, racists, anti-Semites, and irrational reactionaries. These errors were corrected by Norman Pollack and Robert Durden in careful studies of Populism as a political movement. Others studied Populism as a social and cultural movement, much broader than its party goals; see Lawrence Goodwyn, *Democratic Promise: The Populist Moment in America* (New York, 1976); Bruce Palmer, *Man over Money: The Southern Populist Critique of American Capitalism* (Chapel Hill, 1980); Robert McMath, *American Populism, A Social History, 1877–1898* (New York, 1992).

286. Henry George, *Progress and Poverty* (New York, 1884), ch. 24.

287. Omaha Platform, St. Louis Platform, Lorenzo Dow Lewelling, "The Tramp Circular," *Topeka Daily Capital,* 5 Dec. 1893, http://history.smsu.edu/wrmiller/populism.

288. Michel Chevalier, *Lettres sur l'Amerique du Nord* (Paris, 1836). It appeared in an expanded "special edition" in 1837 and a third edition in 1838, which was published in a flawed English translation as *Society, Manners, and Politics in the United States* (Boston, 1939). A modern translation, with many corrections but without Chevalier's notes was edited by John William Ward (Ithaca, N.Y., 1961). The law of liberty and order appears on p. 142.

289. Robert H. Wiebe, *The Search for Order, 1877–1920* (New York, 1967); *Businessmen and Reform: A Study of the Progressive Movement* (Cambridge, 1962); *The Segmented Society: An Historical Preface to the Meaning of America* (Oxford, 1975); *Who We Are: A History of Popular Nationalism* (Princeton, 2002).

290. John Baer, *The Pledge of Allegiance, A Centennial History, 1892–1992* (Annapolis, 1992); Marguerite Miller, *Twenty-three Words* (Portsmouth, Va., 1976).

291. *New York Times,* 27 June 2002.

292. William Jennings Bryan, speech at the Democratic National Convention, Chicago, 1896; the text was an earlier speech (22 Dec. 1894) in the House of Representatives, "I shall not help crucify mankind upon a cross of gold. I shall not aid in pressing down upon the bleeding brow of labor this crown of thorns."

293. Arthur M. Schlesinger and Fred L. Israel, eds., *Running for President: The Candidates and Their Images, 1900–1992* (New York, 1995), 2:15, 17.

294. Among many excellent books on the presidential election, several of the most outstanding are John M. Cooper, *The Warrior and the Priest: Woodrow Wilson and Theodore Roosevelt* (Cambridge, 1983); Arthur S. Link, *The Road to the White House* (Princeton 1947); and George E. Mowry, *Theodore Roosevelt and the Progressive Movement* (1946).

295. The best biography is still Henry F. Pringle, *The Life and Times of William Howard Taft,* 2 vols. (New York, 1939).

296. William H. Taft, *Popular Government: Its Essence, Its Performance, and Its Perils* (New Haven, 1913), 85–91.

297. Taft, Annual Message to Congress, 5 Dec. 1911, in Arthur M. Schlesinger and Fred Israel, eds., *The State of the Union Messages of the Presidents, 1790–1966,* 3 vols. (New York, 1966), 3:2443.

298. Debs, "This Is Our Year," July 1912, in Arthur Schlesinger and Joseph Bernstein, eds., *Writings and Speeches of Eugene V. Debs* (New York, 1948), 358–60.

299. Ray Ginger, *The Bending Cross: A Biography of Eugene Victor Debs* (New Brunswick, 1949); H. Wayne Morgan, *Eugene V. Debs, Socialist for President* (1962).

300. Debs, "This Is Our Year," July, 1912; "Speech of Acceptance," Oct. 1912; "Speech in Canton, Ohio," 16 June 1918; all in Schlesinger and Bernstein, *Writings and Speeches of Eugene V. Debs,* 358–60, 361–64, 432–33.

301. Theodore Roosevelt, *The New Nationalism* (New York, 1910; rev. ed., William E. Leuchtenberg, Englewood Cliffs, N.J., 1961), 25.

302. Ibid., 21–39

303. Ibid., 12.

304. Roosevelt, "We Stand at Armageddon," 1912.

305. Roosevelt, *New Nationalism,* 26, 171.

306. Ibid., 37.

307. Woodrow Wilson, *The New Freedom* (New York, 1913, 1918), 281–84, 253, 294, 49, 58, 69.

A World at War

1. The resolution authorized the president to accept the Statue of Liberty and to make "suitable regulations" for "its future maintenance as a beacon, and for the permanent care and preservation thereof as a monument of art." President Ulysses Grant signed the resolution into law on his last day in office.

2. *New York Times,* 3 Dec. 1916, qtd in Rudolph Vecoli, "The Lady and the Huddled Masses," in W. S. Dillon and N. G. Kotler, eds., *The Statue of Liberty Revisited* (Washington, 1994), 51.

3. *New York Times,* 3 Dec. 1916.

4. Holger Herwig, *The First World War: Germany and Austria-Hungary, 1914–1918* (London, 1997), and Hew Strachan, *The First World War,* vol. 1, *To Arms* (Oxford, 2001), review this very large literature.

5. John Keegan, *The First World War* (New York, 1998); Niall Ferguson, *The Pity of War* (London, 1998).

6. For evidence of German atrocities, including the murder of 6,500 Belgian and French citizens, see John Horne and Alan Kramer, *German Atrocities, 1914: A History of Denial* (New Haven, 2001).

7. Edward Coffman, *The War to End All Wars: The American Military Experience in World War I* (New York, 1968); Ronald Schaffer, *America in the Great War* (New York, 1991); David F. Trask, *The AEF and Coalition War-Making, 1917–1918* (Lawrence, Kans., 1993).

8. Woodrow Wilson, Address to Congress, 2 April 1917.

9. George Creel, *How We Advertised America* (New York, 1920); James R. Mock and Cedric Larson, *Words That Won the War: The Story of the Committee on Public Information, 1917–1919* (Princeton, 1939); Stephen Vaughan, *Holding Fast the Inner Lines: Democracy, Nationalism, and the Committee on Public Information* (Chapel Hill, 1980).

10. George Creel, *Rebel at Large: Fifty Crowded Years* (New York, 1947).

11. Thomas Fleming, "When the United States Entered World War I . . . ," *Military History,* Dec 1995; Creel, *Rebel at Large,* 156–59; Robert Lansing, *War Memoirs of Robert Lansing* (Indianapolis, 1935), 322–24.

12.	George Creel et al., *Complete Report of the Chairman of the Committee on Public Information* (Washington, 1920).

13.	George T. Blakey, *Historians on the Homefront: American Propagandists for the Great War* (Lexington, Ky., 1970).

14.	Creel, *Rebel at Large*, 168.

15.	H. L. Mencken, "Star-Spangled Men," *New Republic*, 29 Sept. 1920; I. F. Stone, "Creel's Crusade," *Nation*, 9 Dec. 1939.

16.	*Leslie's Weekly*, 6 July 1916.

17.	C. R. Macauley, "You Buy a Liberty Bond . . . ," 1917, in the collections of the National Park Service, Statue of Liberty National Monument; reproduced in Bertrand Dard, "Liberty as Image and Icon," in Dillon and Kotler, *Statue of Liberty Revisited* 74.

18.	For many years this poster hung in the men's room of the American Antiquarian Society.

19.	Joseph C. Leyendecker, "Weapons for Liberty," in the Huntington Library and Art Gallery, n.d.; Susan I. Fort, *The Flag Paintings of Childe Hassam* (Los Angeles and New York, 1988), 10.

20.	Joseph Pennell, "That Liberty Shall Not Perish from the Earth," poster, Smithsonian Museum of American History.

21.	Fort, *Flag Paintings*, 21, 24.

22.	For eighteenth-century ideas of freedom from fear see above, 92.

23.	Human Statue of Liberty, Camp Dodge, Iowa, in Pierre Oriovoyeur and June Hargrove, eds., *Liberty: The French American Statue in Art and History* (New York, 1986), 279.

24.	Kit Hinrichs, Delphine Hirasuna, and Terry Heffernan, *Long May She Wave: A Graphic History of the American Flag* (Berkeley and Toronto, 2001), 22–23.

25.	Living Flag Postcards, ca. 1909, in ibid., 22.

26.	Qtd. in Arthur Garfield Hays, *City Lawyer: The Autobiography of a Law Practice* (New York, 1942), 219.

27.	Woodrow Wilson, "Spurious Versus Real Patriotism in Education," *School Review*, Dec. 1899, 603–4, qtd. in Robert Justin Goldstein, *Saving "Old Glory": The History of the American Flag Desecration Controversy* (Boulder, Colo., 1995), 70–71.

28.	Qtd. in Arthur Schlesinger and Joseph Bernstein, eds., *Writings and Speeches of Eugene V. Debs* (New York, 1948), xi.

29.	Goldstein, *Saving "Old Glory,"* 82.

30.	Ibid., 84–86; citing New York Times, 27 March, 2, 3 June 1916; 3–8, 10, 13–15, 18 March 1917.

31.	From a quantitative survey in ibid., 75–80.

32.	Ibid., 79.

33.	Robert Murray, *Red Scare: A Study in National Hysteria* (Minneapolis, 1955), 12; cited in John M. Barry, *Rising Tide: The Great Mississippi Flood of 1927 and How It Changed America* (New York, 1997), 137.

34.	Goldstein, *Saving "Old Glory,"* 83.

35.	*U.S. v. Spirit of '76*; Bill Kauffman, "Muskets and Misfires," *Wall Street Journal*, 9 June 2000.

36. V. E. Tarrant, *Jutland: The German Perspective* (Annapolis, 1995), 252.

37. Robert Wiebe et al., *The Great Republic* (Lexington, Mass., 1977), 946.

38. Eric Foner, *The Story of American Freedom* (New York, 1988), 175.

39. Ibid.

40. Ibid., 172–74.

41. Katherine Ruschenberger, "Suffrage Liberty Bell," *New York Times,* 31 March 1915.

42. Jane Addams, *The Second Twenty Years at Hull House* (New York, 1910), 103.

43. Theodore Draper, *Roots of American Communism* (New York, 1957); Richard Drinnon, *Rebel in Paradise: A Biography of Emma Goldman* (Boston, 1961).

44. Murray, *Red Scare;* William K. Preston Jr., *Aliens and Dissenters: Federal Suppression of Radicals, 1903–1933* (Cambridge, 1963).

45. *Schenck v. U.S.,* 249 U.S. 47 (1919); *Debs v. U.S.,* 249 U.S. 211 (1919); *Frowerk v. U.S.,* 249 U.S. 204 (1919); Wallace Mendelson, "Clear and Present Danger: From Schenck to Dennis," *Columbia Law Review* 52 (1952), 313–17.

46. *Whitney v. California,* 274 U.S. 357 (1927); Henry J. Abraham, *Freedom and the Court: Civil Rights and Liberties in the United States* (New York, 1967), 125.

47. Robert Cottrell, *Roger Nash Baldwin and the American Civil Liberties Union* (New York, 2001); Samuel Walker, *In Defense of American Liberties: A History of the ACLU* (Carbondale, Ill., 1999); Donald L. Johnson, *The Challenge to American Freedoms: World War I and the Rise of the American Civil Liberties Union* (Lexington, Ky., 1963); Charles l. Markmann, *The Noblest Cry: A History of the American Civil Liberties Union* (New York, 1965).

48. Paul L. Murphy, *The Constitution in Crisis Times, 1918–1969* (New York, 1972), 69–70; Roger N. Baldwin and Clarence B. Randall, *Civil Liberties and Industrial Conflict* (Cambridge, 1938).

49. Andrew Sinclair, *Era of Excess: A Social History of the Prohibition Movement,* 2d ed. (New York, 1964), 136.

50. Michael Kammen, *Spheres of Liberty* (Madison, Wisc., 1986), 81.

51. Richmond Pearson Hobson, *The Great Destroyer* (Washington, 1911); Sinclair, *Era of Excess,* 48.

52. H. L. Mencken to James Beck, 12 Dec. 1924, qtd. in Michael Kammen, *A Machine That Would Go of Itself* (New York, 1987), 337.

53. George Wolfskill, *The Revolt of the Conservatives: A History of the American Liberty League* (Boston: Houghton, Mifflin, 1962), ch. 2.

54. Sinclair, *Age of Excess,* 58, 213.

55. Schopenhauer was so fond of this thought that he kept a group of porcelain porcupines on his writing desk. See Deborah Luepnitz, *Schopenhauer's Porcupines: Intimacy and Its Dilemma* (New York, 2002).

56. Hays, *City Lawyer,* 470.

57. Hays, *City Lawyer;* idem, *Let Freedom Ring* (New York, 1928; rev. ed., 1937), 51. His papers are in the Princeton University Library.

58. Hays, *Let Freedom Ring;* idem, *Trial by Prejudice* (New York, 1933).

59. Hays, *Let Freedom Ring,* 25.

60. For firsthand accounts, see Hays, *Let Freedom Ring,* 25–88. Leading studies are Edward J. Larson, *Summer for the Gods: The Scopes Trial and America's Continuing Debate over Science and Religion* (New York, 1997); and Ray Ginger, *Six Days or*

Forever? Tennessee v. John Thomas Scopes (New York, 1958), an excellent account of the trial.

61. Hays, *Let Freedom Ring,* 70, 76.

62. Ibid., 71, 74.

63. Ibid., 192.

64. Paul Avrich, *Sacco and Vanzetti: The Anarchist Background* (Princeton, 1991); Francis Russell, *Sacco and Vanzetti: The Case Resolved* (New York, 1986); Hays, *Let Freedom Ring,* 143–46.

65. Hays, *City Lawyer.*

66. Hays, *Let Freedom Ring,* 103–27, 128–29.

67. Dan T. Carter, *Scottsboro: A Tragedy of the American South* (Baton Rouge, 1969; rev. ed., 1979); James Goodman, *Stories of Scottsboro* (New York, 1994).

68. Charles L. Markmann, *The Noblest Cry: A History of the Civil Liberties Union* (New York, 1965); Alan Reitman, ed., *The Pulse of Freedom: American Liberties, 1920–1970s* (New York, 1975), 74–77; Hays, *Let Freedom Ring,* 127.

69. Hays, *City Lawyer,* 234–35.

70. Albert Hirschfeld, "Ernest Hemingway," reproduced in Ron Tyler, *The Image of America in Caricature and Cartoon* (Fort Worth, 1975), 137.

71. Hemingway to Ivan Kashkin, 19 Aug. 1935, in Carlos Baker, ed., *Ernest Hemingway: Selected Letters* (New York, 1981), 419; Keneth Kinnamon, "Hemingway and Politics," in Scott Donaldson, ed., *The Cambridge Companion to Ernest Hemingway* (Cambridge, 1996), 159.

72. Hemingway to John Dos Passos, in Baker, *Selected Letters,* 375.

73. Dorothy Parker, "The Artist's Reward," *New Yorker,* 30 Nov. 1929.

74. Two excellent and very different biographies are Nancy Milford, *Savage Beauty: The Life of Edna St. Vincent Millay* (New York, 2001); Daniel Mark Epstein, *What Lips My Lips Have Kissed: The Loves and Love Poems of Edna St. Vincent Millay* (New York, 2001).

75. Epstein, *What Lips My Lips Have Kissed,* 35, 51.

76. Millay, *Renascence and Other Poems* (New York, 1917); Milford, *Savage Beauty,* 167.

77. Milford, *Savage Beauty,* 162, 163.

78. Allan Ross MacDougall, ed., *The Letters of Edna St. Vincent Millay* (New York, 1952), 99–100; Epstein, *What Lips My Lips Have Kissed,* 136.

79. Edmund Wilson, *The Shores of Light* (New York, 1952), Ross Wetzteon, *Republic of Dreams: Greenwich Village: The American Bohemia, 1910–1960* (New York, 2002), 272.

80. Edna St. Vincent Millay, *A Few Figs from Thistles: Poems and Four Sonnets, Salvo One* (New York, 1920); idem, *Second April* (New York, 1921); idem, *The Harp-Weaver and Other Poems* (New York, 1923); Wetzteon, *Republic of Dreams,* 269.

81. Colin Falck, ed., *Edna St. Vincent Millay: Selected Poems* (New York, 1992, 1999), foreword.

82. Epstein, *What Lips My Lips Have Kissed,* 199.

83. Millay, *Harp-Weaver and Other Poems.*

84. Foner, *Story of American Freedom,* 147.

85. Edward A. Filene, *The Way Out: A Forecast of Coming Changes in American Business and Industry* (Garden City, N.Y., 1924); idem, *Speaking of Change* (New York, 1939).

86. "Armed with New Knowledge—Sure of Her New Skill," *Saturday Evening Post*, 1928; Foner, *Story of American Freedom*, 150.

87. William Leach, *Land of Desire* (New York, 1993); "Notes from New York," *Merchants Record and Show Window, An Illustrated Monthly Journal for Merchants, Display Managers, and Advertising Men*, Dec. 1924.

88. Goldstein, *Saving "Old Glory*,*"* 91; T. H. Watkins, *The Great Depression* (Boston, 1993), 157–58.

89. Fireside Chat, 30 Sept. 1934, in Samuel I. Rosenman, comp., *The Public Papers and Addresses of Franklin D. Roosevelt* (New York, 1938–50), 3:422; Kammen, *Spheres of Liberty*, 149.

90. See also Jerry Mangione, *The Dream and the Deal: The Federal Writers Project, 1933–1945* (Boston, 1972).

91. "American Labor Party, Roosevelt and Lehman," poster, New York American Labor Party, 1936, collection of David and Janice Frent.

92. Franklin D. Roosevelt, State of the Union Address, 1935, in Arthur M. Schlesinger and Fred Israel, eds., *The State of the Union Messages of the Presidents, 1790–1966*. 3 vols. (New York, 1966), 3:2811.

93. "The America Way: Liberty and Justice for All," manufacturer unknown, ca. 1940, in Gerald E. Czulewicz Sr., *The Foremost Guide to Uncle Sam Collectibles* (Paducah, Ky., 1995), 26.

94. George Wolfskill, *The Revolt of the Conservatives: A History of the American Liberty League, 1934–1940* (Boston, 1962), 20–21; *New York Times*, 23 Aug. 1934.

95. James T. Patterson, *Congressional Conservatism and the New Deal: The Growth of the Conservative Coalition in Congress* (Lexington, 1967); Clyde P. Weed, *The Nemesis of Reform: The Republican Party During the New Deal* (New York, 1994).

96. "The Lilliputian New Deal," Condé-Nast Publications, 1935, in Bernard Schwartz, ed., *The American Heritage History of the Law in America* (New York, 1974), 221.

97. Wolfskill, *Revolt of the Conservatives*, 196.

98. Ibid., 62–65.

99. Oscar Handlin, *Al Smith and His America* (Boston, 1958); Wolfskill, *Revolt of the Conservatives*, 160, 152.

100. Wolfskill, *Revolt of the Conservatives*, 287.

101. Ibid., 124.

102. Carey Orr, "The Trojan Horse at Our Gate," *Chicago Tribune*, 17 Sept. 1935, in Stephen Hess and Milton Kaplan, *The Ungentlemanly Art: A History of Political Cartoons* (New York, 1968), 217.

103. Wolfskill, *Revolt of the Conservatives*, 177.

104. James A. Farley, *Behind the Ballots: The Personal History of a Politician* (New York, 1938), 292ff.

105. Wolfskill, *Revolt of the Conservatives*, 212–13.

106. In Rosenman, *Public Papers and Addresses of Franklin D. Roosevelt* 4:283–85.

107. Sinclair Lewis, *It Can't Happen Here* (New York, 1935, 1936), 3, 83, 410.

108. Wolfskill, *Revolt of the Conservatives*, 83–85.

109. In 2002, the Target Corporation discovered that it was selling caps and clothing marked with the Fascist symbol 88, which it speedily withdrew from its stores.

110. William Gropper, "Come Up and See Me Sometime," 1934, in Tyler, *Image of America in Caricature and Cartoon,* 130.

111. Irving Howe and Louis Coser, *The American Communist Party* (New York, 1962).

112. Foner, *Story of American Freedom,* 213.

113. Harvey Klehr and John Haynes, *The American Communist Movement: Storming Heaven Itself* (New York, 1992).

114. E.g., Louis Hartz, *The Liberal Tradition in America* (New York, 1955).

115. Francis Townsend, *New Horizons: An Autobiography* (Chicago, 1943).

116. Jackson Putnam, *Old Age Politics in California, from Richardson to Reagan* (Stanford, 1970).

117. David Hackett Fischer, *Growing Old in America* (New York, 1977, 1978), 182–83.

118. Charles J. Tull, *Father Coughlin and the New Deal* (Syracuse, 1965).

119. Alan Brinkley, *Voices of Protest: Huey Long, Father Coughlin, and the Great Depression* (New York, 1982).

120. T. Harry Williams, *Huey Long* (New York, 1969).

121. Ibid.

122. Brinkley, *Voices of Protest,* 173.

123. This was *Morehead v. New York ex rel. Tipaldo,* 298 U.S. 587 (1936); see Paul L. Murphy, *The Constitution in Crisis Times* (New York, 1969), 114.

124. John W. Chambers, "The Big Switch: Justice Roberts and the Minimum Wage Cases," *Labor History* 10 (1969), 44–73.

125. Kammen, *Machine That Would Go of Itself,* 28.

126. Ibid.

127. Ibid., 127.

128. Ibid., 153.

129. *Marion* (Ohio) *Star,* 3 May 1913; Eric Goldman, *Rendezvous with Destiny* (New York, 1952), 154.

130. Sol Bloom, *The Autobiography of Sol Bloom* (New York, 1948), 220–24.

131. Kammen, *Machine That Would Go of Itself,* 311.

132. Ibid., 73; David C. Mearns and Verner W. Clapp, *The Constitution of the United States with an Account of Its Travels* (Washington, 1952), 11.

133. Arthur Garfield Hays, *Democracy Works* (New York, 1939); idem, *City Lawyer,* 242, 263, 277.

134. Hays, *City Lawyer,* 276–77.

135. Kammen, *Machine That Would Go of Itself,* 336–56.

136. Robert K. Carr, *Federal Protection of Civil Rights* (Ithaca, 1947); Jerold S. Auerbach, *Labor and Liberty: The La Follette Committee and the New Deal* (Indianapolis, 1966); Murphy, *Constitution in Crisis Times,* 176–79; *U.S. v. Classic,* 313 U.S. 299 (1941).

137. National Resources Planning Board, *Security, Work, and Relief Policies* (Washington, 1942); idem, *Report for 1943,* 3 vols. (Washington, 1943); Alan Brinkley, *The End of Reform* (New York, 1995); Keith Olsen, "The American Beveridge Plan," *Mid-America* 65 (1983), 87–100; Foner, *Story of American Freedom,* 232–34, 247, 257, 321.

138. "Liberty's Crown," *Los Angeles Herald Examiner,* 8 Dec. 1976, in Roger A. Fischer, *Them Damned Pictures: Explorations in American Political Cartoon Art* (North Haven, Conn., 1996), 161.

139. Learned Hand, "The Spirit of Liberty," speech in Central Park, 21 May 1944, in Irving Dilliard, ed., *Learned Hand, The Spirit of Liberty: Papers and Addresses* (New York, 1952), 189–92.

140. Henry Ashby Turner Jr., *Hitler's Thirty Days: January 1933* (Reading, Mass., 1996), 110.

141. USS *Iowa*, after-action report, 28 March 1944, Naval Historical Center, as noted in Malcolm Muir, *The Iowa Class Battleships* (Poole and New York, 1987, 1988), 48.

142. Hand, "Spirit of Liberty," in Dilliard, *Learned Hand,* 189–92.

143. Ibid.

144. Martin Jacobs, *World War II Homefront Collectibles* (Iola, Wisc., 2000), 21.

145. "Lest We Forget: World War II; Roosevelt's Pearl Harbor Speech," transcript and recording, http://www.pearlharbor.org/speeches; see also Emily S. Rosenberg, *A Date Which Will Live: Pearl Harbor in American Memory* (Durham, 2003).

146. "Remember Pearl Harbor," words by Don Reid, music by Don Reid and Sammy Kaye; many versions of the song are available in transcript and recordings on the Internet, among them http://www.pearlharbor.org/speeches-songs-music-asp.

147. Jacobs, *World War II Homefront Collectibles,* 22, 23. One of the manufacturers and sellers of these items was Jack Ruby, who in 1963 assassinated Lee Harvey Oswald. In 1941, he and a friend founded the Spartan Novelty Company in Chicago, and after Pearl Harbor he designed and patented plaques commemorating the attack. He also sold busts of his hero Franklin Roosevelt. Ruby was a hustler, close to many figures in organized crime. He was also described as a "cuckoo nut" on the subject of patriotism, and so devoted to Franklin Roosevelt that he wept when he heard of the president's death.

148. "The condition upon which God hath given liberty to man is eternal vigilance." John Philpot Curran, *Speech upon the Right of Election of the Lord Mayor of Dublin, July 10, 1790* (Dublin, 1790).

149. John Morton Blum, *V was for Victory: Politics and American Culture During World War II* (New York, 1976), 16.

150. An account was published by the *Monterey County Herald*, 16 Aug. 1945, in an interview with Mallory, then living in Chico, California. Mallory said that he confided in a few of his closest friends, and when reports began to spread he returned to Tojo, asked to check the dentures and removed the Morse code, and narrowly escaped a court-martial. I found no other evidence.

151. For overviews see Alan S. Milward, *War, Economy, and Society, 1939–1945* (Berkeley, 1977, 1979); and Mark Harrison, ed., *The Economics of World War II: Six Great Powers in Comparison* (Cambridge, 1998). Both works give little attention to forced labor. On Germany the leading work on slave labor has been done by foreign scholars; see Edward L. Homze, *Foreign Labor in Nazi Germany* (Princeton, 1967); and Martin Kitchen, *Nazi Germany at War* (London, 1995), an important work, but unhappily its value for students and scholars is gravely weakened by the decision of the Oxford University Press to publish without notes. Also useful is R. J. Overy, *War and Economy in the Third Reich* (Oxford, 1988). On Japan see J. R. Cohen, *Japan's Economy in War and Reconstruction* (Minneapolis, 1949).

152. Edwin Bacon, *The Gulag at War* (London, 1994); Galina Mikhailovna Ivanova, *Labor Camp Socialism: The Gulag in the Soviet Totalitarian System* (Armonk, N.Y.,

2000); and a large Russian literature, notably, N. G. Okhotin and A. B. Roginsky, eds., *Sistema Ispravitelno-Trudovikh Lagerei v SSSR, 1923–1960: Spravochnik* [The System of Labor Camps in the USSR, 1923–1960: A Guide] (Moscow, 1999?); also Angus MacQueen, *Gulag,* BBC2 documentary, July 1999, with many interviews of camp survivors, which were published by Angus MacQueen, "Survivors," *Granta* 64 (1998), 37–53; Stéphane Courtois et al., *Le Livre noir du communisme: Crimes, terreur, répression* (Paris, 1997), 8–48, 285–98.

153. The story emerges from official histories. For Australia: Paul Hasluck, *The Government and the People,* 2 vols. (Canberra, 1952, 1970); and S.J. Butlin, *War Economy, 1939–1942* (Canberra, 1955); S. J. Butlin and C. B. Schedvin, *War Economy, 1942–1945* (Canberra, 1977). For Britain: H.M.D. Parker, *Manpower* (London, 1957). For New Zealand: F.L.W. Wood, *The New Zealand People at War: Political and External Affairs* (Wellington, 1958); J.V.T. Baker, *War Economy* (Wellington, 1965), 97–104 [176,000 conscripted workers in New Zealand; other numbers elusive].

154. A Gallup Poll in January 1942 showed strong support (68 percent) for a "labor draft" for American women. Among young adult women (21–35) approval rose to 73 percent. In the election year of 1944, Roosevelt half-heartedly asked Congress for a labor draft for women. Labor and business both opposed it, as did many in both political parties. The idea died in committee. William O'Neill, *A Democracy at War* (New York, 1993), 132.

155. Blum, *V Was for Victory,* 27.

156. Cowles initially refused, and the president said in that case he would be appointed ambassador to Australia, where he would have to work with MacArthur. Cowles changed his mind. Personal communication.

157. Robert Griffith, "The Selling of America: The Advertising Council and American Politics, 1942–1960," *Business History Review* 57 (1983), 321–46.

158. Foner, *Story of American Freedom,* 222.

159. Barry Moreno, *The Statue of Liberty Encyclopedia* (New York, 2000), 236–38.

160. "RVI à 50 ans," http://www.kvi.be/fr/allesivoi/50jaar.html.

161. Ken Weigel, "V-Campaign," *World of Wireless,* http://home.luna.nl/~arjan-muil/radio/history/history-frame.html.

162. Ibid.

163. Some variations were not positive. Prostitutes who gathered round Army camps were called V-girls.

164. Penny Colman, *Rosie the Riveter* (New York, 1995), 12; Stan Cohen, *V for Victory: America's Home Front During World War II* (Missoula, Mont., 1991).

165. Gerhard L. Weinberg, *A World at Arms: A Global History of World War II* (Cambridge, 1994), 439; Robert Dallek, *Franklin D. Roosevelt and American Foreign Policy, 1932–1945* (New York, 1979), 373.

166. Dallek, *Franklin D. Roosevelt and American Foreign Policy,* 373.

167. Foner, *Story of American Freedom,* 243.

168. Goldman, *Rendezvous with Destiny,* 399.

169. Francis Biddle, *A Casual Past* (New York, 1961); idem, *In Brief Authority* (New York, 1962); also *Annual Report of the Attorney General* (Washington, 1942).

170. Biddle's play on William Penn is in the Francis B. Biddle Papers, Special Collections, Georgetown University.

171. Franklin Roosevelt, in *New York Times*, 18 April 1941; Murphy, *Constitution in Crisis Times*, 225n.

172. Richard Norton Smith, *The Colonel: The Life and Legend of Robert R. McCormick* (Boston, 1997), 428–37.

173. *New York Times*, 21 Dec. 1941; Murphy, *Constitution in Crisis Times*, 225.

174. Ralph James and Estelle James, "The Purge of the Trotskyites from the Teamsters," *Western Political Quarterly* 19 (1966), 5–15.

175. David M. Kennedy, *Freedom from Fear* (New York, 1999), 642; Thomas Fleming, *The New Dealers' War* (New York, 2001).

176. O'Neill, *Democracy at War*, 232; Kennedy, *Freedom from Fear*, 751–52.

177. Roger Daniels, *Prisoners Without Trial: Japanese Americans in World War II* (New York, 1992), 46.

178. Kennedy, *Freedom from Fear*, 752.

179. *New York Times*, 2 June 1997.

180. For early discussion of the Michelangelo model see *Kansas City Star*, 6 June 1943; for general discussions see Penny Colman, *Rosie the Riveter: Women Working on the Home Front in World War II* (New York, 1995); Lara Claridge, *Norman Rockwell: A Life* (New York, 2001); Sotheby's, *Norman Rockwell, Rosie the Riveter* (New York, 22 May 2002), on the occasion of the painting's auction.

181. Ulysses Lee, *The Employment of Negro Troops* (Washington, 1966), 689–705.

182. Kennedy, *Freedom from Fear*, 768.

183. "Why Should We March," broadside, 1943, LC.

184. Ernie Pyle, *Here Is Your War* (1943; rpt. New York, 1989), 298.

185. Ibid., 297.

186. Jeffrey L. Ethell, *World War II Nose Art in Color* (Osceola, Wisc., 1993), 88.

187. Ibid., 54.

188. Ibid., 77.

189. Roland Gaul, *The Battle of the Bulge in Luxembourg*, 2 vols. (Atglen, Pa., 1995), 2:354–57.

190. Ibid., 355.

191. In 2001, the Smithsonian Institution sponsored an exhibition of these magazine covers from the summer of 1942, collected by Marguerite Storm of Pacific Palisades, California. For a catalogue see Peter Gwillim, Kreitler, *United We Stand: Flying the American Flag* (San Francisco, 2001).

192. John Faber, ed., *Raising the Flag on Iwo Jima* (audiobook, Washington, 2002), is an interview with photographer Joseph Rosenthal, taped in 1957. Allegations that the flag-raising was a fraud, staged by the photographer, were made by reporter Robert Sherrod in 1945 and published in *Time*. The accusations were entirely false, and Sherrod issued a retraction, but they were repeated in an iconoclastic work by Karal Ann Marling and John Wetenhall, *Iwo Jima: Monuments, Memorials, and the American Hero* (Cambridge, Mass., 1991). The record is set straight by Parker Bishop Albee and Keller Cushing Freeman, *Shadow of Suribachi: Raising the Flags on Iwo Jima* (New York, 1995); and Tedd Thomey, *Immortal Images, A Personal History of Two Photographers and the Flag Raising on Iwo Jima* (Annapolis, 1996).

193. Norman Rockwell, *My Adventures as an Illustrator* (Garden City, N.Y., 1960).

194. Ibid., 323.

195. Ibid., 338.

196. Franklin D. Roosevelt, speech to Congress on Lend-Lease, fifth typed draft with changes in his own hand, Franklin D. Roosevelt Presidential Library, Hyde Park, N.Y.

197. Stuart Murray, James McCabe, et al., *Norman Rockwell's Four Freedoms* (Stockbridge, Mass., 1993), 38–43.

198. Rockwell, *My Adventures,* 339.

199. Ibid., 341.

200. Murray, McCabe, et al., *Norman Rockwell's Four Freedoms,* 59.

201. Ibid., 65.

202. Ibid., 67.

A People Among Others

1. David Behrens, "It's Official: Peace at Last, Long Island Marks V-J Day," http://www.lihistory.com/7/hs739a.htm; Naomi Bliven, "V-J Night: The Way It Was," *New Yorker,* 14 Aug. 1995; Chalmers Roberts, "Peace at Last! Cheers Erupt in Washington," *Washington Post,* 26 July 1995; Eric F. Goldman, *The Crucial Decade—And After: America, 1945–1960* (New York, 1973), 3–15.

2. Behrens, "It's Official: Peace at Last"; Bliven, "V-J Night." Some of the most vivid accounts of V-J Day were the eyewitness reports of radio journalists: NBC's Ben Grauer from Times Square, Don Eldridge from Chicago's Loop, and others can be heard on the Web at "Radio News—V-J Day," http://www.otr.com/vj.html.

3. "The Smack Seen Round the World, 1945"; "Edith Shain Says She's the V-J Nurse"; "Eleven Sailors and Three Nurses Say They're the True Smoochers," *Life,* Aug. 1980, http://www.life.com/Life/special/kiss01.html.

4. Two weeks later, on September 2, 1945, the instrument of surrender was signed aboard the battleship *Missouri,* and President Truman proclaimed another official V-J Day, which was observed in a more solemn way, with church services and reflective speeches. But when Americans of that generation spoke of V-J Day, they remembered the first spontaneous celebrations, which remained as vivid in their minds as the day of Pearl Harbor.

5. "VJ Day," http://members.aol.com/clarcoog/auto34.html.

6. Lucinda Eddy, "War Comes to San Diego," *Journal of San Diego History* 39 (1993), 114–19.

7. William T. Paull, "Memoirs," http://www.sihope.com/~tipi/chap18.html.

8. *San Francisco Examiner,* qtd. in "V-J Day (Victory over Japan)," http://www.vikingphoenix.com.

9. Goldman, *Crucial Decade—And After,* 4.

10. Alonzo L. Hamby, *Man of the People: A Life of Harry S. Truman* (New York, 1995), 295.

11. "Who Is the Kissing Sailor?" *Life,* Oct. 1980, http://www.life.com/Life/special/kiss03.html.

12. Michael J. Bennett, *When the Dreams Came True: The GI Bill and the Making of Modern America* (London and Washington, 1996), 125.

13. Morton Keller and Phyllis Keller, *Making Harvard Modern* (New York, 2001), 30; David M. Kennedy, *Freedom from Fear: The American People in Depression and War, 1929–1945* (New York, 1999), 787; Keith W. Olson, *The GI Bill, the Veterans, and the Colleges* (Louisville, Ky., 1974), 25.

14. Olson, *GI Bill*, 42–49; Bennett, *When the Dreams Came True*, 237–76.

15. President George W. Bush signed legislation for expanded loans for any veteran who served at least ninety days on active duty in time of war, effective as of January 1, 2002. See "For Veterans a Higher Limit on No-Down-Payment Loans," *Boston Globe*, 5 Jan. 2002, E1.

16. Conversation of James B. Conant with John Henry Fischer.

17. Olson, *GI Bill*; Goldman, *Crucial Decade—and After*, 4–14, 49–50; Kennedy, *Freedom from Fear*, 787.

18. For histories from different perspectives see James G. Bradsher, "Taking America's Heritage to the People: The Freedom Train Story," *Prologue* 17 (1985), 228–45; Stuart L. Little, "The Freedom Train: Citizenship and Postwar Political Culture, 1946–1949," *American Studies* 34 (1993), 35–67; Michael Kammen, *Mystic Chords of Memory* (New York, 1991); 576–79; Eric Foner, *The Story of American Freedom* (New York, 1998), 249–52.

19. Little, "Freedom Train," 41.

20. Bradsher, "Taking America's Heritage to the People," 230.

21. Little, "Freedom Train," 40.

22. Ibid., 48.

23. Ibid., 60.

24. Ibid., 36, 42.

25. "Freedom Train Tours America," *National Geographic* 96 (Oct. 1949), 529–42.

26. Ibid.

27. Langston Hughes, "Freedom Train," in *Selected Poems* (New York, 1981), 276–78, and idem, "Freedom Train," 78 rpm recording by Paul Robeson, 1947.

28. Manuscript or first printing of Langston Hughes, "Freedom Train," in *Selected Poems* (New York, 1981), 276–78

29. Bradsher, "Taking America's Heritage to the People," 231–37.

30. Since 1990, a new historiography of the Cold War has developed throughout the world. It has revised the American revisionists who argued (1960–90) that Soviet leaders were pursuing the traditional goals of Russian nationalism and that the United States caused the Cold War to protect its hegemony, to promote capitalist imperialism, and to prevent third world nations from becoming independent. The revisionists believed that the United States and the Soviet Union were on the same moral plane, or even that the United States was the more culpable. In foreign affairs they thought that the United States recklessly engaged in nuclear diplomacy for its own selfish interests. In domestic affairs they believed that Alger Hiss and the Rosenbergs were innocent victims of right-wing "Red-baiting" in a great repression of civil liberties. This interpretation appeared during the late 1950s and 1960s in the work of Gabriel Kolko, Gar Alperovitz, William Appleman Williams, and Barton Bernstein, and in even more extreme forms after Vietnam, from a second generation of New Left historians in the United States, who began to call themselves Marxists, shortly before the fall of the Soviet Union.

At the same time, American writers on the far right created another revisionist historiography. It excoriated centrist leaders in the United States from Roosevelt to Kennedy and Johnson for failing to stand strongly against Stalin at Yalta, for the loss of eastern Europe and China, for the defeat in Vietnam, and for the loss of the Cold War.

Then came the collapse of the Soviet Union and the liberation of eastern Europe by its own people. After 1989, many materials emerged from Soviet archives and from classified American sources such as the Venona transcripts. This evidence documented the depth of evil in the Communist regimes, the primary role of Soviet leaders in the origins of the Cold War, and the guilt of Alger Hiss and the Rosenbergs. It also produced more sympathetic understandings of American leaders and a more positive view of their policies. See Stéphane Courtois et al., *Le Livre noir du communisme: Crimes, terreur, répression* (Paris, 1997); John Lewis Gaddis, *We Now Know: Rethinking Cold War History* (Oxford, 1997); Alexander Fursenko and Timothy Naftali, *"One Hell of a Gamble": Khrushchev, Castro, and Kennedy, 1958–1964* (New York, 1997); Walter Isaacson and Evan Thomas, *The Wise Men* (New York, 1986); Mary L. Dudziak, *Cold War Civil Rights: Race and the Image of American Democracy* (Princeton, 2000).

31. Courtois et al., *Le Livre noir*, 14; an English translation is promised from the Harvard University Press.

32. Qtd. in Sidney Webb and Beatrice Webb, *Soviet Communism: A New Civilization?* (London, 1936), 1036.

33. Robert Conquest, *Stalin* (London, 1991), 265.

34. Hamby, *Man of the People*, 270–71.

35. Isaacson and Thomas, *Wise Men*, 644–45.

36. Forrest C. Pogue, *George C. Marshall: Statesman, 1945–59* (New York, 1987), 514.

37. Harry S. Truman, "Memorandum," May 23, 1945, reproduced in Hamby, *Man of the People*, 313; "Farewell Address," 15 Jan. 1953, *Public Papers, 1952–53*, 1197; George Marshall, "Washington Birthday Remarks at Princeton University, February 22, 1947," and "Address at Harvard University, June 5, 1947," rpt. as appendices to Pogue, *George C. Marshall: Statesman*, 523–28; Dean Acheson, *Present at the Creation* (New York, 1969); John McCloy, *The Atlantic Alliance* (New York, 1969); George Kennan, *Memoirs, 1925–1950* (Boston, 1967); Charles Bohlen, *The Transformation of American Foreign Policy* (New York, 1969).

38. Isaacson and Thomas, *The Wise Men*, 350.

39. The Long Telegram appears as "Chargé in the Soviet Union (Kennan) to the Secretary of State, February 22, 1946," *Foreign Relations of the United States, 1946*, vol. 6, *Eastern Europe, the Soviet Union* (Washington, 1969), 696–709; "X" [George F. Kennan], "The Sources of Soviet Conduct," *Foreign Affairs* 24 (1947), 566–82.

40. In World War I, the United States insisted on being an associated rather than an allied power. In the Second World War no formal alliance was made by the United States. President Franklin Roosevelt feared that the response of Republicans and conservative Democrats in the Senate might disrupt the war effort.

41. David Hackett Fischer, *Paul Revere's Ride* (New York, 1994).

42. An extraordinary collection of Minuteman artifacts has been assembled by Brad Bigham, Concord, Mass.

43. Alonzo L. Hamby, ed., *Harry S. Truman and the Fair Deal* (Lexington, Mass., 1974), 175.

44. Cissie Dore Hill, "Voices of Hope: The Story of Radio Free Europe and Radio Liberty," *Hoover Digest,* Fall 2001; http://www.hoover.stanford.edu/publications/digest/014/dorehill.html.

45. Dwight Eisenhower, "Farewell Address," 17 Jan. 1961, *Public Papers of the Presidents, 1960* (Washington, 1961), 1035–45.

46. Louis Smith, *American Democracy and Military Power* (Chicago, 1951); Gordon B. Turner, ed., *A History of Military Affairs in Western Society Since the Eighteenth Century* (New York, 1952, 1953), required reading in service academies and ROTC programs during the Cold War.

47. Richard Rovere, *The General and the President and the Future of American Foreign Policy* (New York, 1951); D. Clayton James, *The Years of MacArthur,* 3 vols. (Boston, 1970–85); Hamby, *Man of the People;* David McCullough, *Truman* (New York, 1992).

48. Paul L. Murphy, *The Constitution in Crisis Times* (New York, 1972), 257–59.

49. David Caute, *The Great Fear: The Anti-Communist Purge Under Truman and Eisenhower* (New York, 1978); Ellen Schrecker, *Many Are the Crimes: McCarthyism in America* (Boston, 1998).

50. Goldman, *Crucial Decade—And After,* 145.

51. A pathbreaking book of high importance is Mary L. Dudziak, *Cold War Civil Rights: Race and the Image of American Democracy* (Princeton, 2000)

52. Gunnar Myrdal, *An American Dilemma* (New York, 1944); For Baltimore, see Elinor Pancoast et al., The Report of a Study on Desegregation of the Baltimore City Schools (Baltimore, 1956).

53. James T. Patterson, *Brown v. Board of Education* (New York, 2001); Richard Kluger, *Simple Justice: The History of* Brown v. Board of Education *and Black America's Struggle for Equality* (New York, 1983).

54. Langston Hughes, "Refugee in America," in *Selected Poems* (New York, 1959), 290.

55. Hamby, *Man of the People,* 433.

56. President's Committee on Civil Rights, *To Secure These Rights* (Washington, 1948); Dudziak, *Cold War Civil Rights,* 79.

57. Dudziak, *Cold War Civil Rights,* 90, 94.

58. Ira Glass, *Visions of Liberty: The Bill of Rights for All Americans* (New York, 1991), 221–23.

59. For primary materials see Howell Raines, ed., *My Soul Is Rested: Movement Days in the Deep South Remembered* (New York, 1977); David J. Garrow, ed., *The Walking City: The Montgomery Bus Boycott, 1955–56* (Brooklyn, 1989); Stewart Burns, ed., *Daybreak of Freedom: The Montgomery Bus Boycott* (Chapel Hill, 1997).

60. Rosa Parks with Jim Haskins, *Rosa Parks: My Story* (New York, 1992); Douglas Brinkley, *Rosa Parks* (New York, 2000).

61. *Gayle v. Browder,* 352 U.S. 903 (1856).

62. Rosa Parks statue, sculpture sold by Ebenezer Baptist Church color illustration on their Web site, www.ebenezer.org

63. Parks, *Rosa Parks: My Story* (New York, 1982); Brinkley, *Rosa Parks.* Memoirs of close friends include Johnnie Carr, *Johnnie: The Life of Johnnie Rebecca Carr*

(Montgomery, Ala., 1995); Virginia Durr, *Outside the Magic Circle* (Tuscaloosa, Ala., 1985); and Jo Ann Robinson, *The Montgomery Bus Boycott and the Women Who Started It* (Knoxville, 1989).

64. Frank Adams with Myles Horton, *Unearthing Seeds of Fire: The Idea of Highlander* (Winston-Salem, N.C., 1975); Aimee Horton, *The Highlander Folk School: A History of Its Major Programs* (New York, 1989); John Glen, *Highlander: No Ordinary School* (Knoxville, 1996); Aldon D. Morris, *Origins of the Civil Rights Movement: Black Communities Organizing for Change* (New York, 1984).

65. Robinson, *The Montgomery Bus Boycott and the Women Who Started It;* Charles M. Payne, *I've Got the Light of Freedom* (Berkeley, 1996), 416.

66. Rosa Parks with Gregory J. Reed, *Quiet Strength* (Grand Rapids, 1994); Rosa Parks, *Dear Mrs. Parks* (New York, 1996).

67. For general works: David Garrow, *Bearing the Cross: Martin Luther King Jr. and the Southern Christian Leadership Conference* (New York, 1986); Taylor Branch, *Parting the Waters: America in the King Years, 1954–63* (New York, 1988).

68. Martin Luther King Jr., *Autobiography*, ed. Clayborne Carson (New York, 1998), 20, 23.

69. Ibid., 23.

70. Martin Luther King Jr., *Stride Toward Freedom: The Montgomery Story* (New York, 1958).

71. King, *Autobiography,* 60

72. Ibid., 60–61.

73. John Lewis, interview, 23 Feb. 1999, http://www.time.com/time/community/tran scripts/1999/022399lewis.html.

74. Martin Luther King, "I Have a Dream," in James M. Washington, ed., *Martin Luther King: I Have a Dream, Writings and Speeches That Changed the World* (New York, 1996), 102–6; as pub. in *Negro History Bulletin* 21 (May 1968), 16–17.

75. The mass media also popularized a simplified history in which King "launched the civil rights movement," much to the resentment of others and to the embarrassment of King himself. Richard Lentz, *Symbols, the Newsmagazine, and Martin Luther King* (Baton Rouge, 1990).

76. Payne, *I've Got the Light of Freedom,* 397.

77. Branch, *Parting the Waters;* David Garrow, *Protest at Selma* (New Haven, 1978); John J. Ansbro, *Martin Luther King Jr.: The Making of a Mind* (1982).

78. Dudziak, *Cold War Civil Rights,* 158–59; Harris Wofford, *Of Kennedys and Kings: Making Sense of the Sixties* (New York, 1980), 125; Richard Reeves, *President Kennedy: Profile of Power* (New York, 1994), 123; James T. Patterson, *Grand Expectations: The United States, 1945–1974* (New York, 1996), 475; Todd Gitlin, *The Sixties* (1987; rev. trade ed., New York, 1993), 140–43. See also Jonathan Rosenberg and Zachary Karabell, *Kennedy, Johnson, and the Quest for Justice: The Civil Rights Tapes* (New York, 2003), 32, which conclude that "on the whole, relations between civil rights leaders and the Kennedy administration became increasingly strained in 1961 and 1962. John Kennedy simply was not that interested in civil rights. From his vantage point, the denial of black rights was an old wrong that would take many years to fix, compared to the challenges of the international situation."

79. Cecil J. Williams, *Freedom and Justice: Four Decades of the Civil Rights Struggle, as Seen by a Black Photographer of the Deep South* (Macon, Ga., 1996), 27.

80. Ibid., 146, 214.

81. Sara Evans, *Personal Politics: The Roots of Women's Liberation in the Civil Rights Movement and the New Left* (New York, 1979).

82. Barbara Deckard, *The Women's Movement* (New York, 1979), 332.

83. Betty Friedan, *The Feminine Mystique* (New York, 1963); Nancy Cott and Elizabeth Pleck, *A Heritage of Her Own: Toward a New Social History of American Women* (New York, 1979).

84. Bruno Bettelheim, "Individual and Mass Behavior in Extreme Situations," *Journal of Abnormal Psychology* 38 (1943), 432–50; Eugen Kogon, *The Theory and Practice of Hell* (New York, 1946); Olga Lengyel, *Five Chimneys: The Story of Auschwitz* (Chicago, 1947). For other work influenced by this literature see Stanley Elkins, *Slavery* (Chicago, 1959; 2d ed., 1968).

85. Judith Hole and Ellen Levine, *Rebirth of Feminism* (New York, 1971), 81.

86. Gerda Lerner, *The Majority Finds Its Past* (New York, 1979), 38–39 and "Women's Rights and American Feminism," *American Scholar* 40 (1971), 235–48; for an understanding of the movement centered on equality see William H. Chafe, *Women and Equality: Changing Patterns in American Culture* (New York, 1977).

87. Evans, *Personal Politics*, 214–15.

88. William Wordsworth, *The French Revolution as It Appears to Enthusiasts* (London, 1804); also in "The Prelude," bk. 11., l. 108.

89. Foner, *Story of American Freedom*, 308, 234; F. A. Hayek, *The Road to Serfdom* (1944; new ed., Chicago, 1994).

90. Foner, *Story of American Freedom*, 236, 308; John Gray, *Hayek on Liberty* (Oxford, 1984); George H. Nash, *The Conservative Intellectual Movement in America Since 1945* (New York, 1976); Jerome Himelstein, *To the Right: The Transformation of American Conservatism* (Berkeley, 1990).

91. For general histories of high quality (but with different taxonomies of conservative groups) see Jonathan M. Schoenwald, *A Time for Choosing: The Rise of Modern American Conservatism* (New York, 2001); William B. Hixson Jr., *Search for the American Right Wing* (Princeton, 1992); Nash, *Conservative Intellectual Movement in America*.

92. Milton Friedman, *Capitalism and Freedom* (Chicago, 1962).

93. George M. Marsden, *Fundamentalism and American Culture: The Shaping of Twentieth-Century Evangelicalism, 1870–1925* (New York, 1980).

94. Kenneth Durr, "When Southern Politics Came North: The Roots of White Working Class Conservatism in Baltimore, 1940–1964," *Labor History* 37 (1996), 309–31.

95. Schoenwald, *Time for Choosing*, 100–123.

96. William F. Buckley Jr., *God and Man at Yale* (Chicago, 1951); on Young Americans for Freedom see Lawrence F. Schiff, "The Obedient Rebels: A Study of College Conversions to Conservatism," *Journal of Social Issues* 20 (1964); and Richard G. Braungart, "SDS and YAF: A Comparison of Two Student Radical Groups in the Mid-1960s," *Youth and Society* 2 (1971).

97. Barry Goldwater, *Conscience of a Conservative* (Washington: 1960); autobiogra-

phies include *With No Apologies* (New York, 1979), and *Goldwater* (New York, 1988); leading biographies are Robert A. Goldberg, *Barry Goldwater* (New Haven, 1995), and Lee Edwards, *Goldwater* (Washington, 1995). On the election, F. Clifton White and William J. Gill, *Suite 3505* (New Rochelle, N.Y., 1967), and Theodore White, *The Making of the President—1964* (New York, 1965).

98. Todd Gitlin et al., "Port Huron Statement," 1962; Kirkpatrick Sale, *SDS* (New York, 1973); Foner, *Story of American Freedom,* 287–91; Massimo Teodori, ed., *The New Left: A Documentary History* (Indianapolis, 1969).

99. For general works, Sale, *SDS;* Teodori, *New Left;* John Diggins, *The American Left in the Twentieth Century* (New York, 1973); Paul Berman, *A Tale of Two Utopias: The Political Journey of the Generation of 1968* (New York, 1996).

100. Ann Charters, *Kerouac* (New York, 1973).

101. Ibid., 43–63; Michael Schumacher, *Dharma Lion: A Critical Biography of Allen Ginsberg* (New York, 1992), 23–66; James Grauerholz and Ira Silverberg, eds., *Word Virus: The William S. Burroughs Reader* (New York, 1999). Silverberg knew Burroughs for many years at the Grove Press.

102. Carolyn Cassady, *Off the Road: My Years with Cassady, Kerouac, and Ginsberg* (New York, 1990), 385.

103. John Clellon Holmes, "This Is the Beat Generation," *New York Times Magazine,* 16 Nov. 1952; idem, "The Game of the Name," (1965), in Ann Charters, ed., *The Portable Beat Reader* (New York, 1992), 619–26; Jack Kerouac, "Origins of the Beat Generation," *Playboy,* June 1959, also recorded on *The Jack Kerouac Collection* (Rhino Records, 1990); Allen Ginsberg, "A Definition of the Beat Generation," *Friction* 1 (Winter 1982–83), 50–52, rpt. in Bill Morgan ed., *Deliberate Prose, Selected Essays 1952–1995: Allen Ginsberg* (New York, 2000), 236–39.

104. Jack Kerouac, *On the Road* (New York, 1957); also idem, *The Dharma Bums* (New York, 1958) and *The Subterraneans* (New York, 1958); an excellent collection of primary materials on the beat movement by its leading scholar is Ann Charters's *Portable Beat Reader.*

105. Charters, *Kerouac,* 288.

106. Jack Kerouac, *Selected Letters, 1940–1956* (New York, 1995), vii; also idem, *Selected Letters, 1957–1969* (New York, 1999), ix; on his historical method, see Charters, *Kerouac,* 360.

107. Among many accounts of the Six Gallery reading are Michael McClure, *Scratching the Beat Surface* (San Francisco, 1982); Allen Ginsberg and Gregory Corso, "The Six Gallery Reading," *Deliberate Prose,* 239–42; Kerouac, *Dharma Bums,* ch. 2.

108. Allen Ginsberg, *Howl, Original Draft Facsimile, Transcript and Variant versions, Fully Annotated by the Author, with Contemporaneous Correspondence, Account of First Public Reading, Legal Skirmishes, Precursor Texts, and Bibliography* (New York, 1986); idem, *Howl of the Censor* (San Carlos, Calif., 1956).

109. Gary Susman, "Word Virus," *Boston Phoenix,* 8 Feb. 1999; Grauerholz and Silverberg, *Word Virus.*

110. Charters, *Kerouac,* 365.

111. Jay Stevens, *Storming Heaven: LSD and the American Dream* (New York, 1987)

112. Jonah Raskin, *For the Hell of It: The Life and Times of Abbie Hoffman* (Berkeley, 1996).

113. Paul Goodman, *Communitas* (New York, 1960).

114. A major work is forthcoming from Fred Turner of Stanford University.

115. Timothy Miller, *The Hippies and American Values* (Knoxville, 1991), 61–62.

116. Ibid., 61.

117. The promoters' story is told in Joel Rosenman, John Roberts, and Robert Pilpel, *Young Men with Unlimited Capital: The Story of Woodstock* (1974; Houston, 1999).

118. Laura Joplin, *Love, Janis* (New York, 1992), a memoir by her sister; Myra Friedman, *Buried Alive: The Biography of Janis Joplin* (New York, 1973), an account by an acquaintance who worked for Joplin's manager; David Dalton, *Piece of My Heart: The Life, Times, and Legend of Janis Joplin* (New York, 1985), by an editor of *Rolling Stone.*

119. Friedman, *Buried Alive,* 24–33; Joplin, *Love, Janis,* 54–55; Dalton, *Piece of My Heart,* 151–52.

120. Dalton, *Piece of My Heart,* 169, 241.

121. Janis Joplin, "Me and Bobby McGee," by Kris Kristofferson, on *Pearl,* Columbia CD KC30322; Colleen O'Conner, "Kris Kristofferson . . . ," *Dallas Morning News,* 4 March 1990; Maurice Isserman and Michael Kazin, *America Divided* (New York, 2000), 161–63.

122. Curtis Knight, *Jimi: An Intimate Biography of Jimi Hendrix* (New York, 1974), 12, 190; Knight was a close friend, who often performed with Hendrix.

123. Jimi Hendrix, "Stone Free," on *Stone Free: A Tribute to Jimi Hendrix* Warner Brothers CD45438; lyrics from LeosLyrics.com.

124. Jerry Rubin, *Do It,* Echols, 17.

125. David Hackett Fischer, *The Great Wave: Price Revolutions in World History* (New York, 1996).

126. Philip M. Isaacson, *The American Eagle* (Boston: Little, Brown, 1975).

127. Robert Justin Goldstein, *Saving "Old Glory": The History of the American Flag Desecration Controversy* (Boulder, Colo., 1995), 99–194.

128. Scot Guenter, "The Hippies and the Hardhats: The Struggle for Semiotic Control of the Flag of the United States in the 1960s," *Flag Bulletin* 130 (1989), 139.

128. Songs from Bob Dylan, *Lyrics, 1962–1985* (New York, 1990).

129. Charters, *Portable Beat Reader,* 370–71.

130. Gitlin, *Sixties,* 200–201.

131. Alex Weiner and Deanne Stillman, *Woodstock Census: The Nationwide Survey of the Sixties Generation* (New York, 1979), 242–43.

132. Gitlin, *Sixties,* 199.

134. Flip Schulke, *He Had a Dream: Martin Luther King and the Civil Rights Movement* (New York, 1995), 44, 45, 98; Williams, *Freedom and Justice,* 77–126, 143–66, 193–238.

135. Irene Dispatch, "A Family Divided," http://www.ustrek.org/odyssey.

136. Stokely Carmichael, speech at Garfield High School, Seattle, 19 April 1967; transcript on the IRC's Stokely Carmichael Page, http://courses.washington.edu/spcmu/carmichael.

137. Ibid.

138. John Lewis, interview, 23 Feb. 1999, http://www.time.com/time/community/transcripts/ 1999/02239lewis.html.

139. *New York Times,* 16 Nov. 1998.

140. Robert Conot, *Rivers of Blood, Years of Darkness: The Unforgettable Classic Account of the Watts Riot* (New York, 1968), an excellent history; Robert Fogelson, *The Los Angeles Riots* (New York, 1969); Governor's Commission on the Los Angeles Riots, *Violence in the City—An End or a Beginning* (Los Angeles, 1965); Audrey Rawitscher, *Riots in the City: An Addendum to the McCone Commission Report* (Los Angeles, 1967).

141. David Wallechinsky, *The Complete Book of the Olympics* (Boston, 1991); Rebecca Nelson and Marie J. MacNee, *The Olympic Factbook* (1996).

142. Wallechinsky, *Complete Book of the Olympics.*

143. Ibid., Steven W. Pope, "Ethnicity and Race in North American Sport," *Sporting Traditions* 12 (1996), 99–106; Jim McKay, "'Just Do It': Corporate Sports Slogans and the Political Economy of Enlightened Racism," *Discourse: Studies in the Cultural Politics of Education* 16 (1995), 191–205.

144. Rudolph Vecoli, "The Lady and the Huddled Masses," in Wilton S. Dillon and Neil G. Kotler, eds., *The Statue of Liberty Revisited* (Washington, 1994), 68n.

145. Robert Asher and Charles Stephenson, eds., *Labor Divided: Race and Ethnicity in United States Labor Struggles, 1835–1960* (Albany, 1990), 3.

146. Ronald Formisano, *Boston Against Busing: Race, Class, and Ethnicity in the 1960s and 1970s* (Chapel Hill, 1991).

147. What follows is taken from a two-part story by Thomas Farragher, "Image of an Era," *Boston Sunday Globe*, 1 April 2001; and "Beyond the Flag's Fury," *Boston Globe*, 2 April 2001.

148. Ibid.

149. Stanley Forman, "Photo of Incident in City Hall Plaza, *Boston Herald*, 6 April 1976

150. U.S. Bureau of the Census, *Historical Statistics of the United States;* U.S. Bureau of Labor Statistics, *Employment and Earnings* (Washington, 2001).

151. Patterson, *Grand Expectations*, 644.

152. Ibid., 647.

153. Weiner and Stillman, *Woodstock Census*, 174.

154. Ibid., 174–75.

155. Echols, *Daring to Be Bad*, 105.

156. Ibid., 205.

157. National Organization for Women, "1998 Declaration of Sentiments," http://www.rtpnet.org/ncnow.

158. Echols, *Daring to Be Bad*, 16.

159. Foner, *Story of American Freedom*, 271.

160. Ibid., 272.

161. R. Fischer, *Them Damned Pictures*, 204.

162. Qtd. in David Gergen, *Eyewitness to Power* (New York, 2000), 19.

163. These examples are taken from R. Fischer, *Them Damned Pictures*, 201–25.

164. See Gerald R. Ford, *A Time to Heal: The Autobiography of Gerald Ford* (New York, 1979); John Robert Greene, *The Presidency of Gerald Ford* (Lawrence, Kansas, 1995); Erwin C. Hargrove, *Jimmy Carter as President: Leadership and Politics of the Public Good* (Baton Rouge, 1988); Gaddis Smith, *Morality, Reason, Power: American Diplomacy in the Carter Years* (New York, 1986); Jimmy Carter, *Keeping Faith: Memoirs of a President* (New York, 1982).

165. *Newsweek,* 13 Oct. 1980, 83, qtd. in R. Fischer, *Them Damned Pictures,* xii, 17.

166. Gallup Organization, "State of the Nation," 6 Aug. 2002.

167. D. H. Fischer, *Great Wave,* 217–28; data on inflation, unemployment, crime, drug use, and family disruption in *Statistical Abstract of the United States* (1993), tables 101, 102, 208, 220, 300, 756; also Federal Bureau of Investigation, *Uniform Crime Reports* (1993–94). For violent crime precisely the same patterns appear in crime reports and mortality data, which are independently derived.

168. R. Fischer, *Them Damned Pictures,* 166, 167; Dani Aguila, ed. and comp., *Taking Liberty with the Lady* (McLean, Va., 1986).

169. Peter Novick, *That Noble Dream: The "Objectivity Question" and the American Historical Profession* (Cambridge, 1988).

170. Roderick P. Hart, *Verbal Style and the Presidency* (Orlando, Fla., 1984), 214.

171. Fischer, *Them Damned Pictures,* 123.

172. Hart, *Verbal Style and the Presidency,* 217, 221.

173. Ibid., 221.

174. *New York Times,* 28 Aug. 2000.

175. *Boston Globe,* 29 June 1997.

176. Richard Seth Hayden and Thierry W. Despont, *Restoring the Statue of Liberty: Sculpture, Structure, Symbol* (New York, 1986), 59.

177. "Being in Total Control of Herself" quilt by Yvonne Wells, in Maude S. D. Wahlman, *Signs and Symbols: African Images in African American Quilts* (New York, 1993), 74.

178. Herman Melville, *Redburn* (1849; Boston, 1924), 169–70.

179. Ralph Henry Gabriel, *The Course of American Democratic Thought* (New York, 1940, 1956), 46.

180. Horace M. Kallen, *Cultural Pluralism and the American Idea* (Philadelphia, 1956).

181. Ibid., 113.

182. Lawrence H. Fuchs, *The American Kaleidoscope: Race, Ethnicity, and the Civic Culture* (Hanover, 1990), 273.

183. Ibid., 77, 126.

184. *Boston Globe,* 3 Nov. 1993.

185. *New York Times,* 4 Nov. 1993.

186. Ibid.

187. Ibid.

188. Something similar had happened twice before. From 1789 to 1837, every American president but one (John Quincy Adams) had held high office or served in uniform during the American Revolution. From 1861 to 1901, every president had held high office or served in uniform during the Civil War. Altogether men who served in those wars led the country for 154 of 218 years from 1776 to 1993.

189. Clinton, "Stand Up for Peace," speech at Dundalk, Ireland, 12 Dec. 2000, CNN.com, 13 Dec. 2000.

190. Clinton, "Shared Values and Soaring Spirit," *USIA Electronic Journal* 3 (June 1998), 1–2.

191. Clinton, "One America in the 21st Century," commencement address, University of California at San Diego, 14 June 1997.

192. *New York Times,* 18 Aug. 2001.

193. David Maraniss, *First in His Class* (New York, 1995, 1996), 237–38.

194.   Molly Ivins, *Shrub* (New York, 2000), 194.

195.   Ibid., 195.

196.   On the PBS *NewsHour with Jim Lehrer,* 27 April 2000.

197.   Myron Magnet, *The Dream and the Nightmare: The Sixties' Legacy to the Underclass* (New York, 1993); Peter Collier and David Horowitz, *Destructive Generation: Second Thoughts about the '60s* (New York, 1996); Bill Minutaglio, *First Son: George W. Bush and the Bush Family Dynasty* (New York, 1999, 2001), 167, 290, 314.

198.   George W. Bush, speech at Al Smith Memorial Dinner, New York City, 19 Oct. 2000, CNN.com, 20 Oct. 2000.

199.   Minutaglio, *First Son,* 256.

200.   Marvin Olasky, *The Tragedy of American Compassion* (Wheaton, Ill., and Washington, 1992).

201.   A recording of the pilot's interview appears on CNN.com, "Witnesses to the Moment: Worker's Voices," 11 Sept. 2001, posted 9:11 P.M. EDT; http://www.cnn.com/2001/CAREER?trends/09/11/witnesses/index.html.

202.   For weeks afterward, the *New York Times* published a daily revision of the casualty list.

203.   *New York Times,* 12 Sep 2001.

204.   This from a team of investigative reporters for the *New York Times,* 16 Sept. 2001, 16.

205.   On Adams and Hancock see D. H. Fischer, *Paul Revere's Ride,* 174–83; on Madison see Anthony S. Pitch, *The Burning of Washington* (Annapolis, 1998), 96–97, 125–33; Irving Brant, *James Madison, Commander in Chief* (Indianapolis, 1961), 298–315.

206.   Interview with Jane Garvey, *Boston Globe Magazine,* 4 Nov. 2001.

207.   Neil Lewis and David Johnston, "Jubilant Calls on Sept. 11 Led to F.B.I. Arrests," *New York Times,* 28 Oct. 2001.

208.   For Madeline Sweeney, *Boston Globe,* 21 Sept. 2001.

209.   See the examples in D. H. Fischer, *Paul Revere's Ride.*

210.   Benjamin Rush to John Adams, 13 July 1780, in Lyman Butterfield, ed., *Letters of Benjamin Rush,* 2 vols. (Princeton, 1951), 1:253.

211.   On April 19, 1775, at least fifty Americans were killed by British troops in a population of 3 million. On September 11, 2001, 3,119 people were killed by terrorists in a population of 300 million. The death rate was a little more than 17 per million in 1775, compared with a little more than 10 per million in 2001. In the attack on Pearl Harbor, 2,403 people were killed, missing, or died of wounds in a population of 133 million; the Pearl Harbor death rate was 18 per million. For sources see D. H. Fischer, *Paul Revere's Ride,* app.; and Samuel Eliot Morison, *The Rising Sun in the Pacific,* vol. 3 of his *History of United States Naval Operations in World War II,* 126–27. Estimates of 9/11 casualties are revised to 5 Jan. 2002 and appear in the *New York Times,* 7 Jan. 2002. All of these numbers shrank from earlier estimates.

   Relative losses were much greater in earlier surprise attacks. When a large force of French and Indians attacked the town of Deerfield on the night of February 28–29, 1704, the number killed was reckoned in two lists at 47 or 53. Another 111 were captured, and some suffered a fate worse than death. In a total colonial population of about 300,000, the death rate was 156 per million, much larger relative to population than the World Trade Center. The Virginia massacre of 1622 killed 347 people in a colonial population of 1,240, which in relative terms was incomparably more than the victims of terrorism in 2001.

See also Pitch, *Burning of Washington;* Kenneth Stampp, *And the War Came: The North and the Secession Crisis* (New Haven, 1942); Richard Current, *Lincoln and the First Shot* (Philadelphia, 1963); W. A. Swanberg, *First Blood: The Story of Fort Sumter* (New York, 1957).

212. Jay Winik, "Security Comes First," *Wall Street Journal,* 23 Oct. 2001; Ronald K. L. Collins et al., "Liberty Comes First, War or No," *Wall Street Journal,* 30 Oct. 2001.

213. "Re: Attack on World Trade Center," http://www.wwwomen.com/talk, with 29 other postings.

214. Deborah Solomon, "Once Again, Patriotic Themes Ring True as Art," *New York Times,* 28 Oct. 2001.

215. Revision of Norman Rockwell's "Freedom from Fear," *New York Times,* 2 Nov. 2001, B12.

216. Patricia Leigh Brown, "Facing Fear and Finding Freedom on the Road," *New York Times*, 10 Oct. 2001.

217. *New York Times,* 26 Sept. 2001.

218. Cornel Nistorescu, "An Ode to America," http://www.expres.ro/evz/editori al_en.html.

Conclusion

1. André Jardin, ed., *Correspondance d'Alexis de Tocqueville et de Pierre-Paul Royer-Collard; Correspondance d'Alexis de Tocqueville et Jean Jacques Ampère* in *Oeuvres Complètes,* ed. J. P. Mayer (Paris, 1970), 11:443.

2. Ibid.

3. Jean Jacques Ampère was about to embark on the same mission. He visited America in 1851 and published his reflections as *Promenade en Amerique* (new ed., Paris, 1874).

4. Tocqueville, *L'ancien Régime et la Révolution ed André Jardin, Oeuvres, Papiers et Correspondances d'Alexis de Tocqueville, Edition définitive,* 2 vols. (Paris, 1953), 1:217; a very loose English translation appears in Stuart Gilbert, tr., *The Old Régime and the French Revolution* (Garden City, N.Y., 1955), 169.

5. Ibid.

6. *Moeurs,* usually used in the plural, is a complex French noun, sometimes rendered into English as "mores." Often it is translated as "morals," and so appears in many English and American editions of Tocqueville's works. A more accurate translation would be "customs" or "folkways."

7. Alexis de Tocqueville, "Pocket Notebook Number 3," in *Journey to America: Alexis de Tocqueville,* tr. George Lawrence, ed. J. P. Mayer (Garden City, N.Y., 1971), 149, where *moeurs* is inaccurately translated "morals." On Tocqueville and habits of the heart see James T. Schleifer, "Tocqueville and Some American Views of Liberty," in Joseph Klaits and Michael H. Haltzel, eds., *Liberty/Liberté; The American and French Experiences* (Washington and Baltimore, 1991), 51–69; also Marvin Meyers, *The Jacksonian Persuasion* (Palo Alto, 1957).

8. At the time of this writing academic historiography is still moving in the opposite direction. It is still fashionable for historians to talk of the "invention of tradition" and "imagined communities." These relativist models come mainly from Marxist scholars. They rest on a foundation of historical materialism and are mindlessly repeated by scholars who have no memory of their origins, and no understanding of their consequences, long after Marxist models that inspired them have been abandoned.

9. Tsao Hsingyuan and Fang Li Zhi, "Chinese Perspectives: A Beijing Chronicle and Chinese Views of Liberty, Democracy, and the Pursuit of Scientific Knowledge," in Wilton S. Diller and Neil G. Kotler, eds., *The Statue of Liberty Revisited* (Washington, 1994), 108.

10. Joseph D'Souza, "India, the New Word for Freedom," *Relay Magazine,* http://www.om.org/relay/stories/4-97IndiaFree.html.

11. Kanchan Banerjee, "Let Us Celebrate Freedom," Freedom Festival 1997, http://www.freeindia.org/ff97/celebrat.htm.

12. Nehru, "Awake to Freedom," 15 Aug. 1947, http://www.itihaas.com/independent/speech.html and other Web sites.

13. D'Souza, "India, the New Word for freedom."

14. "Swami Vivekananda and American Independence," http://www.vedanta-atlanta.org.

15. Ibid.

16. Bisheshwar Mishra, "Different Communities Viewed Freedom Variously . . . ," speech at Nehru University, 16 Oct. 1996; *Times of India,* 17 Oct. 1996.

17. Tagore, "Song of Free India," http://www.kamat.com/kalranga/freedom/meaning.htm.

18. Dhananjay Keer, *Dr. Ambedkar: Life and Mission* (Bombay, 1962).

19. Joanna Rogers Macy and Eleanor Zelliot, "Tradition and Innovation in Contemporary Indian Buddhism," in A. K. Narain, ed., *Studies in the History of Buddhism* (Delhi, 1980), 133–53.

20. D. S. Sesharaghavachar, "Dr. B. R. Ambedkar," http://www.freeindia.org/biographies/greatleaders/ambedkar.

21. G. M. Tartakov, "Art and Identity: The Rise of a New Buddhist Imagery," *Art Journal* 49 (1990), 409–16.

22. Ibid.

23. Mishra, "Different Communities."

24. Mary Kaldor, "Bringing Peace and Human Rights Together," public lecture, London School of Economics, 20 Oct. 1999, http://www.lse.ac.uk/Depts/global/Kaldor89.htm.

25. William Coxe, *Travels into Poland, Russia, Sweden, etc.* (1792).

26. Adam Michnik, "The Rebirth of Civil Society," public lecture, London School of Economics, 20 Oct. 1999, http://www.lse.ac.uk/Depts/global/Michnik89.htm.

27. Lech Walesa, *Lech Walesa: A Way of Hope* (New York, 1988).

28. Kaldor, "Bringing Peace and Human Rights Together."

29. *Guardian,* 8 March 1999.

30. Jonathan Steele et al, "What Price Freedom?" *Guardian,* 8 March 1999.

A PLAN OF THE SERIES

THIS BOOK is part of a series that will comprise a cultural history of the United States. The first volume, *Albion's Seed,* was about four great migrations from Britain and Ireland to America (1630–1775) and the origins of regional cultures in what is now the United States. The second volume, *American Plantations,* is still in progress. It is about the meeting of Africans and Europeans in America and the cultural consequences of that encounter.

The volume before you is the third in this series. It takes up a problem introduced in *Albion's Seed,* about the many different folk-cultures of liberty and freedom that took root in the New World. We follow them as they flowered in the Revolution, expanded in the early republic, and multiplied even to our own time. The fourth volume, *Deep Change,* also in preparation, is about a cultural transformation that followed.

Each volume is complete in itself, but all of them are part of a single enterprise. They share many features that set them apart from much academic writing in recent years.

Most important, they all address the same question, which is about the origins of an opening society in the United States; that is, a society increasingly organized on ideals of liberty and freedom. For many generations this was the central problem in American history. After the troubled years of Vietnam and Watergate many historians lost interest in it, because they lost the faith on which it rested. They no longer asked why America is an opening society, but why it is not more open. Some wrote of their own country as a closed or closing society. This series returns to the old problem. It combines a deep affirmation of American values, with something of the critical edge in more recent work.

To that end, all of my books seek a way forward by combining the strengths of two schools of historical scholarship. In the late nineteenth and early twentieth century, an old school of political and military history centered on leaders and events. In the late twentieth century, a new social history rejected *histoire evenimentielle,* and turned to problems of structure, process, and the experience of ordinary people. Much was gained in this effort, but something was lost. The new social history of the 1960s greatly expanded historical thinking in many dimensions, but it lost interest in events, contingencies, and individual choices. It grew heavily deterministic, and its protagonists too often became the objects of history rather than its agents or authors.

From that mixed record of success and failure, a question arises. What comes after the new history? This series seeks to combine elements that the old and new history tended to keep apart. It is about both elites and ordinary people, individual choices and collective experience, exceptional events and normative patterns, vernacular culture and high culture, the problem of the state and the problem of society. To those ends, it tries to keep alive the ideal of *histoire totale* by employing a concept of culture as a coherent and comprehensive whole. It also has an abiding interest in historical contingency, in the sense of people making choices and choices making a difference in the world.

In terms of epistemology, this work also tries to move forward in another way. The old history was idealist in its epistemic assumptions. Its major findings were offered as "interpretations" that tended to be discovered by intuition and supported by testimony. The founders of the new social history aspired to a more empirical method, but the epistemic revolution was incomplete, and something of the old interpretative sweep was lost in the process. This series tries to combine the interpretative thrust of the old history with the empiricism of the new—interpretative sails and empirical anchors. Every volume gives much attention to empirical evidence. The first and second volumes are ethnographic in different ways. The third volume is iconographic. It uses images, artifacts, and material culture as empirical evidence. The fourth combines quantitative data with the evidence of individual experience. In that respect, the series might be understood as a set of experiments. It tries to use empirical methods in ways that might engage both a scholar and a reader.

In the temporal dimension of historical inquiry, the Whig practitioners of the old political history recognized a close connection between the past and present. An epigram by E. A. Freeman appeared on the wall of the seminar room at Johns Hopkins, where I trained as a graduate student: "History is past politics, and politics are present history." Social historians went another way. They liked to say that "the past is a foreign country." They insisted that every period of the past should be reconstructed with respect for its integrity, rather than its relevance to the present. Something was profoundly right in that idea of integrity in the past, but something went wrong in its separation of past and present. The result was an academic antiquarianism that took a heavy toll of historical scholarship. Here again this inquiry seeks a third way. The past is not a foreign country. Our own ancestors lived there. Their acts and thoughts are an important part of our own world, and we have much to learn from their experience. This series rests on that assumption. Each volume centers on a period in the American past, and follows its problem and theme into the present.

In terms of writing, this work attempts a reunion of the old and new histories. The old political history tended to be a narrative discipline. It told stories. The new social history was more analytical. It became a problem-solving discipline, and a favorite vehicle was an academic monograph that did not take a narrative form. The empirical and analytical requirements of social history made simple storytelling difficult and even impossible in some cases. The books in this series take another approach. They are braided narratives that combine analytic writing with a story line. In all of those ways, these books seek a third way forward in historical scholarship.

A PLAN OF THE BOOK

A WORLD AT WAR: A FREE SOCIETY AND ITS ENEMIES, 1916–1945

ACKNOWLEDGMENTS

This history of liberty and freedom developed in an appropriately free and open way, with much help from many people. It began at Brandeis with two unexpected discoveries in 1995. I was gathering materials for a lecture on the iconography of the American Revolution. As the sources came together, I was surprised to discover the strength of an empirical connection between revolutionary symbols and the regional cultures that I had studied in *Albion's Seed*. My very bright Brandeis undergraduates were quick to see the interpretative possibilities, and they helped me to explore them. In particular I remember Jeremy Stern, who was full of ideas and suggestions.

A second discovery emerged from a search for the ancient origins of our modern words *liberty* and *freedom*. This ignited another train of thought. Especially helpful in that connection were conversations with my Brandeis colleague Tzvi Abusch, now at the Princeton Institute of Advanced Study and a leading expert on Middle Eastern languages. Tzvi helped me to explore the oldest known words on liberty and freedom in Mesopotamian sources, and their unexpected meanings.

From these beginnings, a book began to grow. As it did so, three colleagues invited me to do three trial runs. Charles Dew asked me to give a lecture at Williams College. I am grateful to him for that opportunity and to Charles Fuqua for suggestions about Greek and Roman materials. Ray Arsenault invited me to talk at the University of South Florida, Robert Reich gave me a chance to test some of my ideas in his faculty seminar at Brandeis, and Ralph Thaxton invited me to speak at Mary Washington College. The Templeton Foundation also invited me to present the major themes of the book to a conference of philosophers and historians at Newport. Special thanks go to Robert Nozick and Joseph Raz, who helped to refine the conceptual architecture of the book.

As the book developed, it occurred to me that the materials might lend themselves to a traveling exhibition on images of liberty and freedom. I called James Kelly, Director of Museums at the Virginia Historical Society. Jim is a leader in his field, and we have been friends for many years. He has a deep knowledge of history and an extraordinary familiarity with public and private collections of American and European art and artifacts. His wonderful exhibitions are works of art in their own right. I have formed the highest respect for his judgment, and I cherish his friendship. Jim supported the project in many ways, and we worked closely together in its development. He found many materials, reshaped the conceptual design of the book, and read the manuscript in several drafts with close attention to detail. I am deeply in his debt.

Jeffrey Ruggles at the Virginia Historical Society had a major role in this project. He turned up many materials and obtained permissions for their use. Jeffrey also became an active collaborator in the design of the book and the exhibition. It is a pleasure to work with him. Heather Beattie at the Virginia Historical Society did much of the scanning of images.

Special thanks go to Charles Bryan, very able president and CEO of the Virginia Historical Society, a first-class historian and a good friend. He has made the Society into one of the most vibrant historical institutions in the world. In the midst of his many responsibilities, Charles sat with us in our meetings and was very generous with his advice and support. The Virginia Historical Society also contributed a subvention that helped to meet the cost of the color illustrations in this book. I am very grateful to Charles and to James Kelly for their help.

Thanks also to Bertie and Bill Selvey for taking me into their gracious home on my trips to Richmond. I remember with pleasure their table talk, and their wonderful seven-headed shower that started the day with a mighty splash.

The National Endowment for the Humanities gave us a major grant for the exhibition. We are very grateful to Bruce Cole, Director of the Endowment. His intervention at a critical moment may have saved the project. Program Officer Clay Lewis helped us to refine our proposal, and he helped it through the difficult processes of review. Additional support for the exhibition came from the E. Rhodes and Leona B. Carpenter Foundation. Furthermore: A Program of the J. M. Kaplan Fund provided a grant toward the production of the book.

We were fortunate to have the advice, support, and criticism of four leading American historians of liberty and freedom. Nearly all of Eric Foner's many books have been about liberty and freedom in one way or another. He shared his expertise with us, read this book in manuscript, became an advisor to the exhibition, and was very generous with his counsel. We also have a major debt to Michael Kammen, who has written many important works on the history of liberty and freedom. Through the years, I have learned much from his creative scholarship. He gave the manuscript a rigorous reading and helped us to improve it in many ways. James McPherson also read the manuscript and helped us with problems of liberty and freedom in the nineteenth century. Pauline Maier gave us the benefit of her knowledge of the Revolutionary era and suggested ways of refining our conceptual thinking on iconographic problems.

Experts in other disciplines were very generous in helping us. I had an opportunity to consult with Whitney Smith, the leading authority in the world on vexillology, the science of flags. I remember a conversation that continued through a winter afternoon, and also an opportunity to explore his library, the best on its subject. He and his Flag Research Institute were very helpful in many ways.

Robert Hoge and Elena Stolyarik of the American Numismatic Society helped us with coins and medals, as did Philip Attwood and David Ward in the Department of Coins and

Medals at the British Museum. Scott Dolson also assisted us with political medals and badges, and Barry Jason Stein allowed us to use military insignia in his collections.

On quilts and quilting we are grateful to Barbara Barber of Westerly, Rhode Island; Julia K. Swan of Cambridge, Ohio; Carol Wagner of Roseville, Minnesota; Rebekkah Seigel in Owenton, Kentucky; and Yvonne Wells of Tuscaloosa, Alabama. Robert Hunter of *Ceramics in America* helped with ceramic materials.

Mary Haskell gave us access to her extraordinary collection of American posters, printed materials, and drawings of the twentieth century and was very generous in sharing her knowledge and her materials in that genre. I remember a happy afternoon when four of us were crawling across her living room floor, amid piles of wonderful materials that she had collected. It was a delight to work with her.

David Frent was very helpful with his unrivalled collection of political artifacts, and his unrivalled knowledge of American political artifacts. Gerald E. Czulewicz allowed us to use some of the extraordinary treasures in his collection, and he taught me much about them in our conversations on the telephone.

Michael and Pat Del Castello allowed us access to their collection of American art. Joe Kindig III gave us permission to reproduce one of the greatest early American sculptures. Joel Kopp helped us with Indian artifacts in his collection. Martin Jacobs and Stan Clark allowed us to reproduce images from their collections of artifacts from the Second World War.

Others who helped us were Alistair McMillan at Nuffield College, Oxford, who gave us permission to use his photographs of Ambedkar's shrine in India; Stanley Forman, who allowed us to reproduce his Pulitzer Prize–winning photography; and Monica Karales, who helped us get access to the original photographs of her husband, James Karales. We also wish to thank Frank Mauran of Providence, Rhode Island; Marcia Spark in Tucson, Arizona; Mr. and Mrs. Rex Starke, Gardner, Massachusetts; Elizabeth Enfield of Rockport, Massachusetts; Richard Hume; Ann Marie and Robert Cotton; the Dietrich Foundation; the Thomas Ross Collection; the Daniel J. Terra Foundation; the Chipstone Foundation; the Benjamin and Susan Shapell Foundation; and the Norman Rockwell Family Agency.

Many artists helped us with their work. Philip Ratner allowed us to reproduce his brilliant sculptures at the Statue of Liberty. Hudson Talbott was very helpful with his joyous paintings of Miss Liberty. Edward Sorel allowed us to use one of his caricatures. We are grateful to Jennifer Howard for permission to use her graphic arts, to James Mann for his mural paintings, and to Martha Cooper for her photography.

The staffs at many institutions gave us access to their holdings and permission to reproduce them in the book and exhibition. In New England, our thanks go to Leonard Brooks of the United Society of Shakers at Sabbathday Lake, in New Gloucester, Maine. We are also grateful to Hope Alswang and Barbara Rathburn at the Shelburne Museum in Vermont. In Massachusetts, we had the help of Joyce Woodman at the Concord Free Public Library, Ronald Frazier at Dedham Historical Society, Joanne Davis at the Wayland Historical Society, Leslie Morris and Susan Halpert at Harvard's Houghton Library, Kim Pashko at the Boston Museum of Fine Arts, Richard Nylander and Adrienne Sage at the Society for the Preservation of New England Antiquities, Peter Drummey and Anne E. Bentley at the Massachusetts Historical Society, Rainy Tisdale and Sue Goganian at the Bostonian Society, John R. Grimes, Marylou Curran and Claudia Scoville at the Peabody Essex Museum in Salem, and Georgia Brady Barnhill at the American Antiquarian Society in Worcester. We are also grateful to the curatorial staff of the New Bedford Whaling Museum, the Mead Art Museum at Amherst College, the Connecticut Historical Society, the Wadsworth Atheneum in Hartford, the Yale University Art Gallery in New Haven, and the John Carter Brown Library in Providence.

In New York, Morrison Heckscher went out of his way to help us with materials at the Metropolitan Museum of Art. We also wish to thank Jeri Wagner at the Met, Nicole Wells at the New-York Historical Society, Anne-Marie Reilly and Stacy Hollander at the American Museum of Folk Art, Kerry L. McGinnity in the Museum of the City of New York, Claudia Nahson at the Jewish Museum, Dr. Joshua Brown at the American Social History Project in the City University of New York, Martha Cooper of the Municipal Art League of New York, Leslie De Georges at Scalamandré in New York City, Mark Hunt at the Franklin D. Roosevelt Library and Museum, Bob Sullivan of the Schenectady County Public Library, William Dimpelfeld and Jo Mordecai at the Schenectady Historical Society, Kim Yi at W. W. Norton & Co., Fred Allen at American Heritage Publishing Company, Jeff Dosik in the library of the Statue of Liberty National Monument, and the staffs of Condé-Nast Publications, St. Paul's Chapel, the Trinity Church Archives in New York City, and the New York State Museum.

In Pennsylvania, Andrea Ashby Leraris at Independence National Historical Park was as always a model of efficiency and grace. Also very helpful were Susan Drinan at the Atwater Kent Museum in Philadelphia, Adjutant Tom Farley Jr. of the First Troop Philadelphia City Cavalry, Lee Arnold and Kerry McLaughlin at the Historical Society of Pennsylvania, Herbert K. Zearfoss of the Pennsylvania Society of the Sons of the Revolution, Dr. Fred Rude of the Philadelphia Chapter of the Sons of the American Revolution, Don Creswell at the Philadelphia Print Shop, Nicholas Ciotola at the Historical Society of Western Pennsylvania, Paula L. Stefano at the Bucks County Historical Society, and the staffs of the Library Company of Philadelphia, the Pennsylvania Historical and Museum Commission in Harrisburg, and the Mussellman Library at Gettysburg College. Thanks also go to Leslie Bowman and Grace Eleazer at the Winterthur Museum and to Nancy Davis and Louise Brownell at the Maryland Historical Society.

In Washington, we had much help from Ellen McCallister Clark of the Society of Cincinnati, Beth Rae Richardson at the National Geographic Society, Beverly Cox and Kristin Smith of the National Portrait Gallery, Lisa Kathleen Graddy of the Political Historical Collection in the Smithsonian National Museum of American History, and Tambra Johnson at the Library of Congress. Thanks also go to the curatorial staff of the U.S. Senate Collection, the White House Historical Association, and the National Archives.

In Virginia, we thank Wallace Gusler in Williamsburg, Dr. John Coski at the Museum of the Confederacy, Claire Christophe and Bettie Lee Gaskins of the Robert E. Lee Memorial Association, Ensign Brian J. Hoyt, Public Affairs Officer on the staff of the commanding officer, Atlantic Fleet, United States Navy in Norfolk, and the staffs of the Library of Virginia and the Valentine Richmond History Center.

In the Carolinas, thanks go to Johanna M. Brown at the Museum of Early Southern Decorative Arts at Winston-Salem, J. Graham Long at the Charleston Museum, Carl Steen of Diachronic Research in Charleston, Diane Smith at the University of South Carolina Press, the South Carolina Department of Natural Resources, the South Carolina Department of Archives and History, the South Carolina Historical Society in Charleston, and the Charlotte Museum of History in North Carolina.

In Tennessee, we are grateful to Edwin S. Gleaves at the Tennessee State Library and Archives, and Dr. Candace J. Adelson and Dan E. Pomeroy at the Tennessee State Museum. Also we thank Robert Cason, Alabama Department of Archives and History; Robert Cargo, of the Robert Cargo Folk Art Gallery, in Tuscaloosa; Warren J. Woods at the Historic New Orleans Collection; Sally Boitnott at the Pelican Publishing Company, Gretna, Louisiana; and Gary Truman at the Flip Schulke Archives in Florida.

In the West, we wish to acknowledge Carla Rickerson at the University of Washington Libraries; Terri Raburn at Nebraska State Historical Society; Carolyn Ducey at the International Quilt Study Center in the University of Nebraska; Eli Paul, Doran Cart and Jonathan Casey at the Liberty Memorial Museum of World War I in Kansas City, Missouri; Cowan's Auctions in Cincinnati; Debra Armstrong-Morgan and David Leopold at the Harry Ransom Center, University of Texas at Austin; the Texas State Preservation Board; Elizabeth M. Holmes at the Buffalo Bill Historical Center; Ovid Need and the staff at Motorbooks International, St. Paul, Minnesota; Roni Lubliner at Universal Studios in Los Angeles, and the staff of the Chicago Historical Society, and the Art Institute of Chicago; Greenfield Village and Henry Ford Museum in Dearborn, Michigan; and the Wisconsin State Historical Society.

We are also grateful to the staffs of the British Library, British Museum, and the Victoria and Albert Museum in London; the Musées de la Ville de Paris; Thomas Ross Ltd. in Binfield, Berkshire; Helen Dahinden of Diogenes Verlag AG in Zurich; the Polish Poster Gallery in Warsaw; and Dr. He Qi of Nanjing, China.

Our thanks go to Elizabeth Barnett for granting permission to reprint excerpts from "E. St. V. M." (self-portrait, 1920), "First Fig," and "What Lips My Lips Have Kissed," by Edna St. Vincent Millay, copyright 1920, 1922, 1923, 1950, 1951, 1980, by Edna St. Vincent Millay and Norma Millay Ellis, all rights reserved. We also thank Mimi Ross at Henry Holt & Co. for permission to use Robert Frost's poem "Black Cottage," copyright by Robert Frost and Lesley Frost Ballantine.

Corbis generously allowed us to use many photographs from the Bettmann Archive without fee through the Corbis Image Donation Program. We are grateful for their support, and for the assistance of Rachel Wright and Susan Kim. Rebecca Hirsch at Art Assist helped us locate owners and copyright holders and obtain permission for use.

One of our largest debts is to Marianne Litty and the team at Pure Imaging in Watertown, Massachusetts. They made the creation of digital images into an art form, refined many of our materials, constructed collages and flag plates, and solved many problems with the illustrations. Marianne did all of these things with superb skill and unfailing grace, often under heavy pressure of deadlines. We are deeply grateful for her help, and it was a joy to work with her.

At Oxford University Press, two very able editors had major roles in this project. Sheldon Meyer has been a friend and advisor for many years and offered helpful counsel for this book. Peter Ginna was deeply involved on a daily basis. Peter gave the manuscript a very close critical reading, and greatly improved it. India Cooper was once again a superb copy editor. Joellyn Ausanka was the managing editor and did an excellent job, as always. Joellyn brought the pieces together, refined the text, organized the illustrations, caught errors that had eluded everybody else, and presided over a five-ring circus with extraordinary skill, tact, judgment, rigor, and good humor.

At Brandeis, Dona Delorenzo and Judy Brown ran the office with high efficiency and grace. Thanks go to Jehuda Reinharz, our excellent president, historian, colleague, and good friend. And thanks also to my colleague Paul Jankowsky for his interest and support, and especially for the civility and decency that he brings to the academy.

In the family, my father, John Henry Fischer, was my most trusted advisor on this book, and helped me to improve it. My brother Miles talked through some of the difficult problems. Susanna, Erik, Anne, and Fred offered much encouragement and support. My wife, Judith, was a very active collaborator on this project. She read the manuscript, suggested many improvements, assisted in finding materials, made helpful suggestions regarding the design of the book and jacket, and did much more besides. Our inspiration in this work was Thea Turner, our granddaughter. This book is dedicated to Thea, and to her free and happy spirit.

Wayland, Massachusetts, and Bar Harbor, Maine   D.H.F.
June 2004

INDEX

Page numbers in **bold** refer to illustrations.